Getting Business to Come to You

SECOND EDITION

Other books by Paul and Sarah Edwards

Best Home Businesses for the 90s

Finding Your Perfect Work

Home Businesses You Can Buy
(with Walter Zooi)

Making Money with Your Computer at Home

Secrets of Self-Employment

Teaming Up
(with Rick Benzel)

Working From Home

Getting Business to Come to You

SECOND EDITION

A Complete Do-It-Yourself Guide to Attracting All the Business You Can Enjoy

Paul and Sarah Edwards
and Laura Clampitt Douglas

Jeremy P. Tarcher/Putnam
a member of
Penguin Putnam Inc.
New York

We acknowledge the sponsorship of the color insert by PaperDirect™. Most of the marketing materials pictured on pages three through eight of the color insert are from PaperDirect's *Great Idea Book* and catalogs. These include letterheads, envelopes, business cards, novelties, portfolios, binders, postcards, door hangers, gift certificates, and presentation folders. Displays created by PaperDirect are copyrighted by PaperDirect, Inc. You can contact PaperDirect by phoning 1-800-A-PAPERS (800-272-7377) or on the Web at www.paperdirect.com

Most Tarcher/Putnam books are available at special quantity discounts for bulk purchases for sales promotions, premiums, fund-raising, and educational needs. Special books or book excerpts also can be created to fit specific needs. For details, write or telephone Special Markets, The Putnam Publishing Group, 200 Madison Avenue, New York, NY 10016; (212) 951-8891.

Jeremy P. Tarcher/Putnam
a member of
Penguin Putnam Inc.
200 Madison Avenue
New York, NY 10016
www.penguinputnam.com

First Trade Paperback Edition 1998

Library of Congress Cataloging-in-Publication Data
Edwards, Paul, date.
Getting business to come to you : a complete do-it-yourself guide to attracting all the business you can enjoy / by Paul and Sarah Edwards and Laura Clampitt Douglas.—2nd. rev. ed.
p. cm.
Includes bibliographical references and index.
ISBN 0-87477-845-X
1. Home-based businesses. 2. Advertising. 3. Marketing.
I. Edwards, Sarah (Sarah A.) II. Douglas, Laura Clampitt.
HD2341.E38 1998 97-42596 CIP
658.8—dc21

Book design by Lee Fukui
Cover design by Lee Fukui

Printed in the United States of America

10 9 8 7 6 5 4 3 2 1

Acknowledgments

As we have often said, success is always a joint venture. Only through the help and support of many others have we been able to complete the two-year process of incorporating all the updates, ideas, concepts, and experiences garnered since the first edition into this new edition of *Getting Business to Come to You.* We are truly blessed for the creativity, understanding, insight, and leadership of our publisher, Joel Fotinos. The insight and clarity of our editors, Mitch Horowitz and Rick Benzel, have served as an ongoing compass, keeping us from losing our way in the forest of detail this book involves. A major thank-you to Jocelyn Wright for taking on the not-inconsiderable task of taming the complexities of the artwork in this book and to David Groff. To Claire Vaccaro and Coral Tysliava, thanks for providing a user-friendly look and feel for our book.

We are most grateful for the feedback and support of the readers of our books and the many self-employed individuals and small-business owners who have so graciously shared their mistakes, masterpieces, hurdles, hassles, victories, and triumphs with us. With your support and the help of our invaluable assistant, Joyce Acosta, we are able to pursue the grander mission of which this book is a pivotal part: to serve those with the heart to dream of a more meaningful and rewarding life and the courage to create it.

Contents

PREFACE

Tailor-Made, Top-of-the-Mind, Word-of-Mouth Marketing

In the first edition of *Getting Business to Come to You* we dispelled many myths about what's required to get all the business you can enjoy coming to you. We presented a new perspective on how happily self-employed individuals can get plenty of business while leaving themselves free to do what they do best and enjoy most. And the results have been exciting.

Many people wanting to start their own business have used *Getting Business to Come to You* to turn their goals into reality. Elio Samame, for example, was working as an independent fitness trainer meeting his clients in their homes or at Gold's Gym, but he wanted to have his own gym. He decided to implement one idea from our book every day and in 1991, he opened a 2,500-square-foot gym, Elio's Fitness for Success. One year later he expanded to a 10,000-square-foot-facility where he is today.

Others have used the first edition to expand and build their businesses. Julie Tenenbaum wrote to tell how she had increased her word-processing business, Final Draft, by 50 percent by using just one idea she got from *Getting Business to Come to You*. Photographer Helen Garber wanted to turn her lifelong love and sideline business into a full-time income. Using concepts from this book, she developed an innovative marketing plan for getting more business by doing what she enjoys most: photographing art gallery openings and charity events.

She's carved out a special niche that's keeping her so busy she has had to move from her home studio into an artist's studio.

In this expanded edition, we've added a wealth of insights garnered from the experiences of thousands of people like these. You'll not only find many years' worth of practical, low-cost marketing ideas; you'll also discover an entire approach to knowing when, how, and in what way you can best attract all the business you can enjoy. You'll discover what you can do to get most, if not all, of your business from the one, single most effective way successful businesses tell us they get their business—by word of mouth. With a steady flow of business coming to you at the recommendation of others, you will be free to spend your time doing what you enjoy most and do best, serving your clients and customers.

You won't need to worry unduly about competition, because you will know how to keep yourself on the top of the minds of those you are best suited to serve by establishing yourself in your own unique niche where you can truly shine.

Best of all, you'll discover that marketing yourself to get business coming to you won't need to be a dreaded or difficult aspect of your work. If there is one thing we've learned since writing the last edition of this book, it is that there are effective marketing methods for virtually every personality. You do not need to become someone you're not to market yourself successfully. Nor will you need to do things you find uncomfortable or distasteful. You'll find that you have been doing the very things that can bring you a steady flow of business since you were in kindergarten. And you can find ways to tailor what you do to fit naturally into your schedule, your budget, and the way you enjoy working.

Whether you are just getting started or already established and want more or a better quality of business, we know that this tailor-made, top-of-the-mind marketing approach can help take your business to the next level. The ideas in this book have been tested in countless seminars throughout the country. This comprehensive, new, and exciting marketing approach can prepare you to meet the challenge of attracting a steady flow of business.

To begin applying the ideas you'll be reading as quickly as possible, we invite you to use the checklist on the next page to identify the most pressing marketing challenges you're facing right now. Later, if you encounter other challenges to having plenty of business, you can return to this book again and again for the ideas you need to move on to new levels of success. You'll find it to be a valuable tool at each step along the way in achieving your goals.

What are Your Current Challenges?

Check any of the following statements that apply to you:

___ I need some business. I don't have any yet.

___ I need more business. I have some, but I need more.

___ I need steady business. I have plenty of business sometimes but then I hit dry spells.

___ I have business, but I'm having to spend too much time, energy, and money marketing myself. I need to free my time to do income-producing work.

___ I'm getting business, but it's not the kind of work or clients I want.

___ I have plenty of business but I'm working too hard for too little money.

___ I need to do less work but be able to charge more for it.

At whatever stage you are in your independent career, as long as you have a business that people need and will pay for, if you Get Ready, Get Set, and Go as outlined in this book and use this approach consistently over time, you will have business coming to you.

Here's to all the business you can enjoy!

PART I

GET READY:

Positioning Yourself to Be in Demand and Sought After

You have to be talked about to get work.

—Georgia O'Keeffe

One call was of particular interest to orga- nizational development consultant Marilyn Miller as she took the phone messages off her answering machine. The city of Malibu was planning to hire a California organizational development (OD) consultant and they wanted to talk with her. As she promptly returned the call, she learned that city council members had wanted to identify a variety of consultants, ask for proposals, and then select someone to work with them on a long-term team-building program. But, they told her, in seeking out the names of possible consultants, every person they spoke with advised that the consultant they needed was Marilyn Miller. So, now all they wanted to know was when she could come in to work out the details of a contract so they could start working together.

Isn't this the kind of message we'd all like to find waiting on our voice mail, in our e-mail, or our mailbox? Well, this is the kind of contact you can expect once you're in demand and sought after. But how did this happen? How was it that every person the council members talked with recommended Marilyn Miller? It didn't happen for the reasons you might think.

It isn't luck. When you hear about someone getting an opportunity like this, it's easy to think, "Boy, is she ever lucky." And, yes, sometimes people are in the right place at just the right time, so it looks as though luck tapped them on the shoulder and propelled them to a level of success unattainable by all the rest of us who aren't so blessed. But if you look a little deeper at such serendipity, usually you'll discover that, as the saying goes, "Luck is what happens when preparation meets opportunity."

Luck alone is far too fickle to rely on as a source of steady income. While business may fall into your lap once in a while, no one can count on it to happen week after week, month after month, and year after year. And it wasn't chance that caused the city council to contact Miller. She often gets business in this way.

It isn't being the very best. If it wasn't luck, then, you may be tempted to think Marilyn must be one of best OD consultants around. She must be so good that no one else can hold a candle to her. But no, while Marilyn is good at what she does, so are many other people the council could have called.

You've undoubtedly noticed yourself that the most successful individuals aren't necessarily the very best at what they do. Usually successful people do a good job for their clients, but not necessarily the best possible job. In fact, you may even have had the experience of knowing you're as good, or maybe better, than someone else who gets business you would love to have.

It's not money. If it's not luck or superior abilities, then it must be money. Miller must have spent big bucks on costly advertising and promotions. But, no, actually Marilyn spends very little money on marketing. While money can buy the chance to get your name out, it rarely convinces others that you're the best person to work with. In fact, we've found that having lots of money to spend on getting business can be a surefire way to lose a lot of money fast. The most expensive ad campaign won't get people to send a steady stream of business your way until you've proven to them that they should.

It's not bargain basement prices. Oh, then, you may be tempted to think Miller offers the lowest price in town. That's why she gets business so easily. But, no. She charges a substantial, but fair, fee for her services. When you're self-employed, charging bargain basement prices may keep you busy, or even too busy, but it won't bring you the income you need or the loyal following that will keep you in business. To make a decent living, you'll eventually have to raise your prices and when you do, your bargain basement customers will flee to the lowest bidder.

So how did Marilyn get this business? She got it the same way market researcher Eleanor Duggan got a steady flow of business coming to her after leaving her job. Within the first year on her own, Duggan was working to her full capacity. She did it the same way instructional designer Mike Greer got business coming to him. After leaving his job, Greer tripled his income working only five hours a day. He did this the same way a San Francisco man we met on a radio talk show got his new business plan writing service under way in only three months. Within three months, this weapons-designer-turned-business-plan-writer was making more money than he had from his salary as an engineer. And he already had several people working for him.

These individuals were able to get plenty of business coming to them because they'd each become *well known* to those who should know them as someone who understands and can address the needs and problems of the clients they serve. In other words, they have developed a *reputation:* a favorable, recognized standing as people who can serve their particular clients. What they do, whom they do it for, and when they're the best choice is clear to those who need to use their product or service, or those who are sources of referrals and recommendations. They've achieved top-of-the-mind status so that they have tapped into the best possible source of steady, ongoing business: *word of mouth.*

Tapping into the #1 Best Source of Steady, Ongoing Business

Have you ever had this experience? Someone you'd like to do business with tells you, "I sure wish we'd known about you sooner. We would have loved to work with you. Maybe next time." Unfortunately, most us of have had more than one experience like this because it's virtually impossible to anticipate the precise moment when a potential client or customer you've never met will be ready to do business with you. But when that moment comes, they'll do business with whoever's in the right place at the right time. So how do you make sure you're the one who's there when that magic moment arrives?

> **Your Goal: Stand Out from the Crowd and Distinguish Yourself**
>
> *You need find a way to stand out from the crowd and distinguish yourself. You need to become so well known in the right circles that when someone needs what you have to offer, your name will either immediately come to mind or be the first one mentioned whenever they turn to others to find what they need.*

That's top-of-the-mind, word-of-mouth marketing. And that's what this section is about. It's about how you can lay the foundation for building a business-generating reputation for yourself, even if you're just starting out in your business. It's about how to position yourself to be in demand by the people who need to know about you. It's about how to develop a plan for making sure people know who you are, what you do, and why they should work with you.

Are You Ready?

If you want to get business to come to you instead of having to spend your time drumming it up, chances are you're eager to get top-of-the-mind, word-of-mouth marketing working for you. But are you ready to do what you'll need to do to get it? To find out, complete this checklist and then read chapters 1 through 4. You may be surprised to find you're not as ready as you think. You may realize why you don't yet have all the business you can enjoy. And, you'll also know what you can do right now to get going.

___ 1. Have you decided on the **one** thing you want to become well known for?

___Or are you straddling the fence, still offering a variety of things to get by or until you see what takes off?

___ 2. Are you willing to commit 100 percent of your *available* time, energy, and money to developing this **one** thing?

___Or are you dividing your available time among various ideas or possibilities?

___ 3. Do you have your own niche, your own specialty, that capitalizes on your unique combination of interests, skills, talents, experience, background, and contacts?

___Or are you doing pretty much what others in your field are doing?

___ 4. Can you demonstrate why you're the best choice for your clients or customers?

___Or are you hoping people will believe in and want to do business with you?

___ 5. Do you have a plan for how you'll become known to the people who need to know about you? Will your plan keep you on the top of these people's minds?

___Or are your efforts at marketing catch-as-catch-can?

___ 6. Are you able to follow your plan consistently and frequently enough to actually have the impact you're seeking?

___Or do your marketing efforts slip through the cracks due to lack of time or because you really don't like doing them?

Unless you're already exceptionally well positioned, getting business coming to you will take some time. How long will depend on how ready you are. You may be ready to take off right now. Or you could find that you have several months of work to do before you'll be in a position to be in demand and sought after. Taking the time you need to get in position to be in demand will be worth the investment. If you rush into trying to get business without positioning yourself solidly, you'll just have to go back later and get in a better position. So why not start now?

But What If You Desperately Need Business Right Now?

If you need business right now, you may be feeling somewhat anxious about the prospect of needing to take preparatory steps before you'll be ready to get business coming to you. This concern is the single most common reason people bypass the steps they need to take and then wonder why they can't get the level of business they need and want. Trying to get business from a position of desperation is a tremendous challenge and too often leads to less than desirable decisions. You've undoubtedly met people yourself who seem so hungry for business that you feel sorry for them. Chances are, though, you're not particularly interested in doing business with them.

Instead, you may wonder why they don't have plenty of business if they're any good at what they do. You may be concerned that they'll go under or take a job instead of completing their work with you. You may worry they won't be around to provide customer support or to stand behind their product or service. Chances are you'd prefer to do business with people who have ample business, because it suggests they must be doing something right.

So, if you need business right now, you owe it to yourself to do something to get some business fast so you won't be feeling, sounding, and looking desperate. Here are some emergency stopgap measures you can take to generate enough income, time, and energy to stay afloat while you take the steps you need to get a more reliable, steady stream of business coming to you.

Five Ways to Get Stopgap Business Fast

1. Turn your ex-employer into your client. Your former employer already knows your capability and has a proven need for it. Often you can negotiate to do on a part-time or contractual basis what you did on a full-time salary. Or perhaps you can negotiate a contract to train your replacement. This can be a viable strategy even if you are going into an entirely different type of business.

2. ***Subcontract or do overload.*** Your competitors can be an excellent source of business. Our surveys show that successful businesses get as much as 25 percent of their business from their competition. So, offer to do work they can't take or don't want to do.

3. ***Work as a temporary employee in a field related to what you'll be doing in your business.*** Working for a temporary agency can provide valuable experience and excellent contacts. At the same time, it provides a flexible source of immediate income while you're building your business.

4. ***Make an offer they can't refuse.*** Some income beats no income. So identify people who need your skills and make them a "special" offer that's so tempting they simply can't say no. Be sure they know this is a "special" price, not what you regularly charge, and be sure you can at least cover all your costs, including some value for your time. Also ask them to serve as a reference for you in the future.

5. ***Volunteer.*** Some work beats no work, and work tends to beget more work. There's nothing worse for your morale than having your skills lie dormant. Valued volunteer efforts can turn into paying efforts. Many volunteers find their experience leads to paying contracts or orders. At the very least, volunteer efforts can be a source of experience, contacts, and references that you can leverage into other business you might not otherwise know about or be able to get.

CHAPTER 1

Focusing—Clearly Defining What You Do

"What business am I in?" "What exactly is it that I'm about?" Answering these questions is the first step on the road to success.

—Peter Drucker, Management Consultant

Imagine for a moment that you're attending a business networking event and you meet several individuals for the first time. Each one tells you what he or she does as follows:

Person A: "I've started a business doing market research, selling business information, and writing promotional materials for public relations firms."

Person B: "I do a variety of things: word processing, résumé writing, editing, and business writing. I've also done some technical writing and written articles for magazines and newsletters."

Person C: "I am a professional organizer. I'm also a real estate agent. And lately I've gotten involved in selling a great line of skin care products."

What's your reaction to these individuals? Are you impressed? Would you be interested in doing business with them? Do you think you'll be referring others to them? A month from now, if you were to find their business cards lying on your desk, do you think you'd remember who they were? Would you keep their cards?

Chances are, based on these introductions alone, you would not. And you probably wouldn't be surprised to learn that these individuals are all having difficulty getting enough business. They, however, are baffled. They don't understand why the few clients they have always seem satisfied with their work but have yet to provide any referrals. They don't understand why, when it comes to discussing prices, their customers always seem to expect a super bargain. Do you understand why they're having these reactions?

What's Wrong with This Picture?

Why do you think these people are having trouble achieving the success they're seeking? While they may do excellent work, be honest and trustworthy, hardworking and fair, it will probably be difficult for any of them to generate a steady flow of well-paying clients.

These people are making one of the most common, but least talked about, marketing mistakes: they haven't decided what business they're in. Actually, they're trying to run a variety of different businesses in hopes of being versatile and picking up as much work as possible. Yet they're having a hard time getting business because in order to spread the word about you, people must be crystal clear about what business you're in. They must *perceive* that you know what you're doing, that you're fully committed to it, and that you take it seriously.

The more scattered someone is, the easier it is to recognize this problem. For example, we received a direct-mail piece from someone who indicated that he could provide fifteen different services from business systems analysis and management consulting to custom programming, bookkeeping, and computer training. And, indeed, he may be able to do all these things, but from the perspective of generating business, chances are he won't get many opportunities to do any of them.

YOUR GOAL
Let Others Know What Business You're In

Why You Must Focus

Lack of focus is actually quite common among self-employed individuals. When we wrote the first edition of *Working from Home* we noticed so many people carrying on multiple businesses simultaneously that we coined the term *patchwork professions* to refer to this phenomenon. We met a yoga teacher who also does word processing, a pet-sitter who was selling diet products, and a consultant who did photography on weekends. At first glance it seemed as though this was an ingenious way for people to patch together a way to become their own boss. Later, however, we reached a dramatically different conclusion.

In 1989, we conducted a nationwide survey that included in-depth interviews with over 100 successfully self-employed individuals. We were startled to discover that these individuals were different in almost every conceivable way but one. They were men and women of different ages from different ethnic groups. They had diverse educational backgrounds. Some had had years of experience in their fields before going out on their own, while others had entered entirely new fields. They had different motivations for being their own boss. Some wanted to be home with children, others wanted to pursue their passion, while still others were on their own as a result of a life-altering crisis like an illness or losing their job. Some had started with a carefully prepared and detailed business plan. Others had operated successfully without a plan, flying intuitively by the seat of their pants.

Among all these differences, all but two individuals had one thing in common: they were highly focused. Over and over and over again we heard the same message. At some point along the way, they had each realized that they had to make a commitment to ***one*** business. And, in fact, many of them talked about having to make difficult choices and let go of some possibilities that seemed appealing.

It was at this point we realized that, generally speaking, self-employed individuals in patchwork careers have a significantly more difficult time getting business than those who are focused. Although usually they don't realize why, they experience a variety of chronic problems.

- ***Not being taken seriously.*** Often those who are trying to do a variety of things complain that their clients, customers, suppliers, friends, family and/or relatives don't treat their businesses with respect. Customers haggle over prices and drag out payment. Suppliers resist extending credit. Family members send them job clippings from the want ads and joke about when they'll be getting a "real job."

When we ask audiences their reaction to people who do multiple types of work, the common responses we hear again and again are:

> *"If they were successful at doing any one of these things, they wouldn't have time to do the others."*
>
> *"They couldn't be very good at* **all** *these things."*
>
> *"I wouldn't want to count on them. They're too scattered."*
>
> *"Jack of all trades, master of none."*
>
> *"Not professional. They sound flaky."*

Of course, these observations may be completely unjustified, but they are nonetheless real. A large company, like Sears or Wal-Mart, that has lots of employees can offer lots of divergent things from insurance to tires and women's clothing to optometry without losing credibility. But it's more difficult for people to believe that a self-employed individual working alone or with an assistant or two could have the time, expertise, resources, and experience to do a high-quality, reliable job at an array of divergent things, even if they can.

Generally when people choose to do business with someone who's self-employed, it's because they believe the individual will have more in-depth knowledge and background in a particular area and will provide more personalized and individual attention than a larger, more impersonal company. So, doing a multiplicity of things shatters one of the most appealing assets that gives us an advantage as self-employed individuals or very small companies. And now, even big businesses are finding they need to stick closer to their knitting. Many larger companies that diversified broadly in the eighties returned in the nineties to their "core" function, pulling back to provide the products and services for which they are best known and most respected.

- ***The constant expectation of low, low prices.*** While those who are more focused can command significant fees and prices, people who are patching together a variety of businesses report that they have trouble charging more than the most modest of fees. Comments like the following are a common refrain, "I charge much less than most similar services, but when people hear my fees, they just hang up. They seem to be shopping for the lowest possible price."

- ***Not enough time or money to reach a critical mass.*** People providing multiple products and services have to divide whatever time, money, and energy they have among the various things they're doing, so it's more difficult to get enough momentum going for any one activity to really take off. Instead, each aspect of their work tends to end up limping along.

- ***Confusion about who you are and what you do.*** It's not uncommon that whatever aspect of one's multifocus business is mentioned, people will say, "Oh, I thought you did . . ." or "Aren't you the same person who does . . . ?" "Oh, you're not doing . . . anymore?" This can happen even when someone is successfully established in one focused business and then decides to launch new ventures.

For example, Mary G, a successful wedding makeup artist, decided to sell a line of skin products at a local trade show as a way to bring in some extra income. This venture turned into a marketing nightmare. When her previous clients and referral sources came by her booth, they expressed concern and disappointment. "Oh, you're not doing wedding makeup anymore?" they asked. Even though she explained that she was selling the skin care products as an adjunct to her wedding makeup business, months later she was still getting comments like "I heard you had changed businesses" or "I didn't know you were in business anymore." She has no way to measure the full extent of the business she's lost.

- ***Endless other marketing dilemmas.*** When you're involved in more than one type of business, you're faced with a perpetual dilemma of how to introduce yourself, how to refer to your business, and what to put on your business card. Unfortunately there is no ideal answer to these marketing dilemmas. Some people try having different business names, cards, and introductions for each of their different business activities. But invariably they discover they have the wrong card at the wrong time and end up crossing off and writing in information on the card, saying something like "This card is for my . . . business, but you can still reach me there."

To avoid this, we've even seen people carry a card case filled with their various business cards and pull out whichever one is appropriate to the circumstances. But this doesn't leave the best of impressions. When we demonstrate this approach in our seminars, many people roll their eyes. Others snicker.

Another popular alternative is to use a generic card, name, or introduction that doesn't give any clues about what you do; i.e., KJL Services or John Jones and Associates. While this doesn't leave anyone confused, it leaves almost everyone nonplussed. It makes no memorable impression, so the tremendous marketing advantage a business name, introduction, or card can provide is lost.

Why People Don't Focus

With all these headaches, it's surprising that many people remain so unfocused. But having many ways to earn a living simultaneously is very tempting for a number of reasons.

- ***We Fear Failure.*** Ironically, the most common reason people fail to focus despite the problems it presents is that they're afraid they won't have enough business. It's like having a safety net, something you can fall back on. If one business activity doesn't take off, maybe another one will.

That's what happened with Harriet K., the professional organizer/ real estate agent/skin care salesperson. After studying for several years, she finally got her real estate license and at first things went well. She made a good living for two years. Then the real estate market tightened up. Her sales were few and far between, so she started looking for other things to do. Being a highly organized person by nature, when she heard about the emerging field of professional organizing it seemed like an obvious way to supplement her income. But, as is usually the case, she found getting clients for that business to be equally challenging, so when a friend introduced her to a multilevel marketing opportunity selling skin care, it sounded like a godsend.

Unfortunately, Harriet was barely eking out a living from these three businesses. Had she put all her time, money and energy into any one of them she might have fared better, but by operating from fear, she fell into the trap of chasing opportunity. Without her full attention, no one business could flourish. And worst of all, people began writing her off as someone who wasn't serious about what she did.

It's far better to take a part-time, temporary, or even full-time job, if necessary, while you invest in getting **one** business up and running than to juggle three marginal businesses.

- ***We Don't Want to Miss an Opportunity.*** When you're on your own it's hard to say "no" to business, but if you want a steady stream of the right kind of business, sometimes you have to. Too many people take on any kind of business they can get and then end up inadvertently juggling multiple businesses. That's what happened to Aaron M. He'd been a high school teacher who decided to become a marriage, family, and child counselor (MFCC). After going to night school and getting his credentials and license, he left his teaching position and opened a psychotherapy practice.

At first, of course, he wasn't busy full time, so when a colleague asked him to consult for the school system he jumped at the opportunity. That led to another small consulting job. Then his neighbor needed help setting up her computer and hired Aaron to help. Soon the neighbor had referred two other people who needed a computer consultant. Within three months, Aaron had the seeds of three businesses taking root: marriage and family counseling, educational consulting, and computer consulting.

At first this arrangement seemed great. He was amazed at all the opportunities coming his way. His counseling practice, however, was suffering. The consulting jobs left little time to market his fledgling practice and, before long, he realized that the seedlings of each business would have to be watered if he wanted any of them to grow. He knew he had to make a choice. If he intended to get any more consulting contracts, he'd have to get business cards and start marketing that service. Clearly he'd gotten off track and by trying to seize every opportunity, he'd lost sight of his original goal, to have a thriving therapy practice.

• ***We Have Multiple Interests.*** Another common reason we don't focus when we become self-employed is that we're multifaceted human beings with lots and interests and abilities. We want to do some of this and some of that. I know I, Sarah, certainly did. I was interested in biofeedback so I wanted to do that. I was interested in child development and I loved speaking and doing seminars so I wanted to teach parenting classes. I was fascinated with portable video equipment when it first came onto the market so I wanted to teach public speaking to politicians and executives. And, believe it or not, for a time I was doing all those things and more.

Actually doing all those things was fun and stimulating. I was learning and growing as I mastered those activities, but I was also frustrated because it took so much time and effort to line up the chance to get paid to do any of them. Getting scheduled to do one parenting seminar might take three months. Getting a contract to teach public speaking might take six months. I realized if I was ever going to get a steady stream of business, I'd have to decide what I wanted to focus on and give it my all.

Fortunately, since we decided some fifteen years ago to focus on providing information, resources, and support for achieving a more balanced and rewarding life through self-employment, we've been able to do many of the things we'd previously enjoyed. We teach and speak, counsel and do seminars and make videos, but now all these activities have one focus. So every effort we undertake to further any one aspect of our work automatically increases our success in all the others.

• ***We Think Generally, Not Specifically.*** Finally, often people don't focus because to them the many businesses they're involved in are so related that they seem like one business. This is the case with many of the people who come to our seminars. When we discuss the importance of focusing, they agree and think they are focused. It's not until they try to explain what they do to the audience that they realize others perceive them as scattered.

That was the case with Kingston G. Since technical writing, business-plan writing, résumé writing, and newsletter writing are all forms of writing and he's a writer, it never occurred to him that potential clients would be confused or put off by the diversity of his business, *Words Say It All*. He was disappointed with the level of business he'd been able to attract, however, and it wasn't until he tried explaining what he does at a seminar that he realized why he wasn't getting the response he wanted.

Essentially Kingston was presenting people with a cafeteria of writing choices and hoping they'd find one that interested them. But these days most people prefer theme restaurants to cafeterias. When they want pizza, they go to their favorite pizza parlor. When they want Chinese, they go to their favorite Chinese restaurant. If they want steak, they go to a steak house. And so it is with getting business. When people want to have a résumé done, they go to a résumé writer. If they need a business plan, they want to work with a business plan writer.

So, Kingston's cards and brochures featuring a list of "writing services" he can provide is the equivalent of a restaurant advertising that they serve "food." He's is not positioning himself to be in demand and sought after. He's not helping people remember who he is and what he does. And he's not standing out from the crowd.

One Notable Exception

We mentioned that all but two of the successfully self-employed individuals we interviewed were highly focused. These two individuals shared one notable quality that made them exceptional. They are true geniuses. Geniuses frequently undertake multiple projects, including businesses, simultaneously yet they do not suffer from their lack of a single focus. They and others like them we've met since do not have a problem rising above the perception of being scattered; people accept them, classifying them generically as inventors, entrepreneurs, or sages.

Inventor Stanley Mason is one such individual. He creates an array of concepts and products and solves problems for major corporations. Chances are you use some of his creations—the granola bar, squeezable ketchup bottles, baby-shaped disposable diapers with stick tabs, stringless Band-Aid wrappers, and microwave cookware (Masonware). Another such individual is Noah BenShea, philosopher, poet, author, consultant to leading think tanks, and owner of Noah's New York Bagels.

Getting a steady stream of business coming to them doesn't seem to be a problem for these true geniuses. They routinely engage in a variety of activities and use their productive intelligence with the intensity of a laser beam to shift their focus from one activity to another. This is different from most of us who, while we may have multiple businesses, need to develop them consecutively over time. Such genius, unfortunately, is rare.

SIGNS YOU'RE NOT FOCUSED

Although there can be other reasons you might encounter any of the following problems, each can be a sign that you are not being perceived as having a clear focus for your business. Check any that apply to you.

___ 1. You have multiple business cards for your different business activities or wonder if you should.

___ 2. You've purposely chosen a general business name that doesn't say what you do so you can use it for all the different things you do.

___ 3. You often feel conflicted about which aspects of what you do you should mention when you introduce yourself.

___ 4. People don't seem to take your business seriously.

___ 5. People are often confused about or can't describe what you do.

___ 6. Clients seem satisfied with your work but rarely refer other business to you.

___ 7. In trying to tell people what you do, you often respond by saying, "I do a lot of things" or ask, "What do you need done?"

___ 8. People have trouble explaining to others what you do or frequently comment that they never can keep up with all the things you're doing.

___ 9. Your business cards and brochures include a list of things that other people are doing as full-time businesses.

___10. You have difficulty summarizing what you do in a simple sentence.

Committing to a Focus

So, unless you're one of those rare individuals who qualify as true geniuses, the first and most important step you can take to position yourself to be in demand and sought after is to focus what you do. Your goal should be to define what you do by depth, not by breadth. As long as you scatter your efforts, chances are you'll have a difficult time getting a steady flow of the right kind of business. But once you commit to focusing all your available time, money, and effort on one endeavor, you'll be in position to become known for that activity; and as your reputation grows, word of mouth will start bringing business to you.

If you're already doing or considering a multiplicity of things, you need to decide what you want your focus to be, what one thing you want to become known for. As we know personally, making such a choice may not be easy. You may feel torn between pursuing what you enjoy doing and what people seem to be most willing to pay you to do. You may have to let go of some of your pet projects in order to pursue only one of them. Making such a choice can be agonizing.

Choosing a focus will open certain doors to you while closing others. But just as you'll never get to see the world if you can't decide which destination to head for first, so it is with committing to one focus for your business. The doors that will open to you once you fully commit to one endeavor will present new opportunities you may never have imagined. Here are three possible ways to define your focus:

*1. **Pick one.*** In some cases the best decision is simply to pick one of the things you've been considering or pursuing and let the others fall by the wayside. That's essentially what we did. We were each doing several things in addition to writing and speaking about working from home and self-employment. But then, through our interviews, we realized that if we wanted to be truly successful, we had to make a commitment to one thing and give it our all. I, Paul, decided to let go of the training business that had been our bread and butter. I, Sarah, stopped marketing my psychotherapy practice and began referring new business to colleagues. I saw the practice I'd worked so hard to develop dwindle to nothing.

Over several years we had developed a successful speaking skills course and a valuable model of interpersonal communication which we'd spent years having statistically validated. Both of these pursuits had been producing income and held even greater promise. Feelers were out to turn them into books. People were talking to us about licensing these materials. But, since we'd also been busy writing and promoting *Working from Home,* we hadn't had the time and energy to give either of these other ventures the effort they needed to realize their full potential.

We knew we had to make a choice, and so with some discomfort we put these projects away in the back of a filing cabinet. But we have never regretted making these difficult decisions, because once we committed to focus our work together on providing information and resources on self-employment, almost as if by magic, our careers took a significant leap forward and have unfolded in rewarding ways. Of course, it wasn't really magic. It was commitment, dedication, hard work, and determination. It was because we were giving this one goal and this one dream everything we had to give.

Interestingly, many years later, we found ways to use our communication model in our work. You can read about it in our book *Teaming Up, A Small-Business Guide to Collaborating with Others.* The speaking course, though, remains buried in the filing cabinet. But who knows? Someday we may find a use for it as well.

High Touch Tip: Tune into Compliments

Your clients and customers, friends, relatives, and colleagues are constantly providing you with clues to where you truly shine. Following these clues can help you to focus on how you can use your unique assets. Listen to their compliments, what they spontaneously praise you for, what they say when they brag about you. Don't slough these comments off. Note them and recognize that these are the very things you want to become known, the very things that will draw business to you.

2. ***Create an Umbrella Concept.*** Sometimes it's not possible to earn a full-time living doing a particular business. There may not be enough demand for what you want to offer, or you may live in an area where there aren't enough people to support such a business full-time. In this case, you can avoid the problems of being unfocused by providing a variety of closely related services under a unifying umbrella concept.

For example, if someone who wants to do proofreading for textbook publishers has a hard time getting enough business or making enough money from proofreading alone, he or she might create a business under the umbrella concept of Textbook Editorial Services and provide editing, proofreading, and indexing.

Mike Chlanda of Yellow Springs, Ohio, built his reputation under the umbrella of Business Support. He provides small businesses with mailing list management, incoming and outgoing fax transmissions, word processing, billing bookkeeping, and computer training. In a larger community, it would probably be difficult to distinguish yourself adequately using an umbrella concept like this, but in the small community of Yellow Springs, it's worked quite well for Chlanda.

In the small New Mexico town of Madrid, we saw a highly imaginative sign for another umbrella business, Jack of All Arts. Four years ago ex–Philadelphia writer Steven Duffy decided to pursue his dream of opening an art gallery. His tastes were quite eclectic and he wasn't sure just who his market would be, so he conceived the idea for Jack of All Arts. This unifying concept conveys the whimsical mix of fun, folk, and fine art he displays in his gallery. As Jack of All Arts, Duffy can openly mix and blend his tastes. You might find an extraordinary $12,000 table next to an interesting $200 print, and yet it all works well.

Singer/songwriter Ellen Bernfeld and her composer/conductor friend Anne Bryant began singing lullabies to soothe and calm their new English springer spaniel puppies. Then their creative juices started flowing, and they decided to produce an entire album of music for dogs and the people who love them. Working out of Anne's Stony Point, New York, home where Ellen has a thirty-two-rack sound studio, they produced a CD and fully illustrated book called *Songs for Dogs*. In order to expand their business, however, they've needed to add other CDs to their line, so now they are creating CDs under the umbrella concept music for pet owners. Their next album is *Songs for Cats and the People Who Love Them.*

As you can see, the secret to creating a successful umbrella concept is providing a cluster of products or services that are clearly related in the minds of those who need the service. If you recall Kingston G., whom we mentioned earlier, was trying to combine résumé writing, business-plan writing, and technical writing in a business called Words Say It All. Although each of these services involves writing, they are sought out by individuals who have quite different needs and circumstances. A more effective umbrella concept might be When Words Matter Most, providing résumé writing, proposal writing and business-plan writing. These three services are needed by people whose futures depend on winning approval from their written materials.

High-Tech Tip: Use Creativity Software

All achievements, all earned riches, have their beginning in an idea. NAPOLEON HILL

Use brainstorming software like *Idea Fisher* by Idea Fisher Systems or *Mind Man* to help you think creatively about how you might develop an umbrella concept or hybrid focus that combines the multiplicity of things you want to do. This software doesn't "think" for you, but it helps you define problems, brainstorm new and creative ideas, evaluate possible solutions, and clarify your thinking. (See Resources at the end of this chapter for details.)

3. ***Develop a Hybrid.*** Some people don't want to choose among the various things they're doing, so instead of doing multiple things, they combine the activities they love most into one hybrid business. Marcy Hamm, for example, has three great loves: mathematics, music, and computers. But instead of trying to offer three different services like tutoring, composing, and computer programming, Hamm left her prestigious job as a software engineer to produce computer-generated music that reduces stress and speeds healing.

Tom Reiter wanted a career in acting, but he found work in computer programming. Then, multimedia technology burst onto the scene and Reiter discovered a way to combine his talents in an entirely new field. He creates multimedia presentations for trial lawyers, including computer-animated reconstructions of crime scenes. His company is called Trial Presentation Technologies.

As Marjorie Bride of Portland, Maine, turned fifty she wanted a sideline business that would provide additional income and the flexibility to care for her family. She also wanted to cultivate her love of travel, art, and the outdoors. So, she's created a hybrid travel business called Maine Experience. With her partner, Betty Scott, of Weston, Massachusetts, she creates tour packages for groups and individuals who want to explore what Maine has to offer in terms of their special interests like sports, art, or history. A group, for example, which is interested in art, might have the opportunity to dine with local artisans as well as to visit art museums and galleries.

In our book *Finding Your Perfect Work, Making a Living, Creating a Life,* we profile dozens of people who have created such hybrid career solutions. Creating a hybrid might be the ideal solution for Harriet K., whom we mentioned earlier. Instead of presenting herself as having three businesses—professional organizer, real estate, and skin care sales—Harriet might create a hybrid business handling all the hassles of moving—from selling the house, to finding a moving company, to coordinating the entire move.

Marketing Mistake: Lots of Visibility Without Recognizability

Maria Y. is ambitious, multitalented, and articulate. She's adept at getting media attention and publicity for her business activities. She's skilled at building trust and conveying her expertise to others in a believable way. Nonetheless, she was frustrated that while her extensive promotional activities stimulated initial interest, after people reviewed her materials and talked with her further, their interest often dropped and only occasionally turned into business.

When we met Maria, she had no idea why she wasn't achieving the success she felt she deserved. After we had scanned her promotional materials and talked with her, however, the problem was apparent to us. In one article, she was featured as an enterprising art agent working in a unique niche with aspiring clothing designers. In the next article, she was cited as a career counselor, offering advice on how to increase your chances of landing a dream job. In still other articles, she was quoted offering business-planning advice for would-be entrepreneurs. In speaking about her work, she mentioned helping companies with their marketing plans. Her business card consisted of her name and a list of services ranging from marketing consulting to copywriting.

You didn't need to talk with her for long before you became completely confused as to what she did and doubtful as to whether she would be the best person to help meet your needs.

As talented and skilled as Maria is at marketing and promoting herself, not only are her efforts producing little business; she's actually losing more business from them than she's getting. An umbrella concept such as being a professional business coach with a name like Your Business Partner or Strategic Business Decisions might help her focus and build a reputation as someone who can help start-up companies get up and going.

Marketing Masterpiece: Focusing Varied Interests

Jerry Sazevich has created an intriguing hybrid career for himself drawing upon his love of history, architecture, and community development. As a freelance architectural historian he researches the history of houses, leads architectural tours of historical areas, does genealogical research, and participates in the restoration of historic buildings. This collection of activities might have appeared somewhat scattered, but early in his business, a clever journalist with the *St. Paul Pioneer Press* dubbed him the House Detective. He's used this nickname ever since. It serves as an easy-to-remember synopsis of what he does and has helped him to get publicity and build a reputation as a leader in this unique field.

Action Steps: Getting Focused

1. Take an honest look at your business and evaluate whether or not you are sufficiently focused. Are you going in too many directions at once? Are you giving what you most want to accomplish a 100 percent effort?

2. If not, take this opportunity to review your original motives for wanting to be your own boss. Explore how you may have gotten sidetracked and why you haven't committed to one activity in which you can become well known, in demand, and sought after.

3. Ask colleagues, friends, clients, or customers to tell you what business they'd say you're in. If they have difficulty being specific or mention a variety of distinct activities, it's a sign you're not as focused as you believe you are.

4. Review your life goals and priorities and think about what focus would be most compatible with what's most important to you in life.

5. To help you decide on the one business you want to become known for, weigh your options by asking yourself:

    Which things do I do best?
    Which activities do I enjoy most?
    What do I do that people need and appreciate most?
    In what areas do I have the greatest expertise and experience?

What am I already best known for?
What do I have the best contacts to do?
What will people most readily pay me for?
What involves the least risk?
What fits best with my lifestyle and personal goals?
What comes most naturally to me?
What am I most eager to promote?

6. Make a commitment to your success by selecting a focus and begin now to devote your full efforts to that focus.

Resources: Focusing

Books

Best Home Businesses for the 90s. Paul and Sarah Edwards. New York: Tarcher/Putnam, 1995.

Finding Your Perfect Work, Making a Living Creating a Life. Paul and Sarah Edwards. New York: Tarcher/Putnam, 1996.

Focus, The Future of Your Company Depends on It. Jack Reis. New York: Harper Business, 1996.

Software

Idea Fisher. Creativity software by Idea Fisher Systems, (714) 474-8111.

MindMan, The Creative MindManager. Visualizing Ideas, P.O. Box 829, Mount Eliza, VIC 3930, Australia, +61-3 9787 6207 www. mindman.com

CHAPTER 2

Niching—Deciding What You Want to Become Known For

Examine yourself; discover where your true chance of greatness lies. Seize that chance and let no power or persuasion deter you from your task.

—Chariots of Fire

"I've belonged to my networking group for over a year now and although I attend all the meetings and have volunteered often to help out at weekly functions, I have yet to get one referral. Everyone is very friendly and they seem to like me. They just don't send me any business."

We could see the hurt and confusion in this woman's eyes despite her valiant effort to present a professional appearance and demeanor. We understood what she was experiencing all too well. She was trying not to take it personally, but inwardly she was tormented by doubts and disappointment. She could feel her dream of a more independent life slipping away, and she was wondering what she was doing wrong. We asked what type of work she did; she told us she was a bookkeeper.

We'd heard far too many similar stories. *"I'm a management consultant,"* the distinguished, well-dressed man told us. *"I have twenty-five years of experience in all areas of management training from communication skills to customer service, presentation skills and negotiation. I can also do turnaround consulting, sales skills, and business development."* He described the extensive contacts he'd made over the years working in upper management for a *Fortune* 500 company, but now his personal calls to the many names in his carefully cultivated Rolodex had led to few projects. Everyone was always very nice, very courteous, and even encouraging, but he wasn't getting business.

"This is my brochure," the event planner explained. *"I've sent out hundreds of them, but no one is calling. When I follow up by phone, no one remembers having received it."* We glanced quickly at the attractive, tasteful brochure she placed in our hands. It appeared to be expensive, probably costing far more than this woman could comfortably afford. The investment spoke well of her commitment and determination, but we could hear an edge creeping into her voice. She, too, was inwardly tormented by her inability to attract the business she needed. The brochure told us that she did event planning for companies large and small, student organizations, and individuals. "No job too small" it read.

Each of these three individuals is experienced, knowledgeable, competent; and *focused*. As you can hear, they know what business they're in: bookkeeping, management consulting, and event planning. But despite having focused their businesses and spent considerable time, effort, and money marketing, they are having difficulty getting enough business.

Based only on how they've described their businesses, if you were to meet them yourself, what would your reaction be? Imagine you're meeting them for the first time and they tell you:

"I'm a bookkeeper."

"I do event planning for large and small businesses, student organizations, and anyone giving a special party. No job is too small."

"I am a management consultant with twenty-five years of experience in all areas of management training from communication skills to customer service, cultural diversity, presentation skills, and negotiation. I also do turnaround consulting, sales skills, and business development."

Based on these introductions, do you feel a desire to do business with them? Do they inspire your trust and confidence? Would you keep their business cards? Have you started thinking about who you know who needs their services?

Unfortunately, if you were to meet these individuals, you'd probably have much the same reaction that most people do. Unless you happen to desperately need what they're offering right at this moment and have nowhere else to turn, you have probably quickly lumped these people in with the hundreds of others who provide similar services and will promptly forget about both them and what they do.

What's Wrong with This Picture?

Like too many people who become self-employed, these individuals are proudly defining themselves as being *one of a million*. What they need to be doing is letting the world know why they're *one in a million*. You can spend many dollars and invest many hours in marketing yourself, but if you don't distinguish what you do from the scores of other people who do something similar, you probably won't get the results you're seeking. You may even end up paving the way for others to get the work you were hoping to do.

So what about you? Are you presenting yourself as one ***of*** a million or one ***in*** a million? In reality you are one in many a million. As our fingerprints and DNA attest, each of us is as unique and different as snowflakes. No one of us is a replica of any other. Each of us has our own talents, abilities, and skills to contribute. Even identical twins develop their own unique identities. But when it comes to telling the world what we do, too often we lump ourselves together with all the many others who do the kind of work we do.

Like the three individuals above, we identify ourselves as someone who does bookkeeping, management consulting, event planning, word processing, editing, computer training, public relations, and so on. By thinking of ourselves and our work in this way, we're saying, "I'm one of many. You know what I do. I do what all bookkeepers, word processors, computer consultants, or public relations specialists, or whatever do." And that's exactly how we get filed away in the minds of those we could be doing business with. If we're remembered at all, we're remembered as "one of those . . ."

If you want to have plenty of work coming to you, however, you need to become known for what makes you stand out from the crowd. In reality, no two computer consultants are the same. Nor are any two word-processing services, editors, or public relations specialists. You know this firsthand if you've ever attempted to replace a valued and trusted product or service you've come to rely upon. While you can probably find other similar products or services, none is just like the other. Each has its strengths, its weaknesses, its quirks and idiosyncrasies that make it more or less the best choice for your particular needs.

So, before undertaking any further marketing, it's vital that you take the time and energy to identify what you want to become known for. What makes you distinctive? What about you stands out from the crowd? Why do people choose you? Who are you best suited to serve and why? These are the fingerprints of your work, and they help define your niche. Once you identify and begin emphasizing the things that can make you notable, you'll instantly become more memorable. You'll begin attracting the clients and customers who are most likely to be satisfied with your work, the ones who will become your most loyal customers and your best referral sources.

Here's a dramatic example of the difference having a niche can make. Marcella was a translator. A Russian immigrant, she spoke several languages fluently. She also had lined up a cadre of other translators who could work in languages she didn't speak. When Marcella opened Translations Services Unlimited, she was confident she could provide virtually any type of translation anyone needed. But, a year later, she admitted things weren't going well. Despite spending every free evening on marketing and every spare dollar on advertising, she was still working at a full-time job and had only intermittent work through her service

What baffled her most, however, was the success of her competition. Maria was a Hispanic and, although there were few Hispanics in the area, she specialized in Spanish translation and had plenty of business. In fact, many of the translators Marcella had lined up to do translations in other languages were getting work through Maria.

"Although it was a difficult decision, " Marcella reported, "I decided to scale back the plans for my business. Instead of trying to offer an array of translation services, I decided I would simply focus on my personal strength, Russian. Many Americans want to do business in Russia, so I thought this might be more realistic." The results were amazing. From the moment she began specializing, Marcella found that "often the first thing people say after I tell them that I do Russian translation is 'Oh, do you do other languages, too?'"

Before long, she had more business than she could handle. She quit her job and was subcontracting work out to other translators just as she had originally hoped. In fact, she and Maria were even referring business to each other. Ironically, instead of trying to provide all kinds of translation services for all kinds of needs, by specializing Marcella found a *niche* that opened doors to the very opportunities she'd been seeking.

YOUR GOAL
Be one in a million.

That's the paradoxical power of having a niche!

Just What Is a Niche?

Technically a *niche* is an architectural term referring to a special place that's designed to display or show off an object of some kind, like an ornament, that's placed in a recess of a wall or an arched area of a room. And that's just what a niche can be for you. Finding your niche will set you off from others who do something similar and draw the best possible attention to you and what you can offer.

The term *niche* is also used in the field of ecology, referring to the function, role, or position an organism has in its community or as part of the whole. And once again, that's what a niche can be for you: work that's so ideally suited to you that it seems almost like your calling in life, your personal role in the scheme of things. Finding such a niche is like having your own special corner of the world, your own place in the marketplace that's custom-tailored to you. Your niche will look, and sound, and feel like right where you belong.

Some people have such a highly unique focus for their work that they've essentially already created a niche of their own. For example, Florence Feldman-Wood is the Spinning Wheel Sleuth. She tracks down unusual spinning wheels and publishes information about them in her newsletter. She teaches spinning and weaving, speaks on textiles, and has created a specialized registry service to link fiber and fabric enthusiasts. This is her focus and her niche.

Del Howison and Sue Duncan have both been fascinated by horror movies, comics, and books all their lives. They've turned that passion into Dark Delicacies, a catalog of horror gifts, books, and other paraphernalia. "It's our niche," Del says. And he adds, not surprisingly, "We're scared to death, but we're having a great time!"

B. C. LaBelle describes herself as a prairie preservationist. Seeing that the prairie lands around her home in rural Nebraska are in sore need of repair, LaBelle plants community prairie gardens and creates prairie art from elements of nature like dried grass and wildflowers. Through her work, which has earned her a national conservation award, she helps to increase people's awareness of the beauty and importance of American prairies.

These are just a few examples of the many unique careers people can design for themselves when they become self-employed. Such "boutique" businesses are, in fact, a "niche."

But what if the work you do is more conventional? What if it seems as if you *are* one of many? There are lots of bookkeepers, computer consultants, word-processing services, editors, writers, and so forth. But that doesn't mean you can't find your niche. Consider this: While there are many word-processing services in most communities, there are not many others like Janis Uhley's Top Drawer Writer's Service. Jan's specializes in typing and preparing television scripts and screenplays. Having a performance background herself, Uhley is no ordinary typist. She edits and adds creative input and knows how to deal with the tight schedules directors, producers, and screenwriters have. She works with them from preproduction through revisions and filming. She can turn around a script in ten to twelve hours.

There may be hundreds of bookkeeping services in a given area, but there are few like Chellie Campbell's. Chellie sees herself as being in the business of financial stress reduction. She not only provides bookkeeping services; she also teaches her clients about how their attitudes toward money directly affect whether they have enough of it or not. You can think of Chellie as a therapist for your bank balance.

There is a growing number of information researchers, but few, if any other, like Jennifer Polhemus. She analyzes litigation, then produces a report with tables, charts, graphics, and written summaries for attorneys. And while there are many computer consultants, there are not many in a given community like Kyle Roth. He installs computer systems for law offices.

Yes, there are many management consultants, too, but there is none other like K. C. Truby, who is known as the Lonesome Cowboy. K. C. provides marketing consulting to accountants during the winter, and during the summer he conducts Wild West Marketing seminars for them on his dude ranch in Fort Casper, Wyoming.

In talking with successfully self-employed individuals, we have invariably found many such interesting specialties. We're continually amazed at the rich variety of niches people have carved out for themselves. It seems that indeed there are as many possible niches as there are snowflakes, fingerprints, or DNA molecules. And once you've found your own niche, it will become infinitely easier to get business coming to you.

Why You Need a Niche

Most successful self-employed individuals offer a highly specialized product or service to a particular market segment or niche that no one else, or few others, is adequately serving. They don't do general management consulting; for example, they consult to the fashion industry on collection problems. They don't have a general billing service; they do billing for anesthesiologists. They don't do public relations; they do public relations for multimedia Internet companies or environmentally conscious businesses. Or perhaps they have a temporary agency exclusively for design professionals or escrow officers.

But why do those who are the most successful seem to specialize almost instinctively? Actually, self-employed individuals niche for the same reasons brothers and sisters usually cultivate distinctive niches within a family: in order to participate and win the attention they need to grow and develop. Within a family, one sibling, for example, might become the "smart" one; while another becomes "the athlete," and still another becomes "the entertainer." One child might identify strongly with the mother, while the other identifies with the father. This phenomenon of family niching is well documented.

In his book *Born to Rebel: Birth Order, Family Dynamics, Creative Lives,* Frank J. Sulloway relates one of the most dramatic stories of "family niche picking" we've heard. In Ralph Nader's family, during adolescence Nader and his three siblings agreed to divide up their studies of the world to minimize direct competition with one another. The eldest brother, Shafeed, undertook studying the United States and Canada. The second sibling, Claire, specialized in studying the Middle East. The third sibling, Laura, selected Mexico and Latin America. Nader, the youngest, chose to study China and the Far East.

As Sulloway points out, children do such selective niching, albeit usually much more subconsciously than the Naders, because it provides certain distinctive advantages: First, given differences in age, younger children will typically lag behind their older siblings in developing similar skills; so to the extent that they can cultivate different skills, younger children can minimize negative comparisons with older siblings. Second, to the extent that children differ in their abilities, parents will find it more difficult to make comparisons. And third, novel abilities not already mastered by other family members make each child a more valued and appreciated family member.

In the business world, niching works in a similar fashion. Why do you suppose Marcella's translation service didn't take off until she decided to specialize? Well, before specializing she wasn't drawing the attention she needed. She wasn't coming out well in comparison with her more niched colleague. Her services weren't perceived as being as valuable (although in actuality, as her later experience showed, they were equally valuable). And because she was trying to offer all types of translation, her competition was less inclined to share business with her.

Here is a summary of the key reasons why whatever stage your business is in, if you want to get business coming to you, you should make it a point to identify your special niche.

• ***Stand Out from the Crowd in a Memorable Way.*** Just as no one leaf stands out in a pile of similarly colored leaves, so it is that no one individual will stand out among many others who are perceived as doing the same kind of work. If you want people to respond to your brochures, take your phone calls, and remember you from networking events—if you want them to seek you out—you have to be perceived as special, not just another interchangeable worker who can be called in or disposed of based on whoever's available or who will work for the cheapest price.

As increasing numbers of people are working on their own and companies are relying more on "contingent workers," it's all the more vital for you to distinguish yourself from the flood of temps, part-timers, contract employees, freelancers, and others who are looking for work. And the best way to distinguish yourself from the crowd is to become known as a *specialist,* someone who's valued for the expertise you've gained through devoting yourself to meeting particular needs of particular clients and customers in particular circumstances. That's precisely what establishing and working in a niche of your own makes possible.

Just think, for example, about your reaction to the following individuals:

GENERALISTS	SPECIALISTS
"I'm a chiropractor. I do general chiropractic . . . my patients are anyone with a back!"	*"You know how many people these day are suffering from stress-related injuries? Well, I'm a chiropractor and I specialize in stress-related aches and pains."*
"I'm a freelance photographer. I can take pictures of just about anything."	*"You know how a lot of families like to have a portrait taken of the entire family? Well, I'm a portrait photographer and I specialize in family portraits that capture the way a family wants to be remembered at a particular time in life."*

"I'm an architect. I do all kinds of projects, residential and commercial, large and small."

"You know how expensive buying a new home has become these days? Well, I'm an architect and I specialize in remodeling projects that enable people to turn their existing home into their dream home."

Which of these people are you most likely to remember? If you needed any of these services, which ones would you be more likely to contact? Whose cards might you keep? As you read these introductions, does anyone come to your mind who could use their services? Can you imagine yourself referring business to any of these people? Which ones?

We've asked hundreds of people questions like these and reactions are uniform throughout the country. Upon hearing the generalist descriptions, people respond with comments like this:

"Too general. Lots of people do that."

"Sounds like they're hungry for business."

"I wonder how good they are."

"I get a sense maybe they're just starting out or still finding their way."

"I'd rather do business with someone more specialized, someone who knows more about what I need."

Uniformly people respond positively, however, to those who are more specialized, making comments like these:

"This person really seems to know what she's talking about."

"This person piques my interest."

"I'll remember this person."

"This hits a nerve. I could use that service."

"I can think of lots of people who need that."

These comments demonstrate why it's so important to decide here and now what you want to specialize in, where your best contribution lies, so you can become known for that kind of work and get business coming to you. That's exactly what architect Don Carter discovered when he went out on his own. Having previously worked at a large firm, Carter knew he could do all kinds of projects, residential or commercial, large or small, so he planned to do them all. But getting business was much more difficult than he had imagined, especially since the Southern California area where he lived was just going into what would be a deep and long recession.

We advised Don to do some deep soul-searching to identify what his favorite projects are and what type of client or customer he felt more interested and qualified to serve. Actually the answer was right in the front of his mind. He has a special ability to envision how an existing structure can be transformed to resemble the ideal structure his client would prefer, but can't afford. This led Carter directly to his niche: turning existing homes into the owner's dream home. And from that point on, marketing his business has become both easier and more effective.

Turnarounds like this are not surprising once you decide to niche. Most people clearly prefer to do business with someone who's a specialist, someone who's made a commitment to truly understand and master serving particular problems and needs. We all want to feel confident that those we do business with know what they're doing from firsthand experience in helping others like us. We look for and seek out specialists, experts, and authorities.

- ***Know to Whom, Where, and How to Best Spread the Word.*** "I'd like to start a desktop publishing business," one woman wrote to us. "I could work with just about anyone, but I don't know where to begin." Clearly she felt bad about herself and her inability to get under way. But, it wasn't her ability that was lacking. Of course, she didn't know where to begin. You can't know where to begin as long as your focus is on working with *anyone*. But once you define precisely who you're most interested in and best suited to serve, almost as if by magic, you'll have an idea about where to begin.

Defining your niche helps you define whom you want to reach, where you will find them, and what you'll need to do to attract their business more quickly and inexpensively. In an effort to get more business, the management consultant we described earlier was running from one networking group to another, attending a small business conference here, sending a newsletter to major industries there, speaking on presentation skills here and negotiations skills there. He felt exhausted and frustrated that no one seemed to remember him or take him seriously. Basically he was scattering his time, money, and resources to the wind in the hope that someone, somewhere, would respond. But by specializing in one type of clientele, as K. C. Truby has done in deciding to work with accountants, and by selecting one aspect of management for which he can become known like marketing, he can better focus his efforts where they will be most effective.

Imagine, for example that you plan to do medical billing for "any" health professional who needs some kind of billing done. Like the general management consultant above, you'll need to reach out to lots of different kinds of professionals, each with different needs, each turning to different sources for information about where to get help. And you'll have other obstacles to overcome as well.

First, you'll have a credibility gap to fill. You'll have to somehow convince a variety of professionals that you have sufficient expertise and knowledge in each of their specialties to understand their problems and meet their needs. But, in addition, reaching such a wide range of professionals will be costly and time-consuming, because they read different journals, turn to different directories and referral sources, and network through different organizations.

If, on the other hand, you decide to specialize in doing billing for physical therapists and orthopedic surgeons, then your task of becoming known and sought after is much simpler. These two professions refer frequently to each other. They work with similar patients who have similar problems and circumstances. They read journals on similar subjects and participate in similar organizations. What you learn in becoming a specialist serving each of these groups will help you become familiar with the needs and problems of the other. Having a good reputation with one will help you earn the respect of the other.

As massage and aroma therapist Janice Kinzer of Graver Beach, California, found out, by serving a niche, you also have a far easier time finding and reaching people who will be ready and willing to do business with you. While it might have been tempting for Kinzer to focus on serving anyone who gets stressed out by life's ups and downs, she realized that trying to reach such a broad group would require greater marketing and advertising efforts than she could afford. So, instead, she chose to serve a very select group. She created Bridal Home Spa, a specialty service catering to brides and their bridal parties.

Her business specializes in helping brides look and feel great on their wedding day through relaxation and relief of prewedding jitters. She offers special wedding party discounts for bridesmaids and other guests. She takes her equipment to homes and hotels so that even using her service is stress-free. And although her clientele is limited at any one time, it is a constantly renewing one and newlyweds can continue using her services after they're married.

This niche enables Kinzer to: 1) target her services to specific needs she can build a reputation for serving; 2) know immediately who, how, where, and when to find customers; and 3) keep her marketing costs down to a bare minimum. In other words, by niching, you can send one clear and consistent message about what you can offer to those who most need to hear it, and you can more easily reach them at the precise time and place they need you. This will be especially true the better known you become for your niche.

• ***Turn Your Competitors into Colleagues and Referral Sources.*** When I, Sarah, began practicing psychotherapy, I was dismayed to discover the large number of other psychotherapists in my community. Not only were there hundreds of psychiatrists, psychologists, clinical social workers, and marriage and family counselors all seeking clients to serve, but many of them were also using the very same specialized psychological techniques and modalities I was using.

What was I to do? How was I ever going to compete with all these other therapists? Although I didn't realize it at the time, I solved the problem by finding a niche where I could shine, a place in the crowded field where I could distinguish myself from all the other therapists in the area. I decided to specialize in working with children.

At that time, there were no other Transactional Analysis/Gestalt therapists in my community who would work with children. But I had seven years of experience working in child-development programs, and I had a young son at home who I was already teaching to use TA concepts to understand his behavior and our family interactions.

From the moment that I made this decision to specialize, suddenly I no longer had any competition. Instead I had a slew of referral sources. The very therapists who had been my competitors were glad to know there was someone available to see the children of their clients who needed treatment. I now could be their colleague. Just as once Marcella began specializing in Russian translation, she could refer business back and forth with Maria, I could now refer parents of my clients to my colleagues and they could refer children of clients to me. And, that's precisely how I built my practice.

So, why fight and battle over who gets the biggest piece of pie when you can bake you own and have it all while everyone else is enjoying theirs?

• ***Generate More Referrals.*** When you have a specialty or niche, not only are colleagues and competitors more comfortable referring to you, but it also becomes easier for everyone you contact to refer to you more easily. A chiropractor, for example, who specializes in stress-related aches and pains or in ergonomic problems will more likely come to mind whenever someone he meets later encounters a friend, colleague, or acquaintance who is suffering from such problems. When someone complains at lunch about needing to send a clever gift, a gift basket company that specializes in chocolate pizzas will be more likely to come up in conversation than a company that does generic gift baskets for anyone who needs one.

So why not get other people to spread the word for you by making what you do so precise and appealing that whenever someone needs what you offer, you're the one who immediately comes to mind?

• ***Command a Better Price.*** Most people want to get the best possible price for whatever they buy. It's human nature. But when we're talking with a specialist, an expert, or an authority, we naturally expect to pay more. And, if we can, we will do so, as long as we believe we're truly getting something special. We recently experienced this firsthand.

While walking through an art store in Taos, New Mexico, we observed an especially beautiful hand-carved buffalo. We asked the price, hoping it would be reasonable. But as the clerk began telling us about the artist who made it, we grew apprehensive, certain it would cost far more than we wanted to pay. She told us about how he specialized in a particular technique his grandfather had pioneered and how this technique created the special glazed appearance that made it so beautiful and unusual. She described the process involved in creating the stunning finish, how long it took and the many steps involved. When she finally told us how much it was, although the price was more than we would have ever imagined paying, it was clearly an excellent value and we happily took it home with us where it sits today in its own special niche in our living room.

By carving out a niche for yourself, as this artist has done, you can become known for your expertise and experience and as you focus more narrowly on your specialty, you'll have the opportunity to learn even more about it so you can perfect and refine your skills and abilities. As your experience and expertise grow with each new client, what you can offer becomes ever more valuable. So, by specializing, you won't need to work for pennies. You won't need to feel tempted to undercut your prices in order to compete. And the more experience you have over the years, the easier it will be to command still-higher prices, if you desire, because you'll be doing a better and better job and your reputation will grow accordingly.

• ***Do More Meaningful, Fulfilling Work.*** Finally, we've been talking primarily about how niching makes it easier to become known so you can get business coming to you, but there is actually a deeper, more profound benefit to niching. Inwardly, most of us are yearning to do more meaningful work—meaningful in the sense of feeling that what you do matters. For some, this means improving the lives of other people. For others, it means improving things around them or making a contribution to their field of work. For still others, it means leaving behind a unique legacy in the form of a body of work. By developing, applying, and honing the capabilities we each possess, we give our work meaning. With meaning come purpose and the ability to feel a sense of importance about what we do for a living,

The process of finding your niche provides the opportunity to discover such meaning and find where you can make your greatest contribution. It calls upon you to uncover your talents, your interests, your callings, and desires to find work you can devote yourself to. By working from such a deep commitment, you may not even feel as though you're working. You'll be excited and motivated both to market what you do and to do it even better. Your success can become self-perpetuating. You'll experience the gratification of knowing that you're making a positive difference in the lives of those you serve. And, even with all the invariable hassles, your work will provide you with the sense that you're fulfilling your destiny.

When researcher Dr. Barrie Yeager spoke with self-employed individuals in writing *The Meaning of Work among the Self-Employed,* she found they frequently described their work in the kind of glowing terms more often used to describe enriching leisure activities. Here are a few examples:

"It's a lot of fun."

"It's a way to find out how big a person I am."

"It's a way to see what I'm made of."

"It's a way for me to serve other people."

"It's my connection to the world."

"It's fulfilling."

"There're not enough hours in the day to have that much of a good time."

"It involves my soul."

"It's exhilarating."

"It really is a great feeling."

"There's a lot of personal satisfaction."

"It doesn't feel like work; it seem more like fun."

What better to become known and sought after for than something that feels this good? And when working feels this good, even otherwise less appealing aspects of being your own boss like marketing and administrative activities become easier and more pleasurable, too.

Why People Don't Niche

Even though finding a niche has so many advantages, many people, nonetheless, resist the idea of niching. Or they fudge a bit on defining their niche, saying something like "Well, I work primarily with lawyers, but I'll also do work for anyone who . . ." Of course, such hedging of your bets negates the value of niching. It's like an eraser that says "Here's what I do, but not really." It's also indicative of how hard deciding to commit to a niche can be sometimes. Here are several of the most tempting reasons you might become niche-resistant and how to overcome them:

- ***Niching Seems Harder.*** The greatest fear of niching is that by narrowing down as tightly as possible what you do and for whom you do it, you will have fewer people to draw upon and therefore fewer people to work with. But, in reality, as we've already indicated, the opposite is true. As long as the niche you have chosen has enough potential customers, the more specialized your business is, the more people will be able to recognize the benefit of what you can offer them. And the more business you'll get coming to you.

So, niching is counterintuitive. While it seems that the more people or industries you serve, the easier it will be to get more business, as we saw in Marcella's situation, for self-employed individuals that's usually not the case. Paradoxically, the more you specialize, the easier it becomes to get more business. So, in order to commit to your niche, you

WAYS TO CARVE OUT A NICHE

Here are a few examples of many combinations of ways you can define what you do and for whom to find a niche:

Where You Work	West Side, East Side, MacArthur Park, Kansas City, California, mobile van, on client's site, via modem, fax, or phone.
Whom You Work With	Children, adults, elderly, men, women, smokers, overeaters, joggers, dog lovers, brides, widows, small businesses, midsize businesses, *Fortune* 500 companies, magicians, sports fans, single parents, two-career couples, ethnic groups, religious groups, collectors.
The Industry You Work In	Health, construction, law, real estate, banking, insurance, medicine, sports, entertainment, tourism, restaurants, banks, beauty salons.
When You Work	At all hours, overnight, fast turnaround, on call, weekends, evenings, for certain life events (e.g., birth, marriage, divorce, death, retirement), at special occasions like conferences or parties.
The Problem You Address	Collections, employee turnover, cash-flow management, drug abuse, having too little time, allergies, PMS, repair, maintenance, marketing, customer relations, training.
The Media You Work In	One-on-one consultations, seminars, books, tapes, telephone, newsletters, video, speeches, products, on-line, mail order, radio, or television.

may have to suspend your disbelief. You may need to resist the temptation to say "I work with anyone."

Usually the smaller and more clearly defined your niche the better. Dr. James St. Ville of Phoenix, Arizona, for example, is an orthopedic surgeon with a very tightly defined niche. He specializes in treating retired professional athletes. While this is indeed a small population, Phoenix is a popular retirement area for professional athletes, and a high percentage of them have serious chronic orthopedic problems, so Dr. St. Ville has ample patients in need of his services.

Of course, a niche can be too small to provide the level of income

Mixing and Matching to Expand or Narrow Your Niche

You can mix and match the elements of a niche to make it more or less specialized. For example,

- **A newsletter** on practice management for medical professionals could be narrowed to become a newsletter on marketing for plastic surgeons in California or expanded to serve health professions nationwide.
- **A graphic-design service** for small business could be narrowed to serve public relations firms in South Florida or expanded to women-owned small businesses in the Southeast.
- **A legal transcription service** could be narrowed to provide after-hours services for litigators via modem or broadened to twenty-four-hour turnaround for all law firms in Bolling Brook, USA.
- **A mobile pet grooming service** could be narrowed by specializing in grooming poodles for dog shows or broadened by serving pets in a given metropolitan area.
- **A video production company** could narrow its niche by specializing in video production for the entertainment industry in Southern California or broaden its niche by providing multimedia production for high-tech businesses on the West Coast.

you need. So, if that's your fear, the solution is not to try to serve "everyone," but instead to broaden your niche just enough to provide an ample pool of specific customers or clients you can draw upon. You can do this by expanding slightly on whom you serve, what you offer, where you offer it, or how you offer it.

For example, if doing medical billing for orthopedic surgeons is too small a niche in your community, you can maintain the integrity of your niche by serving orthopedic surgeons in nearby communities. You could do billing via modem and expand even further geographically. Or you could expand your customer base to serve other biomedical professionals like physical therapists and chiropractors.

Any such approach would be preferable to abandoning or diluting your niche. Here's an example of why. We've watched three health-food bakeries in our area close their doors during this last year after compromising the integrity of their niche. All three started out specializing in low-fat, health-conscious desserts and other delicacies. But none of them were attracting the number of walk-in customers they needed, so gradually they began adding coffees, breakfasts, lunches, and more conventional bakery goods. The more they moved away from serving their "health-conscious" niche, instead of seeing an increase in business, their business dropped off even further. They began to lose the core customers they had already attracted, and they were attracting few new health-conscious customers now that what they offered was so diverse. The general public, on the other hand, didn't find their quasi–health-conscious foods appealing either.

Instead of moving away from their niche, the owners of these bakeries needed to find more innovative ways to expand serving their niche. They could, for example, have sold not only retail but also wholesale to health-food stores and healthy restaurants. They could have taken samples to the offices of cardiologists and other doctors whose patients need to be on restricted diets. They could have sold a healthy cookbook of their most popular recipes, held classes on healthy cooking at their facility, sold gift baskets through hospital gift shops or health-food stores filled with their healthy bakery goods for people recovering from lifestyle-related life-threatening illnesses. They could have created a mail-order catalog or Internet site directed at people who live in smaller communities that can't support a healthy bakery. And so forth.

Some people can serve several niches, but if you take this route, it's important to handle each one with virtually the same care and attention you would give to a single niche. And it will be helpful to find an "umbrella" or unifying concept under which to define and describe what you do (see chapter 1; page 19). Of course, having more than one niche will also take more time, energy, and money. So usually it's best to get yourself established soundly in one before spinning off into others.

Usually, if you don't have enough business, the solution is not to abandon your niche but to capitalize on it still further by serving it more broadly, better, more effectively, or more creatively.

• ***Niching Seems Limiting.*** When I, Sarah, was deciding to specialize in treating children with psychological problems, I was afraid at first that by narrowing myself to such a small niche I would end up working only with children. I was interested in working with lots of different types of people, and I didn't want to lose the chance to work with others whom I could help. Many people feel the way I did when they decide to go out on their own.

When two personnel managers left their jobs at a large department store, for example, they decided to form a partnership that drew upon all their skills. They didn't want to have to choose among the many things that interested them, so they settled upon a general-purpose consulting practice doing training, consulting, marketing, and personal coaching. But they found marketing this business to be difficult. They resorted to having several separate brochures and sending out monthly mailings that emphasized different aspects of their business each month. But these tactics didn't create any greater interest. If anything, potential clients were more confused than ever as to why they'd want to do business with these two women.

A poet made a similar mistake. She wanted to earn her living selling poetry, but fearing she wouldn't be able to earn enough money in this field, she created a business card that listed everything she could do including singing, calligraphy, selling gift items, and coordinating parties, in addition to writing poetry. Needless to say, not only were others confused about what she did, but she herself also became confused about how she should describe what she did. To overcome this confusion she developed a pat answer, "It depends on which hat I'm wearing." Of course, most people weren't interested in helping her find the right hat for them.

We all have a variety of multifaceted interests, talents, and skills. We don't want to be limited to doing the same thing with the same people over and over again day after day. We want to have varied and novel experiences. But just because you establish a niche doesn't mean you can't do a variety of things or serve different types of people. In fact, if you recall, Marcella got more business translating in other languages after she decided to specialize in Russian. This is another paradox about niching. By the very act of specializing, we make ourselves more valuable and appealing to people in general and thus we're able to do more interesting and varied things.

As I, Sarah, became known as a specialist in working with children, for example, soon people wanted to know if I would work with adolescents. And indeed, I got many such referrals and found working with adolescents greatly rewarding. In addition, my work with children often required me to work with the entire family system. Also, some of the parents I worked with would refer other adults they knew to me. Sometimes I would pass these referrals on to other therapists I felt could better serve them, and other times I would work with them myself. Soon my specialty expanded to include dealing with all types of childhood issues, and I was actually seeing more adults than children, working with them to resolve early childhood traumas.

So, rarely does specializing actually have to limit whom you work with or what you do. It simply gives you a doorway, or a niche, through which people can get to know you, trust you, and see what an excellent job you can do. The solution is not to give up your varied interests and skills, but rather to focus your interests on a specialized platform where you can showcase and apply your various skills. The personnel managers, for example, might form a business called Boutique Management Services, providing a wide variety of personnel functions for clothing stores that are too small to have their own personnel department. The poet, on the other hand, might focus her business by becoming Lyrics for Love's Special Occasions, creating invitations, songs, and poems for ceremonies and events like weddings, engagement parties, anniversaries, and bridal showers.

When Larry Barnett completed graduate school and began his video production business, he started marketing to restaurant chains, because although he had never done a professional video project, he had worked his way through school as a manager for a fast-food chain. This experience qualified him to produce his first small low-budget video for a restaurant's training film. This project gave him the experience he needed to find additional clients in the field, and as his experience and reputation grew, each restaurant project he did made it easier to obtain the next one.

Although he was interested in providing many different production functions to many different industries, he avoided the temptation to try being all things to all people. Instead he found that by sticking to his niche of doing commercial films for the restaurant industry, his projects became increasingly challenging and interesting. As his reputation grew still further, he began doing specialty productions and before long other related industries were also seeking him out.

• ***Niching Requires Taking a Stand.*** Often people resist niching because they're afraid to commit to one course of action. As a woman once told us, "I want to be able to roll with the punches. If I settle in on a niche, it may be the wrong choice. I may decide later I want to do something else." Being able to roll with the punches is, indeed, most important in this age of rapid change. But again, paradoxically, you can usually move more swiftly and effectively by taking a stand about who you are and what you do than you can as someone who's an undefined and unknown member of a general pool of people who do something similar.

For example, Tom and Nancy Nickle wanted to start a medical billing company working with doctors and hospitals, but business was slow. Nonetheless, Tom was continuing to pursue this goal when, at a networking event, someone asked him, "Well, if you do billing for doctors, can you also do it for freight departments?" He said yes and before long, based on referrals from this new client, he had all the business he could handle working with freight departments. Suddenly he had a new, thriving niche!

So, sometimes declaring a niche serves as a springboard for what will become your ultimate niche. We've often found you have to take a stand and begin walking down a certain path or you'll never see the appealing opportunities around the corners that lie ahead.

Action Steps: Do You Have a Niche?

Set aside some time to reflect on whether you have a clear and defined niche that you truly enjoy and want to become well known for. Here are several steps you can take to facilitate such reflection:

- Do you have a specialty now or are you hedging your bets? Be honest. Do you think you're specialized but actually you're trying to get whatever work anyone will give you?
- Test yourself: If you can't tell someone what you do in ten seconds or less, odds are you have yet to clearly define your niche. If you can't explain it, people won't understand it and if they don't understand it, they won't remember it. If they don't remember it, they won't call you. Here are a few examples of how you can describe a clearly defined niche in ten seconds or under:

I pack artwork for shipping so it will arrive safely.

I keep law libraries up to date.

I train employees to better appreciate cultural diversity.

I help retail shops attract more customers to malls.

I provide medical care for ill travelers.

I create menus for restaurants.

I develop ride-sharing programs for city and county transportation departments.

I help doctors join group practices.

I design kitchens for gourmet chefs.

I conduct environmental-impact studies for commercial real estate developers.

I help recover funds for burned investors. I write healing music.

- Set aside time to assess how you feel personally about the idea of finding and committing to a niche.
- Do you agree that you have unique qualities, skills, and abilities you can bring to your work?
- If so, when or how did you discover them? Have you always known about them or have you only recently acquired or become aware of them?
- If you don't think of yourself as having unique qualities, how do you feel about the possibility that you have special qualities you're overlooking? Could you entertain the possibility that you do? Or might there be latent abilities you're yearning to develop? Choosing a niche can provide an opportunity for you to do that.

Finding Your Niche

Finding a niche means clearly identifying a group of people who need a particular product or service you're distinctively able to provide. Your niche needs to be small enough that you don't have much competition and can reach most of your potential clients within the limits of your time and budget, yet large enough to include ample clients and customers you can support yourself and your business by serving. Chip Morgan, for example, has found the right balance: he provides full-service design and construction management for radio-station owners who are remodeling or building new facilities. Although there are fewer than one hundred such stations in the country at any time, that's more than enough to keep Morgan busy.

While cleaning her carpet, Cynthia Butcher realized that the fumes from the cleanser were making her dizzy. She figured other people might have sensitivities to commercial cleaning products, too. So she started Cynthia's Clean Team, providing a specialized cleaning service using only nontoxic, homemade, and biodegradable cleaning products. To succeed in this niche, she doesn't need everyone to use her service. She only needs about fifteen steady environmentally sensitive customers a week to do just fine.

Often, finding a niche of the right size to fit your needs is a matter of matching your education or specific job experience to the needs of a particular industry. But it can also be based on a lifelong interest, or hobby, or even a personal tragedy. For example, computer programmer and consultant David Brace's daughter suffered a serious brain injury. In helping her recover, David developed the software for computer-based therapy for brain-trauma patients. This has led to his developing a programming specialty working on projects that retrain accident victims with brain traumas.

We each have or can develop our own unique qualifications such as these. Finding them is a matter of relating experiences from your personal history to people's current needs, then building new experiences that make you even better qualified to meet those needs. In fact, it's at the crossroads of such experiences where you'll most likely find your ideal niche.

Head for the Crossroads

Your ideal niche will lie at the crossroads where your interests and assets intersect with opportunities you have to meet real-life needs around you. Over the years, we've noticed how successfully self-employed individuals invariably find such areas of overlap. They find an overlap of their desires, their assets, and their opportunities. We call the process of combining these three things ***matrixing***, and it provides a formula for finding your niche:

MATRIX FORMULA

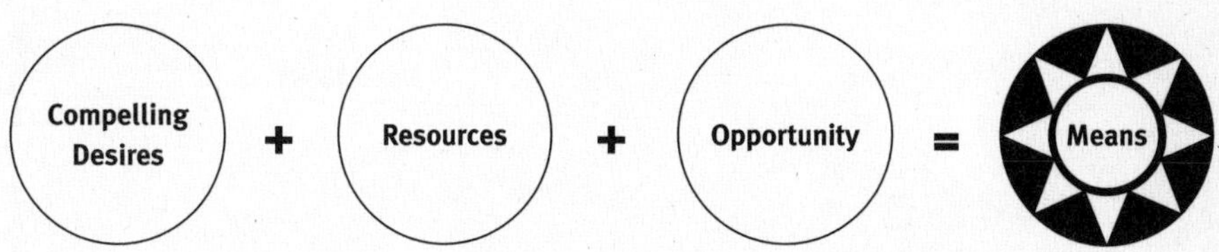

- *Compelling Desires:* the things in life you feel most passionate about, interested in, or concerned for
- *Personal Resources:* your background, experiences, contacts, and other assets
- *Opportunities:* problems, needs, and desires people are willing to pay you to address

We've written extensively about ***matrixing*** in our book ***Finding Your Perfect Work.*** It doesn't matter, however, whether you're already in business or are just starting to look for what type of work you want to do on your own; the process of defining your niche remains the same. Here's an example:

A bodyguard loved photography. It was his passion, but he rarely had time to pursue it and clearly wasn't good enough yet to earn a living from it. So, in looking for his niche, he wanted to combine his skills as a bodyguard with his as yet undeveloped interest in photography. He also had his experience as an emergency medical technician during military service to draw upon. While there are many possibilities for combining these interests and assets, the niche he's carved out for himself is accompanying world-class photographers on dangerous, remote location photo shoots. It's an ideal match because not only can he protect his clients, he can also care for them should they be injured, and best of all for him, he is learning the secrets of photography from the world's best!

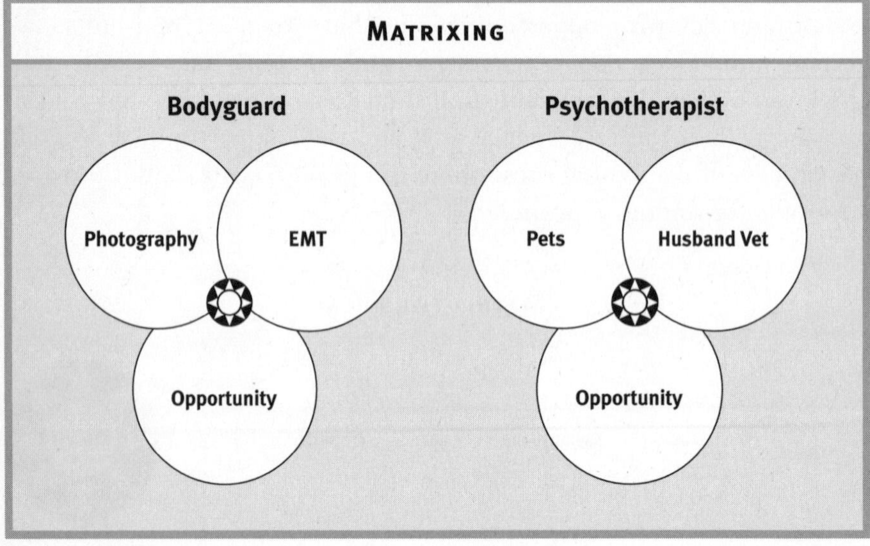

A psychotherapist in private practice was experiencing the tightening of the mental health field when she stumbled upon her niche. Her husband is a veterinarian and they both love animals. She understands personally the pain and desperation people can feel when they lose a beloved pet, so now she specializes in providing bereavement counseling for grieving pet owners. That's her niche and, believe it or not, she has more clients than she did before she decided to specialize.

These are just two of hundreds of matrixing examples profiled in ***Finding Your Perfect Work.*** Here are a few of many other favorites we've discovered since then:

Keith Previte has found his niche by focusing his barber shop on his passion for sports. Yes, he opened The Upper Cuts, a barbershop for sports lovers. The wood floor of the salon looks like a basketball court. The walls are decorated with murals of major sports figures in action. And, of course, a television at every chair provides live broadcasts via satellite of a variety of sports events from hockey to baseball games. And surprisingly, Previte reports that 20 percent of his clients are women sports fans.

There are many personal fitness trainers in Los Angeles, but Cherly Anker-Agata is one of a kind. She's found her niche. An avid traveler and runner, former paralegal Anker-Agata started her unique home business, Off 'N Running Tours, after returning from a vacation where she wished there were local trainers who could take her on guided runs through the streets of Greek cities. So now what she does is create customized runs through scenic side streets for people visiting L.A. She plans out the running route, serves as a running partner for her clients, and provides them with a runner's breakfast of fruit, water, and a bagel.

Freelance writer Megan Edwards and her partner, Mark Sedenquist, are using their professional skills to pursue their wanderlust travel. They publish a newsletter and provide an on-line publication called *Roadtrip America,* which features the novelties of the smallest and most obscure towns in America. They developed this niche after taking a six-month sabbatical on the road with their dog and realizing that they didn't want to stop traveling .

Psychotherapist Gary Soloman has also found a unique niche. He's the "Movie Doctor." Combining his knowledge and experience as a clinical social worker with his interest in movies, he's created a novel approach to helping people heal personal problems: he writes them a prescription to see a movie. Although he never suggests that viewing videos replaces crisis counseling, he believes in the healing power of drama. His slogan is "A picture is worth a thousand sessions." In his private practice, he's had ample opportunity to demonstrate that movies are naturally therapeutic tools. Now he has also written *The Motion Picture Prescription,* volumes one and two, in which he prescribes over four hundred movies as tools for healing psychological challenges in life such as alcoholism or abuse.

Janice Porter-Moffitt has drawn upon her love of literature and her experience doing outside events for bookstores to create a unique mobile business. She travels across the country in her van filled with over three hundred books. She sets up tables outside coffeehouses, fairs, and festivals and offers her books at cut-rate prices to people who'd like to read while sipping lattés and cappuccinos.

Rosita Latham has created an "exercise ministry." An ordained minister in Youth Action for Christ, Latham began this ministry in her garage. She teaches exercise, fitness, health, and nutrition using faith, prayer, and spiritual music. This ministry arose from personal experience. Only five foot five, Latham saw her weight balloon up to 215 pounds after the birth of her last child, but through applying her faith and what she learned about exercise and fitness, she regained her health, self-esteem, and strength. Now she's found her niche by helping others do the same. She says, "When you feel good about yourself, you can do more work for the Lord and be a better person."

Jeffrey Mitchell, a paramedic turned psychologist, has become one of the leading experts on emergency-related stress management. Through his Maryland-based institute, the International Critical Incident Stress Foundation, he's trained rescue workers in more than three hundred communities in how to handle the emotional stress of extreme crises like the 1995 bombing of the Oklahoma City government building.

Action Steps: Exploring Possible Niches

No matter what product or services you now provide, you can carve out a niche by finding the unique overlap of your own interests and passions, your experience, background, contacts, and other resources, and what people need and will pay for. To experiment with finding a variety of possible niches to explore, answer the following questions:

1. Your Desires: Interests, Passions, and Concerns

- What aspects of your work do you find most interesting, appealing, and challenging?
- What type of clients or customers do you most enjoy working with?
- What hobbies, pastimes, and other interests do you enjoy?
- What problems or injustices do you see that you feel compelled to make right? How would you make the world a better place?
- What do you wish you could do more of for your clients and customers?

2. *Your Assets: Background, Experience, and Contacts*

- What kind of things do you do best? What do people compliment you on most frequently? What do others often ask you to help them with?
- Who needs such things most?
- How can you provide that product or service in a way that will give you a chance to draw upon your other interests?
- What industries or types of companies do you have contacts and experience in?
- Whom do you know who needs what you offer or who knows of other people who need it?
- What jargon or industry-specific acronyms, problems, legislation, or technicalities are you most familiar with?

3. *Your Opportunities: Needs People Have and Will Pay For*

- What do you hear your clients and customers, or those around you, complaining about?
- What problems do you see them having? What mistakes do you see them making?
- What trends will be affecting your clients and customers or those around you? What opportunities could these trends provide? What problems are or will these trends be posing for your clients and customers? How could you help?
- What new technology is affecting your clients and customers or those around you? What opportunities could it provide to them? What problems might new technology present for your clients and customers or others you know? How could you help them make the most of these developments?
- What new legislation will be affecting your clients and customers or those around you? What opportunities does this new legislation present? What problems or challenges does it pose? How could you help?

Finding the Intersections

Now, begin mixing and matching to find overlaps between your answers to these questions until you find several possible niches you'd like to consider. To discover various possibilities, draw a circle to represent one of your interests and passions; then draw an overlapping circle to represent some aspect of your background, experience, or contacts; then draw a third circle to represent one of the opportunities you see around you.

Matrixing

Finding the overlap of your desires, your resources, and your opportunities to meet the needs of others.

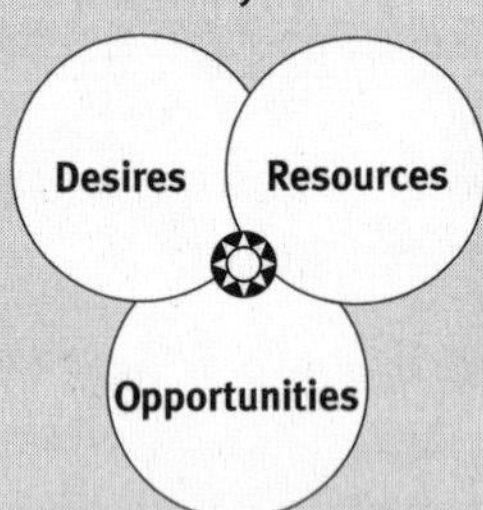

Try out the possibilities you can create by filling in the following statements:

"I could combine my interest in ____________________
with my experience, background, and/or contacts in ____________
to meet the needs __________________________
(type of people, companies, industries)
have for ______________________________.

Sample. A photographer looking for a niche might try this combination:

"I could combine my interest in ***dogs and dog shows***
with my training and experience ***as a photographer***
to meet the need ***thoroughbred dog breeders***
have *for* ***professional photographs of their championship dogs.***

Continue drawing overlapping circles substituting various possibilities from each category until you identify a variety of niches that seem promising. Consider how well each possible niche fits with your goals and lifestyle preferences. Then find out how people respond to the various ideas you are redeveloping.

High Tech Tip: Finding Opportunities by Trend Tracking

To help track trends, special needs, and new legislation and technology related to possible niches in your field, use software that can prepare custom-designed news reports and updates for you such as:

- ***Pointcast,*** free software (http://www.pointcast.com) that's like having a personalized ticker tape and news service running all the time in your PC, providing reports of the latest developments you've selected to know about from CNN, major newspapers, and other publications.
- ***NewsCatcher*** (http://www.globalvillage.com) uses wireless technology to deliver a personal menu of on-line news and information from the Internet to your computer twenty-four hours as day.
- ***Newspage*** (http://www.newspage.com), which turns your individual profile into a custom daily newspaper compiled for you from a variety of sources such as industry trade magazines and the wire services.

High-Touch Tip: When You Just Can't Decide on a Niche

"As in parachuting, if you want to land on your feet in a niche of your own, you've got to have an open mind."

If you're having a difficult time deciding which niche you want to commit yourself to, shift gears and try an alternative way of decision making. Most people use a left-brain approach to logically weigh the pros and cons of their various options and then try to select the one with the most pros and the fewest cons. There is even decision support software like Logic Technology's *BestChoice 3* to help you make such logical choices. But if this left-brain approach

While on vacation in the wilds of Alaska, Johnathon Storm was sitting on a glacier taking in the sights and sounds of nature when he realized what he wanted and needed to do. He's one of the nation's few nature recording artists.

has not produced a satisfactory decision and you're stuck in analysis paralysis, try one or a combination of these right-brain routes to decision making:

- ***Create and consider previously unimagined, seemingly impractical possibilities.*** Often the best niche is not the most logical or apparent option. More often, the best niche is one that involves doing something that other people aren't doing, and perhaps you've never considered doing it either. So allow yourself to imagine different and unusual possibilities. Then refine and test out their actual practicality. You may be surprised at what you discover.

- ***Let your feelings guide you.*** As you consider various options, settle upon the one that feels most appealing, interesting, exciting, rewarding, or satisfying.

- ***Follow your intuition.*** Ask yourself what hunches you have about your niche. Often your intuition can guide you to an excellent choice you might not have considered when evaluating your options logically.

- ***Use visualization, prayer, or meditation.*** Sit quietly, clear your mind, and let yourself become totally relaxed. Visualize your desired outcome in as much detail as possible. Alternatively state your goal, create an affirmation, or pose a question for your mind to meditate upon; e.g., "My ideal niche is becoming clear to me" or "What is the right path for me?" Do not direct your thoughts or pose answers; simply allow images and ideas to come to mind.

One evening while meditating Vera Yahanna, an African immigrant, had a vision that she was to share the experience of African cultures with Americans. Now that's her niche: she hosts cultural events featuring the arts, food, dance, music, and spiritual teaching of different African countries.

- ***Look for coincidences.*** Often people will ask or pray for a sign as to what decision or choice to make and then take note of serendipitous events that could suggest the best direction to pursue. Sometimes the right niche appears in a dream. Or coincidentally someone may call asking for one of the very kinds of services you're considering or someone may contact you to discuss an opportunity that suggests the best direction for your business.

Marketing Mistake: Becoming Known for the Wrong Niche

Be careful of the niche you become known for, because it can be difficult to escape a niche once you've become identified with it. Toni Alessandra discovered this the hard way. Alessandra decided he wanted to become known as the nation's premier sales trainer; instead he became known as the nation's premier listening expert. Here's what happened. While he was in the process of becoming established, he was invited to do a series of audiotapes on listening skills. Since listening is an important sales skill and it was an interesting offer, he decided to do the project. The tapes were such a stunning success, however, that from that point forward Alessandra became known as the "listening expert."

You can just imagine the marketing nightmares this unexpected success caused. When someone would mention his name as a possible sales trainer, the response would often be "Oh, we know who he is. He's the listening expert." When people got his sales-training promotions, they would have a similar response: "Oh, I know who this is. It's that listening guy. I didn't know he did sales training." Actually it took years of concerted marketing efforts and many personal contacts for Alessandra to live down and turn around the fabulous, but unintended, word-of-mouth reputation he had developed.

Fortunately today he has turned this setback to his advantage and has built his reputation as an expert on building business relationships by following the "Platinum Rule": Do unto others as they'd like done unto them. Through his speeches, seminars, and book *The Platinum Rule*, people learn how they can develop rapport with all different types of personalities.

Marketing Masterpiece: Breaking into a Crowded Field

When Greg Schlee graduated from dental school, like many new professionals going into private practice, he faced the challenge of having to develop a clientele. He affiliated with another established dentist with whom he shared office space, but while he got some clients through his associate, if he was going to succeed he knew he'd have to find other sources of business. He settled upon a unique niche. He specialized in working with the kind of patients other dentists don't want to see, like people with severe dental phobias or life-threatening conditions that could be aggravated by the stress of dental treatment. Since other practitioners find these clients challenging and time-consuming, Schlee began spreading the word about his specialty among other dentists, and it didn't take long before he began getting referrals.

Does this mean Schlee works only with difficult clients? Most certainly not. Many people have some trepidation about going to the dentist, so when someone hears from a friend or associate with a dental phobia how great working with Dr. Schlee is, he gets plenty of calls from less seriously anxious patients. Psychotherapists are another source of referrals for Schlee, as are cardiologists whose heart disease patients fear having a heart attack in the dental chair. Schlee has become an expert in the emotional and psychological aspects of dentistry and is teaching classes in dental school on such issues.

Tracking the Life Cycle of Your Niche

No matter what niche you establish for yourself, chances are you'll need to evolve what you do over time in response to the changing needs of your clients, social and economic trends, and your own personal development. In fact, we've found that most niches have a life cycle, starting at some point in a field and evolving to another as the field itself evolves.

Steve West chose his niche at an ideal time. In 1991, he decided it was time to do work at something he loved. He drew on his seven years of experience in running a real estate company to turn his favorite hobby into a livelihood by becoming the exclusive U.S. distributor of Boreal, a rock-climbing shoe. He chose this niche just as climbing gyms were beginning to spring up across the country, so his business in this new field grew along with a trend. Sales shot up from $400,000 in 1991 to over $3 million in 1994. He soon controlled 40 percent of a burgeoning new market.

In establishing your niche you, too, will find yourself somewhere within the life cycle of whatever field you're in. All fields go through a life cycle of from one to five stages and, over the course of your career, you may need to evolve your niche accordingly. Whatever stage you're in at any given time will have an impact on how broadly or narrowly you need to define what you do. So, think about where your field is right now in the following life cycle and project what you think it means in terms of the future for your niche.

Stage One: Pioneering

A new field usually starts as an idea for a niche in the minds of a few innovative individuals. Such pioneers experiment to see if they can provide a solution to a problem or fulfill some unmet need. They have to educate their potential consumers about the value of the new service or product, sell them on the idea of trying something new, and then produce convincing results.

Some niches—like being a prairie preservationist, a spinning wheel sleuth, a nature recording artist, or a catastrophic-weather photographer—are so special that there may never be anyone else who does something similar. In some cases, this an ideal situation, but it can also be a difficult one because you're literally carving your niche from the wilderness. Sue Rugge, for example, pioneered what became the information research industry. She started her business essentially as an independent librarian, and it took many years of marketing before companies readily understood what she did and why they needed it.

As in the case of information research, many innovative niches become the embryos for fledgling new industries. If this happens to you, you'll suddenly have unanticipated competition. That's what image consultant Susan Bixler experienced. When Bixler became a business etiquette consultant, she was one of very few such specialists. Now there are over fifteen hundred etiquette consultants. To maintain her niche she's had to become all the more specialized, and she's done that by establishing herself as an expert on etiquette for today's high-tech workplace that's filled with new technologies like voice mail, E-mail, and cellular phones. If you're pioneering a new niche and it starts growing around and over you, you too will need to evolve your niche in an emerging field.

Stage Two: Emerging

Often when pioneers in a new field succeed, increasing numbers of people begin to recognize the value of using a new product or service and the niche emerges into an up-and-coming industry. And as the word spreads, more people begin offering similar products or services. A professional association may be formed, a newsletter published, and national conferences held. Colleges, universities, trade schools, or private organizations may begin offering training courses in the field.

This is where the medical billing field was, for example, when we included it in ***Best Home Businesses for the 90s.*** Medical practitioners across the country were realizing they could use such a service to save time, money, and hassles. The word spread about the need for this business, and people wanted to learn how they too could do medical billing. Classes and self-study courses were developed. Books and other materials were written to help people get started. As this happened, medical billing itself was no longer a niche. To establish a niche in this field, you had to specialize in some way, either by narrowing the nature of what you did (for example, by providing overnight electronic billing to doctors) or by narrowing the focus on the group you did billing for (for example, by specializing in serving anesthesiologists).

The field of information research, once Sue Rugge's highly specialized niche, now has a national professional-membership association which lists thirty-seven different specialties. Professional organizing, also once a highly specialized consulting niche, has now emerged into a full-blown field with multiple specialties, as has image consulting with many specialties like wardrobe, makeup, color, etiquette, cultural diversity, and professional image.

Stage Three: Sizzling

If the demand continues to grow and many people leap in to take advantage of what appears to be an up-and-coming field, the new industry really begins to sizzle and develop a reputation as a "hot" business! Once a field gets the reputation of being "hot," even more people rush in to participate. Even more books, magazine articles, and newsletters appear outlining how to get involved in the "hot" new field. As has happened with medical billing, often at this point a variety of companies also begin selling business opportunity packages or certification programs designed to help people break into a "hot" business.

This is actually a hard time for everyone in the field and it's the most difficult, but most important, time to develop a new specialty in the field because it's about ready to peak.

Stage Four: Peaking

Once a field has been dubbed "hot," it will eventually begin to cool off. In fact, the hotter it gets, the sooner it will start cooling down. So many people rush into a "hot" field that the competition grows fierce, and quality may become a problem as less experienced opportunity seekers try to enter a field for which they're only marginally prepared. The field becomes highly competitive as more newcomers battle to get the few remaining new customers or try to steal existing ones away from one another. Prices may drop as competitors try to undercut one another, and making a good living in the field becomes more difficult.

If you think back to "hot" industries of the past, you can see this process at work. In the seventies, for example, becoming a psychotherapist in private practice was "hot." There were thousands of private- and public-certification programs across the country. People poured into this field in large numbers. Self-help books proliferated and packed the bookstores. By the eighties, in many areas of the country, there were so many psychotherapists that competition became intense.

Selling real estate, on the other hand, was on the rise and soon it became very "hot." Large crowds of people began packing into hotel rooms to learn how to become real estate agents or buy property for "no money down." Some of those people, by the way, were disillusioned psychotherapists. Then, of course, the real estate market began to cool. Mass-market real estate courses disappeared and people began looking for opportunities elsewhere.

If you find yourself in a peaking field trying to keep from drowning in the flood of others entering the field, you'll have to take steps to hang on to your niche or establish an even more specialized one that's all the better suited to your unique abilities, contacts, and resources.

Stage Five: Maturing

When a field starts cooling, there is a core of people who will stick it out because they love the business or because they are so good, well connected, well established, persistent, or ideally niched that they can ride out the glut. To preserve quality and protect their interest, those in the field often organize to lobby for state or federal licensing programs that require extensive academic training and certification to enter the field. Once this happens, less interested and committed individuals flee to other opportunities. As long as there continues to be some demand, the field then matures and stabilizes, now attracting only those people who are willing to go through the formal or informal credentialing process required to enter a more established career. Prices also usually return to a more attractive level.

Does this model suggest that you shouldn't try to establish a niche in a field that's "hot" or "maturing"? Not necessarily. If it's a good business, there may be new niches emerging. In medical billing, for example, growing numbers of dentists and alternative health practitioners are beginning to qualify for third-party payments. Also, access to this field is still open. You don't need to go through extensive licensing requirements and years of academic training to get started and there are ample high-quality training programs, courses, and business-development packages.

What's important is to assess where you are in the life cycle of your field and also to look at what's motivating you to establish your particular niche in it. Is it is a passion, calling, intense interest, or special talent of yours? Are you particularly well connected in the field already through family, friends, contacts, or previous experience so you'll have an inside edge in getting clients or customers? Would you be willing and able to carve out your niche serving clients who aren't being served in some innovative way? Are you willing to apprentice or work under or through others to build a reputation in this field? These are all ways to survive and thrive in a mature industry.

If you can answer any of these questions in the affirmative, then it can be well worth your while to pursue such a niche. But if you're looking for something that's so "hot" you can walk right into a flood of clients, look somewhere else, because whatever niche you choose, if you want to get and keep business coming to you, you'll need to make a long-term commitment and stick with it through good times and bad.

Your best niche will always be the one that you're most motivated to work hard at, learn as much as possible about for years to come, and evolve with as it matures and develops.

Think Ahead: Protect Yourself from Fads

Sometimes a "hot" idea for a niche will actually be a fad of temporary interest to those who initially clamor for it. Of course, you can't always tell beforehand when something is going to be a fad, but you don't want to spend a lot of time and money becoming known for something that will be here today and gone tomorrow. So right from the start, explore where you can go with a niche if it should turn out to be a fad. This way you can approach all your marketing from the perspective of what your niche can become, not only what it is right now.

A designer, for example, wanted to break out on her own and had a hot idea. The emerging women's fashion at the time was to have large shoulder pads in everything from blouses to overcoats. Well, many women couldn't afford to replace their entire wardrobe, so her idea was to create and sell a line of shoulder pads in a variety of shapes and sizes that women could place in their existing clothing. Her shoulder pads sold like hotcakes, but cooled off just as quickly. So, while she made money her first year in business, she was left shortly thereafter with a reputation for an outdated fashion.

Had she thought this niche through in the beginning, she could have positioned herself as a designer who specialized in creating accessories to help women update their clothing. Then, everything she did to promote her line of shoulder pads would have paved the way for even greater success with her next fashion-savvy line of items, which is ultimately what she did.

Action Steps: Evaluating Your Niche

If you think you've identified a niche for yourself, you can use the following criteria to evaluate it and decide if you need to widen, narrow, or otherwise refine it.

1. Do you enjoy this particular type of work? Signs that you will enjoy your niche include:

    ___ Looking forward to getting to work each morning, especially on Mondays.

    ___ Noticing that time seems to fly when you're working in your niche.

    ___ Feeling satisfied after a day of hard work.

    ___ Liking the clients and customers you work with.

    ___ Feeling enthusiastic about letting others know about your work, even if you don't especially like marketing.

    ___ Wanting to keep learning as much as possible about and get better at what you do.

    ___ Preferring to do this type of work even if you could get paid more or have more clients doing something else.

2. Do you feel that you are good at and well suited for this niche? Signs that you are include:

   ___ Your niche feels like an expression of the essence of who you are as a person.

   ___ The niche makes good use of your abilities and presents opportunities for you to grow.

   ___ Even if you know you still have much to learn, you feel capable most of the time while you're working.

   ___ Many aspects of your work come naturally to you, even if they're challenging at times, and you feel renewed from your work.

   ___ You like and enjoy the company of your colleagues in this field.

   ___ You like talking with others about the development of your work

   ___ Your niche fits well with your desired lifestyle and your personal life goals.

3. Is your niche narrow enough to clearly distinguish you from others? Signs that your niche isn't narrow enough include:

   ___ Frequent comments by others like: "Oh, I know lots of people who are doing that" or "That certainly is a popular field right now."

   ___ Clients and customers frequently call to get price estimates so they can do comparison shopping.

   ___ Frequent haggling over prices.

   ___ Frequently losing business to a competitor.

   ___ Having difficulty explaining how what you do is different from what others can offer.

4. Is your niche large enough to support you? Signs that you need to broaden your niche include:

   ___ You have difficulty finding enough clients and customers you can market to.

___ Clients and customers are happy with your work but can rarely make referrals or offer suggestions for how you could contact others with needs like theirs.

___ No matter how much or how effectively you market, you rarely have enough business.

___ The people who would most likely be able to put you in contact with your clients or customers tell you they rarely or only occasionally encounter someone needing what you offer.

5. Can you cost-effectively and dependably reach people in the niche you've identified?

6. Does your niche have a future and can you foresee it evolving with emerging trends and changes in the economy?

Resources: Niching

Books

Aha! 10 Ways to Free Your Creative Spirit and Find Your Great Ideas. Jordan Ayan. New York: Crown Trade Paperback, 1997.

Brainstyles. Marlane Miller. New York: Simon & Schuster, 1996.

Discovering the Gift of You. Nikki Nemerouf. Westminister, Calif.: 1996.

Finding Your Life Mission. Naomi Stephan. Walpole, N.H.: Stillpoint, 1995.

Finding Your Perfect Work. Paul and Sarah Edwards. New York: Tarcher/Putnam, 1996.

Nichecraft. Dr. Lynda Falkenstein. New York: HarperCollins, 1996.

A Whack on the Side of the Head. Roger von Oech. New York: Warner, 1988.

Software

BestChoice3, by Logic Technologies. Decision support software for analyzing and weighing alternatives. 56925 Yucca Trail, Ste. 254, Yucca Valley, CA 92284, (800) 776-3818 or (760) 228-9653, www.logic-gem.com

Organizations

Life Purpose Institute, 5755 Oberlin, Suite 208, San Diego, CA 92121, (888) 311-5005. Provides referrals to certified Life Purpose/Perfect Work consultants who can assist individuals in finding and defining their focus and niche. Consulting is available in person, by phone, or on-line.

CHAPTER 3

Mastery—Demonstrating Why You're the Best Choice

How did I get so good at this? Probably by working with 25,000 clients. —BEN SHIELDS, Rolfer

How did I get so good at this? I don't know. I've always understood color ever since I was a little girl." —DIANE VITORINO, Colorist

Don't you wish that somehow people would just know that you're good at what you do and that hands down you're the one to do business with? It should be obvious, right? But, of course, it's not. When you're employed, your position within the company usually carries with it an assumption of expertise. But when you're on your own, everyone claims to be an expert. So, unless you and your niche are already well known, people have no way of knowing if you're the best person to do business with until you demonstrate it to them in some way. And when you do that, if you do it well, the results can be dramatic.

Randy Merrell creates custom-fitted cowboy boots. His motto is "boots that will fit, endure, and satisfy like no others." And he means it. The result: a nationwide reputation and a never-ending waiting list for his $1,000+-a-pair boots. And that's especially amazing because to get fitted for your first pair of Merrell boots, you have to travel to Vernal, Utah, near the Colorado border. Once there, Merrell will spend three to four hours videotaping your stride, measuring your feet, and making a rubber stamp of your footprint on paper. Then you wait a year for your boots to arrive! Merrell is a master bootmaker. He makes about seventy-five pairs of boots in a good year.

You may not yet be as great a master as Merrell. Most of us aren't. You may not even be expert yet at what you do, let alone a leading authority in your field. In fact, you may not even truly be a specialist at this point. But if you've found the right niche, whether you're a novice or an old hand at what you do, you're in the ideal position to achieve a level of mastery and excellence that will make you a true specialist, expert, and ultimately an authority whom people will seek out and gladly pay well for your work.

It's rare for anyone to talk about mastery in the context of getting business because being good at what you do is no guarantee that business will come your way. You may be outstanding at what you do, but if no one knows about it, others with far less skill and expertise may get the business you're best suited to do. Still, ultimately, in one form or another, it's your mastery of what you can accomplish for others that you'll need to be showcasing if you want to get business coming to you.

YOUR GOAL
Develop and Demonstrate Your Expertise

You need to acquire expertise at what you do and understand its value so you can lead others to recognize and understand it, too.

Often, we may aspire to achieve levels of excellence in our work, but we don't know how to attain it, let alone how to explain it. "I'm just a run-of-the-mill typist," one woman told us at a workshop, "but I get the job done for my clients when they need it, the way they need it." In this one sentence we've learned this woman doesn't see herself as special, so chances are others won't either. But more important, if you read between the lines, she's also told us that she's not really as run-of-the-mill as she thinks. While she could be more specialized and expert at what she offers, she would see that she already has a great deal to offer if she were to examine how and why she's able to get a job done when it's needed the way it's needed.

Even if you are a great master at your line of work, you may not know just how to describe what makes your work so outstanding. Yet, that's precisely what will help you get and keep a steady stream of good-paying business coming to you. Whatever your current level of expertise you owe it to yourself and your work to recognize and develop your abilities to the fullest and to find ways you can comfortably explain and describe what you're good at so people will know when and why you're the best choice.

You need to know and be able to articulate what makes you special. That's how you'll become well known and valued for what you do. Yet like most people, you may not have a clue about how to demonstrate why you're the best choice. Too often we just hope somehow that people will recognize our value and figure out that they need us. And we're sorely disappointed when they don't. But honing your specialty, truly becoming a master at it, and building on the knowledge and skill you gain is actually the best foundation you can build to assure that your work will become praised and sought after. Your expertise, your special know-how, can be what makes your marketing efforts memorable and distinctive. And, it is the best way we know to make sure you can give yourself a regular promotion every year along with a regular increase in your income.

Becoming Preeminent in Your Niche

The better known you are as a leader in your field, the easier it will be to attract business. However, most of the self-employed individuals earning over $100,000-plus we've spoken with were not well known in their fields when they started out. But most of them have become well known by doing one of three things:

- Furthering the knowledge in their field
- Assuming a leadership role in their field
- Pioneering a new field

Management consultant Dave Jamison became prominent in his field by serving as the president of a local chapter, then at the national and international levels of his professional organization. Psychologist Dr. Linda De Villars became a leading authority on the relationship between sexual satisfaction and exercise by undertaking a groundbreaking study. Pat Hardy became a prominent bed-and-breakfast innkeeper by editing a newsletter, co-founding and serving as executive director of a trade association, and co-authoring a definitive book for innkeepers.

Anyone who is the first to offer a product or service in an area of need is a pioneer and thereby can become a leader in the field. Gene

Call became the country's first private-practice consultant, helping professionals market their businesses. Howard L. Shenson was one of the first to provide information about how to become a professional consultant and became known as the "consultant's consultant." Judy and Shell Norris started the first reunion-planning business and remain preeminent despite a proliferation of such services. When Boyd and Felice Willat created the Day Runner Time Management System, they became the pioneers and leaders of what was to become the burgeoning field of personal organizers.

Following a personal interest, Dana May Casperson has established herself as a tea etiquette expert by tracking down the long-lost traditions, history, customs, and etiquette of formal tea-dining protocols. Through her company, Everyone's Cup of Tea, she has now delivered more than forty two-hour tea presentations at exclusive hotels and resorts across North America. She also trains aspiring bed-and-breakfast and tearoom owners.

James Murray Elwood has established himself as an expert by developing a custom-designed career program for lawyers. Stockbroker Ted Rodosovich has become known as the Mobile Stockbroker. An expert at pioneering new ways to deliver his services to recent retirees and busy entrepreneurs, he takes his office to them! He says, "I want to dispel the churn 'em and burn 'em idea that most people think of when you mention stockbrokers. I'm a prototype," he says of his new approach.

Becoming preeminent in your field as these individuals have means people will think of you first. It's the ideal way to get business, especially for anyone who doesn't like or have the time to do a lot of marketing. You can become well known and sought after, not by spending lots of time and money on marketing, but by doing what you do and like best. You can gain access to gatekeepers, establish yourself in your niche, and create the momentum you need that gets people to seek you out—all by doing what you're in business to do.

Becoming a true specialist in your niche puts you on the road to preeminence. Your visibility automatically makes it easier and more compelling for people to seek you out. Simultaneously, your perceived value goes up and you can command higher fees without resistance. As you build on what you learn as a specialist, your reputation will grow further and you'll become known as an expert and then as an authority. With each step up this specialist pyramid, you can become more memorable, more visible, and more valuable.

While the idea of becoming a preeminent expert or authority may seem a bit overwhelming at first, actually it's not too much to expect of

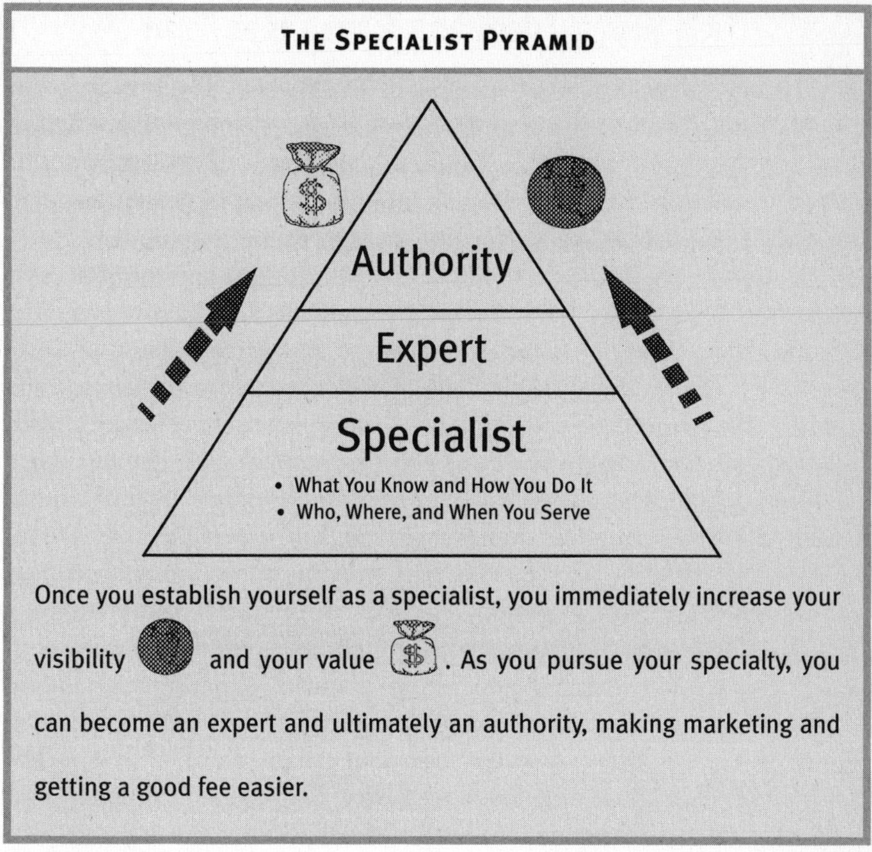

yourself. No one else can possibly know what you have the opportunity to learn once you commit yourself to becoming an expert in your custom-tailored niche. Also, knowing how you're special and being able to communicate why you're the best choice is a prerequisite of being effective in any business-generating activities. It will help you know which marketing methods to select and what message you want to convey through your marketing efforts.

THE SPECIALIST PYRAMID
Authority
Expert
Specialist
• What You Know and How You Do It
• Who, Where, and When You Serve
Once you establish yourself as a specialist, you immediately increase your visibility and your value. As you pursue your specialty, you can become an expert and ultimately an authority, making marketing and getting a good fee easier.

But how do you go about becoming a preeminent specialist in your niche? And how do you articulate your expertise in a way that enables people to understand, appreciate, and value what you can do? That's what this chapter is about. It's about how to obtain the added expertise you need as quickly as possible and how to collect and pull together evidence of your expertise so you can articulate it to others through various marketing activities. By taking the steps outlined in this chapter, you'll know what to say about who you are and what you do. Whether you're introducing yourself, writing winning ad copy, or leaving a message on-line, you'll never be at a loss for words.

Eight Steps to Establishing Yourself as an Expert

After Nancy Bonus sold her successful weight-loss business to a nationwide firm, she decided it was time for a career change. Upon investigating a variety of possibilities, she decided on a new direction: she wanted to become an image consultant specializing in helping women look their best. While she had many years of experience doing before-and-after makeovers with her clients, she was entering an entirely new and fast-growing field. She knew the basics of doing makeup, selecting clothing styles, and coordinating a wardrobe, but she also knew she was far from being an expert and she had a lot more to learn. But to gain the expertise she aspired to achieve, she needed experience working with clients so she could begin building a reputation based on her results.

Many people who go out on their own find themselves in a similar situation. They know what they want to do, but they don't yet have all the specialized skills and expertise they need to attract ample business and deliver results of the quality that will bring clients and customers back again and again. Fortunately, although each career field differs in terms of what you need to master before you can attract and satisfactorily serve clients and customers, today you can usually develop the expertise you need more quickly than you might think. Here is the Eight-Step Program we suggested to Nancy. We've seen it produce dramatic success again and again.

EIGHT STEPS TO BECOMING AN EXPERT

Step 1. Assess and outline your current expertise.
Step 2. Get the lay of the land.
Step 3. Build on your strengths and fill in the gaps.
Step 4. Articulate a point of view for how you work.
Step 5. Collect evidence to support your point of view.
Step 6. Review and begin documenting your experience.
Step 7. Identify the patterns suggested by your experience.
Step 8. Explain and articulate what you've discovered.

Step 1. Assess and outline your current expertise.

If you've chosen the right niche, you'll be able to draw on much of your existing background and experience to establish yourself as an expert, even if you're entering a new field. What is expertise, after all, but skill and knowledge acquired through experience? But often we don't acknowledge how expert we are at something unless we've obtained our expertise through formal education or actual job experience. For example, a woman wrote us to say, "After researching my son's chronic illness for the last five years, I would like to go into medical information research, but I don't have any experience." Obviously, she had considerable experience, but she was discounting the experience she had because she didn't have any formal academic or on-the-job training.

Vocal coach Ivan Borodin didn't make this mistake. He became an accent specialist out of necessity. While studying acting, he was told that if he wanted to work, he'd have to lose his pronounced New York accent. He immediately sought out the services of several speech coaches, but he wasn't happy with their help. Instead, he decided to train himself, using books on the subject. His own success in learning to adopt a nonregional "standard American" accent ultimately led him to teaching others what he'd learned. He's developed his own theories and techniques and teaches classes and offers private counseling on accents and dialects.

So, review all the experience you've had that's relative in any way to your niche, be it from previous jobs, your education, hobbies, or personal life. Then assess the level of your expertise in terms of what you ***know***, what you ***understand***, what you can ***do***, and what you can **teach**.

> ***Knowing*** refers to what you're aware of and have information on relative to your niche: the facts and figures, so to speak.
>
> ***Understanding*** means that you comprehend the significance and implications of what you know, its effects, how it operates, and why.
>
> ***Doing*** means that you can apply or use what you know to help yourself or others achieve specific outcomes. This level of knowledge comes from experiencing firsthand the various implications of what you know and understand.
>
> ***Teaching*** refers to whether you can enable others to know, understand, and use information in the same or similar ways you do.

The great masters in any field not only know a great deal about what they're doing and do it flawlessly; they also understand it intimately, and can explain and even teach others about it. In assessing your existing level of expertise, however, you may find that from your formal education or personal interest, you know a great deal about your field but have little experience actually doing it. Or, based on your job experiences or innate talents, you may be good at what you do but have minimal understanding of how you do it. You may even know and understand your work thoroughly and be able to do it expertly but be at a loss when it comes to explaining or teaching it to others.

To truly become a specialist and expert in your field you must know and understand what you do at a level considerably beyond what most people know. And while unless you wish to, you don't need to teach others to do what you do, you do need to understand what you do to the point that you can explain it to others and help them understand it, too. If you can teach people about your work, it can become an additional source of income and an important aspect of your marketing efforts. Teaching can increase your credibility and the perceived value of your product or service as the best choice. And even if those you teach don't need what you offer, if they understand it they're more likely to refer or tell others about you.

William Lupinacci, founder and head of The Programmers' Consortium, a $2-million-a-year home-based service business in Oakton, Virginia, puts it this way: "The most unusual thing we have done to market our business successfully is to spend every spare dime and every spare hour we have on the quality of the products and services we deliver. When you have a better product, customers tend to come to you rather than the other way around. Instead of spending one to two hours per day commuting, our programmers spend some of that time improving the quality of their work. We pour money that would have gone to overhead costs back into better quality." In other words, they're investing in developing their expertise.

As the German philosopher Goethe urged, "Knowing is not enough; we must apply. Willing is not enough; we must do." We cannot wait until we're totally prepared experts. We'll only become experts by beginning our quest for expertise through actually doing our work and building upon whatever expertise we have at the moment. The list on the following page can help assess your expertise so you can begin articulating your own point of view, your unique take on the products and services you are offering.

Step 2. Get the lay of the land.

If you have experience in your field, you have a decided advantage because you already have a map of the territory. You probably know what others are doing, for example. You know what's involved in providing a

Action Steps: Assessing Your Current Level of Expertise

How would you describe your current level of expertise in your niche? Check any of the following statements that apply:

___ I admit I'm a total novice. I don't know much yet, and I don't have the skills I will need. But I'm eager and willing to learn.

___ I know a lot about the niche I want to develop, but I don't have much experience at actually doing it.

___ I have some experience, but there's still more I can learn.

___ I'm good at what I do, but I can't really explain it to others. I'm not sure I understand how I do it.

___ I'm good at what I do, but it doesn't seem to be what people want to pay for. I need to find how I can make what I do more marketable.

___ I've mastered my work to the point where I now have my own philosophy, methodology, and system for doing it.

___ I'm so knowledgeable and experienced at what I do that I could, or do, teach others how to do it.

___ I have assumed a leadership role in my field.

___ I'm pioneering a new field. No one else is really offering what I do at this point.

high-quality service, who needs what you can offer, and what people are currently paying for it. You may even have a good reputation in your field and specific contacts you can build upon.

However, if you're carving out a niche in a field that's new to you, you'll first need to master what you'll be offering. You'll need to establish contacts in your new field and feel out your own special corner by exploring the neighborhood, so to speak. You'll want to find out as much as you can about who's doing anything that's related to the niche you want to establish.

For example, Toby Young had always wanted to be her own boss. Since her background included having worked as a legal secretary and as an English teacher, she first thought about starting a word-processing service. While that seemed like a practical option, in her heart Young wanted to do something new and different. So, she decided to do something she found fascinating instead: oral histories.

To get the lay of the land, she read everything she could find about this field, including books designed to help people preserve their own family memories. She took a course through the Oral History Program at California State University at Fullerton, which also offers referrals and transcription services to oral historians and provides a brochure and other materials on how to set up oral history interviews. Through the Cal State Fullerton program, she learned about the Oral History Association, which has an Internet site through which she can communicate with oral historians all over the country.

With such contacts, Young found that although she was new to the field, she was able to get her business, TDY Life Stories, under way quickly. She specializes in written personal and family histories and says of her new business, "I adore it. I'm in seventh heaven because I love people and I love to write. Everybody enjoys telling their life story, and I make a good listener." Often people tell her they wish they'd known about her services before their own relatives died. With people over the age of eighty-five being the fastest-growing segment of the population, it looks as though Young has found a niche with a promising future.

William Lupinacci gets an overview of his field and keeps tabs on developments in his industry via computer with the help of his associates. He and the 130 freelance programmers who work through his home-based company, The Programmers' Consortium, monitor, search, review, and disseminate information from over fifty different industry-related Web sites, forums, and Internet news groups. In addition, each programmer, who also works from his or her home, subscribes to at least one unique industry publication and circulates important information among the others via E-mail. They regularly share their observations and impressions with one another via E-mail.

Here are several ways you can get the lay of the land as you set out to establish yourself in your new niche:

• ***Join one or more relevant professional or trade associations.*** You can locate local, state, and national trade and professional associations by networking with mentors and gatekeepers or at the library through Gale's *Encyclopedia of Associations*. Gale's is on-line now, too, through subscription (see the Resources listed at the end of this chapter for more information). As Nancy Bonus began exploring the field of image consulting, she discovered a local chapter of the Association of

Image Consultants International (AICI), which has a mentor program for new people entering the field. Through AICI she met a mentor, Jole Andre, who has been guiding Nancy through the ins and outs of her new field.

• ***Read the trade journals, newsletters, and magazines.*** By reading key publications in your field, you can identify the current leaders and top authorities to find out what they and others are saying that's relative to your niche. You can identify the hot issues, the key concerns, problems, and trends in the field. Nancy Bonus, for example, has discovered that there are many specialties now in the field of image consulting and this is enabling her to define one that's best suited to her unique background in weight loss and beauty.

• ***Read books and other materials that provide an overview of the field.*** Most professional trade associations have a suggested reading list. Alternatively you can work with your local reference librarian in person or by phone or search the Internet for sites related to your field. Industry-specific Internet sites will not only have suggestions for further reading, they can also be a rich source of inside information about what's going on in the field.

• ***Attend an annual conference.*** Essentially an annual conference is like taking a snapshot of any field. It can give you a quick overview of the key issues, concerns, and trends. It can provide easy access to the leaders and their viewpoints. When we spoke at the national conference of the Association of Independent Information Providers (AIIP), for example, we met a number of individuals who had come because they had decided to carve out a niche in information research and saw attending the annual meeting to be one of the quickest and most cost-effective ways to become familiar with the entire field. At this three-day conference they were making important contacts with new peers and learning firsthand about the latest developments in the industry.

• ***Attend trade shows.*** Like a conference, a trade show can also give you a snapshot of the totality of a field—its issues, concerns, trends, and leaders. It can also give you a perspective on what clients and customers are most interested in. Look for the most crowded booths. Observe which booths are attracting attendees and which ones are deserted. Listen to the conversations of attendees who gather around exhibits that are relevant to your specialty. Observe which sessions are well attended and which ones aren't.

• ***Sample competitors.*** Madelaine Crowe started her business as a facialist by becoming a consumer. She got a facial from all her future competitors, making careful note after each session about what she liked and disliked about each experience. When she opened her salon, she incorporated all the things she liked and made sure to avoid all the things she disliked. Not surprisingly, she quickly became known for offering a consummate service. You can do the same. Become an expert on your competitions' services and you'll know better how to define and describe your expertise.

When Teresa Pastorius first dreamed of opening a bed-and-breakfast inn, she got the lay of the land by checking into—and checking out—a variety of inns. She studied everything: their brochures, promotional materials, decor, and room costs. This helped her identify what she liked and didn't like. When she finally bought a B&B in Klamath Falls, Oregon, she used what she'd learned to redecorate and refocus the inn to feature what she believed would work best.

So, sample the services of your colleagues and competitors. Notice what works and what doesn't. Listen to what the clients or customers are saying. Watch what they do and how they react. Call and request competitors' brochures and other sales materials. Get price quotes. But don't just be a copycat. If you copy others, you'll never be an original. Don't set yourself up to get the overruns and leftovers of others. Use what you learn to hone your unique niche and make it better.

As you shop, ask yourself the following questions:

> What is this person or company doing that sets them apart?
>
> What's special about what they're doing?
>
> Who are their customers? Who are they best suited to serve?
>
> How well are they doing at providing the product or service they claim to offer?
>
> How do you feel about the product or service? How could what they do be improved? How could you do a better job?

• ***Talk to Founders and Innovators.*** To get the inside scoop on your field and where you stand in relation to it, interview the pioneers and leaders in the field, those who have made and are making the field what it is today. Read and talk also with industry analysts and consultants. Find out their particular points of view as well as their perspective on the important issues and needs facing the industry.

There are many ways for you to reach these individuals. Of course, whenever possible, it's better to attend their speeches and seminars at conferences and trade shows, read their books, or buy their audio programs. But you can also interview them personally for an article, schedule and host a chat with them for an on-line forum or news group, or if they'll be attending your trade or professional meetings, volunteer to host a party in their honor or to chauffeur them to and from the hotel and the airport.

When you talk with such leaders find out:

Who they consider to be the authorities and industry leaders.

What they're saying about the kind of work you do.

What they consider to be the most important issues in this field.

Who they see as the up-and-comers and why.

The information and background available through the above resources can serve as the starting point for defining how what you do is similar and different from what others are doing. It will help you talk knowledgeably about your niche and where you stand within the scheme of things.

Step 3: Build on your strengths and fill in the gaps

In the past, the number of years of experience you'd had doing something was everything. The longer you'd been working in a field, the more respected and valued your expertise was. Today, that has changed considerably. Expertise today is not so much about longevity as it is about results. People are interested in results. If you can produce masterful results, you'll be respected whether you're a gifted novice or a third-generation expert, whether you've been in business for seventeen years or are just beginning.

So, after assessing your level of expertise, identify what additional information and experience you need to get the kind of results both you and your clients expect. Then take whatever courses you need to take, obtain whatever certification and credentials you're missing, or otherwise line up ways to gain the particular knowledge and experience you need. Here are six of the many options available today for gaining expertise.

1. Formal education programs. The majority of students enrolled in formal education today are working adults. Colleges and universities have designed flexible programs to account for the busy

Action Steps: Develop Your Own White Paper

One of the best ways to fully explore and research your niche is to write your own "White Paper" on the history and future of your industry. In this paper briefly outline the origins of your field, how it has changed over time, the prevailing controversies, and the accepted ways of operating. Explain the basic assumptions, needs, and clientele. If you're pioneering a new field, explore these same issues in regard to its origins and any other related fields. Here's a guideline you can use in preparing your White Paper:

1. Summarize the history of your field, when it started, the ups and downs, and significant developments throughout its evolution. How has it changed? How is it changing today?
2. Identify what you believe have been the three most important trends affecting the nature and success of your industry over the last ten to twenty years.
3. Describe how you think the following are currently affecting your field:

   The U.S. and, if appropriate, the global economy

   government policies

   prevailing social and cultural values

   lifestyle trends

   technology
4. Create at least three possible scenarios for the future of your field and explain how each would most likely affect your niche.
5. Identify what you consider to be the top three adverse developments that could negatively affect the future of your field
6. Identify what you consider to be the top three developments that could open the doors for exciting new opportunities in your field.
7. Summarize what you consider to be the major challenges, opportunities, and developments in the field that people should know about and take into consideration when buying your product or service.

schedules of their working students. There are even home-study, online, and schools-without-walls programs. For example, when production accountant Krystin Hermann decided to make a career change, she enrolled in Antioch College's marriage and family counseling program to develop expertise in her newly chosen field. Antioch is a nontraditional university that draws on both life and classroom experience.

Long-distance learning opportunities abound as well. Interactive on-line correspondence courses, real-time classrooms, and personal counseling on a vast array of topics are available on the Internet. Most colleges and universities are either offering or will soon be offering individual courses and full degree programs electronically in subjects that range from computer science and engineering to business administration, education, psychology, and health sciences.

High Tech Tip: Long-Distance Learning

Individual courses, professional certification programs, and even full-degree programs are now available on-line from accredited institutions of higher learning. If learning on-line is appealing, you can start by contacting the university of your choice directly. Chances are they have a growing variety of on-line programs. If you don't have a particular school in mind, or the school of your choice doesn't offer course work in the subject area you're seeking, look through *The Electronic University, A Guide to Distance Learning Programs* listed in the Resources at the end of this chapter, or use any Internet "search engine" such as Yahoo! to search through the wide variety of programs available on-line. In searching, use the key words "on-line education" or "distance learning." Also the Electronic University Network is available on America Online at http://www.petersons.com.

2. ***Training and certification programs.*** You can often gain the expertise you need without enrolling in a formal education program by tapping instead into a wealth of more informal training and certification programs. Some of these programs are offered by colleges and universities; others are run by private organizations or individuals. Some are packaged as self-study correspondence courses, while others are live seminars and classes; and still others are available on-line.

As Alan Salisbury, president of Learning Tree International, a company that offers 117 classes and 17 professional certification programs, told the *L.A. Times,* "A college degree is a foundation. To stay current, professional certification is very important . . . (It) provides a portable credential." In fact, a recent study by International Data Corp. demonstrates the value of enhancing your expertise through a certification program. The study found that people who complete a series of related, specialized courses to earn a professional certificate made nearly 12 percent more money than their uncertified counterparts.

Here are just a few examples of the kind of training opportunities self-employed individuals are using to fill in the gaps and further their expertise:

Denise Conklin had worked for a public relations firm for ten years when she decided to go out on her own as a PR specialist. To update her knowledge and enhance her expertise, she enrolled in the University of California at Los Angeles Public Relations certificate program. This program involves completing about a dozen courses over a period of one and a half years.

Software companies offer certification in their products. Web designer Todd Cranston-Cuebas has built his expertise and credibility by becoming certified in Adobe's Framemaker. Ogeddi Adigwe is certified by Microsoft as a Solutions Provider for Windows 95 and Windows NT, with the result that Microsoft refers clients to him. Many professional associations offer such training programs. The American Society of Training and Development, for example, offers course work at the local chapter level for beginning trainers, as well as advanced course work and certification in specialties like instructional design.

After twenty years as an editor and writer, Rick Benzel decided to apply his writing and editing experience to pursuing his lifelong dream of becoming a screenwriter. While he had a theater background from college, to hone the craft he's long aspired to master he enrolled in a variety of screenwriting courses through UCLA Extension.

A practicing psychotherapist in New Orleans, J. B. Anderson had discovered that people coming to the stress management center where he worked primarily had three problems: addictions, relationship problems, and job burnout. He felt they did quite well in helping people with the first two problems, but in the area of job burnout they were giving people new skills and then sending them back to the same stressful job situations. So, to expand his expertise, he decided to attend the Life Purpose Institute in San Diego, California, and become a certified life purpose counselor.

This training enabled Anderson to begin helping clients find less stressful and more enjoyable work and led him to open the Career Development Institute. Since acquiring this added expertise and developing this specialty, his practice has grown by 30 percent.

Chances are you can find learning programs in even the most specialized fields. At Home Professions of Boulder, Colorado, for example, offers an eighteen-month home-study course for those wanting to develop their skills as scopists, people who transcribe court reporters' notes. Berea College in Kentucky is a mecca for individuals seeking to master regional crafts. They offer courses in blacksmithing, weaving, pottery, wood shop and broom making. Part of their program involves working as an apprentice with an established local artisan. Vermont College of Norwich University offers a novel low-residency certification program in children's writing. Australasian College of Herbal Studies of Lake Oswego, Oregon, offers a home-study course in aromatherapy, nutritional herbal medicine, and more. The Feng-Shui Institute of America of Wabasso, Florida, conducts nationwide intensive workshops and home-study programs leading to professional status as a Feng-Shui consultant.

Sometimes the best course of study is one offered by an individual who himself or herself is a master of what you're seeking to learn. Often those who are the very best in a field will have established formal training programs. Boot maker Randy Merrell, for example, whom we mentioned earlier, teaches bootmaking classes to others wanting to master his craft. Each year thirty-some people enroll in two-week sessions at the Merrell Institute of Bootmaking. Enrollees come from across the country often looking for a second career. Their backgrounds range from business executives to computer technicians and other professionals.

Tim Somerville runs one of the country's three top independent golf colleges. His institution is not designed to help students become professional golfers but to enable people who love golf to work in the field pursuing such specialties as golf course management, teaching golf, and golf club technician.

So as you identify the authorities you most admire in yours or a related field, explore possibilities for studying with them personally. That's what Cheryl Morris has done. A ceremonial artist and healer, Morris had read a variety of books by shamanic healer Lynn Andrews and decided to contact her. She discovered that Andrews offers a four-year self-study program and ongoing week-long trainings through the Lynn Andrews Center for Sacred Arts and Healing. Morris has been studying with Andrews now for nine years.

3. ***Licenses or Franchises.*** Another way to develop your expertise is to purchase a franchise or business opportunity from someone who has developed a proven winning system. Many companies offer business opportunity licenses and franchises. The best of such companies

High-Touch Tip: Turn Learning Assignments into Expertise Building

Turn class assignments, student projects, dissertations, or theses into an opportunity to gather the information, data, and expertise you need to become an expert in your niche. Turn the results of your assignments and projects into evidence of your expertise that you can use in your marketing activities and materials.

Career counselor Adele Scheele turned her doctoral dissertation into an opportunity to discover and articulate her theory of successful careering. She interviewed successful leaders in a wide range of fields to determine what contributed to their success. From these interviews, she was able to identify six critical career competencies. These competencies became building blocks for her own success as a career specialist. Her dissertation also became the blueprint for her popular book *Skills for Success.*

offer comprehensive training as part of the package you purchase. This was the answer for Nancie Lee Cummins.

Three years ago Cummins was married to a successful contractor and living a comfortable life selling group health and life insurance to corporations. She and her husband owned several homes, and it seemed as though they had it made. Then things began to unravel. Her husband's business filed for bankruptcy, and their marriage began to fall apart. "At this point I knew I needed to figure something out quickly," she said. "Although I had never considered it before, I began to look at buying a business that I could run myself, and I started doing some serious research. I knew that my home situation was near the breaking point. I went from having everything in terms of material wealth to almost nothing."

Not allowing herself to fall prey to the adversity of her situation, Nancie began to take stock of what she *did* have. She had the drive to succeed, she had a depth of experience in the group insurance business, she had researched home-business opportunities, and she had her engagement ring. She decided to buy a medical billing business opportunity from Medical Management Software, Inc., of San Mateo, California. From her phone conversations with Merry Schiff, president of Medical Management Software, and other information she gathered, Nancie felt this was the right way for her to quickly develop a new specialty. To finance the purchase of the business, she sold her engagement ring.

Medical Management Software provided three days of training in the use of the medical billing software, a one-year support contract, software for lead management, related books and other resource materials, a business plan, and 1,000 leads within Nancie's territory. Having received the training and materials, Nancie began marketing herself and within the week she got her first call from a doctor wanting to use her services. "Believe it or not," she reports, "I haven't sent out a marketing letter since."

While not everyone has such dramatic success, buying the right business opportunity or franchise can be a way to quickly acquire needed expertise and assistance for carving out a new niche.

4. ***Hands-on Experience.*** Often the type of additional experience and information you need isn't the kind you can learn from further study. Some of the gaps in your background may have more to do with not knowing how to use or apply the knowledge you already have rather than with needing to obtain additional information. In other words, you may need more specific kinds of direct experience, not more book or classroom learning. Fortunately there is a variety of ways you can gain hands-on experience.

Action Steps: Form an Advisory Committee

To test your ideas and fill in the gaps, consider forming a committee of advisors from among people you respect and admire. Begin by initiating contact with these individuals through personal contact, E-mail, or by phone. Approach them as colleagues whose work you respect and want to collaborate with. Start your dialog informally and then, as your own ideas and thinking progress, ask them if they would be willing to serve on your advisory board.

I, Sarah, created an advisory board for my Los Angeles–based radio show, *Here's to Your Success*. Through this advisory board, I shared ideas and tapped into the expertise and support of entrepreneurs like Wally Amos, self-esteem and motivational experts like Jack Canfield and Mark Victor Hanson (before they authored the *Chicken Soup for the Soul* series), and best-selling fiction author Dean Koontz.

You can think of such an advisory committee as a sounding board—ask them to react to your ideas, plans, observations, and conclusions; send them reports of your progress; get feedback from them on your products and services. And, of course, take every opportunity to credit and promote their work in the process of promoting yours.

Marketing Mistake: Reaching Beyond Your Expertise

Alex was ecstatic to have landed a contract to do his first video project. It was a big project. His fee was substantial. It was a coup that could launch his career. Although he had little experience, he'd done enough reading and student projects to have been able to talk his way into an opportunity to gain some high-prestige experience fast. Things went OK at first, but before long Alex found himself in over his head. Editing was taking much longer than he had imagined. He was missing some of the footage he needed. He discovered his equipment couldn't do some of the things he'd promised, so he had to lease new equipment. As he got further behind, he began cutting corners, pasting things together, covering up that the project was at risk, running seriously behind schedule and over budget.

Ultimately Alex was unable to produce the video by the date it was needed. The angry client demanded that Alex turn the raw footage over so they could try to salvage it by going elsewhere. Actually the project never was finished. The client had lost money and was embarrassed professionally; Alex, too, had lost money and been embarrassed professionally. But he lost even more. He had lost the chance to gain respect in his field. Instead he started off his career with a negative reputation that required years to turn around.

As former Canadian Prime Minister Trudeau reminds us, "You can't go any higher than your foundation is deep." Alex's mistake was not having not achieved a higher level of mastery, but what he had marketed himself as being able to deliver. His reach had exceeded his grasp. His grand coup ended up being a debacle. Since he had the ability to get the job in the first place, when the problems began cropping up, he should have brought in someone who could finish the project for him and paid them to do it. Then he could have delivered the video while learning from a master what to do next time.

CONSULTATIONS WITH INDUSTRY EXPERTS AND LEADERS. When sales trainer Helen Berman decided to start her own business, she chose working in the publishing field as her niche. Although she had experience in the field, she knew she needed additional expertise if she was going to become known and respected among publishers, so she sought out one of the leading authorities in that field. He was teaching a course she could take, but Berman had neither the time nor the patience to sit through a semester of course work. She needed to be in clients' offices, not the classroom. So, she called the instructor, explained her situation, and asked if she could hire him by the hour as a consultant or supervisor. He said yes and went on to become a mentor for Berman, helping her understand what she should be learning from her experience with clients.

Sandy McKnight faced a similar situation when she decided to establish herself as a voice coach. She even attended a four-day workshop with one of the industry professionals she most admired. While she left the workshop more knowledgeable, she still had many questions about how to apply what she had learned to her circumstances, so she, too, called the instructor to arrange for private counseling sessions. Thus began a relationship that stretched over years. Every couple of years McKnight would take a refresher course from her mentor and whenever she found herself dead-ended with an issue, she would schedule a private consultation.

MENTORING, INTERNSHIPS, AND APPRENTICESHIPS WITH INDUSTRY LEADERS. Finding a mentor is a matter of being willing to participate in activities that will put you in proximity with people who can help you and then reaching out to ask for the guidance you need. Professional and trade associations are one of the best places to find mentors. Many organizations have mentor programs in which new members are assigned to an established member. The Association of Image Consultants International (AICI), for example, has such a program nationwide. As mentioned above, that's how Nancy Bonus found a mentor when she decided to develop a new specialty as an image consultant.

When there is no formal mentoring program available, there is a variety of other ways to establish a mentor relationship. Start by attending meetings, trade shows, or other activities where you can identify the leaders and movers and shakers in your field. Then make a point to participate in their seminars, volunteer for committees they serve on, or assist on a project they're involved with. Alternatively you can contact such individuals personally by phone, mail, or E-mail and request a consultation or the opportunity to study with them.

Most successful people are eager to help others, but often they're also busy, so be prepared to pay mentors for a consultation, at least at first. Later you might volunteer to assist them in some way in exchange for the opportunity to learn more from them. Professional potter Virginia Cartwright is a good example of how the mentoring process can work. Aspiring to be a world-class potter, Cartwright especially admired the work of one prominent potter. To study his technique, she enrolled in courses he offered at the community college. Over several semesters, her teacher began to see the potential in her work and took an interest in her professional success. He invited her to begin assisting and eventually conducting some of his classes. Under his tutelage, her skills and contacts in the art world grew and she has, indeed, become established as a world-class potter.

As Denise Conklin was completing the UCLA certificate program in public relations, she knew she needed hands-on experience and a client list. So she signed up at the school for an internship, and that's how we met her. We called UCLA looking for an intern. Over several months, she worked with us on several PR projects, and we became her first client. Since she was knowledgeable and eager to learn, her expertise grew rapidly and we were more than happy to contribute a testimonial and serve as a reference for future clients.

Professional photographer Andrew Gillies found his mentor by apprenticing. "I was good enough at what I did to get some business, but having enough steady business was always a struggle," he told us. "When I looked at the person whose work I admired most, he never seemed at a loss for work, so I decided I wanted to become so good at what I did that people gave me rave notices." To hone his skills as a publicity photographer, Gillies offered to apprentice himself to the photographer whose work he so admired. At first he volunteered to assist on shoots for free; later, as his expertise grew, he received a nominal fee. Ultimately, he began taking on shoots his mentor was too busy to accept, keeping the full fee.

For more information about finding mentors, see **chapter 10**.

5. *Volunteering.* There's no expertise like that which comes from having lots of direct experience, but often gaining experience can be difficult for a novice attempting to establish a particular niche. When I, Sarah, began to specialize in treating children with emotional problems, I volunteered to do programs for a nursery school and to provide free consultations once a week at a pediatrician's office.

My (Paul) first business was political consulting. I became a political consultant through the same route most others have taken. I came up through the ranks of volunteers. From the time I was a teenager I had a passion for politics and I had worked many hours on campaigns for free. Later, I volunteered to manage several campaigns for underdogs, and they won. As my reputation grew as a campaign strategist and manager, I decided it was time to offer my services as a professional consultant.

For more information about volunteering as a way to build your business, see **chapter 9**.

6. ***Let Your Marketing Activities Do Double Duty.*** The best way to establish yourself as an expert is often to collect information and experience with large numbers of clients and customers so you can speak with authority about their needs, problems, concerns, and the variety of possible solutions that will work well for them under varied circumstances. But gathering that much information can take a long time—years, actually—if you have to rely on getting it from working directly with your own clientele. Of course, if you've been in business for some time and are now focusing on a niche, you can survey or interview past clients from over the years who fall into your new niche. But one way to speed up the process is to make double duty of whatever marketing methods you'll be using. You can use speeches, seminars, surveys, trade show exhibits, articles, newsletters, focus groups, and on-line chat polls to gather pertinent information quickly.

For example, you can arrange to speak for your professional or trade association and incorporate a survey or poll into your presentation to gather data about the needs and problems in the field. You can do a seminar for an adult-education program for potential clients or customers and then structure class activities or homework to gather relevant insights into and data about their needs and circumstances. If you do an article for a trade publication or consumer magazine, you can arrange to include a contest or poll of readers. You can host an on-line chat and poll participants on their key needs and common concerns.

Although focus groups are usually used to gather market research, they can be equally useful as a way to increase your expertise. We frequently hold informal focus groups to find out from prospective readers of our books the kinds of problems they're experiencing and the most innovative solutions they've found. Usually we invite individuals to an informal evening of networking and discussion in our home, but occasionally we have hosted a dinner party at a neighborhood restaurant.

For more information on using these marketing methods as a route to building your expertise, see **chapters 9** through **12** in which these methods, as well as mentoring and volunteering, are described in greater detail.

Composer Irving Berlin pointed out that "the toughest thing about success is that you've got to keep on being a success. Talent is only the starting point." And so it is with being a specialist. Establishing yourself as an expert in your niche is a lifelong learning-by-doing process. It's never too early or too late to claim and build upon your expertise.

Step 4. Articulate a point of view about how you work.

"Good prices," "Top Service," "We deliver for you." While the words may differ, we've all seen and heard endless promotions like this. While these are things everyone wants when they buy a service or product, they're also things everyone expects. Regardless of how desirable they may be, there's nothing noteworthy about these promises. If you want to stand out from the crowd, you need to stand *for* something. You need to take a position on the issues you feel are important to your clients and customers. You need to have your own *point of view*.

After all, if everyone else in your field is saying about the same thing you're saying, why should anyone take note of you? Let's imagine for a moment that your new puppy is misbehaving in the house and you decide to seek the services of a dog trainer. In the process of interviewing possible trainers over the phone, you gather information about price and convenience, but chances are you want to know something about what they'll be doing, too—their philosophy, their approach to their work. Let's say you interview four people and get the following four different responses:

Trainer #1: Emphasizes her training and background, years of experience, and describes the number and length of sessions she usually holds, but volunteers nothing about her approach to dog training. When asked, she tells you that you can trust her to accomplish the results you want within six sessions on your premises.

Trainer #2: Points out that he won't really be training your dog, he'll be training you. He explains that he'll be teaching you how to discipline your dog by withholding affection until the dog produces the desired behavior.

Trainer #3: Tells you that she believes in carrots instead of sticks. She calls her technique "affection training" because she will be teaching you to use your dog's natural desire to please to teach it to behave. She wants to come over to meet you and the dog first so she can show you how you'll be working together.

Trainer #4: Explains that their company will take your dog to their facilities, teach it all the kinds of behavior you desire, and return it to you fully trained in two weeks. "We lay down the basics with the dog; then you step in to follow through," she promises.

What is your response to these four individuals? Who will you be more likely to remember? Which approach is most appealing to you? Who would you most likely do business with? If you're like most people, you won't give much thought to Trainer #1. She has not articulated her point of view, although she has one. We all have a point of view about the way we do our work. Like many of us, however, she may be unaware of her point of view, not having taken the time to discover and think out how to describe it. Or perhaps, she didn't articulate her point of view for fear of alienating a prospective client.

Have you ever done that? Have you ever made yourself so milquetoast plain that anyone could find what you do palatable, but few find it appealing?

As far as the other three trainers are concerned, they have each articulated a clear point of view. Most likely you'll remember all three of them because they've each taken a stand. They use three very different approaches to dog training. Chances are they're working to master their particular approach. And you will know whether they have or not. You will be able to see if it's working the way they explained that it would. If they're good at their approach, you'll see positive results and you'll conclude that they are, indeed, experts in their approach.

Will they lose business by having a point of view and taking a stand? Of course. But they will also get business. Of course. Those who find their approach appealing will be attracted to them. Those who don't will look elsewhere. That's what getting business to come to you is all about. Those who find your point of view and what you have to offer appealing will be drawn to seek you out. You won't have to twist their arms or use time-consuming, clever sales techniques. Getting business to come to you is a matter of self-selection. People who don't find what you're offering appealing will go elsewhere, as they should. But people who like your point of view will be predisposed to satisfaction. You'll get less price resistance and more referrals because you stand for what your particular clients and customers want.

In the case of the four dog trainers, personally we were put off by Trainer #2. His approach is not consistent with the kind of relationship we want to have with our dogs. We were skeptical of Trainer #4's approach. We believed our dogs probably would be trained at the kennel, but we weren't sure that the training would carry over to our household once the dogs got home. Also we didn't want to be separated from our dogs for two weeks, and we were concerned that they might pick up bad habits at the kennel like excessive barking. Trainer #3, however, seemed perfect for us. We hired her and have been happy with the results. We've talked about her services a lot and referred others to her.

You might have made an entirely different choice, and that's good. It means that these trainers have defined their points of view clearly enough so that each of us could pick the best services for our different situations. We hope that, having picked the most suitable expert for your situation, you would be as happy with your choice as we are with ours. No one likes taking potluck when it comes to finding the right service or product. When you have several clear points of view to choose from, however, you don't need to. With the right information, customers can custom-order their products and services by selecting the best ones for them.

Action Steps: Developing Your Point of View

Step 1. Notice other experts' points of view.

You can begin developing your point of view by taking note of how other experts express their points of view. Whether you agree with the experts you hear or read about is not the issue. The issue is to notice how they're articulating their niche so that those who are interested in it can recognize them and seek them out.

The following, for example, are experts from a wide variety of fields, but they have one thing in common. They are articulating a particular point of view about their area of expertise. They're often quoted in newspapers, magazines, etc., because they're willing to take a stand that sets them apart from the crowd. People reading their comments may or may not agree with them, but they will know where they stand. Those who agree and could benefit from their viewpoints will be attracted to do business with them. If they were saying the same thing everyone else is saying, however, they wouldn't get quoted and they wouldn't be enjoying the benefits of free publicity.

—"Physicians have been getting much more tense and much angrier in the past few years," psychologist Jack Singer told *USA Today*. As a specialist in teaching stress-management techniques to medical professionals, Singer reports he's seen a lot more anger, tension, and hopelessness among his physician patients in recent years. He claims that "managed care has introduced a new set of things that increase stress. When physicians are angry or tense, the probability of their committing malpractice is much greater."

—"Most people can live with far less by shedding conspicuous consumption," Charles Long told the *Los Angeles Times*. Having written the book *How to Survive Without a Salary*, Long is an expert on what he calls the conserver lifestyle. "We've bought into the myth of competition for so long that being downsized can feel like personal failure . . ." But Long says, as a conserver, he works harder now than he did as a civil servant but enjoys a better quality of life.

—Big shots have entourages to cater to their every whim. But what's an ordinary person to do? Sharon Stevens, owner of Green Iris Day Spa in Batavia, Illinois, suggests a massage, aromatherapy, manicure, and pedicure. She told *Home Office Computing* magazine, "Everyone needs a little pampering now and then. Women who don't consider themselves to be drop-dead gorgeous might feel intimidated in some spas when they should fee relaxed and rejuvenated."

—Supermarket trendmeister Phil Lampert believes that the average supermarket has too many products. "We don't really need all these different spaghetti sauces, for example," he told *USA Today*, "or two different brands of salt with a three-cent price difference. We just shut down and buy the same thing week after week." He believes store owners should get to know the people who come to their stores personally by asking them questions. "They should be like family."

—Parenting expert Nancy Samalin, author of *Loving Each One Best*, told a *Los Angeles Times* reporter that "parents often ask how they can get the kids to listen more. The answer is simple to understand, difficult to do. It's talk less. What you can say in a paragraph, say in a sentence. What you can say in a sentence, say in a word."

Step 2. Review the points of view of others in your field.

You may already know exactly what your point of view is, but if not, think over what you discovered by getting the lay of the land in your field. How are your opinions and viewpoints different from those of others? Read articles, papers, and marketing materials from experts in your field. Attend their seminars, lectures, and speeches. Listen for their point of view. What do you agree with? What do you disagree with?

Step 3. Develop a position statement

What is your position? Your point of view? Write a one-page position paper for your own use only, describing the following:

- What is your philosophy about the service or product you offer?
- Why is it needed?
- Why is it different from what can be found elsewhere?
- Why do you do things the way you do?
- What are your beliefs about the needs of your clients and about what you have to offer them?
- What are the most common problems, needs, mistakes, and concerns your product or service addresses?
- What needs to be done about these problems, needs, mistakes, and concerns? What are you doing about them?

Sample Position Statement

As you've probably realized, we have a particular point of view about marketing and it's not one that you're likely to read elsewhere. Here's a summary of our point of view on what self-employed individuals and very small businesses need to do to make sure they have ample business.

Our Position on Marketing

Year after year having a steady flow of clients and customers remains the number-one challenge for home-based and small businesses. As a self-employed individual who is selling your time or making the products or services you offer yourself, most likely you simply don't have the time, resources, or interest to undertake large-scale marketing efforts. You can't afford to spend vast amounts of time or money getting business. You need to get business coming to you.

At first, this will mean focusing your time, energy, and money on building your reputation and image as a specialist, expert, and authority in your own niche. As long as there's demand for what you offer, once you've become well known in your specialty, business will begin coming to you. The better known you become, the more momentum you'll have and the less time you'll need to spend generating business.

But you don't need to change who you are or do marketing activities that you find distasteful in order to become well known. There is a wide variety of marketing activities that you can choose and tailor to your personality, interests, time constraints, resources, and the nature of your business. If you consistently initiate and follow through on enough of these activities in proportion to how much business you need, as long as there is a demand for what you offer and you satisfy the clients you get, more business will start coming to you.

Step 4. Collect evidence to support your point of view.

In listening to experts or reading their quotes, have you ever noticed that their comments are usually interspersed with facts, figures, examples, metaphors, and stories that illustrate their viewpoint in dramatic and compelling ways? Well, once you've assessed and identified your expertise, it's important that you, too, begin gathering supporting evidence you can draw upon to demonstrate that expertise and support your viewpoint. You will be able to use this evidence in any of the business-generating activities you undertake. You can sprinkle it throughout the content of your marketing and publicity materials, sales presentations, and personal conversations with potential clients and customers, mentors, and gatekeepers.

Earlier we mentioned supermarket guru Phil Lampert, who believes that most stores stock too many products. Lampert writes a syndicated column for the *Chicago Tribune*, is a correspondent for NBC's *Today* show, and has written the book *Phil Lampert's Supermarket Shopping and Value Guide*. His opinions and viewpoints are always supported with interesting statistics about grocery stores. For example, he told *USA Today*, "A typical store stocks 35,000 or more products. Each week new ones are added and old ones are axed. Last year more than 20,000 new products were introduced, but only about 1,500 make it onto shelves. Of those, only about 300 will be around three years later." As you can see, Lampert has the facts and figures to support his expertise.

Electrical engineer Julian Goldstein had struggled most of his life with diabetes. Four years ago he started taking yoga classes to relieve the pain of a herniated disk. Before his back got better, he was surprised to discover that his blood sugar levels had improved and within five months he was insulin-free! Now Goldstein has a new career teaching yoga classes to Type II diabetics in Encino, California. The results, he tells *Self* magazine, are dramatic. "A lot of diabetics see their blood sugar levels drop 50 to 100 points during the first week. Some can reduce their insulin intake by as much as 40 percent within 40 days."

To support his belief that doctors are experiencing more stress these days, psychologist Jack Singer, whom we mentioned earlier, conducted a survey of 500 doctors in eleven states and found that almost all of them complain of added stress in their practices. Singer, who teaches health-care techniques to cope with stress, found top stresses include dealing with insurance companies and managed-care organizations, coping with regulations, and fearing malpractice litigation. These findings now provide him with facts he can use to back up his viewpoint.

Steven Mitchell Sack, author of *The Hiring and Firing Book,* has a private practice as a plaintiff's advocate specializing in employment law. It's his viewpoint that the legal climate has shifted in favor of employees, and to support his position he points out that employment-related lawsuits have increased over 500 percent.

Elisabeth Howard and Howard Austin have a mission to teach the world to sing. It's their position that "anyone with a normal speaking voice can sing." Their Born to Sing courses and audio and video programs provide ample evidence to support their claim through testimonials like this one from actress Tracy Wells, who says, "I can now call myself a singer."

In 1995 after Felice Willat left Day Runner, the phenomenally successful company she launched from her home with husband, Boyd, she started a new company, Tools for the Heart, with partner Ilene Segalove. Their goal was to create personal products for women that inspire self-discovery and well-being. Their first product is *Woman's Book of Changes,* a guided journal for women. To support their belief that reflecting on the changes taking place in one's life can open opportunities for a more balanced and joyful life, they cite the work of Dr. Mark Goulston, a UCLA psychiatrist who specialized in women's issues. They quote Goulston as having found that "journaling helps women look back without regret and forward without fear, which increases contentment, joy, and calmness."

Willat also cites studies by Southern Methodist University in Dallas where researchers have found that keeping a journal has physical benefits as well. She quotes the July/August 1996 issue of *Health* magazine as reporting that studies at the university suggest people who write about upsetting events have stronger immunity and visit their doctors half as often as those who write only about trivial events.

Business consultant and author of *Wide Angle Vision,* Wayne Burkan has a contrarian viewpoint. While conventional wisdom says that if we want to succeed, we must listen closely to our biggest and best customers, Burkan tells us, "Conventional wisdom is wrong! To delight your customers of today, you need to deliver *more* than they expect tomorrow. But they can't tell you what they will want next. The group that knows what your best customers will want tomorrow are your lost customers of today." To back up this viewpoint he makes comparisons among the track records of companies like Apple Computer, Dell Computers, IBM, Smith Corona, and Sun Microsystems and cites testimonials from CEOs at companies like Motorola and Southwest Air.

Colene Sawyer has developed her own evidence. A marriage and family counselor whose mission is to help people understand the mysterious and powerful process of falling in love, Sawyer has established herself as an expert by writing a book entitled *Fishing by Moonlight: The Art of Choosing Intimate Partners.* A six-year project, the book became the platform for thoroughly researching her specialty. She searched through books, case studies, her personal experience and experience with her clients, interviews with couples and hundreds of workshop participants, distilling a broad range of information, until she discovered and accumulated ample evidence for what has become her point of view that not only can we make better choices in selecting a mate; we can also learn and grow within whatever choices we make.

Even if you consider yourself to be a master at what you do, you can benefit from finding and using evidence like this to support your approach. People often need help in understanding why what you do is so special and more than worth the fee you are charging. They may need help understanding the significance of what you do, why what you do is different, and why it's particularly valuable to them.

You've probably had the experience yourself of not appreciating how special a good service was until you had to find someone else to perform it. We had such an experience in working with sound studios. We were happy with the studio we'd been using locally, but we had no idea how special their service was until we had to use sound studios in other cities. Suddenly we could have written a sales brochure for our neighborhood studio. Being the perfectionist that the owner was, perhaps even he had no idea how many things could go wrong in a less professional studio! Knowing these things can help him communicate why his methods work so well.

So, begin now gathering evidence that will support your position and your point of view. Here's how:

Action Steps: Collecting Your Evidence

Search for and gather as much evidence as you can to support your position about your approach to your work and validate your point of view. Who else agrees with you? What studies and research provide proof of your beliefs and experience? Begin building your case using as many of the following types of evidence as you can find:

Types of Evidence

Examples	Hypothetical cases
Visual aids	Charts, samples, objects, pictures
Incidents	Real personal experiences and anecdotes
Demonstrations	Using objects or people to show and tell
Expert and client testimony	Quotes of other experts' opinions, eyewitness accounts
Statistics	Demographics, sales figures, research findings, studies, market surveys
Comparisons	With others or by analogy and metaphor
Facts and Figures	Historical, geological, laws, the Constitution

Where to look

- Review demographics, statistics, surveys, and research findings.
- Scan for supporting quotes from other well-known authorities.
- Conduct your own surveys or interviews with clients and customers.
- Hold informal focus groups.

Step 5. Review and begin documenting your experience.

Probably the most important evidence you can gather will come from documenting and codifying your own experience. Often this is done intuitively. We accumulate experience, learn from it, and reach conclusions about it that are usually out of our awareness. This is how over time we get better and better at what we do. But if you haven't been tracking your experience and learning from it consciously, you can't use what you've gained to help your clients and customers better understand your work, nor can you use it in your marketing materials and other activities.

We talked earlier, for example, about the artist who created the beautiful buffalo we bought in Santa Fe, New Mexico. Obviously, he had thought about his craft. Each piece was indeed an inspired creation, but he also understood the nature of the process he'd used to create it. He knew its history and its evolution. He was working to improve upon it, watching the results, always refining and improving.

Jose Garza had a similar experience. He provides computer consulting via modem to his clients using software that allows him to access the clients' computers over the phone and make needed fixes. "At first I noticed my clients seemed to have certain concerns about remote assistance, so I began keeping a record of the concerns they expressed. Almost 100 percent were concerned about security; 80 percent were concerned about the complexities of using the technology. This helped me learn not only how to best present what I could do, but also how to adjust the process I used to make it less intimidating and more user-friendly."

Ten years ago when we started our radio show *Working from Home*, we developed a list of questions we wanted to ask all the successfully self-employed individuals we had as guests on our show. We've also asked the same questions of hundreds of others we've interviewed for our books, columns, and magazine articles. We've found over the years that we can return to these answers again and again to find patterns of problems and solutions we were unaware of at the time we began asking the questions. In fact, much of the philosophy and many of the methods contained in this book have developed as a result of the information we've gathered from consistently asking these simple questions.

Here's what you can do to begin tracking your results:

- Identify five to ten issues you want to track; i.e., in an effort to answer questions like these:

What are the most common problems in my field?

What do people usually do?

What are the most common mistakes people make over and over again?

What do people perceive themselves as needing most? Do I concur? Is there something important that they're overlooking?

What's growing? What's fading away?

What works? What doesn't? Why?

- Create a computer-based or paper form or checklist you can use to systematically gather information on these key issues.
- Keep careful client and customer records. Identify when you will collect the information you're seeking on each client and file the records for easy review, access, comparison, and analysis. Using a free-form database like *askSam* by askSam Systems or a spreadsheet like Microsoft's *Excel* can help you do this.
- Ask for feedback frequently. Talk with existing, past, and potential clients, customers, referral sources, and colleagues about the issues you're tracking. Their insights, reactions, and input can provide you with added perspective.

Action Steps: Keep a Mastery Journal

Start using a journal to record your observations as you work to achieve greater and greater mastery of your work. Set aside a quiet time each day to contemplate the experiences of your day. This might be at night before going to bed, or in the morning upon awakening. If you work out regularly, you might use that time to let your mind reflect on patterns you're noticing. Or, if you meditate or pray regularly, you might allow time afterward to think about your work. Ask yourself what you're noticing. What observations have you made over the day or week? Jot down in your journal any patterns you see. Go back periodically to reflect and reread past observations and comments. This may stimulate new observations and lead you to new conclusions.

Step 6. Identify the patterns suggested by your experience.

Gathering and collecting information is meaningless unless you also begin to see the implications and meaning that lie hidden within the information you've gathered and the observations you've made. As detective Alex Cross in James Patterson's popular novels says, "Data gets collected, data runs loose in the brain and eventually connections are made." Or, as American Indian Joe Leaphorn in Tony Hillerman's popular murder mysteries advises his protégé, Jim Chee, "You have to look for the patterns."

When we did a pilot test of our *Hire Yourself* course with psychologist Dr. Jessica Schairer, for example, we observed that people wanting to become self-employed who had recently been laid off from a job were significantly more likely to be depressed than others taking the course. We also noticed that people who were depressed while taking the course were less likely to complete their assignments and follow through on the activities they needed to undertake to actually become self-employed. And their lack of progress led them to become even more depressed.

From these observations we were able to incorporate into the course several new elements to address this problem. We added tools to help people assess their level of motivation to be self-employed, so that each person could better assess whether becoming self-employed was a last-ditch act of desperation or a career goal they actually wanted to achieve. We also began alerting participants to the signs of depression and helping them to understand that it's a natural and common reaction to job loss. You can identify similar key patterns as follows:

Action Steps: Identifying Significant Patterns

After you have been tracking the key issues identified in Step 5 for some time, you will begin seeing the patterns and you can begin reaching conclusions as to their meaning. Here's an example of how such patterns emerge. You can use this same process for identifying such patterns in your work.

Sample: Identifying Patterns

Voice coach Sandy McKnight conducts Theater of Life training programs for private individuals and corporate staff. Five years ago she began tracking the needs among her clients and customers. Using the same questions we suggest for tracking your key issues from pages 97–98, here's how she used the information she'd been gathering to create a new niche for herself that draws on her unique background in improvisational theater to improve her clients' business and personal relationship skills.

- **What are the most common problems?** As McKnight worked with clients to develop their voices, she realized that one of the biggest problems they faced in using the skills they were learning was that they had no place to rehearse their roles in life. Interacting in every important personal and professional relationship was always like opening night. There was no chance to practice, no place to get your part down before facing the audience, no place to learn how to think on your feet.
- **What do people usually do?** As a result, her clients were forever winging it, learning the important skills of life on the fly, pretending they knew what they were doing, trying to put up a good front, and having to live with the dire consequences of being ill prepared for their parts. This would never happen in the theater. No director would ever put a cast up before an audience without having given them a chance to rehearse.
- **What mistakes do people make over and over again?** To avoid dire consequences and prevent disaster, she found that most people stay in a tiny comfort zone of behavior, taking as few risks and trying as few innovations as possible, hoping for the best.
- **What do people perceive themselves as needing?** Although they were not always able to articulate it directly, she could tell that her clients were hungry for a safe place to take risks, to try out new behaviors and develop new personal and interpersonal skills that would improve their business and personal relationships.
- **What's growing? What's fading away?** In the past, she experienced people as being less willing to try something "touchy feely" like her Theater of Life class. Now she finds that people are desperately seeking a way out of the chaos of their lives. They're juggling so much that they're willing to try something new and different, even if it means feeling uncomfortable at first in the class. The old rules aren't working, and so more people are willing to loosen up if it will help them to become more centered and at peace in the midst of the chaos around them.

- **What works? What doesn't? Why?** Winging it isn't working. Instead, McKnight believes, people have to take personal responsibility for mastering their own lives. "We all must learn to walk our talk, develop our own voice, and put out the message we want to send to the world in a way that enables us to get what we want from life."
- **What have you noticed that no one else is talking about? What's been overlooked?** McKnight finds that most people don't speak up for themselves. In fact, she points out, research from Stanford University indicates that 40 percent of people consider themselves to be shy at any given time and 70 percent have been shy at some time in their lives. In fact, McKnight believes, our schools have taught us to be shy, telling us to shut up and listen. As a result, most people don't have their own voice.

Calling upon years of observations and experience helping people find their voice, McKnight has developed the Theater of Life as a safe place to try out new behaviors, master new interpersonal skills, and rehearse using them effectively. The response has been dramatic from both organizations and individuals. As she begins taking the program nationwide, McKnight is continuing to gather data and observe patterns of what works and what doesn't so her programs can continue to evolve and grow.

These are the kinds of patterns you can discover relevant to your field to establish yourself as an expert and ultimately as an authority. The process of finding the answers to questions like these is what will enable you to acquire the expertise to build a reputation for yourself as someone others will want to seek out.

Step 7. Explain and articulate what you've discovered.

Once you've begun to notice patterns and gained new understanding into the needs and circumstances of your clients and the nature of your work, it's important that you find words, metaphors, illustrations, graphics, or stories that will help others better understand what they need to do and how you can help them do it. Whatever methods you decide upon to get business coming to you, the best way to demonstrate your expertise will always be by helping people understand what they're experiencing, what they need to do, and how you can help them achieve it.

You can think of your marketing activities as an opportunity to tell the story of what you've learned about your customers' world, how it works, and how what you know can help them. Notice, for example, how the following experts have become successful by making it easier to understand complex and mysterious or otherwise unfathomable or unpalatable aspects of life.

Information broker Seena Sharp helps companies understand the critical need for ongoing strategic research. She finds that her clients often don't realize they're making decisions without key information. They don't always know what information they need, how to get what they need, or what to make of the avalanche of information they have.

Seminar leader and author of the best-selling book *Men Are from Mars, Women Are from Venus,* John Grey, has achieved acclaim by helping men and women understand and bridge otherwise seemingly impossible differences in their points of view.

Tana and Alfred Brinnand of Scotts Valley, California, used information about how to protect themselves from carpal tunnel syndrome to create MouseMitts, unique and colorful half-glove wrist protectors. The mitts are designed to protect against all four aspects of stress related to this all-too-common injury: irritation, cold, strain from repetitive motion on the keyboard, and carpal misalignment.

For thirteen years Sandra Schrift owned and operated the Podium Speakers Bureau. But in 1996, based on what she was learning about the needs of her clients, she shifted direction and became The Shift Coach, a personal coach for professional speakers. She works as a combination cheerleader, advocate, partner, taskmaster, and sounding board to help them grow from "part-time to full-time to big-time." She finds that "my clients don't have time anymore to do it alone. They need to partner with others. By partnering with a coach, things get going faster."

Dimitri Vazelakis felt left out of the birthing experience when his wife, Elsie, became pregnant with their son, Alexander. He found that although childbirth was a time of joy and excitement, it was also a time of stress and anxiety. Both Dimitri and Elsie thought a little humor would help him and other fathers feel more a part of the experience. So they came up with the idea for the Labor Coach (TLC) Kit, which is filled with both humorous and practical items for the father-to-be who's helping his wife through delivery.

Stephen Gordon, founder of Restoration Hardware, is reinterpreting the hardware store. He's created an upscale tool-and-home-furnishing chain that appeals equally to men and women. The story of the store and the items in it are told through folksy curatorial labels posted on the merchandise like this one on a $2.75 metal spatula which reads, "I remember a particular sandwich spreader from my summer sandwich-making noontimes at the lake-front house on Indian Bay in upstate New York." Reminiscent of the *Old Farmer's Almanac* and the highly successful J. Peterman catalog, Gordon's deeply personal, nostalgic point of view pervades the store and is highly appealing to baby boomers and younger shoppers. Based in Eureka, California, the chain has already grown to twenty-two stores and is now spreading back east.

Speaking of the Peterman catalog, if you haven't seen it, you should. It, too, is a masterpiece of mastery. It features hard-to-find classic clothing in a magazine-like catalog that exudes a personal point of view. Each item, be it a velvet floor-length hooded cape, a leather military jacket, or safari shirt and pith helmet, is accompanied by a personalized message from Peterman explaining such things as the history, origin, and nature of the item, how he found it, and why he chose it. As you browse through the catalog, you feel assured that he is indeed a master at locating and selecting these unusual pieces.

Here are several steps you can take to begin telling the story of what you're learning and discovering through your work:

- ***Develop new terminology*** that will help your customers and potential clients make sense of what they're experiencing and how what you have to offer will help. We're not suggesting that you create more "jargon." Jargon only makes your message more intimidating and remote. It creates more distance between you and people who could otherwise be interested in what you do. Instead, you want to coin a turn of phrase or find words that capture the essence of what people need to know to better understand their experience and how it relates to what you're doing.

You may have noticed that experts and leading authorities often coin new terms or turns of phrase that help their clients and customers better understand their experience.

Career coach Adele Scheele, for example, whom we mentioned earlier, has coined a variety of terms to help people understand the skills needed for career success. She divides the workforce into *sustainers* and *achievers* as a way to explain to her clients the reason some people who do excellent work get passed over again and again for promotions. She talks about the importance of learning how to "*magnify your accomplishments*," by broadening your expertise in order to make yourself more valuable. She developed the idea of "*catapulting*" your relationships into opportunities you wouldn't have access to on your own.

Peak performance expert John Garfield coined the term *peak performance* as a way to help athletes and other achievement-oriented individuals understand how to attain optimal mental and physical performance levels. Jim Newman coined the term *comfort zone*.

Through her work with organizations, professional trainer Cherie Carter-Scott noticed a rising tide of negativism in the workplace. To help her clients recognize and reverse these disastrous patterns, she coined the term *negaholic* as a way to describe colleagues, managers, and organizations that pull us all down. She has developed her own point of view about how to identify negaholics, be they a boss, a spouse, co-worker, or employee, as well as how to cope with your own case of *negaholism*.

Psychiatrist Eric Berne was a true master of popularizing terms that can help people understand otherwise mysterious psychological experiences. You may recognize many of the terms he coined. Some are now in the dictionary, e.g., *positive and negative strokes*, *life script*, and *psychological games* in which people create drama in their lives by shifting roles as victim/rescuer/persecutor. Other terms Berne coined with which you may be less familiar include:

> *rubberbanding* refers to times in the present that cause us to re-experience a similar time in the past. For example, when a client yells at you disapprovingly, you might rubberband back to a time when as a child your father would yell at you and feel as small and powerless as you did then.
>
> *reachback* refers to how far back from a dreaded event you begin anticipating and worrying about it. For example, how long before having to give an important speech do you start feeling nervous? For some people, the reachback is only moments; for others, it can be days or weeks.
>
> *afterburn* refers to how long a negative experience continues to eat away at you after the fact. For example if you flub your speech, how long afterward do you continue to feel bad about it?

To describe the growing numbers of self-employed people who are working from home, we coined the term *open collar worker*. Later, in reviewing the patterns of self-employed individuals we've interviewed, we noticed that four out of five people going out on their own today are not your classic entrepreneur. In fact, most self-employed individuals don't identify with the word *entrepreneur*. So, we coined the term *propreneur* to describe the new breed of workers who are going out on their own "for" (*pro*) some reason other than the love of business enterprise per se. We've noticed that propreneurs are quite different from entrepreneurs in terms of their motivation and how they want and need to run their businesses. Many things that work for entrepreneurs don't work at all for propreneurs.

• ***Find metaphors, stories, and examples that produce "Ahas"*** and help your clients understand complexities, mistakes, misperceptions or oversights.

Management consultant Kenneth Blanchard has helped millions of managers to better understand the complexities of motivating their employees. To tell the story of the management principles he has discovered, Blanchard, along with Spencer Johnson, chose to use an allegory and the result was their best-selling book *The One Minute Manager.*

The creators of MouseMitts, mentioned above, use analogies to explain the benefits of their product. They point out that any dancer or athlete will agree that warming up is important and that performing "cold" is inviting trouble. So it is, they contend, with computer keyboarding. MouseMitts keep the wrist warm and relaxed while leaving the palm cool and dry. The Mitts' Lycra fabric wicks away any perspiration, just as it does in swimsuits, biking pants, and aerobic outfits. Likewise, when doctors prescribe elastic bandages for aching feet, knees, and wrists, they know elastic provides needed support to bones and muscles. But while wearing an elastic bandage is ugly and bulky, MouseMitts give the same gentle support attractively, comfortably, and in a way that fits in with an office environment.

Organizational development specialist Warren Bennis, a nationally acknowledged expert, helps managers and CEOs understand leadership. He has interviewed and studied the great leaders in our society and uses their stories to illustrate the patterns of leadership he's discovered. He also makes use of metaphors, for example, comparing the times we live in with "Chinese baseball" in which after the ball leaves the pitcher's hand, the fielders can all do anything they wish like moving the bases around or having everyone run into the infield.

He also uses turns of phrase like *"the commitment gap," "unwarranted optimism,"* and *"creative deployment of self"* to explain the characteristics of true leaders and makes use of quotes like this one from Abigail Adams: "These are hard times in which a genius would wish to live. Great necessities call forth great leaders."

• ***Write an article, booklet, or informative brochure*** that outlines your philosophy, methodology, or point of view. Support each point with the evidence you've gathered. Few things go so far as an article, booklet, or book to establish someone as an expert. And there's good reason for this. The process of writing forces you to think about what you believe, define what's important, and find ways to explain it so that others can understand.

We suggest beginning small. You can start by writing a brief treatise or informative brochure, for example, using your white paper (see page 78) and notes from your mastery journal as a guide. Then move on to write an article, a booklet and ultimately, if you wish, a book. Write the first draft of your first attempt for yourself. If you can articulate your expertise to yourself, you're well on your way to being able to describe it to others. Then rewrite your treatise as a conversation with your clients or customers. Start with what you think they know and experience, then explain what you do in terms that help them understand and deal with their situations.

For example, if you design and create pins using American Indian beadwork, in your first draft you might write about what attracted you to this craft, its history, and importance to you. You might describe your particular approach, the type of materials and designs you use and why, along with information about how your approach is similar to and different from other beadwork. Then, in the second draft, you might shift gears and explain what has attracted people to Indian beadwork throughout time, misconceptions people have about this art form, different approaches to it, and finally your approach and what it offers that's unique.

Even if you never let anyone else read what you've written, we guarantee that writing about your work will help you talk more easily and clearly about what you do. Marriage and family counselor Colene Sawyer, whom we mentioned earlier, says of having written her book, "Writing the book clarified my ideas and my treatment philosophy. It helped me define a focus for my work and create a niche." If you like what you've created, though, it can also become your calling card. You can incorporate it into most of the marketing activities you will be doing. It could even become an additional source of income for you at some point.

For more information about writing informative brochures and articles, see chapter 11. And by the way, if you don't like writing or find typing too time-consuming, try talking out ideas about your work into a tape recorder. Then, have your thoughts transcribed by a transcribing service and review and edit them until you feel you've clarified your thinking and captured the essence of your point of view about the work you're striving to master.

Nothing Sells Like Results

Obviously the mastery required to become preeminent in your field is not an overnight process. It's more like a lifelong journey. Your point of view and mastery will evolve as your work evolves. If you consciously set out to become a leader in your field, the patterns you observe and the understandings you reach will make your viewpoint richer and more compelling with each passing year.

You'll be developing a body of experience and knowledge that can serve as a blueprint for any business-generating activities you want to undertake. Whatever marketing methods you choose can become an ongoing conversation between yourself and those who need or will enjoy what you're offering. Your marketing efforts can be much more than a sales pitch; they can become a way for you to let people know what you're discovering about how to enhance or improve their lives.

Whether you're already established in your field or are entering an entirely new niche, by taking these eight steps, you won't need to twist arms or develop slick marketing angles. You'll be able to communicate to your clients and customers with the kind of credibility, integrity, and sincerity that inspire people to seek you out and tell others about you.

The Best-Known Resource Usually Gets the First Call

Whether you're Dr. Joyce Brothers, Stephen Hawking, or Fine Tailoring by Harry, if you are known as the leader, you will find it easier to attract business. You will be positioned as preeminent in your field. This doesn't mean you have to be "the best," although that helps. It means that people will think of you first. How can you do it? Try the following: (Check off any steps you've already taken and star the ones you want to work on now.)

___ Further the knowledge in your field. Discover something new. Tackle a previously unadvised area of need.

___ Develop a new process or enhancement for your product or service.

___ Create an on-line forum or news group.

___ Pioneer a new niche. Synthesize your previous experience into an entirely new area of expertise.

Becoming preeminent in your field gives you access to gatekeepers, establishes you in your niche, and creates the momentum you need without expensive, time-consuming marketing. ***First usually remains foremost.***

Marketing Masterpiece: A Master of Mastery

Julia Cameron believes that human beings are naturally creative. Unfortunately, however, in the process of growing up and getting educated, many of us conclude otherwise. We conclude that creativity is limited to those special, rare individuals our society calls artists and that we're not one of them. Cameron's mission over the past fifteen years has been to help her clients eradicate this misunderstanding. Over the years, she has developed, refined, and honed her craft of teaching people to unleash their creativity and in the process has established herself as one of the world's leading authorities on how to break through blocks to creativity.

Cameron's philosophy and methods are outlined in the word-of-mouth best-selling book *The Artist's Way,* which she wrote with Mark Bryan. In her live workshops and the book, Cameron and Bryan help people from all walks of life understand why they don't think they're creative and how to unleash their innate creativity. They have identified ten basic principles of creativity along with exercises and Rules for the Road people can use to begin a journey back to their natural creativity. They've developed two basic tools for what she calls "creativity recovery," The Morning Pages and the Artist's Date.

To help people understand what they're experiencing and what they can do to change, Cameron has created terms and metaphors like "filling the well," "creative U-turns," "gain disguised as loss," "imaginary lives," and "poisonous playmates." Her message is sprinkled through and through with inspiring and insightful quotes that bring home her point of view, such as Anaïs Nin's admonition that "life shrinks or expands in proportion to one's courage," Einstein's observation that "in the middle of difficulty lies opportunity," and composer Billy May's warning that "you've got one hundred creative horses. If forty are off wondering what the critics will say, you've only got sixty left to work with. Call your horses back!"

All her methods and concepts come from her own personal experiences. Her results speak for themselves. She says, "I doubt that I can convey to you the feeling of the miraculous that I experience as a teacher, witnessing the before and after in the lives of students . . . the sheer physical transformation . . . the students' faces take on a glow as they contact their creative energies."

Action Steps: Developing a Mastery Plan

Whether you're just starting out or have already been on your own for many years, if you haven't already done so, develop a plan for continually enhancing your expertise.

Make sure your plan addresses only those aspects of your work that you're interested in, motivated by, and curious about. If you try to implement a plan based on what you believe you should be doing instead of what you want to be doing, chances are you won't do it and then you'll be disappointed in yourself and your plan.

- **Set up a system to track your client's needs and progress.** Identify up to ten factors you want to track. Keep notes or other records for each client documenting what you've observed about these factors;

  e.g., "I want to know whether most of the clients for my line of evening wear for overweight women feel embarrassed to show off their bodies."

- **Set forth two to five hypotheses you want to test to determine what works or doesn't.** Track your results with clients. Collect evidence about whether your results match these hypotheses or if they suggest new hypotheses you can test out;

  e.g., "I believe that most of my clients are spending more money than they need to be spending to get their inventories done."

- **Single out one area of expertise at a time that you can focus on and become more proficient at.** You might want to set aside time to practice a particular aspect of what you do regularly at free demonstrations or charity events;

  e.g., "Right now I'm working on getting better at using a razor instead of scissors to create cut layers for customers with long hair."

- **Identify one area of study to explore each quarter.** Read, take course work or classes in a particular area of expertise you wish to enhance. Aim to invest at least four hours a quarter in such continuing education. That's equivalent to the continuing-education hours required in many states to maintain a professional license;

  e.g., "This quarter my goal is to read through the research that's been done on why so many Internet Web sites are abandoned."

- **Consider taking a poll, conducting a survey, or doing at least one informal focus group each year;**

  e.g., "This year I'm going to do a telephone poll of all my past and present clients to find out whether they anticipate doing more or less PR this year."

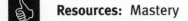

Resources: Mastery

Books

Encyclopedia of Associations, Gale Research Company, Detroit, annual. www.gale.com.

Home Businesses You Can Buy, The Definitive Guide to Exploring Franchises, Multilevel Marketing, and Business Opportunities. Paul and Sarah Edwards. New York: Tarcher/Putnam: 1997.

The Electronic University, A Guide to Distance Learning Programs, National University Continuing Education Association. Princeton, N.J.: 1996.

Peak Learning, How to Create Your Own Lifelong Education Program for Personal Enjoyment and Professional Success. Ronald Gross. New York:Tarcher/Putnam, 1991.

The Power of Mindful Learning. Ellen J. Langer. New York: Addison Wesley, 1997.

Trade Shows and Professional Exhibits Directory. Gale Research Company, Detroit, annual.

Wide Angle Vision. Wayne Burkan. New York: Wiley, 1996.

Research Sources

Finding the Competition

The Internet is increasingly the place to begin researching the competition. We have listed many such resources throughout this book. However, because the Internet is an evolving medium, you will find a significant turnover in sites and resources. Many resources we identified at earlier stages of this manuscript had disappeared as we checked them several months later. So it's wise to use search engines like Hotbot (www.hotbot.com), Yahoo (www.yahoo.com), Alta Vista (www.altavista.com), Lycos (www.lycos.com), and Excite (www.excite.com) yourself to find directories of the businessess like yours and other resources for locating both competitors and potential colleagues. Or use MetaCrawler (www.metacrawler.com), which will search five of the largest directories simultaneously.

In addition to industry lists on the Internet, here are other sources of information for researching the competition:

Directories

Directory of Directories, Detroit: Gale Research. Annual. This directory does what it says. It describes directories of all kinds. Usually available in libraries; however, you may save yourself a trip as some libraries will answer questions by phone.

Dun's Electronic Business Directory, published by Dun & Bradstreet (www.dbisna.com), produces information on companies in multiple formats. It contains information on over 8.5 million businesses and professionals in the U.S., including both public and private companies of all sizes and types. The company information available includes the name, address, telephone number, type of business, number of employees, and its Standard Industrial Code (called the SIC, a seven-digit number developed by the Office of Management and Budget and the Census Bureau, although some databases have modified the last few digits since the codes have not been updated regularly and therefore do not include some new technologies). You can search according to a specific company name, or by product or service, SIC code, city, county, SMSA (Standard Metropolitan Statistical Area) code, geographic location, telephone number, zip code, or number of employees. There is a small per-record charge for each company, and it is available on CompuServe and Dialog. More extensive information on more than 160,000 private and public U.S. companies is available in the *D & B Million Dollar Directory® Series*, available on CD-ROM and in a bound series of books.

On-line Yellow Pages

BigBook (www.bigbook.com)

Bigfoot (www.bigfoot.com)

Four11 (www.four11.com)

GTE SuperPages (www.superpages.gte.net)

ON'VILLAGE (www.onvillage.com) and WhoWhere? (www.whowhere.com).

Researching Products

The Catalog of Catalogs V: The Complete Mail-Order Directory. Edward L. Palder, Bethesda, Md.: Woodbine House, 1997.

Catalogs on the Net! Find who is making their products available on the Internet in catalog form (www.catalog.thelinks.com).

Thomas Register of American Manufacturers. Available on the Internet and in libraries, this is the world's largest industrial source for finding products, services, and companies (155,000 of them). With thousands of supplier catalogs available from the Web site, you can get detailed buying and specifying information (www.thomasregister.com).

Tracking Trends

Newsletters and magazines are two of the best ways to review what the trend watchers are saying. Among the leading publications are:

American Demographics. A magazine focusing on consumer trends. P.O. Box 10580, Riverton, NJ 08076, (800) 529-7502. (www.demographics.com)

Trends Journal, published by The Trends Research Institute, the director of which is the noted futurist Gerald Celente. P.O. Box 660, Rhinebeck, NY 12572-06, (888)ON-TREND and (914-876-6700), fax: (914) 758-5252. (www.trendsresearch.com)

Trend Letter. Global Network, 1101 30th Street, N.W., Ste. 130, Washington, DC 20007, (800)368-0115 or (202) 337-5960, fax: (202) 337-1512. (www.trendletter.com)

The Public Pulse. The Roper Organization, 205 East 42nd Street, 17th Floor, New York, NY 10017, (212) 599-0700, fax: (212) 682-2102. (www.lib.uconn.edu/roper.com)

Government Publications:

Government publications are a good source of information for tracking demographic trends.

Statistical Abstract of the United States. Over a thousand pages summarizing social, political, and economic data from multiple government agencies. Published annually.

United States Industrial Outlook. Forecasts for selected manufacturing and service industries. Published periodically.

Government publications are available from government bookstores as well as on the web at www.access.gpo/su-docs/sale and from private distributors such as www.bernan.com.

In addition, Standard and Poor's Ratings publishes surveys of major domestic industries. For information, contact the company at 25 Broadway, New York, NY 10004-1064, (212) 412-0100.

CHAPTER 4

Developing Your Tailor-Made Marketing Campaign

Good work counts to your advantage only if it is seen, heard and somehow recognized . . . Gilbert of Gilbert and Sullivan even wrote about it: "Toot your own trumpet, or brother, you haven't a chance." —ADELE SCHEELE, *Skills for Success*

"I'm just not cut out to be a salesperson."

"I don't like promoting myself."

"I'm too busy to spend my time marketing."

"I don't have any money for marketing."

"I've been running the same ad for nearly a year now, but I don't get much business from it.

"I've been networking like crazy, morning, noon, and night, but I'm not getting any business from it."

At one time or another we've all had concerns like these. They are real. We're not all suited to sell and promote ourselves in the ways others do so well. We often don't have funds for the kind of marketing we'd like to do. Once we get busy, it's hard to squeeze time for marketing in between the paying work we have to deliver on. And there are perfectly fine marketing activities that are effective for others but just don't work for us.

Fortunately, to get business to come to you, you don't have to have a sales personality. You don't have to try to become someone you're not or grit your teeth to do things that you find offensive. And you won't have to spend more time or money than you have. But, until you become known and sought after, you will need to find ways to "toot your own horn" that you're comfortable with, have the time and money to do, and will produce the results you want.

YOUR GOAL

Enjoy Letting People Know What You Can Offer

In other words, you need a tailor-made plan that suits your personality, your schedule, your budget, and your business. That's what this chapter will help you do. It will walk you through how to decide which marketing activities are best suited to you and your business and how to make doing them appealing, practical, and effective. You'll also learn how you can use the remainder of this book as a tool for creating and implementing your plan and as a resource you can return to again and again to make sure you have ample business coming to you. It starts with taking a look at the way you think about getting business.

Developing a Marketing Mindset

The way you think about the fact that you'll only have as much business as you can generate will have a great deal to do with how much business you get and how easy, or difficult, it is for you to get it. To many people, having to get business is a drag. They feel like career counselor Richard Bolles, who has said that being self-employed is like being on a perpetual job search. Unfortunately, if this is how you feel about getting business, if it feels like a burden or a chore you'd rather not do, it will be difficult, if not impossible, for you to communicate the kind of enthusiasm and excitement that will draw clients and customers to you. Or, if marketing is something you only think about when you're desperately in need of business and you must force yourself to do it begrudgingly, you'll have a hard time developing a creative and effective plan for getting the business you want and need.

We've found that people who have plenty of business don't think about marketing as a drag. Whether they're shy and retiring or outgoing and effervescent, they're so excited about what they have to offer that they *want* to make sure people know about it. In fact, they feel eager, almost compelled, to reach out and make contact in whatever ways come naturally to them so people will know about their work and its benefits.

Lessons from $100,000-Plus Home-Based and Small Businesses

When we set out to discover how successful self-employed people get business, we decided to begin our search with people who have plenty of opportunity to do the kind of work they find most meaningful and earn a good living from it—over $100,000 a year. What we found was that, in addition to focusing, niching, and mastering their work, they do a number of additional things that others usually don't do. First, they're not willing to leave success to chance. They're not willing to wait and see if business comes to them. They're determined to make sure people know about what they do and are motivated to do business with them. Here are the seven lessons we've learned from them:

1. **Develop a Marketing Mindset.** Shift your thinking about getting business so that you're excited, eager, and motivated to do it.

2. **Do What Comes Naturally.** Don't try to be someone else. Choose activities you feel comfortable with and can enjoy doing and that you have the time, money, and motivation to do.

3. **Market in Fertile Ground.** Don't waste your resources marketing in barren fields. Target your efforts to reach people who actually need what you offer.

4. **Take the Initiative . . . and Follow Through.** Don't wait. Initiate enough activity on a regular basis and follow through so that when people need what you offer, you'll be the one who comes to mind.

5. **Don't Bet Everything on One Horse.** Create momentum and critical mass for your business by simultaneously using more than one marketing technique in more than one media. Make sure people hear about you, read about you, and see what you have to offer.

6. **Find a Marketing Platform.** Don't make getting business difficult. Find a platform from which the word can spread about you and your service or product.
7. **Prepare for Results and Let Them Be Your Guide.** Don't lose out on getting business you've generated. Prepare for results. Track what you're doing and let the results be your guide. Experiment to find what works.

This internal drive spurs their creativity and makes them want to find imaginative, and comfortable, ways to spread the word.

So even if you have no marketing or business background, even if you're starting out in a brand-new community without any existing relationships, even if you're competent but not yet outstanding at your work, you can develop a positive marketing mindset that will enable you to create effective and affordable ways to attract business. By making the following three mental shifts in how you think about getting business, you, too, can project a positive mindset and make getting business easier and infinitely more enjoyable.

1. Think Opportunity, Not Obligation

Instead of thinking about what a drag it is to have to get business or how difficult, unpleasant, time-consuming, and costly it is to market yourself, shift your attention instead to how eager you are to let others know about what you offer. If you've chosen the right niche for yourself, you like your work and think it's important. You know it's needed and that it improves the lives or the businesses of your customers. Your work is more than a good idea or a way to make some money; it's a benefit to those you serve.

Without the funds to pay for elaborate marketing efforts and the ability to hire top-notch professionals, your own compelling sense of passion for your work will be the most essential element in attracting business to you. This kind of passion is contagious. It will come through in all your spoken and written communication whether you're introducing yourself or have created a classified ad. So, start to think about marketing as a way to share your enthusiasm for what you do.

Imagine, for example, that you have a wonderful secret. This secret will make all the difference in the world to those who know about it. And by telling others about this secret, you'll get to do what you most want to do and earn a living from doing it. Wouldn't you feel excited to share such a secret? Wouldn't you want to find every way possible to let others know about it? Wouldn't you want to use every spare moment you have to make sure people find out about it? If you've chosen the right niche, this is precisely what you have the opportunity to do.

When you focus on your own needs, problems, and concerns, it's easy to become discouraged, frustrated, self-conscious, or even angry that things aren't going better or faster. But when you're focused on what you can accomplish for others through your work and the positive difference you can make in their lives, you'll start feeling motivated to reach out, to communicate and demonstrate to others in the most effective ways possible. So, shift your attention away from yourself to the value and importance of your work. Instead of focusing on worrying about being rejected or not having enough time or money, shift your attention to what you'll be able to accomplish through your work. Suddenly marketing will take on a whole new meaning for you.

If you don't feel motivated like this by your work, go back to chapters 1 and 2. Think again about how you can niche your work and develop your expertise so that it feels like a valuable secret you just can't wait to pass on to others. The right niche feels like it's your baby. You're proud of it. You want to promote it. You want to bring it forth and share it with the world. It's something you care enough about to fight for, because you may need to.

The right niche is also like a demanding child; it won't leave you alone. It'll pester you to take good care of it. In a way, you won't be able to live with yourself if you don't do justice to it. Amanda McBroom knows this all too well. She enjoyed writing songs and lyrics for her friends and loved ones, but she didn't want to get involved in marketing them in the dog-eat-dog music industry. She thought that would take all the joy out of creating them, but her music began to develop a life of its own. Those who heard it badgered her endlessly to get it into the marketplace so more people could hear it. She resisted. They badgered. She resisted, until slowly over time, she realized her music deserved to be heard and the world deserved to hear it. She knew that unless she took on the task of getting it to market, though, it would never happen.

She took up the challenge, and her music is no longer a well-kept secret among friends. It's been heard on her album *Amanda McBroom—Dreaming,* on Steven Bochco's groundbreaking television series *Cop Rock,* and at the world-famous Pasadena Playhouse in her one-woman show, *Heartbeats.* We now often read about her appearing on Broadway.

To ignite this drive within yourself, remember why you went out on your own in the first place and why you've chosen your particular niche. Reconnect with how much you want to do what you're doing. Remind yourself of how important it is to you and why. When you get bogged down, you might ask yourself, Would I want to go back to work for someone else? If your answer to this question doesn't motivate you to get busy getting the word out, rethink the nature of your business.

2. Think Communication, Not Manipulation

Often people think marketing is about being cute and clever, creating a lot of hype or sizzle. Worse, they fear it's about being manipulative. In fact, at least for self-employed individuals, marketing that will get business coming to you is not about any of those things. Sizzling cute and clever hype may attract attention, but it doesn't build trust, respect, or value. It doesn't foster long-term relationships. That's what you'll need to get and keep business coming to you. That's what you'll need to attract people who are willing to pay your price for the work of your choice. That's what you'll need to get them coming back again and again and sending referrals to you.

So instead of worrying about being cute and clever or manipulative, think about getting your message across. Shift your attention to what it is about what you do that's important to your buyers. Think about how you can communicate your "secret" to them in terms they'll understand. Think about how you can help them see the benefits of what you offer. Hopefully by now you know what it is that makes what you do special, but those who need it will only care about such things if they understand what it'll do for them. They have one thing on their mind—WIIFM: What's in It for Me? Your job is to answer that one basic question. WIIFM is the most popular radio station in the world. If you focus your attention on communicating what's in it for your clients and customers, they'll start tuning in to you. Otherwise, they'll surf right on by.

Your clients and customers want to know how what you provide will meet their needs; what they can count on from you; and what they will get for their money in terms of improvements or benefits to their life, job, or business. Can you save your customers money, time, or effort? Can you increase their ability to compete in their market? Can you make your buyers look good to their bosses? Can you help your clients correct others' mistakes and save their jobs? Can you give them peace of mind? Put yourself in the customer's shoes, and you won't have to twist any arms or come up with dazzlingly clever ways to hype what you do. If you talk about, promote, and advertise from their perspective, your potential customers will be motivated to take notice, get interested, and decide to buy from you.

To help shift your thinking from a seller's to a buyer's perspective, pretend you're buying what you offer from someone else. Talk with people who need and use your service. Hold an informal focus group with your customers. Attend conferences, meetings, and events where your customers gather to discuss their issues. Don't talk; listen. Read what they read. Watch what they watch. Go where they go. Listen and look for their needs and concerns. Notice how they talk about them, the words and phrases they use. Think about how you can explain what you do so it addresses those needs and concerns. Then communicate your message in terms they understand. Use their own words to open their eyes to new vistas that will help them understand and live better in their world.

3. Think about Contact, Not Activity

The gentleman in the first row of the audience we were speaking to had been running a classified ad for a year with little or no response. Several rows back a woman was burned out on networking. Both these individuals were fed up with having to market themselves and their business. But the problem wasn't marketing. The problem was, as is too often the case, that they were confusing activity with contact.

Marketing is about making contact with people who need what you offer. It's not about keeping busy. Both these individuals were busy marketing. They were going through the motions, thinking they were doing everything right. They could probably present a class on how to write catchy ads or networking etiquette, but as good as they were at these marketing activities, they weren't making contact. All ninety-one of the business-generating activities described in part III of this book are potential ways to make contact. But unless doing them actually results in your making contact with the people who need what you offer, they're a waste of your time.

If you're offering a product or service that addresses an unmet need or solves a problem, you probably have a pool of potential customers who need what you have to offer right at this very minute. But chances are they all don't know about you and you don't know about all of them. Somehow you need to find each other. And that's what marketing is about. Marketing is like your flag, your bullhorn, your neon sign that enables you to make contact with people who need what you offer.

Often people ask us, "What's the best way for me to market what I do?" They're looking for *the one* steady, reliable way they can count on for making contact with clients and customers. But there is no single business-getting route that's guaranteed to reach everyone. As you'll discover later in this chapter, there is probably a wealth of activities that will work well for you and your business. Finding the ones that will work best for you is an experiment. In fact, marketing is an experiment. People who are motivated to make contact with those who need them are always experimenting with new possibilities to get their message out.

What works when you're first starting your business may be different from what will work later when you have a waiting list of customers backed up. What will work in a time of economic growth may not work during a recession. What worked using last year's technology may not work this year now that people are turning to still newer technology.

To get business coming to you, you'll need to be willing to experiment, trying several activities, then letting the results be your guide. If, over time, you're not getting the results you want, if you're not making contact, there's no sense in getting bummed out about it; you simply need to keep experimenting further, until you do.

Action Steps: How Do You Feel about Marketing?

What's your attitude toward marketing? Do you need to adjust the way you think about it? Check off any of the following statements that describe you. The higher the numbers you check, the more likely it is that you need to change the way you think about getting business.

___ 1. I love marketing my business. I like letting people know about my products or services. It's fun, interesting, and rewarding.

___ 2. Marketing is OK. It's a natural part of being your own boss, and I don't mind doing it.

___ 3. Marketing is not my favorite thing to do, but it's necessary so I do it. I have to exert a concentrated effort, though, to make sure I don't get so distracted or busy that I forget to do it.

___ 4. Marketing is one of the most difficult aspects of being self-employed. If it weren't for marketing I would really enjoy being my own boss. But having to get business is an ongoing drag.

___ 5. I'd rather have a root canal than do marketing activities. But if I want to be my own boss, I have to grit my teeth, summon up the courage, and do it anyway.

Doing What Comes Naturally

As a self-employed individual or small business, chances are you'll be your own best promoter. In truth, no one else can do it quite as well, or as believably, as you. Not that there aren't professionals or others who can advise and assist you, but you know best what you can do, the benefits your product or service offers, and which marketing activities you feel most comfortable with and adept at. Here's an example of what we mean.

George, a programmer and high school teacher, had developed an administrative management software program for boutique owners. The idea of calling on boutique owners in person caused his palms to sweat and his knees to buckle, so he decided to develop the software and hire a salesperson to market and sell it for him. Once the software was complete, however, he went through one salesperson after another. No one could sell this software, not the retired boutique owner, not the professional sales trainer, and not the computer consultant. All the other marketing activities he suggested to this parade of sales personnel were also of little avail. His funds exhausted, George had a difficult choice to make. He had to either forget about his idea or try marketing it himself.

Convinced that he'd gone too far to turn back, George began thinking about how he could at least sell off his existing inventory. His mother was a boutique owner and had been the one who'd inspired him to develop the program in the first place, so he prevailed upon her to set up a free, two-hour evening seminar for her colleagues on how to increase sales by computerizing their boutique. This he knew he could do comfortably. He was a good teacher and enjoyed teaching. He would simply explain the elements and benefits of computerizing their boutiques and then, to illustrate his points, demonstrate how his software carries out each of the key tasks.

Sure enough, the evening went well. Half the people at the first seminar bought the software that evening. Others placed an order later. He asked those who bought the software for the names of others he could invite to future seminars. Using this approach, before long he had multiple evening seminars each week and plans to make similar presentations at retail trade shows. "I realized," he recalls, "that until *I* could sell this product, no one else could either. Now I'm confident that if I wanted to, I could teach others to sell it, but I'm doing fine on my own at this point."

George was successful because he gave up trying to market his program according to some preconceived notion of what marketing had to be and found a way to make it comfortable, practical, effective—even enjoyable—for him. And that's what each of us must do. Some of the most successfully self-employed individuals are painfully shy and retiring. Others have extremely limited funds. Most have tight schedules. Often they don't think of what they're doing as selling, or even as marketing. Yet they get business by doing what they do naturally in the course of providing their products or services.

So, you don't have to be a great salesperson. And you don't need to try to be someone you're not. In fact, far from it. Usually, the more your marketing reflects the best of your own nature, the more successful you will be. Of course, at times you may want to experiment by doing something that's new and challenging—if so, that's great. But as the owner of a small or home-based business, you will discover that the best marketing methods—at least initially—will always be those that reflect your personality and style: your personal, customized touch.

You never have to use marketing methods that feel uncomfortable or awkward to you.

All marketing activities come down to doing one or more of four things that we've all done since kindergarten: WALK, TALK, SHOW, and TELL. Some of us like to talk. For us, marketing activities from networking to making sales calls allow us to talk to our heart's content. Others of us enjoy being in the limelight, up on the stage, so to speak. Activities like giving speeches or seminars can be our forte. Still others of us prefer to remain in the background and communicate through the written word in brochures, advertising, direct mail and so forth. Some of us work best one-on-one through others like mentors and gatekeepers. Many of us want our work to speak for itself, and it can. We simply have to find ways to let those who might need or want it experience what we do firsthand through demonstrations, exhibits, or samples.

The best marketing activities will be those that enable you to be most fully yourself. Effective marketing is a matter of identifying what you enjoy doing most, what comes naturally to you, and what best fits into your schedule and your budget. There are plenty of options for us all. In Part III of this book, we feature ninety-one different ways to Walk, Talk, Show, and Tell your way to generating business. To help you identify which ones might be best suited to you, you'll find symbols throughout various chapters of the book indicating which activities are which. So you can walk, talk, show, and tell your way to success.

Think about it now, for example: What suits you best? Do you like to make personal one-on-one contact with potential clients and customers? Or do you prefer to stay in the background and put your work in the spotlight? Would you prefer to work through influencers? Do you

WALK, TALK, SHOW, TELL ICONS

Since all business-getting activities are simply one or more of four things we've all been doing since kindergarten, as you read about the various activities for getting business coming to you, you'll find WALK, TALK, SHOW, and TELL icons throughout the book to help you decide which activities will be most suited to and effective for you and your business. In fact, one way you can use this book is to thumb through it at any time and, by looking for the ICONS, pick out one of the kinds of activities you feel most like doing at the moment.

WALK—Activities you can get out and literally do on foot.

TALK—Activities you do by talking to people in person or on the phone.

SHOW—Activities that let people see your work firsthand.

TELL—Activities that provide people with materials that enable them to learn about what you do.

like to tell others about what you do through written materials of some kind? With today's technology there is a proliferation of ways you can give your message a personal touch either in person or without ever making personal contact. Whatever activities you choose, feel free to tailor them to your personality, your business, and you. Make your marketing a reflection of who you are and what you do, because, after all, that's precisely what people will find most engaging.

Since you probably will be the one to implement whatever marketing you do, you need to be sure you enjoy doing the tasks involved and can fit them into your schedule. So, invest your time, money, and energy in business-getting activities that you look forward to trying out.

Don't force yourself to use methods that are unduly stressful, time-consuming, or expensive; you'll probably just end up abandoning them. If, for example, you hate public speaking, don't talk yourself into using seminars as a key marketing tool; there are many other workable methods more suitable to your personality and talents.

Many people find that when they begin doing marketing activities they enjoy, they gain more and more confidence and begin wanting to try out other activities that initially would have seemed intimidating. As your confidence grows, you, too, may want to give your business a boost by trying out various new ways to let people know about you.

Action Steps: What Marketing Methods Are Best Suited to You?

To find which kinds of business-generating activities are most comfortable and interesting to you, take the following quiz. Check the statements that best describe you and select the activities that would be most appealing and easiest to fit into your schedule and your budget. In part III, you'll find the ins and outs for carrying out the business-generating activities you find most applicable.

Making Personal Contact (Chapter 9)

___ I like to meet people person-to-person.

___ I enjoy personally letting people know what I do and how I can help them.

___ I work well when I'm the center of attention, even in the spotlight.

___ I feel comfortable and would enjoy using (check any of the following):

- ___ *Direct solicitation: selling in person or by phone or modem*
- ___ *Free consultations: working directly with prospective clients and customers*
- ___ *Networking: making business contacts at meetings and social gatherings*
- ___ *Sales speeches and seminars: selling to a group*
- ___ *Volunteering: contributing what I offer to trade, civic, or business concerns*
- ___ *Walking around the neighborhood: going door-to-door to meet my clients and customers*

EXAMPLE: Barbara Sacker's secret for getting business to come to her is breakfast. Barbara, the president of Sacker Training Company, woos corporate prospects by inviting them to monthly networking breakfasts she hosts at elegant downtown restaurants. Each month she invites six people who don't know one another. She never gives a sales presentation but, instead, facilitates engaging discussions that highlight her expertise and experience.

Getting Others to Talk About You (Chapter 10)

___ I feel more comfortable letting other people promote and sell what I offer.

___ I enjoy working through and with peers and colleagues.

___ I like letting others know why they should promote my work.

___ I feel comfortable with and would enjoy using (check any that apply):

- ___ *Gatekeepers and mentors*
- ___ *Gift certificates and coupons*
- ___ *Letters of reference, endorsements, and testimonials*
- ___ *Referrals*
- ___ *Sponsorships, donations, and events*
- ___ *Publicity*:
  - ___ *Newspaper*
  - ___ *Newsletter*
  - ___ *Magazine*
  - ___ *Radio and TV*
  - ___ *Business and trade publications*
  - ___ *Cyberspace*

EXAMPLE: Wade and Chery Hudson have a unique niche. As Just Us Books, they publish books for African American children. Publicity has been their best business generator. As the first African American–owned children's publishing company, they've been featured in *Essence, Black Enterprise* and *Emerge* magazines, appeared on African American talk shows, and been covered by the *Washington Post,* the *Detroit Free Press, and the Chicago Sun-Times.*

Telling People All About It (Chapter 11)

___ I enjoy writing about what I do.

___ I'm good at explaining what I do in terms others can easily understand.

___ I'm good at motivating people with words.

___ I feel comfortable and would enjoy creating (check any of the following):

- ___ *Advertising*
- ___ *Articles and columns*
- ___ *Bounce-backs*
- ___ *Brochures and flyers*
- ___ *Bulletin boards, tear pads, take-ones, and door hangers*
- ___ *Card decks and coupon packs*
- ___ *Catalogs*
- ___ *Direct mail*
- ___ *Fax-back, broadcast fax, and E-mail*
- ___ *Flyers*
- ___ *Inserts*
- ___ *Newsletters*
- ___ *Phone and hold button messages*
- ___ *Postcards*
- ___ *Product packaging and point-of-sale displays*
- ___ *Sales letters and proposals*
- ___ *Reply cards*
- ___ *Web site*
- ___ *Yellow page and other directory listings*
- ___ *Your own book*

EXAMPLE: Ed Voil's business is Vertical Systems Analysis. He helps companies evaluate and improve their elevator service. With the help of marketing consultant Carol Milano, Voil created an inexpensive fourteen-page booklet called "Owner's Guide to Better Elevator Service," which features charts and a form he uses to evaluate elevator service. These booklets are his calling card. He uses them as handouts at trade shows, at speeches he gives, and to get publicity in trade publications targeted at residential and commercial property managers and co-op and condominium board members.

Showing Off What You Can Do (Chapter 12)

___ I primarily enjoy doing what I do, and I do it well.

___ I feel more comfortable letting my work speak for itself, and I don't mind finding ways to show it off.

___ I don't mind being the center of attention as long as the focus is on the work I'm doing or have done.

___ I feel comfortable and would enjoy using (check any of the following):

- ___ *Audiotapes*
- ___ *Business cards as samples*
- ___ *Compact discs*
- ___ *Demonstrations*
- ___ *Displays*
- ___ *House parties, open houses, and occasion events*
- ___ *Media appearances*
- ___ *Multimedia Web sites*
- ___ *Photos and portfolios*
- ___ *Radio advertising*
- ___ *Having my own radio show*
- ___ *Samples and giveaways*
- ___ *Television—advertising*
- ___ *Having my own television show*
- ___ *Trade shows and special events*
- ___ *Video brochures*

EXAMPLE: Erica Gjersvik deals wholesale in handmade Mexican crafts, and they sell themselves when the right people see them. She makes sure they do so by taking a booth each year at the semiannual International Gift Fair in New York. This show puts her crafts in front of important buyers and boosts her credibility. By seeing her there year after year, buyers who are choosing gifts that will be featured in catalogs know her company stands for quality and beauty.

Marketing Mistake: Forcing Yourself to Do Marketing You Dread

Janet was so excited. Having just opened her business in private arbitration and negotiations counseling, she had found her perfect work. She had always been expert at helping people resolve disputes and had just completed her formal training to become an arbitrator. Now, through a serendipitous relationship, she'd been invited to speak to one of the major national trade associations. The exposure and relationships she could build at this conference could launch her career, so she leaped at the opportunity.

As the event approached, however, she began to feel increasingly apprehensive. She had virtually no public-speaking experience, and just the thought of climbing onto the podium to address a crowd of hundreds was making her heart pound and her palms sweat. She even began having nightmares that she lost her voice at the beginning of the speech. This opportunity was too good to pass up, however, so she strengthened her resolve to press ahead and began preparing her presentation and rehearsing it with a vengeance.

By the day before the event she felt sure she could have given the presentation standing on her head, but that night after a cross-country flight, she had a grand bout of nerves that left her sleepless. Exhausted and filled with anxiety the next morning, she headed off to the conference hall. As the presiding official began to introduce her, she thought she was going to faint and when she stepped to the podium, her nightmare turned to reality. She began to speak and then her mind went blank. She froze. Pausing, she started again. Again she froze. Just as she thought she had surely died and gone to hell, someone in the audience called out to her, "Just take a breath, and relax. We're all eager to hear what you have to say." She took a breath, and this kind gentleman continued to walk her through her anxiety for four or five minutes until she was finally able to finish her speech.

It was an hour she would never forget. She'd made a lasting impression, but not the one she'd hoped for. While the audience was kind (many of those present reached out to express their support), for years to come she was remembered as the woman who lost her voice. She had made the classic mistake of not tailoring her marketing efforts to her personality. Yes, it was a great opportunity, but she had no experience in public speaking and, like so many of us, was highly fearful of it. Had she listened to her feelings (and her dreams), she would have had ample warning of possible problems ahead and could have arranged for a way to participate at the conference that would have been more in keeping with her skills and comfort level.

Since she works well with small groups, she could have offered to host a roundtable at the luncheon, instead of speaking to a large crowd, for example. She could have offered to pull together a panel presentation that included her mentor and other colleagues she respected. Or drawing on her strength as an arbitrator, she might have presented her speech as a demonstration in which she illustrated her approach to arbitrating. Certainly any of these approaches would have greatly reduced her anxiety and boosted her confidence.

Marketing Masterpiece: Getting Business Doing What You Love

Psychiatrist Dr. John Schairer describes himself as relatively introverted. He hadn't been marketing his practice because he just didn't like doing the type of marketing psychiatrists typically do to build their practices; i.e., giving talks and attending meetings to network with other psychiatrists. He doesn't like to hype his practice, and his point of view is somewhat unique: instead of trying to convince clients to adopt his philosophy of life, health, and well-being, Schairer strives to listen very carefully to his clients to understand their point of view, the truth of their experience. Then, he helps them resolve their difficulties within their own perspective, thus enabling them to achieve their goals with the least amount of catastrophic change.

The idea of tailor-made marketing fit right in with the nature of his practice and, like most mental health professionals these days, Schairer knew he needed to find an innovative way to fill and build a self-sustaining practice. Here's the tailor-made campaign he developed for himself: Since he gets most of his clients through referrals from other professionals, he's always sought to develop his reputation by having satisfied clients return to their referral source and explain the positive results they've gotten by working with him. To build upon this approach, he decided to host a workshop in his home with a highly regarded teacher of meditative techniques and invite his existing and potential referral sources to attend.

He was completely comfortable inviting colleagues to be his guest at a workshop he himself was eagerly looking forward to experiencing. The nature of the workshop made a statement about his interests and his point of view as a practitioner. It enabled him to become "Top of the Mind" with existing referral sources and gave him the opportunity to make contacts with new like-minded practitioners. Even though some people he invited couldn't attend the workshop, Schairer still had the opportunity to call and talk with professionals he'd been wanting to meet, all without having to step into the traditional sales and marketing role he finds uncomfortable.

The results were dramatic. From the contacts he made through this tailor-made approach, he filled his practice within two months. Over the following year, he reached a critical mass and his practice has remained full for the past two years.

To follow up and track his results, Schairer has created a billing program that includes a referral tree. He can track his income according to referral sources, and he can track referrals from any branch on the tree. Now he's linking this program to his US Robotics Pilot hand-held computer, so the information he enters during sessions with new clients will be automatically entered into the billing program and transferred to his desktop computer for storage and analysis.

Finding Fertile Ground

Georgina is outgoing, friendly, and engaging. She loves to network. It's a natural for her, but the results of her efforts have been disappointing. She creates elegant, trendy, custom-designed women's clothing and laments, "I've been networking like crazy for months. I went to five meetings this week alone. But I'm not getting any business. What's wrong?"

It would seem Georgina is doing all the right things. She's been attending small-businesswomen's organizations because she had noticed how plain and dowdy their wardrobes usually are. "They really need me!" she explained. But the response she's getting suggests otherwise. The women she's meeting may need her, but from what she tells us, they don't know it. The women Georgina has been networking with were not particularly image conscious. At their luncheon tables they talk about their new office equipment, hiring practices, and investment opportunities, not the latest fashions. Georgina has been networking in barren fields.

For your marketing efforts to pay off, you have to market in fertile ground. You need to be making contact with people who are actually experiencing a need for what you offer. It's certainly harder to earn a living as a missionary than by helping people achieve something they already desire. Your marketing efforts need to be suited to your business and your customers' needs as well as to you and your needs. In Georgina's case, we urged her to stick with networking, but to target her activities at women in professions where image and personal appearance are vital to success, like professional speakers, ad agency executives, or public relations specialists.

To reach such individuals, instead of running around madly to lots of business and professional meetings, we suggested that she work through gatekeepers like facialists, hairstylists, and makeup artists who could refer her to women who would be interested in attending a by-invitation-only private showing and networking event which she can host each month at her studio.

Charles was also marketing in barren fields. He was trying to start a scholarship matching service. "This is a lot harder than I thought," he told us. "I've been advertising in the newspaper every weekend for the past four months, and I've had very few calls. I'm not giving up, though. I'll give it a year and if it doesn't work by then, I'll have to look at doing some other business."

While there are many parents who need to find scholarship funds for their college-bound children, how likely would they be to look in the newspaper for help in finding such scholarships? Most parents would be more likely to contact a school counselor, a college testing service, teachers, or maybe a parents' magazine or school newspaper. Seeing an ad in the newspaper and knowing nothing about the company offering the service, they might fear that they'd be taken in by some kind of scam. So Charles, too, needs to start marketing in more fertile ground.

Let results be your guide.

While you need to allow time for your marketing efforts to produce results, you also need to see some signs of results and, if you're not getting any, adjust your efforts as soon as possible. Instead of advertising all year in one newspaper, Charles could sample a variety of marketing activities until he finds fertile ground, something that's suited to both him and his business. Charles could set up a Web site for parents of college-bound high-school students, for example, network with school counselors, or even try a classified ad in a parents' magazine.

Finding the best business-generating activities for your business

To find the best marketing strategies for your business, identify which type of business you are, a service or a product business, and whether your clients and customers are primarily consumers or other businesses. You can use the chart and examples on the following page as a guide. Then as you read about the activities you're most interested in doing in Part III, you'll see sections called ***Best Bets*** which will tell you what type of business each activity is best suited for.

Tip: Also review the methods your competition is using. Investigate what people in your field both locally and from other parts of the country are doing. Find out what seems to be working best for them. If you find that most of them are continually using the same one or two methods over others, this is generally a sign that these methods work well in your field. Find ways to tailor this approach to your personality and your niche.

If no one is using a marketing approach you find appealing, don't automatically discard it. If it's plausible, try it out. What works for others may not be the best approach for you, and they are not you.

Initially the best methods of promoting your business will tend to require a relatively low investment of cash in exchange for a greater investment of your time and energy.

Marketing activities also vary significantly in terms of how much time, money, and energy they require. Networking and building a referral program, for example, require considerably more time and energy than using direct mail and advertising, but they cost less. Marketing methods also vary according to how quickly they produce results. Directly soliciting business in person usually produces results more quickly than getting business to come to you through referrals. Writing personal letters, sitting down at the phone, or calling on prospective customers door-to-door will probably be quicker than using networking or public relations.

Many people are so averse to selling, however, that they would rather use more indirect methods that take a little more time. But if you don't have time and need business fast, sales promotions are probably your best bet, because they encourage people to buy immediately! Here's

SERVICE BUSINESSES

Consumer	Business
Bed and breakfast	Bookkeeping/Accounting service
Carpet cleaning/Window washing	Computer programmer
Day care for children or adults	Equipment repair
Hair styling/Beautician	Information brokering
Lawn/Landscape maintenance	Medical transcription
Plumbing/Electrician	Public relations/Publicity
Repairs/Refinishing	Sales training
Resume service	Secretarial/Word Processing service
Tax preparation service	Translation service
Wedding planning	Webmaster

SERVICE/PRODUCT BUSINESSES

Consumer	Business
Balloon delivery	Architecture/Building contracting
Cabinetmaking	Commercial art
Calligraphy	Computer consulting
Catering	Desktop publishing
Couturier	Import/Export
Gift-basket service	Industrial video production
Home remodeling	Instructional design
Jewelry design	Security consulting/Installation
Photography	Trade show exhibit building

PRODUCT BUSINESSES

Consumer	Business
Antiques	Audio and video training programs
Bootmaking	Corporate specialty gifts
Crafts	Customized business cards
Embroidery	Customizing cameras
Herb growing	Custom office furniture
Jewelry making	Small clothing manufacturing
Knitting supplies	Software publishing
Mushroom growing	Toolmaking
Perfume	Wholesale catering
Web store	Wholesale nursery

a comparison of how the various methods addressed in this book relate on the time/money continuum.

THE TIME/MONEY MARKETING CONTINUUM

More Time	Networking		Public Relations		Direct Mail		More Money
Less Money		Referrals		Sales Promotions		Advertising	Less Time

Until your business is well under way, you should be willing to spend at least 40 percent of your time and money on marketing. This means that since successful self-employed individuals work an average of sixty-one hours a week, you could spend twenty-four hours or more each week marketing. If you don't have any business yet, you should spend your entire week marketing until the business you generate starts filling your time. Then, even when you get busy, we recommend setting aside at least 20 percent of your time and money for marketing. The wisest time to market is when you have business, because if you wait until a slow time, you may have to endure a long dry spell while your marketing efforts take effect. And, you'll be trying to get business from a needy position. That makes it more difficult to project the self-confidence required for others to place their confidence in you.

Choose marketing methods that will provide you with the easiest and least costly access to the specific people you want to reach.

As your business grows and you have ample customers to fill your time, you may want to shift the balance of your marketing efforts to activities that may cost a little more but free your time for billable work. So to find the right balance on the time/money continuum, ask yourself

1. How much business do I need?
2. What can I afford to do?
3. How much time do I have to invest?
4. How much effort will the activity I undertake require relative to the business it will generate?
5. What will I be motivated to do?

THE FOUR MOST EFFECTIVE LOW-COST MARKETING METHODS

There is clearly no single marketing approach that's guaranteed to work for everyone or every type of business. What will work best for you will most likely be a variety of activities that are best suited both to you and your business. Nonetheless, we've found there are four methods of attracting business that seem to produce the best results for the most people relative to the time, energy, and money they involve.

The Fastest: WALK Around the Neighborhood.

For those who feel comfortable meeting people face-to-face, one of the fastest ways to get business to come to you is to pick out a target building, street, area, or type of establishment where you'll find people who need your services or who serve people who do. Then simply walk from office to office, booth to booth, or store to store introducing yourself and leaving your materials. Repeat this process regularly. By the third visit, those you meet will probably remember you.

EXAMPLE: When Rosemarie Vega started her pet-sitting service in Deer Lake, New York, she began by dropping by pet food stores, veterinarians, and dog groomers, one by one, introducing herself and her service repeatedly until she developed a number of such gatekeepers. She says, "This is the best source of business for me. When I get a referral from one of these sources, the client almost always hires me." For more information on this business-generating method, see page 346.

The Least Threatening: TALK to Gatekeepers.

If you hate to sell, working through gatekeepers is one of the easiest and least threatening ways of getting business. Gatekeepers are people who in the process of what they do every day come into regular contact with people who are in need of your service or product. You can get plenty of business by developing relationships with such gatekeepers.

EXAMPLE: When draftsman Michael McCormick decided he wanted to do freelance work, he approached several contractors he knew, showed them his work, and expressed his desire to work with them. Now he gets all his business through referrals from three of these contractors.

For more about this low-risk marketing method, see page 400.

The Most Fun: SHOW What You Do by Sampling

If you love the work you do, sampling is one of the best ways to make getting business fun. If you find a way to let prospective clients and customers sample what you offer, your work can sell itself and your marketing efforts become additional opportunities to do what you like most. Whether you offer a service or product, there is always some way you can stimulate interest by providing a sample that gives people a taste of what's to come that whets their appetite.

EXAMPLE: Marla Harper has been fascinated with gargoyles since childhood, and she's turned her passion into a livelihood. She hand-paints gargoyles from reproductions of famous buildings throughout the world on T-shirts, tote bags, sweatshirts, and other items. And as you might imagine, she promotes her business by wearing her creations.

For more about this nonthreatening marketing method, see page 618.

The Most Exposure for Your Money: TELL Your Story Through the Media

Tell
NEWS
Articles
Direct Mail
Newsletters
Publicity
Yellow Pages

Publicity can be one of the best low-cost ways to become well known. Studies have shown that an editorial mention is often more effective than paying for advertising in that same media. The best publicity, be it in trade journals, newsletters, magazines, on-line, or on radio and television, can tell your story to the very people who are most interested in hearing it.

EXAMPLE: When Judy and Shell Norris decided to start a reunion planning business they were pioneers, they could find no one else doing it. To help spread the word they sent a news release about their new service, and it was picked up by the *Wall Street Journal.* Within no time what they thought would be a part-time business became full-time employment for them both. In the process, they launched an entirely new industry.

For more information on gathering publicity, see page 372.

Taking the Initiative ... and Following Through

"I put every extra penny I had into a beautiful direct-mail campaign. I hired a designer and a copywriter. I used four-color printing. I bought a targeted list. I did everything according to the book. But the only call I've gotten so far was from someone who wanted to do the printing for my next mailing!"

This comment was from the owner of a public affairs consulting firm, but we hear many similar stories. In selecting business-generating activities, it's easy to lean toward the more passive methods like direct mail, advertising, directory listings, Yellow Page ads, and so forth, where you hope people will see it and wait for them to call you. These methods are quite appealing because they're relatively nonthreatening and don't require a lot of our time. And after all, aren't these the methods most often used by corporate America? If they work for the big guys, why not for us? As one woman said, "I just want to put in some ads and have the phone start ringing." But, too often the phone won't ring.

Don't wait.

While there are circumstances when more passive methods like advertisements and directory listings do work for self-employed individuals, they usually work better as an adjunct to other more active methods, like networking, meeting gatekeepers, giving speeches, or going where you actually make personal contact with potential clients or otherwise making sure people personally experience your product or service or get a recommendation from someone who has. Particularly at first, it's difficult to rely on more passive methods for your primary source of business. Chances are you'll end up spending more money than you can afford, and you'll be disappointed with the results.

Think of your own reaction to flyers, brochures, advertising, and direct-mail solicitations you receive from someone you've never met or heard of. When was the last time you personally hired a complete stranger from a directory listing? When you receive a mailing for a particular product or service, what are you most likely to do with it? Unless you already know about the person or company who sent it, chances are it went straight into the trash; much unsolicited mail is never even opened. But let's say you did open it and were even interested in the product or service. Would you call or might you decide to seek out someone you already know who does something similar? Or would you get a referral from a colleague or merchant you trust?

More often than not, the kind of products and services self-employed individuals provide aren't the type that people will buy from an ad or a mailing. Of course, there are exceptions, but think again of your own reaction. If you needed to hire a lawyer, accountant, management consultant, or event planner for your business, would you be likely to hire such an individual based on an ad? If you needed a pet-sitter, investment counselor, facialist, real estate appraiser, or even a bed-and-breakfast inn, how would you go about finding one? You'd be more likely to seek a referral from a friend or colleague than to respond to a flyer you received in the mail. Here's an example:

"We saw an ad in a travel magazine for a bed-and-breakfast inn in Aspen," our friend told us. "It looked great, but pictures can be deceiving. So, we called a referral service and got several names. Coincidentally one of the inns we were referred to got a positive review the following week by a travel writer for our local paper. That cinched it. We made the reservation and we loved the inn."

As this story illustrates, a more active, personal, multi-pronged approach usually gets the best results. The most successful methods for getting a steady stream of word-of-mouth business are usually those that create visibility and credibility and build personal relationships. More passive methods can be used to follow up on contacts or as visual reminders of a relationship you've already initiated through other means. In other words, to build relationships and credibility, you need to do active things you can enjoy and do naturally, be they networking with gatekeepers, doing direct solicitation in person or by phone, giving free consultations or demonstrations, or speaking or exhibiting at trade shows. Then, if your budget allows, you can use more passive methods like mailings, advertising, and directory listings to keep yourself and your business in the minds of prospective customers so that when the moment comes when they need you, they will think of you immediately and be able to find you.

This is how "top of the mind" marketing works. The public affairs specialist, for example, who spent all his money on a direct-mail piece would be better served investing his time and money in networking or presenting at professional meetings and then following up each month by sending a newsletter to the potential clients he's met. This newsletter might feature tips on how to create an effective public affairs program.

Mark Johnson couldn't wait for someone to call. He couldn't afford to. He was fired from his job without warning or any severance package at 4 P.M. on a Friday. Over the weekend he decided to go out on his own. He didn't ever again want his financial security to ride on the whims of corporate downsizing. So, in debt and without savings, he set a goal on Monday morning: he wasn't going to sleep until he'd generated \$300 in personal income. He spent the day calling potential clients and signed up his first consulting assignment that day. The next day he set the same goal. Within about ten days he was well on his way to what became a \$75,000-a-year business.

High-Tech Tip: Tailor-Make Your Marketing with Technology

Today, there's never an excuse for not reaching out to connect with potential clients and customers. Today's technology, from faxes and modems to E-mail and voice mail, opens a wealth of opportunities to communicate more quickly, easily, and personally than ever before. In future chapters, you'll find many examples of how technology is making it easier every day to WALK, TALK, SHOW, and TELL your way to lots more business. Here are three steps, however, that can help you develop a more effective tailor-made plan.

Find Prospective Clients and Customer Lists on the Web

Visit sites like LookupUSA (www.lookupusa.com) and iMarketing Center (www.imarketinc.com) to find free and fee-based services to help you locate new customers. LookupUSA has 88 million household addresses and 10 million business listings, and you can see the listings on maps that you can print out. iMarketing Center includes a database of 10 million prospects from which you can search and select the precise names you want, as well as profiles of more than 10,000 industries and a directory of over 100,000 professionals categorized by specialty and geography. It's also available on CD-ROM as *D&B MarketPlace*.

Use Electronic Post-It Notes

Are you tired of having sticky yellow reminder notes tacked up all over your office but have never found a better way to make sure you follow through on what you need to do? Well, try *Post-It* Software Notes by 3M. This software package puts the convenience of those pesky Post-It Notes inside your computer. Posting electronic Post-Its on an electronic Memoboard will not only be certain to tidy up your desk; you can also print them out if you wish and attach them as personalized notes to your mailings. In fact, you can even E-mail them as reminder notes to others or attach an alarm to any note you make that will notify you when it's time to take follow-up action.

Know When Enough's Enough

Of course, it is possible to spend too much time and money trying to line up a particular client or customer. But how do you know when enough's enough? Small-business consultant Amy Skolen of Strategic Solutions suggests dividing the amount of time and money you spend on each customer by the revenue each brings in to determine what you can afford to invest. Using a program like Intuit's *Quickbooks,* you can track your hours and overhead on a project-by-project or client-by-client basis and gather the data you need to make such marketing decisions.

Think about the activities you're using now and those you've used in the past. How many of these activities are more impersonal and passive in nature? As you explore the methods in part III, see if you can include a wider range of activities that involve taking personal initiative. It won't mean that you'll have to use methods you're uncomfortable with. If you don't like to network in person, for example, you can network online. If you don't like giving speeches, you can host a Web site that gives people a glimpse of your personality and style and a chance to interact with you.

Until you're well known and readily recognizable, we recommend an 80/20 mix of active to passive methods.

Set a goal to initiate a specific number of personal contacts each day, week, or month. Then make sure you follow up on them. If you don't, you could end up warming up the sale so that someone else can step in and take the order. That's what happened to Marjorie. She came up to us during a break at a seminar we were giving to share her disappointment. She was selling advertising specialties. Several months before, she'd met someone at a conference who seemed quite interested in her service, but only that week she'd learned that he had placed a large order with her competition. "I don't understand it," she said, shaking her head. "He told me he'd call as soon as their budget was approved. I gave him my card. He'd even picked out the items he wanted. We filled out the order form together."

Marjorie had done everything right up to a point. She had sold her contact on placing an order, and he did. Unfortunately he placed it with someone else. She did the work; the competition got the business. She had come face-to-face with the old saying "Out of sight, out of mind." Has this happened to you? You may never know. It was only by accident that Marjorie ran into her competitor at a networking meeting and learned of her misfortune. Often you never realize how much business you've lost unless you follow up later and find that someone else walked in to complete your sale.

Don't let others get the business you've generated.

To make sure contacts actually do call you when the moment comes that they need you, you have to follow through and keep in touch. Follow-through is part two of "top-of-the-mind marketing." Give out your business cards but, more important, get the cards of those you contact or find other ways to be sure you can follow up. If you've taken a booth at a trade show, get the names and addresses, phone, fax, or E-mail addresses of those who express interest in your service. Then follow up immediately. We attend several trade shows each year, but we can count on one hand the number of people who made a follow-up contact based on interest we expressed at a booth. Often they could have gotten our business. All they would have needed to do was remind us of our interest and make it easy for us to buy.

Of course, we all get busy. We forget. We don't want to be bothersome. We misplace the name and number. So, we tend to just wait and hope she'll call us. "After all, she said she would call when she was ready." Don't leave your success to chance. Think of how many other people may be contacting those you've gotten interested in your product or service while you're waiting. Think of Marjorie. Take action to keep your name ever-present in the minds of your prospective clients. Nothing is colder than a long-forgotten contact, no matter how eager the person seemed when you first talked.

Don't just keep churning up new contacts, month after month, leaving sales you've already made lying around for others to collect. What a waste. Allocate equal time and money for following up on what you've initiated. Create a database of contacts using mailing-list, contact-management, or personal-information-management software. Use this software to send your past, present, and prospective contacts something at least quarterly or contact them via fax, modem, or E-mail whenever you have a spare minute or need to give your business a boost.

Reasons for Not Following Up

Following up is easy to forget. But by not following up on interest you've generated, you're leaving the door open for someone else to walk in to business you left on the table. Here are some of the most common reasons for not following through and what you can do to avoid them.

1. **I'm too busy.** Well, you may not be too busy for long if you don't follow through on getting work for the future. To make sure you don't forget about follow-up, use contact or personal information management software like *Act!, Ascend, Lotus Organizer,* or *Microsoft Outlook* to schedule your follow-up. Most of these programs have alarms, tickler systems or reminder features that will alert you to the follow-up tasks you need to do.

2. **There's no reason to make contact.** There's always some reason to make contact with anyone who's already expressed interest. You can call with added information. You can find out if there are further questions. You can simply convey that you want to follow up.

3. **I don't want to seem pushy.** You never have to be pushy to make a follow-up contact. Be friendly. Be helpful. Be thoughtful. Be curious. Many people respond positively to persistence and determination. It conveys that you're sincerely interested in doing business.

4. **I don't know what to say.** When you're at a loss for words, simply remind the person you're talking with of your last conversation and tell her that you're calling to follow up. You might ask if she's given any further thought to your conversation, if she has any further questions, if you can provide her with any additional information.

5. **He may not remember me.** It doesn't matter if he remembers you or not. It's nothing personal. Everyone is flooded with information. Everyone has his own priorities and pressures. After you remind him of your last contact, if he still doesn't recall, simply tell him again about what he was interested in and proceed as if you were making a new contact.

Yes, it takes time to set up and keep up such a database. But it's worth the investment. This list can become one of your most valued assets. Once you have the system set up, you can send out a mailing or send a broadcast fax in less time than it would take to go to a network-

PURGING YOUR MAILING LIST

According to Linda Rohrbough, author of the prize-winning book *Mailing List Services on Your Home-Based PC* (McGraw-Hill), 20 percent of mailing list addresses more than one year old are probably incorrect. Keeping your list purged and updated is something you can do yourself or hire a mailing list service to do for you. If you decide to do it yourself, here are some suggestions from Rohrbough:

1. **Update routinely.** When mailings are returned and phone numbers, faxes, or E-mail change, enter the changes or remove outdated contacts at the time. Don't let such changes accumulate in your in-box or some special file "to get around to updating some day." They'll get misplaced or the job of entering them all will grow too large to fit conveniently into your schedule. If you have a lot of updates, you might want to hire someone to come in regularly to enter them or hire a mailing list service to do them for you.

2. **Clean your list periodically.** First, you need to clean your list using a software package like *My MailManager* for Windows 95 or *My Deluxe MailingList* for Windows 3.1, by My Software. This software includes the U.S. Postal Service CD-ROM which compares your database with 11 million delivery points in the U.S. to see if the addresses are still current. My Software Company is located at 1259 El Camino Real, Suite 167, Menlo Park, CA 94025-4227, 650/473-3600), or visit their Web Page at http://www.mymaillist.com.

3. **Poll your cleaned list.** Once you have a clean list, you can periodically poll the list to determine if they're still interested in receiving your mailings. The most cost-effective way to do this would be to send a First Class postcard with an attached business reply card that people can return to request your newest free catalog or other giveaway. By sending your postcards First Class, you can have "address correction requested" printed on the front of the card. The post office will then notify you of any address changes.

   Make sending the reply card back as easy as possible. Those wanting to continue getting your catalogs should be able to simply tear off the reply card and pop it in the mail postage-paid. You can call your nearest U.S. Postal Service Postal Business Center to find out whether it will be cheaper to put a stamp on each business-reply card or to apply for a Business Reply Permit, in which case you will only have to pay postage on the reply cards that are actually returned.

Rohrbough also suggests asking on the business-reply card for the names and addresses of others who might want to receive your catalogs.

ing meeting. So, keep your list up-to-date and, to save time and money, purge it regularly.

No matter how busy you get, keep plenty of business in the pipeline.

Until you become so well established that you've consistently had a waiting list for several years, don't let your initiative slip. Of course, as your business grows, you won't have to initiate as much activity and you can rely more heavily on passive marketing methods. Once you're consistently busy year after year, you can try reversing the 80/20 formula, if you wish, to 80 percent more passive activities and 20 percent more active ones. Just be sure the passive activities you choose are actually having an impact. Otherwise, they're a waste of money and leave you with a false sense of security.

Most important, however, is to keep initiating. Getting business is much like riding a bike. You have to pump and pump at first to get up to speed, then you can coast. But, not for too long, or you'll end up at a standstill again. That's what happened to computer consultant Bill Slavinsky. After a stunningly successfully first year, Slavinsky was so busy that he had little time to market. But he wasn't worried. In fact, he withdrew the surplus money from his company and took a well-earned vacation. He returned to an empty desk and no business in the pipeline. It took several months to prime the pump and get business flowing again. But, he's never made that mistake again. Now he always has several marketing activities under way, no matter how busy he gets.

Telecommunications consultant Mark McKibben had never done much marketing. Right from the start, he had one large client who kept him busy . . . until they decided to pull the plug on his contract. Fortunately he was protected until the contract ended, but he never again wanted to risk his fate on a canceled contract or a fickle client. He immediately launched his first marketing campaign and hasn't been without one since. His rule of thumb is simple: he never allows his monthly expenses to be covered by income from a single account. This philosophy has paid off. He now runs a seven-person 1.25-million-dollar business, McKibben Communications of Chatsworth, California.

In other words, if you want to keep coasting, you've got to pedal periodically. As a past client explained to Slavinsky why he'd taken his business elsewhere, "I haven't seen or heard from you in so long, I figured you were either too busy or out of business." So reach out on a regular basis, at least quarterly, even after you're busy and well established. Make sure people keep you in mind. Should you generate more business than you can handle, set up referral agreements with colleagues who can handle your overflow. You can do the same for them when your business is slow.

Tip: To avoid the risk of large client defections, financial expert Ashok B. Abbott of West Virginia University suggests this for self-employed individuals:

Balance long-term and short-term projects. Long-term clients provide a base of ongoing steady business; short-term projects free your time to market and protect your income from sudden cancellations. Aim for a 40/60 split: 40 long-term, 60 short-term.

High-Touch Tip: Keeping Your Marketing on Track

It's easy to think you're doing enough of the right kind of marketing, yet end up wondering why you don't have more business. To help solve this problem, we've developed ***The Business Generator,*** a marketing kit to keep your marketing efforts on track and make sure you're initiating and following through frequently enough on the right kind of activities. This multimedia kit helps you get on a regular schedule and continually adjust the amount of marketing you do to the amount of business you need.

It also guides you to the activities that are best suited to you and your business and provides a way for you to check out if you're implementing your activities with the frequency you need. Available through Nightingale Conant, 7300 North Lehigh Avenue, Niles, Illinois, 60714, (800) 323-5552 ($129.95) or Brubaker Tapes, 410 Gatewood Terrace, Sierra Madre, CA 91024, (800) 561-8990. Also available on CD-ROM ($49.95), through Brubaker Tapes.

Don't Place All Your Bets on One Horse: Create a Critical-Mass Marketing Campaign

"I was looking for someone to help us design a rec room. My neighbor recommended someone they'd used, but I didn't get around to calling him. Then when I was reading an article in the paper about remodeling, I noticed that this same man was quoted in the article. That very afternoon while I was at the hardware store I saw a flyer announcing a class on remodeling. It was being taught by this same man! I couldn't escape it. Obviously this was the person to call. I did, and we've been very happy with his work."

You've probably had an experience like this yourself. It illustrates why you can't rely on only one approach to getting business. To get business coming to you, you need to initiate a combination of activities so those who need your services and their referral sources will see you, hear about you, and read about you repeatedly in as many different ways as possible. This is what we call *critical-mass marketing,* and it enables you to develop a sufficiently high profile that your name becomes a powerful magnet that will draw business to you. By creating a critical mass of attention, people will think of you first and foremost.

When Helen Berman decided to become a consultant and sales trainer for the publishing industry, she found that the competition was tough. There were already a number of well-known consultants serving this industry. So how was she to break in? She knew that calling a list of potential customers would be costly both in time and in money. The people on such lists wouldn't know who she was or what her training programs involved, so she would have to place lots of calls to make even one sale.

So, instead, she sought to build a high profile for herself and her programs that would cause interested, qualified individuals to identify themselves to her. Then when she contacted them, they would already know who she was and be motivated to talk with her. In this way, the same number of contacts would lead to many more sales.

Having researched what the hot sales topics would be, she contacted meeting planners for upcoming conferences in the publishing field and proposed that she provide seminars that addressed these topics using her sales methods. She got several bookings. Simultaneously she began calling the trade magazines in the field to explore writing a sales column for them. Soon, based on the reputation she was building through the trade shows, she was writing a column for *Folio,* the magazine publishing industry's leading trade magazine.

From attendees at her workshops and contacts made as a result of her column, she identified potential clients who would immediately recognize her as a credible professional. She contacted them by phone and mail, and soon her training calendar begin filling up. By the following January, Helen was booked ahead for the entire year.

You've heard the saying "Success attracts success." Critical-mass marketing operates on that principle. It assumes that if you create enough momentum around yourself and your work and then follow through by providing a top-quality service or product, your success will grow.

Here's another example of critical-mass marketing. When aspiring movie director David Beaird came to Los Angeles, everyone told him Hollywood didn't need another director. And indeed he found the studio doors closed tight. Having taught acting and having built a theater company in Chicago several years before, however, he decided to use that experience to get into film directing. He rented a theater and began teaching acting classes there on Monday evenings. Soon he put on a play he'd written, starring students from his classes. He then invited the press and industry representatives to see it. Many liked it. It received several drama awards from a local trade paper. The momentum was building. Based on the response to his play, he was able to attract backing for a low-budget film.

Although the film was never distributed, he did get to show it at the Cannes Film Festival and received some attention. That led to further backing. After his second low-budget film, he reached his critical mass and was placed on the directors' list for a major studio. Three years later, he finished the film version of the original play he had put on at the theater. It's called *Scorchers*. It stars Faye Dunaway and after having been released in movie theaters, it's now available on video. David was able to create the critical mass he needed to leap to a level of success that might have taken many years to accomplish via more traditional routes.

Here's how to build a critical mass like these for your product or service.

Never rely on only one marketing method at a time.

Instead of putting all your marketing efforts into one activity, as Charles did by pinning all his hopes on one regular newspaper ad or as Georgina did by trying to rely on attending lots of the same networking meetings each month, draw on a variety of coordinated activities that will establish you as preeminent in your niche. Allocate whatever time and money you have to several methods simultaneously to find out which ones produce the best results and have the maximum impact. Don't risk running out of money and energy before you get known well enough that business starts coming to you.

Select a variety of complementary activities.

Have at least five compatible marketing activities under way at all times so people will repeatedly see you, read about you, and hear about you wherever you turn. Select a mix of activities that suit your goals, your personality, your business, your time, and your budget that you can carry on simultaneously over a specified period of time. Try to include a variety of ways clients and customers can experience you: (1) through some form of personal contact, (2) through others who sing your praises and recommend you, (3) through reading about what you do, and (4) by directly seeing or experiencing the results you produce.

In other words, think of your business-generating efforts as a *campaign*. That's an ideal word to describe what you're wanting to accomplish. A campaign is a systematic course of activities coordinated to accomplish some specific purpose. And indeed, that's exactly what your marketing efforts need to be: a systematic course of activities that are coordinated for the purpose of getting business to come to you. Consider, for example, this six-month campaign for how Grace, the woman we described earlier who wants to earn her living as a poet, might promote her niche business: Lyrics for Love's Special Occasions.

Grace might select a six-month promotional theme, "Love Is in the Air," focused on sponsoring a gala fashion show in conjunction with a local bridal boutique. She and the boutique owner could begin their campaign by promoting the show three months in advance by taking out ads in the local paper, setting up an in-store promotional display, lining up donated prizes of romantic dinners from local restaurants, and getting the restaurants to give away coupons for the fashion show. Then, of course, they could send a news release to the local media about the upcoming show.

During the show itself, Grace could disseminate gift cards with love lyrics to those present, sing the lyrics as the bridal models walk down the runway, and generally promote her services. She could offer a special price to anyone who registers for a new class she'll will be offering on How to Keep Romance Alive. With any luck and a lot of personal communication with the editor of the daily living section of the local paper, this joint effort will draw a feature story either before or after the show in the local paper. Similarly she might get television coverage of the event, especially if it's a slow news night, has a Valentine's Day or June Bride theme, or she can arrange for local celebrities or other dignitaries to participate.

During the three months after the show, Grace might send those who attended a series of postcards featuring special seasonal offers like "Why Not Have a Romantic Saint Patrick's Day?" or "Make Summer the Time for Romance." A certain number of those who signed up for her class may want her to plan events or provide other services for them. So she can offer a free initial consultation for class members. At the end of the six months, Grace should review the return on her efforts and make plans for the next six months' campaign.

Action Steps: Develop Your Five-Star Campaign

In creating critical mass, five seems to be the magic number. If you can mix and match five WALK, TALK, SHOW, and TELL activities simultaneously, you can create lots of momentum while keeping your marketing efforts manageable. In the above example, Grace's Five-Star Campaign includes: (1. SHOW) a special event, (2. TELL) a public relations effort, (3. SHOW) sample gift cards, (4. TALK) seminars, and (5. TELL) follow-up postcards featuring special offers.

In creating your first campaign, we recommend starting with a combination of the kind of activities you like doing and feel most comfortable with from pages 125–28. Read about the pros and cons of the various marketing methods you've selected in the following chapters and choose five that best suit your market, personality, interests, skills, time, and budget. Then begin experimenting with the activities you've selected, keeping in mind this fundamental rule of successful marketing:

> ***The measure of a successful marketing campaign is the extent to which it reaches at the lowest possible cost the greatest number of people who can and will buy your product or service.***

Based on your results, you can continually add new activities to your mix, dropping some and adding others, to obtain the greatest impact and maximum exposure for your niche.

Aliza Sherman is the founder and creator of Cybergrrl Webstation (http://www.cybergrrl.com), a source of on-line information and resources for women. To attract women to her site, she (1. SHOW) relies on publicity both on-line and off, (2. TELL) writes articles about women and technology, (3. TALK) networks through her local Webgrrl chapters, (4. TELL) sends out direct mail, and (5. TELL) publishes a cybergrrl newsletter.

J. Murray Elwood of Stratford, Pennsylvania, has carved out a niche providing career counseling to lawyers. He is a lawyer himself, and his five-star marketing plan consists of (1. TALK) establishing personal relationships with the directors of career development at the four local law schools where he also offers workshops (SHOW), (2. TELL) placing his brochures at legal and professional meetings, (3. TALK) networking at Chamber of Commerce and Bar Association events, (4. TELL) placing ads in the weekly suburban edition of the legal newspaper, and (5. TELL) sending regular mailings to human resource directors, priests, pastors, adult-education directors, and recent graduates listed in law school alumni directories.

Don Holcombe's five-star marketing plan is a mix of high-touch and high-tech approaches for attracting the public's eye to his one-of-a-kind painted rock and mineral artworks. Based in Payson, Arizona, he (1. SHOW) exhibits at consumer and trade shows, (2. SHOW) makes week-long appearances at the Grand Canyon Lodge, (3. SHOW) arranges for his artwork to be displayed at tourist facilities, and (4. TELL) sends mailings to a targeted list of art-loving celebrities and collectors. To make sure the right people actually see his mailings, (5. TALK) he establishes a relationship with key gatekeepers and sends them personal handwritten notes.

Maximize Your Marketing Efforts

Since any marketing activity you undertake requires some investment of valuable time and money, make the most of each investment you make by piggybacking as many other marketing activities onto it as you can. In other words, take advantage of as many of the opportunities a given marketing activity presents as possible. When you undertake any one activity in your five-star marketing plan, go through the list of methods above on pages 125–28—or browse through the table of contents—and identify as many other activities as you can that could dovetail with or augment your efforts. Then, mix and match suitable methods for maximum impact.

If, for example, you're planning to speak at a major conference that many of your prospective clients will be attending, don't just show up and go home with a pocketful of business cards to follow up on. Before the conference, send a news release about your appearance to the newsletter of your appropriate trade association. Talk with the editor about a feature story on your topic to help boost conference attendance. Plan to advertise in the conference program guide, so that everyone attending will read about you even if they don't attend your presentation.

If you've already established yourself as an expert and are on the way to becoming well known, you can offer to sign copies of your book, if you have one, at the conference or to host a roundtable discussion. This will help the conference planners attract registrations and give you added exposure on the program.

Do a mailing inviting key individuals you want to meet to attend your speech. You might send them your news release or a postcard. Hand out samples or free materials at the speech that provide information about your product or service and include some special offer good for the week of the conference.

After the conference, you might write an article for your trade journal summarizing issues of note that arose from discussions during the workshop. Send a copy of the article, whether you get it published or not, to your past, present, and prospective client list.

Again, one of the most rewarding aspects of using critical-mass marketing is that, like riding a bicycle, once you get the momentum going it enables you to go further faster with less and less effort. Activity you generate develops a life of its own, and you find that not only do you have to call fewer people, but a growing number of people are also calling you. Efforts from months and years ago continue to bear fruit.

We still get calls from articles that people clipped five years ago. That's why we use the term *critical mass*. Once you achieve it, the momentum will keep your business going, and growing.

Finding a Marketing Platform

While other health-oriented bakeries on Los Angeles's upscale Westside have failed or floundered, Alaine Carnegie's sales are soaring. What's the difference? Her baked goods are delicious, but so are others'. She's busy marketing, but so are others. There is one dramatic difference, however: While others are struggling for visibility in a crowded marketplace, Alaine found a platform from which to market Alaine's Bakery. She's actively involved in the vegan movement. Vegans are total vegetarians who eat no meat or dairy foods. She speaks to their groups, brings samples to their meetings and conferences, exhibits at their expos, does joint demonstrations with their representatives at local health-food stores, and much more. While, of course, not all Alaine's customers are vegans, they're an organized community, all highly committed, vocal spokespersons for their lifestyle, so they readily and eagerly spread the word about good health-conscious food that meets their requirements.

Recently, Alaine's high-energy Rain Forest Cake has become a big hit with cyclists, so cycling circles have become a second platform from which she can gain new advotees. An avid networker, Alaine is finding that these platforms provide ample opportunities to use a wide variety of marketing activities effectively while doing things that come naturally to her and for which she has an abiding passion herself.

You can build a critical mass much more quickly with less investment of your time and effort if you find a platform like these from which you can launch your business-generating activities. For sales trainer Helen Berman, annual trade shows for the publishing industry and her column in *Folio* was her platform. Director David Beaird's platform was the small theater he rented. For Dave Lakhani, owner of the Computer Clearance Center, a used-computer store in Boise, Idaho, it's sponsoring an annual swap meet.

Lakhani's annual swap meet has become a popular event at which attendees either trade or buy used and new equipment. He uses it as a springboard for publicity and other promotional activities like radio spots, participating in promotional card packs, and getting feature stories in newspapers, one of which generated 1,200 phone calls in one day! From those calls 120 people came by his store and 70 made a purchase. Lakhani also co-hosts a radio show now that serves as another platform for his business.

Based on his own training program, cyclist Johnny Goldberg created a forty-minute fitness program called Spinning. At first he tried opening his own Spinning gym, but this didn't work out. So he moved his classes from one gym to another and finally home to his garage. Having to compete with a plethora of fitness centers, he needed a platform and in 1994 he found it. He contacted Schwinn about making a new-and-improved Spinning cycle and began showing off his program at industry trade shows. These demonstrations still attract large crowds and serve as the platform for what is now a worldwide network of trained instructors who teach his program in more than a thousand fitness clubs worldwide.

Teaching trade-school classes was the platform for the programmer James Milburn. Milburn began his career as an accountant, so he understood what small-business people needed in customized software. He spoke their language and could get the computer to speak it, too. But how was anyone else to know he was any different from any other programmer? He showed them by offering low-cost classes in custom programming for small businesses. These classes became his marketing platform. Some of his students soon learned how difficult programming customized software could be, and they knew they didn't want to do it themselves. Since they could see that Milburn understood their needs, he got their business.

Free consultations for corporate employees became the platform for Teri Goehring. An image and color consultant, Goehring offers free image seminars for corporation employees during the lunch hour and sells products to those who attend. The Science of Mind Church became a platform for Jerry Florence. Instead of waiting for a record company to produce his first musical album, he produced it himself and sold copies at church performances. Within two years he'd sold over thirty thousand copies and was booked to sing concerts across the country. The Internet has been the platform for Bill Vick. Vick operates an executive recruiting firm and by being among the first to offer and promote his services online, he's become a leader in his field.

Think of what could serve as a platform for you launching your marketing activities. Don't wait, however, until you find a platform to begin implementing your five-star plan. Often you'll find the ideal platform in the process of initiating and following through on business-generating activities.

Making Your Marketing Efforts Self-Liquidating

Most self-employed individuals have limited marketing funds. Yet they have a pressing need to generate income. So why not arrange for your marketing activities so they not only generate business but also pay for themselves. In other words, when possible, turn your marketing activities into profit centers.

Computer guru Dave Lakhani, for example, rents advertising display tables at his annual swap meet to small-business owners for $50 each. Fees from the advertising cover the costs of his event.

Sometimes sales trainer Helen Berman is paid to make presentations at the trade-association meetings where she markets her programs. Or she may be offered a free booth at a convention. Even when she is simply reimbursed for her expenses, most of her marketing costs are being paid for. Sometimes she's paid to write for trade magazines and journals. But even if she contributes an article for free, she can arrange to barter for ad space in exchange for her article.

By a similar token, Director David Beaird can charge for his acting classes and thereby cover the cost of the theater through which he is able to promote his work. Charging admission to plays also helps offset his marketing costs.

Preparing for Results and Letting Them Be Your Guide

Here's a nightmare that's so awful you'll probably think it could never happen to you, but in fact in one way or another it happens too often. Tanya had spent several months lining up a special segment featuring her makeup seminars on one of the most popular radio stations in town. After sending a dynamic media kit, she followed up by phone and courted the producer through weeks of telephone tag. Once she'd piqued interest, she sent segment outlines, did a guest appearance to "test the waters," and repeatedly followed through until the feature segment was actually scheduled.

You can imagine her excitement when the segment was finally aired. And sure enough, it generated a stream of calls all day long at the center where she conducted her seminars. Only one problem: Her seminars weren't part of the regular schedule of programs offered at the center and although the center administrator knew about the upcoming promotion, no one had alerted the receptionist. Not having been informed about Tanya's seminars or the promotion, callers were told there were no such programs being offered!

Not only did Tanya miss out on a lot of business before this misunderstanding was corrected, but a deluge of calls from disgruntled listeners complaining to the radio station about not being able to find the seminars strained what would otherwise have been an excellent ongoing media contact.

The lesson here comes through loud and clear. Whatever marketing activities you plan to undertake, don't initiate them until you're set up to respond successfully to the business they generate. To do otherwise is to waste your time and money and risk your reputation. Here's how to avoid a number of the most common ways people inadvertently miss the very business they've worked so hard to generate.

Have your product or service ready. Planning to launch an innovative Web-based service for entrepreneurs, Craig sent out a media release. As is so often the case, he ran into a few glitches in developing the site. As a result, when editors and producers tried to visit the site, it wasn't up and running. He made an impression all right, but not the one he wanted to make. Don't let this happen to you. Make sure your product or service is ready to go before announcing it to the world.

Have your phone system in place. Have your phone service set up and prepared to be answered professionally either by you or knowledgeable, trained personnel. If clients expect to respond by fax or E-mail, have these in place as well. The proprietor of a cleaning service we spoke with recently lost a major contract because he didn't have a fax so he couldn't receive their specifications quickly enough to submit a bid. A carpenter found an answering machine full of hang-ups after taking out his first classified ad in a suburban weekly. He solved the problem by getting a cellular phone and having incoming calls forwarded to him wherever he was working.

Consider a business telephone listing. No matter how people find out about you, they may lose track of your phone number. If you have a business phone listing, however, they can find you by calling information or looking you up in the Yellow Pages.

Have promotional materials ready to send out. When Brian decided to do travel consulting as a sideline business, he wasn't sure if he would be able to make money, so he didn't want to invest in printing business cards, brochures, or other materials until he tested the waters. So when he introduced himself at a local Chamber of Commerce event, he was unprepared for the many people who asked for his card, brochure, fee schedule, and so forth. At first he told people he was too new at it to have any materials, but since he could see that was making the wrong impression, he had to improvise.

He told those who approached him that if they would give him their cards, he would send material to them in the mail and call the following week to answer any questions. Then, he did what he should have done in the first place. Using *Microsoft Publisher* and paper he ordered by phone for overnight delivery from Paper Direct, he created interim cards and stationery and promptly followed up on his contacts.

Action Steps: Tracking Your Results

As John Schairer did with his software program, set up some way to track how each new contact learned about you so you'll know which of your marketing efforts are working and which ones aren't. Then invest more of your time and money in those methods that are producing the best results. Keep in mind, though, that volume is not always the best measure of success. If one activity generates thirty contacts but only two sales, it's not as effective as an activity that generates only ten contacts and six sales. Likewise an activity that generates six clients who spend $100 for a one-time consultation isn't nearly as effective as an activity that generates one $10,000 year-long contract. So in tracking your results, you have to track:

Response— How many contacts you made.

Sales— The percentage of contacts that actually resulted in sales.

Income— How much income was generated from each sale.

Quality of Sales— Such factors as how soon the client pays, how long or frequently they'll need you, and whether they are in a position to refer other business to you.

Public relations specialist Suzanne Tanner learned the importance of such analysis early in her business. She had a choice to focus her marketing on two different industries. One was for a fast-growing industry with many eager start-up companies, but often cash strapped like herself, these companies generally had a forty-five-day accounts payable policy. The other industry was unstable and overcrowded, but the industry norm was to pay fees up-front. Eager to get some cash flow going, she went with the quick-pay industry. Unfortunately, however, because the field was so volatile, the projects she got were usually short-lived and due to the competitive nature of the industry, they rarely led to other referrals. She quickly realized she needed to refocus her marketing efforts on the more dependable, albeit slower-paying, industry.

Contact management and financial software like Intuit's *Quickbooks* can be helpful to you in collecting the variety of data you need in order to measure your results. The key, however, is that you have your own system for knowing where each order, sale, client, or customer came from. Without this you can't correlate your results with the marketing activities that produced them. Here are several possibilities:

1. When a prospective client or customer calls, always ask how he or she heard about you and immediately open a contact management file where you can record the response. If you do this using contact management software or some other type of database, you can set it up so you'll be able to sort the database by marketing method and see how many contacts and ultimate business each method is generating.
2. Code all your ads, flyers, newsletters, and other written materials with different department numbers; e.g., John L. Johns, Computer Consulting, 1234 Main Street, Department D, Central City, N.Y. Then by making sure to request the department number, you'll be able to sort order forms or calls by which marketing activity each person is responding to.
3. Ask how clients heard about you on all order forms or agreement forms they fill out when they begin doing business with you.

Are You Ready?

You don't have to wait until all the things mentioned in chapters 1 through 4 are in place before you start getting business. Often you can't. Many of the steps we've outlined in these first four chapters will be an ongoing process. Some will take time for you to implement. Nonetheless, we've been surprised to discover how many people print up cards and stationery, choose a business name, and start marketing themselves without having thought through and committed to a particular niche, without having identified their expertise, and without having outlined a plan for how they'll get business that they'll be comfortable with implementing.

So, in these chapters, we've presented an overall philosophy for how you can become well known and sought after. You can use this philosophy as a guide throughout the life of your independent career to assure that you have ample business coming to you. Whether you're already in business or just beginning, you need to start building your success from wherever you are now. As you get each of these elements in place, however, you'll find that getting business becomes increasingly easy. Before long, you'll be one of those individuals who says, "Oh, I don't have to do much marketing; plenty of business is coming my way. Most of it comes to me by word of mouth."

To check on your progress to date review this list:

___ 1. Are you focused? Have you committed to one specific identifiable business that people can clearly understand?

___ 2. Have you found your niche, something people need that you can become known for?

___ 3. Are you known as a specialist or expert in your niche? If not, have you worked out a plan for developing your expertise and demonstrating why you're the best choice?

___ 4. Do you have a Tailor-Made Marketing Campaign?
- ___Have you identified what type of marketing activities you enjoy and do most naturally?
- ___Are you marketing in fertile ground?
- ___Do you have a Five-Star Marketing Campaign?
- ___Does your marketing include ways for clients and customers to have personal contact?
- ___Are others starting to talk about you?
- ___Do people have a chance read about you?
- ___Have you found ways to show off what you do?
- ___Have you found a platform for your marketing activities?
- ___Are you tracking your marketing results so you know what's working and what isn't?

PART II

GET SET:

Creating a Winning Marketing Message

The end of understanding is not to prove and find reasons but to know and believe.

—Thomas Carlyle

"Our hands are always in the spotlight," the attractive woman told the group of businesswomen, "from the first handshake to the one that seals the deal. What do your hands say about you?" Background luncheon chatter ceased. Everyone was looking at the speaker; their eyes dropped down quickly to glance at folded hands, most of which were clean but sporting chipped, chewed or otherwise neglected fingernails. "As a manicurist," she went on, "I understand most businesswomen don't have the time or money for a weekly manicure. So, I've created a way women can care for their own nails at home. It's called Natural Nails and in less than thirty minutes a week, you can look like you've spent hours at the salon."

Her hands, which were beautifully manicured, held a book. The cover design was simple, elegant, and clean. It mirrored her hands holding a single pink rose. The title read *Natural Nails.* She said no more. The mistress of ceremonies had asked everyone to keep their introductions short. Within moments the sound of whispered side conversations returned and the meeting proceeded. But when the formal program ended, it was obvious few had forgotten about Natural Nails. A large crowd formed quickly around the manicurist. She was busy passing out her business cards which matched the cover design of her book, as did the catalog she was handing out that explained her various nail- and skin-care products in a friendly, personal tone.

Isn't that how we'd all like our message to be received? Loud, clear, and compelling, even magnetic. Yet compare this impression with those you more typically see and hear. How often do those you meet introduce themselves with nothing more than their name and the field they're in? How many times has someone handed you a generic business card sporting a generic business name and looking nothing like the attached brochure? How often have you seen people attract initial interest in what they do only to see that interest wane right before their eyes as they stammer when they try to further explain their business? How often do you hear those you meet apologize awkwardly for not yet having a brochure to leave behind or explain nervously why they're crossing out the telephone number on their card to fill in the current one?

When it comes to making the right impression, it's often little things like these that matter most. There's a saying that you don't get a second chance to make a first impression. Nowhere is this adage more true than in your business life. Whether you're writing a letter, sending a direct-mail piece, placing an advertisement, making a simple telephone call, or introducing yourself at a networking meeting, you have mere seconds, if that, to make people want to see or hear more. Therefore, it is up to you not only to create a good product or service but also to make sure that your first impression is a positive one.

Whether your first contact is in person or in print, on-line or via the mail, making a positive first impression begins with communicating your message in a distinctive and impacting way. Since you often have only seconds to do this, you must make sure people instantly grasp what you do. Who needs you and why must come through loud and clear in the way you introduce yourself, in the name you choose for your business, and in the visual images you select for your business cards, stationery, and marketing materials.

In our rush to get established, it's easy to cut corners and try to scrape by. In an effort to make the best possible impression, it's equally easy to waste needless dollars preparing fancy materials that miss the mark. Making a clear, consistent, and compelling impression is not about spending a lot of money. It's about thinking out what you want to say and finding cost-effective ways to attract interest and instill confidence and trust. That's what this section is about: how to craft your message so that it gets to the heart of what makes you special. It's about choosing the right words and the right visual images to make a name for yourself and leave an unforgettable impression.

Are You Set?

You may be ready to do the business that comes to you, but are you set up to make the kind of impression that will attract it to you? To find out, complete this checklist and then read chapters 5 through 8. You may be surprised to find that by taking a few simple steps you can boost your business dramatically without having to greatly increase what you're doing or how much time you're spending to market yourself.

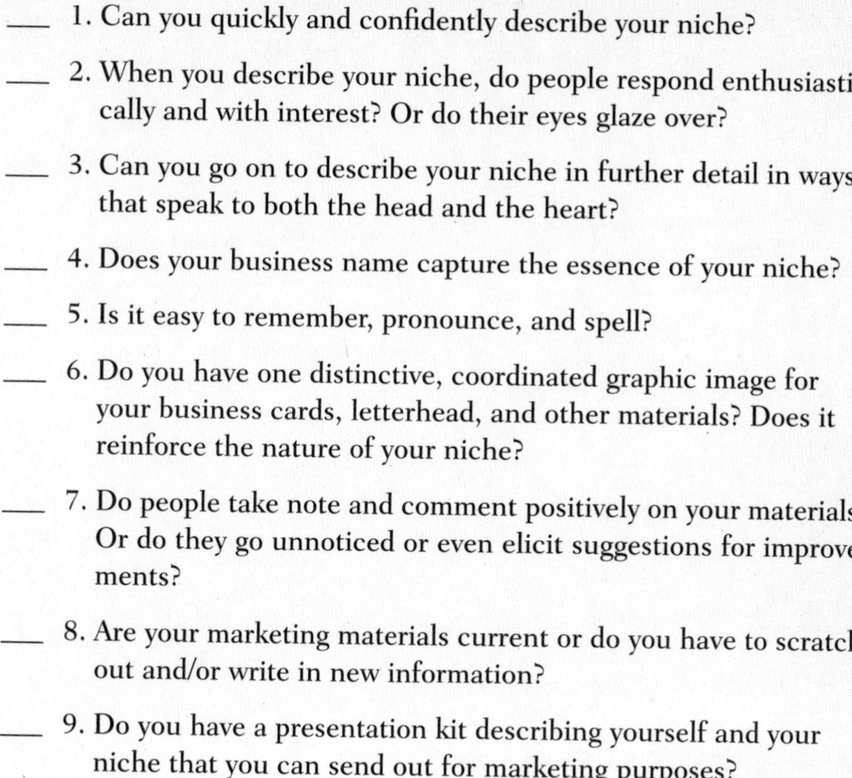

___ 1. Can you quickly and confidently describe your niche?

___ 2. When you describe your niche, do people respond enthusiastically and with interest? Or do their eyes glaze over?

___ 3. Can you go on to describe your niche in further detail in ways that speak to both the head and the heart?

___ 4. Does your business name capture the essence of your niche?

___ 5. Is it easy to remember, pronounce, and spell?

___ 6. Do you have one distinctive, coordinated graphic image for your business cards, letterhead, and other materials? Does it reinforce the nature of your niche?

___ 7. Do people take note and comment positively on your materials? Or do they go unnoticed or even elicit suggestions for improvements?

___ 8. Are your marketing materials current or do you have to scratch out and/or write in new information?

___ 9. Do you have a presentation kit describing yourself and your niche that you can send out for marketing purposes?

As you read through the following chapters, you will find that the most important aspects of creating a winning marketing message will usually involve little or no additional cost and, if done correctly, whatever you invest will come back to you again and again in increased business.

CHAPTER 5

Describing What You Do in a Memorable Way

If you can't say what you mean, you can't mean what you say.
—BABYLON 5

The new member seemed friendly and confident as he extended his hand to introduce himself to the informal group gathered around refreshments. He was greeted pleasantly, but as he explained what he did, everyone was momentarily at a loss for words. They recovered quickly, however. "Nice to meet you," several mumbled, introducing themselves and returning to continue their previous conversations.

Have you ever had an experience like this in meeting someone for the first time? Do you every find yourself at a loss for words because as the person tries to describe who he is and what he does, you have no idea what he's talking about? Such conversations usually end quickly. No one likes to appear foolish or ignorant, and we don't want to embarrass others by implying that we can't understand what they're saying.

Similarly, you've probably opened an advertising flyer or been handed a brochure or business card, but, try as you might, you don't have a clue as to what service or product is being described or why on earth you'd be interested in it. What happens to such mailings, brochures, and cards? Of course, they end up in the trash.

Most of us have many experiences like these, yet when it comes to our own businesses, we're confident no one would ever have such a reaction. Nonetheless, overgeneralized or overly technical and professional jargon have put an instant end to more conversations and landed more marketing materials in the trash than just about any other marketing mistake. Unfortunately, this problem is a lot like bad breath. It's hard to know when you've got it because while what you're saying is clear to you, few people will tell you when it's not clear to them.

But just think of all the opportunities you have to explain to people what you do. Every time you introduce yourself to someone, in person or through your printed materials, on your voice mail message, your written communication, and every marketing activity you initiate, each of these activities presents the opportunity to attract interest and stimulate desire for your services and products. Yet, how easy it is to stumble over such explanations on the spur of the moment or to simply settle for the more conventional or mundane solutions. Or, on the other hand, how perplexing it can be to sit down and try to craft what you do into one clear, concise, attention-getting, appealing, thought-provoking, and compelling statement! With a little forethought, though, it need not be such a challenge.

If you truly want your marketing efforts to start bringing business your way, how you describe your niche needs to send one consistent message that gets right to the heart of the matter from the perspective of those you're communicating with. Your marketing message needs to capture the essence of what makes you special in a way that 1) gets attention, 2) makes an impression, and 3) sparks a desire in those who would be your customers, clients, or referral sources. No matter how great you are at what you do, no matter how many marketing activities you initiate, or how much money you spend doing them, unless you accomplish these three things, you'll be wondering why you don't have more business. Describing your niche effectively is what this chapter is designed to help you do.

Once you have a winning description that captures the essence of what makes you special, it can become the theme that runs through all your promotional and marketing activities. Having one winning core description can work for you like a set of Russian nesting dolls. Have you ever seen a set of these brightly colored lacquered dolls? At first you see one large doll. Then you discover you can open the doll and inside you'll find another smaller doll virtually identical to the first. This doll can also be opened to display a still-smaller doll, which can be opened to a still-smaller one, and so on down to the tiniest possible doll. Well, once you find an effective way to describe the heart and guts of your niche, the kernel of that thought can work just like a nesting doll. It can become the blueprint for how to present yourself in all contexts. You can boil it

YOUR GOAL

Let People Know Where You Shine

down to a one- or two-word business name or expand it to a one-line slogan, a sizzling seventeen-second introduction, a powerful display ad, a multiple-page brochure, a Web site, a full-blown presentation, or even a book. It all starts with getting down to the heart of the matter.

Getting to the Heart of Your Message

Whatever medium you'll be communicating in, if you want people to seek you out, your message will need to strike some chord within them, something that wakes them up for a moment and takes them out of their routine, away from whatever's on their mind at the time, and rivets their attention on what you're communicating. Here's an example of what we mean.

Before attending one of our "Getting Business to Come to You" seminars in Seattle, Gayle Larson had been describing herself as:

> *"a computer applications consultant, specializing in applications training, program installation, macros and template design and program selection and solutions."*

She wasn't happy with the response she'd been getting when she described her work in this way and at the seminar, she discovered why. She perceived herself as a user-friendly computer trainer, a specialist at putting people's fears and concerns about technology and software to rest. But the way she'd been introducing herself in person, on her business card, and in her other marketing efforts was intimidating to the computer novice and the technophobic. She was actually sending the opposite message to what she wanted to be communicating.

At the seminar, she clarified her focus and designed her message. A new name for her company was born on the spot: Terror-Free Computing. Later, she discovered that her hunch was right. By introducing herself as a user-friendly software trainer, she got the response she wanted. She could focus her message in this way without losing other types of related business. This response gave her the courage to print new business cards and adopt a new image. Her business card now reads:

Terror-Free Computing,
Specializing in Software Training.

Using this same theme on flyers and throughout all her marketing efforts began producing dramatically improved results.

By taking similar steps, secretarial business owner Julie Tennenbaum of Kansas City, Missouri, was able to increase her business by 50 percent. She went from projecting an image as a generic service to a specialist who could take her clients' projects from conception to final draft. Final Draft is now the name of her business.

Had these people changed? Had their skills increased? Did they have to spend a fortune on fancier, more expensive marketing? No. What changed was that they started describing their special skills in a way that got to the heart of the matter.

Speak to Me Where I Live

If you can speak to people at the heart of where they live, you'll get their attention, pique their interest, and spark their desire. So, to get your message across, you need to speak first to the heart, then to the head. Many marketing experts refer to this process as focusing on the *benefits* of what you offer instead of the *features* of what you do.

Unfortunately, too often Features/Benefits discussions degenerate into a prime example of the very mistake they're trying to prevent. By focusing on abstract or complex terminology and concepts, they leave you feeling confused and dazed. So instead of focusing on the difference between features and benefits per se, we're going to talk about how they can help you get right to the heart of the matter for those who would be your customers and then reassure them by getting down to the facts of the matter.

Features are the facts about what you do, how you do it, and why you do it the way you do. Benefits, however, are the positive results someone will get from using your product or service, whatever it is you offer that "does their heart good." It's the promise of these results that sparks desire. Here's why.

Benefits address the heart of the matter. All the following are statements of fact about a particular product or service.

- The VCR programs itself.
- The car has a steel frame.
- The accountant is a CPA.
- The attorney is a Harvard graduate.
- The milk is pasteurized.
- The gold is eighteen karat.

- The cleaning service is bonded.
- The printer uses four separate color cartridges.
- The flatware is sterling.
- The speech teacher helps you speak clearly and confidently.
- The software provides easy reporting.
- The temp agency screens applicants thoroughly.
- The designer has won awards.
- The publication has 1,000 target readers.
- The computer is a Pentium II.

All these statements speak to the head. Are they important? Probably. But what's missing when you're focusing on such facts is *why* they're important. What "value" are they to the user? That's where "benefits" come in. They get to the heart of the matter. The facts about what you offer address the *inquiring mind* that's asking, "What will it do?"; the benefits answer the *hungry heart* that wants to know, "What will it do *for me*?" Features address "What?" Benefits address "So what?"

Finding benefits in the facts. Let's take a look at what's significant about the facts we've listed above. What kind of issues lie at the heart of the matter for each of them?

FACT:	HEART OF THE MATTER
The VCR programs itself.	You don't have to read instructions. The clock won't blink at you. You won't feel stupid. You'll get to see the program you want.
The car has a steel frame.	You won't get hurt.
The accountant is a CPA.	You can rely on her knowledge. You won't go to jail or lose everything you have.
The attorney is a Harvard graduate	He's gotta be sharp, so you'll win the case.

The milk is pasteurized	Your family won't get sick.
The gold is eighteen karat.	You'll be envied and admired. She'll be happy with you. You'll feel good seeing her happy.
The cleaning service is bonded.	You don't have to worry about theft or damage.
The printer uses four separate color cartridges.	You won't waste ink and, therefore, money. It will be easier to change. You won't waste your time.
The flatware is sterling.	You'll impress your guests. You'll feel more important. You'll enjoy its beauty.
The speech teacher helps you speak clearly and confidently.	You can sell more of your products/services. You'll be liked or admired. You'll be more successful.
The software provides easy reporting.	You'll get the information you need. You'll stop getting frustrated. You'll save time. You'll service your customers better.
The temp agency screens all applicants thoroughly.	Your work won't suffer. You won't get behind. You'll get exactly the work done you need.
The designer has won awards.	You'll get more business. Your materials will be better than your competitors'. More people will pay attention to your company.

The publication has 1,000 target readers.	You'll get more calls, more business. You'll feel successful.
The computer is a Pentium II.	It will be faster, therefore, you will be faster. You'll be able to get more things done. You'll look good to your boss and make more money. You'll feel proud having the latest and whizbang-best.

As you can see, the facts focus on the product or service, while getting to the heart of the matter addresses the inner needs and concerns of the user. This is a critical distinction. The facts are pretty clear-cut, but what lies at the heart of the matter can be highly personal. Think, for example, about why you bought the car you are driving now. Did you buy it because of its gas mileage? Its price? Its color? Its image? Its powerful engine? Its cup holder? Actually, even if one or more of these features figured into your decision, it wasn't really these facts that sold you; it was the benefits you perceived from these facts. For example:

It wasn't the gas mileage; it was the additional money you'd have each month/year to invest or spend on something else.

It wasn't the price; it was having less debt or being able to pay off the loan faster.

It wasn't the color; it was how that color makes you feel—excited, sophisticated, elegant, etc.

It wasn't the car's image; it was how you'll appear to other people by owning this car: successful, economical, young, carefree, etc.

It wasn't the engine's power; it was the sense of power you feel as you accelerate.

It wasn't the cup holder; it was knowing you won't spill your morning coffee all over your slacks or skirt on the way to meet a client.

There are undoubtedly a variety of meaningful benefits from what you offer, but you need to know specifically which ones will get to the heart of the matter for your particular clients and customers. That's why it's so important to understand the needs and concerns of the people you hope will buy your products or services. Usually, it's not enough to talk in glittering generalities. You must get specific.

Get Specific

Psychologists assert that all human needs fall into a hierarchy of five separate and distinct needs:

- SURVIVAL
  Food, clothing, shelter
  Other necessities
- COMFORT
  The security of knowing you'll be safe and secure
  Luxury and indulgences
- KINSHIP
  Friends and family
  A sense of belonging to a group
- STATUS
  To be admired and looked up to
  The authority to get things done
- SELF-FULFILLMENT
  Finding inner meaning, pursuing dreams, achieving excellence
  Becoming "all that you can be"

In general, all needs and concerns can be boiled down to meeting one or more of these five basic needs. So, it's useful to think about which of these needs your product or service can help people achieve, but then you must go to the next step. If you want people to realize that you understand *their* needs, you must address their specific situations and perceptions.

Generally speaking, the more generalized your benefits, the more suspicious knowledgeable people will be about your legitimacy and the more they will want you to give them specific facts to support your claims.

For example, let's say you have a specialized temporary-help agency. The fact that your agency prescreens all applicants thoroughly could mean that when the temp arrives, the office manager's boss won't scream at him because the phone wasn't answered on the second ring, but the manager will probably never tell you about her irate boss. You have to know enough about the specifics of having a demanding boss to know that they jump down the throats of their office managers when the phone isn't answered. By mentioning that you understand this, you'll be talking to the office manager right where he lives and he'll know that you understand the heart of the matter for him.

If you're selling a product to *Fortune* 500 companies, you'll need to know about the specific kind of concerns that purchasing agents share in common, such things as "Will it help get me a bonus?" "Will it save my job?" "Will it make me a hero?" "Will it make me feel in control?" Will it make me feel important?" "Will it get me an award?" "Will it stop so-and-so from complaining all the time?" On the other hand, if upper-level managers will be making the purchasing decision, you'll want your marketing message to address their concerns, things like: "Will it make the sales force more effective?" "Will it help increase the price of the stock?" "Will it get the board off my back?" "Will it keep me from having to deal with layoffs?" "Will it help me sleep at night?"

If you don't already know the kind of people you hope will be seeking you out, it will take some time and effort to get to know them well enough to find out specific key issues, concerns, hopes, and dreams they share. Doing so, however, will be well worth your effort. If you've completed the Action Steps at the end of chapters 2 and 3, you should have a pretty good idea of the issues you need to address to speak directly to where your clients and customers live. But, to make sure you do, it's helpful to take the time to describe your ideal client or customer in as much detail as possible. (See the action step on the next page.) Later in this chapter, you'll also find a simple test you can use to determine if you've gotten to the heart of the matter.

Just Give Me the Facts

Unless someone believes you're able to address the heart of the matter, they probably won't seek you out; but there are times when people aren't interested in hearing about benefits. They just want to know the facts, sometimes very specific facts. This happens whenever someone is quite knowledgeable about a product or service. We, for example, have given up responding to generalized promises like "Healthy Gourmet Food."

Action Step: Develop Your Ideal Customer Profile

Describe your ideal client or customer in detail. Who are these individuals? What do they do? What is their life like? What are their goals? What's most important to them? What are their most common problems? What bugs them the most? What do they complain about? What do they praise? What would they consider to be the ideal solutions to their problems? To the extent possible, use the same words to describe your customers that they use in talking about themselves, their goals, and their problems. Think about the words and phrases you hear them using as they talk about the issues your product or service addresses.

After you've written your profile, you may want to have several clients or customers read your description and see if they agree. Find out what they'd add and what they'd change.

EXAMPLE: As a family day-care provider, my ideal customer is a busy two-career couple who have one or more children under five. They want to earn a good livelihood and pursue their careers, but they also want their children to be well cared for and to have the chance to learn and develop in a healthy, safe atmosphere. The ideal for them is to have their children taken care of while they're at work in a loving home setting by a well-educated professional. But usually their income is tight. They can't afford a full-time nanny. Their biggest problem is finding high-quality child care at a price they can afford. Also, they have erratic hours, so they can't always pick their children up right at 5:30 every evening.

But we'll try out a restaurant immediately if it advertises "Low Fat, No Wheat, No Dairy." We don't want to read that a new computer model will increase our productivity and make our home office more efficient, although that's the outcome we seek. What we want to know is whether it's a multimedia Pentium with thirty-two megabytes of RAM and a three-year warranty with an on-site or next-day turnaround repair policy.

In such circumstances, the features have become synonymous with their benefits, so people are "feature shopping." They know what they're looking for and they want to do their own evaluation based on qualifications, specifications, or other basic facts. "Don't tell me about how great I'll look after plastic surgery," the educated consumer says. "Tell me if you are a board-certified plastic surgeon." "Don't tell me you'll help me quit smoking. Tell me what methods you'll be using to help me stop." "Don't tell me your training program will boost our bottom line. Tell me how you're going to do that."

So, it's important to determine just how much your prospective clients and customers already know about what you're offering. If it's something new that most people know little about, you'll want to focus your marketing message on the benefits you're offering. If people are already quite familiar with what you're offering, you'll want to emphasize the most important features. But since the decision to buy anything will always ultimately be based on how well you get to the heart of the matter, you'll want to be able to readily and clearly communicate both the facts and the benefits of what you do.

Finding a Happy Balance

You want to find a happy balance between addressing the heart of the matter and getting to the most important facts of the matter. Addressing the heart of the matter lets the heart know you understand where it lives. Presenting the most important facts proves to a skeptical and dis-

A Warm Heart and a Satisfied Mind
If you speak only to the heart, the mind becomes suspicious. If you speak only to the mind, the heart will become indifferent. So you want to describe what you do in a way that both warms the heart and convinces the mind.
Specific Facts and Features
Bold General Promises
Indifference
Confusion
Boredom
Turnoff
Interest
Desire
Trust
Confidence
Doubt
Suspicion
Disbelief
Turnoff

cerning mind that you can do something about whatever's at the heart of the matter. When you lean too far in either direction, you risk losing credibility or interest. Focusing primarily on the facts risks confusing or boring people, or losing their attention. Think, for example, of your own reaction to the following two sets of descriptions:

FACTS, FACTS, FACTS	PROMISES, PROMISES, PROMISES
"I'm a CLU and ChFC. I specialize in strategic business succession planning."	*"I take people down the road to financial independence. I'm a financial planner."*
"I specialize in electronic component engineering and radiation effects."	*"I'm a hypnotherapist. I'll make sure you'll never have to worry about your weight ever again."*
"I've worked in human resource development for twenty years at IBM. Now I have my own company, consulting on employee benefit packages and retirement planning."	*"We provide low-cost, reliable, top-quality service."*

For most people, the first set of descriptions is too technical and complex, too focused on specific facts, while the second set sounds too good to be true. Chances are the first group of individuals leaves you feeling confused or uncertain, or uninterested in what they do, while the second set leaves you thinking it's just more hype or that they couldn't possibly understand the complexity or reality of your situation.

Actually, finding a balance between these two extremes isn't as difficult as it may seem. We've found a simple but highly effective formula for putting your finger on the heart of the matter and backing it up with the most important facts about what you do. That's the winning combination for having a dynamic marketing message. Taking the following Actions Steps will provide you with the basic ingredients you'll need to craft a message that will create desire, build trust, and inspire confidence.

Action Steps: Deciding What Matters Most

1. *Finding the Benefits Behind the Facts*

There are a variety of things that make you a valued specialist in your niche. Your challenge is to let your clients, customers, and referral sources know why you're the ideal choice for *them*. So, practice finding three benefits for the following sample list of facts. Then develop your own list of what you consider to be the most important facts about what you can offer and identify three specific benefits for each that get to the heart of the matter from your clients' and customers' perspective.

EXAMPLE: I am an expert in my field.
You'll be working personally with a knowledgeable professional.
You'll be able to depend on top-quality work.
You won't have to spend a lot of time supervising my progress.

I have twenty-five years of experience.

My product is the best quality on the market.

My product/service is the cheapest in the field.

My product/service has more bells and whistles than any other.

I use top-quality materials.

I am available to you twenty-four hours a day.

I guarantee my work and will replace it free of charge.

I offer free return shipping.

I am a licensed practitioner.

2. *Developing Facts to Address Desired Benefits*

Now, reverse this process. Having identified the specific benefits of your most important assets, think about the most common needs of your clients and customers and work backward to identify what you offer that addresses them. You may find that you want to add certain features to what you offer in order to better meet some of your customers' needs.

Here's a list of typical benefits that are as close to universal as possible. Check off those your product or service addresses and identify at least two *specific* features you offer, or could offer, that address these needs. To the extent possible, use the very words and terms your clients and customers use or are most familiar with.

BUSINESS-TO-CONSUMER

Saves time
Saves energy
Saves effort
Exclusivity
Elegance
Affordable
Pretty
Luxurious
Tight control
Feels good
Looks Good
Tastes good
Smells good
Sounds good
Restful
Energized
Sexy
Fun
Happy
Amusing
Will save your marriage
Keeps my kids out of trouble
Immediately available
Low cost

BUSINESS-TO-BUSINESS

Saves time
Saves energy
Saves effort
Customized service
Visibility
Sells more product
Makes product faster
Efficient
Lower overhead
Raises profit
Lowers expenses
Turns over inventory faster
Higher stock prices
Happy investors
Happy board
High margin
Worry-free
On time
Top quality
Reliability
CYA (Cover Your Anatomy)
Looks good to my customers/clients
Low Cost

3. Getting Down to the Heart of the Matter

Review the above lists of your fact/benefit combinations and **select the one aspect** you think most directly hits the nerve of where your clients and customers live.

EXAMPLE: In the case of the licensed family day-care provider in our sample above, the one key aspect of her business that addresses her ideal customer's deepest need is her background. She's a trained nurse, an early-childhood educator, and a mom herself. She can provide a safe, loving, and educationally rich second home for their children during the times when they can't.

OK, so you know your ideal customer in as much detail as possible. You've identified all the various aspects of what you do that are of benefit to these individuals and you've identified what you think is the one most important issue for your clients and customers. Now, it's time to turn what you've discovered into a specific message that will (1) get attention (2) hook interest, and (3) make a compelling impression.

Crafting Your Message

We're all bombarded with a virtual avalanche of messages every day. From the time we turn on the TV while getting dressed or are reading the newspaper over breakfast, to the time we spend listening to the radio in the car, sorting through the mail we find on our desks or waiting for us on our computers, to the myriad of personal and business contacts we make throughout the day, the shops we browse through and the reading we catch up on before we go to bed, we come across literally thousands of marketing messages every day. What on earth are we to do with all this information? Well, most of us sort it out, discard what's of no interest or importance to us (which is usually most of it), and then mentally file away anything we believe to be important, hopefully flagging the things we want to add to our "To Do" lists.

This is the very process you want to tap into when you describe what you do. Whether you're meeting someone in person for the first time or crafting a classified ad, whether you're calling someone on the phone or setting up a booth at a trade show, you want people to take note of your message, quickly decide if what you do has any relevance to them and, if so, help them find a way to mentally take note of it and flag it for action. Here is our formula for doing this easily and quickly. It begins with getting attention by using a One-Line Attention Grabber and then making a lasting impression with a File-Opening Sound Byte.

Getting Attention—The One-Line Attention Grabber

You should have a handy One-Line Attention Grabber you can use like a neon sign when you need to attract interest and pique curiosity in the midst of a flood of other messages. The purpose of an Attention Grabber is to wake people up, startle them out of whatever they're preoccupied with, and stimulate an almost irresistible desire to find out more. Your Attention Grabber should raise questions and leave people eager for the answers. Here are a few examples:

> *"I get paid to shoot things and blow them up."* Photographer Jonathon Cohon, Chicago, Ill.
>
> *"You can call me the Idea Man."* Ab Mobasher, marketing consultant, Kirkland, Wash.
>
> *"I do financial stress reduction."* Chellie Campbell, financial management seminars, Los Angeles, Calif.
>
> *"I'm the original party animal."* R. David Hackenbruch, bartender, Indianapolis, Ind.
>
> *"I clown around."* Claude Palmer, Clowns, Clowns, Clowns. Ontario, Canada.
>
> *"Let me take the world off your shoulders."* Sharon Howard, massage therapist, Cleveland, Tenn.
>
> *"I buy houses."* M.J. "Duke" Perrson, real estate broker, San Diego, Calif.
>
> *"I'm the Professional Type,"* Madelaine Fishman, The Professional Type, Hollywood, Fla.
>
> *"We put ❤ in your home."* Betty Janes, gifts and decorative accessories, Kearney, Neb.
>
> *"We make time."* Ace Secretarial Overload, Downey, Calif.
>
> *"I'm the Table Doctor."* Tony Columbie, chiropractic equipment repair, Miami, Fla.
>
> *"I give you credit."* Maria Metcalf, credit counseling and secured credit cards, Bonita, Calif.
>
> *"Let me put you in control of your remote control."* Wrenn Goe, Manufacturer, Remote Control Holders, Coconut, Grove, Fla.

"I specialize in confidence." Barbara Babcock Chizmas, Imagine Consulting and Business Etiquette, Redlands, Calif.

"We do good deeds." Shane Liedtke, Meridian Title Company, Murray, Utah.

"We make your money work as hard as you do." Bob Cullen, financial planner, Covina, Calif.

Of course, your Attention Grabber doesn't have to be limited to words. It can be something you wear, a sample, even your business card (see chapters 6 and 12). But having a slogan, tag line, or one-liner can be a useful way to be sure you get someone's attention so you can introduce what you do.

High-Touch Tip: Think Outside the Box

Dennis R. Green of Farming Hills, Michigan, loves bold ties. In fact, he has a collection of close to 100 wild ties in a wide variety of colors and patterns. Since he's in the creativity business (he owns an advertising agency), Green decided to use his ties as his Attention Grabber. He's become known as "the creative guy with the creative tie." This novel approach to attracting attention works wonders for him in person, on-line and on paper. We met him, for example, at a business conference sponsored by the University of Wisconsin at Whitewater and, like most people he meets, our first comment to him as a stranger in the crowd was "Wow! What an interesting tie!" The door was open. So when it comes to creating an Attention Grabber, don't limit your imagination; think outside the box.

What if you don't feel creative?

If you don't feel that you're clever enough to create a novel Attention Grabber, don't despair. Most of us feel that way. According to Ivan Misner, founder of Business Network International and author of *Seven Second Marketing* (Bard Press, Austin, Tex.), the best grabbers appeal to the basic senses—sight, hearing, taste, smell, and touch—and there are many ways to create one. Here are a few of Misner's suggestions:

- TICKLE THE FUNNY BONE. USE HUMOR.
  "We check your shorts." Dean Georgiana, electrician

- Pluck at the heartstrings.
  "We provide life after death." Jack Knight, insurance agent, Yucaipa, Calif.

- Use verse. Make a rhyme.
  "You are not alone when you need a loan." Jim Nassor, mortgage broker, Holland, Ohio.

- Rephrase a familiar saying.
  "I believe in the tooth, the whole tooth and nothing but the tooth, so help me God." Joe Wilson, dentist, Glendale, Calif.

- Use wordplay.
  "A business without a sign is a sign of no business." Ray DeLeone, sign company, Cottonwood, Ariz.

- Shock 'em.
  "I have a criminal mind. I break into your house . . . so I can show you how a real criminal can do it." Security consultant.

- Do a play on your name.
  "Sweat's my name; air conditioning is my game." Tim Sweat, heating and air-conditioning specialist, Dallas, Tex.

Don't let the prospect of creating an Attention Grabber intimidate you. Play with it. Sometimes the best ideas pop out when you're horsing around, or when you're trying to describe to someone what you do. Misner tells about this story of how Thomas Teixeira, a personal injury attorney in Groton, Connecticut, found a memorable way to introduce himself.

"I developed my memory hook after settling a very significant case for a middle-aged man who had suffered a traumatic brain injury in an automobile accident. While I certainly felt euphoric that I had played a role in getting this kind man enough money to ensure that he could live comfortably for the rest of his life, I was profoundly saddened that I could do nothing to . . . give him back the life he had before the accident." His Grabber came to him in a flash one night while taking a shower after reading his kids a bedtime story—Humpty-Dumpty! Here it is—

"I can't put Humpty-Dumpty back together again, but I can sue the person who pushed him off the wall."

Teixeira likes this hook because it explains exactly what kind of legal work he does; it says he's an approachable, caring human being with a sense of humor, not a stuffed shirt. It also reminds him of his limited role in the lives of injured people. He says, "I can't make everything right, but I can make someone pay."

High-Tech Tip

To tap into your creativity, visit the Creativity Forum on CompuServe Interactive (GO CREATE). There you'll find a special section on Business Creativity, Creative Ads, and much more.

To spur your imagination and generate lots of possibilities, you'll find Misner's book *Seven Second Marketing* is full of great examples like this one. Also review **Appendix 1:** Creating Messages That Sell, which is available on-line without charge as a special report at www.paulandsarah.com on the Great Ideas for Getting Business page. Use books like Roger von Och's *A Whack on the Side of the Brain* or try creativity software like *Idea Fisher* or *Mindman*. (See **Resources** at the end of this chapter. Hiring a marketing or creativity consultant for a couple of hours of creative brainstorming can be useful as well. You might experiment with a variety of ideas until you find one that works well. Then use it repeatedly. Let it work for you like an advertising jingle.

Keep in mind, however:

Your Attention Grabber can't say it all; it just opens the door.

Never think your Attention Grabber is all you need to introduce yourself and describe what you do. It's not. Your Attention Grabber is like a sneak preview of the benefits you offer. It opens the door, so you'll be invited in to say more. There are times when you won't need to use an Attention Grabber because the door's wide open and you already have everyone's rapt attention. Often, however, you won't. Usually there will be a myriad of other things vying for the attention of those you want to communicate with, everything from luncheon table side conversations to noisy exhibit booths or a crowded page of other Yellow Page ads. That's when an Attention Grabber will come in most handy.

You can use your Attention Grabber as a segue to introducing yourself to a group of fellow networkers at the refreshment table during the social hour. You can incorporate it into the headline of a news release, use it to attract attention to a display ad or feature it as a motto or slogan on your business card. You might even include it as part of a voice mail greeting the way Muscle Movers of Seattle does: "Hi, you've reached Muscle Movers," the message announces, followed by instructions for leaving a message and closing with the slogan "Let Our Muscles Do Your Moving." And of course, you can always also use your Grabber as a quick reminder of your specialty in situations where everyone already knows who you are.

Sharrie Long, of Madre Hill Travel in Sierra Madre, California, has had her Grabber made into a rubber stamp. She stamps it on the back of her business cards, invoices, or correspondence.

Action Step: Take Note of What Works

Attend one or more networking groups where members stand and introduce themselves. Listen to how people introduce themselves and note your own reactions. Which introductions cause you to sit up and take notice? Whom do you want to make a point to meet later? Which ones cause your attention to drift? Which ones do you quickly file away as "another one of those"? Whom can you recall on your way home and why?

Also notice how others are responding to other people. Which introductions set off a twitter around the room? Which ones prompt questions or comments? Which ones seem to hit a nerve for lots of people? Who has people approaching them after the formal part of the meeting? Are some so overly cute and clever that they attract interest, but not business?

Ask yourself what the most effective introductions have in common. Why do they work so well? Think about how you could incorporate such characteristics into the way you describe your business.

Once you have everyone's attention, however, you need to develop the interest you've piqued so that those you're communicating with will fully grasp what you can do for them and want to keep track of it by keeping your business card, filing your brochure, and most important, creating a mental file folder for you in their minds where they'll be able to recall who you are and what you do when they need you.

Making a Lasting Impression—The File-Opening Sound Byte

To deal with the avalanche of information we're deluged with every day, we quickly discard most of the things we see and hear as unimportant, even if it's cute or clever; but if something impresses us as important, we stop briefly to create a mental file folder where we record and store the information for quick recall. So, once you have someone's attention, you want to help her quickly decide if she's one of your ideal customers, or possibly a referral source. If so, you want her to feel compelled to open a mental file folder 🗁 just for you. If you're providing written materials like a business card, flyer, brochure, or ad, you also want her to literally create a file for you in her database, Rolodex, or file cabinet.

That's the reaction you want. Here's what you *don't* want: "Oh, she's one of those marketing consultants. I can always find one of those." No file. "Oh, he's an electrical engineer. I can't imagine needing that." No file. "I don't have a clue what she's talking about." No file. "Should I know what that means?" No file. To avoid reactions like these, you need what we call a File-Opening Sound Byte, a brief way to find out if those you're communicating with are tuned in to what you're saying, appreciate its importance, and understand what you can do about it for them. Creating such a Sound Byte is a three-step process. Here's how to do it.

Step 1: Ask A Specific Question to Open a Mental File Folder 🗁

Before telling people what you do, you want to be sure they have a mental file folder open for you and are ready to take note of who you are and what you do. The quickest and easiest way we've found to do this is to ask a very specific question to determine if they know about, understand, and can relate to the ***one most important issue*** your product or service addresses. You can start your question with something like "You know how . . . ?" followed by a description of the one most important problem or need that your product or service meets. Here are several examples:

"You know how agonizing it is to be at work and constantly be worrying about what your kids are doing and if they're OK?"

"You know how it always seems like your computer goes down at night or on weekends when all the 'help lines' are closed?"

"You know how a lot of people are afraid to go to the dentist?"

"You know how time-consuming and stressful doing your taxes can be?"

"You know how hard it is to work when you desk is buried in piles of paperwork?"

"Do you ever sit and stare at your pet and wonder what it's thinking?"

"You know how difficult it can be to find a good publisher when you're a first-time author?"

"Have you ever cherished a special piece of heirloom jewelry?"

"You know how difficult it can be to find attractive, affordable clothes for formal occasions when you're pregnant?"

"You know how your eyes get tired and sore sometimes when you work for long hours at the computer or spend long hours on the road?"

"You know how sometimes you just can't find the right words to say what you want to say?"

"You know how sometimes you wish you knew what your competition knows?"

"Have you ever enjoyed the splendor of a Nebraska prairie?"

As you read through these questions, can you relate to these experiences personally? If not, can you empathize with people who do? Might you know others who feel this way? Do you find yourself nodding and saying something like "Yeah, I know about that," "Boy, do I know what you mean," "Yeah, I've heard about that," "A friend was just talking to me about that," or "I can imagine that." If so, these questions have hit a nerve, struck you momentarily as something that could be important and you've opened a file folder in your mind where you can store the information you're about to hear, under a heading like *Working Parents Worrying about Kids, First-Time Authors Getting a Book Published, Eyestrain at Work, Getting Stressed Out Doing Taxes,* and so forth. And now you're ready to hear more.

Don't say anything more until you see proof that such a folder is open and waiting.

Step 2: Watch and Listen for Recognition

Before describing what you do, watch and listen for a sign that the person you're talking with can relate to the problem you've posed. It might be a head nod, an uh-huh, a laugh, or a comment of some kind. The moment you see or hear such a confirming reaction, you know that he's opened a file folder 🗁 in his mind where he can put what you're about to say about your niche and you can proceed with describing what you do.

If you're not getting any acknowledgment, if he's looking puzzled or blank, if his eyes have glazed over, try rephrasing your question and probing until you find a way to state the problem so he can relate to it. If he's unfamiliar with what you're talking about, take a moment to explain it to him using a brief example or a quick fact. Then, again watch for some indication that he understands what you mean . . . before you proceed to tell him what you can do about it.

Step 3: Put Yourself in the Mental Folder by Solving the Problem

Once you're sure people have opened a mental file folder for the key problem you address, tell them what you do to solve that problem or meet the need in a way that's unique and different from what others do. For example:

> *"You know how agonizing it is to be at work and constantly be worrying about what your kids are doing and if they're OK?* **Well, what I do is provide a safe and loving second home for preschool kids while their parents are at work. I'm a licensed family day-care provider."**

> *"You know how it always seems like your computer goes down at night or on weekends when all the 'help lines' are closed?* **Well, I have a twenty-four-hour computer help line, and my lines are never closed. You can call me anytime day or night and get hooked up immediately with a computer consultant."**

> *"You know how a lot of people are afraid to go to the dentist?* **Well, I'm a dentist and I specialize in working with people who have dental phobias."**

> *"You know how time-consuming and stressful doing your taxes can be?* **Well, you can bring your tax headaches to me. I'm an enrolled agent and I'll take the stress out of the tax season for you."**

> *"You know how hard it is to work when your desk is buried in piles of paperwork?* **Well, I'm a professional organizer and I've developed a way to clear off a desk and put everything on it in order in just one hour."**

> *"Do you ever sit and stare at your pet and wonder what it's thinking?* **Well, I'm a pet psychic. I can tell you what's on your pet's mind and why it behaves the way it does."**

> *"Have you ever cherished a special piece of heirloom jewelry?* **Well, I'm a jewelry designer and I create heirlooms."**

> *"You know how difficult, and expensive, it can be to find attractive and affordable clothes for formal occasions when you're pregnant?* **Well, I've designed a collection of formal wear pregnant women can rent for formal occasions."**

"You know how your eyes get tired and sore sometimes when you work for long hours at the computer or spend long hours on the road? **Well, I'm an optometrist and after years of work with people who suffer with eyestrain, I've created a visual aerobics program that can eliminate eyestrain while you work."**

"You know how sometimes you just can't find the right words to say what you want to say? **Well, I have a way with words and what I do is 'wordcrafting.' I help people find just the right words to get their message across."**

"You know how difficult it can be to find a good publisher when you're a first-time writer? **Well, I know most of the editors at the major publishing houses and I can help you get their ear. I'm a literary agent."**

"You know how sometimes you wish you knew what your competition knows? **Well, I can find out. I'm an information broker. I specialize in strategic intelligence."**

"Have you ever enjoyed the splendor of a Nebraska prairie? **Well, I create Prairie Art from the flora and fauna of the Nebraska prairie."**

Using a File-Opening Sound Byte Accomplishes Five Key Things

1. It makes sure people are listening and tracking what you're saying.

2. It lets people know that you know where they live and truly understand their needs and problems.

3. It illustrates that you have something special that will address their specific needs.

4. It creates a mental "tab" to help people remember you later when they or someone else they know needs what you offer; e.g., "Oh, I remember this lady who's a pet psychic. I kept her card."

5. It "anchors" or connects you and your message with a specific pressing problem they can relate to, so the next time they encounter that problem, chances are you'll come to mind.

Action Step: Creating and Testing Your File-Opening Sound Byte

As we mentioned earlier, there's a simple test you can use to determine if you've gotten to the heart of the matter as far as your clients and customers are concerned. Finding the right File-Opening Sound Byte can be that test. If you've gotten to the heart of the matter, your Sound Byte will get an immediate dramatic and positive reaction from your ideal customer. A powerful Sound Byte will elicit a laugh, a chuckle, a "Wow!" or perhaps a whole story about how what you're saying applies to them. As one woman told us, "I've been using my Sound Byte for six months now. In a group I always get a laugh of recognition. Sometimes it even gets a round of applause! Many of my new clients start off like good friends because from my Sound Byte they know immediately that we're on the same path."

When you hit upon a heartfelt "Ain't It Awful" in the lives of your clients and customers, they know you truly understand their situation and they will feel an immediate rapport. If you get a lukewarm reaction to your Sound Byte, however, that tells you you're not quite on target yet. A cool or aloof reaction says you're off the mark and you need to rethink what your clients and customers believe to be at the heart of the matter for them. So keep experimenting with different ways to word your Sound Byte until you get a response that tells you you've hit a nerve.

Avoid asking the obvious.

One common mistake people make in creating a File-Opening Sound Byte is to ask the obvious. They might say, "You know how people need to have their bookkeeping done?" or "You know how people want their written documents to be done well?" These are not key problems. They won't open any folders. You have to get down to the heart of the matter, into the real world where your clients and customers live. You have to let them know you know the thorns in their side, the crux of the matter, the little things, and the big things, that drive them crazy.

Instead, you might say, "You know how sometimes it seems there's too much month for the money?" or "You know how even though you're using financial management software, your checking account balance still never matches with your bank statements?" "You know how no matter how many times you go over your documents you still miss those pesky little spelling errors and grammatical mistakes?" Or "You know how when you need to get something off to a client, you need it right away, not sometime next week?"

If you watch and listen carefully, you'll know if your Sound Byte is hitting people where they live. If they are simply polite, you haven't reached them where it counts.

Make sure your solution is as specific, noteworthy, and unique as possible.

Another common mistake people make is to present a mundane solution. They say something like "You know how even though you're using accounting software, your checking account balance still never matches your bank statements? Well, I'm a bookkeeper and I can help you solve your money management problems." Or "You know how when you need to get something off to a client, you need it right away, not sometime next week? Well, I have a word-processing service and I'll work with you to meet your needs."

You may get people to open a mental folder with Sound Bytes like these, but chances are they'll close it back up without putting your message in it. These solutions are too general. They don't present anything special about what you can do to solve the problem. They don't convey why you'll be any different from all the other bookkeeping and word-processing services.

So, instead you might say, "You know how even though you're using accounting software, your checking account balance still never matches your bank statements? Well, I do remote bookkeeping. Through the phone lines I can work on your files and track down those minute and elusive errors you don't have the time to find." Or "You know how when you need to get something off to a client, you need it right away, not sometime next week? Well, I'm part of a network of professional word-processing services and when you call I can put you in touch with someone who can start on your project right away."

Don't forget to pause, wait, and watch for a response.

Again, if you watch and listen carefully, you'll be able to notice if your message has made it into the file folder. People will make comments like "That's just what I need," "I sure could use that!" and "That would be great!" They may want to know more or ask for your card. These are all signs that they've registered your message in a special mental file folder that may well come to mind the next time they're in the midst of the very problem or issue you've described.

But you have to pause after you ask your opening question and wait for a response. If none follows, reword or explain and wait again. Think of using your Sound Byte as like playing tennis with a friend. When you hit the ball over to her side of the net, you wait for her to take a swing at the ball before you hit over another one.

Practice until you find a real zinger.

Test out your Sound Byte in person where you can get direct feedback before using it on printed materials and in other media. Nothing is more reliable or more revealing than person-to-person reactions. They provide a chance for you to hear and see the reaction to your Sound Byte firsthand with all the accompanying body language and facial expressions. So, test out a variety of possibilities until you consistently get a clear-cut, full-bodied response that tells you you've hit a vital nerve. The more of a zinger your Sound Byte is, the more likely people who hear or read it will think of you the next time they have a need for what you offer.

Once a Sound Byte is consistently getting the response you want, then you can begin using it in print, on-line, and elsewhere where you don't have the opportunity to see the readers' reactions firsthand.

Use different Sound Bytes in different contexts.

Since your Sound Byte needs to hit a personal nerve with those you're communicating with, often one Sound Byte will not work in every context. For example, you may need one Sound Byte for talking with people who already know your field well and another for those who are generally unfamiliar with it. A software engineer, for example, might refer to "fuzzy logic" in talking to fellow engineers about cross-referring, but in talking with the small-business people who will use his software, he might talk about how your software saves you time by doing a lot of the calculations for you automatically behind the scenes.

Or since different types of clients have differing needs, you may need to tailor your Sound Bytes to the particular needs of the individuals you're talking with. If you're selling identification tags for pets, for example, you might need one Sound Byte for pet owners who will be buying your tags and another Sound Byte for the retail store owners who will be stocking them:

To consumers you might say, "You know how easy it is for your pet to slip out the door without your noticing? Well, I've created a pet ID tag with a built-in computer chip that authorities can use to quickly track down a lost pet."

To the retailer you might say: "You know how people will buy something that attracts their attention on the spur of the moment while they're waiting at the cash register? Well, I have a product that pet owners find irresistible. I've created a pet ID tag with a built-in computer chip authorities can use to quickly track down a lost pet. When people read the rescue stories on our display, they have to have one too."

So, start by developing a Sound Byte for the one characteristic that's most important to most of your clients and customers, then you can develop and test others that address special needs of particular clients. As a caterer, for example, you might have an all-purpose Sound Byte like the one Carol Zapadka, who owns Full-Service Catering in Vernon, Connecticut, uses: *You know how sometimes when you give a great party everyone has a great time but you?* Well, Zapadka says, with her help, *"You can be a guest at your own party."* Then in addition to this general Sound Byte that most people can relate to, you might have other Sound Bytes that are addressed to partyers with special needs.

To apartment dwellers you might say, "Do your guests hate to come to your parties because they can never find a place to park? Well, as your caterer, I take care of all the arrangements for your party, including valet parking services." Or, to a group of hip trendsetters, you might say, "Are you tired of serving the same old culinary fare at your parties? Well, exotic menus are my specialty. I'll make your party memorable. I'm a caterer."

Expanding Your Message for Maximum Effect–Introductions, Slogans, Headlines, and More

Once you have an Attention Grabber and Sound Byte that work well for you, you can use them as a blueprint or template for describing what you do in virtually any medium. The more times someone sees it and hears it, the better. Each impression will reinforce the other and make your mental file folder all the more accessible. The elements in your Grabber and Sound Byte can become like your signature. Use them as part of your standard introduction. Incorporate them into a slogan for your business card and other marketing materials. Use them as part of your voice-mail message. Build them into headlines for your ads, news releases, brochures, speeches, flyers, or newsletters.

Right after Tom Ahern, Lisa Bousquet and John Horton started their advertising agency, the economy went into one of the worst recessions in history. Their very survival was at stake, but they realized their clients and customers were in the same boat. The economy was at the heart of the matter for them, too. So, they built their identity as a company that could help others do more business in the worst economy since 1929. They developed a marketing campaign around the following theme. See if you can relate. You know how tough the economy has been over the past few years? Well, "In the worst economy since 1929, we decided to open a new business to help *you* do *more* business. Either we're idiots. Or geniuses. You decide. We're Horton Ahern Bousquet. We do smart marketing, public relations, and advertising for less."

This unique thematic approach worked well because it struck a chord with most small businesses. By the end of their first year in business, Horton Ahern Bousquet had landed twenty-two clients and $225,000 in revenue.

Marketing Mistake: A Sound Byte That Bit Back

When psychologist Karen Dresser started her company consulting with managers on how to reduce stress in the workplace, she had an agenda of her own: Managers needed to stop stressing out their employees. She was convinced managers were unknowingly causing most workplace stress. In fact her first Sound Byte was something like this: "Did you know you cause most of the stress that keeps your workers from being as productive as you want them to be? I can show you how, by easing up on your staff, you can reduce sick days and absenteeism and boost your workers' output dramatically."

She was quite disappointed with the response she got from this theme. She wasn't attracting business; but worse yet, several of the managers she met became openly angry and hostile when she introduced herself in this way. At first, she didn't understand. She had their best interest at heart, and she was convinced she had gotten right to the heart of the matter. What she discovered, however, was that the managers themselves were tremendously stressed-out. The last thing they needed was to feel guilty about creating stress for others, too, even if they were the cause. They were coping as well as they could with pressures of their own.

From her point of view the managers' behavior was at the heart of the matter, but from their perspective, their own pressures were the heart of the matter. When she shifted her focus to address their needs, *as they perceived them,* she saw a dramatic shift in results. "I had to learn to walk in their shoes," she recalls. "To do this, I offered to do free day-long consultations so I could better understand their needs. The experience really woke me up." These days her Sound Byte is more like this: "You know how stressful it is to manage a downsized, right-sized workforce in which everyone's having to do more with less? Well, I teach managers how to manage stress so they'll have the energy they need to manage their business."

Marketing Masterpiece: Expanding Your Message for Maximum Effect

"You know how often a new software program will come out months after the date when it was announced and then it doesn't always do what it was supposed to do? Well, that's because getting the bugs out of the last 10 percent is more difficult than anyone imagines. What I've done is develop a planning process that enables software companies to avoid such bugs and cut their development time by more than half."

This is how software engineer Rick Hubbard introduces himself and his company, Professional Resources Co., to the public. While Hubbard's business is highly technical, he's found a way to describe it so most people can understand what he does, even if they have little technical background or experience.

"Words really make a difference," Hubbard says, and so he's built his business around explaining his work in terms the listener can understand. Although he had a negligible marketing or sales background, he has built upon his twenty-five years of training and experience in software engineering by learning about developing team consensus, group dynamics, and software quality assurance to develop a consulting process that telescopes what usually takes weeks of planning into a four-to-six-day consultation that addresses the four most serious problems software developers face.

In talking to prospective clients, he speaks right to the heart of their greatest concerns using their terminology:

> *"You know how the requirements collections phase*
> *of a software project can take months to complete*

and then delivers poor results? What I do is help project teams capture their requirements in two to three days *with 90 percent-plus completeness."*

"Every software developer can relate to this," he says. Invariably they're interested in the prospect of cutting their development time dramatically. After having gotten their interest, Hubbard elaborates on his program for Accelerated Processes, expanding his Sound Byte into a full-scale computer-based slide presentation in which he outlines:

The four key barriers to top-quality software
The five problems these barriers create
His solutions to each of these problems
How his process is different, and better, than others
The time frame of the normal planning process compared to his Accelerated Processes
A description of the process
His experience with over 150 business-oriented software development projects
A summary of the benefits

Having gotten to the heart of the matter and clarified the issues for his clients, Hubbard can use these same concepts as the basis for a brochure, a Web page, a newsletter, an article, or any other marketing activity he wants to undertake as his business grows.

Following the steps outlined in this chapter, you, too, can craft your message that speaks to the heart of what makes your products or services special and important and leave a lasting impression that will draw business to you.

Resources

 ***Brief Descriptions.*** Ron Richards. Results Lab, 2175 Green St., San Francisco, CA 94123, (415) 563-5300, E-mail: ronr@resultslab.com

Idea Fisher, creativity software by Idea Fisher Systems. 2222 Martin, Irvine, CA 92612; (714) 474-8111, E-mail www.ideafisher.com

MindMan, The Creative MindManager, Visualizing Ideas, P.O. Box 829, Mount Eliza, VIC 3930, Australia, +61-3 9787 6207, E-mail www. mindman.com

Seven Second Marketing, How to Use Memory Hooks to Make You Instantly Stand Out in a Crowd. Ivan Misner. Ph.D. Austin, Tex.: Bard Press, 1996.

Whack on the Right Side of the Head. Roger von Oech. New York: Warner, 1988.

CHAPTER 6

Making a Name for Yourself

In real life, unlike in Shakespeare, the sweetness of the rose depends upon the name it bears.

—FORMER VICE PRESIDENT HUBERT H. HUMPHREY

The first thing you hope *will* come to someone's mind when they need what you offer is your name or the name of your service, product, or company. Major mass-market manufacturers spend millions on developing what is called brand identity for their products. As a small or home business, your business name is your brand identity, but of course you probably can't spend millions to make sure it comes to mind.

Nonetheless, if the people you meet can't remember your name when they need to call you or refer to you, all your business-getting efforts go down the drain. "A bad name," says Al Ries in his book *Focus,* "is a millstone around your neck." If, however, when someone needs to reach you, your name pops instantly to mind, you will be on your way to a new client or customer. An aptly chosen name used effectively on all your marketing materials can play a vital role in getting ample business coming to you . . . and you won't need to spend a million dollars to make a name for yourself.

Here's an example of just how powerful a business name can be. A Los Angeles man found a name that, by itself, brought him all the business he needed. He named his hauling company Grunt and Dump. This name holds a special appeal to those turning to the Yellow Pages in need of having something hauled. The Starving Students moving-van company has a similar story. The rates their company could charge were essentially fixed by state law, so using Starving Students has never cost appreciably less than other moving companies, but again the name has special appeal to people who need help in moving.

While your business may never stand on its name alone, it can and will stand, or fall, on the image it creates. Imagine, for example, that you find the following word-processing services listed in the Yellow Pages or a professional directory. What impression do you get about these companies as you scan their names? What does it tell you about what they do and who they are? Which company would you call if you needed to hire a word-processing service? Why would you choose that company over others?

YOUR GOAL

Choose a Name That Means Business

AAA Secretarial
Affordable Word Processing
At All Hours
Britannica Publishing, Inc.
Burdiss, Rita K.
Executive Business Services
Main Street Desktop Publishing
Joanne's Secretarial
Keystrokes
Letter Perfect
Marion Chadsworth Office Services
9 to 5
Paper Tiger
Professional Transcribers
Rogers and Cassidy
While You Wait Word Processing

Chances are you're attracted to certain of these businesses, nonplussed by others, and clearly not interested in some. Not only does each of these business names make a statement about the business, they also create an image, be it accurate or not, about what the service is, the quality or nature of the service, and even the price you can expect to pay. Some of these names like Rogers and Cassidy are obscure. (Is this a law firm?) Other like Professional Transcribers target a particular niche, as does Executive Business Services, which aims for an upscale clientele. Still others like Affordable Word Processing, At All Hours, and While You Wait highlight an appealing benefit. Keystrokes and Paper Tiger are memorable because they elicit an interesting visual image, while a name like 9 to 5 may unintentionally send an undesirable message (e.g., Don't expect me to go the extra mile by putting in any extra hours).

Is Main Street Desktop Publishing limiting its clientele by identifying so closely with one geographical area? Or does its proximity attract business? By using her name alone, is Rita K. Burdiss losing business unnecessarily? Or does this suggest someone who is well known?

Which service do you expect will charge more: Joanne's Secretarial or Marion Chadsworth Office Services? Most people we've surveyed expect that Joanne will be charging less than Marion. That's fine if this difference reflects a pricing decision Joanne has chosen; it's not so fine if her name is giving the wrong impression to prospective customers. If her prices are similar to Marion's, she's probably wondering why she encounters price resistance.

In this chapter, you'll discover how to select a name that will convey the message you want to send about your business. You'll see how making the right choice can magnify and multiply all your other marketing efforts and attract more of the kind of business you want.

Elements of Business Names That Sell

Once you're self-employed, whether you are a small business, home business, or independent contractor, you will be operating under some business name even if you've decided to simply use your personal name. Your business name identifies you on your letterhead, cards, and stationery. It's the name that appears on your business bank account and on your business license. From a marketing standpoint, however, the name you choose is anything but a formality.

The choice of your company name can be the single most important marketing decision you make—and one with the lowest cost. The name you choose can be an important sales tool and a crucial factor in developing a positive image, or it can be a source of confusion to potential customers. Your company name may even have effects, either positive or negative, that you never intended.

Therefore, before setting out to get customers and make yourself more visible, it's wise to evaluate your company name to determine whether it's a help or a hindrance to you. If you're interested in getting more business, now is a good time to review the effects of your name, because it is far easier to modify or change a name when you're starting out than after you've become better known.

Is Your Name Working for You?

Although your business name can be one of your most effective and least expensive marketing tools, people often choose a business name without giving thought to its marketing value. As a result, many business names actually hurt business instead of helping to get it. Some people select obscure, clever, or confusing names that may have special meaning to them, but to no one else, such as: HalVir Products, a combination of a husband/wife team named Hal and Virginia; Gossamer Wings Consulting, selected from a line of the owner's favorite poetry; or Flying Ace Frame Shop, the choice of a picture framer with a love of aviation. Oddly enough, even someone who has created the most interesting attention grabbers and sound bytes to describe their business may have chosen the most mundane and forgettable of names for that business. The most common mistakes we've observed are selecting a name that is:

1. **Vague**—like ABC Quality Services, Flintrade, Symtec, or Moonlighting, Inc.

2. **Misleading**—like calling a boat-detailing company Safety Car Care or referring to a company that creates medical procedure manuals as Freeland Writing Services

3. **Similar** to others—like Desktop Publishing Unlimited, Custom Photography, or Management Consulting Associates

4. **Forgettable**—like Gowner Cleaning, Executrue, or R & S Design

5. **Hard to spell or pronounce**—like Ardrurdel Transcription, Beauxvilla Baskets, or Teknique Komputer Training

6. **Sounds bad to the ear**—like Klapock Consulting, or Yusu Catering

Here are four ways you can decide whether your business name is working for or against you and what you can do if it isn't:

1. Does Your Name Clearly Identify What You Do? A name like ABE Enterprises doesn't provide a clue as to what the business offers. Therefore, it has little or no marketing value. A name like Your Limousine Service, however, tells what the business is. Such a name can attract business and referrals. The more precise your name, the more likely it will be that potential customers will understand what you do, keep your business card, and be able to reach you through the phone book or by calling information.

Think, for example, about how the following names leave no doubt as to what services they provide. Steven Benson of the Northern California Bay Area has named his company Classy Glass Window Cleaning, which he describes as "a cut above the rest." A computer consultant in Eugene, Oregon, calls his business Rent-a-Nerd. Ted Rodosovich of San Diego is The Mobile Stockbroker. Ellen Lieber counsels people with disabilities. She calls her business Access/Abilities. Like HoldEverything, the popular chain of stores that sell containers for storing just about anything you'd need to organize in your home or office, Access/Abilities is one of those names that may not be instantly recognizable on its own, but once it has been identified by a tag line, the imagery of the name locks in and is easy to remember.

A few other examples of crystal-clear names are Flowers Just Because, a flower shop in Milpitas, California; Funds for You, used by a fund-raiser in Broadview Heights, Ohio; and Pictures on Porcelain, created by an artist in Overland Park, Kansas.

Keep in mind, though, that what seems clear to you may be confusing to others who don't understand the ins and outs of what you do. Why Quality Marketing is a good name for selling customized airbrushed garments, for example, may be clear to the owner but leaves us feeling confused. While upon reflection ProtoType may be a clever name for a résumé and career-planning service, at first glance it seems more like a print or design shop.

2. ***Does Your Name Distinguish You from All Others?*** A name like Jones and Jones Towing Services or AMBA Travel clearly conveys what the business does but doesn't set these businesses apart in a notable way from other towing services or travel agencies. Such names have less marketing value than names like Low Dough Tow in Sacramento, California, or Dirt Cheap Travel, Michael McGlothlin's San Francisco–based travel agency for price-conscious travelers. While McGlothlin will book hotels and car rentals, he specializes in "Dirt Cheap Plane Tickets to Anywhere." His name features the benefit of his niche. Featuring a benefit is often a good idea. It helps him attract the particular kind of customer he wants to serve.

So does Mo' Hotta Mo'Betta. This mail-order and Internet company sells—you guessed it—hot, hot, hot sauce. Commuter Cleaners was the brainchild of Paul McDonald. He had been spending ten hours a week commuting by rail from his Connecticut residence to his accounting job in New York City when he had the idea for a unique dry cleaning service. As the name conveys, his service picks up from and delivers dry cleaning to commuter stops for weary travelers who don't want to spend their weekends taking care of errands like the laundry.

3. ***Is Your Name Memorable?*** The best business names make an indelible impression. Who can forget Grunt and Dump, for example? Or, how about Totally Twisted, a Rockville, Maryland, pretzel company?

One of our other favorites is Now Showing, a lingerie shop in Oklahoma that's located in a converted movie theater. The great thing about this name is that not only do you remember the image it conjures up in your mind, but it also reminds you of where the shop is located once you've been there.

Here's another memorable example: Wreck-a-Mended is an auto body shop in Orlando, Florida. It was the grand prize winner of small business columnist and author Jane Applegate's Best/Worst Small Business Name Contest. What we like most about this name is that it not only describes what the service does in a memorable way; it also conveys that it has a good reputation.

4. Is Your Name Simple to Pronounce, Pleasing to the Ear, Easy to Spell and Look Up? No matter how clever, precise, or creative your name may be, if people can't understand, spell, and pronounce it, you'll most likely lose some business because of your name. Case in point: We recently received a great mail-order catalog which inadvertently got misplaced. Its name was one of those jazzy multiple-consonant, few-vowel words. Try as we can, we can't conjure up what it was called. Not only have we wanted to order a number of items ourselves; we've also wanted to tell several other people about some of their clever gift ideas. We can only hope that one day soon they'll send us another catalog.

So, avoid names like Anatomorphex, a special-effects company, mNemoDex™ Group, and Aesculapian. *Aesculapian* is a Greek word for healing medicine. To Dr. Martin Groder it seemed like an appropriate name for his psychiatric treatment center. But you can just imagine the difficulty someone would have trying to refer people to his clinic, or to any of these three businesses.

JERYWIL Consulting cleverly combines the owners' names, Jerry and William, but it will most likely be hard to spell and pronounce, difficult to look up in the phone book, and very easy to forget. Kritter Sitter, on the other hand, is a clear and memorable name for a pet-sitting service. However, by cleverly changing the "C" in *Critter* to "K," the owners may lose some potential customers who will remember the name but won't be able to find it in the phone book or from directory assistance because they or the operator will be looking under "C."

Hire Expectations, a temp agency, and Faults Alarm, an earthquake preparedness company of Pasadena, California (and finalist in Jane Applegate's Best/Worst Small-Business Name Contest), have a similar problem. When hearing these names, everyone we tested them on thought they would be spelled "Higher Expectations" and "False Alarm." Even the award-winning Wreck-a-Mended could present problems for people who hear the name and look for it in the phone book under "Recommended."

We, too, were surprised to discover that people understand the name we selected for our audiotape line of products just fine when they see it in type but don't understand it when they hear it verbally. The company name is Here's How. Looks fine, but try saying it over the phone. We found that people frequently ask, "Here's Hal?" so we have to spell it out: "That's two words, H-E-R-E'-S H-O-W."

How a name sounds matters, too. Al Ries in his book *Focus,* for example, advises to be careful of words that end in vowels. He points out that *A, E,* and *O* can work, but he asserts that *I* and particularly *U* can be treacherous. He gives examples of major corporations who have spent millions of dollars on advertising that cannot make up for a name that sounds bad. Names ending in consonants sound best, though *K* (as in *turkey*) can be tricky.

If your name, or one you're considering, violates any of these four criteria, don't despair; you're in good company. When Kimberly Clark, the tissue company, tried adding a tissue that contained Vitamin C derivatives that would reportedly kill germs as people sneezed or blew into them, they named their new tissue Avert Virucidal Tissues. The product bombed in large part, analysts say, because "Virucidal" sounds like "homicidal" or "patricidal." Since then other tissues with additives have been successful, most notably Puffs Plus, a name most people who have had a sore, runny nose can relate to.

The *Wall Street Journal* reported how over thirty years ago famed psychologist Abraham Maslow, renowned for developing the concept of a man's psychological "hierarchy of needs," wrote a disarmingly farsighted book on self-actualized management. Although groundbreaking at the time, the book never caught on—principally, the writer related, because Maslow had coined the term *eupsychia* to describe a more desirable type of work group and insisted, against the advice of peers like management consultant Peter Drucker, on calling the book *Eupsychian Management.* Now, three decades later, *Eupsychian Management* is making a comeback. The book has been republished under a new name, *Future Visions.*

Fortunately, as you'll see, you can not only avoid such naming problems but also correct them quickly and with less difficulty than you might think.

You can put as little or as much effort into selecting an effective

Marketing Mistake: An Image-Building Effort Backfires

When Kate Ambrose began offering graphic design to advertising agencies thirteen years ago, she registered her name as Kate Ambrose and Associates, with the intention of creating a more professional image. She wrote to us at *Home Office Computing* magazine, concerned when a few of her newer clients discovered she was a one-person firm and expressed surprise as if they'd been misled. "Am I misleading potential clients?" she asked.

Ambrose's problem is a common one. Adding "and Associates" to one's name is a popular image-building strategy. Usually it's meant to convey that while you're a one-person company, you have a cadre of associates you can draw on to extend the range, size, and/or scope of your services. Sometimes single-person companies will even include the names or specialties of associates in brochures, proposals, and other marketing materials.

So, it's understandable that some of Ambrose's clients were surprised to discover she had no associates. Even though her name hadn't prevented her from getting ample business over the years, should she risk unintentionally misleading or confusing any future clients? Since she didn't have or intend to have any associates, we suggested that she drop "and Associates" from her business name.

To add greater substance to her business image, we suggested giving her business a name other than her own that highlights one of the unique qualities her clients find most valuable about her services. Or, since she has successfully established a reputation based on her name, she can capitalize on her reputation as a solo practitioner and use either her personal name in conjunction with a tag line, like Kate Ambrose, Advertising Design Services, or incorporate "Advertising Design Services" into the business name itself; e.g., Kate Ambrose Advertising Design Services. Any of these names leaves the issue of company size out of the equation entirely. Alternatively, some people incorporate their business and add "Inc." to their name to communicate substance.

name as you choose, but the choice you make will have a bearing on how hard or easy it will be for you to market your business. For marketing purposes, the more specific you can be about your business, the more easily your name will sell itself. That is precisely what home inspector Pat Thiel discovered. Prior to attending our *Getting Business to Come to You* seminar in Wisconsin, Thiel had been using the name Thiel Associates for his company. After hearing our criteria for a good business name, he decided to change his company name to Affordable Home Inspection, Inc. He's been pleased with the difference. "Now," he told us, "it's much clearer to everyone what I offer." He even gets calls from the Yellow Pages because his name sells his service.

Using Your Own Name

That's not to say that using your own name will never work. After all, in many cases *you* are the service. Let's suppose you are a well-known hairstylist like Edward Salazar, who has established his reputation over the past twelve years through his own cable-television show. In such a case you might want to name your salon simply Salazar, because your name says it all. Alternatively, for people who haven't heard of you yet, you might call your business Hairstyles by Salazar. A byline like this featuring their own name is a common choice among artists, consultants, and people providing creative or professional services. Keep in mind, however, that unless you are already quite well known, you will need to invest time and money to make your name sufficiently well known that it can stand on its own, as Donna Karan, Carole Little, Ralph Lauren, Vidal Sassoon, and Tommy Hilfiger have done so well.

Information researcher Seena Sharp of Hermosa Beach, California, uses her own name effectively; her company is Sharp Information. Likewise, Susan Taylor of Sumner, Washington, provides business services as Taylored Business Assistance. Our favorite example, however, was one from Jane Applegate's Best/Worst Small-Business Name Contest: Cheatham Tax Service of Oceanside, California. Dean Cheatham wrote to say that he's has been making an honest living from his work for thirty years and that many of his clients came to him because of his name. "They love to tell their friends that Cheatham Tax Service does their returns," he told Applegate.

People Shouldn't Have to Make Notes on Your Business Card

William and Erma Gardner of North Kingstown, Rhode Island, began their business as EW Gardner, Golf Car Sale and Repairs. Motorized golf car services is certainly a niche in and of itself, but the Gardners have an even more unique specialty. They primarily sell and repair golf cars for elderly or disabled individuals. So, when we met them at one of our seminars, we took notes on the back of their business card to be sure we'd remember their unique specialty. After the seminar they decided to refine their name and their card. Now no one needs to take notes to remember precisely what they do.

Of course, you don't want to unduly limit your business because of the name you select. If you envision growing your trucking company to include shipping services, for example, you'll be better off calling yourself FastFleet instead of Speedy Trucking.

Your Business Name Should Tell Your Story

As when you describe what you do, your name should get to the heart of the matter. The more a business name conveys the particular benefits you offer, the more you will stand out from the others. Let's reconsider, for example, the names for the word-processing service we listed at the beginning of the chapter:

AAA Secretarial	Keystrokes
Affordable Word Processing	Letter Perfect
At All Hours	Marion Chadsworth Office Services
Britannica Publishing, Inc.	9 to 5
Burdiss, Rita K.	Paper Tiger
Executive Business Services	Professional Transcribers
Main Street Desktop Publishing	Rogers and Cassidy
Joanne's Secretarial	While-You-Wait Word Processing

Each of these names tells a story, and each story appeals more to some than to others. Someone with a low budget, for example, might be attracted to Affordable Word Processing or Joanne's Secretarial. Executive Business Services and Rogers and Cassidy sound top-of-the-line. Certainly there's an attraction to "perfect" letters and to anyone who works like a "paper tiger." Someone living or working near Main Street might find that location convenient, although a study by ABC Nameback Insertions of New York found that of all types of business names, those carrying geographic connotations were declining most rapidly: not surprising in a world where a company of any size can go national or international via fax, the Internet, or voice mail.

If Rita K. Burdiss is known and respected in her community, her name will be appealing, but if those needing her services have never heard of her, using her own name isn't likely to be helpful. If you're in a hurry, While-You-Wait Word Processing sounds great. And if you don't

Does It Pay to Be First?

In most phone directories you'll find there's fierce competition to be the first name listed under any particular heading. Here's an example someone sent us via E-mail from a local phone directory.

A (that's it—just "A")	A Aaaaaaabsolute
A A	A Aaaaaaawesome
A-AA	A AAAABlooming
A AA	A-AAAAbrupt
A-AAA	A Aaaabsolute
A Aaaaa-1	A Aaaamerican
A Aaaaaaaaaaaaaabsolute	A Aaaanytime
A Aaaaaaaaaaaaaahsome	A Aaaaardvark
A Aaaaaaaaaaaah	A Aaaawsome
A Aaaaaaaaaaadorable	A-AAABCOT
A Aaaaaaaaaaall	AA-AAAKEY
A Aaaaaaaaaaanytime	A Abacadadrabra

Is it worth convoluting your name in such silly ways just to be the first listing in a directory? Only if the vast majority of your business comes from such directory listings and those who would be calling you don't care about much else other than the convenience of calling the first listing. We've polled over a hundred audiences throughout the country, asking how many people would call AAA Secretarial first. In each audience consisting of 150 to 500 people, only three to five people indicate that they would. So before building your name around the alphabet, think about where your clients and customers will be most likely to find out about you and what their most important criteria for selection will be.

want to bother with making a decision about who to call, you might just call the first name on the list, AAA Secretarial.

As you can see, your choice of a name can and will appeal to certain types of clients or customers, so it's important to make sure it attracts the particular clientele you're interested in. We recognize, for example, that you may not always agree with our analysis of a particular name in this chapter. You may not like some that we think are effective, or vice versa. Different people often react quite differently to a business name, so it's all the more important to test the effect of any name you're considering on those you wish to attract.

Marketing Masterpiece: Two Simple Names That Say It All

A business name doesn't need to be flashy or make a big splash to be a winner. Here's proof. In our *Getting Business to Come to You* seminars, we always put up on an overhead screen a list of forty-some names of word-processing services taken from the Los Angeles Yellow Pages. The names are very similar to those we used as examples at the beginning of this chapter. We ask our audiences, usually 150 to 500 people, which of these businesses they would call if they needed to use a word-processing service. Much to our surprise and amazement, the result is *always* the same, from Wisconsin to Florida, Missouri to New Mexico, New York to California. See if you can pick out the winning name. It's among those on this list you've seen before:

AAA Secretarial
Affordable Word Processing
At All Hours
Britannica Publishing Inc.
Burdiss, Rita K.
Executive Business Services
Main Street Desktop Publishing
Joanne's Secretarial
Keystrokes
Letter Perfect
Marion Chadsworth Office Services
9 to 5
Paper Tiger
Professional Transcribers
Rogers and Cassidy
While You Wait Word Processing

The answer is Keystrokes. It has an inexplicable magic that appeals to small- and home-business owners. While they can never tell us why they like this name so much, they sure do. It's simple and memorable and since we've been doing these workshops for over ten years, seemingly timeless.

Another simple name that works wonders was the brainchild of Bash Dibra. A dog trainer on Long Island, New York, Dibra calls his program Simple Solutions. The beauty of this name is in part that it's simple, easy to remember, and the number-one benefit of his services to frustrated owners of ill-behaved dogs. But, in addition, he gets to use the name of his business over and over again whenever he writes or talks about what he does. A frequent guest on local and national television, Dibra talks about his "simple solutions" for excessive barking, his "simple solutions" for housebreaking, and so forth. Naturally his book and video are also called *Simple Solutions.*

Action Step: Recognizing Winning Names

Make a point to notice business names that others are using. Which names grab your attention? Which ones can you recall the next morning or the following week? What makes these names memorable? Review cards you've collected to recall which names failed to register at all. Why do some appeal to you while others leave you cold? Here is a list of actual business names. Can you identify what these people do? Would you remember these names? Why? See below for the answers:

Absolute Rubbish
Becoming Baby
CardSenders
Changing Creatively
Destination Directors
Ebbets Field Flannels
Fashion after Passion
Finders Keepers
Flowers Just Because
Fotogenic Felines
Furniture Medic®
Idea Lab
Investigative Services for Attorneys
Let's Do It Again, Resale Fashions
Martin Cantor, Manufacturer of Embroidered Emblems
Muster's Last Stand
On the Map
Party Time DJ's
Portraits on Location
ProClaim
Ritual Adornments
Sewing for You
The Critical Guest
The Flicker Shoppe
The Rolling Market
Vision Aerobics
Watermark Impressions
Words Are My Business
Writer's Bloc
Wiser Choices, Low Fat Cooking

Although at first glance you may not know precisely what each of these businesses do, chances are you have a reasonably good impression. If nothing else you're probably curious to know more about them. When coupled with a tag line, Sound Byte, or Grabber, these names nail down precisely what the owners do in a memorable way.

- **Absolute Rubbish,** a rural waste disposal recycling company in Oregon and a finalist in the Jane Applegate Best Small-Business Names Contest
- **Becoming Baby,** maternity clothes for big, beautiful, pregnant, and nursing women, Cumberland, Rhode Island

- **CardSenders,** a professional greeting card marketing service that mails greeting cards to a client's mailing list throughout the year, Petaluma, California
- **Changing Creatively,** counseling to manage life transitions and conflicts
- **Destination Directors,** meeting and event managers for out-of-town events
- **Ebbets Field Flannels,** historic baseball apparel, Seattle, Washington
- **Fashion after Passion,** Jaye Yaksic's maternity garments and baby accessories shop in Alameda, California, and a *Business 96* Great Name Winner
- **Finders Keepers,** collectibles in Panama City, Florida.
- **Flowers Just Because,** a flower shop in Milpitas, California
- **Fotogenic Felines,** a photographer specializing in cat portraits, especially champion felines, Santa Monica, California
- **Furniture Medic®,** furniture restoration, refinishing, and repair, Warwick, Rhode Island
- **Idea Lab,** a think tank for marketing campaigns, Los Angeles, California
- **Investigative Services for Attorneys,** a private investigator for attorneys
- **Let's Do It Again, Resale Fashions,** previously owned clothing, Phoenix, Arizona
- **Martin Cantor, Manufacturer of Your Design Embroidered Emblems,** puts your company's designs on ball caps and other items
- **Muster's Last Stand,** a hot dog stand in Mountain View, California, and fifth-place winner in the *Business 96* Great Name contest
- **On the Map,** colorful maps of local business districts featuring the location of merchants' shops created by J. Victor Booney of Leawood, Kansas. His slogan is "Put Your Business on the Map."
- **Party Time DJ's,** mobile disk jockey, Miami, Florida

- **ProClaim,** medical claims processing service in Tustin, California
- **Ritual Adornments,** ethnic jewelry, beads, and folk art in Santa Monica, California
- **Sewing for You,** custom sewing and embroidering, specializing in golf knickers, Baden, Pennsylvania
- **The Critical Guest,** a hotel evaluation service in Stamford, Connecticut
- **The Flicker Shoppe,** unique hand-dipped candles in Lincoln, Nebraska
- **The Rolling Market,** mobile seafood and meats delivery to restaurants and markets in rural towns and communities, Gering, Nebraska
- **Vision Aerobics,** a program for reducing eyestrain, Red Bank, New Jersey
- **Watermark Impressions,** commercial printing and business forms, Santee, California
- **Words Are My Business,** promotional brochures, newsletters, and reports
- **Wiser Choices, Low Fat Cooking,** cookbook and newsletter for eating more healthfully, Singlehouse, Pennsylvania
- **Writer's Bloc,** writing and editing specialist, Vancouver, Washington

Five Choices for Naming Your Business

As you can see, you have a variety of options when it comes to the name you select. The best decision will depend upon how well known you and your product or service already are, the nature of your niche, and what kind of business you want to attract. Here are the pros and cons of five choices for naming your business. See which ones best match your circumstances, goals, and objectives.

1. Your Own Name

Examples: Barabas & Covey
Judith August Company
Fleming, Ltd.

Martin Wallach & Associates
The Silverman Group
G.G. Bean, Inc.

PROS: Useful when *you* are the business, as in a specialized consulting service, or when your reputation makes you a major asset because you're well known and respected in your field or you want to become personally well known for your work. It's also the safest name choice from a legal standpoint, because usually, although not always, no one else will challenge the use of your name.

CONS: Doesn't tell what you do or what your business has to offer. Unless you are already well known you will need to spend considerable time and money to establish your name as a recognizable fixture in your industry. Some names are also hard to spell, remember, or pronounce. Others like Jones, Hernandez, and Williams are so common you may be mistaken for someone else's business (or reputation).

2. Your Name with Tag Line Describing What Your Company Does

Examples: Clampitt Paper Company
Karelson Custom Boats
Lenberg & Associates, Computerized Litigation Support
Liana, Haute Couture Wardrobes
Pat Mann, Animal Behavior Specialist
Susan Block's Match-Nite

PROS: Identifies your name with what you do. Often used by and expected of professionals.

CONS: Might not allow you to expand into other areas or, unless your field is unusual in itself, to be specific about how you are unique.

3. A Name That Communicates the Primary Benefit

Examples: Rent-to-Own Computers
One-Hour Messenger Service
Guaranteed Roommate Finder
Day & Night Pest Control
No Mess Chimney Sweep
Safe & Sound Security Patrol

PROS: Your name is an ad, selling your key benefit. It reflects something people want, so it's easy to remember, will be more likely to come to mind when needed, and can more easily attract the eyes or ears of those who need it.

CONS: You've got to live up to your name, and focusing on one benefit can limit expansion possibilities or flexibility should other benefits become more valued.

4. A Description of Your Niche

Examples: Class Reunions, Inc.
Law Library Management, Inc.
Latté Dah
Notary on Wheels
The Newsletter Factory
Roof Leak Detector Co., Inc.
In Absentia Pet and Plant Care

PROS: Your name can become a mini-billboard for your company. It will allow you to convey specifically what your business does in a way that sets you off from others.

CONS: A highly specialized name can limit expansion into other niches. If for some reason your niche becomes passé, you will need to adopt a new business name.

5. A Made-up Name

Examples: The ADD Group
ReViva
Whiskering Heights
ECM Limited Partnership
Profitivity

PROS: A well-chosen original name can be sufficiently unique or clever to be particularly memorable. Since it's one of a kind, it can distinguish you from everyone else. Also, an original nonspecific name can be useful when the company name will be an umbrella for several diverse business activities or product lines.

CONS: An original coined name has no meaning in and of itself and so provides no signal as to who you are or what you do. It will be up to you to create any meaning it is to acquire. Because it doesn't rely on familiar words, an original creation can also be harder to remember, spell, and pronounce. Of course, it can be done; e.g., Clorox, Gore-Tex, Polaroid, Reebok, and Xerox.

Action Steps: Creating a Winning Name

If you have completed the Action Steps in chapter 5, you are already well prepared to create a winning name. The work you did to create an Attention Grabber and a File-Opening Sound Byte will have prepared you to create a name that gets right to the heart of the matter, letting your clients know precisely when and why you are the best choice.

Paradoxically, however, we've noticed that rarely do people who have good Attention Grabbers or Sound Bytes also have good business names. Perhaps their less-than-effective names have motivated them to develop a winning way to describe what they offer. But why not use your name to lead into or reinforce the same theme that underlies all your other marketing messages?

Here's a six-step process for creating a winning name:

1. Gather the Ingredients. Generate a long list of words that describe what you want your business to reflect. You could start with the list of benefits you generated in chapter 5 (pages 179–80). Select a variety of adjectives, times, places, uses, feelings, features, humorous aspects of what you do, and other images you have of your work, the results you produce, and products you offer. As a help in doing this, you may want to use creativity software like *Idea Fisher, IdeaBank,* and *QBank Name Development* modules.

SAMPLE: *Landscape Gardener*

backyard	formal	ornamental
beauty	fruit	patio
breeze	garden party	peaceful
ecological	gate	pest-free
Eden	green	plants
English	grounds	roses
floating	herbal	sculpture
flowers	hummingbirds	seasons
shade	summer	water
springtime	sunlight	weeds
stress-free	trees	year-round

2. Brainstorm Possibilities. Piece together the various words you've collected. Play with them. Consider alliterations or phonetically pleasing names or words that together make up an acronym. Don't censor or judge; just generate possibilities. A poor name could be the seed for a winning one. You might also want to solicit ideas from colleagues, family or friends. Ask for ideas from on-line user groups and forums where you're active. You may not like or use any of these ideas, but they can help stimulate your imagination and expand your options.

SAMPLE POSSIBILITIES: *Landscape Gardener*

Ecological Gardens
Edible Gardens
Eternal Spring Gardening
Floating Garden Pond Service
Flower Gardens All Year
Forever Green Lawn and Garden Service
Formal English Gardens
Four-Seasons Gardening
Garden Gate
Garden of Eden Landscaping
Garden Party Perfect
Green Grounds, Inc.
Old-Fashioned Gardens
Patio Gardens
Peaceful Breeze Landscaping
Pest-Free Plants
Professional Grounds
Rose Gardens and More
Rooftop Gardens
Shady Nook Landscaping
Summer Daze
Tiny Gardens
Your Personal Garden

3. Evaluate the Options. Review your creations in relation to what you know about your target client or customer and the people who would or do buy from you. The closer to the heart of the matter your name is, the more impact it will have. But consider your options from all perspectives. Who might take offense? How could the names you're considering be misinterpreted? Does this name have other connotations than what you intend? Don't make the mistake we made when Paul started his public affairs consulting firm. We named the firm PAA, Public Affairs Assistance. Not a week went by that we didn't get calls from someone wanting information about how to get on welfare!

This faux pas, as irritating as it was, pales in the shadow of others we've encountered like SID'S Baby Furniture or two winners of Jane Applegate's Worst Small-Business Name contest: Amigone (pronounced "am-I-gone") Funeral Home and, the all-time winner from a nine-year old's point of view, a Thai restaurant named after the palace of the royal family in Thailand, the Poo-Ping Palace.

SAMPLE EVALUATION: *Landscape Design*

If our landscaper is targeting work with office or apartment managers, Green Grounds, Inc., or Professional Grounds might work well. For the busy two-career couple who want year-round attractive landscaping with no effort names like Four-Seasons Gardening, Garden Party Perfect, Forever Green Lawn, and Garden Services might be appealing. For the person who wants to hire a garden consultant, Shady Nook, Peaceful Breeze, or Summer Daze get more to the heart of the matter. Practical clients might be attracted to Pest-Free Plant and Lawn. There is a variety of highly niched names in this list like Edible Gardens, Ecological Gardens, Floating Gardens, and Patio Gardens if our landscaper wants to specialize his business. Tiny Gardens or Rooftop Gardens might be an appealing name for landscaping services in Manhattan or other high-rise urban areas.

4. **Get Feedback.** Use a laser printer and desktop publishing software like Microsoft *Publisher* to create a selection of mock business cards that feature the names you think hold the most promise. Ask twenty-five existing or potential customers to look over your stack of mock cards and tell you which company they'd be most inclined to contact and why. You can also gather such feedback from networking groups and on-line forums and user groups you frequent.

5. **Make Your Choice.** Incorporating the feedback you've gotten, select your favorite name. Then do a final check to make sure the name you've selected meets as many of the criteria for a winning name mentioned above as possible and make any final adjustments:

___ Does it identify what you do?

___ Does it distinguish you from all others?

___ Is it easily remembered?

___ Is simple to spell and pronounce?

EXAMPLES: Jim Walters of Orlando, Florida, does advertising specialties. His business name, In Your Face! Name Recognition Specialists, meets all four of these criteria. It describes precisely what he does. It distinguishes him from other more staid and laid-back advertising specialty companies. It gets right to the heart of the matter for his target customers: dynamic, highly motivated business owners who want to make sure their name stays in the front of their customers' minds. It's certainly easy to remember and it leads right into a fuller description of what he does: "We keep your business name, logo, and phone number in the face of your clients and prospects, so they'll call you instead of your competition."

Might there be people who don't like this name? Of course. People who want to project a low-key, understated image will most likely not be attracted to this name. But it's not addressed to those folks. In other words, those to whom a name doesn't speak, won't like it. If you've chosen well, that will be true of your name as well. You don't need to come up with a name that's acceptable to everyone. Such a name would most likely have all the juice taken out of it and be truly appealing to few. You want to select a name that will speak to the particular clients and customers in your niche.

6. Check Legal Availability and Protect Your Name. Before you take any formal steps to use the business name of your choice, make sure no one else is using it in your trade area or that no one owns a trademark or service mark for that name. The last thing you want is a lawsuit, or the threat of one, after you've invested time and money in promoting a business name. And even if using a name similar to someone else's never draws a lawsuit, for obvious reasons you don't want your business to be confused with any other. If the name you want is available, be sure to take steps immediately to protect it from others who might want to use it in the future.

Checking Whether a Business Name Is Available

There is one caveat whenever you use a business name other than your own proper name: the name you're considering may already be in use and may even be the name of a product or service that is protected by a trademark or service mark. There can be serious legal consequences of even inadvertently using a name already in use. You may be forced to change your name and have to start rebuilding your identity and, of course, reprinting all your materials. But whether there would be legal consequences or not, using the same name as someone else can confuse potential customers and result in business going elsewhere.

In most cases, if your business will operate only in your local area (township, city, or county), you may be OK by simply determining whether or not the name you desire is being used in your trade area. But don't be surprised if you're not the only one who has come up with your bright idea for a name. Great names can have many parents. Doing a quick search through *WhoWhere?* on the Web, for example, for the name

High-Touch Tip: Getting an Objective Reaction to Your Name

To get immediate direct feedback on your business name, when appropriate, ask people you meet for the first time if they would be willing to do you a favor and write on the back of your business card what they think you do and for whom. Ask them to be totally honest, even if it means telling you they don't have a clue what you do. You may be surprised at the feedback you get. Many of the people who have done this exercise in our workshops are amazed at how others perceive a business name they thought was perfectly clear.

Also, when you meet someone whose business name leaves you in the dark as to what he does or who he is, don't just nod politely. Do him a favor and ask, "What do you do exactly?" Not only will you possibly find a hidden prospect or referral source, you may make a friend and learn something new as well.

Keystrokes produced thirty word-processing services using some form of that name throughout the country. Here's another prime example:

In searching *Biz*File* for the award-winning Wreck-a-Mended Auto and Body Shop of Prior Lake, Minnesota, we found it shares its name with many other body shops across the country. There is a Wreck-a-Mended Auto Body in Tempe, Arizona, Carterville, Illinois, Colfax, Iowa, and Revere, Massachusetts. Then there are Wreck-a-Mended Frame & Body in Section, Alabama; Wreck-a-Mended Collision in Johnston, Iowa; Wreck-a-Mended Body Works in Gordon, Nebraska; Wreck-Amended Auto Collisions in Central Islip, New York; and a Wreck-a-Mended Auto Collision in Dallas, Texas. Finders Keepers has over 120 users who are running a range of businesses from antiques, collectibles, sports memorabilia, and souvenir shops to private investigators, nurseries, gift and consignment shops, apartment finder services, and a service for locating metal equipment.

So, you'll want to find out if anyone else is using the name you've selected or one that sounds like it, even though it's spelled differently, or is otherwise so similar that a problem might arise. Start by checking out the name's local availability. That's the easiest thing to do. Then if you plan to do any advertising or promotion outside your local area, you need to take further measures to ensure your right to use the name. Here are a number of steps you can take:

1. Check your local phone books and yellow pages and call information for more recent listings. Libraries have good collections of phone directories if you live in a metropolitan area with multiple directories.

2. Check at your county courthouse for fictitious name registrations, also referred to as "dba's"—"doing business as." At some time, it will be possible to do this kind of checking on the Internet, but at this writing, that's not the case for most people.

3. Write to the state office that handles corporate names, usually the secretary of state, to determine whether someone has reserved or taken the name for corporate use.

4. Search on the Web through national white- and yellow-page directories like *BigBook, Bigfoot, Four11, GTE SuperPages, ON'-VILLAGE,* or *WhoWhere?* (See **Resources** for specific Web addresses.) Or use a CD-ROM like *PhoneDisc PowerFinder* by Digital Directory Assistance. These databases list millions of business names from coast to coast compiled from the nation's telephone directories and other sources. On-line services like CompuServe also offer directories like *Biz*File* which offer more in-depth information. Search through several such databases, because what you can't find on one often turns up on another.

5. If you plan to have a Web site for your business, check the availability of various versions of your name through a company like InterNIC, which regulates Web site names (see **Resources**) to see what's available and what's already been taken.

6. To be sure that the name you want to use does not violate someone else's claim on it as a trademark or service mark, even if you plan to operate only locally, you will need to do a trademark search. A trademark is a word or logo that identifies a product; a service mark offers the same protection to a service. You can do the search yourself (see the High-Tech Tip that follows) or have it done for you. A trademark search firm (you can find them on the Web) can search for you, but a trademark and patent attorney can advise you whether your name is the type that can be registered as well as conduct the trademark search. The attorney will check for legally similar names as well as exact duplicates at the federal level and in all fifty states. Expect to pay a trademark search firm several hundred dollars; an attorney will cost more.

High-Tech Tip: On-line Trademark Searches

A trademark search was once a costly and time-consuming process best done only with an attorney or a trademark search firm, but today providers of trademark searches are available on the Web at reasonable cost or you can do your own search. A search using *www.webcrawler.com* yields dozens of services, including attorneys and search firms, with prices ranging from five dollars (www.trademark-search.com) to the hundreds of dollars and accomplishable within twenty-four hours. You can also do a trademark search yourself by going to a U.S. Patent Depository Library and using *Cassis,* the government database, free. Or for a fee, on your own PC, you can do a trademark search using a database like *Trademarkscan,* available on CompuServe (GO: TRADEMARK) and subscriptions services like Dialog.

If you are seeking to register a trade or service mark, we recommend consulting with an attorney who specializes in intellectual property even if you conduct the search yourself. By providing the attorney with the results of your own on-line searches (be sure to record your entire search session), you can save on your legal costs.

Four Signs That You Should Change Your Name

If you're already using a particular name, before starting a concerted business generating effort, make sure your company name is an asset and not a liability in terms of helping you get more business. Have you been having any of the following problems?

1. Customers can never seem to remember the name of your company. It may be too abstract, complex, or unusual.
2. When you introduce yourself with your company name, it doesn't register, or people repeatedly say, "You do what?"
3. People are surprised when they hear your prices. Your company name may imply higher or lower prices than you charge.
4. People are constantly confusing you with another company with a similar name.

PROTECTING YOUR BUSINESS NAME

Once you've found a name you wish to use that's available, there are steps you can take to protect it from use by others. Contrary to what most people believe, however, registering your name as a dba does not in itself protect you from others using use your business name. To protect your name, you can:

1. Incorporate and reserve your name with the state office that handles corporate names, usually the secretary of state. This will reserve your name in that state only. If you wish to protect it in other states as well, you must register your corporate name separately in those states.
2. Determine if you can register your name and logo as a trademark or service mark. If so, this will offer still broader protection. You can get the information you need to do this, including the forms you need to use, through the U.S. Patent and Trademark Office (See **Resources** at the end of this chapter.) Alternatively, you might want to refer to *Trademark, How to Name a Business and Product & Trademark* by intellectual property lawyers Kate McGrath and Stephen Elias for Nolo Press. It also includes forms, statutes, and other resources.

NOTE: Taking these steps, however, will not protect your name from being used by others as an Internet Web address. Even if the use of your name is otherwise reserved, to reserve its use on the World Wide Web you will have to apply for domain registration through a company like InterNIC.

If you consistently encounter any of these problems, consider changing your business name. Unless you've spent years building a reputation and therefore have high name recognition, it is rarely too late to change it. Company name changes are common: About one out of ten corporations change their names each year.

Name Changes Made Easy

If you could be attracting more business by changing your company name, there is a way to do so without losing the investment you've already made in your current name. You can use the new, more effective name you've chosen as a slogan or tag line to your existing name, such

THREE STEPS TO EASING YOUR WAY INTO A NAME CHANGE

If you know you need to change your name but you've already invested considerable time and money in establishing and promoting your existing name, rather than scrapping all your efforts and starting fresh with a new name, you can change your name in stages by taking the following three steps.

Step 1. Use a verbal tag line. Begin verbally using your new name as an add-on or tag line to your existing name. Never cross out your existing name or write in the tag line on your card or other materials, however. If you wish, you can add it to your materials as a personal note on the back of your card or at the bottom of your correspondence; e.g., "Remember, I'm your 24-hour help line." or "Let me be there when you can't be."

Step 2. Add your tag line in print. When you're ready to reprint your business cards and stationery or when you do a new marketing piece, add your new name as a tag line to your existing name. Alternatively, you can use your new name as your primary identity and add your old name as the tag line. This interim step gives everyone a chance to associate your new name with your old name.

Step 3. Formally adopt your new name. As people become increasingly familiar with your new identity, if your tag line is working well for you, the next time you print your materials, switch to using it exclusively as your official business name. By this time, people will most likely be familiar with it and won't become confused. They probably won't even notice the change, unless it's accompanied by a dramatic change in your graphic image. If you do change your overall look, do it when you can do all your materials at once. You don't want to have one set of business cards and another set of stationery. This could be confusing, and definitely won't look professional.

NOTE: Officially changing your business name will involve obtaining or changing your dba (Doing Business As) or your corporate registration in your state. If you have been using your own name, you will need to obtain a dba or register as a corporation for the first time.

as Betty Blevin's Business Services, Your Personal Administrative Assistant. Add your new name as a tag to all your materials and advertising. List your business with the phone company under both names. As you become known by the new name, demote the old one to the slogan or tag line until, if you wish, you can drop it altogether.

Adding a tag line that describes what you do can make a substantial change in the impact of your name. For example, The Bohle Company adds to all its printed material a line that reads Corporate Marketing and Public Relations. Helen Trent Designs is clarified by Glorious Interiors; Lee James is enhanced by Web Graphic Designs. In each case, without changing the name, what the business offers becomes quite clear. The tag line establishes a definable image.

You might want to consider using elements from your Attention Grabber or Sound Byte as the tag line. For example, the family day-care provider whose Sound Byte we described in chapter 5 could add the words When You Can't Be There or A Second Home to the generic tag line Family Day Care Provider she uses after her name. The twenty-four-hour computer consultant could add Your 24-Hour Help Line to the generic Computer Consultant label that follows his name. The dentist specializing in dental phobias could add "Stressless Dentistry" after his professional title, or, as a California dentist does, "We Serve Dental Chickens."

Here are a few other examples from chapter 5 of how a name or tag line can be used to reinforce your Sound Byte:

> *"You know how hard it is to work when your desk is buried in piles of paperwork?" Well, I'm a professional organizer, and I've developed a way to clear off a desk and put everything on it in order in just sixty minutes.* ***My company*** **is One-Hour Organizing."**
>
> *"Do you ever sit and stare at your pet and wonder what it's thinking? Well, I'm a pet psychic. I can tell you what's on your pet's mind and why it behaves the way it does.* ***My company name*** **is Pet Talk."**
>
> *"Have you ever cherished a special piece of heirloom jewelry? Well, I'm a jewelry designer and I create heirlooms.* ***My company*** **is Customed Heirloom Jewelry."**
>
> *"You know how sometimes you just can't find the right words to say what you want to say? Well, I have a way with words.* ***My business*** **is Wordcrafting.** ***I help people find just the right words to get their message across."***

Getting Your Name Out There

Essentially all marketing is about getting your name out. So once you have a winning name, it can serve as the cornerstone for all your marketing efforts. You can think of all your business-generating activities as one concerted effort to make a name for your name!

Resources

Books

How to Register Your Own Trademark. Mark Warda. Sourcebooks: Naperville, Ill., 1997.

Trademark: How to Name Your Business and Product. Kate McGrath and Stephen Elias. Nolo Press: Berkeley, Calif., 1996, (800) 992-6656, www.nolo.com

Trademark: Legal Care for Your Business and Product Name. Kate McGrath and Stephen Elias. Berkeley, Calif. Nolo Press, 1997.

Software

Idea Fisher, creativity software by Idea Fisher Systems. 2222 Martin, Ste. 360, Irvine, CA 92612, (714) 474-8111, www.ideafisher.com

The Name Stormers. 2811 Declaration Cr., Lago Vista, TX 78645, (214) 350-6214, www.namestormers.com

MindMan, The Creative MindManager. Visualizing Ideas, P.O. Box 829, Mount Eliza, VIC 3930, Australia, +61-3 9787 6207 www.mindman.com

On-Line Services

Biz*File is produced by American Business Information, 5711 South 86th Circle, Omaha, NE 68127, (402) 593-4500, fax: (402) 331-1505. Available on CompuServe, 5000 Arlington Centre Boulevard, Columbus, OH 43220, (800) 848-8990, www.compuserve.com

Trademarkscan is produced by Thomson and Thomson, 500 Victory Road, North Quincy, MA 02175, (800) 692-8833, www.thomson-thomson.com

Web Name Registration

Network Solutions, Inc. (InterNic), www.internic.net

U.S. Patent and Trademark Office

Washington, D.C. 20231
General information: (703) 308- HELP
Automated: (703) 557-INFO
Web address: (http://www.uspto.gov/web/offices/tac/doc/basic/)
Provides information on registering your trademark including:

- Basic Facts about Registering a Trademark
- Information Numbers
- The Registration Process
- Filing Requirements
- Written Application Form [PTO Form 1478]
- The Drawing Page
- Fees
- Specimens
- Additional Requirements for Intent-to-Use Applications
- Trademark Services

White and Yellow Pages on the Web

- BigBook (http://www.bigbook.com)
- Bigfoot (http://www.bigfoot.com)
- Four11 (http://www.four11.com)
- GTE SuperPages (http://www.superpages.gte.net)
- ON'VILLAGE (http://www.onvillage.com)
- WhoWhere? (http://www.whowhere.com)

CHAPTER 7

Creating an Unforgettable Impression

Things are not only what they are. They are, in very important respects, what they seem to be.

—Former Vice President Hubert H. Humphrey

Would you hire a sloppily dressed, poorly groomed individual to sell your products or services? Of course not. But your marketing materials are as much your sales force as any personnel you hire. For someone who is self-employed, they may be your only sales force, other than yourself.

Your materials represent you when you're not there. Sometimes they precede you onto the desks and into the homes or offices of your clients and customers, communicating who you are, what you do, and how much it's worth. Often they determine whether or not you'll get an appointment or a phone call. They're what you leave behind as a reminder to those you meet of what you can offer them and serve as a way they can tell others about you. So, it's vital that your graphic image speak well of you.

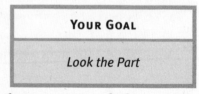

Your Goal
Look the Part

When publicist Kim Freilich started her company, Kim from L.A., she was a one-woman company operating from home in the highly competitive, primarily New York City–based world of book promotions. She knew right from the start that image would be vital to her success. If publishers thought of her as a second-rate alternative to bigger, more established New York firms, she would either get passed over for work or have to discount the value of her services. So, she decided to invest time, energy, and money in creating a powerful graphic image for her company. That investment paid off. She recalls, "My clients figured anyone who has invested that much in her business image is serious about what she's doing."

Fortunately, to have that kind of impact today, you won't need to dress your business image in the equivalent of an Armani suit. You needn't spend a fortune to make an unforgettable positive impression. By investing time, attention, ingenuity, and as much money as you can afford, you can create an image that your clients and customers will take seriously and that will make you, your niche, and your business name all the more memorable. With an effective visual identity, every letter you send, every business card you present, and every piece of material that comes from your office serves as a mini-billboard for your company, reinforcing and enhancing all your marketing efforts with one impactful impression.

GRAPHIC IDENTITIES

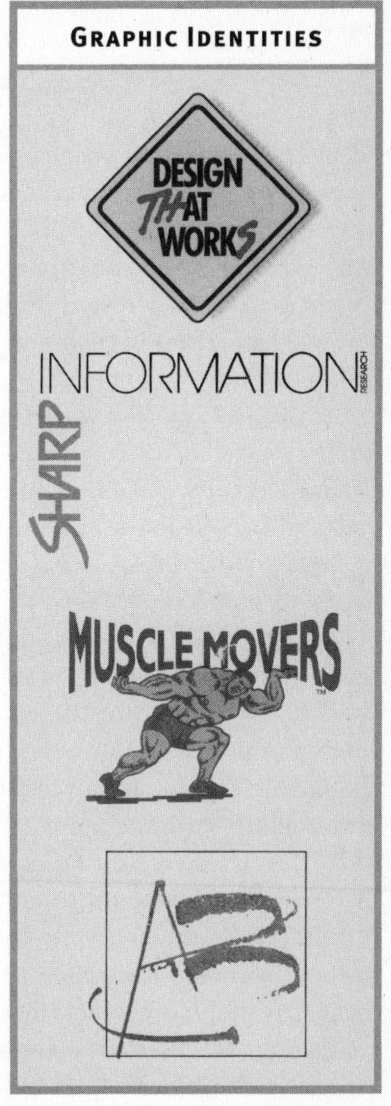

Notice, for example, how dramatically different these graphic identities are and yet how clearly each tells the story of the company it represents.

From bold and dramatic to humorous or businesslike, each of these graphic identities relies on a visual symbol image or unique typeface to communicate its message. While you can't see the colors here, Design That Works with its bright yellow road sign in red and black ink symbolizes Linda McCulloch's work as a corporate marketing communication designer in Tucker, Georgia.

Sharp Information's crisp black and gray tones on white is the look Seena Sharp has chosen to present her work as a business researcher in Hermosa Beach, California. The graphic for Muscle Movers in brown and maroon on cream says it all for Brionne Corbry's moving company in the Seattle area. And Anne Cowie's copper and steel graphic illustrates her calligraphy and design work in Belmont, North Carolina.

Each of these images creates an impression that communicates the nature of the business that's appropriate and effective with their particular clientele. This is precisely what you want to do in creating a graphic identity for your work. Your image should reinforce your business name and niche and help distinguish you from all others, all the while saying "I'm professional, knowledgeable and capable."

Do You Need a New Look?

An effective business image will draw a second glance. Then the person looking at your materials will give you and what you offer a second look as well. If your image is working for you, those receiving your materials will sometimes say something about them, but more likely they will simply be more interested in finding out about you and your business. You will have risen in their esteem because your graphic image has proclaimed, "This is a person to note."

Is this the reaction you're getting? By these criteria, how do the materials you're using now stack up? Do your mini-billboards turn any heads? Do they make one consistent impression or are they a hodgepodge of various looks, typefaces, and colors? Whatever business you're in, your graphic image needs to be unique, attractive, and impactful. It needs to stand on its own, because often you won't be there when people get their first impression of your company. Your materials will be representing you, serving as your ambassador.

If you're not getting the positive response you could be getting from your graphic image, now is the time to change it. Most companies change the design of their letterhead, cards, and other materials several times before settling on one that fully expresses the message they wish to convey. If you're getting an acceptable response, but not a noteworthy one, you might want to wait until you run out of your existing stock of materials or the next time you need to change a phone number or address. But in the meantime, start thinking about what you want your image to communicate and how you could do that most effectively.

As you will discover, an effective graphic image does not need to be expensive. With desktop publishing software, preprinted four-color papers and the wealth of clip art available today on-line or on CD-ROM, you can create your own graphic look if you feel so inclined. Or, on the pages that follow, you'll find a host of other cost-effective options for enlisting the expertise of others to help you create the right design. Give yourself permission to experiment with the ideas that follow until

Action Steps: Collecting Looks You Like

Spend some time looking at the graphic images other businesses have created for themselves. Networking events and trade shows are two places where you can collect a variety of samples of graphic images. Peruse networking tables or trade show booths and notice which materials stand out, which ones catch your eye. You might also look through a printer's sample books, which contain many examples of possible designs. Make a point to specifically identify what impresses you. What turns you off? What is noteworthy? What do you overlook or pass over without noticing? Think about how you could incorporate the elements you like into a distinctive look of your own.

As you consider the many possibilities, keep in mind who your clients or customers are. What do they expect from a business like yours? The creative and unusual? The tried, true, and trusted? The highly professional and classy? A matter-of-fact and down-to-business attitude? Design your materials to communicate your message in a way that also meets their expectations.

you find a graphic identity that makes your business stand out in the way you want it to.

Elements of Graphic Images That Sell

Imagine that you have found the business cards pictured in the color insert in a stack on your desk. Since they've been piling up for a while, you may or may not remember when or where you got these cards or who these people were. So you lay them out on your desk to decide what you'll do with them. Which ones communicate most clearly and effectively? Which ones draw your attention? To which ones do you give a second glance?

In evaluating the impact of these cards, notice that there are actually six elements involved in creating a graphic image: • Design concept, • Name or logo, • Color choices, • Paper choice, • Layout of the information and images, • Typeface and font selection. Let's take a look at each of these elements in terms of why some images work so well while other don't.

Design Concept

Think of your graphic image as a visual representation of your business. Notice how each of the sample cards conveys a concept about the business it represents. Each graphic concept, for better or worse, reflects who the business is and what it does. If done well, the message conveyed by the visual image will match the message of the words and they both will match your idea of who you are, your niche, and what you offer. Kritter Sitter, for example, both looks as though they care and says that they do. Profitivity, with its metallic copper on black design, matches the quality Kathryn Dager is striving to help her clients achieve through her customer service training programs.

If done haphazardly or without forethought, however, your visual concept may send a conflicting or confusing image. Suppose, for example, that Brownfox Enterprises* coordinates nature adventures and Arnold Cimmons himself, albeit a practical man, is a wildlife expert and outdoor tour guide. The visual image he's chosen for his card, most likely done quickly on a tight budget, sends an entirely different message about the nature of who he is and what he does. As a result, he may be missing opportunities or raising doubts in the minds of potential clients.

Mary Rinkles's* clients most likely won't want their newsletters or events to be as nondescript as the look she's chosen to represent her business. Her lack of any design concept works against her. After all, she's in the business of providing services that will make her clients more memorable, but her own business image is not.

Whereas Dager and Taylor have chosen a design concept that gets right to the heart of the matter for their business, both Brownfox's and Rinkles's graphics miss the the point of the message they want to send. Just as in selecting your business name and deciding how you'll describe what you do, your overall design concept needs to provide a glimpse into the heart of what you're able to provide those you serve.

Name or Logo

A logo is a unique typeface and format or graphic design that represents your company or product. It provides an immediate visual identity that distinguishes you from other businesses. You can use a logo as a design element in all your advertising and promotion. You can also use it in

---

* Fictitious examples reflective of many business images we have seen.

lieu of or in conjunction with your company name as your proprietary trademark or service mark. It's like a visual signature for your business.

You'll notice that two of the cards from the samples in the color insert have no logo: Brownfox Enterprises and Litigation Support.* The others have either a unique graphic rendition of the business name itself as their logo (Dollmaker's Journal, and Michael Faircloth) or they have used a visual image of some kind that represents their business. Kritter Sitters, for example, features a passel of friendly critters; Don Aslett sparkles with soap bubbles, Mary Rinkles uses an open book, and Profitivity has a custom design. Note that Michael Faircloth has used both a unique graphic rendition of his business name and a distinctive visual image of a grand piano.

Notice also that Faircloth and Aslett don't actually say on their cards what their business is. Instead they use their visual image to communicate that message. Faircloth is a pianist and piano teacher. Aslett is "cleaning the world." He provides cleaning services, books, tapes, videos, and other materials on housecleaning.

These examples illustrate dramatically the added impact having a logo can provide for any business. According to a study by the Schechter Group, a New York corporate identity firm, people responded more positively to a company name combined with a logo than to a name alone. You can see that the logo one selects can communicate a wealth of material about the personality and nature of a business that can't necessarily be said with the name alone. Kritter Sitters, for example, communicates a warmth and friendliness that's highly appealing to pet owners. It says Jan and Lyn love animals, will take good care of them, and both they and the animals will have a good time in the process. On the other hand, without a logo, we get very little impression about the personality or ability of Arnold Cimmons of Brownfox Enterprises.

But by looking at Mary Rinkles's card, you can see that using just any logo is not much better than none at all, and sometimes worse. An effective logo is unique and impactful. It says something important and memorable about you and what you do. The open book Rinkles uses is taken from a standard clip-art library and is used by thousands of others in a wide variety of ways. It's similar, for example, to the icon we use in the **Resources** section of this book. Even such a commonly used image, however, could work better for Rinkles if she used it in some unique way, or if it had a more direct connection to what she does. If she were a freelance proofreader for book publishers, for example, it might be somewhat more effective.

When we show the fictitious Brownfox and Rinkles cards to people, the general reaction is "Well, they're probably just starting out and don't have much money to invest." Even if this is true, it's not the message anyone wants to send with their materials and with the options available today, there's no need for this kind of reaction to your graphic identity.

Dr. Cosoven's image for Litigation Support, on the other hand, may look graphically plain. But before discarding it as ineffective, consider who his clients are as a legal medical consultant. They are lawyers. Cosoven has purposely chosen to tailor his card to look identical to those used by the law firms to whom he markets. Therefore his is a more effective business image than one might think.

As you can see, the best use of your name and logo will communicate who you are to those who need you in a way that will be appealing and noteworthy to them.

Color Choice

As you can see from the color on the sample cards, color plays an important role in the impact of a business card. Mary Rinkles, Litigation Support, and Brownfox Enterprises are simply black ink on white stock. Although this is usually the most inexpensive choice, generally it's a look you should try to avoid. Two-color printing, while more expensive, carries considerably more impact. Michael Faircloth, for example, has added a touch of color to his basically black-and-white image by including a single red line under his name. Kritter Sitter had added color to their otherwise black-and-white card by adding green to the foliage around the animals in the logo.

Don Aslett has gone all out on color, using more expensive, but

PROTECTING YOUR LOGO

Others may be tempted to borrow a good logo. AT&T learned this the hard way. They failed to register their clever Yellow Pages walking fingers. Now all Yellow Pages companies can use the graphic, and many do. Thus sometimes people receiving solicitations from these companies think they're dealing with AT&T. As in protecting your business name, to protect your logo so others can't use it, you must initiate a search to make sure your design is available for use. If the design you're proposing is available, you can then protect it by registering your logo with your state, if it provides for trademark protection, or with the United States Patent and Trademark Office. (See page 227) attention-arresting four-color printing. His card has an off-white background with a horizontal purple stripe and purple ink for all the type except Aslett's name, which is in orange. The soap bubbles and globe are a pale rainbow of pastel yellow, blue, and pink.

If your budget is extremely tight, there are ways you can stick to one color of print and still create an interesting visual image. Here are just a few:

Reverses and screens. To provide variety and interest, you can use reverses (white on black) or screens (gray tones like the Sharp Information logo at the beginning of the chapter). In fact, if you look at Michael Faircloth's design, you will see the use of a reverse (his first name is white on black) and a screen (the piano is a light gray tone).

Colored ink on colored paper. For a more distinctive look that costs little more, you can use a colored-paper stock for your materials, perhaps with a colored ink. That's what Dollmaker's Journal has done. Editor Barbara Johnston has chosen pale blue paper with a blue ink. Blue ink also looks good on gray paper. A deep burgundy on ivory or gray paper is also attractive. If you can spend just a little more, think about using two colors of ink. For example, you could keep the same deep burgundy and add black or gray ink on bright white paper or use brown and blue inks on ivory. Profitivity has chosen black and copper metallic ink on ivory.

Preprinted papers. Another way to add color to your image is to select among the many choices of four-color preprinted papers. Such papers are usually available for printing matching business cards, stationery, brochures, and presentation materials. See the color insert for examples.

Paper Choice

The paper you choose for your collateral materials is a good deal more important than most people realize. After the look you choose for your name or logo, the choice of paper is the next most important decision you'll make in creating a successful business image.

In many instances, your envelope is the first thing people see with your company name on it; the letterhead is the second. In other cases, your business card is someone's first introduction to you. Not only do they see these materials, they also touch and feel them. Studies done on various types of letterheads that get through an assistant's hands to his or her boss show that the better the quality of the paper, the more likely it is to make it to the desk of those you want to reach. So paper is not a place you want to scrimp, and usually there's no need to.

The difference in cost between an average letterhead stock (which is called a #1 bond with watermark) and an expensive high-quality letterhead stock (100 percent cotton content) is approximately one penny per sheet! That's only $10 per thousand sheets, but that $10 can make a big difference. How much you want to invest in your materials will depend, of course, on the cost of your product or service. But make sure that you use either a watermarked bond, a 25 percent rag bond, or a good fancy-finish text sheet and that your second sheets are the same as the letterhead itself. Photocopy paper for letterhead or second sheets won't do. Envelopes, too, must match your letterhead stock, as in most cases should your business card.

To convey substance, we recommend using a 70-pound bond paper for letterhead, brochures, newsletters, and flyers and a heavy card stock for your business cards if at all possible. Lesser-weight paper feels flimsy and doesn't hold up well in the mail or with handling. The paper selected by Profitivity not only has weight, it also has texture. You can feel a subtle horizontal pinstripe pattern ingrained in the paper. This sense of texture is enhanced by the fact that the copper ink of the logo and business name is embossed; that is, it's slightly raised off the surface of the paper.

Selecting a coated paper is another way to add pizzazz to your cards, brochure, flyers, and business cards. A bright white coated paper, for example, really makes the red and black ink on Michael Faircloth's card stand out. Don Aslett's off-white coated stock adds an extra sheen to his four-color card. If you use coated stock on some of your materials, however, keep in mind that ink colors look somewhat different on coated paper, so check to be sure the inks you use on coated paper are still compatible with the colors of your other materials.

Typeface Selection

If you look carefully at the sample cards, you'll notice the variety of typefaces their owners have chosen and the distinctive effects each typeface has. Some are more formal; others are more informal and thus warm, friendly, or fun. Some command your attention; others are less interesting or even difficult to read. Also notice that the size of type fonts varies widely. The smaller the type, the more difficult it is to read and thus the easier to pass over unnoticed. Compare Dollmaker's Journal to Mary Rinkles, for example. Whereas Dollmaker's is larger and easy to read,

Rinkles, in an effort to get in lots of text, has made her card hard to read. Also, notice that while Dr. Cosoven's card is nearly as nondescript as Brownfox Enterprises', by use of a larger more stretched type font, Litigation Support stands out more clearly and looks more professional.

So, in designing your cards take time to look over various typeface options available through desktop publishing or graphics software. Specialized software for custom designing your own marketing materials also includes many type-style options (see **Resources** at end of the chapter), including software for creating 3-D fonts. For an even wider selection, peruse typeface books at print shops and find a typeface that suits the image you want to convey for your company. Beware, however, of unusually interesting typefaces that may look intriguing but are difficult if not impossible to read. Check both upper and lower cases of fonts you're considering and take particular note of how the letter combinations you'll be using will look.

The Impact of Color

Your graphic image has only seconds to make an impression. Market studies have determined that color is vital to what gets noticed and each color sends its own subtle psychological messages. They find that:

- **Red** suggests power, life and vitality.
- **Yellow,** the most visible of all colors, conveys warmth, happiness, and a bargain.
- **Blue** suggests purity, serenity, prestige, confidence, cleanliness, and knowledge.
- **Green** is associated with being natural and healthy.
- **White** represents freshness and light.
- **Black** communicates elegance and sophistication.

Layout Creation

The next element of your graphic image is the layout of the various other elements we've just discussed along with the other information you want to include. Layout refers to the way the elements are positioned in relation to one another and to the total space that's available. The way you arrange these items on the paper makes a statement about your business, whether you want it to or not. The layout can detract from or assist in creating the image you want to convey. In fact, all the other elements may be just fine when considered separately but fail to achieve your objectives when laid out ineffectively.

Look at the elements that have been included on the sample cards.

Notice the use of open space, the way the various elements of each are combined, and their proportional size. The Brownfox image seems barren, for example, while Mary Rinkles's seems too crowded. Don Aslett includes more information than Kritter Sitter or Profitvity. What information does each image highlight? Barbara Johnston of Dollmaker's Journal, for example, has featured her phone number because she wants people to be able to find it quickly and easily. Kritter Sitters emphasizes their motto, "Care is our concern," and the fact that their service is bonded.

High-Touch Tip: Use Layout to Make Sure You Get Your Calls

Have you ever tried calling someone and reached their fax number by accident? Who hasn't? Why do you suppose this happens so often? It's a design problem. It happens because the name, address, and phone number are laid out so that the eye automatically goes to the fax number instead of the voice-mail number. Studies show that the eye goes from the upper left of a piece of paper to what's in the lower right-hand corner. Notice how your own eyes automatically scan a card diagonally from the top left to the lower right. But just as layout creates the problem, layout can also solve the problem. You can put the fax on the left side of the page and the phone on the right or, as we've done on our materials, you can separate the fax number from the phone number by placing them on separate lines, making the phone number one point-size larger and printing it in bold or another color of ink.

Coordinating Your Graphic Identity for Maximum Effect

Once you've taken the time and spent the money to conceive, test, and create the image you want, you can use it again and again, everywhere. Actually, sticking with one consistent graphic image can save, not cost, you money and it will make you more memorable.

So, once you've selected an image, use the basic elements of your design on every piece of printed material you produce, from business cards to presentation packets, invoices to mailing labels, fax cover

Marketing Masterpiece: Business Image to the Rescue

Sometimes the right graphic image can cut right through misconceptions and other problems than would otherwise make getting business more difficult. Benjamin Shield, for example, has used a graphic image as a goodwill ambassador for his private practice as a Certified Rolfer.

Rolfing is a form of therapeutic bodywork; and if you've ever heard of it, like everyone else who has, chances are the first thought that comes to your mind is "pain." Rolfing has a reputation for being a very painful, albeit effective, treatment.

Shield, however, has worked with over 25,000 patients in his career, and his calendar is booked solid six months in advance because he uses a virtually pain-free approach to Rolfing. And his business card makes it clear he's not your everyday Rolfer.

ROLFING
TM
BENJAMIN SHIELD, PH.D.
Certified Rolfer®
Pacific Health Resources
1137 Second Street, Suite 100
Santa Monica, California 90403
(310) 458-1800
(310) 451-7815 fax

His logo, which is imprinted in maroon on a soft warm ivory stock, has the word ROLFING along the top and features a graphic portrait of two smiling bears. One, dressed in a striped T-shirt and shorts, is gently rubbing the shoulders of the other, who is seated comfortably on a small wooden stool in a pair of heart-patterned boxer shorts. Below the portrait are Shield's name and his designation as a registered Certified Rolfer, followed by his address and phone number. Of course, he uses this graphic on all his materials, including his annual holiday card to past and present patients.

This masterful graphic image clearly demonstrates what Shield does in an unforgettable way. It distinguishes him from other Rolfers and, best of all, it overcomes the number-one objection wary patients have to using his service!

sheets to Web-site design. Put your graphic signature on everything that goes out from or otherwise represents your company. Keep the same color theme, the same typeface, and the same layout concepts for all the materials you use to represent your business. This consistency will reinforces the identity you're working to create. (See color insert for examples of how others have created one consistent graphic identity.)

Action Steps: Coming Up with a Winning Look

It takes a long time for people to recognize a company image and even more time to get accustomed to a new one. So, whether you're creating an image for the first time or doing a makeover, you'll want to use whatever design choices you make for some time to come. You'll also want to use your new image as often as possible in as many ways as possible to make the most memorable impression. So don't just turn the project over to a designer and let her come up with something.

If you've completed the action steps in chapters 1 through 6, you're well prepared to create a winning design for your business. Even if you're planning to use the services of a professional designer or illustrator, take time to think through the key message you want to communicate about the nature of your niche and how you could best do that graphically. Then, share your conclusions and convictions with any professional you'll be working with. Here are three steps you can take to be sure you get the results you want:

1. Generate visual images that capture the essence of your niche. Reflect on your File Opening Sound Byte, your Attention Grabber, your business name, and any tag line you use to describe your business. They all should be sending one consistent message. Now you want to carry that same theme into a visual design. In the color insert you'll find a gallery of business cards that show how people whose names and Sound Bytes you've read about previously have translated the heart of their niche into a visual image. Review these examples and begin imagining possible visual themes for your business. What colors, images, symbols, and so forth come to mind as representative of your business?

2. Stimulate your imagination. To get your visual creativity going, ask yourself questions like:

- If my business were a color, what color would it be?
- What common objects or images does my business remind me of?
- If I couldn't use any words but I wanted to communicate the nature of my business, how could I do so?

After J. T. Taylor suffered a physical ailment that prevented her from continuing her work as an interior designer, she tailored a new career for herself. A longtime collector of rare artifacts, she was inspired by the golden giraffe she kept on display in her bedroom to begin selling items like those she collected to interior decorators. The golden giraffe became the symbol for her business, One of a Kind. Located in Irvine, California, Taylor says people often comment on the beauty of her card, which is gold foil on forest green.

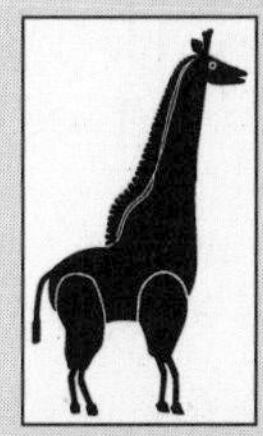

The motto of Peter Vizzusi's Magic Sands Class Studio in Aptos, California, is "Hand Made." He wanted his graphic image to depict the physical act of blowing and opening glass by hand over a fire. Working with illustrator Mott Jordan, he developed a pen-and-ink drawing for his logo reminiscent of a WPA ink block that reflects the light and the heat of the furnace as the men work.

Jack Ferguson's nickname is "Rhino," and his business name is Rhino Real Estate. The image that came to the mind of his designer, Bob Lawry, was the word *Rhino* sculpted into the plated shape of a rhinoceros.

3. Test your best concepts. Whether you're designing your own materials or using the services of a designer, you'll want to get reactions to your ideas. Designers will often give you mock-ups of several options, or you can create your own mock-ups using desktop publishing software. Show your choices to associates, colleagues, clients, and customers. Get their reactions. Listen for observations about details you may have overlooked: like "That gray paper is depressing"; "That looks great, but I can't read the phone number."

Put your logo on everything.

Every piece of advertising, promotional material, or collateral you use should carry your logo, if you have one, or your company name in its characteristic layout and type font. If you've designed your own logo on your computer, of course, it's already available to use on any document you create or to upload to your on-line or Internet presence. If you're using a designer, ask for an electronic version of your image, or scan your image into your computer yourself. If you don't own a scanner, you can have the image scanned at a print shop like Kinko's. Alternatively, your printer can prepare what are known as slicks of your design. These special coated sheets have your logo in various sizes printed on them in heavy black ink, which can then be cut out and stripped onto camera-ready art for various advertising and promotional purposes.

Put your name, addresses, and phone numbers on everything.

Yes, everything. Leaving your name, address, and phone number off any element of your graphic sales force is an all-too-common oversight that can cost you business. Worst of all, you'll never even know how much business you've lost!

Think of your own experience. How often have you said to yourself, "This is really great. I'd like to get another one"? But search as you may, you can't find a phone number or address to order more? How often has someone asked you how he could get in touch with a service you've used in the past and although you'd love to refer him, you can't find a phone number or address to provide? How often have you thought, "Oh, no problem, I remember the company name and city, so I'll just call information," but, alas, you find no listing under that name?

Occasionally, even large businesses make mistakes like these, but it's much more common among self-employed individuals. It's easy to think, "Well, all the information is on my business card, so if they need me they'll call." Or "It's all in my brochure or in my proposal." Well, cards get misplaced. Proposals get tossed. The solution is simple: put your name, address, phone number E-mail and Web addresses, if you have them, on everything!!! Not just your letterhead, cards, and stationery. Not just on your invoices and brochures. Even if these things don't get lost or thrown away, they may get filed . . . somewhere. Think how much time it can take to dig through past records to find an old receipt or invoice. It's too easy for someone to say, "Well, I'll look for that later" or "I'll look that up as soon as I can get to it." "Later" can become never—and your prospective new client, customer, or referral source may never get around to contacting you.

So put your name, address, phone number, and fax and E-mail addresses on the product itself (if you have a product) and on the package, box, or material it comes in. If you have a service, put all this information on each page of everything you send out, hand out, or post. Put it all on giveaways like bookmarks, calendars, refrigerator magnets, pens, sticky notepads, anything you can give to everyone who uses your service that they will keep in a handy place. And, even though it will cost a little more, pay to have a separate telephone listing under your

Your Graphic Sales Force

The following is a basic inventory of paper and electronic tools you can use for marketing purposes. Not all businesses need all these tools, but it's a good idea to think through which ones you may be using before you make a final decision on an image for your company. You'll want to be sure the look you select is suitable and practical for all possible uses. So, check off from the list below the ones you anticipate using and make it a point to present one coordinated graphic image on them all.

___ Business cards
___ Letterhead
___ Second sheets
___ Envelopes
___ Mailing labels
___ Invoices
___ Fax cover sheet
___ Flyers and brochures
___ Samples and giveaways
___ Statements
___ Business checks
___ Trade show booths
___ Product and price lists
___ Newsletters
___ Presentation packages
___ Press release mastheads
___ Product packaging
___ Point-of-purchase displays
___ Postcards
___ Quote sheet
___ Thank-you notes
___ Service agreement
___ Signs and banners
___ Web page

If for some reason it's not possible, or desirable, for all the elements in your graphic sales force to have an identical look and feel, select compatible alternatives that are as consistent as possible with your chosen graphic image.

Note: You'll find specifics on how to design and use business cards, brochures, news releases, product packaging, point-of-purchase displays, and trade show booths as marketing tools in chapters 10 and 11.

business name, as well as your service or product name. The little extra money you spend will come back again and again in clients, customers, and referral sources who can find you.

Cost-Effective Solutions for a High-Quality Look

If you're thinking no matter how much you might want to there's no way you could afford to create the kind of coordinated graphic image we've been suggesting, think again.There are at least four options for creating top-quality materials. Each of these options has its own pros and cons and some cost more than others, but there is a viable option for everyone.

1. Have a graphic designer, illustrator, or desktop publisher create your graphic identity. Then have the your basic materials printed by a professional printer, adding additional pieces as your budget allows.

PROS: The advantage of this approach is that you are getting expert advice and professional skill. You also will have maximum flexibility in choosing unique design elements. There are few limits to what you can create. So if you make the right choices, you'll have a winning look you can use forever. Also, especially in color printing, professional print quality still has an edge and most people can still tell a do-it-yourself or mass-produced design from one done by professionals.

CONS: Using the services of professional designers and printers will cost more up-front. Sometimes designers have their own ideas of what looks good and it may or may not match what your clients, customers, and referral sources will find appealing. To be cost-effective, professional printing requires that you place quantity orders, and you may not need large quantities of some of your materials. You may also want to test your design in small quantities before investing in a large order.

TIPS: There is a variety of ways you can save on professional design and printing costs:

- Use the services of a novice designer or even arrange to have your logo and graphic image designed by an intern or college art or design class.
- Select and purchase your own paper at a discount paper house and provide it as "customer stock" to the printer. Such stores are listed in the Yellow Pages under paper dealers.

- Get estimates from several printers, because prices will vary substantially.
- Consider using an out-of-state printer through mail order. To find mail-order sources, pick up a free copy of the *Horsetrader,* a tabloid found at paper houses.
- Have your professionally created graphic scanned into your computer so you can print out your own materials as you need them on a laser printer if they're in black, white, and gray tones or if you're using one or more colors, on a color ink jet printer.

2. ***Desktop publish your own materials.*** Using a computer along with some combination of desktop publishing, clip art, and graphics software and a laser-quality printer, you can create your own materials and print them on an as-needed basis in whatever quantities you need.

PROS: Certainly, if you own or have access to the necessary software and equipment, this option clearly provides a cost advantage upfront. You can pick out and purchase your own paper at discount paper stores. You can cost-effectively test a variety of design options over short periods of time to see which ones are most effective. You can even customize or tailor the content or look of your materials to particular clients or referral sources or to different fields or industries. Some software includes predesigned templates to help guide your design decisions.

CONS: You may not have the time, skill, or interest to create your own materials. Graphic design requires time, education, skill, and talent that not everyone is blessed with. Using the necessary software and equipment also takes time, knowledge, experience, and patience. In all honesty, your own designs may look too amateurish to convey the professional image you're seeking. Affordable software may have an array of built-in design limitations like the number of type fonts or layout options. Customizing layout may be complex and time consuming.

TIPS: There are Web sites like iPrint (www.iprint.com) that allow you to create your own graphic image on-line. You can see what you'll get and once you like what you see, you can order the finished product. To acquire the skills for producing your own high-quality graphics, you can read **Appendix I: Writing and Designing Materials That Sell,** which is available on-line without charge as a Special Report at www.paulandsarah.com on the Great Ideas for Getting business page and the **Resources** listed there or take design courses. Alternatively, you can create your own design concept and then hire a professional to execute it properly.

3. ***Do-it-yourself with preprinted papers.*** There is a variety of companies through which you can purchase complete sets of coordinated four-color papers for most of your printed materials from cards and letterheads to presentation folders and brochures. You then simply add your logo and other graphic content to their four-color graphic papers. Some preprinted paper companies like Paper Direct also offer customized design services to do this for you. (See color insert for example.)

PROS: You can purchase attractively designed four-color materials in smaller quantities than you could afford to purchase from a print shop. There are many designs to choose among. You can add various components as your budget allows, customize, and test material. Software templates are available to help you coordinate the design of your content with the preprinted design.

CONS: The paper quality, particularly of the business cards, tends to be less substantial than ideal. Preprinted papers may not be available

PRINTING PRICE COMPARISONS

The following chart shows the estimated cost of three options for printing your marketing materials based on going rates at the time of this writing. Of course, prices will vary considerably at local print shops, and mail-order houses change prices periodically. These figures do not include design costs and are based on ordering letterhead, stationery, and business cards. They do include the price of the paper.

Printing Option	100 of Each	500 of Each	1,000 of Each
Professional Quick Print Shop	$19.00/$72.00	$50.00/$108.00	$90.00/$153.00
Business Form Company	Not Available	$93.00/$124.75	$121.50/$173.00
Do-It-Yourself on Pre-printed Paper	$21.95	$99.75	$179.50

for all the marketing materials you'll need, like invoices, labels, or trade show banners. Others will be available only in certain designs Some designs may not fax well. You will still need to have a graphic sense to add your logo and material in an aesthetically pleasing way. Preprinted paper can get expensive when ordered in quantity and, perhaps worst of all, there will be others using elements of your graphic image and most likely this will be noticeable.

TIPS: To avoid looking like everyone else who has selected the preprinted paper design of your choice, take the paper you've chosen to a designer and get professional help in incorporating your name, logo, and other information into the paper design in a unique way. If you have a scanner and color ink-jet printer, you may be able to scan elements of your preprinted design into your computer so you can use them on other materials not available through the catalog, although print quality will not be as good as on those you purchase from the company.

4. *Have your materials custom-designed by a business forms company.* Mail-order business forms companies like Nebs can customize an entire look for your business and incorporate it into their literally hundreds of forms from cards, stationery, and presentation packets, to labels, statements, invoices, and checks. They also offer many specialized forms designed for particular industries like contractors, repair services, cleaning services, photographers, and so forth.

PROS: This is a one-stop service. They can do the design, provide the materials, and do the printing for virtually any form or materials you need. You can start with ordering the most important items and then add others as your budget allows.

CONS: The design choices may be more conventional and less creative than what would make an unforgettable impression of the essence of your business niche. You will get the best prices for larger-quantity orders than you may need as a small business. There may be no customized forms for your particular industry.

TIP: Some companies will allow you to provide your own custom logo and design, which they then add to any form you want to order.

With good-quality materials on hand, you'll always be prepared to make the most of whatever marketing opportunities are presented to you. They can make a positive, unforgettable impression that will get more business coming to you.

High-Tech Tip: Owning a Color Printer Can Save You Money

A color printer can save you thousands of dollars in printing and copying costs over the course of your business. With a color printer, prices for which now begin under $300, you can create or scan your color logo into your computer and include it as part of any document. You can include it on proposal cover sheets, or add it to the opening slide of presentations you give. You might even tuck it into the lower right-hand corner of each slide. You can add it to your name tag or imprint it onto news clippings you send to clients and customers to let them know you're thinking about them, or include it on clippings in your media kit. You can print out the opening page of your Web site and include it along with your mailings to clients or media. The possibilities are limitless.

Marketing Mistake: A Hand-Me-Down That Didn't Fit

To the extent that it's possible, you want your business image to stand as visual evidence that you're an expert in your niche. That means you have to walk your talk through the look you choose. Personal shopper Maxine Hubbell learned this the hard way. While the way she dressed always made a positive statement about her sense of style and taste, she didn't dress her business with the same care.

To help save on start-up costs, Hubbell's father had volunteered to donate several reams of second sheets from the stationery he'd used in a business he closed down years before. He also worked out an arrangement with a retired friend of his whose son owned a print shop to create letterhead, stationery, cards, and a simple brochure for Hubbell's new business. Naturally she was appreciative, but little did she know that paper and graphic design can look as hopelessly outdated as the clothing and hairstyles in old photographs.

What she did notice was that while people responded enthusiastically to her personally, their reaction to her materials was lukewarm at best. When she put her materials out on the networking tables at business events, few would be picked up. When she handed people her card or brochure, it wasn't unusual for someone to ask if she worked from home or if her business was a full-time venture. "I love having a home business," she explained. "Since I do a good job, where my business was located or how much time I spend shouldn't be an issue." But obviously, her materials weren't inspiring confidence in her abilities.

In hopes of getting to the root of the problem, Hubbell submitted her materials to a graphic designer in the networking group she belonged to. To promote his business, the designer was running a contest to find the member most in need of a graphic makeover. Sure enough, Hubbell won a free consultation.

What she learned was that like clothing styles, paper colors, textures, and typefaces go in and out of fashion and since Hubbell was in a fashion-related business, it was especially important that her image have a contemporary, modern look. In fact, paper makers closely monitor trends in the fashion, interior design, and carpet industries to ensure that their styles remain current. But unlike the quixotic fashion industry where styles change from season to season, papers and type fonts, we're told, have a longer shelf life of two to three years.

Dressed in its newly designed wardrobe, Hubbell's business image immediately drew a better response. "The whole thing cost no more than I customarily spend on a couple of nice suits," Hubbell points out. "And paying for the redesign was worth it, even if I have to put my own wardrobe on hold for a while to cover the costs." Her brochures have started to disappear from the networking tables and people she meets often comment positively on her cards.

Resources

Additional resources for designing specific marketing materials such as media kits, Web pages, and brochures can be found in chapters 8, 10, and 12, as well as **Appendix I: Writing and Designing Materials That Sell,** which is available on-line without charge as a Special Report at www.paulandsarah.com on the Great Ideas for Getting Business page.

Books

The Business Card Book, by Dr. Lynella Grant. Scottsdale, Ariz.: Off the Page Press, 1998.

The Complete Stationery Guide and Design Book. Val Cooper. Special Marketing Group, 1995. Specialty Marketing Group, (800) 698-7781. Includes over 1,000 designs, tips, and work sheets for creating a graphic image for your business. CD-ROM also available with four-color designs.

Desktop Publishing and Graphics Software

Adobe Pagemaker and *Adobe Illustrator.* Adobe Systems, 345 Park Avenue, San Jose, CA 95110, (800)-42ADOBE, www.adobe.com

Microsoft Publisher. Microsoft Corp., One Microsoft Way, Redmond, WA 98052-6399, (800) 426-9400, www.microsoft.com/publisher/

Master Publisher Suite, by IMSI. 1895 Francisco Boulevard East, San Rafael, CA 94901, (415) 454-7101, www.imsisoft.com

CorelDraw. Corel Corporation, 1600 Carling Avenue, Ottawa, Ontario K1Z8R7, (800) 772-6735, www.corel.com

Free Design Ideas

S.D. One Idea Exchange, a Massachusetts-based paper manufacturer, will send you a dozen examples of other companies' projects from its library of thousands of printed pieces, (800) 882-IDEA, www.warren-idea-exchange.com

Specialized Software for Custom Designing Marketing Materials

Custom Business Stationery. My Software Company, 1259 El Camino, Ste. 167, Menlo Park, CA 94025, (650) 473-3600, www.mysoftware.com. Includes preprinted paper for creating custom letterhead, envelopes, and business cards.

Font FX. DCSi. 3775 Iris Avenue, Ste. 1B, Boulder, CO, 80301, (303) 447-9251, www.dcsifx.com. 3-D fonts for creating company logos, designs, or text in print or electronic form.

My Professional Marketing Materials. My Software Company, 1259 El Camino, Ste. 167, Menlo Park, CA 94025, (650) 473-3600, www.mysoftware.com. Includes 5,000 graphic images, 500 color photos, hundreds of layouts, and 125 fonts for creating cards, letterheads, brochures, postcards, and a wealth of other marketing materials.

Print Artist Professional. Sierra On-line, 3380 146th Pl. SE #300, Bellevue, WA 98007, (425) 649-9800, www.sierra.com. Includes 1,500 professionally designed layouts, 10,000 full-color graphics, 300 type styles, and 600 photos for creating cards, stationery, labels, banners, and more.

ProVenture Custom Business Stationery. My Software Company, 1259 El Camino, Ste. 167, Menlo Park, CA 94025, (650) 473-3600, www.mysoftware.com. Hundreds of professional layouts and designs for letterheads, envelopes, and business cards; for designing stationery from scratch.

Clip Art Software

Art Explosion 125,000. Nova Development, includes 125,000 pieces of clip art on CD-ROM, 23801 Calabasas Road, Ste. 2005, Calabasas, CA 91302-1547, (800) 395-6682, www.novadevcorp.doc

ClickArt, by Broderbund, has 125,000 images, photos, fonts, etc. Broderbund, P.O. Box 6121, Novato, CA 94948, (415) 382-4400, www.broderbund.com

Form Design Software

Delrina FormFlow. Jetform Corporation, 560 Rochester St., Ottawa, Ontario Canada KIS 5K2, (800) JETFORM, www.jetform.com

Microsoft Electronic Form Designer. Microsoft Corp., One Microsoft Way, Redmond, WA 98052-6399, (800) 426-9400, www.microsoft.com

Presto! Forms. New Soft, Inc., 3353 Gateway Blvd., Fremont, CA 94538, (800) 214-7059, www.tophat.com

Preprinted Paper Houses

(Call or write for a free catalog)

Paper Direct
100 Plaza Drive
Secaucus, NJ 07094
(800) A-PAPERS

Idea Art
P.O. Box 291505
Nashville, TN 37229
(800) 433-2278

Queblo Images
150 Kingswood Rd.
Mankato, MN 56002
(800) 523-9080

Mail-Order Business Forms Companies

These companies will design your logo, letterhead and stationery, business card, and other promotional material to create an overall coordinated look. (Call or write for a free catalog.)

ImageDirect,™ by Paper Direct. 100 Plaza Drive, Secaucus, NJ 07094, (800) A-PAPERS, (800) 272-7377, www.paperdirect.com

NEBS. 500 Main Street, Groton, MA 01471, (800) 225-6380.

CHAPTER 8

Developing Your Promotional Package

Image creates desire. You will want what you image.

—J. G. GALLIMORE

Imagine you've been invited to speak at a meeting of potential clients. Or a prospective client calls to say they want to consider you for a large project. Perhaps you hear someone wants to interview you for an article in your trade journal or the local newspaper. You know that any one of these opportunities could lead to considerable business, and they're all signs that your reputation is growing and your marketing activities are paying off. But, just as your heart begins to leap for joy, you hear the inevitable question, "Would you send us some material on your business ASAP? We don't have much time to make a decision."

Are you ready? Do you have materials you can pull together into a professional package and get out to them quickly and easily? If not, it could take days to create background and promotional materials that will make the impression you're hoping for. After spending your time, money, and energy to attract interest, you don't want to have to pull something together haphazardly and hope for the best.

Whether you're sending a proposal, making a sales presentation, following up with materials for an interested client, or responding to a request from the media, someone will invariably ask you to send out a promotional package. And, of course, that person will need it immediately! Having such a packet of materials seems to be like the cover charge you must pay to see a popular performer, but often it's the magic password that will open doors to the opportunities you've been seeking. It's presumed that you will have such a packet, ready and waiting, and if you don't, you're likely to be passed over for someone who does.

So, you'll want to have several key promotional materials on hand and a way to put them together quickly into an attractive, inviting, and easily understood package. This can be as simple as having a presentation folder or a cover page with your logo on it, or you may want to create a more custom-designed way to present your materials in print, on CD-ROM, or on your Web site. Such a package of materials is sometimes referred to as a publicity kit, but since you'll have the opportunity to use it for far more than getting publicity, we refer to it as a promotional package.

Whatever stage your business is in—whether you're a family day-care provider who needs materials to give parents seeking child care, a management consulting bidding on a *Fortune* 500 contract, or a professional speaker wanting to get booked as a guest on radio and television programs—you can benefit from having a basic promotional package on hand. Even if you don't plan to launch a promotional campaign anytime in the near future, we advise putting together the components for a promotional package now and maintaining it. You never know when opportunity will tap you on the shoulder unexpectedly, and when it does, you'll want to be ready to respond. It's inevitable that someday someone will ask you to provide some material about your business ASAP. So, don't be caught short.

This chapter is designed to help you decide what you should have handy and how to package it most effectively. Whether you're sending out an entire kit of materials or only using bits and pieces as the circumstances require, a promotional package is a valuable tool you should keep up-to-date and always have at hand. And now is the time to build it if you haven't already—not sometime in the future when you have a specific need for it. As you will see, an effective promotional package is usually not something you can easily throw together at the last minute. Done properly, however, creating a kit can be a highly cost-effective investment of your time, energy, and money that will serve you well in a wide range of situations.

YOUR GOAL
Promotional Materials That Speak for You

Components of a Basic Promotional Package

The materials you want to have handy to include in your promotional kit will depend on the nature of your business and the expectations of your clients and customers. Whatever you include, however, should to the extent possible present one coordinated graphic image. Then you will be able to mix and match and customize what you provide to the needs of the situation. You can use the checklist below to identify what you think you should have on hand. The rules of thumb for producing these materials—what they should look like and how best to put them together physically—follow. (For free ideas on writing winning news releases and query letters, see our Web site at www.paulandsarah.com.) As you read about each element, you may be surprised to discover additional materials you'll want to have available for your promotional package.

Your Biographical Profile

A biographical profile is a brief, thumbnail sketch of your personal résumé with such facts as your accomplishments, career and educational background, and fundamental goals in relation to your company or the particular event you are publicizing. If you can add a pithy or substantive quote, so much the better. And be sure to include reference to any media coverage you have had and any awards or other professional acknowledgment you've received. You may also want to have a profile of any other key individuals involved in your company.

WHAT MATERIALS DO YOU NEED?

The following is a list of items frequently found in a presentation package. Check off the elements you think apply to your business.

___ 1. Your biographical profile

___ 2. A description and history of your business

___ 3. A vision or mission statement

___ 4. A product or service description (including technical specifications)

___ 5. A sell sheet or mini-brochure

___ 6. A publicity photo (of you, your work or product)

___ 7. Copies of articles, testimonials, or endorsements

___ 8. A broadcast résumé

___ 9. A sample or novelty

___10. A newsworthy news release, cover letter, or query letter

High-Tech Tip: Why Limit Yourself to Paper?

While we are talking primarily about print promotional materials, today there is no reason to limit yourself to this one medium only. You can provide your promotional materials on a CD-ROM, a computer disk, an audiotape, or a video. Bill Herz, whose company is Magicorp Productions, teaches executives how to use magic to better communicate a sales or business message. He gets most of his new business from referrals, so when people call requesting information, he sends a videotape of his performance along with his printed promotional materials which include his brochure, twenty to twenty-five letters of recent references, article reprints, his bio, and a two-page client list.

Others are turning their promotional package into an interactive multimedia presentation and making it available on computer disk. A small San Marcos, California–based ad agency pops their multimedia promo in the mail along with a bag of popcorn and a note that says, "Sit back and enjoy." You can make your own multimedia CD-ROM presentation with equipment like Smart Friendly's CD-R 1002, which costs under $800, Hewlett-Packard's Sure-Store CD-Writer, at a bit over $1,000, and Pinnacle Micro's RCD 5040.

And, of course, growing numbers of people, us included, are using their Web sites as a promotional package. On our site, paulandsarah.com, along with daily messages, chats, and Q&A, we have samples from our books, seminars, radio shows, our bio, and ordering information. Dr. Ethan Welch uses his Web site simply to promote Medical Sea Packs, the emergency kits he has developed and sells for charter and leisure boats. Quilt maker David Walker's site is almost like a public service announcement, introducing visitors to the art of quilting and featuring the work of a different quilter each month.

There are several different formats you can use for your profile. You may be advised to use the same format for your profile as you would for a news release, including a headline and date. We advise against this format, however, unless you have a large production budget. We suggest instead that unless you have hired a public relations firm and will therefore be using their logo, you print your profile directly onto your letterhead or on a special abbreviated version of it that includes only your logo. Place your name at the top as the headline or title. This format will allow you to print larger quantities of your profile to use for multiple purposes at different times.

Using your letterhead for this and other items in your promotional kit, as we recommend, will require having a high-quality, well-designed letterhead similar to those described in chapter 7, preferably two color. Since you will be using your letterhead for many purposes, you can justify spending more money to produce it and having larger quantities printed, which will help keep costs down. (Also see color insert.)

Your profile should not exceed a single page unless there is a compelling reason for it to do so. If it contains more material than you can fit on a single sheet, use the excess material to create ideas for news features.

Company Description and History

Your company description provides a thumbnail sketch of the history of your company. Again use your letterhead, and follow the same one-page format you used for your profile. Your company name should serve as the headline or title. Keep the description simple and to the point; do not overembellish. Stick to the facts, beginning with the year of the company's inception. Cover pertinent data such as the guiding principle behind the business, your primary activities, and general plans for the future. Be sure to include reference to any publicity your company has received from the media by using a line such as "as featured in the *Journal Northwest* magazine."

Vision or Mission Statement

In recent years, it has become common for customers and clients to request a company's Vision and Mission Statement. This is the result of recent emphasis on TQM (Total Quality Management), Empowerment, Legendary Service, and other management theories and techniques being utilized by larger companies to improve their ability to compete in the marketplace. Therefore, even if you are a one-person business, you too may want to include or be asked for such a statement.

A vision statement is a concise description of your company's aspirations—a sort of "what we want to be when we grow up" statement. Having done the work of defining your niche and what makes your special, you should be well prepared to write such a statement, focusing on the issues that lie at the heart of the matter of what you do for your clients and customers. For example, Is your business built on personal service? Speed? Innovation? Are you a pioneer breaking new ground or a solid resource for critical activities? A vision statement provides answers to such questions. One of the most familiar vision statements you're undoubtedly familiar with is heard on television almost every day somewhere in the world: ". . to seek out new life, new civilizations, to boldly go where no one has gone before." In case you don't recognize this vision statement, it is part of the opening lines for the ever-popular *Star Trek* series.

Our vision statement is "to help people make the transition from a time when most people had the security of a lifelong salaried job to a time when we can create more balanced, satisfying, and harmonious lives by creating our own independent careers."

A mission statement is a brief list of goals that illustrate how you are going to achieve your vision. If your vision is to provide innovative solutions to marketing problems for your clients, your mission might include maintaining access to instant communications, developing alliances with unique sources of creativity, and providing cost-effective outlets for your client's message.

Our mission statement is "to provide information, resources, and support through books, seminars, radio, television, and a nationwide network of Perfect Work consultants to people seeking to create more balanced, satisfying, and harmonious lives by becoming self-employed." Elements of this mission are incorporated into the design of our business cards and letterhead.

Even if you don't use your vision or mission statements in your promotional materials, you should have them both in mind when preparing your marketing materials. These statements can help you make the right decisions day-to-day and keep you on track toward your goals. One caveat, however: Although your vision and mission statements should we well thought out and provide a foundation for your business activities, you must revisit them on a regular basis to ensure that they remain dynamic and pertinent to your business and your industry.

Product/Service Description

If you have a narrow or highly technical product line, this sheet will detail your products' specifications. You can title it Fact Sheet or Technical Specifications. Again, you can use your letterhead and follow the same format, using the same design features to match the other pieces in your promotional kit.

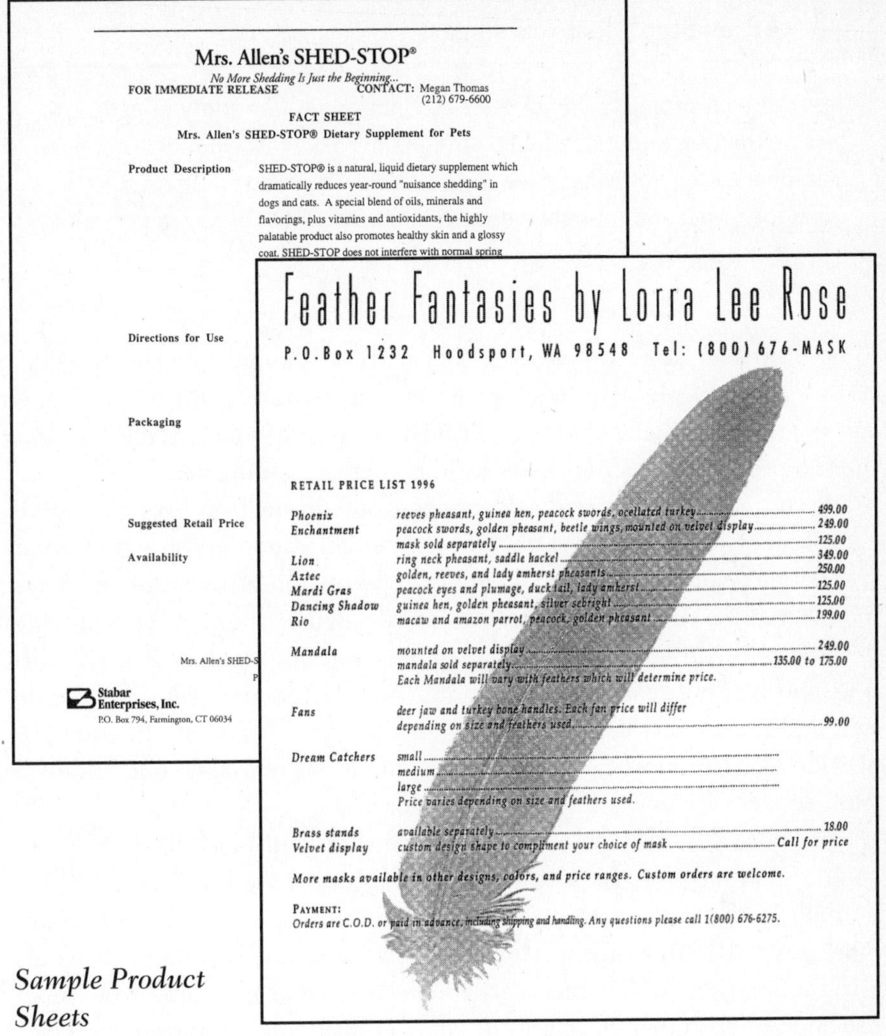

Mrs. Allen's SHED-STOP®

No More Shedding Is Just the Beginning...

FOR IMMEDIATE RELEASE CONTACT: Megan Thomas (212) 679-6600

FACT SHEET

Mrs. Allen's SHED-STOP® Dietary Supplement for Pets

Product Description SHED-STOP® is a natural, liquid dietary supplement which dramatically reduces year-round "nuisance shedding" in dogs and cats. A special blend of oils, minerals and flavorings, plus vitamins and antioxidants, the highly palatable product also promotes healthy skin and a glossy coat. SHED-STOP does not interfere with normal spring

Directions for Use

Packaging

Suggested Retail Price

Availability

Mrs. Allen's SHED-S

P

Stabar Enterprises, Inc.
P.O. Box 794, Farmington, CT 06034

Feather Fantasies by Lorra Lee Rose

P.O.Box 1232 Hoodsport, WA 98548 Tel: (800) 676-MASK

RETAIL PRICE LIST 1996

Phoenix	*reeves pheasant, guinea hen, peacock swords, ocellated turkey*	499.00
Enchantment	*peacock swords, golden pheasant, beetle wings, mounted on velvet display*	249.00
	mask sold separately	125.00
Lion	*ring neck pheasant, saddle hackel*	349.00
Aztec	*golden, reeves, and lady amherst pheasants*	250.00
Mardi Gras	*peacock eyes and plumage, duck tail, lady amherst*	125.00
Dancing Shadow	*guinea hen, golden pheasant, silver sebright*	125.00
Rio	*macaw and amazon parrot, peacock, golden pheasant*	199.00
Mandala	*mounted on velvet display*	249.00
	mandala sold separately	135.00 to 175.00
	Each Mandala will vary with feathers which will determine price.	
Fans	*deer jaw and turkey bone handles. Each fan price will differ depending on size and feathers used*	99.00
Dream Catchers	*small*	
	medium	
	large	
	Price varies depending on size and feathers used.	
Brass stands	*available separately*	18.00
Velvet display	*custom design shape to compliment your choice of mask*	*Call for price*

More masks available in other designs, colors, and price ranges. Custom orders are welcome.

PAYMENT:
Orders are C.O.D. or paid in advance, including shipping and handling. Any questions please call 1(800) 676-6275.

Sample Product Sheets

If you are promoting a varied product line, this sheet will serve as a sample list of items, each with a few words describing the items as vividly as possible. The amount of detail in the descriptions needs to be enough for a reader to picture what you are talking about without photographs, yet short enough to fit on a single page.

If, however, it's necessary to use multiple sheets for technical specifications such as benchmark tests on computer hardware, then do so. Here, again, do not use extraneous descriptive adjectives—keep each description as short and to the point as possible. In describing a product line, you can begin with a short paragraph detailing the focus of your merchandise followed by a sample list of items, as Mrs. Allen's

Action Step: Test Your Impact

Test out your product and service descriptions with a variety of people to be sure they are understandable. After people have read your descriptions, ask them to tell you what they think you do. You may be amazed to discover that what you thought was clear has left readers who are unfamiliar with your field in a fog.

Shed-Stop has done on page 259. Lee Rose simply itemizes and describes each art piece in her line of Feather Fantasies. Both companies can incorporate these sheets in with their promotional materials or use them on their own as handouts or in response to inquiries.

If your company provides a service, you will need to list or describe each aspect of that service to give the reader a general grasp of what you do and whom you serve. Don't use abbreviations or acronyms your reader may be unfamiliar with unless you define them. If you provide desktop publishing services, for example, your sheet might list: typesetting, layout and design, pasteup, and newsletter preparation. Include any additional services your company provides as well. If you also provide word-processing services or mailing-list management, indicate such services in an equally clear manner.

Suppose you provide a single service that is difficult to describe in such a manner. Systemax Computer Graphics, based in New York, for example, provides a customized computer animation service. That statement says little or nothing to someone who is not familiar with computer animation, so it's necessary to describe what it is and, if possible, provide either drawings or photographs of a sample computer screen.

Sell Sheet or Mini-Brochure

A "sell sheet" is simply a one-page brochure that features a product or product line. It usually contains a photograph or graphic of some sort and whatever generic specifications are common to the various products you provide. It is designed as a reminder to a customer of the breadth or depth of your product line. If you use sell sheets, you should have one for each of your principal products.

Similarly, a mini-brochure features the services one provides. It should provide separate information on each of the services you offer. For example, a creative design company might have a mini-brochure on

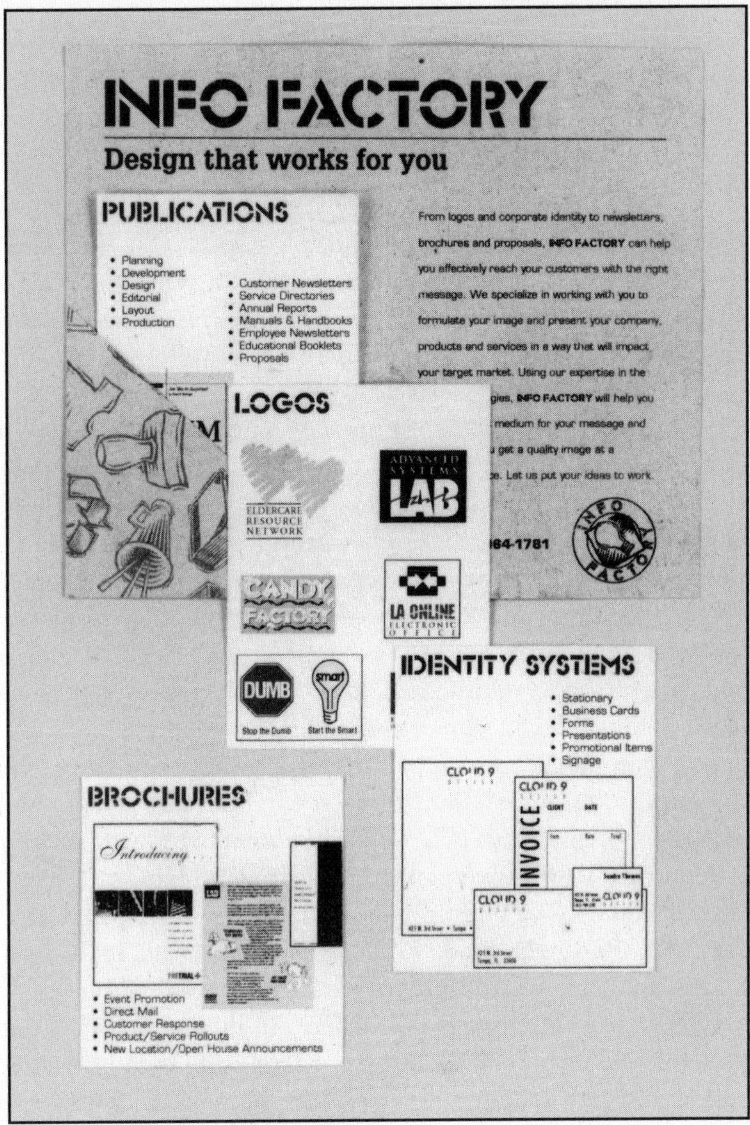

SAMPLE MINI-BROCHURE *Jeff Kauzlaric has created a versatile mini-brochure with easily changeable inserts that describe the various services available from his design company, the Info Factory.*

newsletter production services, another on image enhancement material design, and a third on advertising prep services. Info Factory of Los Angeles, featured above, has created a unique one-page mini-brochure that includes four small cards, one for each of their services: Publications, Logos, Identity Systems, and Brochures. These cards are tucked into a slot in the left-hand corner while the text on the right provides Info Factory's mission, their specialty, and the benefits of using their services.

Publicity Photos

We recommend that everyone have multiple copies of at least one photograph of themselves or their product. In your own business, a picture isn't only worth a thousand words; it may be worth thousands of dollars. Often a flattering photo of you will increase the effectiveness of your promotional package a hundredfold.

People love pictures. Brochures, mailers, newsletters, and newspaper articles attract more attention when they include pictures. Think of your own response when you receive a mailer or read an article. Don't you enjoy seeing the writer? Yet unlike entertainers and performers who know all too well the magical power of a photo, businesspeople only rarely have a ready supply of professionally photographed black-and-white or color glossies on hand.

Suppose you have volunteered to give a speech or workshop for your local trade or professional association and the program director tells you, "If you can send us a picture right away, we'll feature you on the front page of our newsletter." Since it can take three weeks or more to have professional photos taken and developed, you will have missed a great opportunity unless you already have one on hand.

Let's say you receive a direct-mail solicitation to be listed in a new directory. The offer looks good, so you apply. The listing includes a picture but the application, with photo, must be received within the week. Again, if you have no photo handy, when the directory comes out, instead of having your picture next to your name there will be an empty gray square or a stylized directory logo, leaving you wondering whether the listing was really worth the money.

We used to be all too familiar with situations like these. Not only were we missing these opportunities; it was also embarrassing having to apologize for not being able to provide a photo. Since it seems that some of the best promotional opportunities often arise on the spot, have publicity photographs made as soon as possible. Then, when an unexpected publicity opportunity comes along, you will be able to say with confidence, "I'll Fedex you my publicity kit with the photo this afternoon."

The best photograph to include in your kit depends on your particular business and the product or service for which you are trying to gain recognition. We suggest having at least two types of photos on hand: a

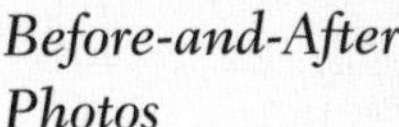

Before-and-After Photos

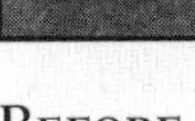

BEFORE

AFTER

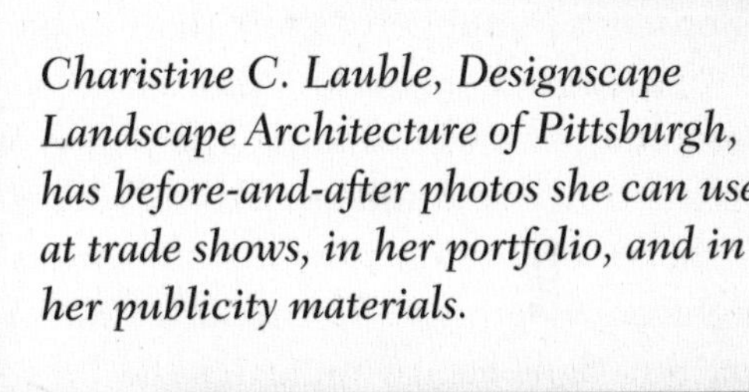

Charistine C. Lauble, Designscape Landscape Architecture of Pittsburgh, has before-and-after photos she can use at trade shows, in her portfolio, and in her publicity materials.

BEFORE

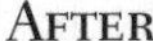

AFTER

professional-quality head shot of yourself and either a photo of your product or product line, a candid shot of yourself in action providing your service or before-and-after photos demonstrating your results. We strongly advise against sending a snapshot, as they don't reproduce well and don't show you or your products off in a professional light.

Once you have head shots taken you will probably find many uses for them. If you speak at a professional association, for example, the program may include pictures of the presenters. If you are receiving an award, the organization will often include a photo in its mailing about the upcoming recipients. If you write a column or article for a publication in your field, you may be asked to send a photo to appear next to your byline. In such cases a formal head shot is expected. (And if it isn't requested, you should ask to have one appear.) See Les Brown's head shot on page 268.

If your promotional kit is primarily to showcase a single product, a package shot showing off the product is essential. Magazines are likely to require a package shot if they plan to review the product, and it is important for a consumer to be familiar not only with the name of the item but also with what it will look like on the shelf. So a software publishing company, for example, should be more interested in showing off its product in publicity shots than in picturing the people who created it. A package shot is also a solution if your product itself does not photograph well, as with a bowl of potpourri or a computer software program. For a creative solution see Mrs. Allen's Shed-Stop photos on page 268.

In the event that you have a business with a broad product line, you might consider a group product shot. A photograph of assorted birdhouse designs clearly indicates the breadth of the line. However, don't try to include a sample of every product you make in the photograph. Squeezing everything in will reduce the size of each item substantially, making the photo too busy, and items will be difficult to recognize. Three to five items are probably all you will need to give an idea of the breadth and quality of your product line.

Newsletters, newspapers, and magazines, however, are usually more interested in candid action shots than in a formal head shot, particularly for reviews and feature stories. They may want to see a unique product or capture you engaged in some aspect of what you do. Sometimes they will even send a photographer out to take a picture of you in action. But you will increase the likelihood of a publication including your story or news release by including an intriguing photo.

When promoting a service business, the type of photograph to use will depend on the results of the application of your service. For instance, if you design custom wedding gowns, a photograph of a sample gown you've created or a collage of candids showing your gowns is the best way to go. On the other hand, if you are a computer consultant, the important thing to promote is you and your skill. Therefore, you might choose to include a photograph of yourself working with a client and a computer. If you are a landscape designer, you might use a picture of yourself sitting on a forklift with a huge ornamental bush on it or working at a garden bench in front of a beautifully manicured lawn. Landscape architect Christine Caspary Lauble of Pittsburgh features before-and-after photos in her promotional materials. (See page 263.)

Although four-by-five inches is an accepted size for your photos, most people still prefer a five-by-seven or the older standard of eight-by-ten. A smaller size can get lost if it's in with a lot of other materials. If newspapers and newsletters comprise the bulk of your contacts, black-and-white photos are preferred; magazines, and many other promotional activities however, often require color. The results can be stunning and can be used in many ways. For example, see Lorra Lee Rose's Feather Fantasies in the color insert. It does not cost much more when having your photo taken to ask the photographer to take a roll of color shots, so you can have a supply of both on hand.

Each photograph you include with your materials must be captioned with a brief typed description. This is particularly helpful for product photos and action shots. There are two methods of applying the caption: affix it to the center back of the photograph, which requires the recipient to flip the photo over to see the caption, or tape it to drop from the bottom of the photo. The former is neater, but most people find the latter more convenient. Sometimes a caption on the back will be overlooked. It never hurts to check with the person to whom you will be sending photos to see which caption style he prefers. Another alternative is to have the caption printed on the photo, although this will add to your cost. (See examples on page 268.)

We have used our pictures for every one of these activities at one time or another, although when we had them taken we never dreamed so many photo opportunities would arise. By using a scanner, you can place your photos in a myriad of documents, edit them, and turn them into cards, banners, calendars, business cards, and more. (To find photo-editing software for doing these things, see **Resources** at the end of this chapter.) Here are a few tips for making the most of such opportunities:

*1. **Have your photographs professionally done.*** It costs more to use professional photographers, but it's worth the investment. You've

FIFTEEN USES FOR A PUBLICITY PHOTO

To determine whether having publicity photos taken is truly worth the time, energy, and money, we consulted Los Angeles photographer Charles Behrman and discovered at least fifteen reasons why you should have a professional photos on hand:

1. To accompany an article you have written
2. To accompany articles written about you
3. To include in brochures, newsletters, and other promotional pieces
4. As part of your advertising
5. To send out with a news release
6. To accompany your listing in professional- and trade-association membership directories
7. To use on cards, letterhead, or postcards
8. To accompany announcements about you or your business in club and organizational newsletters
9. As part of direct-mail pieces about your product or service
10. To include on invitations to open houses or promotional events you hold
11. To use on a book or booklet cover or jacket
12. To mount on an easel to promote your speeches, workshops, or booths at trade shows or conferences
13. To use in a portfolio or presentation of your work or to show you in action working with clients
14. To include on your Website
15. To be included in a program guide with a description of workshops or speeches you give

probably seen muddy, fuzzy pictures in directory listings or newsletters. These are usually the result of using snapshots someone submitted because they didn't have a professional photo.

2. ***Select a photographer with an excellent track record.*** Get referrals from satisfied colleagues in your field. Always review the photographers' portfolios and decide whether they shoot the type of look you want for yourself and your business. Since you can expect to invest several hundred dollars in your pictures, you don't want to have to do

them over again. Worse than having to select between the lesser of two evils is having to select from a proof sheet of fifty evils. Good photographers provide proof sheets with a variety of great shots among which you may choose.

3. *Have your hair and makeup done professionally.* It is worth the investment for both men and women. Some photographers provide these services themselves or make other professionals available to you; alternatively you can hire your own. The best photos may look as though they were snapped at an impromptu moment, but they weren't. Every detail of hair, clothing, makeup, lighting, and shading was attended to before the spontaneous moment was captured. When deciding on hair and makeup styles, avoid trendy looks that will look outdated quickly.

4. *Expect to spend several hours with your photographer.* Having a good photograph taken is like going to your accountant at tax time: it always takes longer than you expect. Don't expect to be in and out in an hour—set aside a morning or afternoon.

5. *Order a decent supply of black-and-white or color glossies to have on hand.* Don't think twenty-five or more is too many. You don't want to have to wait to order prints when an opportunity arises to send out your materials. Also, ordering in quantity saves money. Glossies need to be crisp and clear with a high contrast between the background and your image.

6. *When including your photo on printed promotional materials, always have a high-quality screen made.* A photograph has continuous tones that blend into one another, but printing processes can reproduce only discrete lines or dots. Therefore anytime you print your photo on a brochure, bio, product sheet, or any other printed material, you need to have it screened into a halftone prior to printing so that it will reproduce properly. The halftone needs to match the type of paper and printing process you will be using so that the photos don't look grainy or fuzzy. Photographer Charles Behrman of Los Angeles recommends a 65-dots-per-inch screen for newsprint quality, a 135-dots-per-inch screen for magazine quality, and a 150-dots-per-inch screen for brochure quality. The printer you choose will make a big difference, too. As a rule, he says, "Print houses can provide 50 percent higher resolution than instant print shops."

Les Brown
Mrs. Allen's Shed-Stop is a new and unique, all-natural dietary supplement that eliminates non-seasonal shedding in animals and promotes healthier, glossier coats. For more information contact Megan Thomas, Hunter & Associates, (212) 679-6600.
Barbara Allen, Founder and CEO of Stabar Enterprises, and her dog, Jano.
For more information contact Megan Thomas, Hunter & Associates, (212) 679-6600.

Publicity photos can be 4 x 5, 5 x 7, or 8 x 10-inch head shots, package shots, or informal shots. Including your name on the photo is desirable. **Top left:** *motivational speaker and author Les Brown.* **Right:** *Barbara Allen, founder and CEO of Stabar Enterprises, and her dog, Jano. The caption reads: "For more information, contact Megan Thomas, Hunter & Associates, (212) 679-6600."* **Left:** *Shed-Stop products. The caption reads: "Mrs. Allen's Shed-Stop is a unique, all-natural dietary supplement that eliminates non-seasonal shedding in animals and promotes healthier, glossier coats. For more information, contact Megan Thomas, Hunter & Associates, (212) 679-6600."*

7. ***Keep your photo up-to-date.*** You want people to recognize that you are the person in the photo, so take new photos to account for major changes in your appearance: hairstyle and color, clothing style, and age.

Once you have good photographs on hand, not only can you respond to promotional opportunities more readily, but you also are apt to create more opportunities for their use.

Copies of Articles, Testimonials, or Endorsements

As soon as possible, your promotional package should include copies of testimonial letters from satisfied customers and clients, endorsements from authorities or other credible sources, as well as clippings of recent articles that have been written about you. We all like to do business with people we know or at least know of. If we don't know them, then we want to know who does. This sort of information can serve as a substitute for personal referrals and give substance to your reputation. Including such documents provides evidence that there is in fact already an interest in you, your work, and your company. This is an example of how promotion begets more promotion.

A collection of good testimonials, endorsements, and articles may take you some time to build, but if you keep at it, you will eventually have an excellent set. (See pages 270 and 387 for examples) You might begin your efforts by agreeing to speak for free to a local civic group and requesting that they do an article about you in their newsletter to promote the program. You might ask a client if you may reproduce a letter of appreciation they have written to you. Or you might send a news release (see **Resources**) to your small community newspaper, as such papers are often looking for newsworthy articles about local residents. In other words, start building your collection with articles from whatever small publications you can get to write about you and advancing toward coverage in the most influential publications in your field or community.

Once you've gotten permission to reproduce testimonial letters or endorsements and collected any articles that have been written about you, we recommend photocopying these materials on a high-quality paper such as Hammermill Laser Print, Mead Moistrite X02, or Union Camp's York Town. If you have a copy shop do your printing, ask them to show you a test copy before proceeding with your order. You can get great-looking copies from newsprint (even with pictures) from top-notch, well-maintained machines. Find a copy shop that produces the quality you seek. Initially use one sheet for each article. As your print portfolio grows, however, copy news clippings on both the back and front. If you are printing on both sides of the page, investigate some of the #1 offset sheets.

While you only have a small number of articles to duplicate for your kit, you can save money by investing in a copy machine, which you can get today for under $300 yet produce high-quality copies for only pennies. This will also save you the time of running out repeatedly to the copy store.

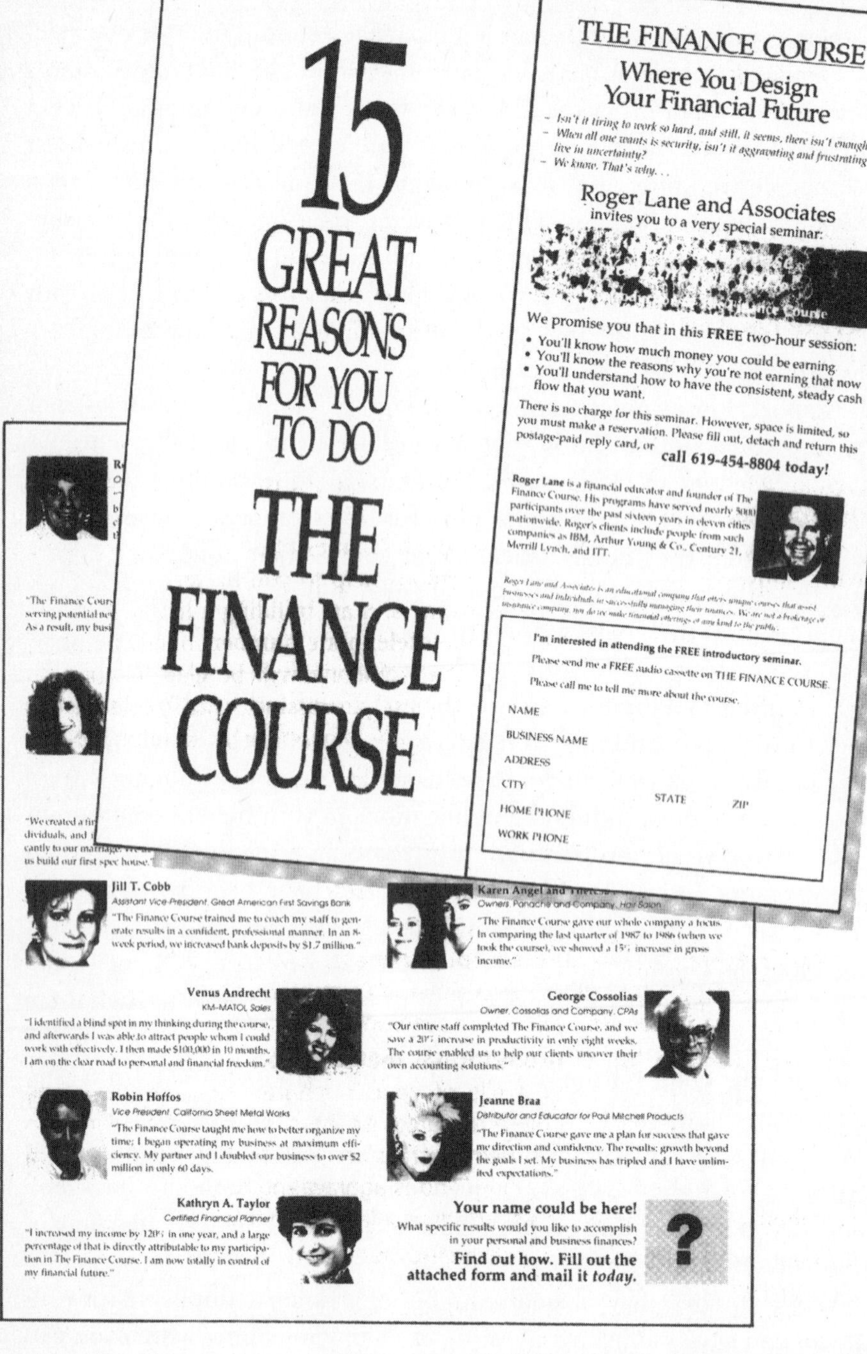

Sample Endorsement Letters *Letters of endorsement or testimonials like these from clients, customers, and colleagues dramatize the results from your product or service.*

High-Touch Tip: Using Ad Reprints

If either print or broadcast advertising is a part of your promotional efforts, do not forget to get reprints of your advertising as well as any editorial copy. Use them as you would article reprints—to enhance your visibility. Black-and-white copies of print advertising and either color or black-and-white reproductions of slides or frames from film or video work equally well.

The special advantage to using your advertising as part of your promotional kit is that it's the one other place you can toot your own horn with impunity. So go for it and make the most of your advertising dollars. It also will make your ad all the more familiar when your contact actually encounters the advertising in its own milieu.

Your Broadcast Résumé

Just as knowing what's been written about you boosts your reputation, so knowing about any media appearances you've made on radio or television can build confidence in your expertise and demonstrate that you can handle a promotional opportunity articulately without freezing up. This is particularly true if you are seeking more publicity in the media. So, you will want to begin building a history of these appearances and include a list of them in with your promotional materials.

Again, it may take you awhile to build this résumé. Should you not yet have any broadcast experience, listing public appearances might be equally acceptable. You can include a list of any professional presentations you have made, courses or seminars you have offered, or speeches or other public appearances where you in essence held the spotlight.

Like Harriet Schechter's media list on page 272, your broadcast résumé should include a listing with dates, times, and sources of all such events, programs, and stations where you have appeared.

Sample or Novelty

Whenever possible, include some type of sample or novelty in your promotional kit to further attract attention and create a fascination with your message. The lace maker might include a small swatch of inexpensive but attractive and unusual lace. The wedding-dress designer could include a small booklet of tips for a memorable wedding or on how to select a suitable dress style. The professional organizer could enclose a

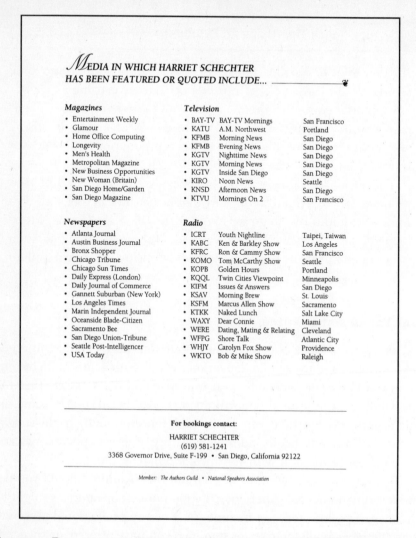

MEDIA IN WHICH HARRIET SCHECHTER HAS BEEN FEATURED OR QUOTED INCLUDE...

Magazines

- Entertainment Weekly
- Glamour
- Home Office Computing
- Longevity
- Men's Health
- Metropolitan Magazine
- New Business Opportunities
- New Woman (Britain)
- San Diego Home/Garden
- San Diego Magazine

Television

• BAY-TV	BAY-TV Mornings	San Francisco
• KATU	A.M. Northwest	Portland
• KFMB	Morning News	San Diego
• KFMB	Evening News	San Diego
• KGTV	Nighttime News	San Diego
• KGTV	Morning News	San Diego
• KGTV	Inside San Diego	San Diego
• KIRO	Noon News	Seattle
• KNSD	Afternoon News	San Diego
• KTVU	Mornings On 2	San Francisco

Newspapers

- Atlanta Journal
- Austin Business Journal
- Bronx Shopper
- Chicago Tribune
- Chicago Sun Times
- Daily Express (London)
- Daily Journal of Commerce
- Gannett Suburban (New York)
- Los Angeles Times
- Marin Independent Journal
- Oceanside Blade-Citizen
- Sacramento Bee
- San Diego Union-Tribune
- Seattle Post-Intelligencer
- USA Today

Radio

• ICRT	Youth Nightline	Taipei, Taiwan
• KABC	Ken & Barkley Show	Los Angeles
• KFRC	Ron & Cammy Show	San Francisco
• KOMO	Tom McCarthy Show	Seattle
• KOPB	Golden Hours	Portland
• KQQL	Twin Cities Viewpoint	Minneapolis
• KIFM	Issues & Answers	San Diego
• KSAV	Morning Brew	St. Louis
• KSFM	Marcus Allen Show	Sacramento
• KTKK	Naked Lunch	Salt Lake City
• WAXY	Dear Connie	Miami
• WERE	Dating, Mating & Relating	Cleveland
• WFPG	Shore Talk	Atlantic City
• WHJY	Carolyn Fox Show	Providence
• WKTO	Bob & Mike Show	Raleigh

For bookings contact:

HARRIET SCHECHTER
(619) 581-1241
3368 Governor Drive, Suite F-199 • San Diego, California 92122

Member: The Authors Guild • National Speakers Association

SAMPLE BROADCAST RÉSUMÉ *This broadcast résumé by professional organizer Harriet Schechter lists cities where she has been featured in the media and mentions specific shows she's appeared on. Her résumé is unique in that it is printed on the back of her media presentation kit.*

brightly colored button that says "I'm Organized for Success!" This would be especially effective if the name of her business were Organized for Success and the button colors matched her logo.

One of the most clever kits we have received was from author Peter McWilliams and seminar leader John-Roger. In promoting their book *Life 101*, in which they write about "everything you wish you'd learned about life in school but didn't," McWilliams and Roger filled their publicity kit with crayons and such other timeless elementary-school supplies as wide-margin paper and flash cards. Similarly, when Michael Cahlin created the Chocolate Software Company, he included a real chocolate disk those receiving his materials could snack on while reviewing information about his new computer software that features hundreds of recipes for chocolate lovers. Of course, he sent materials out right before the Christmas holidays!

MAX International, which produces rolls of paper for printers, created a kit using an actual mini-version of their product box to promote their recycled paper line. They filled it with a sample of the product and a recycled paper notepad in the shape of a roll along with a folded sheet of product information headlined "We're NUTS about recycling." Also in the kit was a can of soda for sipping while reading and a stack of bar coasters specially printed on both sides to illustrate *How Recycling Works* (see illustration). The entire kit was packed with peanuts—REAL PEANUTS in their shells—for nibbling. (See color insert for another example of a clever peanut bag novelty.)

To stimulate ideas for clever novelties, flip through a catalog from one or more of the advertising premium companies like Stucker Specialty Advertising of Chatsworth, California, or AdAnswer of Silver Spring, Maryland. Although an actual sample of what you do is best, it is not always possible or cost-effective to provide one. Be sure, however, that any novelty you use creates interest in you and your work. See **chapter 12**, page 618, for more information about selecting and using samples and giveaways.

Packaging Your Promotional Materials

Once you have assembled all the elements for your kit, you need to decide how to package them. Even when someone has requested your kit or you have notified someone that you are sending one, you still need to make sure your materials get attention once they arrive. Can you imagine having up to two thousand pieces of mail cross your desk every day, all asking you to consider them and take action? That's what many of the people who will be receiving your kit are faced with, so how you present your materials can be just as important as what is in it.

In order to get attention for their clients, major public relations firms have been known to use every tactic in the book and more to make sure they stand out from the crowd. From sending a release in a gift-wrapped box to having pop-up art that jumps out when the kit is opened to announcing the arrival of the release with the sound of trumpets, there isn't much that hasn't been tried. One of the most notorious (and least popular with most people receiving them) is materials that are folded in with glitter or confetti that sprinkles out all over everything when the package is opened.

As a small or home-based business, you may not have the budget to use overly dramatic tactics (although we'll describe some who have done so quite effectively), such extremes are not necessary, and can backfire. What is necessary is a professional look and a personal touch and that can be achieved simply by using an attractive presentation folder to enclose all the materials in your kit.

Marketing Masterpiece: A Perfect Package

We receive a lot of promotional packages from people wishing to be guests on our radio or television shows. Most are pretty run-of-the mill. One, however, stands out as a true masterpiece. When it first arrived in the mail, our assistant called out gleefully that someone had send us a gift. Intrigued, we stopped what we were doing and went right down with eager anticipation to see what it was.

When we opened the package, gift wrapped with ribbon and a handwritten card "to Paul and Sarah," there was a book called *Present Perfect, The Essential Guide to Gift Giving* by Sherri and Larry Athay. It came with a newsletter-like sell sheet with a caption that read "Have YOU ever experienced the pressures of gift giving?" The newsletter proceeded to provide samples from the book of humorous but useful advice for gift-giving like "Present Danger! Gifts You Should Never Give Anyone" and teasers that direct you to certain pages of the book like one with a chart that reported the number-one gift preference for both men and women. We couldn't resist looking that up. (Surprise! It was money.) The newsletter also featured background on the authors and testimonials from the media and satisfied readers. Tied to the package was a handwritten enclosure card that read, "We'll talk to you soon."

And, indeed, they did! While they may have planned on calling us, we didn't wait for their call. We called them right away to arrange for an interview. This was such a marketing masterpiece because it not only got our attention delightfully, it was a perfect sample of its own message—the perfect present!

The Presentation Folder

There are at least five options for creating a professional presentation folder to organize and hold selected promotional materials. Some will fit into the tightest of budgets, while others will involve more of an investment. You can have:

1. Your logo, picture, or slogan custom-printed onto a folder. You can have such folders printed at your print shop or companies like Paper Direct and NEBS will do such printings for you matching your stationery and business cards (see sample in color insert).
2. Your logo printed on adhesive labels that you then place on standard die-cut folders that are available in most office-supply stores or mail-order catalogs.
3. The cover of a book, workbook, or product package added to the front of a standard folder. When such covers are printed, consider ordering extra copies and affixing them to standard die-cut folders. Or, you can affix a four-color glossy photo of your product or service with the name of your company printed on it.
4. Your cover sheet or any other item in the kit itself serve as the cover by using a see-through vinyl folder or binder.
5. A customized die-cut folder or display designed just for you as Info Factory has done by turning their mini-brochure into an all-in-one promotional piece (page 261).

Make sure that the folders you select are color coordinated to complement and enhance the colors of your logo and stationery (see color insert). Carry out your color scheme throughout the entire kit. Have plenty of copies of all materials on hand. Promotional opportunities often require immediate action. Reporters and writers, bookers and editors are all on deadlines, so they may need your material "yesterday." By having ample materials collated and handy you won't have to drop everything and rush round pulling your materials together when an opportunity arises.

Make up enough copies to cover a three-month period. Somewhere between ten and fifty sets should be adequate. Each time you have additional sets duplicated, add copies of your most recent articles or testimonials and drop less current ones unless they are from very prominent publications. Don't actually assemble the kits, however, until you need them, because which elements to include in a kit will depend on the person to whom and the purpose for which you are sending it.

Like many people these days, marketing and public relations consultant Daniel Dern customizes his kit to the particular client or customer by using standard boiler-plate copy which he edits and personalizes with select samples, testimonials, etc. The entire process takes him no more than fifteen or thirty minutes.

In assembling your kit, insert the key elements in the right-hand pockets of your folder with a cover letter, news release, or query letter on top and include your business card in the precut slot. Place any photographs, testimonials, or articles about you in the left-hand pocket. And if you're sending your materials by mail, send them in a large envelope imprinted or clearly marked with your company logo or other identification. A printed mailing label is perfectly acceptable with the name and address of the person or organization to whom you are sending your kit.

Action Steps: Selecting a Folder on a Tight Budget

Do some shopping at office-supply stores to find an inexpensive folder that you can use to display your promotional materials. If you find several possibilities that are constructed differently, get one of each, assemble your presentation materials into kits, and test the response to each one. Also try different options for customizing the front jacket of your folder. Present each one to at least five different people and ask each group the following questions:

A. How long has this company been in business?
B. How many people work for this company?
C. Describe briefly the level of expertise this company projects.
D. What level of sales does this company achieve annually?
E. How long will it take for them to respond to an information request? A service call? A complaint?
F. What is your gut reaction to this company?

Select the one that gets the best response. If you get consistently less-than-positive responses, ask what about the kit gives them that impression. Then make appropriate changes.

Making the Most of Your Package

Once you have all the promotional materials you need on hand, don't sit by and wait passively for someone to request them. Incorporate them in as many ways as you can into any of the types of marketing activities you initiate like those in the chapters that follow. Here are a few rules of thumb about making the best use of your materials:

1. Don't send your entire kit in response to general, routine requests for materials. These requests are usually obligatory in nature and sending an entire promotional kit is too expensive unless you know there is actual interest. Reserve your promotional kit for those who have actually shown interest in what you have to offer.
2. Unless you're undertaking a media campaign, make it a point to have spoken personally with anyone you send an entire kit to so you can assess if there is real interest.
3. Always include a cover letter with your presentation kit to remind the recipient of your conversation or reason for sending the materials.
4. Save your presentation kit for the end of an interview or sales call. No need to distract them with reading material during the conversation.
5. Avoid distributing your presentation kits en masse. Aim to customize what you send for each recipient, and make it clear that it has been assembled just for them.
6. Always have a generic presentation kit in the event an unplanned opportunity presents itself.
7. Whenever possible, provide a personalized "walk-through" of the materials in the kit, showing the prospect each piece and explaining what it is, before leaving it with them.
8. Avoid putting all your materials in the initial kit you provide. You want the opportunity to make a series of contacts and provide additional pieces of information each time.

Are You Set?

Having completed the last four chapters, you have the information and the tools for creating a winning marketing message that will begin attracting business for your niche. Use the following checklist to track your progress to date:

___ 1. Do you have an Attention Grabber you can count on to get people listening eagerly and with curiosity to what you have to say about your business?

___ 2. Can you describe your niche using a File-Opening Sound Byte that people respond to enthusiastically and with interest?

___ 3. Can you go on to describe your niche in further detail in ways that speak to both the head and the heart?

___ 4. Does your business name capture the essence of your niche?

___ 5. Is it easy to remember, pronounce, and spell?

___ 6. Do you have one distinctive, coordinated graphic image for your business cards, letterhead, and other materials? Does it reinforce the nature of your niche?

___ 7. Do people note and comment positively on your materials? Or do they go unnoticed or even elicit suggestions for improvements?

___ 8. Is the information on your marketing materials current so you don't have to scratch out and/or write in new information?

___ 9. Have you built a promotional package that shows off and describes you and your niche that you can use for a variety of marketing purposes?

___10. Are you beginning to get business or referrals from people who have heard you describe your business, seen your businees name, or read your card or other materials?

If you can answer these questions positively, you are ready and set to go forward with your marketing plans, initiating and following through on as many activities as your need for business requires.

Resources

Do-It-Yourself Custom Folders

To customize your presentation folders you can use preprinted papers like those listed below or you can custom-design your own using a template from *The Desktop Publisher's Idea Book,* by Chuck Green, New York: Random House, 1997, www.randomhouse.com/

Photo-Editing Software

Adobe Photoshop and ***PhotoDeluxe,*** Adobe Systems, 345 Park Avenue, San Jose, CA 95110, (800) 42ADOBE, www.adobe.com

Kai's Photo Soap, MetaCreations Corp., 6303 Carpinteria Avenue, Carpinteria, CA 93013, (800) 472-9025, (805) 566-6200, www.metatools.com

LivePix, Live Picture, Inc., 910 E. Hamilton, Ste. 300, Campbell, CA 95008, (800)724-7900, (408) 371-4455, www.livepicture.com

Picture It, Microsoft Corp., One Microsoft Way, Redmond, WA 98052, (800) 426-9400, www.microsoft.com

Preprinted Papers

Avery Dennison, 20955 Pathfinder Rd., Diamond Bar, CA 91765, (800) 525-7064; (909) 869-7711.

Paper Direct, 100 Plaza Drive, Secaucus, NJ 07094, (800) A-PAPERS, (800) 272-7377, www.paperdirect.com

Queblo, 150 Kingswood Road, Mankato, MN 56002, (800) 523-9080, www.catalog.orders.com

Professionally Created Custom Folders

If you don't have the time, technology, or inclination to produce your presentation folder materials, you can, of course, have them designed and printed by a local desktop publisher, graphic artist, or print shop. Alternatively, you can use mail-order design services like:

NEBS, 500 Main Street, Groton, MA 01471, (800) 225-6380.

Specialty Printers

Gentile Brothers Folder Factory, 116-A High Street, P.O. Box 429, Edinburgh, VA 22824, (800) 368-5270.

PART III

GO:

Choosing Tailor-Made Marketing Methods

Passion persuades. —Anita Roddick

The following four chapters provide a wealth of marketing activities for getting business to come to you. As we suggested in chapter 4, most people find they do best focusing their business-generating efforts on activities that are personally enjoyable and that they can do reasonably well with ease. Therefore, we've organized the most popular and effective methods of successful small and home-based businesses into four types of activities so you can identify the ones that will be best suited to your personality and your business:

- Making Personal Contacts (**chapter 9**)
- Getting Others Talking About You (**chapter 10**)
- Telling All About It (**chapter 11**)
- Showing What You Can Do (**chapter 12**)

In picking activities to initiate and follow through on, we suggest starting with whichever chapter is most reflective of the kind of interaction you would most enjoy having with the people who will be buying your products and services. If you like face-to-face interaction, begin by picking activities in chapter 9. If you'd rather have others promoting you, turn to chapter 10. If you like writing about what you do, turn to chapter 11. If you're more comfortable letting your work speak for itself, start with chapter 12 to identify ways in which you can showcase your work. To assist you further in choosing the activities best suited to you, you'll also find icons that indicate whether they consist mainly of WALKING, TALKING, SHOWING, or TELLING.

Generally we recommend selecting five activities you can be initiating in conjunction with one another during a given period of time, as outlined in chapter 4. But many people tell us they prefer to simply start with their favorite chapter and initiate and follow through on something from that chapter every day, week, or month. Either of these approaches seems to work well if you initiate something frequently and consistently enough and follow through religiously.

If you're comfortable undertaking activities from all four chapters, it can be ideal to select at least one activity from each chapter and do them in conjunction with one another. This is ideal because people will get the opportunity to meet you, hear about you from others, read about you, and see or experience what you do. Such a multimedia approach can have a powerful impact.

After trying out various activities over time, you may find that one or more work marvelously for you, and so you'll want to stick with those activities until they no longer draw business for you. When Lynne Frances started her cleaning service, for example, she tried various methods of generating business but found that most of her business came from a simple classified ad she had placed in the community newspaper. From that point on she relied exclusively on this activity for years, even after most all of her business came from word-of-mouth referrals.

On the other hand, you may find that you need to change the type of activities you initiate frequently to reach different people in different ways. Many people find that mixing and matching a variety of activities throughout the year is most effective.

To assist you in deciding which activities to use, we describe each marketing method, what it involves, and its pros and cons along with a variety of examples of how others are using it. We then provide step-by-step guidelines for how to get the best results from each marketing activity.

Are You Going Yet?

Often people think they're marketing their business, but in fact, they're not doing anywhere near enough business-generating activity to create the kind of momentum they need to get business coming to them through word of mouth. So, here is a checklist you can use to determine whether or not you're maximizing your marketing activities:

___ 1. Have you identified the kind of marketing activities that you enjoy most, you do best, and are most suited to your business?

___ 2. Have you picked five activities you want to focus on for a specific period of time?

___ 3. Are you initiating five activities a day, week, or month, depending on how much business you need?

___ 4. Are you following through on each activity? Or are your contacts growing cold?

___ 5. Do you feel enthusiastic about the marketing you're doing?

___ 6. Are you keeping track of the results you get from each activity so you can decide whether it's worth your time and money?

___ 7. Are you getting a positive response from the activities you are doing or do you need to do them differently or try something else?

___ 8. Are you beginning to have the experience of people you meet or call for the first time telling you that they know who you are because they have already read or heard about you?

___ 9. Are you beginning to get business coming to you through word of mouth only indirectly related to any specific business-generating activity you've done?

CHAPTER 9

Making Personal Contacts

All business is relationship.

—Paul and Sarah Edwards

Some people love interacting with other people. They love to meet them and talk to them. Making personal contact comes naturally to them, and they would be doing it whether they needed to or not. Grace Gottlieb is such a person. If Grace has a moment free, she's on the phone. She fills her mornings and evenings with civic and social activities. She's also a bit of a ham. She likes to joke and kid around and enjoys being the center of attention. She has plenty of business coming to her because getting business by interacting with people is as natural to her as breathing. She has no qualms about calling someone on the phone to introduce herself and her gift basket business. She likes visiting with prospective clients and consulting with them on the gift basket programs she could design. She belongs to lots of organizations and takes an active part in most of them. Someone once said about her, "I think just about everyone knows Grace."

Your Goal: Get Personally Acquainted

- ___ *Direct solicitation*
- ___ *Free consultations*
- ___ *Networking*
- ___ *Speeches and seminars*
- ___ *Volunteering*
- ___ *Walking around the neighborhood*

While you may not be as outgoing as Grace, if you enjoy talking and interacting with others, either in groups or one-on-one, the marketing activities in this chapter can be an enjoyable way for you to get business coming to you by doing things you do naturally. Read through and select those approaches that are most appealing to you and are best suited to your business.

Direct Solicitation

Talking personally to people who need what you offer is the quickest and most reliable way to get business. Of course, the dreaded words *cold calling* can send a shiver down the spine of even experienced salespeople. But we've been surprised to find how many self-employed individuals successfully market their businesses by initiating personal contact to acquaint people in their market niche with what they have to offer.

David Goodfellow is a good example. When he decided to sell mailing list services to small businesses, Goodfellow got started by going through the Yellow Pages and calling small companies in his community to determine whether they needed his services. He started with those listed under the letter *A* and never got past *K*. He generated a steady flow of business from the first half of the alphabet!

Ray Bidenost of Pasadena, California, also built BaLooney Balloons, his gift balloon and event decoration company, by mastering the art of cold calling. He started by calling on restaurants and bars where he had been a patron. He found he picked up one client for every eight calls. Sometimes people ordered right over the phone. With over 550 clients in his database now, he belongs to many community organizations and warms up his sales calls by sending postcards to people on their membership lists. Averaging up to fifty calls a week, he says, "I just call people and act like I know them." He has a list of the type of businesses he'll be calling throughout the year. He says, "Right now, for example, I'm focusing on hotels."

So while it may take a bit of confidence and ingenuity to get through to the people you want to contact, if you like relating to others and promoting your product or service, direct solicitation can be a successful route to getting your business off the ground and establishing yourself so that business starts coming to you.

Pros and Cons of Direct Solicitation

If you like to sell, direct solicitation is without a doubt the quickest and most surefire route for getting business, establishing relationships, becoming known, and building a reputation. But direct solicitation is a numbers game. Since a sale usually isn't made until after the fifth call, the key is to keep at it. You have to be willing to hear a lot of "nos" and figure that every "no" will bring you that much closer to a "yes."

It helps to think about sales calls as relationship building, because after all, that's what they are. You are introducing yourself to people who could use what you have to offer, getting acquainted with them, and finding out about their needs. What's the worst thing that can happen from a sales call? They don't need you now. Okay, but they may in the future. Or they may run into someone who does. And you'll be foremost on their mind!

Best Bets: Direct solicitation is particularly useful for unique services or products that fill a pressing need. It is appropriate when what you have to offer is of a high enough price to justify contacting people individually. It is less effective when there is a flood of similar products or services all of which are inundating potential customers with sales calls.

Tips for Getting Results from Direct Solicitation

Since direct solicitation is a numbers game, here's what you can do to save yourself time and effort and make the entire sales process less intimidating. Since at some point, everyone has to make the sale or close the deal, you'll also find many additional ideas for effectively selling your product or service in chapter 13, Turning Interest into Business Again and Again. Here, however, are some ways you can save time and money in contacting people person-to-person.

Warm up your calls. There are many ways you can "warm up" your sales contacts and thereby increase your success rate. Whenever possible build your list of contacts from people who have already met you through other activities. This isn't always possible, however, so here are some other routes.

- You can build your list from members of an organization to which you belong, as business coach Tova Feder did by calling the list of fellow NAWBO members.
- You can collect names of people to contact from colleagues and associates and, if they agree, use them as an introduction.
- You can send those you intend to contact something in advance as a conversation opener. It might be a newsletter, a sales letter, a direct-mail piece, or flyer (see chapter 11, Telling All About It). Whether they read it and remember you is less important than that you can open your conversation by inquiring whether they received your materials and letting them know you want to follow up.

Marketing Masterpiece: Getting Business by Phone

When Tova Feder of Sherman Oaks, California, decided to open her business providing coaching services to small businesses, she built her business quickly using direct solicitation. She joined the National Association of Women Business Owners (NAWBO) and set a goal to call seventy-five people from the local chapter directory by devoting three days per week to making marketing calls. We, Paul and Sarah, met her when she placed a call to us, told us about her services, and offered a free consultation. Although we were not in need of her services, we were most impressed with her warm and friendly, yet authoritative, approach and invited her to join us as a guest on our radio show.

Here are the key points we learned about the offer she makes when she places her marketing calls. She explains that she provides her services to professional women who want to become more successful and accelerate progress in their careers. She points out that she has personally learned the ropes of small business start-up and development over twenty-five years through her own business and by working with successful companies. "I have lived through the joys and heartaches of small-business growth and can help you navigate those same waters," she says, going on to add: "I would like to introduce you to my services by offering a free consultation/coaching session so you can experience for yourself how my services can help you achieve greater success."

Using this approach, Feder was able to make appointments from her marketing calls for five free consultations each week. Two of those five people go on to become clients. As a result, Feder had a thriving full-time business within six months.

My (Sarah) favorite way to warm up calls is to build my list from among companies or individuals whose services I use and/or admire most. This way I can start off my conversations by defining myself as a customer or advocate and communicate why I like their services or products and would like to work with them.

Create visibility for yourself beforehand. Arrange to have made some impression on those you will be contacting before making your sales calls. For example, you might speak to their professional association. You might write an article for their trade paper. You might have exhibited at a trade show in their field or provide a donation or sponsor an event you know they are involved with. Of course, those you contact may not have seen your name in conjunction with any of these activities, but the fact that you can reference them when you make the contact helps build a bridge between strangers and increases the chances that they will put out a welcome mat for you.

Get personal. Always try to have the specific name and title of the person you wish to talk to. You will have a much harder time trying to talk to "the proprietor" or "the person in charge of ______." Being able to ask for the person you wish to talk to by name will increase your success dramatically. Often you can find the names of those you wish to speak to through searching on-line yellow pages or CD-ROMs (See page 111 for a list of such resources).

A financial consultant we interviewed has an intriguing way to warm up his calls. He looks at name plates on the desks of businesses he visits and then places phone calls using the names at a later time. Or he calls the company and tells the secretary, "I'm supposed to mail something to a man I met at your company and I can't remember his name. He was about thirty-five and his name was something like—" The operator offers twenty names, while he takes notes so he can call them back.

Follow the rules. The Federal Trade Commission has issued stringent rules on when and how businesses can use the telephone to solicit customers. They can levy heavy fines against anyone who violates their rules, which include:

- Calling only between 8 A.M. and 9 P.M.
- Informing consumers that it's a sales call
- Describing the nature of the good or services you're selling
- If a prize is involved, explaining the odds of winning and that no purchase is required to win

Also, many communities have regulations limiting door-to-door solicitation and many buildings have NO SOLICITING signs. Always respect all such limitations.

Focus your contacts on those who you know actually need what you offer. You will be much more successful in your sales contacts if you limit your calls to people or companies who you already know clearly need what you are offering. Many mailing list services, for example, are able to get the business by dropping by establishments that have guest books or customer sign-up cards at expos. Once they see that someone is collecting names, they can ask what the potential client plans to do with the lists and offer to help them set up their mailing list.

A marketing consultant who specializes in representing seminar companies uses this approach to direct sales. She attends as many such events of potential clients as possible as a participant and makes a checklist of the kinds of things they could have done to improve their attendance. Shortly after the event, she contacts the company, introduces herself as having attended and enjoyed one of their events, and asks if they would be interested in her ideas for how to boost attendance.

A graphic designer collects brochures, flyers, and other marketing pieces handed out or displayed at networking groups, expos, and conventions. When he finds one that could use some improvement, he contacts the owner, compliments her on the value of her product or service, and asks if he could meet with her briefly to share some ideas on how she could increase the business she attracts from her marketing materials. Usually the owners agree and often at some point in the future they hire him to redesign their materials or create new ones.

Collect background information. Find out as much as you can about a company or the type of individuals you will be contacting before calling on them. Much of the kind of information you need is available on-line (see page 111). But libraries, personal contacts, the newspapers, and trend magazines and newsletters (see pages 112–13) can also be helpful. Such information can make your initial contacts much easier. For example, the ergonomics specialist who knows the number of worker's comp claims per company in a certain industry might have an easier time establishing rapport with companies in that industry. The public relations specialist who knows about a company's newest line or previous image problems could have an easier time making a personal appointment.

For additional sources of information, see **Sources of Market Data to Help Close Sales** in chapter 13.

Ask open-ended questions and listen carefully. Once you make personal contact with prospective clients, get them talking about their experience, needs, and interests as soon as possible by asking questions like:

- Are you familiar with this product/service?
- Have you seen or used something like this before?
- Do you have or are you using something like this now?
- Have you ever thought of using something like this?
- How has your experience been having or using something like this?

Such questions can serve many purposes. First, people love to talk about themselves and/or their businesses, so such questions build rapport. Second, in the process of asking such questions, you may find out quickly that this person is not actually a prospective client. He may be completely satisfied with another similar service. He may have just used such a service and have no need for another one at this time. Or his sister-in-law may be offering the same thing you are. The sooner you find out such things the quicker you can get on to serving someone who does need what you're offering.

In addition, however, the answers to such questions will give you many clues you can use to more clearly explain how what you can offer will help them and provide opportunities to demonstrate your mastery of issues that are important to them.

Don't talk price; build value. Often the first thing people will want to know is your fees or prices. Do not discuss price, however, until you have more information. Tell those who jump right into asking about price that you will be happy to discuss your prices but since there is a range of things you can offer, first you need to know more about what they need or would be interested in. This will give you the chance to demonstrate why what you can offer is well worth your price. The best time to discuss price is after people are quite interested and are hoping they can afford you.

Turn interest into sales. Oddly enough, few people actually ask for business. They wait around hoping to take an order. Don't fall into this trap. Once you sense interest, ask when and how someone wants to proceed. If you get a firm "no," this is good because you won't need to waste your time further. If you get resistance or objections, that is good too, because it gives you a chance to clarify if and how you could better meet a customer's needs. Corporate event planner Donna Friedman, for example, spends two days each week on sales and marketing. She

SMILE!

Much of your success in making any new personal contact will rely on your ability to establish trust and rapport quickly. Your facial expression can be an important key for building such rapport. Looking engaging, friendly and nonthreatening, however, usually takes some effort on your part. Just take a good look at yourself in the mirror without smiling at yourself and you'll see that the human face in repose is not all that engaging. Facial lines, wrinkles, and contours make some people look tired, others look remote, removed, or superior, while some look a bit depressed, sullen, or even angry.

Now smile at yourself in the mirror. Notice the dramatic transformation that comes over your face. A smile works wonders on everyone. It does take a bit of effort to remember to smile, but if you ever doubt its worth, just walk through a busy airport and notice how differently total strangers react to you when you greet their brief eye contact with a smile. Or listen to how the sound of your voice changes when you're smiling. Noticing how dramatically a smile improves the response you get. Many people, like Barb Tomlin, a communications and marketing specialist in Albuquerque, New Mexico, warm up their sales calls by having a mirror beside their desk to make sure they have put a smile on their face and into their voice. Tomlin has a full-length mirror in her home office. By watching her own facial expressions and body language, she's able to address her phone contacts as though she were talking to them face-to-face. She finds it makes for a livelier, more effective conversation.

There's no doubt about it: if you're marketing person-to-person, a smile is one of your best assets.

finds that every ten calls generate one appointment and every appointment leads to a proposal. If she doesn't get that job, she usually gets a subsequent one from that company.

Don't give up; try, try again. Keeping in touch and following up is often the key to getting business through direct solicitation. Even when someone is interested in or needs your service or product, they may require multiple contacts with you before they decide to buy. Don't let someone else walk in and benefit from all your initial contact; stay in touch. Always present something new or provide added incentives to move ahead. Sometimes you may even want to do something a bit unusual, the way Roy Sloan did. When Sloan started his New York advertising agency in 1979, he was looking for a smart, promising new company he could represent that had the potential to grow into a highly successful business. He targeted a small start-up ice-cream company and tried just about every conventional way of making contact with them from phone calls to letters to meeting company representatives at trade shows—all to no avail.

After a year of frustration, he decided upon a bold strategy. He wrote the president of the company a letter that explained that his company, Advertising Management, "has been assigned as your advertising agency." Shortly after sending the letter, Sloan followed up with a phone call and met with the company president. He got the account, and no one ever asked who assigned him to be their agency. If they had, however, he was prepared. He was going to tell them that God had assigned him and that representing them was his destiny. He went on to represent the company—Haägen-Dazs—for nearly a decade.

For more information on handling objections, following up, and turning interest into business, see chapter 13.

Warming Up Cold Calls

The information we've given so far on selling is based on the concept that your other marketing techniques have opened the door for your sales call. But if you need customers quickly to get or keep your business alive, you may actually have to brave the elements and do some cold calling.

The problem with cold calling and the classic techniques so many of us are taught in books and seminars is that they are miserably uncomfortable not only for you, the seller, but also for the potential customer. Both of you feel forced into some sort of adversarial position. The buyer feels that the seller is trying to wrench dollars from his budget, and the seller feels that the buyer is there not to buy but to keep anybody from buying.

There are several techniques that can make this process not only a lot less onerous but even, possibly, fun and more productive. Doing selling research is one highly effective one. Now that most companies have extensive Web sites and the number of corporate databases abounds, getting the information you need to warm up your cold calls is easier than ever before. So if possible always visit a prospective client's Web site and gather any other on-line background you can find. Much of the best information still comes from making person-to-person contacts like the ones that follow, be they by phone, E-mail, or face-to-face.

In earlier chapters we discussed the fact that the more you know about your target market, the more likely you are to be able to reach it. When you must make a sale, however, you have to deal with individual members of that target market. At this point your research needs to be completely specific. That is, instead of knowing that your target market, for example, consists of small-to-medium-sized manufacturing plants, you must know exactly what a specific company manufactures, what differentiates them from their competition, what they value in a supplier or contractor, how they service their customers, etc. To get this sort of information, you usually have to go to the "horse's mouth." And that is a great place to start.

Sellers usually are afraid that any contact they have with a prospective client or customer is going to be perceived as adversarial. Sometimes it is, but it doesn't have to stay that way. Some years ago a sales rep for a small manufacturing firm contacted the head of purchasing for a major New York bank. Because she had been referred to him by the president of the bank, he grudgingly gave her the appointment. When she arrived, he sat with his arms folded across his chest and asked how she knew the president. She sized up the situation immediately and answered completely honestly, "My best friend in the whole wide world, who lives in Dallas, Texas, is his brother's wife . . . (long pause) . . . and they hate each other's guts!" The purchasing manager nearly fell out of his chair laughing.

That call was a cold call, even though there was a referral. Essentially, every first call is a cold call whether there is interest or not. If there has been interest in the product or service, you still must ensure that the provider will be you. What will set you apart from all others is the way you handle that first contact.

If you use a first contact to present your product or service and try to convince them to buy, you will have missed the greatest opportunity you have to set yourself apart from all your competition. Other than a simple explanation of what you do and why you are there (or want to see to them, in the case of a phone call), the entire first contact should be spent trying to find out the specifics of what they do, the way they do it, and how your product or service might enhance their efforts. It is your job to elicit this information.

Business-to-Business With companies like banks, you usually know what they do, but are you sure you know their specific focus? For example, are they primarily a retail or commercial bank? Where is their growth targeted? How many branches do they have? How deep are they into electronic services? What is their loan focus? What revenue streams are the most profitable for them? Are they a target for merger? What are their long-term plans?

Why do you want to know these things? Let's suppose you are a graphic artist. Until you have this information, you cannot determine what approach to use for spec work. You don't know whether to focus your efforts on consumer incentives or print advertising. And without knowing who their real customers are, you cannot determine how to help the company reach them. There is no way you can collaborate in their efforts unless you know what they are trying to achieve in their marketplace.

With other types of companies, you may not even really know what they do or how they do it. Ask for a brief tour. Most people like to show off what they or their companies do. Ask them about their last training effort. Ask what they find to be their single biggest obstacle to profit. Is it the cost of goods or services? Is it overhead? Find out how they do specific tasks that relate to your product or service. The above sales rep retrieved sample receipts from the trash near the bank's automatic teller machines (ATMs) and discovered that the bank was using what is known as *safety paper*. Safety paper is the same stuff used for checks that prevents alteration. It is very expensive. However, the receipt you get from your ATM is not a legal receipt. She went to the purchasing agent, gave him that information, and suggested an alternative which of course her company could provide. The bank ended up saving over $600,000 per year on that single item alone. Her competitor not only lost that business, but the rest of the bank's business as well. Why? Because she did her homework. By doing so she became, not an adversary, but a trusted partner of the purchasing department. Incidentally, the agent she was working with eventually went to another bank, and she got that business as well.

Doing specific research about a prospective client offers opportunities to tailor your product or service to meet their needs. The training firm, Team Approach® of Lancaster, Pa., for example, analyzed the training needs of their clients and discovered that in several cases the biggest problem was the actual implementation of what they had learned. They modified their consultancy to provide implementation services including monitoring, tracking, and new-habit development. In doing so they developed "an expertise" that completely separated them from their competition as well as created a licensable and franchisable opportunity.

But what if the company you want as a client is huge and you don't even know whom to contact? This situation often offers opportunities beyond your wildest expectations. Your best source of initial information is the receptionist. He or she can tell you much about the company and who is in charge of what. Be sure to get his name and thank him for his help. And be sure, too, to let the next person you speak to know how very courteous and helpful the receptionist was.

Often, because of the nature of many products and services, the person responsible for making such decisions may not be the individual to whom you are first referred. That offers an additional opportunity to get a referral to the right person. Write down every name you are given (be sure to spell correctly). For example, your initial conversation might go something like this:

Receptionist:
"Good morning. Jones & Company. How may I help you?"

You:
"Good morning. My name is Jane Smith of Smith & Associates. To whom am I speaking?"

Receptionist:
"This is Nancy Allen. How may I refer your call?"

You:
"Hello, Ms. Allen. Could you please tell me who is responsible for contracting newsletter production services?"

Nancy:
"I believe that would be Alex Jefferson in Customer Service. I'll transfer you."

You:
"Thank you for your help, Ms. Allen. Yes, I'd like to speak to Mr. Jefferson."

Jefferson:
"Customer Service. Jefferson. How may I help you?"

You:
"Good morning, Mr. Jefferson. My name is Jane Smith of Smith & Associates. I understand you are responsible for contracting newsletter production services. Is that correct?"

Jefferson:
"Well, I do handle the in-house printing plant. Is that what you're looking for?"

You:
"Not exactly. My company handles the coordination, editing, pasteup, and preparation for both internal and customer-oriented newsletters, and I was wondering if you currently publish a newsletter."

Jefferson:
"I know they've been discussed by marketing and human resources because I've gotten requests for printing costs, and I've run a couple for customer service, but not on any regular basis. They did say the customers really liked the ones they saw, though."

You:
"Yes, it's tough to keep them going. That's exactly the service we provide. We get the list of who's to write what, get the information from them, edit it, and get it ready for you to process. Whom do you think I should contact about this in those departments?"

Jefferson:
"Well, in marketing you might talk to James Maxwell, and in H.R. the best contact for this might be Susan Cantwell."

You:
"That's terrific. Thank you so much. By the way, while I have you, what kinds of prep and press equipment do you have in-house? . . ."

Your next call might be to James Maxwell . . .

You:
"Good morning, Mr. Maxwell. Alex Jefferson suggested that you were the person who knows all there is to know about the way you keep in touch with your customer and prospect base."

Maxwell:
"Well, I am in charge of customer service. I guess that's a fair assessment of my responsibilities."

You:
"He also mentioned you had considered a regular customer newsletter but possibly had found that the work involved in publishing it regularly made it impossible to get the rest of your work done."

Maxwell:
"You said a mouthful. Just getting all the materials in from the various areas is incredibly time-consuming much less editing it, getting it laid out and typeset for the print shop!"

You:
"Well, what if you could have all that part done for you? Given the equipment you have in your printing plant, all that is necessary is the coordination, editing, and pasteup, which my company can do quickly and cost-effectively. Then we give Alex a diskette, which is ready to set up and run. *Voilà!* You have a regular means of keeping in touch with your customers . . ."

And so forth. In this example you have managed to create internal referrals even though you didn't know a soul at the company when your phone calls began. And if Maxwell still wasn't the decision maker, you have his name to use with the individual whose name Maxwell gives you. And you can do the same thing for human resources. The process is the same.

The more people you talk to, the more information you gather enabling you to address the specific concerns of the individual you finally reach. And that individual cannot help but be impressed with all the homework you have done.

Business-to-consumer If your potential clients are consumers, it can become somewhat more difficult to acquire the information you seek, but it can be done. For example, a real estate agent looking for homes to list might scour public records to find out which houses were remodeled in the last five years and what sort of construction the permits were for. They can find out what was originally paid for the house and the change in its assessed value. Match those lists with lists of high-school or college graduates, job changes or promotions, weddings, anniversaries, etc. (all available from the local newspapers), to find people who are possibly in transition.

Approaching these people either to upgrade or downsize their housing precisely at the time these transitions are occurring and armed with precise information about the value of the property they currently own gives an agent a special advantage by allowing him to know whom to contact at precisely the best time. If he then confirms the information with the homeowner personally by suggesting an appraisal or the opportunity to realize a return on her principal investment for college expenses, retirement, etc., he creates an impression that inspires trust and reliability. Now the cold call is no longer cold. It is simply a *first* call.

Here again, the more you know about an individual's needs and what his current situation might be, the better your ability to determine how you can provide a product or service he will value. There is one caveat, however: Never, **never** seek or use confidential information. Information that can only be obtained by devious methods will reflect negatively on you. Despite our vulnerability with regard to privacy (computers have enabled almost anyone to find out almost anything about us), no one likes her illusion of privacy invaded. Be ready to give a simple explanation of where you got the information you have—public records, newspapers, their Web site, a neighbor, etc.

Direct Selling Resources

Books

High Probability Selling. Jacques Werth and Nicholas E. Ruben. Dresher, PA: Abba Publishing, 1997.

How to Sell More in Less Time, Vol. 1. Art Sobczak. Business by Phone, Inc., 13254 Stevens Street, Omaha, NE 68137, (402) 895-9339, (800) 326-7721, www.businessbyphone.com, 1995.

Opening Closed Doors, How to Reach Hard to Reach People. C. Richard Weylman. New York: Irwin Books, 1994.

Selling for Dummies. Tommy Hopkins. Foster City, Calif.: IDG Books, 1995.

Telephone Tips That Sell! 501 How-to Ideas and Affirmations to Help Get More Business by Phone. Art Sobczak. Business by Phone, Inc., 13254 Stevens Street, Omaha, NE 68137, (402) 895-9399, (800) 326-7721, www.businessbyphone.com, 1996.

Newsletters

Telephone Selling Report. monthly newsletter, Business by Phone, Inc., 13254 Stevens Street, Omaha, NE 68137, (402) 895-9399, (800) 326-7721, www.businessbyphone.com

Software

Telephone Tips That Sell! 501 How-to Ideas and Affirmations to Help Get More Business by Phone. Art Sobczak. Business by Phone, Inc. 13254 Stevens Street, Omaha, NE 68137, (402) 835-9399, arts@businessbyphone.com, 1996.

Free Consultations

When makeup artist Lori Tabak started offering facial rejuvenation treatments using electrical stimulation, she was excited about the dramatic results this new technique could produce, but most of her clients were hesitant. It sounded strange. Most people had never heard of it before and since you had to come for two sessions a week for six weeks in a row and then once a month after that, the service seemed like quite an investment.

Free consultations became her most effective marketing strategy. She would describe her new service to her makeup clients and then offer them a thirty-minute free consultation. Many of them were curious enough to take her up on the offer. After all, what did they have to lose other than a little of their time? During the consultation, Tabak would assess the client's skin, explain how facial rejuvenation could help, and then apply the treatment to one side of the client's face. The difference was quite dramatic! The mirror told the tale. Clients could see how much better the treated side of their face looked, and usually that sold them on starting the series. To reinforce the process, Tabak takes before-and-after Polaroid photos throughout the treatments so clients can see the impact of her work.

This illustrates just how effective offering a free consultation can be in generating business. Essentially offering a free consultation is like providing your clients or customers with a sneak preview or an appetizer of what you offer. Some people think of it as a nonthreatening way to make a client-oriented sales presentation. It's a chance to serve while selling.

Pros and Cons of Free Consultations

Offering free consultations is a great way to stir up interest, educate your clients as to what you do, and turn initial interest or resistance into paying business. It is one of the easiest ways to get business, especially when your work produces dramatic results. It opens new doors for people or motivates them to act. In these ways, free consultations can make it possible for your work to sell itself. At times it can make proceeding to buy your product or service almost irresistible.

Offering free consultations is an especially effective approach for anyone who enjoys working directly with clients and customers but who hates to sell or market themselves. It's also a good approach when what you're offering is new or different and your potential clients and customers don't know what it is, don't know whether they need it, or have reservations about trying something new.

If you are new to the business world or to your field, another advantage of giving free consultations is that they can provide you with avenues for developing your expertise, discovering what clients and customers need and like most or least about what you offer, enabling you to speak with more authority and to provide generic examples of what you do in other marketing activities.

On the other hand, free consultations are time-consuming. So they work best when you're offering something that involves a serious investment of time or money. And, of course, if you're busy with paying work, free consultations could mean having to turn away paying clients and so would not be a good investment of your time. In some situations, free consultations work better as an initial strategy for launching your independent career than as an ongoing marketing approach.

Also, some people will try to get you to provide your entire service as part of the consultation so they can go away not needing anything additional. Thus you must plan your offer carefully and structure the free consultation to strike a balance between giving a valuable sample of what you do and creating interest that leads to paying business.

Best Bets: Free consultations work especially well when what you're offering requires a personal rapport and/or a lot of explanation, assessment, and education to help the customer make a decision. It also works best when you can provide a firsthand experience of some of the benefits you provide. It is less effective when most people already know about a product or service, have seen or experienced it in many ways, and wouldn't want to take the time to try it out.

Marketing Mistake: Why Didn't This Work?

Elton was a massage therapist. To market his business, he gave free massages at the local health food store. It was excellent exposure. His name and business cards were prominently displayed at the store and lots of customers took him up on his offer for a free massage. Being very service oriented, he gave them a deep, relaxing massage, talking very little so they could experience the full effect of his work. They would leave to finish their shopping fully refreshed. In fact, he was becoming so popular that often there would be a line of people waiting for a massage. Unfortunately, few people called him to set up appointments. He didn't understand what he was doing wrong. Do you? He was making two key mistakes. Read on and see if you have figured them out.

Tips for Getting Business from Free Consultations

It's vital that you distinguish between giving a free consultation that leads to business and giving away your products and services for free. Here are several ways to make a free consultation worth the time and energy it takes:

Sample to sell. When you do a free consultation, you have to create an experience that leaves people wanting more. Therefore, what you offer needs to hold out the promise of something more desirable. When Elton shortened his free massages to three minutes, he started to generate more interest. Although people felt better after three minutes of massage, they got up wanting more.

Marketing consultant Pete Silver of Miami found the right balance by offering "Free Headlines." He invited potential clients to fax him a sample of any marketing project they were working on or wanted to develop and he would create new headlines to fax back to them. "If you hate what I do, you haven't wasted more than a fax," he reminded them. "But if you're like my established clients . . . from IBM to small one-person shops . . . you could be discovering a better source for getting things done."

Prequalify whenever possible. Because free consultations can be time-consuming and represent a considerable investment on your part, don't offer them to just anyone. Talk to prospective clients first, if possible. Ask them about their interests. Try to clarify if they could actually become clients by asking questions like "If you saw that this could help you to . . . would you be in a position to use my service?" Also, if you will be working with a company, make sure you'll be doing the free consultation with the decision maker by asking something like "If you're convinced this would be a good service, are you the one who can decide whether to do this or not, or are there others you would need to talk with?" By asking such questions, all but the most devoted lookie-loos will usually screen themselves out.

In some cases, an alternative would be to offer a ten- or twenty-minute free phone consultation and reserve your in-person free consultation for those who seem seriously committed to exploring working with you further.

Use an assessment or checklist to heighten interest. A free consultation should provide you with an opportunity to show off your expertise, your specialty, and your mastery. It should make clear why not just any service like yours will do. One of the best ways to do this is to help people gain insight into why they need *your* service and motivate them to sign up. In Elton's case, for example, people felt good after a three-minute massage, but they could call any other masseur anytime and get a massage. Elton still wasn't making a case for himself.

After he started explaining to customers what he was doing, however, and why he was choosing particular techniques for them, he began to get clients from the consultation. "You hold your tension here," he would explain. "Does this bother you often?" "Here's how I work on that. If I were to work with you I would . . ." "Do you like that? Is that helpful?" he would ask as he learned more about selling through free consultations. "If you'd like, I can set aside some time for you later today at my office."

Management consultant Taylor Cruise does free consultations which are basically a free assessment of need. He takes his potential clients through a checklist of questions that leads them to an understanding of how he could boost their productivity. "By the end of the consultation," he says, "they know what they need and what it could do for them. So, I just walk them through what the next step would be and usually, if I'm speaking to the right decision-maker, they want to proceed."

Let people experience the results. Like Cruise and Tabak, you want your potential clients to experience or see a glimpse of what they could have. For example, when Martin Louder started his voice coaching business, he gave a free consultation in which clients had the experience of hearing how their voice would sound if they completed the program. If they signed up for a series, that's what they would get. If they didn't, they would have to live with that memory of knowing how much better they could sound. So walk people through the process of what could be during your free consultation. Help your potential clients imagine themselves having the outcome your service will provide them with. When you're offering something someone needs or wants, this can be a powerful, almost irresistible, motivation.

Ask for the business. Just as in direct solicitation, once you see that someone is interested and pleased with what you've presented, it's important to ask for an appointment or a decision to proceed. Essentially this is a matter of saying something like "I have time to see you later this week," or "We could start next week." For more information on turning interest into a sale, see chapter 13.

Add an incentive. If you wish to motivate people to make a decision quickly, you can offer a special discount for starting right away, by saying something like "I can give you a special price on the first session if you sign up early for the seminar." If someone doesn't take you up on the offer but contacts you later asking for the discount, we suggest honoring it. The whole idea of a discount is to get people to make a commitment and, by extending the offer, you are showing goodwill which further builds trust and solidifies rapport.

Resources Free Consultations

Personal Coaching for Results: How to Mentor and Inspire Others to Amazing Growth. Louis E. Tice, Joyce Quick, and Lou Tice. Nashville: Thomas Nelson, 1997.

Networking

A friend once invited us, Paul and Sarah, to lunch with Kathryn Dager, founder and head of Profitivity, a customer-service training firm. Kathryn had been wanting for some time to do a radio show and establish a 900 customer-service number but didn't know whom to contact. We were so excited about her work that we immediately introduced her to someone who offered her the opportunity to be the permanent host on a consumer call-in radio show. We were also able to refer her to someone who was eager to set up a 900 telephone number with her for customer complaints.

This is an example of the power of networking. Networking refers to using face-to-face contact to establish relationships that can lead to business. It is the epitome of "word-of-mouth marketing" because it's based on talking with people about what you do and listening to find out how you might serve them. In one of our favorite networking stories, for example, a sales rep turned around a disappointing out-of-town sales trip into a shining success. As the rep was flying home from a week of meetings that had led nowhere, he was feeling tired, rejected, and discouraged but decided to strike up a conversation with the person sitting next to him on the plane. To his surprise and delight, his seatmate turned out to be in the market for exactly what he was selling, and the encounter rewarded him with a new five-figure client!

While such providence is never a guarantee, getting dramatic results like these from networking face-to-face with others need not be limited by time or space these days. They can take place across the nation and around the world in person via the Internet or through other on-line networking. Jordan Ayan, for example, had just lost a bid on a major contract before attending a national conference for professional consultants. While networking at the conference, he met Deanna Berg, who to his surprise was the one who had won the very contract he'd lost. Since winning the bid, Deanna had decided she needed help with the project and invited Jordan to join her in fulfilling the contract.

Someone visiting the Working from Home Forum on CompuServe left a message celebrating a multimillion-dollar contract he'd secured in the Soviet Union. He was pleased to tell us that every contact he'd made to conclude this deal came from networking on the Forum!

When information broker John Everett from Dallas was looking for someone to co-author a book with him, he looked no further than his computer. He tapped into an electronic network and left a message describing the type of person he needed on the Forum. He quickly had a response from writer Libby Crowe from Huntsville, Alabama, and together they wrote a successful book entitled *Information for Sale*. To this day they have yet to meet in person; the whole book was written through phone and computer contact. In fact, this very book is the result of on-line networking. It's how we, the Edwardses and Clampitt Douglas, met.

Many of the most promising business opportunities come from being in the right place at the right moment, when you serendipitously encounter someone in need of your product or service. And that's the power of networking. As telecommuting consultant Gil Gordon explains, "Everything in my business, whether it's getting an article published or finding a distributor, is a result of networking." I keep in contact with old friends, past co-workers, sales reps who used to call on me. I've joined a couple of carefully chosen small or discussion groups composed of the people I need to meet for my business, and I'm fortunate enough to know a couple of people who pride themselves on being "matchmakers." They love to get people with common interests together. I can't stress this enough. Just as in job hunting, your friends and contacts are your best assets."

Pros and Cons of Networking

We've found networking to be the most popular way for people to start and build a personal or professional service business. It provides a chance to personally convey your interest in a prospective client's needs. It gives you the opportunity to find out what they need and show how you can serve them better. In the process of networking, prospects also have a chance to discover that they like you, and almost everyone likes to do business with someone they like—particularly when dealing with a service business.

Networking is ideal for anyone who finds it easier to sell someone else than to sell themselves, because when done effectively the more you promote others with whom you're networking, the more likely they are to promote you.

On the other hand, even if you enjoy networking, it is one of the more time-consuming marketing activities. If you are quite busy doing paying work, you may not have time to get sufficiently involved in networking activities to build the kind of relationships that will lead to business. Usually casual one-time, press-the-flesh, eat-and-run contact does not help build your reputation or get business coming to you. Also, networking is often a more long-term marketing strategy. Although you may be lucky and make a contact anytime at any event that will lead to immediate business, usually, in order to get business through networking, you need to spend time and energy week after week, month after month, building relationships.

So if you need business fast, networking may not your best choice. Networking is like planting a garden; you don't get to enjoy an ongoing harvest unless you've planted, watered, and nurtured the seeds through the growing season. With networking, however, you never know ahead of time how long the growing season will be. You could serendipitously get a major client on your first foray, or it could be months before your efforts pay off. The adage "A watched pot never boils" applies directly to networking. If your attention is always on when you will get your next referral or contact, you may overlook the best opportunities and you'll most certainly find networking a frustrating and unrewarding process. After all, what seedling can grow to maturity if the farmer is always digging it up to see how it's doing?

But if you have a good product or service that the people you are networking with need, time is on your side. As long as you are networking with people who need and can afford to buy what you have to offer, you can relax and continue participating wholeheartedly until your investment bears fruit. Meanwhile, networking can be working for you in ways that aren't immediately apparent because it provides you with visibility. Visibility begets familiarity; and familiarity begets credibility. When I, Laura, first moved to Lancaster to take over MAX International paper company, I didn't know anyone other than those I worked with in the company. That first spring when MAX tried a direct-mail piece to Chamber of Commerce members promoting our facsimile paper, there was not a single response.

I spent the next year becoming involved in Chamber activities. I started attending breakfast meetings. I volunteered for one Special Interest Group (SIG) committee and served as a Chamber Ambassador working on membership retention. A year and a bit later I was on the Steering Committee of the Small Business SIG and incoming chair of the programs committee. Our next mailing, which went out to the same list, netted fifty-seven new customers in six weeks—a better than 6 percent response rate! The only difference was visibility. But that's not all; I made a lot of good friends, too.

Wherever you are in today's global village, when you're in the right place at the right time, things once thought to be difficult become amazingly simple. Networking, in person or electronically, is one of the most certain means for making sure you are in the right place at the right time. Just think about it. Wouldn't you prefer to do business with someone you know and trust or someone who has come recommended to you by such a person? Most of us would. For this reason, the more people you meet, the more likely you are to find people to do business with. And, of course, out of sight is out of mind. So the more you keep in touch with the people you know, the more likely they will turn into customers and clients. This is the primary advantage of networking your way to more business.

Best Bets: Networking can be effective in almost any type of business as long as you can identify activities and events where you can meet potential clients, customers, and referral sources. It can even work well for product businesses as a way to find reps, distributors, wholesalers, etc.

Tips for Getting Results from Networking

Since networking is time-consuming, you want to make sure you're investing your time wisely. Some people network themselves into exhaustion and wonder why they don't get more business from the efforts. Showing up and pressing the flesh is simply not enough. There is an art to networking effectively. Here are a few key tips:

Network in fertile ground. The key to getting results from networking is to be sure you're networking in fertile ground. By that we mean, you want to choose where you network carefully so that you'll be sure to encounter an ample number of people who need and are interested in the kind of service or product you have to offer. You can network until the cows come home and have some wonderful experiences, but if you're networking in barren fields you won't get business.

To make sure you're networking in fertile ground, identify places and events where your customers and clients gather and arrange to frequent them yourself. Make sure to join organizations whose members are either potential clients themselves or who serve your potential clients. Networking requires too much time and energy to become involved in groups that only marginally or peripherally address your market.

For example, if, like clinical psychologist Art Weingaertner, you do psychological testing, you might want to join an organization whose members include educators or lawyers, both of whom regularly make referrals for such testing. If you sell health and fitness products, you might wish to become active in a sports club or health organization. I,

Laura, am a member of a number of trade organizations including PROMAX (Promotion and Marketing Executives in the Electronic Media) and EFTA (Electronic Funds Transfer Association). Neither of these organizations pertains to paper people but rather to companies who are customers of my company, the MAX. The meetings, seminars, and conferences provide golden opportunities for introductions, connections, and networking. Even when an event provides no new business, it always provides information that will be helpful to me in getting business and serving my clients better.

Of course, informal networking can be and is done just about everywhere, including churches, social gatherings, sports events, and so forth. Often it happens quite coincidentally, as with the aforementioned sales rep on the airplane. But even informal networking need not be left to chance. Here's how artist Carol Steinberg used networking to get her independent career under way. She developed a plan to attend as many shows at local art galleries as possible and was amazed at the business contacts she was able to make. A career counselor developed a similar plan to build her business. She attended every introductory personal-growth seminar she could, because people who attend such events often want to change careers. During each seminar, she made a point of asking a question or making a comment that allowed her to introduce herself and her work. When a seminar ended, several people would invariably approach her to ask about her services.

Both of these networking strategies are ideal for a business that is starting out on a shoestring. The only investment they require is time and the willingness to speak out. And since both these networkers enjoy going to such events anyway, it is a pleasant way to get business. There are more formal channels through which to network, however, ranging from professional and trade organizations to civic groups such as the Rotary; clubs like the Eagles, the Elks, or the Lions; or such business associations as the Chamber of Commerce. Explore various options (see **Where to Network** below) until you find ones that will be fertile ground for your business.

Attend meetings regularly. Simply being listed in a membership directory or showing up at the annual awards dinner is rarely the basis for making lasting business contacts. It takes repeated interaction to build rapport. To use networking effectively, set aside time on your calendar to attend at least two organizational meetings a week. Sometimes individuals who are newly self-employed worry about spending their time in so-called "socializing." But remember, business is a social

Where to Network: Five Types of Networking Groups

As we've said, you can network just about anywhere. Family and friends are the oldest networks of all. They have launched many businesses, as have members of civic and professional organizations. Most communities have a rich array of informal and formal business networking opportunities. In fact, there are basically five different types of networking groups you might want to consider participating in. Any one of them can become a doorway to a rich array of teaming-up activities. For names and addresses of such organizations see the Resource list at the end of this section on networking.

1. **Business Organizations.** The local Chambers of Commerce found in virtually every city around the country are one of the most popular examples of this type of network. Other examples include women's referral networks, singles' or women's business organizations like the National Association of Women Business Owners, home-business associations, and other small-business organizations. Any number of people from all kinds of professions can network through such organizations. Their goals are to share information among members, listen to business presentations of general interest to the entire group, lobby for local legislation that might be useful to the business community, and mingle informally with one another to develop friendships and business leads. They usually meet monthly for lunch or dinner, although they may also sponsor seminars, expos, or conferences throughout the year. Members are free to come to as many or as few meetings as they wish.

2. **Leads Clubs.** These networks exist for the expressed purpose of generating business leads and referrals for the members. Each group or chapter usually restricts membership to one person from any given profession or specialty. In other words, each leads club is open to just one accountant, one lawyer, one management consultant, one dentist, chiropractor, etc. Meetings are usually held weekly over breakfast, lunch, or dinner. Members are expected to attend all meetings, which often follow a formal procedure that begins with a member giving a presentation about his or her business so that other members can make more effective referrals. Members then exchange leads or referrals, and of course there is usually time for informal networking. Some leads groups require members to bring at least one referral to each meeting or pay a fine. Some groups also require chapter members to

carry the business cards of other members with them to further facilitate making referrals. National leads clubs with local chapters throughout the country include such organizations as Business Network International, LEADS Clubs, and Le Tip International. (To contact these organizations, see **Networking Resources** at the end of this section.)

3. **Community-Service Clubs:** Community-service clubs are dedicated to performing public service for various causes through fund-raisers and volunteer activities. These include groups like Rotary International, Lions, and Kiwanis as well as church- or religious-affiliated associations. In general, overt networking for business purposes is discouraged; however, informal networking can still be quite effective. In the process of "giving something back" to your community, you can meet movers and shakers in your area and often, as a byproduct of volunteering time or cash contributions, you can make valuable contacts that lead to future business relationships.

4. **Professional Associations:** Professional associations are a valuable way to establish relationships with colleagues in your field. Such contacts can often be sources of valuable leads, referrals, cutting-edge information, support, and overload exchanges. Contacts can also grow into long-term teaming-up arrangements of a more committed nature. Participation at national, regional, and local levels can provide many teaming-up opportunities. One way to locate professional and trade organizations is through the Gale Research Encyclopedia of Associations or Finderbinder and Sourcebook Directories, which list local media sources and clubs, groups, and associations in major metropolitan areas (see **Networking Resources** below).

5. **On-Line Networking Groups:** A growing wealth of on-line computer networks provides rich opportunities to link up with potential partners and associates across the nation and around the world. Networking through services such as CompuServe, America Online, and the Internet magnifies your ability to make contact a hundredfold. You can join interest groups, chat with people over bulletin boards, access E-mail, and attend live conferences at any time, twenty-four hours a day. The Court Reporter's Forum or the PR and Marketing Forum on CompuServe, or the Medical Transcriptionist bulletin board on America Online are examples of the type of formal on-line network organizations available to business people in almost every profession.

process. If you have joined suitable organizations, there is nothing frivolous about such activity. It is a legitimate marketing task. Any costs involved are business expenses and as such are tax deductible if you've kept proper records.

Even at times when you have plenty of business, you are best advised to remain active in at least one such group, because generating business takes time. If you wait to start networking until you need business, you may face a long dry spell while you get back into circulation and attract more business. And since out of sight is out of mind, you need to be around when someone you talked with six months ago suddenly needs what you offer. If you're not and someone else is, you know who will end up with the business.

Marketing consultant Robbie Bogue finds that getting dressed in professional attire at the beginning of the workday makes it easier for him to actually get out to luncheon and evening networking events because he's already dressed and ready to go when the time comes. He also recommends that once you get to an event, don't stand around with appetizers and drinks in your hands or you won't get much networking done.

Take the initiative to meet new people. To make the most of any networking activity, make a point of meeting new people at whatever events you attend or participate in. Don't allow yourself to fall into the rut of talking, sitting, or E-mailing only with your buddies. Don't latch on to one person and spend all your time with him or her. You both may enjoy yourselves, but you won't get business by huddling with one person. So circulate. Meet as many people as possible. The more people you meet, the more people you can build business relationships with. Balance your time between reconnecting with people you've met before and meeting others. Set a goal to meet at least five new people before you settle in with old friends.

Also, once you make a promising contact, don't monopolize his or her time in an in-depth one-on-one conversation. Save longer, private conversations for a follow-up contact. Strive to include others who approach you in whatever conversations you're having.

By making an effort to meet new people at every event, you will generate a steady stream of new contacts. Encourage your organization to launch an active membership-recruitment drive or guest program. You might even volunteer to serve as chair of the membership committee or act as a greeter at meetings, welcoming first-time visitors and new members. Serving in an official greeting capacity is one of the best ways to overcome networking shyness.

On the other hand, avoid the temptation to press your card into everyone's hand and rush on to the next person or the next event. If you're going to take the time to network, take the time to do it right and show a personal interest in each person you meet.

Become an active member. The best way to build relationships is to interact frequently with other people in goal-directed activities. You can make contacts by attending meetings or sitting in on chat sessions, but getting involved in goal-directed group activities builds relationships that can develop into business. This is why people who work inside a company often build strong and lasting bonds with co-workers. As a self-employed individual, you have to make your own opportunities for such long-term group interaction. So participate in the activities of any organization you join. Serve on a committee. Lead a special-interest section on-line. If a group has a sports team, a community project, a fund-raising event, or a committee structure, volunteer to participate in these events. You'll earn respect and trust from the team effort and from sharing a history of accomplishment.

And when you participate, don't settle for being a faceless body in the crowd; make a noticeable contribution. Stand out by taking a leadership role. Work your way into the power structure of the group and establish yourself as a valued resource. If you ever doubt the rewards of this approach in terms of increased business, just keep track of what happens to someone's business when that person becomes president of a major charity or trade organization. Follow the person's progress over a year or two, and you will see why we advise this strategy.

Follow up on contacts you make. When you are actively seeking business, we suggest scheduling no fewer than two business meals each week; have breakfast, lunch, or dinner with people you've met through networking. At these meetings, find out how you can help them succeed in their business. Take the time to ask questions, and listen to find out more about what they do. Your interest in them is what will make you interesting to them and make them more open to learning about what you do.

When you get busy, you can follow up on networking contacts by phone or by mail. For personal and business services, however, these contacts are rarely as fruitful as personal ones. Some small-business owners decide to do as Chellie Campbell does. Whenever her book-

11 Tips for Face-to-Face Networking

Sometimes people wonder why they don't get better results from their face-to-face networking efforts. Usually it is because they are not making the most of their networking opportunities. Here are a dozen things you can do to improve your track record.

1. **Arrive at meetings and group activities at least fifteen minutes early.** Always attend the social hour if there is one. This is the time when the most networking occurs. Once the program has started, there is usually little time for networking.

2. **Stop waiting for something to happen.** Sometimes we hear people complain that they have attended various events hoping to network but "nothing happened." They didn't meet anyone. In probing further, we find these people are approaching the networking event as if they were guests, waiting for someone to introduce them. Instead, approach the event as if you are the host, greeting people yourself. Strike up a conversation. If you smile and extend your hand, 99 percent of the people you meet will smile back and introduce themselves in return. If not, you can simply add, "I don't think we've met." Don't wait to be introduced or included in conversations. Instead of milling around in the hope that someone will engage you, initiate conversations by asking simple questions like "What do you do?" "How did you hear about this event?" or "Have you heard tonight's speaker before?"

3. **Always use your "File-Opening Sound Byte."** And say it with your head up and a big smile on your face. This is one time you have a chance to toot your own horn and you need to show your pride in what you do. A shy, timid voice stating "Uh, er, well . . . I have a bookkeeping service" will neither be memorable nor give your prospect any confidence in your competence. If you are not confident, your clients won't be either.

4. **Carry a large stack of business cards at all times.** The greatest networking sin of all is to forget or run out of business cards. Keep them wherever it is most convenient, but always have them handy. An efficient system for exchanging business cards is to keep your cards in one jacket or skirt pocket and put those you receive in the other.

5. **Make sure you get a business card from every appropriate contact you make.** Then you can follow up by calling your contacts later. The primary reason for giving out your business card is so you can get the cards of others in return. Never leave it up to those you want to talk with to contact you—always take the initiative yourself.

6. **Have a pen or pencil handy.** Make notes on the cards you collect about where and when you met the people, any special information about them, and what you want to discuss with them in the future. Don't rely on memory. Since most business cards are undistinguished, chances are two weeks after getting a card you'll have no idea who gave it to you or why you kept it.

7. **Make your name tag work for you.** Don't just put your first name on the tag. In large, clear letters, print your full name and the name of your company. Wear your name tag on your **right** side so people can easily see it when they shake hands with you.

8. **Concentrate on talking with one person at a time.** The second greatest sin in networking is the roving eye. Although it is easy to be distracted, focus your entire attention on the conversation at hand, even if the individual is not a prospect. No one wants to get the impression that you are looking for something better to come along. Don't rush madly from person to person. If you are too much of a go-getter, people will get up and go—away. Over the long term, you will do far better talking sincerely with a few people.

   So don't scout the room for who else is around while you're talking with someone. Make eye contact. Listen. Finish your conversation and then scan the room for others you want to talk with. Research shows that three seconds of eye contact is most effective. Less seems inattentive; more signals intimacy or feels intimidating.

   Usually social interaction goes through a natural conversational cycle, so as soon as a conversation winds down of its own accord, feel free to move on to meeting and talking with others. You can wrap up a conversation graciously by concluding with a customary exit line like "I've enjoyed meeting you," "I'll look forward to seeing you at future meetings," or "Let's talk further later." Such exit lines also work well to extricate yourself from a conversation with someone who is talking on endlessly. You might simply comment, "Excuse me, I see someone I need to speak with. It's been a pleasure meeting you."

9. **Stay approximately fifteen minutes after the event.** Don't rush off quickly. Exchange cards with anyone you met earlier, and wrap up any previously unfinished conversations. Take a moment to say good-bye to anyone you met for the first time or haven't seen for a long time. But, unless you are helping with the cleanup, don't hang around forever.

10. ***Follow up fast with a phone call, meeting, or note.*** If someone you met expressed specific interest in doing business with you, you need to follow up immediately. Call the next day and arrange a meeting. Send selected materials from your presentation kit for perusal before the meeting. (See chapter 8 for how to put together such a kit.)

    You probably won't be able to make a follow-up appointment with everyone you have met, but if there might be any future business value from these contacts, you can at least call the next day. First meetings make first impressions, but following up by phone cements them. These short calls can also provide you an opportunity to determine whether an appointment will be a worthwhile investment of your time.

    If you know for sure that a phone call so soon might not be appropriate, send a handwritten note instead. It still shows the personal touch without any pressure. But be sure to incorporate your "Sound Byte" into your note or letter. Then periodically send news clippings, reports, or announcements you think will be of interest to them. Include information about your recent activities.

11. **Always send a thank-you note or place a call of thanks to anyone who sends you a referral.** When someone has sent you several referrals or one that's particularly profitable, give that person an additional special acknowledgment. Take the person to dinner, send flowers, or give a party to introduce him or her to others.

keeping service, Cameron Diversified Management, grows to the point that she has no time left for networking and follow-up, she adds new personnel. Her service has grown from a two-person to a six-person business in six years.

Actively refer business regularly to others. This may be the most important tip of successful networking. People refer business to those who refer business to them. "Givers gain," Ivan Misner, founder of the

Business Network International, emphasizes. So, make a list of every other business service or product your clients and customers need. Locate people who provide each of these needs to whom you can make referrals *with confidence*. Establish a relationship with these people whereby you will refer clients to one another. Then, whenever someone you are talking with needs a service in your network, volunteer to put her in touch with the resource she needs. You'll become a walking Yellow Pages. And the more you give, the more you'll get.

11 Tips for Networking On-Line

1. **Never confuse advertising with networking.** While there are ways to advertise on-line both for fee and for free (see **Advertising On-Line** in **chapter 11**), when networking on-line, you must exercise restraint in promoting yourself. People are looking for ideas, advice, colleagues, and help. Most people resent a sales pitch or even a self-serving promotion.
2. **Think collegial and interactive.** Just as face-to-face networking is a two-way process among colleagues and peers, so is on-line networking. Visit newsgroups and forums and join Internet mailing lists that relate to your field, review ongoing conversations and think about how you could join in the dialogue and make a contribution based on your expertise and your curiosity. Asking good questions is a contribution, too.
3. **Visit promising sites often.** Just as attending in-person networking meetings regularly is important, being visible on-line regularly is also important. You don't build relationships by dropping a message here and there and rushing on to other sites. You will develop on-line business through establishing ongoing relationships.
4. **Provide personal responses.** The more personal you can make your communication the better, so respond to concerns and queries of particular individuals whenever possible.
5. **Provide valued information.** When leaving messages for an entire forum or newsgroup, focus on tips, trends, new information, or recent discoveries you've made in your work that would be of high interest and practical use to others. You might want to post a tip sheet, your newsletter, or segments from your informative booklet if you have one. Just be sure the information you post is informative, and no more than subtly promotional.

6. **Limit your messages to one idea and keep that one idea to one screen.** It's better to leave separate messages than one long message. People avoid reading long messages. So if you have a lot to say, don't say it all at once. On the other hand, being overly terse—saying "Thanks" or "Ditto" with only your signature—is an irritant.

7. **Check in frequently and respond quickly.** There is an immediacy to on-line networking. If someone leaves a message, she wants a quick response. If you have left messages on a board or with a newsgroup, you should check in regularly to read responses and, where appropriate, reply to them.

8. **Post how people can reach you.** Most forums and sites will allow you to follow your signature with your company name and your Web site. Many will allow street and E-mail addresses and phone numbers, and some permit slogans. A descriptive business name helps on-line as much as in the Yellow Pages. Steve O'Keefe, author of ***Publicity on the Internet***, advises, "Let your signature do your selling."

9. **Avoid hassles.** Refrain from personally criticizing anyone and, by all means, stay away from characterizing people with generalizations like "argumentative" and "small-minded." As you would not like to be a victim in a flame war, don't be a persecutor. If you must defend yourself or your product, stick to facts and specifics.

10. **Seek out useful and appropriate forums and groups.** Make sure you're spending your time where people who might buy or influence your business gather. It's virtually always a mistake to think of a subject area that has nothing to do with your business as "virgin" territory. People simply regard the intrusion of content unrelated to their group as obnoxious.

11. **Create your own on-line networking group.** If you don't find a suitable on-line group for your niche, consider establishing your own. This might take the form of an Internet mailing list, a newsgroup, a Web site, or a forum on an on-line service. One benefit of playing the central role is that you can both demonstrate and acquire expertise recognized by others.

High-Touch Tip: Creating Your Own Networking Group

If you can't find a networking group that meets your needs, you can do what so many others have done: form your own. Many of the organizations we've mentioned provide assistance in establishing new chapters, or you simply create your own group. That's what we, Paul and Sarah, did when we moved to Los Angeles many years ago. We began what we called the Community Network, and each month we hosted a potluck dinner for about twenty of our neighbors and suppliers. During the evening all the attendees would introduce themselves to the group, explain what they did, and what kind of contacts they were hoping to make. Through this informal social network, we ended up meeting contacts, some of whom we continue to do business with today. We also formed many friendships that have lasted for years.

When fiber artist Cameron Taylor-Brown moved to Los Angeles, she too found no ready-made networking group to affiliate with. However, when one of her works was published in *Fiber Arts* magazine, she had an idea. Cameron contacted all the other artists whose work had been displayed in that issue of the magazine and invited them to join with her in putting together a portfolio and presentation binder. She then began showing the joint portfolio to galleries in the area. The portfolio attracted the attention of the cultural affairs department of Los Angeles, who agreed to do a show in a Woodland Hills gallery featuring her and her newly created "network" of artists.

Here are seven steps you can take to create your own business-generating group.

1. ***Identify four to six other individuals whose businesses are compatible with yours.*** They can be your suppliers, customers, individuals you have done joint ventures with, other professionals whom your existing clients and customers rely upon, or colleagues who do different aspects of what you do.

2. ***Get to know these individuals well.*** The better you know them and how they work before you form your group, the better your group will be. You must be sure you can recommend them highly, because making a bad referral can damage your own reputation, not to mention destroy your newly formed group.

3. ***Build the group one by one.*** For a personal networking group to work well, each of the members must get along with and respect the others. Getting a mix of professionals who are compatible can be quite a trick, so we suggest that you begin by meeting with one of the key individuals you have in mind to discuss the idea of forming a networking group. Find out in detail what he or she does, what goals and dreams there are for the business, and how you and others could assist in the achievement of those dreams if you formed a group together. If this individual is interested in building a group with you, discuss and agree upon the purpose, process, time, location, and frequency of your regular meetings. Then ask this individual to meet informally with you and another of the professionals you have in mind.

Also offer to meet with any individual whom he or she would like to have as part of the group. The purpose of these meetings is simply for potential group members to meet one another and get acquainted. If, after this exploratory meeting, you mutually decide that a person would be a good addition to your group, invite that person to join you for the next meeting and present him or her with the idea of joining. Continue the process of exploratory meetings, adding one person at a time—three people meeting with a fourth, four with a fifth, and so on—until you have found as many members as you wish with whom everyone would like to network regularly.

Exploratory meetings can in themselves be excellent networking opportunities even if the individuals involved don't fit well into the group.

4. ***Look for successful colleagues who are team players.*** Individuals you include should be reasonably successful already so each can make a contribution to others (unless everyone in your group is just starting on their own). Avoid competitive individuals who have to be the center of attention or want to be sure they are one up on their peers. Select people who believe there is opportunity in the world for everyone to profit and who enjoy sharing their success with others.

5. ***Decide collectively how the meetings should be conducted.*** Since you are forming a group of colleagues and peers, you will want it to develop its own rules and procedures. Essentially, you have taken the leadership role in forming the group and giving it enough structure to get under way. By building it person by person, you

should now have a compatible group of people who share similar goals and objectives. Getting agreement at this point should be easy.

6. ***Keep administrative decisions to a bare minimum.*** There is nothing that will kill a networking group of business professionals quicker than long discussions over time, place, rules, and procedures. Having built the group one by one should prevent this, but if disagreements do arise about details, don't use your meeting time to solve them. You are meeting to assist one another's businesses to flourish. Volunteer to invest time before the next meeting to poll everyone's needs and concerns so a satisfactory solution can be reached quickly at that meeting.

7. ***Serve as a model by making a lot of referrals.*** If you want to get referrals from the group, begin the process by providing them yourself. The referrals you make do not always have to be for potential clients. Be forthcoming with whatever information, resources, contacts, leads, or ideas you can provide to help everyone in the group succeed beyond their expectations. If you have chosen the right people, they will be grateful and eager to reciprocate. There are several processes you can use during meetings to assist one another:

- Each person can identify the one thing he or she would like assistance in achieving. The group can brainstorm possible ideas and referrals.
- Members can describe how they would like their business to be six months from now, and again everyone can offer ideas, leads, and referrals.
- Each person can bring the name of one individual he or she thinks other members of the group would benefit from contacting and describe why.
- Group members can share "wins," positive, exciting news and developments in their business. Often these wins uncover possible opportunities for other members of the group. For example, when one member of a networking group announced enthusiastically that she was going to be speaking at a special series of seminars for a local department store, other members quickly requested how they too might become involved. Phone numbers were exchanged, and ultmately they were all included in this excellent promotional opportunity.

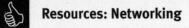

Resources: Networking

Books

Fishing with a Net: How to Do Business on the Internet. 1998, Mike Rounds. Rounds Miller & Associates, 6318 Ridgepath Court, Rancho Palos Verdes, CA 90275, (310) 544-9502.

Guerrilla Marketing On Line. Jay Conrad Levison. New York: Houghton Mifflin, 1995.

Networking for Success, How to Turn Business and Financial Relationships into Fun and Profit. Anne Boe. Deerfield, FL: Health Communications, 1995, (954) 360-0909.

How to Work a Room. Susan RoAne. New York: Warner, 1995.

Power Schmoozing. Terri Mandell. New York: McGraw-Hill, 1996.

The Secrets to Savvy Networking. Susan RoAne. New York: Warner, 1995.

Smart Networking. Anne Baber and Lynne Waymon. Dubuque, IA: Kendall/Hunt Publishing, 1997.

Work-of-Mouth Marketing. Jerry R. Wilson. New York: Wiley, 1994.

National Networking Organizations

Call or write to find out about the chapter nearest you of any of these organizations or for information on starting a new chapter.

Business Network International, 199 South Monte Vista Avenue, Ste. 6, San Dimas, CA 91773-3080, (800) 825-8286, (909) 305-1818, www.bni.com

Leads Club, P.O. Box 279, Carlsbad, CA 92018-0279, (760) 434-3761, (800) 783-3761, www.leadsclub.com

LeTip, International, 4907 Marina Blvd., Ste. 13, San Diego, CA 92117, (800) 255-3847, www.letip.org

Speeches and Seminars

When Harriet Schechter started her business as a professional organizer in San Diego, she had no intention of doing any public speaking or teaching any classes. But she now gets 60 to 75 percent of her business from offering speeches

and workshops on how to clean out the clutter in your life and get and stay organized. Speaking is not only her primary source of clients; it also provides her with an additional source of income. She finds her speaking fees are rising more rapidly than her consulting fees.

Speaking or presenting a seminar on the right topic before the right audience can build both your business and your reputation as an expert in your field. This is particularly true if, like Schechter's, your business is service or information related. If you enjoy speaking and can turn the expertise that makes you effective in your work into a speech, that speech or seminar can bring you valued credibility, exposure, and business.

On any given day there are estimated to be more than nine thousand speaking opportunities in this country. According to *Speak and Grow Rich,* by Dottie and Lilly Walters, associations and corporations alone held nearly one million meetings in 1995. The Walterses predict this number will continue to grow despite the proliferation of electronic communication like video conferencing, on-line classes, and satellite seminars. Of course, these figures don't even include local meetings and conferences or private and church-sponsored events.

Every day, clubs, organizations, and groups in your community, as well as professional and trade associations, are looking for speakers and workshop leaders to give presentations on topics of interest to their members at breakfast and lunch meetings, annual meetings, special events, in-house training programs, conferences, symposiums, and conventions. Informative, entertaining speakers—especially free ones—are in great demand.

Although some of these events may pay their presenters a speaking fee, most such opportunities will either involve no fee or a very low honorarium to cover the speaker's expenses. Unless you intend to develop a full or sideline business from your speaking, however, that should not be considered a drawback. The opportunity to present your expertise before the right groups can be well worth the investment of your time and energy in terms of exposure, credibility, and potential business.

For example, when actress Sandy McKnight decided to create a new business for herself offering speech and diction classes, she built her business almost entirely at first by giving free speeches on how to improve a telephone image to local Chambers of Commerce and other professional business groups. Mike Anderson, creator of Mad Mike's Burger Spread, has used speeches and public appearances to boost sales of his hamburger spread, and Heidi Miller of Heidi's Frozen Yogurt used public appearances extensively to propel her first yogurt shop in Orange County, California, into a national franchise. Mike speaks forcefully on antidrug topics; his theme is "get high on life." Heidi spoke first on health and fitness topics and later on business opportunities, especially for women.

Alternatively, you might want to host your own free or fee seminars for prospective clients and customers. This is how Marie Moran launched her corporate speaking business. She hosted a free day-long seminar at a nice hotel with a luncheon included, for key referral sources, HRD directors, and other prospective clients. The event was by invitation only and was a highly successful way for her to gain high visibility and establish credibility quickly in a new field.

Your seminars and presentations need not be limited to face-to-face experiences. You can provide seminars by satellite and on-line through the Internet or an on-line service. Stormy Knight, for example, was running a mail-order catalog company selling environmentally safe products, but the cost of printing the catalogs was escalating so she decided to investigate selling her products over the World Wide Web. After fourteen months the new business, Net 101, has been "wildly successful" and Knight's number-one promotional method has been to offer free Internet training seminars for the first few months.

Pros and Cons of Giving Speeches and Seminars

Giving a speech or seminar not only positions you as a respected expert; it also gives people the chance to experience your expertise firsthand. You have the chance to establish rapport and build a relationship with an entire group of people all at once. So, in this sense, it's a time-saver that preserves many of the advantages of giving free consultations. Giv-

High-Tech Tip: Satellite Seminars

While certainly not for everyone, satellite seminars are one way to reach customers in major markets throughout the country without the wear and tear and cost of traveling or marketing to each city individually. Via satellite, your workshop or seminar can be uplinked to hotel sites across the country. Sales from your seminars can be augmented with product sales or exhibits on site. For information on setting up satellite seminars, contact FMG Satellite Seminars at 1-800-529-7599.

ing speeches and seminars also gives you a chance to build an excellent list of people with whom you can follow up later in person, by phone, or through the mail. In addition, if you can get paid to speak, even a small honorarium, you can bring in additional income and thereby offset some of your marketing expenses.

Michael Wyland has found this to be true for his business, Sumption and Wyland. He does grant writing, training, and strategic planning for state and local governments, universities, and nonprofit organizations. He promotes his business by appearing as a guest lecturer at local universities, vocational and trade schools, and community colleges. "It's amazing," he says "how many professors are looking to add a little 'spice' to their classes through bringing practitioners into the classroom." He finds guest lecturing provides credibility and stature, entrée to faculty and administrators who may need his services, and referrals from students to their employers.

Offering speeches or seminars is also an excellent way to test out marketing ideas and get instant feedback on the needs, interests, problems, and preferences of your potential clients. In a sense, your seminar or speech can be like a living laboratory for learning and understanding more about the people you want to serve. You can also use general trends and observations you glean from seminars to increase your mastery and as elements in other marketing activities.

On the other hand, getting booked, planning, and arranging for speaking and seminar engagements can be time-consuming. And often it is a long-term process. Some organizations, conventions, and expos book their programs many months and even a full year ahead. So, usually getting an opportunity to speak to groups that have the best potential for generating business will not be a short-term spur-of-the-moment strategy for getting business fast.

Also, it is not worth making a speech or presenting a seminar unless you can do it well and totally professionally. You don't want to risk damaging your reputation by appearing disorganized, inarticulate, or uninformed. This means you will probably need to tailor your speech content to each particular audience and prepare professional handouts and visual aids. It may mean taking a presentation skills course or hiring a speaking coach. Usually in order to get booked to present your speech or seminar, you will need to send a professional presentation kit (see chapter 8) along with descriptions of your proposed speech or seminar. Sometimes you will be asked to provide an audio- or videotape of yourself speaking as well as references or letters of recommendation from other organizations who have heard you speak.

And, of course, while you may get business on the spot, there's no guarantee you will get any business from a particular speech or seminar. In many cases, speaking or giving seminars becomes part of an overall marketing strategy to become known and respected in your field. It can enhance other marketing efforts by giving you credibility and visibility. You may even get business or a referral from someone who was in one of your audiences years ago.

Best Bets: Offering speeches and seminars is most effective as a way to promote service businesses, especially services to business buyers and professionals. It can also be quite effective in offering high-ticket products to businesses.

Tips for Getting Results from Speeches and Seminars

Getting business as a result of making speeches or giving seminars depends to a large extent upon what you say and how you say it. A presentation that receives rave reviews and glowing compliments may not lead to business unless you're talking about the right things with the right people in the right way. Here are several tips for how to give good speeches that also lead to business.

Find a winning topic. The topic you select to speak about will need to be appealing to your potential clientele and show off your unique expertise and experience. Dottie and Lilly Walters, co-authors of the book *Speak and Grow Rich,* recommend that you begin by considering your particular niche or specialty—what you want to become known for—and then survey your potential audience to find out "what hurts." In other words, they suggest identifying the major problems your audience faces and selecting a speech topic that will demonstrate your expertise at solving those problems. Here are a few examples:

- A psychologist who specializes in counseling singles speaks to singles groups on topics related to finding a mate, such as dealing with rejection and understanding the differences between the ways men and women think.
- The owner of an indoor-and-outdoor plant service speaks to business groups about using plants to boost office morale and productivity.
- An accountant speaks to corporations about new changes in the tax law that will affect the corporate bottom line.

- The owner of a gymnastics school for children speaks to parent groups on the positive and negative effects of sports on a child's self-esteem.
- A sales trainer offers a free seminar on how to work a booth for the exhibitors at local trade shows.
- A literary agent speaks to writers' groups on how to get a publisher.
- An information broker speaks to business groups about how to find information on one's competitors through public sources.

One way to test your topics is to present several related ones to meeting planners and let them select the one most appealing to their audience. You'll find that meeting planners will choose your most effective topics again and again. And, of course, you will continually need to develop new topics to stay current and relevant to the issues facing your customers and clients.

If you have trouble identifying a unique topic, experiment with standard ones such as "How to Select a . . . ," "When You Need a . . . ," "What You Should Know about . . . ," or "How to Overcome the Top 10 Problems for . . . ," filling in your particular field of expertise.

Find the right audience. Equally important as identifying your topic is identifying the groups, organizations, and associations to whom you want to speak. Your goal is to speak to groups that include large numbers of your prospective clients or customers. One of the easiest ways to find these groups would be to ask current or prospective clients and customers what organizations they belong to and participate in.

Consulting the *Encyclopedia of Associations,* published by Gale Research, is another way to locate groups to speak before. This directory lists national professional and trade associations, and a second volume includes local and state chapters. Another valuable library resource is *The Directory of United States Trade Shows, Expositions and Conventions,* published by the U.S. Travel Service of the U.S. Department of Commerce. This directory lists when and where the major shows are scheduled throughout the country.

Usually you do not need to be a member of these organizations or groups in order to speak before them. They are looking for speakers or presenters who have information their members need to know. Of course, you can also consider speaking before the civic, trade, professional, and networking organizations to which you do belong. Speaking to local, state, regional, and national organizations of which you are a member will facilitate fellow members' learning more about what you do and make your networking efforts more effective.

Most major urban areas have a variety of continuing-education programs that provide additional opportunities for speaking. Some such programs are affiliated with local colleges and universities. In addition, independent companies such as the Learning Annex provide a catalog of one-to-four-session seminars on a wide variety of topics. Teaching in these programs positions you as an expert. Your name and possibly your picture will be seen by thousands of people who look through the course catalog. Doing such programs also gives those who come a chance to sample your skills and approaches firsthand. You can begin building a relationship with the participants. If you have selected a course title that attracts the right audience, some of them will become customers based upon what they learn and experience from the classes you teach.

Teaching such courses was the sole source of business for computer programmer James Milburn, who taught evening computer-programming classes for small-business owners at a local trade school. Once they found out how difficult programming is, some of his students hired him either to do their programming or to consult with them on customizing off-the-shelf software. Two literary agents in Los Angeles regularly get clients from the class they co-teach on how to get published—so many that they have had to turn away business. And many of the people who attend psychotherapist Dr. Deborah Cooper's classes on relationships sign up for private counseling.

If your speech or seminar consistently does not result in business for you, you need to rethink the topic, the audiences you're speaking to, or the way you're presenting your material. When you talk about something your audience needs and present yourself effectively as someone who has it, at least a few people will want to engage you to provide it.

Here are some sample topics for adult-education seminars and people who might offer them:

The Internet vs. the Intranet, offered by a computer consultant

The Casual Way to Dress for Success, presented by an image/wardrobe consultant

How to Use Your Mouth to Get More Business: Networking Do's and Don'ts, taught by a business networking organizer

Publishing a Newsletter That Means Business, offered by the owner of a desktop publishing service

Collecting Those Bad Debts, presented by the head of a collection service

Get Rid of Clutter, taught by a professional organizer

Getting Anything You Need Without Cash, offered by a business barter service

Protect Your Ideas: Patents, Trademarks, and Copyrights, conducted by a lawyer specializing in intellectual property

Once you have selected your topic and located organizations to which you want to speak, find out the names of their meeting planners or program directors and introduce yourself to these people by phone. Tell them about your background and topic, and if they show some interest, send a presentation kit (**chapter 8**). Follow up with a second phone call to discuss setting up a speaking date.

Surveys from the National Speakers Association suggest that most speakers are hired by word of mouth or from actual experience of having heard a presentation, so speaking can lead to more speaking.

Do more than show and tell. Often getting business from speeches and seminars involves more than simply showing up and telling people what you know. Once your speech has been booked, do everything you can to make sure your presentation will actually lead to future business. Before the presentation, for example, find out as much as you can about your audience so you can tailor your speech to their interests. The more your speech addresses their needs, the more likely they are to want to do business with you.

Also try to arrange to have the organization announce your upcoming speech in a newsletter article that will provide your background, including your business name and your picture. Find out whether they will be sending a news release to local media as well. If they aren't, do so yourself. Such prepublicity helps establish you as an authority to the audience and also assists in attracting to the presentation those individuals who have the most interest in your topic, and thus in your business.

Do not leave the content of your introduction up to the whim of someone who has been asked to introduce you. Often this person is a volunteer who knows little about you and may have had limited experience speaking before a group. Instead, using your bio, write a brief introduction and give it to the meeting planner. A well-written introduction will establish your credibility, set you up as an expert, and predispose your audience to welcome you and your message enthusiastically.

In your introduction, describe your business, your niche, your background, and expertise, and perhaps even give a glowing quote about yourself. Do not be modest in writing your introduction. While you should not overstate your case, it is important to make a strong statement of your qualifications and accomplishments.

If there is no one available to introduce you, don't just launch into your speech. Take the time to welcome the audience and cover the points from your introduction so that people know to whom they will be listening.

Keep in mind that you are not giving a sales pitch, however. Usually even the hint of one will alienate your audience and embarrass and antagonize the program director or meeting planner who booked you to speak—a person who, when pleased with your appearance, becomes a referral source and can write a glowing letter of endorsement to add to promotional materials.

Structure your speech to make sales without selling. Fortunately, you can structure your speech to get business without giving a sales pitch. First, focus your speech on real-life nitty-gritty problems the potential clients in your audience face. Make sure you get to the heart of the matter. Address the reasons these problems occur; let your audience know you understand their situation. Second, provide realistic solutions that demonstrate your expertise, ***but don't tell them how to do everything they need to do.*** If you do, they will appreciate the information, possibly put it to work, but most likely see no need to engage your services.

For example, in her speech on how a business can improve its telephone image, speech-and-diction coach Sandy McKnight outlines the most common mistakes personnel make on the phone and demonstrates the bad image these poor phone skills create. By role-playing scenarios involving such mistakes, she gets her audience laughing and relating to these problems. She then outlines realistic solutions any company can use to train its personnel to speak effectively on the phone. Since few companies have the expertise to conduct this training themselves, however, many are immediately interested in having her give a seminar for their personnel or sending their personnel to attend her public seminars.

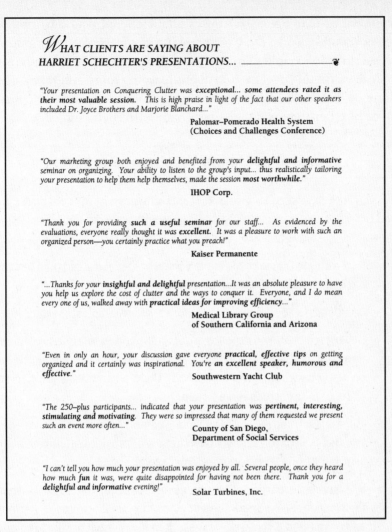

WHAT CLIENTS ARE SAYING ABOUT HARRIET SCHECHTER'S PRESENTATIONS...

"Your presentation on Conquering Clutter was ***exceptional... some attendees rated it as their most valuable session.*** *This is high praise in light of the fact that our other speakers included Dr. Joyce Brothers and Marjorie Blanchard..."*

Palomar–Pomerado Health System
(Choices and Challenges Conference)

"Our marketing group both enjoyed and benefited from your ***delightful and informative*** *seminar on organizing. Your ability to listen to the group's input... thus realistically tailoring your presentation to help them help themselves, made the session* ***most worthwhile.****"*

IHOP Corp.

"Thank you for providing ***such a useful seminar*** *for our staff... As evidenced by the evaluations, everyone really thought it was* ***excellent.*** *It was a pleasure to work with such an organized person—you certainly practice what you preach!"*

Kaiser Permanente

"...Thanks for your ***insightful and delightful*** *presentation...It was an absolute pleasure to have you help us explore the cost of clutter and the ways to conquer it. Everyone, and I do mean every one of us, walked away with* ***practical ideas for improving efficiency...****"*

Medical Library Group
of Southern California and Arizona

"Even in only an hour, your discussion gave everyone ***practical, effective tips*** *on getting organized and it certainly was inspirational. You're* ***an excellent speaker, humorous and effective.****"*

Southwestern Yacht Club

"The 250–plus participants... indicated that your presentation was ***pertinent, interesting, stimulating and motivating.*** *They were so impressed that many of them requested we present such an event more often..."*

County of San Diego,
Department of Social Services

"I can't tell you how much your presentation was enjoyed by all. Several people, once they heard how much ***fun*** *it was, were quite disappointed for having not been there. Thank you for a* ***delightful and informative*** *evening!"*

Solar Turbines, Inc.

SAMPLE ENDORSEMENTS FOR SPEAKING ENGAGEMENTS. *Including testimonials like these in the presentation kit you send to meeting planners helps them feel more confident about booking you to speak at upcoming meetings, conferences, and other events. Harriet Schechter has her endorsements printed on the inside back cover of her presentation kit.*

Similarly, in her speeches for singles groups, psychologist Dr. Deborah Cooper introduces the most common problems singles have in developing lasting, rewarding relationships. She presents these from both the male and the female perspective, and the audience readily identifies themselves and their dates. She then outlines and demonstrates new behaviors that men and women can learn to overcome these problems and describes many success stories about clients who have mastered these new dating skills. Dr. Cooper invites the audience to try out a few of these skills in sample mini-exercises. Once they experience how well her ideas work, they feel excited about learning more and many sign up for one of her seminars, make an appointment for a private consultation, or hire her to present a longer seminar to their company.

Terrified of Speaking? Turn Terror to Terrific!

So, you've been asked to give a speech and you've never spoken before. You can still enjoy the credibility that comes with a successful presentation. Here are some ways to make your debut a little easier.

- Find a single theme or message you want to convey and plan to come back to it again and again. Repetition is a plus.
- Don't make a speech; teach. Tell stories, give examples, use anecdotes.
- Never memorize your speech. You don't need to worry about forgetting what you want to say. You can cue yourself by outlining the key points you want to cover and putting them on an overhead projector, slide, or index card in large bold print.
- Think visual: move away from the podium; take stuff to show-and-tell; use flip charts, slides, or overheads, or provide a multimedia presentation using your notebook computer.
- Use audience participation whenever possible. Get them to share their experiences; break the audience into small groups or partners and have them discuss key issues; then invite them to share their observations and conclusions with the group.
- Check the physical layout at least a full hour ahead of time to avoid surprises and handle last-minute problems with equipment, lighting, climate, etc., so you will be free to concentrate 100 percent on what you have to say.

Stage fright is okay. We all have it. Remember, the audience isn't interested in you . . . they are interested in what you have to tell them. They will only judge you if you withhold your excitement from them. The more fun you have, the better you will be.

Deliver a winning presentation. Even the best information and most-valued expertise loses its impact when the speaker is hard to hear, disorganized, overly complex, or unclear. If you want to speak, you owe it to yourself to learn how to construct and deliver an effective speech. So, a prerequisite for getting business from your speeches is to deliver them in a professional, informative, and entertaining way. If people have thoroughly enjoyed hearing you and are eager for more, they are more likely to become customers.

If you have no experience in speaking, we therefore recommend taking a course in public speaking or presentation skills. Such courses are available from private seminar companies and at many local colleges or universities. In selecting such a course, make sure that it will include the opportunity to actually deliver several mini-speeches. Learning to speak is like learning to drive a car: you can't learn by reading about it or hearing how to do it. So, the more actual speeches you stand up and deliver in the course, the better. We also recommend choosing a course that provides videotape playback so you can review yourself speaking. Don't be intimidated by this. We, Paul and Sarah, have trained hundreds of people to speak effectively and 99 percent of those we've trained are amazed at how much better they look than they expected. As you watch yourself improve, you will develop an increasingly positive image of yourself as a speaker.

Here are a few tips to help you make your presentations sizzle:

1. Do not read your speech. Work from an outline or from note cards with key words that trigger your memory.

2. Be sure to keep within the time limit given to you. Time your talk to leave you some leeway for questions if they are applicable.

3. If you approach your time limit before you reach the end of your speech, skip immediately to your closing statement and end with an upbeat summary.

4. Keep in touch with your audience. If you see eyes starting to glaze over, hear a lot of feet shuffling, or notice people heading for the door, try something different—fast! Ask some engaging questions, invite the audience to share their experiences, or do something dramatic or startling. Even a prolonged pause can bring people's attention back to you.

5. Talk neither over the heads of your audience, using jargon, nor down to them. Respect their intelligence.

Even if a speech does not produce any immediate business, keep in mind that by addressing a group of potential clients or customers you have increased your visibility and your credibility. And you have opened the doors to new contacts with whom you can develop long-term relationships.

Make it easy to buy. Although making a speech is more often a matter of planting a seed that will lead to business later, you can sometimes get business at the speaking event itself. So always have brochures, order forms, or other materials handy. Arranging to take MasterCard or Visa can make signing up right then and there easier as can having a "bill me later" statement. Having a guarantee or making a special offer for attendees can also help.

Follow-up. To generate more business from any speech or seminar, get the name, phone number, address, and E-mail of everyone in your audience. There are several ways to do this. One is to offer a free drawing in which you have all participants place their business cards in a bowl and give away something of value to the lucky winner whose card is drawn; another is to give a special prize to everyone who fills out a questionnaire of some kind. Or you can announce that all who wish to receive further information can leave their cards with you at the close of the program. You will probably get fewer cards using this latter approach, but the cards you get will be more likely to result in business.

Before you close your speech, you can offer to answer remaining questions personally at the back of the room. This is an ideal name- or card-getting opportunity. Many times those who approach you will express interest in your product or service that can be turned immediately into an appointment for a follow-up phone call or meeting. To make the best use of the time you have after a speech, do not get into a long-drawn-out conversation with any individual. Others will become impatient and leave before talking with you. Make contact with as many people as you can and get their names and phone numbers. Then, of course, you must follow up by phone, mail, or E-mail as soon as possible on all the names or cards that you've collected.

Action Steps: Techniques for Tracking Your Contacts

To make the most of the contacts you make, it's essential to set up a method for keeping track of them. This is easy using contract management software like *Act, Ascend, Goldmine,* or *Maximizer* that will store all relevant information and sort and print your mailing lists as well as alert you to when it's time to make a follow-up contact. But even if you prefer to use the old-fashioned hands-on approaches to keeping track of contacts, like a Rolodex or a daily planner like *DayRunner,* here are several important tips for keeping track of those you've met so you can stay in touch and follow up:

1. Create a list of all the marketing activities you undertake. (Remember, we suggest emphasizing five compatible activities simultaneously over a period of time.) When you record the name, address, phone number, and other relevant information for the contacts you make, include information about which marketing activity led to that contact. Keep track of any business, referrals, or leads to other contacts you get through each activity.
2. At least once a month check your list of activities to see which ones are creating results. Compare the results you get from the various activities with the time, energy, and money they require.
3. Drop activities that are not productive and add new ones that arise from the contacts you've made.

Resources: Speeches and Seminars

Books and Magazines

Controlling Stage Fright with Audiences from One to One Thousand. Peter Desberg and George March. Oakland: New Harbinger Publications, 1989.

Flip Charts: How to Draw Them and How to Use Them. Richard Brandt. Brandt Management Group, 8423 Freestone Avenue, Richmond, VA 23229, (804) 747-0816.

How to Run Seminars and Workshops. Robert Jolles. New York: Wiley, 1993.

I Can See You Naked. Ron Huff. Kansas City: Andrews and McMeel, 1992.

Overcoming Stage Fright in Everyday Life. Joyce Ashley. New York: Clarkson Potter, 1996.

Power Presentations. Marjorie Brody. New York: Wiley, 1992.

Powerful Presentation Skill. Debra Smith. CareerTrack, 3085 Center Green Drive, Boulder CO 80301, (800) 334-1018, www.careertrack.com

Sharing Ideas magazine. Walters Speakers Services, Box 1120, Glendora, CA 91740, (626) 335-8069.

Speak and Grow Rich. Dottie and Lilly Walters. Paramus, N.J.: Prentice-Hall, 1997.

Speaking Without Fear or Nervousness. Helen Sutton. CareerTrack, 3085 Center Green Drive, Boulder, CO 80301, (800) 334-1018, www.careertrack.com

Audio

Everything You Wanted to Know about Being Booked by Speakers' Bureaus but Didn't Know Who to Ask. Dottie Walters. Walters Speakers Services, Box 1120, Glendora, CA 91740, (818) 335-8069.

Mega-Success System for Speakers: How to Build a Maximum Income Speaking Business. Dan Kennedy. Empire Communications Corporation, 5818 N. 7th St., Ste. 103, Phoenix, AZ 85014, (602) 997-7707; (800) 223-7180.

Powerful Presentation Skill. Debra Smith. CareerTrack, 3085 Center Green Drive, Boulder, CO 80301, (800) 334-1018, www.careertrack.com. A 4-hour cassette.

Present with Success. Marjorie Brody. Brody Communications, P.O. Box 8868, Elkins Park, PA 19027. (215) 886-1688, www.brodycomm.com

Organizations, Meeting Planners, and Speakers' Bureaus

American Society of Training and Development, 1640 King St., Box 1443, Alexandria, VA 22313, (703) 683-8100. www.astd.org

National Speakers Association, 1500 South Priest Dr., Tempe, AZ 85821, (602) 968-0911, www.nsaspeaker.org

National Trade and Professional Associations of the United States. Columbia Books, 1212 New York Ave. N.W., Ste. 330, Washington, DC 20005, (202) 898-0662, www.d-net.com/columbia

Toastmasters International, Box 9052, Mission Viejo, CA 92690, (714) 858-8255, fax: (714) 858-1207. Toastmasters offers opportunities for people to learn how to speak by participating in Toastmaster groups which can be found in most areas of the country. www.toastmasters.org

Walters Speakers Services, Box 1120, Glendora, CA 91740, (626) 335-8069, www.speakandgrowrich.com, E-mail: Call4Spkr@aol.com. Walters Speakers services offers weekend training workshops on how to speak and get paid for it.

☞ Directories

Directory of Meeting Professionals International, 4455 LBJ Freeway, Suite 1200, Dallas, TX 75544, (972) 702-3000.

The Directory of United States Trade Shows, Expositions and Conventions, published by the U.S. Travel Service of the U.S. Department of Commerce.

Encyclopedia of Associations, Gale Research, 645 Griswold St., 835 Penobscot Bldg., Detroit, MI 48226-4094, (800) 877-4253.

Nationwide Directory of Association Meeting Planners, 1140 Broadway, New York, NY 10001, (800) 223-1797.

Services

Chroma Copy, 12 Channel St., Ste. 802, Boston, MA 02210, (800) 548-8558, chromalabs@aol.com, is a special photo lab that enables you to modem in your photos and they will make up color slides for your presentation and ship them to you within twenty-four hours.

Software

Adobe Illustrator, Adobe Systems, 345 Park Avenue, San Jose, CA 95110, (800) 42-adobe, www.adobe.com

Adobe PageMaker, Adobe Systems, 345 Park Avenue, San Jose, CA 95110, (800) 42-adobe, www.adobe.com

AmiPro, by Lotus Development Corp, 55 Cambridge Pkwy., Cambridge MA 02142, (800) 426-7682, www.lotus.com

ASAP by Software Publishing Corp. Microsoft Corp., One Microsoft Way, Redmond, WA 98052-6399, (800) 426-9400, www.microsoft.com/publisher/

Freehand, by Macromedia, 600 Townsend, Ste. 310 West, San Francisco, CA 94103, (800) 945-9085, www.macromedia.com

Freelance Graphics, by Lotus Development Corp., 55 Cambridge Pkwy, Cambridge MA 02142, (800) 426-7682, www.lotus.com

Kai's Power Goo, MetaCreations, turns photos and graphics into entertaining real-time liquid images, 6303 Carpinteria Avenue, Carpinteria, CA 93013, (805) 566-6200, www.metatools.com

Photoshop, Adobe Systems, 345 Park Avenue, San Jose, CA 95110, 800-42-adobe, www.adobe.com

Quark Express, by Quark, Inc., 5801 Campstool Rd., Cheyenne, WY 84103, (800) 788-7835, www.quark.com

Microsoft PowerPoint, Microsoft Corp., One Microsoft Way, Redmond, WA 98052-6399, (800) 426-9400, www.microsoft.com/publisher/

Microsoft Publisher, Microsoft Corp., One Microsoft Way, Redmond, WA 98052-6399, (800) 426-9400, www.microsoft.com/publisher/

Equipment

You will find a list of do-it-yourself design tools in **Appendix 1: Writing and Designing Materials That Sell,** which is available on-line without charge as a Special Report at www.paulandsarah.com on the Great Gains for Getting Business page. In addition, consider:

Freedomike FM AV4, a self-contained portable microphone and speaker system that can stand alone or operate in conjunction with the house speaker system. Includes a recording option and built-in rechargable power source that makes it self-sufficient for up to twelve hours when no electricity us available. Available from Michael MacFarlane, Walters International Speakers Bureau, 18825 Hicrest Road, Glendora, CA 91740, (626) 335-8069, E-mail: MRMACF@ aol.com

Scan Converter can project sharp text images from your notebook computer onto a television screen. By AverMedia, 47923A Warm

Springs Blvd, Fremont, CA 94539, (510) 770-9899, (800) 863-2332, www.aver.com

Videos

Powerful Presentation Skill, by Debra Smith. CareerTrack, 3085 Center Green Drive, Boulder CO 80301, (800) 334-1018, www.careertrack.com. A four-hour cassette.

Present Like a Pro, by Marjorie Brody, Brody Communications, P.O. Box 8868, Elkins Park, PA 19027, (215) 886-1688, www.brodycomm.com

Speaking Without Fear or Nervousness, by Helen Sutton. CareerTrack, 3085 Center Green Drive, Boulder, CO 80301, (800) 334-1018, www.careertrack.com

Volunteering

When Susan Schatz of Tulsa began her home-based wedding catering business, she decided that donating her artistic one-of-a-kind cakes for charity events was one of the best ways to hook up with wealthy clientele who could afford her services, so she volunteered to create dessert buffets for charity events. Victoria and Richard Turner decided to give away cups of water to promote their Pure Water dealership. They approach country fairs, arts and crafts exhibitions, and other events and offer to distribute cups of water to the patrons. Of course, the cups have their company name on them.

If you are providing a service of some kind, your community provides an excellent venue to make valuable personal contacts with prospective clients by volunteering your expertise to and through civic and community organizations. In fact, this is one of the singularly most effective start-up marketing strategies available for self-employed individuals.

For example, if you are a computer consultant, you might convince a hardware manufacturer or dealer in your area to donate a computer to the organization of your choice. Then you could offer to set it up and install the software needed to do the particular tasks the organization needs. This is essentially what Tom Reiter did, but he did it big time. After Reiter started his own business, called Trial Presentation Technologies, which provides high-tech equipment for courtrooms, he approached the judge for the upcoming O.J. Simpson trial and offered to equip the courtroom and provide his services for free! This was his big break. "It's probably the single best opportunity to educate the legal field to the capabilities of new technology," Reiter said.

Using this approach, a graphic designer could volunteer to design a program guide, a letterhead, or a wall poster for a charity fund-raising event. A public-relations firm might volunteer to do the publicity for the event; a caterer could agree to cater it; a floral designer could do all the floral displays; and a limousine service might contribute a car and driver to pick up award recipients.

Middle Creek Design Group of Lititz, Pa., is a husband-and-wife graphic design and public relations team. Their volunteer work on the Red Rose Run netted them a plum account working with the primary sponsor of the event, Healthguard of Lancaster County.

Whatever your expertise, business or personal, it can be valuable to most volunteer organizations. Although you may get greater media attention from volunteering for civic and charitable activities, you can also offer samples of your work to trade and professional organizations and to other private commercial ventures. An artist, for example, might volunteer to display his or her paintings or sculpture at the opening of a new restaurant. An interior decorator might agree to decorate the office suite of an architectural association. A list broker might volunteer to supply a list of new businesses for a colleague who consults with start-up businesses. All these activities will provide opportunities for valuable exposure, contacts, and referrals.

One of the most popular ways to get business by volunteering is to serve as a committee member in your trade or professional organization or to take on some other volunteer position in the organization. An event planner might volunteer to oversee an annual Chamber of Commerce event. A financial planner might volunteer to do a workshop on retirement planning for his networking group. When Paul's business was teaching presentation skills to corporate executives, we volunteered to do a presentation skills seminar for the leadership team of the local chapter of the American Society for Training and Development, of which we were both members. This gave us a chance to show our program to several key human resource development professionals while contributing to the success of the chapter.

You might even volunteer to help a competitor. Nancy Malvin, publisher of *Keyboard Connection*, a newsletter for self-employed office support professionals, tells this story. A woman called her company asking if she ever subcontracted out overload work when she was too busy to handle it herself. Malvin gets many calls like this, but this call was different. While the caller had no experience, she had just completed a training program and offered to work for free until Malvin was satisfied with the quality of her work. Malvin set up a graduated pay structure for working with this woman, starting at one week's work for free and moving up to hourly fees as her competency went up.

Pros and Cons of Volunteering

Volunteering can be rewarding both for you personally and for your business. In fact, research has shown that volunteering is good for your health. It seems that our immune systems and mood improve when doing good things for others. But volunteering also can mean business because it can enable you to make contacts you could not reach otherwise. It gives people who might be skeptical or unaware of your talents and abilities a chance to experience them firsthand. It also can give you a chance to make a reputation you might otherwise take years to build.

The major limitation of volunteering for most small businesses, however, is scheduling the demands it makes on their time. Volunteering does take time. To do it effectively we suggest that you allow two to four hours per week for your volunteer activities—not too much to take from your week or weekend, yet enough time to be effective in whatever volunteer role you tackle. These hours, however, should not be scheduled as a half hour here and there. Usually to be productive as both a volunteer for the organization and for your business you need to dedicate your time in a block, so you can get to know the people you're meeting and they have a chance to get to know you as well.

Best Bets. Volunteering is most effective for promoting business services and least effective for promoting products to consumers. It works best when what you're offering involves a high level of trust and rapport and when the results are obvious and easily recognized as a valued contribution by people who need what you can offer or refer others to you.

Tips for Getting Results from Volunteering

We've found there are several keys to getting business from giving away what you have to offer:

Make sure the skills you use are the ones you want to sell. Don't show off your one-to-one fund-raising skills if your business is graphic design; design the fund-raising brochure, instead. Of course, if you are making your first foray into volunteering and need to establish yourself as part of an organization or charity event, you may want to learn something about the organization of your choice first by working for a short time at the nitty-gritty functions where volunteers are always most desperately needed. Rarely will you have trouble getting a chance to volunteer for entry-level volunteer activities like:

1. envelope stuffing
2. decorating
3. loading, unloading, moving, setting up, arranging, and carrying
4. typing
5. working directly with service recipients
6. placing phone calls

In order to maximize the benefit to your business, however, as soon as possible, you will need to volunteer your efforts doing functions that allow you to contribute your expertise in some way that will enable potential referral sources or clients to see and meet you. Usually such activities take place at more of a managerial and fund-raising level.

Volunteer for activities that will provide visibility, enhance your reputation, and enable you to meet key contacts. You need to look for ways to contribute that will provide opportunities to meet associates and network effectively in the process of providing a needed service to your community in ways that are related to what you do. Such activities can put you shoulder-to-shoulder and face-to-face with many valuable contacts you could not make otherwise. Some of the more high-profile volunteer work you can do includes:

1. organizing functions
2. speaking on behalf of the organization
3. soliciting cash donations
4. soliciting service/merchandise donations for auctions
5. training volunteers or other personnel
6. providing needed business services for the organization

When Susan Van Lier was beginning her career as an independent producer, for example, she joined Women in Film and volunteered to help with their annual film festival. The specific activity she volunteered for was to chauffeur the keynote speakers and featured seminar leaders to and from the airport, their hotel, and the conference facility. She also escorted them to and from social events at the festival, which provided her with a high profile at these events. This role was an ideal volunteer activity for her because in the process of helping out, she met many high-profile women producers, directors, and actresses she would not have had the opportunity to meet otherwise.

Don't hide your light under a bushel. Be sure to get recognition for what you do. When volunteering in some official capacity, for example, it is appropriate to ask that your name and business cards be on display and that your name be listed as a contributor in menus, program guides, announcements, news releases, or newsletters. Sometimes you can work with the organization to get coverage of your efforts in their newsletter, the local media, or, at the very least, personally, with the movers and shakers in the organization. And, of course, you can send out your own news releases featuring your involvement in such community or professional activities.

Whatever you do, do it well; do it right; and do it all. Since you are volunteering your expertise, be sure to do your best. Even though volunteering can be time-consuming, don't be tempted to just get by with doing a perfunctory job. You'll want to be making contacts, so people will be watching and you'll want to leave the right impression. If you don't have time to do it right, don't do it. Your reputation will rest on your results. Finish the tasks you agree to and follow through to see that those who are affected by your work are satisfied.

Build relationships and make future connections. Be sure to take the initiative to develop a relationship with the people you meet while volunteering. Don't just do what you do in silence and hope people will notice you. Seeing your name on a program guide will probably have little impact compared to the conversations you can initiate and the interests you find in common with the others you're working with. Get to know them and what they do. Think of ways you could assist or work with them professionally and make contact outside the volunteer organization to explore possibilities that could be of mutual benefit.

Also, remember in any area of community or charity work, don't get involved in a particular activity for business reasons alone. Your involvement should be a personal as well as a business investment. Make sure you can be committed to the cause as well as to your own benefit.

Barter instead. Jeff and Mary Freeman of Front Porch Computers in rural Chatsworth, Georgia, have a barter arrangement with a supplier of laser-printer-toner cartridges. They tell their customers about the toner company and, in return, the company gives them referrals and free ads in its 20,000-circulation newsletter. In eight months, this barter arrangement brought the Freemans forty new sales with an average order of $1,500. "The beauty of barter," says Freeman, "is that you supply something to somebody who provides you with something else that you don't have to pay for."

Color consultant Sharon Nelson of Chicago also gets new clients through a barter arrangement. She, however, belongs to a barter club. During the first three years after she joined Chicago Barter, she added about a dozen new clients through bartering. She likes to barter because it allows her to expand her business while keeping her marketing costs low.

Note: although no money changes hands in a barter exchange, the IRS still expects you to pay income tax on the value of the bartered goods or services. But, if you are bartering for a business service, you can deduct the barter activity as a business expense.

Walk Around the Neighborhood

"I do WATN marketing," Mary Maddox told us to explain how she established herself as a successful mobile notary in just a few months. "Whenever I have free time, which at first was every day, I pick out an office building or commercial street and just start walking around the neighborhood. I drop by each office or shop, introduce myself, tell them what I do, ask them something about their business, and leave my card. I go back to the same places about once a month or so just to say hello. Usually it takes about three visits before they remember who I am. After that point, they usually greet me warmly, then we just chat and I'm on my way."

This is the epitome of Top-of-the-Mind marketing. Notice that Mary has mentioned nothing about selling. She never sells during her "visits." She just gets acquainted and makes sure she stays on the top of the minds of the small-business owners she meets. And, as a result, she does get business. This is a fact we can attest to personally because we met Mary at our local print shop. She dropped in, "walking around the neighborhood," while we were picking up a printing order. Two weeks later, we were in the same print shop and a woman walked in and asked, "Do you know where I could find a notary?" Guess whose card they gave her?

About a month later, we had an emergency need for a notary ourselves. It was 11:30 at night, and we had just arrived home late from an out-of-town trip. Guess who we hired to come over on the spot?

Pros and Cons of WATN Marketing

As you can see, WATN marketing can be simple, effective, and nonthreatening. It's ideal for anyone who likes meeting and talking with people. It's a wonderful way to avoid sitting around waiting for business, and it gets you out of the office and actively involved with potential clients and customers. You can do it anytime. You don't have to wait for a scheduled networking meeting or until someone agrees to let you speak to their group. It's immediate, and you can tuck it into your schedule even on busy days by WATN in the areas where your other business activities take you.

Tim Glasby makes planters and mirrors from Victorian tin ceiling tiles. To market his creations he takes photos and samples in the back of his truck and drives to shopping areas with lots of galleries. He drops in on the galleries and introduces himself and his work. Often people buy the samples right off the truck. The contacts he makes "driving around the neighborhood" also lead to other sources of businesses. On a recent excursion to San Francisco, everyone either bought or gave him a referral.

On the other hand, WATN marketing is time-consuming. So, once you are quite busy, you'll probably want to find other activities that don't take you away from paying work. Of course, should you hit a slow time, you can always résumé your "route." You'll reconnect with those who haven't seen you for a while and meet some new people who have come along since your last visit. Also WATN marketing may or may not lead to any immediate business. Sometimes it will take time for those you meet through WATN to have the occasion to use your service or refer someone else to you. But when they do, you can be the one who comes to mind.

While corporate magician Bill Herz now gets all the business he can handle by word of mouth, he started out with no satisfied customers to refer business to him. To get his business going, he walked into office buildings and asked receptionists who was in charge of putting on their meetings. Eventually he picked up a few clients by WATN, and he has gone on to become an internationally popular presenter at corporate functions worldwide.

Best Bets: Clearly WATN marketing works best when you're offering local business services, although if your clients are national or regional, you can arrange to Walk around the Exhibit Hall by attending trade shows, conventions, and expos your clients will be attending. If you do this, however, keep in mind that your clients are at such shows to get business themselves, so respect their needs and only speak with them during a lull when no potential clients are visiting their booths.

While WATN marketing works best with business services, basketball star Dean Tolson actually used WATN to start his own carpet-cleaning business. After retiring from professional basketball, he bought a carpet-cleaning franchise and literally went door-to-door in his neighborhood telling whoever answered the door, "I played for the Seattle SuperSonics. Would you give me a chance to clean your carpets?" Although he no longer uses WATN, after the early success it provided, he went on to form his own company, Glow Carpet Glow, and it has been growing every since.

Tips for Getting Results from Walking Around the Neighborhood

Since WATN is time-consuming, you want to make the most of the contacts you make with people you meet. Here are several tips for how to get business from walking around the neighborhood.

Target the "neighborhood." Select buildings or commercial areas where there is a high concentration of businesses that need what your niche offers. Someone doing medical billing for professionals, for example, could target buildings that have a high occupancy of professional medical practices. A commercial photographer who specializes in fine art might want to walk around the booths at arts-and-crafts fairs, or commercial areas with a high concentration of fine jewelry stores.

Tell; don't sell. Unless you are doing direct solicitation, which you could do by WATN, your goal is not to sell but to introduce yourself, make acquaintances, and keep yourself top-of-the-mind with people who will be needing your services. If you turn the visit into a sales call, you will most definitely encounter a higher level of resistance and you risk running into no-soliciting policies. Once people know you're not selling, however, their defenses will usually drop and they will be more open to making your acquaintance as a fellow business owner and professional. This is a great opportunity to use your File-Opening Sound Byte and/or your Attention Grabber.

Never be a pest. Always keep in mind that you are visiting a business establishment. Make sure you don't interrupt their business activities or interfere in any way with their ability to do business. Wait until customers have completed their business. Come back later if an establishment is particularly busy. Say good-bye quickly if a customer comes in or needs help.

Keep it short. Unless you are prompted by questions from those you meet to talk further, limit your visits to no more than three to five minutes.

Leave literature. Always leave a few business cards or brochures, but don't push those you meet to display or stock your materials unless they express interest in doing so.

Visit repeatedly. As in placing advertising, one visit will probably not do much good. You need to drop by repeatedly until those you're meeting recognize and remember you. Then you need to continue dropping by just to stay on top of their minds. As you get to know the people you meet better, you can ask if they would like additional cards or brochures, or would even be willing to set them out on the counter for their customers' benefit.

Resources: Walk around the Neighborhood

Books

Say It Right: How to Talk in Any Social or Business Situation. Lillian Glass. New York: Putnam, 1991.

Audio

Compelling Brief Descriptions. Ron Richards. ResultsLab, 2175 Green St., San Francisco, CA 94123, (415) 563-5300, E-mail: ronr@resultslab.com

 **Action Steps:** Making Contacts

To start making more contacts that can lead to business:

1. Write a one-sentence description of precisely the type of people you want to reach (e.g., anesthesiologists, working mothers of preschool children, owners of women's boutique dress shops, etc.). These should be the people who most need what you offer in your niche. (See **chapter 5**, p. 176).

2. Alternatively or in addition to the above list, create a list of the people who by the nature of what they do could regularly refer you to contacts in your target market.

3. Now identify ten events, activities, or avenues through which you could make contact with these individuals. What organizations do they belong to? You could join, network, speak before, or volunteer for activities in these organizations. Where might their names appear on a list? You could contact them directly by phone or in person. What civic activities or causes might they be active in? If these causes interest you, too, you could become an active volunteer. Where do they have their offices? You could "walk around their neighborhood." What type of free consultations might they be interested in?

4. From the various possibilities you've created, select one to initiate each day, week, or month, depending on how much additional business you need. One day, you might walk through a professional office building, for example. The next day, you might arrange to participate on a weekly basis in a volunteer activity. The next day, you might contact a meeting planner about the possibility of speaking at a monthly meeting. You might join a particular network group and attend the meetings every Monday morning, etc.

5. Whatever personal contacts you make, use each one as an opportunity to gather as much information as possible about the potential customers or referral sources you meet. Decide on three pieces of information you will acquire to help you get acquainted with each person you meet. Such information might include their favorite spectator sport, the brand of sneakers they wear, their wife's maiden or husband's middle name, their favorite grade-school teacher, a fantasy vacation, their favorite politician and why, what they think is the

most important issue facing voters today, etc. You can select the criteria, but keep away from ordinary topics like what they do, where they went to college, and so on.

TIP: For a good source of the type of information to acquire, check out the "Mackay 66" from Harvey Mackay's book *Swim with the Sharks Without Being Eaten Alive.* You may think that some of the information is too personal, but remember, business IS personal. Mackay says if you cannot answer most of his sixty-six questions about your customers and clients, you really don't know them well enough.

6. Record all the information you gather about your contacts in your contact management files.

Follow-Up Tip: When People Don't Return Your Calls

As you have probably noticed, whatever person-to-person marketing activities you select, follow-up is often key to getting business through your personal contacts. But what if your efforts to follow up leave you lost in voice-mail jail and your valued contacts are not returning your calls?

Professional speaker Ralph Hood has found a clever way to make contact with hard-to-reach contacts. He makes it easy for them to stay in contact. He sends a follow-up letter by mail or fax that asks a few simple but key questions about their needs and best next steps for future contact. He asks the contact to write his or her answers on the letter and send it back via fax or mail. Then, of course, he contacts them in the future in the ways they have indicated will best suit them.

CHAPTER 10

Getting Others Talking About You

You have to get talked about to have your work sell.
—GEORGIA O'KEEFFE, Artist

Think about your most recent decisions to do business with someone. Chances are you make many of your key decisions the way Suzanne does. Suzanne had suffered a severe illness that resulted in needing to change her lifestyle in a significant way.

She needed someone to help her move into her parents' home, for example, while she recovered. Her father recommended someone who could handle the move.

Traditional medicine was not helping her with many of the symptoms that were preventing her from going back to work. A friend recommended a holistic practitioner.

She benefited from his services tremendously, but he also referred her to several other practitioners of holistic medicine, one of whom recommended that she use a slant board, which she ordered from a catalog he provided.

Although she was recovering gradually, she often felt depressed and confused about the future direction of her life because it was becoming increasingly clear that she would have to find a new career. But doing what? She had no idea, until she went to a luncheon at the home of a friend. There she met someone who was talking enthusiastically about a career coaching program she had just enrolled in that was helping her find her purpose in life and create a new livelihood. Suzanne got a referral to that coach and began planning a new life for herself.

Each and every one of these vital products and services came to Suzanne through the recommendation of someone else. Without a storefront that flourishes from walk-by traffic and with little time or money for marketing, all these professionals and small businesses rely on such person-to-person recommendations for most of their business. Finding ways to get others talking about you can be an ideal way to get business, especially if you don't like or have time for selling or other more conventional marketing activities.

But, of course, no one will talk about you unless you give them something to talk about. And who's talking about you, what they say, and whom they say it to will determine whether you will simply become a topic of conversation or someone who is recognized as having a sought-after product or service.

In this chapter you'll find a variety of ways you can develop relationships with others who in essence can become your sales force. Read through and select the activities that are most appealing to you and best suited to your business. As you experiment with these activities, you may find that just one key relationship can lead to all the business you need. Or, you may find that you'll need to build a variety of such relationships to get business coming your way. You may find that you need to combine a core of key supporters with other marketing activities to create the word-of-mouth momentum you need. But without a doubt, getting others to spread the word about you can be a rewarding and effective way to get business coming to you.

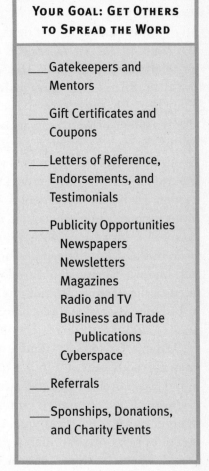

Your Goal: Get Others to Spread the Word

___Gatekeepers and Mentors

___Gift Certificates and Coupons

___Letters of Reference, Endorsements, and Testimonials

___Publicity Opportunities
- Newspapers
- Newsletters
- Magazines
- Radio and TV
- Business and Trade Publications
- Cyberspace

___Referrals

___Sponships, Donations, and Charity Events

Gatekeepers and Mentors

Success in business is almost always a joint venture. And the more support and assistance you have or can create for yourself, the better. That is where mentors and gatekeepers come in. A mentor is a wise and trusted counselor or influential supporter who takes a personal interest in your success. A gatekeeper is an influential individual who in the course of what she does comes into regular contact with people who need what you have to offer. Both are usually experts or authorities in their fields and have a rich array of contacts that can be useful to anyone entering that field.

When Leslie Nichols began doing fashion and product promotions for television game shows, she knew she was entering a very competitive field. She started cautiously, doing a show here and there. While doing one of her first shows, *The Price is Right,* she met Edward Jubert, vice president of what was at the time Goodson Todman Productions, one of the major television game-show producers, now known as Mark Goodson. Jubert was impressed with how every time Nichols was called, she would go the extra mile to come up with whatever prizes they needed. He became her mentor, encouraging her and opening opportunities for her. "He has been and continues to be the kind of person who says, 'All I want from you is your success,'" she says. "When I decided to do this as a full-fledged business with letterhead and all, I called and told him what I was about to do. He said, 'Do it! Do it!'" Twelve years later, Leslie Nichols Promotions is a highly successful firm specializing in fashion promotional placements for film and television. Nichols remains grateful for Jubert's ongoing support.

Virginia Cartwright wanted to be a world-renowned potter, but she knew the odds were not in her favor. Few individuals ever attain recognition as a potter, even if their work is good. Virginia especially admired the work of one prominent potter, so she enrolled in courses he offered in order to study his technique. Gradually, her teacher began to see potential in her work and took a professional interest in her success. He provided her with the opportunity to begin assisting and eventually conducting some of his classes. All the while she continued her studies. Under his tutelage, Virginia set up a studio in her home, and she began exhibiting at art fairs and ultimately in galleries across the country. Over the past ten years she has accomplished what she doubted she could actually do—she is a world-class potter.

Ann Marcarelli watched her carpet-cleaning business fall into decline as the apartment managers with whom she worked stopped cleaning carpets as a routine in their complexes. In studying who else might provide a steady stream of referrals and business, she realized that people who move want to move into places where they would feel comfortable walking around in their bare feet. That included new-home owners, and the gatekeepers to new-home owners are realtors. She contacted some of the top realtors in her area offering their clients a free carpet inspection upon purchase. Word spread among the real estate community and soon she had more business than ever.

In chapter 1, we mentioned a San Francisco man we met on a radio talk show who got his new business-plan-writing service under way in only three months. Within those three months, this weapons-designer-turned-business-plan-writer was making more money than he had from his salary as an engineer. And he already had several people working for him! As you can imagine, we wanted to know how he had become so successful so quickly. The answer was simple: He got all his business from one gatekeeper. Who do you think that gatekeeper was? Who in the course of what they do, day in and day out, comes into regular contact with lots of people who need business-plan writers? Yes, a bank loan officer. This business-plan writer gets all his business from one bank loan officer who refers clients who need a business plan in order to get the loan they're seeking.

If you have contacts or supporters like these, you undoubtedly already know and appreciate their value to you. If you aren't enjoying the support of gatekeepers or mentors as yet, the following can serve as your guide to discover and develop such resources for yourself. Creating an independent career or running a small business can take you into difficult and unfamiliar territory at times. A mentor or gatekeeper can ease your way through tough, competitive waters. They can open doors for you to knowledge, skills, referrals, and contacts you might otherwise need years to access.

Pros and Cons of Gatekeepers and Mentors

From the examples above you can see the many advantages of getting business through gatekeepers and mentors. A referral from a trusted and respected professional right at the moment when someone needs you virtually eliminates the necessity of selling yourself. It is the epitome of getting business to come to you. At least, it makes selling your service or product a snap, because those who contact you are already predisposed in your favor. In essence, gatekeepers and mentors are like a built-in sales force sending you clients or opening doors to people who need you, leaving you free to do the work you do best.

On the other hand, if you aren't already connected to key gatekeepers and mentors, you will have to locate and establish relationships with them. Since they are experts or professionals in their field, they most likely will have many others who are also trying to establish such relationships. So, you will need to distinguish yourself from others and find avenues for making contacts with influential individuals. This can take time and be somewhat elusive. In other words, waiting until you find gatekeepers and mentors can be like waiting for Santa or trying to find a sugar daddy. It isn't something you can count on developing upon demand. Therefore it is best as a long-term strategy that comes about in the course of other marketing activities you undertake.

Best Bets: Using gatekeepers and mentors is an excellent strategy for all categories of business, both products and services being sold to either consumers or business. It works especially well for any kind of business that depends on establishing trust and a personal relationship such as consulting or medical services. It works well when the product or service involves a significant financial investment and is ideally suited to any field that has lots of competition.

Tips for Getting Business from Gatekeepers and Mentors

The biggest stumbling blocks to identifying influential people who believe in you enough to recommend you enthusiastically and will work to help you succeed arise from making faulty assumptions. Too often people think that finding gatekeepers and mentors is all a matter of luck or politics: you either have the connections or you don't. Or they falsely assume that if they do a good job, gatekeepers and mentors will seek them out. And of course, there is just enough truth in these two assumptions to perpetuate them.

Factors like who you know, where you live, who you're related to, and where you went to school can make a difference, but they by no means need to prevent you from finding gatekeepers and mentors. Likewise, while occasionally your work will attract mentors and gatekeepers to you with no additional effort on your part, you simply can't rely on that happening. Usually you will need to take the initiative to make contact with people and bring your product or service to their attention. Here are what we've found to be the key avenues to finding and reaping the benefits of having gatekeepers and mentors.

Put the word out. If you can't find gatekeepers and mentors among your existing contacts, put the word out through the contacts you do have about the kind of people, information, or expertise you need and follow up on every suggestion you get. You will be amazed at how quickly you can gain access to virtually anything you require.

Whenever you need a key resource to assist you in getting business, we recommend building a Networking Tree. Turning an 8½-by-11-inch sheet of paper sideways, write along the left-hand side the names of all

Action Step: Identifying Potential Gatekeepers and Mentors

Look in your own backyard. Many people who could be of invaluable help to you in building your career or business are right under your nose. You may have overlooked them, taken them for granted, or simply been too shy to call upon them. Think back over your lifetime.

Who has taken an interest in you in the past?

For whom have you done a good job at some time?

Who has encouraged you in your career or business?

With whom have you accomplished or overcome something difficult?

Who helped you through a tough time?

Who have you helped through a tough time?

Who do you know of who has done what you want to do?

Previous employers, co-workers, distant relatives, friends of the family, teachers, scoutmasters, ministers or rabbis, long-lost friends and comrades from your past—all these people are possible mentors or gatekeepers for you—or may be able to introduce you to people who will be. Don't be embarrassed to draw help from built-in gatekeepers like family members. Janell Besell's husband, for example, is an anesthesiologist, so when she opened her billing service his office became her first client. Through referrals to his colleagues, her business has grown rapidly. Pet bereavement counselor Diane Kelley of Manhattan Beach is married to a veterinarian. She gets referrals from his office and has ready entrée to other veterinarian's offices.

Most people, whether you're related to them or not, are flattered and even honored to be helpful to others as long as those requesting their help are courteous and respectful of their time and sensibilities. Sometimes, if you need considerable assistance or you are asking for advice that others provide as part of their own business, you should offer to pay for consultation or to take them to lunch in exchange.

Make a list of the people you most admire in your or a related field and find out how you can learn from them. They may provide consultations, do workshops or seminars, or have written a book. They may be willing to allow you to observe, apprentice, or assist them.

When Joanne Gregg decided she wanted to do a particular type of psychotherapy called rebirthing, she turned to her own rebirther, Diane Vaughn, who was one of the best in the field. Joanne asked if she could study with Diane, and Diane agreed. Ultimately she allowed Joanne to assist at her workshops, and as Joanne's skills grew, Diane began referring low-fee clients to her. Thus Joanne was able to begin building a practice of her own.

When Janet Greek was an aspiring television and film director looking for her first opportunity to direct, she learned that a well-known television director whom she greatly admired sometimes allowed new directors to come onto his set to observe. She called him and asked if she could be one of them, and he agreed. After she had been on the set for a while, he offered her an opportunity to direct an episode. That was the break she needed. She has gone on to become a successful director of many popular television programs.

Such mentor arrangements are commonplace. You simply have to have the courage to ask and the willingness to do what it takes to show off your skills by participating in classes, volunteering, assisting, doing grunt work, handling overload, or taking on work the mentor no longer does.

the people you know who might have some information to help you find what you want. Call them one by one. If they can't help you themselves, ask whether they know of anyone who might and write that person's name and telephone number to the right of the person who referred you. Call these people and repeat the process. Soon you will have a whole tree of possibilities that will lead you to precisely what you need.

Imagine, for example, that you are starting a magazine for the suburban business district where you live, to be funded primarily by advertising and distributed free throughout the area. You have prepared a sample issue and begun soliciting advertising from appropriate businesses. Although you have been able to sell a few small ads, many business owners are hesitant to spend the money, and they want to know whether Nolan Glazier Real Estate will be advertising in your magazine. Obviously Nolan Glazier is a gatekeeper, as other business owners take the lead from him. You proceed to try to contact him immediately, but your phone calls and letters fail to get past the secretary.

If this sounds all too familiar, here is how you can get around this roadblock. After building your networking tree, as described above, you discover that:

1. A friend in real estate will invite you to the Board of Realtors' Meeting that Glazier attends each week.

2. A neighbor offers to take you to a meeting of the Chamber of Commerce, to which Glazier belongs, and introduce you to him. He also gives you the name of the Chamber program chairman and will recommend that you speak to the group on how to create effective advertising.

3. A public relations specialist you meet at the first Chamber meeting you attend suggests that you write a short article on community spirit for the local newspaper and interview Glazier for the article. She gives you the editor's phone number.

4. The free-lance designer who helped you do the sample edition of your magazine thinks her best friend knows Glazier's wife. She gives you her friend's name and when you call, the friend just happens to be going to a party in two weeks that is sponsored by the Community Environment Coalition, which Glazier's wife founded.

5. The owner of the shop where you do all your printing thinks Glazier is heading up the committee for the local fire department fund-raiser. He thinks they could use some help.

From this wealth of leads, how can you miss eventually making contact with Glazier? And, if by some chance none of them pan out, you can always create more. This case study also introduces another valuable marketing tool you can use to meet gatekeepers and mentors to bring in more business: community involvement.

Open doors to gatekeepers through community involvement. Community involvement is another way to find gatekeepers and mentors. In addition, it affords you the opportunity to pay back the community that provides you with the means to create your livelihood or build your business. The most successful people always give something back to the community that has supported them. It might involve serving on a board of directors for a charity or community event. It could mean taking part in an initiative to launch a new service or institution or raising funds for a good cause.

Patricia Smith has found community involvement a personally rewarding way to make valuable contacts and develop a reputation for Art Expressions, her gallery in San Diego. She has served as a patron of

University of California art projects, was a founding board member for Quilt San Diego, and co-chaired the Citizens' Advocacy Group to Build University City High School, for which she received a commendation from the mayor. Participating in such community activities provided her with opportunities to contribute to civic causes she believes in while enabling her to meet and interact with leaders in the community interested in art and art collecting.

As Smith has found, the value of community involvement from a marketing perspective is the visibility it provides and the people it enables you to meet. Becoming active in your community can provide visibility in the local media to the general community, a particular segment of the community, and your clients and customers in particular. In the process, it provides avenues through which mentors and gatekeepers can find you.

A second marketing advantage to be derived from community involvement is that whatever publicity, if any, you receive from it is almost guaranteed to be positive. Since publicity is by definition something you cannot control, the more you can do to ensure a positive slant on the exposure you get, the better. (See Publicity, later in this chapter.)

Third, community involvement can put you in touch with the movers and shakers in your marketplace. Meeting and working with the decision makers in various industries is an ideal route to meeting gatekeepers not otherwise available to you. And again in the competition for customers, support of a known and respected colleague can give you an edge.

Look to others who serve those you serve. One of the best ways to identify gatekeepers for your business is to think of all the businesses and professionals who serve or otherwise come in regular contact with your potential clients and customers at the precise time they need your products or services. All such individuals are potential gatekeepers for you. Make a list of them and set about meeting as many of them as possible. If you are a mobile disc jockey, for example, and you specialize in providing music for nonprofit fund-raising events, your gatekeepers would include event planners, florists, caterers, hotels, and tuxedo rental stores, among others. So you would make yourself known to as many such sources as possible.

Woodworker Robert Livingston used this approach when he started a cabinetmaking business as a way to support his work in the theater. He obtains his business from just a few key architects and building contractors who refer their clients to him.

High-Touch Tip: Create an Advisory Board

Creating an advisory board is an excellent way to recruit a group of mentors. When Danny Cox was seeking to become a successful sales manager, he began asking the successful managers he'd read about in trade magazines to lunch. To his surprise, many agreed. Later when left his job to start his own sales-training company, he renewed this lunch habit with a half dozen of the sales people who had become his mentors over the years. They became like an ad hoc advisory board to him.

As we mentioned in **chapter 3,** we (Paul and Sarah) decided to create a more formalized advisory board in 1987 when we started the first all-positive news radio show, *Here's to Your Success.* We identified key people who had been an inspiration to us like Famous Wally Amos, Mark Victor Hanson, Jack Canfield, Dean Koontz, Gerald Jampolski, and Pam Lontos to ask if they would serve on an advisory board for our show. To our surprise, they agreed and their support and ideas helped us to create a successful show that eventually led to our *Working from Home* show, which has run on the Business News Network for the last ten years.

Author and public speaker Jeff Davidson also attributes much of his success to his advisory board. In 1989 when he felt his company had hit a standstill, Davidson decided to invite all his professional contacts—accountants, business professionals, marketing executives, management consultants, and other experts from a variety of fields—to join his advisory board. He sent them formal invitations to a board meeting, and again, to his surprise, most showed up! To this day, he calls on this twenty-six-person board of professionals when he needs advice. To encourage their participation, he hosts a biannual dinner meeting with a printed agenda of issues he is seeking help on.

You notice that we were all surprised when so many of those we approached to serve on our advisory board accepted. So, if you're thinking "Who on earth would serve on an advisory board of mine?" think again. Think specifically of whose expertise and interests parallel yours. Such individuals may be quite willing to help get an effort they believe in off the ground or keep it going and growing.

Developing a Gatekeeper Wheel

To identify valuable gatekeepers for your business, create a wheel with your target client or customer at a hub. Now think of all the other types of businesses that serve the same clientele you're seeking. All these businesses are potential gatekeepers for you, as you are for them.

For example, if you are a wedding makeup artist, all the businesses appearing on the spokes of the wheel below could be gatekeepers for you because they all come into regular contact with brides or mothers of brides. Your gatekeepers could include wedding planners, caterers, tuxedo shops, ministers, hotels, limo companies, bridal shops, florists, mobile disc jockeys.

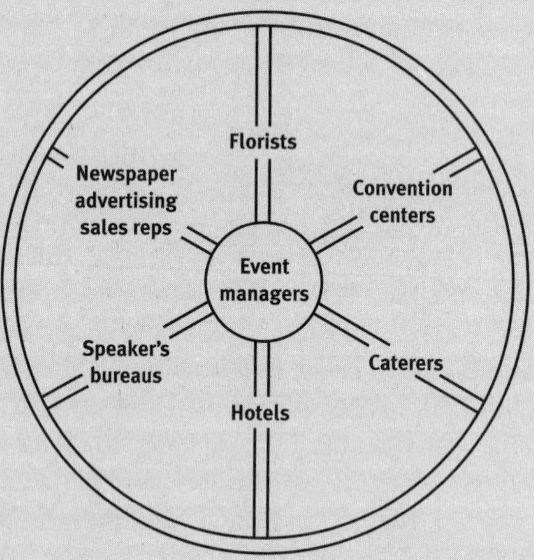

Note that in order to identify your gatekeepers, you need to have defined your target client or customer. In other words, you must have defined your niche. If you're trying to reach "anyone" or "everyone," you will have a difficult, if not impossible, time identifying gatekeepers. So if you are having trouble identifying who your gatekeepers would be, review *Chapter 2: Niching—Deciding What You Want to Become Known For.*

Fourth, gaining a reputation for your community participation increases your credibility in the business marketplace so that making contacts will be easier.

Fifth and finally, community involvement doesn't need to cost a lot

FINDING GATEKEEPERS WHEN YOU NEED BUSINESS FAST

If you are new to a community or for some other reason are starting from scratch and need business fast, try this approach:

1. Identify people in a position to know who needs what you offer.
2. Make face-to-face contact with these people for the purpose of gathering information about who is buying what you're selling.
3. Ask permission to use the name of any person you talk with in contacting the companies or people you learn about.

For example, if you're a landscaper, a painter, or a carpenter, you can talk with bankers about who is getting construction loans. You can contact lumberyards about who is buying material for new homes or major remodeling. Real estate people, property managers, and city personnel involved with zoning and planning are all apt to know of leads for you to pursue. If you live in a major city, you might use a publication called *Contacts Influential* that lists firms and the names of specific contacts.

of money. There are numerous ways to get involved in your community that fit the budget of even the smallest business. Martha Gibson, of M. Power Communications, decided to get involved in a charity event for the Junior Achievement program. The exposure was phenomenal as the event broke all records for attendance. Gibson's contribution to this turnout helped promote both the event and her business. She mailed out Cracker Jack boxes as invitations with her mailing label on one side.

Make mutual-referral agreements. Generally getting referrals from gatekeepers will be a more or less informal arrangement. As long as they like your work and what you offer fits the need of their clients, they may refer regularly or intermittently to you as the occasion arises. As you get better acquainted with your gatekeepers, however, you may want to explore the idea of making a more formal mutual-referral agreement with them. A mutual-referral agreement involves a conscious decision between two or more people to refer business to one another on a regular basis. We find that increasing numbers of individuals and small businesses are developing such agreements.

While most businesspeople make occasional referrals to colleagues and professionals, developing a mutual-referral relationship involves a higher degree of commitment and trust. For example, when I, Sarah, began my private psychotherapy practice, I had an unspoken agreement that I would send clients who needed to work with a male therapist to my colleague Richard Nadeau, and he in turn sent clients who needed to work with a female therapist to me. This arrangement worked quite well for both of us and kept our clients happy. Over the years, our mutual-referral agreement became explicit and we expanded our referral network to include a variety of other types of therapists who could handle special cases neither of us was prepared to undertake. Ultimately we had weekly meetings with key network participants.

Financial planner Dan Silverman has developed an effective mutual-referral agreement with a gatekeeper. He specializes in insurance and estate planning and, in order to provide creative solutions to clients with particularly challenging insurance issues, Silverman has a mutual-referral agreement with insurance agent Julian Movsesian, who specializes in underwriting. Their relationship began with casually referring business to each other on occasion, but over the years as their relationship developed it has become a standard way for them to do business. Movsesian refers smaller clients to Silverman; Silverman refers large, complex cases to Movsesian. They split commissions on the work they refer to each other fifty-fifty. Their arrangement enables both of them to focus on their own specialty without having to limit their business and provides them both with a regular source of new business.

Form a gatekeeper network. You can make mutual-referral agreements on a one-to-one basis with various individuals as Dan has or I, Sarah, have done or you can create a network of gatekeepers and all refer business to one another. Setting up a gatekeeper network with others who serve the same type of clients can be an especially valuable way to generate business for everyone involved. Essentially you can become gatekeepers for one another because virtually every day any one of you may come in contact with people who need what some of the others offer. Such arrangements can be a perfect fit.

To help herself compete as a one-person business with larger production companies, Dena Levy has created such a network for her company, Two-D Productions. She has a pool of gatekeepers who refer to and bring one another in on projects. They include writers, editors, camera people, production managers, and caterers.

If it would be beneficial to all involved, in forming such a network, you might actually meet formally or informally, regularly or intermittently. (See **Forming Your Own Network** in **chapter 9.**) Of course, the more you refer to the gatekeepers in your network, the more likely they will be to refer to you in return. For additional information on etiquette for making referrals among colleagues, see **Referrals,** below.

Resources: Mentors and Gatekeepers

Books

Mentoring: A Success Guide for Mentors and Protégés. Floyd Wickman and Terri Sjodin. New York: McGraw-Hill, 1997.

Mentoring: Confidence in Finding a Mentor & Becoming One. Bobb Biehl. Nashville: Broadman and Holman Publishers, 1997.

Personal Coaching for Results: How to Mentor and Inspire Others to Amazing Growth. Louis E. Tice, Joyce Quick, and Lou Tice. Nashville: Thomas Nelson, 1997.

Gift Certificates and Coupons

Everyone loves a gift. People love getting gifts and people love to give gifts. That's why gift certificates and coupons are such a win/win marketing proposition for everyone. To build her business, massage therapist Marnie Graves gave all her clients gift certificates for a free massage for their friends. When she got too busy to offer many free gift sessions, she began giving clients gift coupons for their friends that entitled them to six sessions for the price of five. Later she sold gift certificates to her clients as special holiday gifts for their friends and loved ones.

Photographer Karen Watson has worked out a clever joint promotion with an orthodontist who presents a gift certificate for a free eight-by-ten portrait to his patients once they have their braces removed. The framed portrait hangs in the dentist's office for three months before the patient can take it home. This way, other patients can admire not only the orthodontist's work but the photographer's as well. Watson gets orders for many reprints and a lot of opportunity for people to see her work and the name of her business.

Hair stylist Edward Salazar also developed a mutually beneficial gift certificate program with a photographer. He gave his best clients a holiday gift certificate for a free portrait with a photographer who gave his VIP clients a holiday gift certificate for a free hairstyling from Salazar.

Gift certificates and coupons need not be limited to personal services, however. Real estate appraiser Larry Church provides home owners selling their home with a coupon for a discount on another appraisal they can pass along to whoever purchases their home. Professional speaker George Morrisey of Meritt Island, Florida, offers a unique variation on offering a gift certificate as an incentive to existing clients. When he does a consulting or training assignment that involves multiple days, he includes telephone consultations for a year as part of the agreement.

These are only a few examples of how you can use gift certificates and coupons. You can mail them, fax them, tuck them in with invoices, brochures, or flyers, include them as an element of an advertisement, give them away at networking events, send them as a follow-up reminder, and use them as a means of generating referrals. In fact, they can be an ideal adjunct to almost any other marketing activity.

Pros and Cons of Gift Certificates and Coupons

Gift certificates and coupons are a versatile way to attract clients and customers who are unfamiliar with what you offer or initially hesitant or uncertain about using your product or service. They are also an excellent customer appreciation tool and serve as an incentive for encouraging forgetful or recalcitrant clients to return. Best of all, they can serve as a way to get your existing clients, customers, and referral sources to spread the word about you.

Coupons and gift certificates are relatively low cost, they don't take a lot of time to create or disseminate, and they can be effective in attracting leads and clients, and you can easily incorporate them in other mailings or personal interaction in the course of doing business. In fact, according to *Research Alert,* studies show that 82 percent of consumers use coupons. Of course, most of these coupon users are buying grocery products, but coupons or gift certificates can be useful to one-person and small businesses as well. They are especially useful if you're not expert at selling and find it difficult or uncomfortable to overcome someone's resistance to buying what you offer. It's a friendly, nonthreatening way to say "Give me a try."

Best of all, however, gift certificates and coupons are a great way to get clients, customers, gatekeepers, or other referral sources talking about you. You can give them gift certificates or coupons that they can give to their friends or customers. And as you've seen from examples above, they're also a great way to do joint promotions with others who will give your coupons or gift certificates to their customers in exchange for your giving theirs to your clients.

On the downside, however, coupons and gift certificates may bring you price-sensitive clients and customers who will resist continuing or paying your full price. So you will want to make sure you use them effectively so you're not spending too much of your time and energy giving away unprofitable products and services.

Best Bets. Gift certificates and coupons work best with consumer products and services, although you can use them for business-to-business services as well. They are most effective when you are offering something people are already familiar with or intrigued by, so that they will be motivated to use them themselves and give them to others who will.

Tips for Getting Business from Gift Certificates and Coupons

While retailers from grocery stores and hair salons make ample use of both gift certificates and coupons, as an individual or very small business you will generally want to use them more strategically instead of trying to hit the mass market. Here are several tips for making the most of coupons and gift certificates.

Target your use. Don't give out gift certificates and coupons indiscriminately. Decide what your marketing goal is for using them and whom you want to attract with them. Do you want to use them as a referral strategy? A customer appreciation campaign? A way to attract new business from a particular type of clientele? Etc.

Make them special. You will increase the quality of the business you get from gift certificates and coupons if you present them as something that is indeed special and desirable, not just a standard promotion to get something for less. So, don't lay them out on the networking table, for example, for everyone to pick up. Give them as a prize for a drawing or as a special gift to anyone in your networking group who makes a referral to you. Don't ask a retailer to set them out on the counter for anyone to pick up; ask him or her to give them out personally as a special part of their own service. A restaurant owner might give a gift certificate along with the bill, for example, as a thank-you for doing business with him. Don't lay them around your own office; give them out personally. Make them special and personal by saying. "I have something I want to give you," or "Because you are such a valued client, I want to give you this gift certificate."

Prequalify. Instead of giving out gift certificates or coupons randomly, ask if the person you're talking with would be interested in your service or know someone who would be. If so, give him a coupon or gift certificate as a special incentive. Personalize it with his name. If you want existing clients to make referrals, ask if they know someone in particular who they think would like to use your service. Then offer them coupons or gift certificates and personalize them too by adding their names. Or when they mention an organization they participate in, you might ask if they think members would appreciate a gift certificate as a prize at their monthly meeting.

Use them to extend business. Instead of giving a client a gift certificate or coupon on her next service, give her one that will encourage her to buy something additional. A manicurist, for example, might give her regular manicure customers a gift certificate for a pedicure. A résumé writer might give a coupon on mailing the résumés.

Tie in with others. Cross-promoting with coupons and gift certificates can be quite effective. If you are a dog trainer, for example, you might tie in with a dog groomer and a veterinarian to do a joint mailing of one another's coupons to your clients. A gatekeeper group (see above) might do a joint coupon mailing together. A networking group (**chapter 9**) might offer gift certificates to one another's clients, and so forth.

Back them up with other kinds of marketing. All publicity and other marketing activities can enhance the value of your gift certificates and coupons. When people have read or heard about you previously in a positive light, they will be all the more excited about getting a gift certificate or responding to a coupon.

High-Tech Tip: Creating Coupons and Gift Certificates

Give your gift certificates and coupons a customized, personalized touch by creating them yourself. You can do this by ordering preprinted certificates from companies like Paper Direct (800/A-Papers) and printing them out on a laser printer (see color insert). Or you can use your own high-quality paper stock and create coupons and gift certificates yourself using templates in software like *Microsoft Publisher.* With preprinted papers or a color ink-jet printer, you can coordinate the look of your coupons and certificates with your business card and stationery. Scan in your logo, graphic, or picture. Add your slogan, the name of the recipient, or an especially meaningful thought.

Resources: Gift Certificates and Coupons

To get your coupons or gift certificates included in value packs sent out with those of many others, contact companies like:

ADVO, 1 Univac Lane, Windsor, CT 06095, (860) 285-6100, www.advo.com

Lifestyle Change Communications, Inc., 1900 the Exchange, Suite #450, Atlanta, GA 30339-2022, (770) 984-1100, www.lifestylechange.com

Money Mailers, 201 Park Place, Altamont, Springs, FL 32701, (407) 831-0022, for names of local representatives.

SRDS, 1700 Higgins Road, Des Plaines, IL, 60018, (800) 851-7737, www.srds.com

Val-Pak, 6456 S. Quebec Street, Building 5, Ste. 550, Englewood, CO, 80111, (303) 843-0943 or look for their local brokers in the white pages of your phone book.

Letters of Reference, Endorsements, and Testimonials

Often gatekeepers, mentors, and satisfied clients and customers will tell you how pleased they are with your product or service, how much it has helped them, or what outstanding results they have seen from working with you. This is an excellent time to ask for their help. Ask whether they would be willing to serve as a reference or assist you by putting their thoughts in writing to use as testimonials or endorsements on your marketing materials. Usually they will be delighted to do what they can.

Whenever a customer calls to rave about one of her products, software publisher Bette Laswell always asks if the caller would write her a letter she could use as a reference. To generate additional testimonials, at times she has sent a note to her entire customer list asking for their comments. She encloses a self-addressed, stamped postcard for them to send their comments and then uses positive quotes people send on her catalog pages, on quote sheets, and along with all orders.

A number of celebrities have bought bake goods from Christine's Kitchen, a healthy gourmet bakery. Christine posts their thank-you notes and letters along with a picture in the store and includes their comments on her order sheets and catering menus. A makeup artist has bound her testimonials in a booklet that she keeps on the coffee table in her waiting room. Jennifer Brown, creator of MouseMitts,™ includes testimonials from overjoyed customers in her publicity materials and gets most of her sales through product reviews of her colorful wrist protectors.

A corporate trainer in Denver always asks clients to send a brief typewritten letter on their letterhead with a few points about how their company has benefited from his training. He then faxes the testimonial letters to companies he's talking with about doing future projects with a personalized note.

Denise Bonfilio specializes in home furnishing made from recycled wood like agricultural salvage of felled trees or damaged buildings. When word of her unique custom-made projects spread, she attracted interest from the White House. Although still awaiting word as to whether they would buy a podium for the president, she included information about her potential customer in publicity interviews, which attracted still more interest in her business.

These are just a few examples of the many creative ways small and home businesses can use testimonials and letters of reference to get others to spread the word about their products and services.

Pros and Cons of Letters of Reference, Endorsements, and Testimonials

Testimonials, endorsements, or letters of reference can be excellent and versatile ways to build credibility. They offer written proof that what you say about yourself or your business in your marketing materials and sales presentations is true. In fact, they make excellent additions to any written marketing piece as well as to your presentation kit. Often prospective clients will ask for the names of others you have worked with. Comments from satisfied clients or testimonials from respected authorities can be of enormous help to you by serving as a reference for prospective clients and customers.

An added benefit is that others can sing your praises in ways that you could not as easily do yourself. A satisfied client with years of experience in her field can say, "He is the best," whereas saying this about yourself would seem entirely self-serving and biased. The samples on pages 270 and 333 illustrate just how powerful testimonial quotes can be.

The only drawbacks to letters of reference, endorsements, and testimonials are if those singing your praises do not have credibility with your clientele or unexpectedly find themselves in the midst of highly negative publicity. Of added concern would be using a testimonial or reference letter from anyone whose comments about you would actually be less than 100 percent complimentary if a client or customer contacted them to discuss doing business with you.

Tips for Getting Business from Letters of Reference, Endorsements, and Testimonials

Use the full names of real people. Identify the sources of your references and testimonials fully. Use their full names, the names of their businesses if appropriate, and their locations: e.g., Samuel T. Weeks, Attorney at Law, Toledo, Ohio. Never use initials like "S.W.," or partial identification like "Toledo lawyer." Such abbreviation simply puts doubts in the minds of your prospective clients, leaving them wondering "Is this a real person?" "Did they make this up?" "Couldn't they get permission from the real person?" "Why didn't they use their full names?"

Always get permission. Never use a testimonial, endorsement, or letter of reference without getting permission first, even if those involved have sent their positive comments to you unsolicited. When you know someone will be glad to serve as a reference, always call to request permission anyway, and from that point forward, let the person know when someone will be calling. No one should ever be surprised to receive a reference call or to see his name used in your publicity.

Say thanks. Corporate trainer and author Dianna Booher always asks clients to document positive comments in a testimonial letter that addresses specific issues they liked and the results they got. Once she receives the letters, she sends the writer of each one a thank-you gift such as an autographed book or audiocassette tapes. They often write back to express their surprise and appreciation for her thoughtful gift.

Make it easy. When clients are willing to provide such an endorsement (and it is permissible to solicit one), make it easy for them to do so. If they've called or spoken to you personally, don't expect them to take the time to compose and mail their thoughts to you themselves; people tend to get instant writer's block or to delay writing. Instead, ask whether they would be willing to dictate a few comments to you on the phone about what your product or service has done for them. Jot down what they say, edit it for grammar and style, and read it back to them for their approval.

If you need an actual letter of endorsement for a publicity kit or proposal package, another alternative is to mail these people a copy of what they have said on the phone and ask them to return it to you on their own stationery. Once your marketing materials are printed, send all the people you have quoted a copy along with a note of appreciation.

Start building a list of such references as soon as you can and have their telephone numbers handy to give out as needed.

Make maximum use of your supporters' comments. Once you have gone to the trouble of getting testimonials and endorsements, use them in as many contexts as possible. You can include them as part of virtually any marketing campaign. Here are just a few ideas:

- Feature them in your brochures, newsletters, flyers, and sales letters and proposals.
- Include them in your advertising, direct mail, news releases, and Web page.
- Feature them on product packaging and point-of-sale displays.
- Include them in your bio, portfolio, and presentation kit, and as part of your introduction when you speak or give seminars.
- You could even use them as a slogan on a business card, banner, or sign: "As seen on KXXX TV," "As featured at the exclusive Get Away Salon," or "Best Pizza of the Year Award from the *Mainland Gazette.*"

Resources: Letters of Reference, Endorsements & Testimonials

Power Schmoozing. Terri Mandell. New York: McGraw-Hill, 1996. Has a chapter on meeting and talking to celebrities.

Publicity Opportunities

How would you like to open the newspaper one morning and find a feature story about you and your product or service? Or imagine that whenever an article, news feature, or story about your field appears anywhere in print or on radio or television, your views are quoted extensively or your products are mentioned prominently. Suppose that anytime your business undertakes an activity or event that you would like people to know about, the media eagerly announces these happenings? That's publicity.

Most people want to do business with someone they know or at least have heard of in a positive light. So when you're just starting out newly on your own, you're confronted with the proverbial chicken-before-the-egg dilemma: you need customers to develop a reputation, and you need a reputation to get customers. One of the fastest ways out of this dilemma is lots of good publicity. Publicity can help you make a high-profile impression as quickly as possible, so that when people need what you have to offer they will think of you and say, "Oh, yes, I've heard of . . ."

That's what Shell and Judy Norris of Chicago did when they opened Class Reunions, Inc., one of the first services for managing college and high-school reunions. They had planned Class Reunions to be a part-time sideline business. But, when the *Wall Street Journal* picked up a story about their new service, a flood of calls kept them busy full-time almost from the start. Similarly, Dan Cassidy was still in college when he started a computerized scholarship-matching service. Having few funds for advertising, he arranged for a guest appearance to talk on a local radio station about his new service, and within a week he had received over a hundred calls from eager listeners. Over the years, he has continued to use radio and television talk-show appearances as his primary means of getting business.

Nathalie Dupree has also benefited from the power of publicity. Twenty years ago, a mention in Delta Airlines' *Sky Magazine* put her tiny Georgia restaurant on the map. She may get calls for years from one piece of publicity. Now having written many books and produced food shows for PBS and the Food Network, she finds that the people whose food products she mentions on her shows get a similar response. She did a show, for example, about a man who makes wooden biscuit bowls. That one show made his business, and ten years later people are still calling for his address.

Kim Jurado of New York had a similar experience when *Brides* magazine mentioned her business Bella Dulce Opulent Marzipan and the handmade peaches she does for wedding cakes. "The phone has been ringing off the hook," she reports. Publicity had turned Robert Stephens's The Geek Squad, an around-the-clock computer repair service, into a national phenomenon. Reading about the Geek Squad in *Time* and other national magazines led Hewlett Packard to contact him about teaming up for a nationwide "Geek of the Year" contest.

Warning: When undertaking any type of contest or drawing for promotional purposes, make sure you aren't inadvertently running an illegal lottery. There are criminal consequences connected with any illegal lottery activity even if it was unintended. Laws regulating lotteries vary from state to state and even county to county, so before holding a promotional contest or drawing, consult with the attorney general's office in your state or the deputy district attorney in the county where you live.

Although the response to publicity is not always this dramatic, these stories are illustrative of the benefits to be derived from well-placed public relations. Once you have this kind of presence working for you, getting business can be easy.

Pros and Cons of Publicity

Next to getting a referral, publicity is the most reliable way to create the reputation necessary to attract business to you. Your reputation is, after all, built on what others say about you. You have undoubtedly read articles featuring businessmen and women in your community and have probably used their services after reading such articles. You also have undoubtedly seen interviews and news stories on television featuring professionals in your community, such as the tax attorney who is interviewed on the local news at tax time, the consultant whose analysis is sought in response to a new technological breakthrough, or the local doctors quoted in the story on advances in plastic surgery. These men and women are enjoying the sweet rewards of publicity. They get so much business from this exposure that many businesses pay thousands of dollars a month to PR firms to make sure that their names get into features like these.

Such exposure is often referred to as "free publicity" because publicity by definition is unpaid for, but it usually isn't actually free. Even if you do all such promotion yourself, you must invest considerable time and energy and a certain amount of money to generate publicity. Time and money are involved, for example, in sending materials to the press in the form of a publicity kit, printing these materials, paying for the postage, and footing the bill for the mileage or phone calls involved in being interviewed. But recent studies show that small businesses increasingly find that, dollar for dollar, they often derive a greater impact from PR than from paid advertising.

Because publicity isn't paid for, however, you never have control

PUBLIC RELATIONS AND PUBLICITY

Pros

! Editorial coverage is more highly regarded than advertising.

! Editorial coverage is more credible than advertising.

! Maintaining a high profile within a specialty increases credibility.

! PR can bring you in contact with peers throughout the business community.

! PR activities open doors to mentors and gatekeepers.

! PR coverage is free.

! Whatever you do for and in your community usually comes back to you tenfold.

Cons

! PR can take a considerable investment of time to create.

! PR takes time to produce results.

! You must develop and commit to a long-range plan.

! Because PR is unpaid, it is also out of your control.

! Media will print and broadcast their impression of you, not necessarily the one you want.

! Postage, kits, and materials require financial investment.

! Getting media attention requires skill, knowledge, and creativity.

over whether you will actually be mentioned or exactly what is and is not said about you if you are mentioned. The media pride themselves on being highly independent and objective. They will use whatever segments and comments they choose and will slant them in whatever way they choose. Also, sometimes scheduled features or segments are dropped at the last minute when unexpected hard-news events occur. Therefore, when you need to know that specific information will definitely appear or need particular sales-oriented information to be announced, advertising is a more dependable route. Of course, the difficulty and unpredictability of publicity is precisely what makes it so valuable. And since publicity often generates more publicity, appearing in the right media can be a very cost-effective investment over time.

Best Bets: You might not be able to imagine getting publicity for your business on national radio or television or even in local newspapers and magazines. Therefore, you might conclude that publicity is not an alternative for your kind of business. This is a common misconception because while many small businesses don't lend themselves to mass media, there is almost always someplace where your business or independent career could benefit from publicity: if not in the local newspaper, then in your trade or professional journal; if not on national public radio, then perhaps in the industry newsletter your clients read. Services and products for both business and consumer can all benefit from getting publicity as long as it appears in a medium your clients and customers read, watch or listen to, value and respect.

So look through the trade magazines, newsletters, and newspapers you receive each week and notice who is quoted in the many articles you read. Who is featured? Who is interviewed in local newscasts? You will be surprised at all the publicity opportunities that are right under your nose. Here are just a few of examples from a single day's reading of our local newspaper and the magazines we received that day in the mail:

- Dan Rosenthal, owner of Way-To-Go travel service, was quoted in a *Los Angeles Times* article advising readers how it can pay to carry extra luggage.
- *Inc* magazine did a human-interest blurb on how Jacki Baker, owner of Mother Myricks' ice-cream shop and mail-order candy business, has offered a free ice-cream-and-cake special to encourage children to read more books.
- The *L.A. Times* announced in its "Save the Date" column that the South Bay Center for Counseling is sponsoring a "Lose Your Blues" benefit.
- "Hot to Shop," another column in the *Times,* responded to a reader inquiry by describing a new product called Wave Webs from Hydro-Fit. Readers were given the 800 number through which they could order these novel gloves for exercising in the water.
- Still another column called "In Brief" announced a nutrition workshop being conducted at a local YWCA by consulting nutritionist Rene Klag.

- A business-section feature on spotting clues to when to sell mutual funds quoted advice from the editors of several financial newsletters in various parts of the country.
- An *L.A. Times Magazine* feature called "Rubbed the Right Way" described a variety of massage salons, including Nice to Be Kneaded, Massage Masters, and Massage Therapy Center, that specialize in serving executive women.
- The Personal Business section of *Business Week* magazine featured several closet-design firms, such as Hold Everything in California and Perfect Closet in Grosse Point Farms, Michigan. They also gave a phone number for requesting a catalog for organizational storage items.

Tips for Getting Business from Publicity

Who wouldn't want publicity like that for their businesses? But would it actually help your business? It's assumed that if your company is mentioned in the newspaper, if you're interviewed on the radio, or if your sign is seen in the middle of a television program, that you will get business. The fact is, not every story generates business. Why not? The answer is simple: The articles you're in, the interviews that you do, the newsletters you're featured in won't necessarily reach your target customer. Publicity is only as valuable as the number of actual potential clients or customers who see it. A home landscape designer interviewed on a show whose audience is composed mostly of sports fans is far less likely to get business than a competing landscaper who is featured in an article entitled "Making Your New House a Home" in a regional consumer magazine.

So before leaping into a campaign to get publicity, ask yourself three questions:

1. What publicity would actually help me reach my target customer in an efficient manner?
2. Might my target customer actually take action to contact me or will he/she recognize my name if I contact him/her as a result of my publicity efforts?
3. Am I willing to commit to the time and effort necessary for a successful publicity campaign?

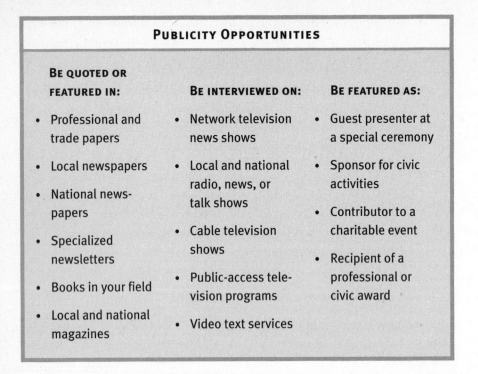

Publicity Opportunities

Be quoted or featured in:	Be interviewed on:	Be featured as:
• Professional and trade papers • Local newspapers • National newspapers • Specialized newsletters • Books in your field • Local and national magazines	• Network television news shows • Local and national radio, news, or talk shows • Cable television shows • Public-access television programs • Video text services	• Guest presenter at a special ceremony • Sponsor for civic activities • Contributor to a charitable event • Recipient of a professional or civic award

After careful consideration of these questions and three answers in the affirmative, set down a series of goals and expectations against which you can measure the results of your publicity effort and you'll be ready to get started. Here are some basics tips for getting your name in the public eye.

Make yourself known to the media. When you read articles or watch news stories quoting and interviewing experts in your field, you may wonder, as we once did, why you weren't mentioned. Often you are just as knowledgeable and interesting as those who are cited. While we once thought that when people became truly expert at what they do, the media will seek them out, we soon learned that even if you're the most expert authority in your field, if the media doesn't know about you and your expertise, they will not call you to talk with you about it. In all but the most unusual of cases, you will need to create publicity yourself by letting the media, or the sources they turn to, know about you.

The most direct way to do this is to contact the media yourself: in person, through your representative, or by mail. A more indirect route is to make sure that the sources to which the media turn for information mention you whenever they are asked for names of people to contact. The customary routes for gaining media attention are to send a news release or a query letter along with your presentation kit.

A news release enables you to announce something you and your company are doing that is newsworthy; a query letter is a means for introducing ideas for stories or interviews about you, your field, or your business. Both news releases and query letters are expected to follow a specific format, so, when you get ready to make contact with the media, see **Writing Effective News Releases and Query Letters**, available on-line without charge at www.paulandsarah.com on the Great Ideas for Getting Business page, or review the other resources on page 398.

When sending your presentation kit to the media, if at all possible, it should include clips from any other publicity you have received, your photo or a sample or photo of your work, and a broadcast résumé if you have one.

Make yourself newsworthy. Keep in mind that an editor of any publication or program receives dozens, if not hundreds, of news releases and publicity kits every day. So you will need to discover how you can make what you are doing newsworthy to the editors, producers, or bookers you will be contacting. Your news release or query letter will need to show them why their audience needs or will want to know about your approach, insights, products, or services. In other words, you must be newsworthy to the viewers, readers, or listeners of the specific medium you are addressing. You must offer something they will find sufficiently meaningful to warrant coverage in the limited time or space of their medium.

What will command extensive coverage in a weekly rural newspaper might not even warrant consideration in the *Kansas City Star,* for example, much less the *New York Times,* so you must tailor your news releases and query letters to the particular publication or program you want to approach. A local community newspaper, for example, might do a story about the opening of an aerobic dance studio if it is the first such service in the community, because before this studio opened people from the community who wanted to attend an aerobics class had to drive out of town. The *New York Times* wouldn't do such an article, however, because there are hundreds of aerobics classes in New York. They might do a story, though, on how attending aerobics classes can affect one's sex life! (See **Marketing Masterpiece: Publicity** below for proof.)

The secret to newsworthiness is relating what is unique about what you are doing to something that people want or need to know. If you have clients and customers who buy your product or service, you must be doing something uniquely valuable. All you have to do is recognize it and find the hook that will makes it newsworthy. Often it involves putting elements from what you do into a newsworthy context. That might involve sponsoring a contest or award, conducting a survey or poll among your clients or within your field, forming an organization or holding an event for people with particular needs addressed by your niche, or announcing a discovery you've made about why people run into the most common problem your clients experience. Here are a few unusual examples:

Now Old Friends Information Services of Orinda, California, wrote to *USA Today* columnist Craig Wilson who writes "The Final Word" about their 70 percent success rate in finding old friends and lovers and how a survey of their customer base indicated that only 4 percent of those located didn't want to be found. The column included the phone number and price in case readers themselves wanted to search for a lost friend. *Andrew Harper's Hideaway Report,* a monthly travel newsletter, drew a feature story in the travel section of their local newspaper based on their reader poll of the most and least favorite travel destinations (Vancouver and Cape Town came in on top, Mexico City and Los Angeles on the bottom). Jack Singer of Las Vegas teaches health-care professionals like medical assistants how to deal with the stress of handling massive paperwork. His survey of 500 doctors in eleven states found that all of them complain about the added stress since the proliferation of managed care, and sharing his findings with the press led to a feature story on him and his business in the *USA Today* Health and Behavior section.

Art dealer Fred Turra got a lot of media attention for his "Magic Bus," which travels across the country hosting workshops and sponsoring charity events featuring noted artists. Pet trainer Miriam Yarden sponsors an annual owner-pooch look-alike contest in Long Beach which draws considerable publicity for her views on dog behavior, including a feature article on fashion accessories for pets.

Professional organizer Harriet Schechter tied in the publicity campaign for her "Time to Get Organized" workshops into National Get Organized Week. Author John Grey, who writes best-selling books on relationships, declared the first Sunday in June to be Marriage Day to help promote the book *1001 Ways to Be Romantic,* and the publisher declared August "Romantic Awareness Month." Marriage Child and Family Counselor Donald Etkes of Claremont, California, created Pleasure Your Mate Month. Marketing consultant Lorrie Walters Marsiglio of St. Charles, Illinois, created Subliminal Marketing Month, September 1–30, and did a publicity campaign throughout the month on this theme.

You, too, can create a holiday for virtually any occasion using *Chase's Calendar of Events* (see **Resources: Publicity**). Or you can dovetail on an existing one by looking at *Chase's*, the *Guinness Book of World Records* or John Dremer's *Celebrate Today.* In hopes of promoting good penmanship, the Writing Instrument Manufacturers Association sponsored National Handwriting Day. The date was chosen because it was the birthday of John Hancock, whose large and legible signature appears on the Declaration of Independence. To piggy-back on the publicity around this occasion, Kay Young of the S.O.S. *Quarterly,* a newsletter for secretarial and office support services, came up with a clever award any secretarial service could use: offer a prize on National Handwriting Day to the client with the best handwriting.

When you create a holiday through *Chase's Calendar,* your holiday is listed in their calendar of events along with how the media or other interested parties can reach you. In fact they have declared March 26 to be "Make Up Your Own Holiday Day"!

Get attention with a hook. The most important part of your message to the media is that hook, or angle, that will stimulate the interest of their readers, viewers, listeners, or Web surfers. So in making contact with the media, you want to lead with your hook and you need to be able to express it right up front in your first few words. In a way, it's

FIFTEEN WAYS TO MAKE YOURSELF NEWSWORTHY

1. Take a poll or conduct a survey.
2. Issue a proclamation or hold a celebration.
3. Announce novel observations and discoveries.
4. Report unusual or human-interest stories.
5. Hold a contest.
6. Sponsor an award.
7. Host or sponsor a special event.
8. Give a valuable but unusual donation.
9. Introduce a novel twist.
10. Create a commemorative month or day.
11. Involve a celebrity.
12. Take on a cause.
13. Establish a Seal of Approval or Best/Worst list.
14. Compile a list of hot tips or fascination facts.
15. Form an organization.

much like having an Attention Grabber (see **chapter 5**) that you create specifically for the particular media contact you want to make. Whether you communicate via the mail, by phone, modem, or fax, you will have only a few seconds to arouse an editor's or producer's interest—about the time it takes to read a headline and the first sentence of your release.

To find a hook that will make you and your business newsworthy, be alert to the issues, events, fads, problems, and concerns being addressed by the media to which your clients and customers tune in, be they trade journals, newspapers, newsletters, radio, or television. Do you have a new product or service that addresses one of your clients' major concerns? Do you offer an improvement on products or services currently being discussed? Have you discovered a new way to do something your competitors have touted already? Are you doing something that hasn't been done before? Have you responded to a community crisis or need? Could you hold an event or sponsor an activity that would call positive attention to your work? Could you do a survey or mini-study related to your work that would provide enlightening, surprising, or intriguing insights? Jump at any opportunity to send a news release about any such development.

Speech and diction coach Sandy McKnight, for example, has found a way for people to reduce or eliminate an unwanted accent. Part-time computer programmer and full-time freelance clown Alan Macy has created a new software program featuring 504 jokes suitable for use in business presentations. Freelance makeup artist Sally Van Swearingen has found that today's brides want to have a magazine-cover-perfect look. There are opportunities for innovation in almost any field. A desktop-publishing company or word-processing service might sponsor a free workshop for local merchants on how the latest technology can give their printed materials a *Fortune* 500 look without increasing expenses. A landscape designer could donate a magnificent rare tree to a local nursing home.

Each of these examples has the material for an effective news release. Where business-related news releases too often fall down, however (and therefore get ignored by the media), is by focusing on technical facts instead of practical or interesting applications to the readers' lives. Announcing a new line of imported lace wedding gowns, for example, is much less newsworthy than announcing that women are choosing more formal wedding attire this spring than at any time in the past thirty years. The new lace gowns, of course, become examples of what today's bride is wearing.

Hairstylist and colorist Gina Furth found an angle that garnered ample attention for her specialty. She made a study of the variations in blond hair-color preferences from coast to coast and compared the regional choices to the looks of Ivana Trump, Madonna, and Candice Bergen. The result was a *Los Angeles Times* feature story entitled "Battle of the Blondes," which included Furth's picture as well as those of the three stars whose looks she was comparing. The name and location of her salon were mentioned as well.

Marketing Masterpiece: Publicity

You might think that conducting a survey or poll as a way to make yourself newsworthy would be too expensive or time-consuming. But that's not necessarily so. When psychologist Linda De Villars of Los Angeles went into private practice as a sex therapist, she needed to establish herself as an authority in her field and gain visibility in the crowded Southern California marketplace where it has been jokingly said that every other person is a therapist. So De Villars came up with a unique strategy for promoting her Loveskills Seminars.

She polled readers of a fitness magazine about the relationship between the amount of time they spent working out at the gym and their frequency of sex. She found that, indeed, there was a relationship. The more people worked out, the more they felt good about their bodies and the more they engaged in sexual relations. There were also interesting differences between the effect of working out on men and women. De Villars presented her findings before the National Association of Psychologists, where her story was picked up by the national media.

Her findings were first reported in *USA Today* and then appeared in numerous national magazines and other media, including the *New York Times*. An evening tabloid television news show featured her as well. More than a year and a half later she was still getting media calls as a consequence of the publicity that came from announcing her survey results.

Present a variety of ideas for stories, interviews, or features. One of the common mistakes people make in trying to get publicity is developing one media hook and sending it out to everyone. Actually you will be more successful if you create a variety of ideas that would be of interest to different media. A custom wedding-gown designer who creates his gowns by combining modern fabrics with rare antique laces he acquires from traveling the world, for example, might be an interesting angle to send to the editor of the travel section of the local newspaper, a travel magazine, or an antiques publication that does features on unusual collections. Another publication, however, might be more interested in a feature story on the history of lace. Other media might be more interested in a story idea on what people wore to the world's wackiest wedding. All of these are possible hooks for this designer.

A professional organizer might suggest ideas for an article or interview on how to bring order to a teenager's room, organizing the closet no one dares to open, or reclaiming your attic, basement, or garage. A financial consultant might propose articles on how couples who budget argue less about money, the one investment that can set your children up financially for life, or the last remaining tax shelter for the middle class. Boil your ideas down to simple eye-catching headlines or a list of attention-grabbing questions. Be sure these ideas are truly of interest to the specific readers, listeners, or viewers of the media to which you will be sending your kit, not just to you. If possible, include a photograph that complements the headline. For example, makeup artist Sally Van Swearingen, who specializes in doing makeup for bridal parties, might create a sheet listing headlines and descriptions such as these:

- Special Faces for Special Occasions
  An eye-catching photo layout of brides-to-be with before-and-after shots that show the different looks makeup can achieve.

- Putting Your Best Face Forward
  A step-by-step guide on makeup application for brides, indicating how much is too much, what the camera will show, and how to bring out the most in one's features.

- The Spring Bride Blossoms
  A detailed discussion of the new colors being used this season for weddings, from attendants' gowns to flowers and accessories, and how to coordinate the bride's makeup to match her choice of colors and enhance her natural beauty.

Including a list of sample leads like these in your publicity kit provides editors and programmers with ideas for ways to include you in their features or programs and makes interviews easier for feature writers and hosts.

Action Steps: Building a Personalized Media List

We suggest building what we call your Personalized Media List that includes the newspapers, magazines, newsletters, and radio and television shows that serve your particular business market. Whatever your potential clients and customers read, watch, or listen to should be on your list. To reach those on your list most easily and quickly, get their addresses, phone numbers, fax numbers and E-mail addresses and, if possible, find out which one they prefer receiving media materials through.

Send your materials to the right person. Considering the time and money involved in producing your news release or query letter and promotional kit, you want to make sure you're sending them to the right person at the right place. And keep in mind that you are no longer limited to sending material by mail or phone. Most media also receive mail by fax and E-mail. Sandra Schrift, a personal coach to professional speakers, sends her news releases via fax, for example. This saves both time and money.

You probably know who some of these contacts are already. To expand your list, ask your customers and clients what they read, watch, and listen to most. Consult directories that list all the major publications and other media along with the names of specific personnel in each position. These directories, found in most libraries, are usually updated on an annual basis. They are especially valuable tools when your promotional plans include national coverage. A sampling of directories is in **Resources** at the end of the book. The reference librarian at your community library can help you locate and use the best ones for your business.

The newsstand is another source of good ideas. Look through all the national, regional, and local publications displayed there and select those you think your potential clients and customers read. Inside these publications will be the names of the editors, columnists, and writers, along with the phone number and address of the publication. Also make a point to read local radio and television listings on a regular basis. Notice the shows that do interviews and news features and what topics they discuss, and watch or listen to those that have topics of interest to your clients or customers. Knowing the format and slant of these shows will be helpful in writing both your news releases and query letters as well as in talking to the person who books the shows.

You can probably use the library to find the editors of all the trade publications for your target market. If the target market for your product or service is, for example, advertising agencies, accountants, or building contractors, you will want to send your materials to any local, regional, or national trade papers and magazines that serve these fields. *Ad Week* and *Advertising Age* are examples of the publications read routinely at ad agencies. Major national trade publications like these often have regional editions as well, in which case you will need to get the names of the editors who deal with your region.

Don't waste your time or your materials by mailing publicity materials to editors who would have no interest in them. A complete package may cost fifteen dollars or more. Although that is a small investment when properly placed, it is far too much money to waste on editors or producers for whom there is no possible interest. For example, the city editors of large urban papers are usually interested only in spot news of general interest, so unless you have a flash release concerned with an event that in your community would warrant front-page or near-front-page coverage, sending him or her your information is the quickest way for it to end up in the circular file. On the other hand, the business or lifestyle editor might be interested in your material for features, product reviews, or events listings.

There are companies and products whose stories would be better suited for other editors. A software company, a custom wedding-gown designer, a landscape consultant, or a building contractor, for example, might send their materials to the technical editor, the fashion editor, the lifestyle editor, or the real estate editor, respectively.

If you are having difficulty finding the time to do the research involved in compiling your Personalized Media List, there is a variety of cost-effective shortcuts:

- ***Buy a media list.*** Companies like Bacon's Information, Inc., and Burelle's Information Services sell media lists (see **Resources: Publicity**). Of course, these lists may include names and addresses that are not suited to your business, but such lists can be a starting point.

- ***Get professional help.*** Instead of hiring a public-relations consultant or publicist to handle all your publicity, hire one simply to select the best media and ask that he or she provide you with such a list, complete with all the pertinent information and mailing labels. But be very careful. Many agencies work on formulas. You need to find an agency that will customize a list for your particular needs.

TREND: Millions, With the Help of Technology, Find They Like Working at Home

Continued from D1

businesses from their converted bedrooms, porches and garages in 1995. Fourteen million more had part-time home businesses, and 8 million telecommuted from home offices. The rest use their home

ger a problem for them. After moving to Sierra Madre in 1976, they gradually began spending less time on their original businesses and more time acting as consultants to the growing legion of home businesses.

There's No Commute, but . . .

Top 10 problems of working from home (according to a survey of home-based businesses):

consulting business in her Long Beach home.

"It looks, feels and smells like a business," said the former insurance and health-care executive. "It has a fax, a computer, a modem, a printer and a fancy-shmancy telephone. I've got a desk, a chair and file and supply cabinets."

Still, Ginty and others say that being taken seriously as a business is one of the biggest hurdles to starting a home office.

"I never hid the fact that my office was in my home, but I didn't broadcast it, either," said Seena Sharp, who started an information broker business in her Hermosa Beach home. Sometimes, though, it was hard to be discreet when clients could hear her children screaming in the background during a telephone conversation.

Recruiting customers is another major obstacle for home businesses.

"The most difficult part is finding the business to do," said Andre Sharp, Seena's husband, who started doing corporate communications and technical writing after he was laid off from a management position with Mattel Inc. in 1986. "I assumed—and wrongfully so—that just because I could do the work meant that I could get the business. In a larger company, the work is

operate a business in one's home. That makes it hard for home-based entrepreneurs to advertise.

"They don't get listed in the Yellow Pages, they don't do publicity, and they don't do enough marketing for people to be able to seek them out," Paul Edwards said.

Some people, like the Edwardses, make a point of living in cities that are friendly to home-based businesses. But many are ignorant of the zoning laws that govern their businesses, and still others prefer to simply ignore them.

Dworman's neighborhood is not zoned for home-based businesses, but three bedrooms and his den are given over to his publishing company, which also produces three conferences a year. He says he doesn't worry about zoning because "we don't have a lot of traffic coming in here, and it's not really a bother to anybody."

On the whole, home business owners say the hassles are far outweighed by the benefits of being able to spend more time with family, control one's hours, dress casually and avoid office politics.

"You lose the stability of the ongoing, predictable, timely paycheck," said Tova Feder, who started a personal and business development coaching service in

he Idea Catches On: Home, Suite Home

ecommuting: Couple quit their day) years ago and liked it. Today they ding a groundswell of 30 million cans who enjoy an easy trip from om to office.

MONICA

RICIA WARD BIEDERMAN
FF WRITER

nty years ago, Sarah Edwards saw her future. e relatively satisfied holder of a government , Edwards had a meeting with a consultant who thing unusual. He worked out of his house. , the mother of a young son, loved the idea. "I ake my life work this way," she thought.

Edwards and her husband Paul, 53, are known ras of the home office. Working out of their onica townhouse, the couple have written five the subject, including the bible of home-based , "Working From Home." More than 35,000 ers participate in their 10-year-old Working me Forum on CompuServe information . And on the radio and in a popular column for azine Home Office Computing, they offer tips on ucceed in business without taking off your fuzzy

3, working at home is an idea whose time has ore than 30 million Americans do it. But as the ecall, it was relatively uncharted territory in en they quit their office jobs to try to make it on n, Sarah as a home-based psychotherapist and political consultant.

ensors told us this was something more and ople were going to be doing," Paul said. But the as unconvinced. "The neighbors thought Paul mployed," Sarah said, laughing.

were few places to turn for advice when they me home business pioneers. Indeed, by quitting jobs before getting their home businesses hed, they broke what has become one of their rules. But, for the most part, they say, their two of working where they live have been a , although there were years, Sarah said, when nt more money than they earned.

are three main reasons home businesses have f, according to Sarah. First, the high-powered, le home computer, the fax and other new gy, she says, "make it possible to have a office in your home." Second, a changing is fueling the trend. Large companies shed 4 mployees during the 1980s, and layoffs continue an upturn in the economy as a whole. This year,

Home office gurus Paul and Sarah Edwards do a radio show from th

Sarah said, there were one-third more corporate layoffs than in 1992. Finally, she believes, working from home (the term they prefer to "working at home") has taken off because Americans don't like working for other people. "Deep in their hearts," she said, "7 out of 10 Americans say they want to be their own boss."

If any single development underpins the homework phenomenon, it's the computer, they say. Sarah recalled that they wrote the first draft of "Working From Home" on an IBM Selectric. The final draft was done on their first computer.

Today publishers routinely accept manuscripts on computer disc, but in that electronic Dark Age—only a decade ago—the publisher wanted only hard copy, and

not copy produced on a Sarah recalled that they computers included in t

Today, 60% of all ho Paul said. Able to in equals, these computer increasingly vital segm minute a new home bus cites Apple and Day Ru home-based businesses

Anticipating a boom Edwardses published " They have been in the

SMALL BUSINESS

Sarah and Paul Edwards, two gurus of the work-at-home movement, have their desks in the loft of their Santa Monica condominium. Sarah resolved to open a home office after a stress-related kidney infection.

PERRY C. RIDDLE / Los Angeles Times

SOUTHERN CALIFORNIA ENTERPRISE

Home Sweet Home Office

Millions, With the Aid of Technology, Find Working There Suits Them Just Fine

By KAREN KAPLAN
SPECIAL TO THE TIMES

PCs Make It Possible

The number of people working from small offices and home offices (SOHOs) continues to grow as personal computers become more powerful, more affordable and easier to use.

PCs AT HOME

Percentage of U.S. households with a

HOME OFFICES

Number of Americans with home offices, in millions:

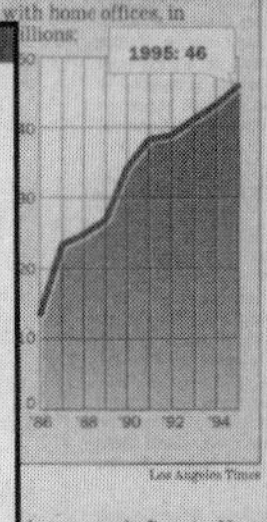

Los Angeles Times

rket research firm in New ricans operated full-time

Please see TREND, D4

SAMPLE NEWS CLIPPINGS. *Articles like these can result from your public-relations efforts.*

Creating Your Own Space

There is much more involved in establishing an effective small office than installing the appropriate computer hardware and software, say Paul and Sarah Edwards, who write extensively on small business and host a weekly network radio show on the subject.

This husband-and-wife team in Santa Monica, Calif., offers *Nation's Business* readers the following tips for establishing a productive work environment at home or in a commercial building:

Plan ahead. Determine how much space you have, and allocate it carefully before buying furniture, filing cabinets, PCs, or other office equipment. Designate and lay out the areas where you will perform basic office tasks such as using the telephone and related accessories, computing, processing mail, handling money, and filing.

For assistance, consider space-planning software such as Planix for Windows

PHOTO: ©BART BARTHOLOMEW

Plan carefully *and be neat, say home-office experts Paul and Sarah Edwards.*

(Foresight Resources Corp.; $99 retail) or 3D Office (Design Ware; $129.95 retail).

Look like a business. Create an air of professionalism for your customers and yourself by minimizing personal items such as laundry and children's toys. And minimize the clutter that inevitably arises as a business grows. If necessary, retain a professional organizer.

Get good furniture. Maximize productivity and minimize the risk of back or repetitive-motion injuries by making your office ergonomically sound. Get a comfortable, adjustable chair with a high back. Also be certain that the computer's keyboard, mouse, and monitor are well designed and positioned at the proper height and angle.

See things clearly. Lighting is a major contributor to high productivity. Daylight is best for your eyes, but even daylight can be enhanced by judicious use of spot lighting and other artificial light. Be sure there is adequate power for lighting and other equipment needs; an energy audit is provided free by many utility companies.

If much of your market is local, the individuals you work with at your selected agency should be personally acquainted with most of the media contacts and can advise you on ways to approach individual media. On the other hand, if you're looking for publicity in national media, you should find a publicist who has personal media contacts with national publications and networks. If you want to publicize yourself on the Web, find one of the growing number of publicists who specialize in Web publicity.

- ***Use a wire service.*** You might also consider using a newswire service to distribute your publicity materials. For several hundred dollars, a company like PR Newswire will send your news release to 1,700 newspapers (see **Resources: Publicity**). Bear in mind, however, that these companies are sending news releases, not an entire media package. So over time, you will be well served to build a list of your own media contacts to whom you can send more personal and customized materials on a regular basis.

Make sure the right person actually gets your materials. Send all materials to editors or producers by name. If you want to increase your chances of avoiding their mail slush pile, send a fax, leave an E-mail message, call in advance, or deliver your material by hand. If you take the time to deliver it yourself, you might make an invaluable personal contact with key personnel.

When sending material to the broadcast media, put both the interviewer's name and the names of the producers and editors of the program on your mailing list, and send your material to all of them. Usually the host will pass along the material to the producer, netting you double exposure.

Always follow up by phone. All media materials should be followed up within a week by a telephone call. Even if your materials were hand-delivered, they may just have been placed on the top of the pile, and there is no guarantee they will be read or considered. A simple phone call helps remind an editor of your materials and brings you to his or her attention more personally. It is not suggested that you pester any editor; one friendly call to check that the materials were received and whether there is any further information that might be helpful is a good beginning that will help establish rapport with your contacts. Several follow-up calls are appropriate when you can't reach someone directly. Those who are most persistent and leave the most intriguing voice-mail messages are the most likely to have their calls returned and get reviews, mentions or bookings.

As you talk to editors, you may discover how to pitch your idea more closely to their specific interests and concerns, and as they get to know you better, they may see opportunities that you had never thought of. So, don't get stuck on the one idea you present. Be open and flexible to all the possibilities. Even if they don't use your material immediately, your relationship can open doors for the placement of future materials.

We continue to be amazed at how many media packages we throw away only to have someone call later and provide us with information that convinces us to do an interview. There are at least two lessons here: that following up can pay off, and that if your materials are routinely getting tossed out, you aren't using the most effective hooks. Follow-up calls can help you learn which hooks work best with whom.

There is yet a third lesson to be learned: Never plan to have a single packet or kit do the job. Allow in your budget for two or three, especially with your most critical media. Some packages will inevitably go astray—to the wrong desk or even at the post office; some will be tossed out (no matter how great they are) simply because there is too large a pile on an editor's desk; and a few will be lost by accident. When you make your follow-up calls, nine out of ten times you will be requested to resend your information. Be prepared.

Persist. CPA and solo practitioner Art Berkowitz, of Laguna Niguel, California, manages to get his name mentioned in the *Herald*'s business section offering tax and financial advice week after week simply by making persistent contact with reporters offering his expertise and then being accessible to return their phone calls promptly.

Don't despair if your news isn't picked up. If you have sent out all this material and no one has chosen to use it, don't despair. Even unused releases bring your name before the media, so consider making the most of your effort by doing at least one of the following:

1. **SEND THE SAME IDEA TO DIFFERENT MEDIA.** Just because an idea is not picked up by one medium does not eliminate its possibilities for others. It may be used with a different approach or at a later date by another medium. So if your subject remains timely, you can send it to another publication, radio program, or television show at a later date.

2. **INTRODUCE YOURSELF AGAIN WITH EACH CHANGE IN PERSONNEL.** When the personnel at a particular media source change, you

can and should resend all materials that weren't used and follow up in person to build a new personal relationship. Actually, turnover of personnel is often a great time to get in on the ground floor working with someone who wants to make his or her own mark by taking a fresh approach.

3. Try, try again. Send out new information you think might be of interest regularly. Or, as long as material remains timely, it may be resent to the same people after a reasonable period of time has passed. However, if some of the material has been given broad coverage elsewhere, it would be wise to eliminate it from the reissue.

Explore alternative routes to media. If you are in an exceptionally large urban area where your press materials are routinely ignored despite being brilliantly written and thoroughly followed up on, there are alternative methods of communicating your message. For example, you might think about writing a letter to the editor, doing an editorial, a piece for the op-ed pages or other commentary, or getting your name in calendar listings in a leading newspaper, magazine, or trade publication.

Letters to the editor. No matter what your company does, there is probably some related issue—business or political—that warrants expressing your opinion. An editor who is presented with a well-written, cogent letter, especially in reply to either a story or a previous editorial, will most likely print it or offer you an opportunity to voice your comment. To get an idea of what is of particular interest to the editor of your local paper, read the Letters to the Editor section regularly and keep up with the features and editorials themselves until you find an opportunity you can effectively comment upon. Make note of broadcast editorials, too, as many radio and television stations provide opportunities for citizens to express opinions over the air.

Nancy Daly, founder of United Friends of the Children, wrote a letter to the editor, for example, thanking the paper for its editorial on the plight of children leaving the foster care system and describing how she and Sandra Rudnick have created a program that provides housing, job training, and other services to such youth. She went on to call for more involvement from the private sector.

Albert Moulton, President and CEO of CADworks, Inc., a software company in Cambridge, Massachusetts, wrote a letter to the editor of *Inc* magazine in response to an article that dubbed Cambridge as the most entrepreneurial place on earth. He opened his letter with "We are one of the firms that has profited from being in East Cambridge: in fact, our software was used to design and/or manage two of the buildings shown in the article's opening photographs." Moulton then proceeded to make his comments.

Similarly, designer Caryl Gorski wrote a letter to the editor of *Publish*, a magazine for graphic communicators, commenting on the design changes in the magazine's layout. Computer consultant James L. Daigle wrote the editor of *PC* magazine describing how one of the software packages reviewed in the magazine had been helpful to one of his clients. Michael Murphy, publisher of the *California Technology Stock Letter*, wrote to the editor of *Business Week* offering additional alternatives to the electric car described in the Science and Technology section of the magazine.

Sports psychology consultant Michael A. Simon wrote the *New York Times* to comment on an article about employee development for professional athletes, pointing out his opinion that long-term development programs need to include mental as well as physical training. New York immigration lawyer David Meyers wrote to the *New York Times* in response to an article proposing the dismantling of the Immigration and Naturalization Service to explain why as an advocate of legitimate immigrants he believes this would be ill-advised.

Editorials. Newspapers also invite citizens to write editorials from time to time. The main criteria for getting an editorial or letter to the editor published are a good writing style and having something important to say. If an editor has samples of your writing from your letters, your chances of receiving such an invitation are increased. Some sample general topics you might consider for discussion in a letter to the editor are:

1. Local government restrictions on your type of business.
2. The advantages of your type of business to the community at large.
3. The positive impact of your type of business on the environment.

Also consider writing to discuss industry-specific topics. For example, a music teacher might decry the decrease in music education in public schools, enumerating the subsequent disadvantages for students. A security consultant might write on the frightening increase in white-collar crime in all businesses and the effect this has on prices to the consumer. Anyone in a repair business can write about the waste generated by our disposable society. Anyone in business might write on the problems of junk facsimile transmissions.

Financial planner Eric Tyson, for example, wrote an editorial for *USA Today*'s Forum entitled "Worries of Boomers' Savings Misplaced," outlining why he thinks people are worrying about having sufficient funds to support themselves after retirement. He points out, by the way, that 25 percent of self-employed people do not have health insurance and that about 43 percent of all Americans don't carry long-term disability coverage!

Op-ed pages or commentary. Op-ed pieces appear on the opposite side of an editorial and present an opposing position. Some papers like *USA Today* do not have op-ed columns, but they do have what they call Guest Columns. Other papers have commentary, essay, or Voices pages.

Kenneth Morris, president of Deigel and Gale, a marketing communications firm, for example, wrote an op-ed piece for the *New York Times* called "Translator-Free Investing," explaining why the securities industry needs to fully embrace plain-English documents and supporting the changes in the Securities and Exchange Commission rules requiring that prospectuses given out to investors be written in "clear, concise, and understandable" language. General contractor Dennis Hathaway wrote a "Speaking Out" piece for the *Los Angeles Times* explaining why homeowners should require contractors to submit itemized bids on residential remodeling and what to look for in such bids.

For information about how to contact op-ed editors, see the *National Directory of Op-Ed Pages,* by Marilyn Ross, listed in **Resources: Publicity.**

All these venues provide an opportunity for people who wish to make key points that a newspaper deems to be of value to their readers. This means you need to present a fresh point of view on a topic you feel passionately about that is related to your work. Developing your own point of view, as described in **chapter 3: Demonstrating Why You're the Best Choice,** can help you to identify what you might want to say in an editorial or commentary.

The more creative you are—and the more responsive to what is currently being written and said in the relevant print and broadcast media—the more likely an editor or producer is to select your letter or commentary for use.

Calendar listings. Most papers have listings of upcoming events. Some have a variety of listings on various days of the week in different sections of the paper. If you have an event of any kind that needs promotion, being listed in one or more of these sections can be invaluable, making more people aware of your event than you might ever be able to afford to reach by sending a direct-mail piece. The added benefit of obtaining a calendar listing is that many people you would like to reach may not be able to attend but will notice your listing, which will help you build your reputation and keep you at the top of their minds.

Keep in mind, however, that all such listings have specific filing procedures and deadlines. So you need to contact the publications you have in mind far in advance and find out what the proper procedure is for being included. If your first attempts at getting listed do not succeed, don't be discouraged. We have found that by persistently sending in listings, along with a personal note to the person who handles them, as long as your events would be of interest to the readers, ultimately they will get in. And once they do, each next time will be easier.

Browsing through the Westside calendar of the *Los Angeles Times,* for example, we found that environmental consultant Don Colburn will be speaking to the California Native Plant Society. Linda Seger will be discussing her book *"When Women Call the Shots"* at Borders Books and Music. BUS Fitness and Dance Center will sponsor free dance and creative movement classes for physically and mentally challenged teens on Saturdays. Landscape architect Shirley Kerins will be offering a talk and tasting on how to liven up your garden and your cooking with herbs at the Huntington Library. The Java Cybercafe will host a free evening seminar called "Getting Started with Yahoo!"

Personal or business features. In addition to calendar listings, most papers have a metro, neighborhood, or business section featuring the achievements of fellow citizens. The *Los Angeles Times,* for example has a "Neighbors" column that features such things as honors people have received, donations they have made, or other accomplishments. They actively solicit readers to send in their news. Marketing consultant Gwen Moran of Farmingdale, New Jersey, contacted the *Asbury Park Press,* the second largest newspaper in New Jersey, and offered herself and her company as an example of a fast-growing trend of companies outsourcing work to independent contractors. It led to a front-page feature story in their Business Monday section called "Flying Solo," which included a half-page photo of Moran in her home office. This one article led Moran to more than $60,000 in new business.

The key to using any of these alternative routes for publicity purposes is focusing your announcements, comments, or opinions on a subject that demonstrates your expertise. Unless you do this, most publications will identify you only by your name and city. If you present yourself as an expert on a subject that's related to your work, they will usually also include either your company name or your line of work. Eric Tyson, for example, was identified as a financial counselor, lecturer, and author of the national best-sellers *Personal Finance for Dummies* and *Investing for Dummies*. For more information on writing pieces for these alternative routes to media see **chapter 11, "Telling All About It."**

Turn your publicity into more publicity. After you have been interviewed, always get the cards, or at least the names, of the writers, editors, producers, and talk-show hosts you have met. Send these people thank-you notes immediately after your interview. To provide a personal touch, you can handwrite your thank-you notes on note cards, preferably imprinted with your logo, name, address, and telephone number. Always add the names of those you contact to your Personalized Media List and continue to keep in touch with these contacts by sending newsletters, pertinent information, and, of course, further news releases about yourself and your business.

Make sure you get a copy of each article and radio or television segment in which you are featured. Add copies of it to your presentation kit and to send a copy to selected clients and referral sources who may not have seen it. Although you can hire a news service to obtain such copies for you, you can do this more cost-effectively yourself. Ask writers how to get a copy of the newspapers, magazines, or newsletters in which you appear; they may offer to send you one. When doing a radio or television interview, take a blank cassette to the studio and before going on the air politely ask the producer or other appropriate person to dub a copy for you. There may be a charge for this, but it is worth the investment, because you never know when someone will ask you for a sample tape.

The more prestigious the media, the more likely they will be to want to see or hear you on a previous show. Before meeting planners invite you to speak at a conference or other program, they may ask to review an audio- or videotape of you in action. Publicity appearances are a relatively easy and inexpensive way to get such demo tapes.

Make sure the media can find you. Since you never know when a key magazine or newspaper may be doing a feature story and need a comment from someone in your field, sometimes the easiest way to get publicity is to position yourself so that the media can always find you.

High-Tech Tip: Publicity in Cyberspace

As the traffic on the "information highway" increases, so does the opportunity for increased visibility. There are entire publications that never see a printing press. They are published on-line on the various local bulletin boards, comprehensive information services, and even on the Internet. Whether your target customer browses the World Wide Web or visits a CompuServe forum or downloads games from a local BBS, there are opportunities for your news releases, stories, and articles to reach a willing market.

If yours is a business that currently uses computers for any type of outreach program—electronic mail, on-line services, research, even marketing, etc.—or if your business depends on clients who do, you may want to make sure any news, newsletter, or other publicity materials you send to traditional media are also made available on-line. Data libraries on many CompuServe forums, for example, contain press releases on new products and services. They also provide a means of uploading your newsletter, often complete with graphics, articles, and letters to the editor. Like the newsgroups on the Internet and various other bulletin board services, it is important that the information you post have value—not just for your promotional purposes—but to readers. Think in terms not of "what they ought to know" but rather "what they want to know." Valuable information on-line has exactly the same effect as valuable information on an editor's desk.

Here, subjects replace headlines. Key word accuracy becomes important. When you post a message that announces your upload, be sure to include not only the title of the article or newsletter, etc., but the actual file name, where it is located, and the key words to find it. Remember, if a reader only knows the title, he or she will try to search using title words as key words. If, in subsequent messages, you mention the title again, be sure to include the rest of the pertinent poop so that lurkers can find it easily.

One of the most valuable aspects of these uploads is the fact that browsing the libraries usually gives you the number of times the file was accessed. Although you may not know who actually downloaded it, you can track the interest it generates. You should also keep track of everyone who asked you about information you post. Then after a couple of weeks, send a message to each one with some questions about the value of the information and how they were able or not able to use it in their businesses or homes. The information you gather in this way helps you know what to cover in future issues.

When the media need an expert or a story idea, they will turn to their favorite sources. They will talk to other reporters, and to friends and colleagues, will look through professional and business directories, and may even scout the Yellow Pages.

Psychologist Dr. Linda De Villars has a one-inch ad running in the Yellow Pages under "Psychologists," featuring her as a specialist in sex and relationship counseling and emphasizing her credentials. A freelance writer seeking an expert to interview for an article he was doing for *Men's Fitness* saw the ad and called her. Not only did Dr. De Villars appear in that article, but he was so pleased with their interview that he decided to pitch additional stories featuring her on related topics to several other national magazines. Based on these magazine articles, she received requests from two literary agents to write a book.

So don't overlook the Yellow Pages as a publicity tool. Also list yourself in targeted directories, and join select professional and trade organizations in order to be included on their membership rosters. Appear on panels, attend meetings, and when possible give presentations at conferences and other gatherings that the press will attend. You know you are doing good public relations when members of the press begin to refer you to one another. For more on on-line publicity See **Resources: Publicity**, below and Web Sites in **chapter 11.**

Extend the impact of your publicity. Once you get publicity, you can extend its impact in many ways for months and even years to come. You can send copies to past, present, and potential clients, your gatekeepers and mentors and other referral sources. You can include copies in proposals and your promotional kit. You can even use it to reach out and make new contacts. Here's an example. Alice M. Yardum-Hunter is a lawyer who specializes in immigration and nationality law. When her comments on changes in the immigration law appeared in the *Los Angeles Lawyer* magazine, she sent a copy of the article to the entire membership of the Los Angeles chapter of Women Business Owners along with a letter explaining to her fellow NAWBO members that she thought they might be interested to know about the significant changes taking place in immigration law and offering to answer any questions they might have regarding their business or the needs of their associates, family, and friends.

Action Steps: Publicity

1. Through your networking activities, you probably have met one or more people who have been successful with a publicity campaign. Interview them to find out what worked, what didn't, and why, and what results they have gotten. Or whenever you see or read publicity about people you know of, send them a congratulatory note via E-mail, fax, or postcard, introduce yourself if necessary, and follow up to ask if they would be so kind as to tell you how such publicity came about.
2. Make a list of all the editors and producers who have shown interest in material similar to yours. Contact each one individually and ask what it is they are looking for in material that crosses their desks. Be sure to send a thank-you note to each one after the contact for helping you understand their needs. Then see if there is something about your company that, if not strong enough to generate a full feature article, is at least interesting enough that it might be included as an example of an issue that could be covered. For example, the editor might not choose to do an article on your house-painting business but might do a feature on getting homes ready to sell and interview you regarding inside and outside colors and what will make the best enhancement for the least money.
3. Based on the information you've gathered, find something newsworthy about your business and develop a release to send to one highly targeted publication. Follow up with the editor to find out why the publication used it or not. Apply what you learned by sending a new release to another publication.
4. Write a short article or tip sheet with advice you would give your clients, and post it on each on-line bulletin board or Internet site you frequent. Track the downloads and contact each person who asks about it to assess its value to them. Compare each site as to the business it brings in over three months' time.

Resources: Publicity

Books

Celebrate Today. John Kremer. Prima Publishing, 3875 Atherton Rd., Rocklin, CA 95765, (916) 632-4400, (800) 632-8676, 1996.

Chase's Calendar of Events, NTC Contemporary Publishing Co., 4255 W. Touhy Ave., Lincolnwood, IL 60646, (312) 540-4500. Annual edition, chronicles more than 10,000 American and international holidays, festivals, celebrations, anniversaries, dates of astronomical phenomena and other similar events, by subject and location. Enables you to submit holidays of your own creation for future editions.

The Consultant's Guide to Publicity. Reece A Franklin. New York: Wiley, 1996.

Effective Public Relations. Allen H. Center, Clen M Broomm, Ph.D., and Scott M. Cutlip. Paramus, N.J.: Prentice-Hall, 1994.

Handbook for Public Relations Writing. Thomas H. Bivins. Lincolnwood, IL: NTC Business Books, 1996.

How to Conduct Your Own Survey. Priscilla Salant and Don A. Dillman. New York: Wiley, 1994.

National Directory of Newspaper Op-Ed Pages. Marilyn Ross. Communications Creativity, Box 909, Buena Vista, CO 81211, (719) 395-8659, 1994.

Marketing Your Arts & Crafts. Janice West. Fort Worth, Tex.: The Summit Group, 1997.

Publicity on the Internet. Steve O'Keefe. New York: Wiley, 1997.

Media Lists

Bacon's Information, Inc., 332 South Michigan Ave., Suite 900, Chicago, IL 60604, (800) 621-0561 or (312) 922-2400, www.baconsinfo.com

Burelle's Information Services, 75 East Northfield Road, Livingston, NJ 07039, (800) 631-1160, www.burelles.com

Gale Research, 835 Penobscot Building, Detroit, MI, (800) 877-4253, www.gale.com

Gebbie's Press All-in-One-Directory. Names and addresses of daily and weekly newspapers, AM-FM radio stations, general consumer magazines, business papers, parade press and news syndicates by specific category of interest.

Oxbridge Communications, 150 Fifth Avenue, Suite 302, NY, NY 10011, (800) 955-0231, www.mediafinders.com

Writer's Digest, F & W Publications, 1507 Dana Avenue, Cincinnati, OH 45207, (513) 531-2222.

Newswire Services

Business Wire, 1990 S. Bundy , Los Angeles, CA 90025, (310) 820-9473.

News USA, 198 Van Buren St., Suite 420, Herndon, VA 20170, (800) 355-9500 or (703) 834-1818.

PR Newswire, 810 7th Ave. 35th Flr., NY, NY 10019, (800) 832-5522.

On-line Resources

A Business Researcher's Interests. Journals and Magazines section provides links to over 800 business-related magazines and research journals: www.brint.com/interest.html http://www.enews.com/monster. A comprehensive site that allows you to search for on-line magazines by name, subject, and category.

CyberPulse. On-line marketing resourse covering newsgroups, mailing lists, promotions and more: www.cyberpulse.com

The Delphi Group. Provides links between Web site development and on-line marketing: www.cam.org/~delphig/index.html

Internet Publicity Services (www.olympus.nt/okeefe/PI). Has a large collection of do-it-yourself Internet publicity.

Multimedia Marketing Group/WebStep. Press releases and Web marketing consulting: www.mmgco.com

NetPost. Specializes in Web site awareness, including news releases and announcements: www.netpost.com

Writing Effective News Releases and Query Letters. A free Special Report on www.paulandsarah.com on the Great Ideas for Getting Business page.

Software

Decisive Survey. Decisive Technology, 1991 Landings Drive, Mountain View, CA 94043, (650) 428-4300, (800) 987-9995, http://www.decisive.com

Publicity Blitz Media Directory-On-Disc. Bradley Communications, Box 1206, Lansdowne, PA 19050, (800) 989-1400, lists 20,000 print and broadcast media contacts in 75 subject categories.

Question. Solutions for Science, (800) 622-3345, www.scitechint.com

Survey EZ3. Atkeison Consulting, (610) 594-9977, (800) 964-4655.

Survey Pro. Apian Software, (206) 547-8394, (800) 237-4565.

Referrals

A steady stream of referrals is, of course, what you will have once you get business coming to you. In fact, Howard L. Shenson, known as the consultant's consultant, has said that the creative professional practitioner should be able to derive 80 percent or more of his or her new business from referrals, follow-up, or add-on business from existing clients. Once you are able to do this, you have a self-sustaining business. And that is the goal of all people who venture out on their own: to be so well established that the business they have produces all the business they need.

Once your business is self-sustaining, you are free to concentrate your time primarily on developing your craft, whether it involves creating products or services, expanding your business, or launching a new venture. So, in a sense you could say that ultimately all your networking, promotions, advertising, and direct mail—all your marketing efforts—are focused on attaining the goal of getting a steady steam of referrals that will make your business self-sustaining.

You don't have to wait until other methods create a referral stream, however. You can make generating referrals a key part of your marketing plan by focusing on the three referral-generating activities described in this section.

Pros and Cons of Referrals

There really is no better way to get business than from referrals. You don't have to find them; they find you. You don't have to stir up their interest because they're already interested when they contact you. You've been endorsed and prequalified. You don't have to work all that hard to convince them that you'll do a good job and be reliable and trustworthy, because your referral source is recommending you. Of course, you will have to establish rapport, answer questions, and otherwise demonstrate that you are what you've been represented to be, but the presumption will be in your favor right from the start.

Those who rely on referrals find they have larger initial orders or projects and a shorter sales cycle. So building your marketing strategy around getting referrals saves you time and costs you little. Marketing experts claim that one referral-generated call is the equivalent of making twelve cold calls. The downside is that it takes time to develop referral sources. If you don't have them already in place, you must build a cadre of satisfied clients and customers and other business relationships who will refer others to you. Market research indicates, for example, that while 80 percent of your customers would recommend you, only 20 percent are asked to. So even if you do have good relationships in place, there is no guarantee they will actually refer to you unless you take the initiative to get referrals coming your way.

There is a wealth of reasons why you may not get referrals even when you have the contacts, satisfied customers, a good reputation, and results to generate them. Your referral sources may not encounter people who need what you offer, for example. They may not recognize when people need you. They may forget about you. They may think you're too busy. They may not know how or if to refer. They may even send you the wrong kind of people. So you will need to invest time, money, and energy in establishing good referral sources, staying in touch with them, and helping them understand when and how to refer to you.

Still, getting referrals can be an ideal way to get business, especially if you dislike selling or are too busy to do other forms of marketing or don't have the knowledge or resources to market yourself. By following the tips below, you'll find you can increase your referral rate dramatically by stimulating referrals instead of leaving whether you get them to chance.

Best Bets: If you're providing a product or service to other businesses, referrals offer perhaps your best chance for success. Most of the businesses polled in a *Venture* magazine survey, for example, reported that they relied heavily on word-of-mouth referrals from business associates in purchasing professional business services: 44 percent chose a lawyer by word of mouth; 45 percent, an accountant; 45 percent, an advertising agency; 42 percent, a business consultant; and 42 percent, a marketing firm. It is a safe bet that this percentage would hold consistently for most service businesses. Although not quite as effective for selling products or services to consumers, referrals can also be a valuable marketing strategy there as well.

Tips for Getting Referrals

A common misunderstanding about getting referrals is to assume that if you do a good job for your customers, referrals will come automatically. Sometimes this happens, but not usually. Typically, getting referrals business relatively quickly is the result of a concerted effort to build and generate referrals. It's like priming a pump. If you pump away at generating referral business, it will begin flowing in more quickly.

In other words, even after producing excellent results, you can never take referrals for granted. Without a specific effort to generate referrals, you may get only a trickle of referral business unless you are in a high-demand business. If, however, you concentrate specifically on ways to prime the referral pump, you can speed up or even jump-start the referral process. Once you learn how to develop and generate referrals purposefully, they start coming more frequently.

Another common myth about getting referrals is that once your business becomes self-sustaining, it will remain so. Occasionally it does, and of course that is what we would all prefer. Many things can interrupt a well-established, steady flow of customers, however. The market can change, making what you offer less in demand. Your client base can change, and clients may begin seeking features you don't provide. Technology can change, rendering your service obsolete. Key referral sources may move or change positions. Their needs or priorities may change. Key personnel who have purchased from you may leave the company. Your competition may undercut your prices.

Keeping a consistent referral-generating effort under way will enable you to pick up on such changes quickly. By responding to them immediately with necessary adjustments and additional marketing activities, you can often short-circuit any drastic drop in your business. In fact, as a one-person or small business, the relative ease with which you can respond quickly to changes in the marketplace is one of your strongest assets. Large businesses usually can't redirect their efforts on a dime, but you probably could—if you attend to your referral network. Well attended to, it can do a masterful job of reconnaissance for you.

As discussed above, your gatekeepers and mentors are excellent referrals sources. But there are three other referral-generating strategies.

You can stimulate referrals from your colleagues or competitors, from your clients and customers, or through your clients' or customers' contacts. Here are tips for making effective use of these three business-generating activities.

Getting Referrals from Colleagues and Competitors

At first blush it might not seem as though people in the same business or field would be a very promising source of referrals. After all, they're your competitors. You might wonder why they would refer business to a competitor, and vice versa. But we've found that up to 25 percent of those we poll find referrals from competitors to be one of their best and more dependable sources of business. Referrals among colleagues work very well in two situations:

Sharing overload One of the challenges every one-person or small business faces is what to do if you suddenly have the opportunity to do more business than you can handle. Instead of turning down work or disappointing your clients or customers by getting behind with extra work, it can make sense to line up colleagues who can handle your overflow. And in return, you can work out an arrangement that when they have more work than they can do, they'll refer their overflow to you. Everyone wins in such an ad hoc arrangement. You each can rest assured that you'll have backup when you've got more work than you can do or when an emergency occurs. Also, when times are slow, you've got a ready-made prospect for getting new business. Of course, in some fields where fee splitting or commissions are allowed, you may share in the revenue generated from the business you refer.

Referring among specialties As we discussed in **chapter 2: Niching—Deciding What You Want to Become Known For**, often the more specialized your business, the more successful you'll be; but by specializing, there may be times when you would need to decline business that doesn't fit with your expertise. By setting up mutual-referral agreements, however, like those discussed above, you won't need to lose out when business that doesn't fall within your specialty comes your way. You can refer that type of business to a colleague whose specialty is more in line with the client's needs and arrange to get referrals in return when his or her clients need what you have to offer. Giving mutual referrals among highly specialized businesses can be a win/win situation for everyone, including the clients who get reliable referrals without having to spend time locating professionals who can offer what they need.

Referral etiquette Of course, making mutual-referral arrangements involves more commitment than simply networking with colleagues and associates or referring casually to one another. When you make referrals to someone regularly, you expect that he will serve the customer or client well, just as he will expect you to do a good job for his customers. Both your reputations are on the line. Also if the level of referrals doesn't live up to your expectations, you or your colleagues will be disappointed. Likewise, if referrals aren't roughly equal in number or quality between you, hard feeling may develop. Whoever is on the short end of the stick may become angry, bitter, or suspicious, thus jeopardizing your future relationship. So you'll want to be careful to make sure no one inadvertently steps on anyone else's toes. While there are no cut-and-dried formulas for how to manage these issues, the following tips can help.

Start small and take it slow. Begin referring business to one another more informally until you get to know the individuals involved and feel confident you have shared goals and expectations, can rely on them to provide high-quality products and services, and can expect reciprocity. Then you can consider making a more formalized agreement and perhaps creating a referral network among those with whom you work well.

Spell out the details of how you'll refer to one another and write them down in a letter. Discuss how you want each other to contact the people you will be referring. Do you want to give your clients the phone number of your associate and let them initiate the client contact, or do you feel more comfortable getting permission to give the clients' phone numbers to your associate directly? It's important to clarify what you consider a "referral" to be. Sometimes people have very different ideas of what constitutes a referral. For instance, consider these situations:

- Jane is a desktop publisher and one day, her client happens to mention that he is about to buy new office furniture. Jane has an informal agreement with an interior designer, so she calls him to let him know the potential customer's name. The problem is, Jane has never mentioned to her client that she's making this referral, so when the designer calls, the client is confused and indicates that he's already shopping elsewhere. This isn't a useful referral. It's not even a very good lead.

- Robert is a career counselor. He has made a mutual-referral arrangement with a psychotherapist. In thinking about people he could refer to get the relationship off the ground, he concludes that since his sister has been having lots of problems with her teenage son, he'll give her the psychotherapist's name and phone number. This, too, isn't a true referral: the sister has yet to express a need for a psychotherapist.
- Marjory is a bookkeeper. In the process of serving one of her clients, she discovers that he has yet to computerize the accounting system for his dry cleaning business, so she gives the dry cleaner's name to a computer consultant in her referral group network. But again, this isn't a true "referral." This will be little more than a cold call for the computer consultant because the dry cleaner has yet to decide that he wants to computerize and Marjory hasn't talked with her client to find out if he wants a referral.

As you can see, there is plenty of room for misunderstandings in making referrals, so always be sure to clarify the referral process you and your associates will be using. Similarly, be sure your customers are aware that you're making a referral—and that they want one—so they won't be surprised when they get a call from your colleague seeking their business. A good-quality referral is one in which the person not only needs the product or service but also realizes the need for it and is actively seeking it. A good-quality referral also involves asking the person if she would like a referral and, if so, telling her something about the person you'll be referring her to, along with why you believe this is the right person for her.

Clarify your expectations. Make sure each of you understands when and to whom you'll be referring. Don't just assume that you will get the number and type of referrals you want to serve. And check to be sure each of you can expect to make such referrals.

Being precise will avoid misunderstandings. Connie, for example, is a massage therapist. She met a facialist at a networking meeting, and they talked about making mutual referrals. Soon Connie had sent her colleague several new clients but had gotten no referrals yet in return. So finally she raised the issue and discovered the facialist felt she could only refer people whom the massage therapist at the salon where she rented space was too busy to take on or didn't want to see.

Always make a referral immediately when an opportunity arises. Don't let a hot lead turn cold with time—or worse, don't think you have helped your colleague by referring someone to him who never calls. From the colleague's point of view, if the person never contacts him, there's been no referral. So when you give an associate's phone number to someone, call and tell him the person's name and that he can expect to get a call.

Don't give a referral to more than one business, unless the person asks for several names. When you have a mutual-referral agreement, it's your job to make sure you perceive a good fit for the people you're referring. If you can't wholeheartedly recommend your colleague's products or services, don't refer to them. And if you can endorse them wholeheartedly, don't put them in competition with others, thinking they're getting an exclusive referral.

When you get a referral from a colleague, follow up right away. No matter how busy you are, always call the person who's been referred to you immediately to discuss his or her needs. Never give the impression you're too busy to respond to your colleague's referrals.

Express appreciation for each referral you get. Always thank your colleague for each referral you get. In fact, thank her frequently. A thank-you note or phone call will usually suffice, but if your colleague has sent you a lot of business or a very substantial piece of business, you may want to send an appropriate gift or express your appreciation by inviting her to be your guest for dinner.

Adjust your referral arrangements as needed. When problems develop, approach them openly from a problem-solving perspective. (See **Resources for Getting Referrals**.) But if a referral relationship doesn't appear to be working out, ending it can be an uncomfortable situation that should be handled with care. If the arrangement has been a casual one, chances are you can let it die a natural death while keeping your relationship cordial. If the person continues referring to you, however, or if you have an explicit agreement to refer to each other exclusively, you'll need to diplomatically let the person know you need to change your plans. Otherwise, you'll risk his becoming bitter, disgruntled, or even vindictive.

In ending your relationship, unless the person has behaved unethically or improperly, there is nothing to be gained from itemizing all the "reasons" you don't want to work with him. Of course, if you're really unhappy it may be tempting to complain. You'll be best served to simply let him know that your situation has changed and that while you can no longer be counted on to make regular referrals, you do continue to wish him the best.

High-Tech High Touch Tip

Giving referrals is one of the best ways to get them, but how do you make sure that those you refer to know about the referrals you are making on their behalf? Well, you can call them or drop them a note or you can subscribe to FollowUp Net. For only $15 a month, FollowUp Net will automatically send a note via E-mail or fax to anyone you've made a referral to and they will provide end-of-the-month reports to any and all of a subscriber's referral targets. For more information, see http://www.followup.net or call (203) 226-5853.

Getting Clients and Customers to Refer Others to You

Ultimately, your most reliable source of business can be your existing clients or customers. Your clients can speak more effectively than any other medium about why someone else should buy what you have to offer; they know better than anyone what you can do. Approached properly, they can become a walking, talking sales force for you. Here is how you can get them to do that:

Make sure that each experience customers have with your business is positive. Although word-of-mouth marketing is not something you can control directly, what people say about you—positive or negative—results from your customers' contacts with you, your personnel, and your product or service. Thus if you want referrals, "The customer is always right."

On the average, a satisfied customer will tell three people about his or her positive experience over the period of a month. But, on the average, an unhappy customer will tell seven people of a bad experience within one week. So while realistically it may be impossible for everyone to have only positive experiences with you and your business, that should be the goal toward which you strive. Always provide the very best quality you can, and if anything goes wrong on your end, be willing to accept full responsibility and do what it takes to make it right. Stand behind your product or service.

If there is a problem, fix it fast. Of course, many of the problems that develop in a business are beyond your control. Your child gets sick; a supplier or subcontractor does not deliver on schedule; a file or bill gets lost. These, however, are your problems, not your customers'. If you want customers to make referrals, you must rectify any problem to the customers' satisfaction. The good news is that customers are just like all of us. We all know about Murphy's Law—that if anything can go wrong, it will. Often it is the way you handle problems that can create your most loyal and dedicated customers.

You probably can think of times when someone lost your business due to a shortsighted desire to be right or to save a little money. We know of a decorator who lost thousands of dollars in future business and referrals because she wouldn't offer to pay a few hundred dollars to cover the cost when a fabric she recommended cracked after only a few months of wear. A freelance writer lost thousands of dollars of work and suffered a lot of negative word of mouth after she turned in a project incomplete when a larger project came her way. Worst of all, when the person who had referred her the business heard what happened, the freelancer's name went from the referral list to the never, never list.

In the first case, eating the loss and, in the second, turning down other work or at least seeing to it that the first project was complete would have paid for itself over and over again. The same holds true for problems that are clearly caused by your customers. Perhaps they change their mind or forget to tell you something critical to your task. Or maybe they're unhappy about their bill. Think how grateful and appreciative you have been when others have gone out of their way to make a last-minute change or adjustment for you as a result of your own oversight. Such goodwill can't be bought.

So while you can't let customers walk all over you, you must find amicable ways to resolve any misunderstandings or conflicts. When no amicable solution can be found, let a lawyer, business manager, or collection agency be the bad guy for you. Their efforts, however, should always be the last resort, and ideally they will simply open the door for you to enter once again as the good guy who is willing to work things out.

Make customers so happy they want to go out and shout about it. Nothing sells like results. Whenever possible, don't just leave customers feeling positive; leave them feeling ecstatic! A customer who is thrilled can't stop telling others about how great you are. And whenever such customers hear of someone else who has a need for your service or product, they can't wait to suggest you.

Often this involves honing your skills and going the extra mile to exceed your customers' expectations. When editor Sherry Glanville left her job to freelance, she found business to be frighteningly slow. One small publisher told her they wouldn't hire her themselves but would recommend her to an author who they thought needed editorial help. But the author didn't think her book needed editing, so she was willing to pay only a low hourly fee for cursory copy editing. Sherry took the job, but as she got into the project she could see that the book needed major surgery. Instead of trying to back out or talk the author into more money, she decided to do the best job she could and several weeks later turned over a beautifully completed manuscript.

The author was overjoyed! Her book now read like a masterpiece. She was so grateful that her check was double the amount agreed upon. She has gone on to write additional books and always hires Sherry. Of course, she also recommends Sherry to all other authors she meets who are seeking editors, and the publisher has referred Sherry to others as well.

Although every extra effort will not produce such dramatic results, the results are cumulative. In business, it is true that the more you give, the more you get.

Let your clients know you want referrals. Often clients do not realize that they can provide you with valued referrals. And even when they do, they often won't refer without some sign or gesture from you. Therefore, while you never want to beg, pressure, or imply an obligation to refer, it is important that you convey to your clients that your business is based on referrals by saying something like "I get most of my business by referrals. It's the best way I know to spread the word about what I do, so your recommendations are important to me."

Fill them in on how and when to refer. Some individuals who are perfectly happy to refer may not do so simply because they don't know when or how to go about it. Some professionals actually prepare a "When to Refer" or "When Someone Needs Me" sheet that spells out how to recognize when someone needs their service.

One way to do this is to write an article for a local newspaper, magazine, or newsletter entitled "How to Know When You Need . . ." Then have reprints made up of the article and give them away to customers; send them in the mail with bills or have them sitting out in your office for people to read or take while they wait. A public relations specialist might write an article called "When You Need PR"; a psychologist might write "When Does a Child Need Professional Help through the Trauma of Divorce?"

Be sure to provide easy opportunities for people to provide you with names of potential customers or clients. Use gift certificates or special-offer coupons as discussed above that customers can fill out for you to send to others whom they think might be interested. Such a certificate might have a blank line that you can fill out in longhand, noting that the person who recommended your service thought the recipient might enjoy it. Or you can ask for names to include on your mailing list or let the recipient know you are willing to receive or make calls. Also make sure everyone you work with has your phone number and address. Using an imprinted giveaway can come in handy for this purpose.

Listen for and act on referral flags. Many times clients will actually mention situations that we call referral flags. You have heard them yourself when someone has said, "I have a friend who . . ." or "So-and-so tried something like this but . . ." Sometimes we let these signals go by or simply assume that a referral is going to follow. Usually, however, nothing will develop unless you pick up on a flag and take the initiative to suggest the next step. Listen carefully for such referral flags and offer to help by saying something like "Perhaps I could be of help to them" or "I could probably help them with that." Then proceed to suggest a next step such as, "I would be glad to call them," "I would be glad to send them our brochure," or "I would love to invite them to our free introductory session." Since your customers are busy and likely to forget your offer, arrange, when possible, to be the one to make the contact.

Provide an advantage for making referrals. You might want to offer an incentive in the form of discounts, gift certificates, and specials to those who refer new customers to you. This is a common practice among many businesses. A seminar leader could offer discounted enrollments when someone brings a friend or a free second audit of the course with the referral of two other enrollees.

Norm Dominquez has built his Phoenix mobile-communications company by generating referrals. He offers his customers credit on their account for free service when they refer someone who becomes a new customer. He calls this "cheap marketing," and fully 80 percent of his business comes from customer referrals. Optometrist Dr. Michael Levin of Pacific Palisades, California, also creates referral possibilities by offering an appealing incentive. He sends his clients a letter (shown below) telling them about ACUVUE disposable contact lenses and offering to provide a free pair to everyone they refer. Then in appreciation, he'll send them a free pack for each person they refer.

Jeanne Mitchell, who operates Tee's, a wholesale quilted-design

Sample Referral Request Letter

Dear Mrs. Sarah Edwards,

Since I began recommending ACUVUE Disposable Contact Lenses to my patients, I've discovered that ACUVUE patients are the most enthusiastic contact lens wearers in my practice. And if you love your lenses as much as my other ACUVUE patients, I'm sure you are already recommending them to your family and friends.

In order for you to share the advantages of ACUVUE, I've enclosed three certificates for free ACUVUE lenses that you can pass along to others. Simply fill in your name and theirs and have them call my office for an appointment. If ACUVUE is right for them, I'll give them a free pair to wear for a trial period.

And to thank you, I'll give you a FREE ACUVUE multipack for every person you refer to me who becomes a contact lens patient in my practice.

Thank you in advance for sharing your enthusiasm for ACUVUE and confidence in me—with people important to you. You can be assured that I'll provide them with the same quality of service that you have come to expect from me. I look forward to meeting them and introducing them to ACUVUE.

Sincerely,
Dr. Michael I. Levin

T-shirt company in Perry, Oklahoma, came up with her own incentive plan after her book club reminded her for the umpteenth time that she could get a free book by referring a friend. She sent postcards promising her current retailers: "We will reward you for your efforts if you help us get the word out." She send out one free T-shirt for every twelve ordered by a referral. She also places these cards in with the orders she sends out. It works, she says, because retailers are always exchanging ideas on merchandise.

Get frequent feedback. To make sure you aren't getting negative word of mouth, convey in person, on a sign, or in your written product information that customer satisfaction is important to you and that you want to know about any complaints. For example, a sign in our local car wash reads, "If you aren't satisfied with the job, we aren't either. Let us know and we'll take your car through again."

Research shows the majority of dissatisfied customers never report their dissatisfaction. They do, however, feel free to express their unhappiness to others. The designer we mentioned earlier who lost thousands of dollars of additional business by not offering to pay for damaged fabric never knew what she had lost. The person who told us about the incident had been too embarrassed to bring the issue up with the designer.

One way to avoid this is to offer guaranteed satisfaction on your products or service. Another is to use feedback forms or to ask directly whether someone is satisfied. A time-management consultant was doing a two-day program for a large government agency. He felt the project was going well but noticed a less-than-enthusiastic response from the project director. He wisely picked up on this body language and asked the director how she felt the program was going. Although at first she said everything was fine, when the consultant emphasized how much he wanted to meet his clients' specific needs, she told him about several things she felt needed to be changed. He was more than happy to comply. Without such a diligent approach, he would have finished the day, collected his fee, and never known his clients were less than satisfied. By correcting midstream, the project was a success and the consultant was invited back to conduct future programs.

Whenever someone who has been a regular client suddenly stops doing business with you, take the time to contact him or her and find out why. This will give you a chance to repair any broken fences or simply let your clients know you are thinking of them.

Stay in touch. Out of sight is out of mind, so to stay top of mind, make some type of regular contact with past clients. Send them something like a clipping, newsletter, flyer, postcard, or note via mail, fax, or E-mail. Or call periodically by phone if you prefer. Marcy Tudor, who runs the Weatherbury Farm Bed and Breakfast in Avella, Pennsylvania, gets 50 percent of her business from repeat or referral business by keeping in touch with her guests via computer. She sends gift certificates, livestock birth announcements, a quarterly *Weatherbury Moos* newsletter, and a monthly calendar of events.

Getting Referrals from Your Clients' Networks

In addition to getting referrals directly from your clients and customers, often you can tap into their referral networks. For example, if you have a bookkeeping service, each of your clients probably uses an attorney who makes referrals from time to time to bookkeepers. Similarly, you occasionally have access to people who need an attorney. Such contacts can be mutually beneficial. Here are some ideas for establishing such referral relationships.

Find out the names of professionals and other services your clients recommend to others. Often, depending on the nature of your business, there will be occasions when you will want or need to interact with other professionals who serve your clients. A family day-care provider, for example, needs to know the name of each child's pediatrician. A psychotherapist needs to know the name of a client's medical doctor. Often these professional contacts can assist you in better serving your customers, but ultimately they can also become excellent sources of referrals. So think of the other businesses or professions you could be interfacing with to best serve your clients.

One way to gather these valuable contacts would be to build into any client information sheet a section requesting the names, addresses, and phone numbers of the other major professionals they use that relate to your work with them. Alternatively, you can simply ask clients when the opportunity arises for the names of specific services you're wanting to establish contacts with. Usually a client who is happy with your work will be glad to make a referral.

While such an approach will not work for every business, most businesses can find some way to connect with the other professionals, suppliers, and business services their clients rely on. This can be as simple as mentioning that you occasionally have clients who need a certain kind of product or service and asking whether they have someone they would recommend. Here are some ideas for how to build referrals through such contacts:

Build bridges. Call and establish contact with the other businesses whose names you get from clients. Do not ask for business or referrals; this would most likely appear presumptuous or imply that you're either a hustler or desperate for business. Anyone appearing too eager inadvertently raises a question as to why they don't have more business. So, instead call to find out two things: more information about what the business is and when and how you can refer clients to them. If they are interested in networking with you, they will inquire about your services as well. Unless the person is a crucial gatekeeper, don't waste your time with a contact who isn't responsive to your offer. Look for those who are eager to network.

Always ask how your clients and customers heard about you. Often the referral will be from someone else with whom your client is doing business. Not only does this help you track the results of your marketing efforts, it also enables you to thank those who are sending you business and gives you the opportunity to meet and network further with new colleagues.

Let your work speak for itself by making sure it's visible. Often referral sources are hesitant to refer someone they don't know well. If, however, they have heard about you or read about you in the local media, they will have more confidence in you, knowing that others have recognized your talents and abilities. Such exposure is one of the primary benefits of a solid public-relations effort. For more information on how to increase the visibility of your product or service, see chapters 5 through 8. Also, any materials you send out should convey an image that engenders confidence in your ability. See chapter 5 for how to create a business image that will help you sell yourself.

Of course, no matter what you offer, if people cannot in good conscience recommend you, your product, or your service, they will not do so. Therefore, again it is your responsibility to make sure that your product or service not only accomplishes the purpose it is designed for but also does it well.

Emphasize your niche, your unique expertise. The more generally you describe your business, the more difficult it is for others to know how to refer people to you. Suppose you meet two dentists, one of whom tells you she works with anyone who has teeth and the other,

Three Referral Taboos

1. ***Never focus on your need for business.*** Focus on how you can benefit others. Present yourself as successful and competent. Build mutually satisfying business relationships in which everyone wins.
2. ***Never dump a lot of promotional materials on referral sources.*** Do not mail or drop by with a pile of your brochures, cards, or newsletters unless a person requests these resources or there is some particular opportunity for him or her to use them, such as an open house or seminar. This is a waste of your money and time and it's aggravating to those who must do something with the materials. They usually end up being thrown away.
3. ***Never speak poorly of a competitor or client.*** Whoever is listening can only wonder whether they will be next.

that he specializes in seeing patients who have dental anxieties. To which dentist will you be more likely to go or refer? Or perhaps you meet two professional speakers, one who says he speaks on any motivational topic and the other, that he talks on how to save money on business travel. Or you meet two chiropractors, one of whom describes himself as a holistic practitioner, while the other says she specializes in treating women with PMS-related problems.

In order to make a referral, most people need some hook to hang you on in their minds. Once they get your hook, you will be someone who comes to mind when there is a need for what you do. People have very specific needs; thus they want very specific referrals. A bookkeeper who specializes in serving doctors' offices, for example, and is recognized for having designed special systems for medical-patient tracking will find it easier to get referrals than someone who does general bookkeeping. A psychotherapist who specializes in treating adolescents with drug problems is more likely to get referrals than one who works with children of all ages. (See chapters 2 and 5 for more information on how to find and best describe your niche.)

Build an image of yourself as a knowledgeable leader in your field. The more you can do to build your reputation as a leader in a given specialty, the easier it will be for others to turn to you. Establish yourself as a source of the latest information in your specialty, someone who knows the meaning of the latest trends and developments and is advancing the state of your field. Usually this will require that you do more than read your trade journals.

You can, for example, conduct informal surveys or polls, advance your own theories, and write articles or even books on your work. Send copies of relevant news clippings and summaries of survey results to your referral sources. Always be ready and willing to provide key information and act as a clearinghouse for giving excellent referrals. With such a reputation, you will be the one people call when they need any resource in your area of expertise. That means business is just around the corner.

Another way to have influence among your peers is to know people in other fields. Research has shown that professionals take advice from the people in their field who have widespread contacts outside the field. By joining networking and civic organizations, you can become a center of influence. (For additional information on building your expertise as a leader in your field, see **chapter 3, Mastery:—Demonstrating Why You're the Best Choice.**

Ten Tips for Boosting Referrals

1. **Build your own mailing list** of all past and present clients and other referral sources.
2. **Send a mailing to everyone** on your list monthly or at least quarterly: a newsletter, copies of news clippings or articles, announcements, flyers, gift certificates, news of appearances you will be making, information on new products or services, and special offers.
3. **Keep your mailing list up-to-date** with a database management system or a professional-contact management software program such as *Act!* by Contact Software International. Be sure to purge outdated names regularly.
4. **Be positive and enthusiastic** about your business. Your enthusiasm will be contagious and will generate business. People like to do business with others who make them feel confident, positive, and optimistic.
5. **Build a glowing reputation.** Be prompt, reliable, ethical, polite, and competent. Never accept work you are not qualified to do; refer it to someone else.
6. **Include an information-request card** in your brochures, newsletters, and other mailings so people can make additional contact with you easily.
7. **Track all your referrals.** Ask all your new clients how they heard about you. Once you've done business with clients and the relationship is well established, ask them what prompted them to use your product or service instead of alternatives in the market.
8. **Always send a thank-you note** immediately to everyone who provides you with a referral. Express your gratitude to those who are especially helpful by sending appropriate gifts of appreciation.
9. **Provide a special referral slip** for your customers to give to others. This slip should have a place for the referring name and offer an incentive such as a discount or special gift to customers for turning it in with their orders. Also provide special gifts or incentives for your customers to give out these slips. Then send a thank-you with the

gift for every referral you receive. Give exceptional rewards to those of your clients who provide lots of successful referrals.

10. **Follow the 80/20 rule** which would suggest that 20 percent of your referral sources will most likely produce 80 percent of your referrals. So, invest your time, energy, and money in the 20 percent of individuals, organizations, and activities that provide you with the best response.

Be a promoter, mentor, or gatekeeper for others. Those who help others succeed will reap even greater success. Take every opportunity you can to promote those who can be of help to you, and help people who are just starting out in fields related to yours. Often you can even feel comfortable supporting your competitors' success, because, as we said before, as much as 20 percent of new business in many fields comes from the competition, who refers business out when they are too busy, need to subcontract, or get calls for areas of business outside their own.

Action Steps: Getting More Referrals

1. Study your market carefully. Ask yourself what types of individuals or businesses might be a key to your doing business with that market. Select one category and explore what you could do to enhance their business by referring you.
2. Build a list of ten things you and your business could do for such referral sources to enhance their business.
3. Select two community organizations dear to your best referral sources and spend two hours per week volunteering with those organizations. Make sure you, also, believe in the organizations' work. Commit to one year with each organization, which should give you enough time to evaluate both your interests, the connections it provides, and your dedication to the premises of the organization.
4. Make a list of current customers who have given you positive feedback. Approach them according to the tenets in this chapter and ask if they would be kind enough to act as a reference.

Resources: Getting Referrals

Books

Endless Referrals, Network Your Everyday Contacts into Sales. Bob Burg. New York: McGraw-Hill, 1994.

How to Get More and Better Referrals. Howard Shenson. Center for Consulting and Professional Practices, William Associates, Box 6159, Torrance, CA 90504, (310) 324-2386, wmooneya@ix.netcom.com

Teaming Up: The Small-Business Guide to Collaborating. Paul and Sarah Edwards and Rick Benzel. New York: Tarcher/Putnam, 1997.

Audio

Referral Business Builder Training Tapes. KC Truby. Bridge 21, 232 E. 2nd St., Suite 203, Casper, WY 82601, (307) 472-1941, Fax (307) 472-1950, www.bridge21.com

Services

FollowUp Net, One Glendinning Place, Westport, CT 06880, (203) 226-5853, http://www.followup.net

Sponsorships, Donations, and Charity Events

Making a donation or participating as a sponsor or contributor to community activities or charity events is a fine, but often overlooked, way to get people talking about you. Of course, large companies like Nike and Virginia Slims have sponsored major sports events like golf tournaments, tennis matches, or marathons. But you need not sponsor an entire event to create visibility for your work. You can, for example, sponsor one runner in a charity race or a booth at a community health fair or environmental exposition.

Art gallery owner Patricia Smith has served as a sponsor for two organizations that are near and dear to her heart, San Diego's Sister City Society and the International Arts Organization's Quilt San Diego. Participating in both these projects is personally rewarding and enables her to make valuable business contacts and provide visibility for her business.

Financial planner Gordon Curry from Northern British Columbia prides himself on using innovative marketing strategies. Noticing that the local stock-car races were drawing large crowds but that racers were struggling to get sponsors for their cars, he offered to sponsor a car for one of the races. He paid only $50 and in return had his name and company name printed on the trunk of the car. Because the spectators sit looking down on the track, everyone watching the race saw his name again and again as the car raced around the track. And much to his surprise, the car he sponsored won the race, so his name was also prominently displayed during the victory lap! He picked up three sales from this exposure and netted a total of $935.

There are many opportunities like these to contribute to a worthy cause that will also help you market your work. You might sponsor a showing for a struggling artist, fund a trip for the local high-school wrestling team, or support the school's marching band. You can sponsor a local soccer or little-league baseball team. All these events present public-relations opportunities as well, because local newspapers and even TV news programs often do features on this type of community activity.

Pros and Cons of Sponsorships, Donations, and Charity Events

Sponsoring or contributing to charity events is an excellent way to make your marketing efforts enjoyable and meaningful. One of the most common reasons people dislike marketing is that it makes them feel so materialistic. It seems very "Me, Me, Me" oriented. Of course, if you care about your work and truly believe in its value, you know you must call attention to yourself or your work so people will know about it and be able to benefit from it. But if at the same time that you're marketing yourself, you can also be doing good for your community and for causes you believe in, what could be better?

And, of course, those who contribute to their community are perceived as leaders, so not only will people see or hear about you, but this kind of exposure will also boost your reputation as a serious, trusted, and valued professional who is willing to support those things you believe in.

On the other hand, simply getting your name listed in ten-point type among several dozen contributors in a program guide will not help get people talking about you. Chances are, few if any will notice. To get the marketing benefit from participating in such activities, you'll need to make sure your potential clients, customers, or referral sources will have some way to know about your participation. This may take extra effort on your part to tie in with publicity or to otherwise get information out in a meaningful way. You may also have to negotiate precisely how your materials or contributions will be acknowledged or featured.

If done effectively, making donations to a community or charity can help build your reputation and standing in the community while contributing to something you believe in. It can provide you with access or exposure to key gatekeepers or mentors. But particularly when it comes to making a donation, you may need to be creative to get recognition for making a donation of the size that you can afford. One alternative is to contribute to a charity that is less well known and well supported than the mainstream ones. Or you can donate something unusual or unique related to your work that will attract media attention.

A landscape designer, for example, donated a rare shade tree to a local nursing home. A balloon-bouquet service donated balloons for a charity event for a hospital—the name of his service was artfully woven into the design on the balloons. When a large event was canceled at the last minute, a catering service donated the party with all the trimmings to a local shelter for battered women.

Sometimes the best contributions of this nature arise from something you simply want to see changed. Before the homeless had received much media attention, attorney Kenny Kahn of Santa Monica was watching these people wandering through the park below his window during the holiday season. Suddenly he had a great idea: he decided to pay these individuals to clean up the park. This quickly became popular with the homeless, and others in the office building began contributing too. A program called People Helping People grew out of this idea. Kahn's story was featured in several newspaper and radio stories.

Occasionally the sudden abundance of a windfall will provide the opportunity to make a donation. When Michael Colyar won the $100,000 1990 Star Search comedy award, he donated 50 percent of his winnings to organizations serving the homeless in Venice, California, where Colyar had worked as a street performer on the boardwalk for five years before his victory. Short of such an opportunity, various businesses in Dallas, Texas, discovered a way to make a reasonable cash donation do far more for their image than the same amount of money in advertising could have produced. They turned to their local public radio station's biannual pledge drive as a way to make a difference.

Instead of making a simple donation, these businesses offered a challenge to the listeners: they offered to make donations ranging from $500 to $2,000, depending on the time of day and the program, if the

Marketing Mistake: Not Overseeing Event Activities

After Jim German developed a line of hypoallergenic flea shampoo and other pet care products, he needed to create name recognition for his product line to draw more people into the retail shops that carry them. A variety of community organizations were holding an Animal Rescue Day, so he thought that signing on as a sponsor would be a excellent way to create visibility for his new products. He paid a thousand dollars to become one of the event sponsors in exchange for which it was agreed that a sample of his flea bath, along with a "Keep Your Pet Safe" pamphlet he prepared to inform people about the allergic reactions pets can have to grooming products, would be made available to each person who came to the event.

It seemed like a win/win arrangement. His company name and logo were included on the program guide and there was a banner near the entrance with his logo on it along with the banners of other sponsors. But to his dismay, when he arrived at the event, he could find neither hide nor hair of his product samples or pamphlets. None of the volunteers or officials at the event seemed to know what he was referring to. His heart sank. Sure enough, after looking diligently for his samples, he found them in a big bin over in a corner alongside a table filled with stacks of free handouts. By the end of the day, only a handful of the thousands of participants had picked up a sample of his product or pamphlet.

He raised the issue with officials after the event, and they assured him that they had indeed made his materials available as promised. Of course, since he was sponsoring a charity fund-raising event, there was no advantage whatsoever to throwing a fit or trying to take legal recourse against the community organizations for not meeting his expectations. He had to swallow his loss and vow to see to it that if he ever sponsored a future event, he would not only get a clear agreement *in writing* but would also arrange to oversee and participate in the distribution of his material to make sure it got into the hands of all those in attendance as intended.

pledges received over a fixed period of time reached a certain level. Such a donation could double the amount of the pledges during that time. Throughout the specified time period, the businesses involved got what amounted to a continuous radio commercial and some even got the opportunity to participate on the air in the pledge drive itself, while the station benefited from greatly increased subscription rates. So everyone wins from a challenge like this.

Of course, this type of donation will not suit every business. A great deal depends on the demographics of your particular marketplace. For instance, in Dallas the public radio station plays an eclectic array of music, whereas in other markets it may be limited to classical music. This changes the listening audience substantially. However, there are programs that are universal to most affiliates of National Public Radio that may pull in listeners who fit the demographic profile of your market.

Another avenue for making donations that can be of great value to the small-business person is a televised auction, usually designed to benefit the arts. These auctions are always in need of products and services to sell to the highest bidder as part of a fund-raiser for local organizations. The value of these items covers a wide range. Since these programs run for many hours, they generally have three or four boards of ten items each with values from $10 to $200. A board is scanned with descriptions about three times before it is closed to bids and then is refilled with new items. There may be one or two mini-boards of ten items with values ranging from $200 to $500, which are scanned with descriptions about six times before each board is closed and then refilled. Last, the maxi-board may have fifteen to twenty-five items ranging from $500 up. This board is rarely closed. Items are closed and replaced from time to time during the course of the auction.

Obviously, there is a spot for almost any product or service. Any service business could offer a few hours of its service as an item for bidding: the computer consultant, for example, could offer a special consultation for home or business of one or two hours; a bed-and-breakfast inn could offer a weekend for two. Even if there is no televised auction in your area, many charities hold an annual fund-raising auction. Donating to these auctions also gets you an invitation to the function at which the auction is held. Such events are excellent routes to meeting gatekeepers or key people in your community.

You can also make a donation offer as part of a special advertising campaign. For example, Les Trois Petit Cochons, a maker of superb pâtés, terrines, and other delicacies in New York, donates a flat amount on all full loaves of pâté or terrine sold during the Christmas season to the Coalition for the Homeless. They simply send a letter to their current customers and any prospects on their mailing list explaining how a portion of every sale will be donated to the Coalition. Gary Linkon, owner of the Sports Trader, tied in with a Say No to Drugs and Say Yes to Sport Campaign in his community by offering T-shirts featuring the campaign's slogan and offering a 5 percent discount to kids involved in the program. Doing something similar in your marketplace for your favorite cause could be the one thing that makes a customer decide to buy from you instead of your competitor.

Best Bets: Sponsoring or contributing to the right organization, event, or cause can be effective whether you're selling products or services to businesses or to consumers because it provides visibility for your work and places you in the circle of community leaders. Toba Burg of Los Angeles actually sells her designer robes and PJs exclusively through fund-raising boutiques. Charities in the area sponsor an array of merchandise boutiques throughout the year and 20 to 25 percent of Burg's sales goes to the charity sponsoring the events. On a good day she makes about $1,000 and participates in anywhere from one to five events a week.

Tips for Getting Business from Sponsorships, Donations, and Charity Events

There are four criteria for deciding to use your marketing funds to sponsor a community or charity event:

- Does the event attract attendees from your target market?
- Would your participation in the event enhance your image or the positioning of your company?
- Will there be publicity for the event in which you could be included?
- Does it coordinate well with the rest of your marketing plans?
- Is it cost-effective, and can you afford it?

If you do choose to sponsor a sports team or similar activity, be sure you attend at least some of the events. First, you want to monitor whether the sponsorship is actually reaching your target market; and, second, you want to be sure to root for your team or support your cause. Your contribution is always more than monetary, and attending or participating in the events gives you the opportunity to meet potential customers and clients as well.

Photographer Helen Garber of Santa Monica, California, has found that contributing her services to charity events held at art galleries is the ideal marketing activity for her. Since she loves art and would want to be supporting these events anyway, attending them to take the publicity photos for the charity event enables her to promote her work while combining two things that she loves most, photography and art.

You don't have to do these activities alone. Fund-raising and other sponsored events offer opportunities for you to approach people who otherwise might be out of your immediate circle or whom you might be uncomfortable approaching on your own behalf. It also offers you an excellent opportunity to work *with* rather than *for* your customers. Ask good customers if they would like to join you in sponsoring a particular event. Partnerships developed through serving the community often develop into good business relationships.

Resource: Sponsorships, Donations, and Events

Books

Special Events, Inside and Out. Steven Wood Schmader and Robert Jackson. Champaign, IL: Sagamore Publishing, 1997. A comprehensive guide to special-event planning.

Action Steps: Choosing an Event to Sponsor

Make a list of every event in your market area that might be attended by your target clients or customers. Include sporting events, charity affairs, pledge drives, et al. This list should be very long. Then narrow your list by limiting it to those most likely to attract a high percentage of people who fit your customer profile (see Ideal Customer Profile, **chapter 5**, page 176). From this narrowed list, select three events to investigate thoroughly. Find out what it would take to be a sponsor of these events: what it costs, what a sponsor's responsibilities are, how your company name would be displayed or credited, who would see it, what publicity it might attract there, etc. Select one to try based on its meeting the four criteria above. Then do it! Track the results and if you like them, then incorporate it in your future marketing plans.

CHAPTER 11

Telling All About It

Ninety-one percent of small businesses use printed material to market their business.

—Impulse Research Corporation

Some people have a gift for words. If that's you, there are many ways you can use that gift to write about what you do so that people will have the chance to better understand what you do and get excited about using your products and services. Printed materials of all kinds are the most popular marketing tools among small businesses according to a nationwide poll by Impulse Research Corporation for Okidata. Seventy-eight percent of those polled reported they used printed materials more than any other method to promote their business, and an overwhelming majority found it to be a "very effective" way to get business. Half reported using brochures and flyers, a third do some type of direct mail, and one in five has some type of printed leave-behind material.

In this chapter, you'll find over forty different ways people can read or hear about what you do. Many of the methods are the more tried and true ways that companies have traditionally marketed themselves. Polished catalogs and brochures, product packaging and displays, direct mail and print advertising, for example, have been primary business generators for the majority of American corporations. Only lately, however, with the advent of computer technology have they become as affordable and feasible for the smallest of businesses and self-employed individuals.

Other methods in this chapter like flyers, newsletters, coupons, and postcards were once thought of as second cousins to the more traditional means of marketing. But in today's information-intensive climate, these approaches to getting business can sometimes outperform their more expensive cousins. A good number of the methods in this chapter—like Web sites, on-line advertising, and fax-back services—didn't even exist only a few years ago. Now each of these marketing methods, be they more traditional or cutting-edge, can be part of your five-star marketing plan or excellent adjuncts to supplement other marketing strategies you're using. And, if you wish, or your budget requires, you can do them yourself. According to the Impulse Research survey, 72 percent of small-business owners produce their own materials using their PC and printer!

The popularity of the methods you'll find in this chapter lies in the fact that once you prepare them and get them into the hands of the right people, they do much of the work of getting business for you, leaving you free to do paying work and respond to the business they produce. As you will see, though, they usually work best as introductions or reminders, leading to a more steady flow of business only after you are known and established or when they are adjuncts to other more personal marketing methods.

Advertising

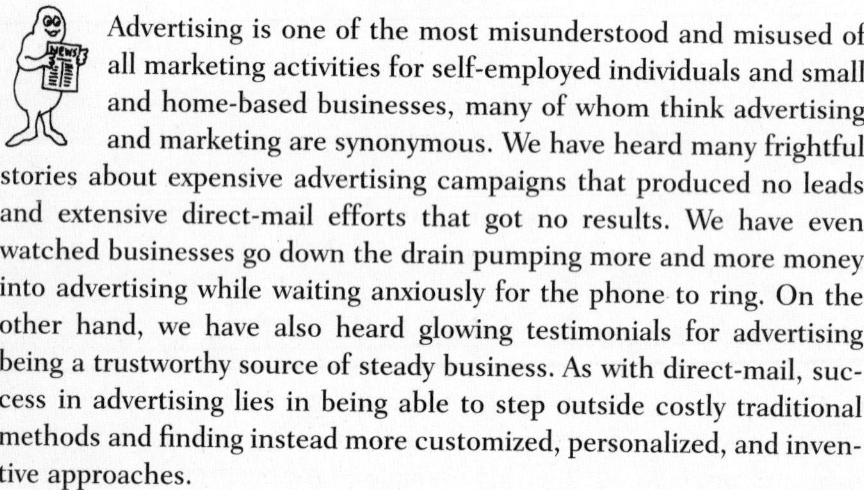

Advertising is one of the most misunderstood and misused of all marketing activities for self-employed individuals and small and home-based businesses, many of whom think advertising and marketing are synonymous. We have heard many frightful stories about expensive advertising campaigns that produced no leads and extensive direct-mail efforts that got no results. We have even watched businesses go down the drain pumping more and more money into advertising while waiting anxiously for the phone to ring. On the other hand, we have also heard glowing testimonials for advertising being a trustworthy source of steady business. As with direct-mail, success in advertising lies in being able to step outside costly traditional methods and finding instead more customized, personalized, and inventive approaches.

Advertising can be especially effective, for example, when you are selling a product such as soap or potato chips to the general public. For a mass-market consumer product, advertising is the most efficient method for reaching the largest number of people. Since most self-employed individuals are selling more specialized products and services, however, using a mass-market advertising approach to get business is like using a forklift to pick up a toaster. A small or home-based business must determine if and how advertising could be a cost-effective medium for reaching its targeted market. Here are three examples.

Judy Wunderlich runs a temporary agency for graphic designers in Schaumburg, Illinois. She gets all her business by sending direct mail to firms that are too small to have an in-house graphic-design staff. Cheryl Myer runs Word Processed Pages from her home in Algonquin, Illinois. She gets most of her business from the Yellow Pages. Roland Sutton of Conway, South Carolina, gets the majority of his parking-lot-maintenance service business from sending out his own newsletters.

Each of these businesses has several aspects in common that make them good candidates for advertising: They all provide a service people know they need. There is an immediate demand for each of them, and what they provide is relatively clear-cut and easy to understand. Also the quality of each of these services is relatively easy to measure. Despite these apparent similarities, however, only one of these businesses has chosen advertising as its primary promotional technique. Each owner has selected the marketing method that is best suited to the nature of his or her particular business.

YOUR GOAL: GIVE PEOPLE A CHANCE TO READ AND HEAR ABOUT WHAT YOU CAN DO

___Advertising
- Classified and display print ads
  - Newspapers
  - Consumer magazines
  - Business and trade publications
  - Independent newsletters
- Directory listings and ads
  - Yellow Pages
  - Trade and specialty directories
- Direct-response advertising:
  - Reply cards, inserts, card decks, coupon packs, and bounce backs
- On-line advertising

___Articles and columns
___Brochures and flyers
___Bulletin boards, tear pads, take ones and door-hangers
___Catalogs
___Direct mail
___Fax back, broadcast fax, and E-mail
___Newsletters
___Phone and hold button messages
___Postcards
___Product packaging and point of sale displays
___Sales letters and proposals
___Web site
___Your own book

Since Judy's company is the first in the Chicago area to offer a service providing temporary personnel in the graphics field, people aren't apt to look for it in the Yellow Pages, nor would the brevity essential to any advertising medium be conducive to explaining her unique service. Thus advertising would not be a cost-effective selection for her, whereas a mail campaign sent directly to businesses who need such services works well. On the other hand, almost everyone in business today knows about word-processing services, so they are apt to turn straight to the Yellow Pages when they need one. Thus, this form of advertising is effective for Cheryl. But since parking-lot maintenance is a highly competitive field, Roland needs some means of distinguishing himself from his competitors. A newsletter provides him with ample space to inform, educate, and sell, which would be too expensive to accomplish through an ad.

The first secret to making advertising work is knowing whether your business is one that is suited to it and, if so, selecting the best kind of advertising for you.

Selecting among Advertising Options

In this information-rich age, the number of avenues for advertising continues to proliferate. Here we will explore a variety of print advertising options that work well for many small, home-based and one-person businesses and professional practices: classified and display print advertising in newspapers, magazines, and newsletters, directory listings like Yellow Pages, direct-response advertising of various kinds, and advertising on-line. For ideas on how you could make use of radio and television advertising opportunities, see **chapter 12.** As we have done in other chapters, we will present the pros and cons of each option and provide tips for how to get business using them. Before we do that, however, there is a variety of myths and other general issues you should be familiar with to make the best choice about whether to advertise and, if so, in which medium.

Avoiding Five Common Myths about Advertising

Before deciding whether advertising will be a good method for you and, if so, which kinds will work best, we want to talk about five common misconceptions we often encountered when people think about advertising. Getting the facts in regard to these myths will help you appreciate what advertising actually can and cannot do.

Myth 1: Advertising is what you have to do to get business. Fact: advertising is only one of many ways to get business. Advertising is simply the purchase of time or space in order to promote a product or service. There are many other marketing methods available to you that do not involve buying time or space, some of which might be better for you than the purchase of any kind of advertising. On the other hand, advertising may be the best method for you.

Much depends on what specific results you expect advertising to get for you. Your expectations are the key to advertising success. First you have to understand how most advertising works. Whether you are thumbing through a magazine, cheering for your team on a cable station, or listening to Dr. Laura on the radio, your brain is absorbing a wide variety of information of which you are not even aware. You may not think you heard or saw that ad for computer software (let's call it DOMFLATCH), but when you receive a direct-mail piece on DOMFLATCH two weeks later, your brain makes a connection and you find that the name is familiar to you.

You still may not be interested until someone you are chatting with says he or she is looking for a program for a particular task and asks you if you've heard of DOMFLATCH. Suddenly, you recall, not where or how you heard about it, but rather the simple fact that you did hear about it. And you mention that to your contact. Now DOMFLATCH has an image, intentional or otherwise, that you received from the previous two messages. It may take several more encounters with the message before the day comes that you are sitting at your computer trying to solve a problem and, suddenly, the solution pops into your head. What you need is a program to do exactly what—now, what was its name?—you know, that one you heard about.

Two days later, there in the mail or on the radio is the ad for DOMFLATCH. This time you make the call or memorize the number to call as soon as you reach a phone. Advertising works the same way for every product and service you buy. Somewhere, somehow, you received an impression about that product or service, deep within the recesses of your brain. The simpler the message, the easier and clearer it will imprint in your unconscious. If the message clicks with your needs and your values, it will surface in your conscious mind when you are reminded at a time when you need the solution the product or service will provide.

Myth 2: Advertising is too expensive for small businesses. Fact: Advertising doesn't have to break your budget. The high cost of much of what you see in various media has actually opened the door for many less costly avenues and techniques that can be just as effective for small businesses. With the proliferation of niches in both print and broadcast media, various media are hungry enough for advertising dollars that both time and space can be purchased for far less than you might imagine. Additionally, there are many creative promotional alternatives, some using techniques similar to advertising.

What tends to make traditional advertising media too expensive for many small businesses is the tendency to try to sell every point you have. Experts say that there are only three things that should be included in your message:

1. Your company name or your brand
2. How to reach you or where to find it
3. One and only one message sent to the inner self of your customer

The more complex your message is, the less likely it will be retained or recalled. So, to keep your advertising cost-effective, keep the message simple.

Myth 3: There is one best advertising method. Fact: Advertising always begins as an experiment. Because most individuals who are in business for themselves don't have a lot of money to spend, too often they begin by putting it all into one approach to advertising that they heard worked well for someone else, hoping it will provide the business they need. In actuality, finding the right advertising medium for your business is similar to concocting a new recipe by trial and error.

Marketing consultant Cork Platt claims that success as a marketer lies in how much you fail. He cautions start-up sole proprietors to avoid the trap of using one advertising approach or outlet at a time, urging instead that they sample several approaches or outlets on a small scale simultaneously. Unless you try combinations until you find the right formula, he warns, you are apt to run out of money before finding the one or two avenues or techniques that will work for you.

Not realizing this nearly put Bobby and Jody Feinstein out of business. When they opened a referral service for household help, on the advice of a business consultant they spent every penny they had on a massive print-ad campaign. They hired an advertising consultant and an excellent designer, carefully selected targeted newspapers and magazines, and blanketed the area with their top-notch ads. You can imagine their horror when virtually no one called from these ads. They later discovered that when people pay for a referral, they want to know the person making it. Ultimately, the Feinsteins discovered they could get an excellent response at trade shows, but they went seriously in debt before doing so. In hindsight, they realized they should have put a little of their money into testing the responses to a variety of marketing approaches, perhaps by starting with a few classified ads while simultaneously experimenting with trade shows or networking. By using such a shotgun approach, they would have found out what worked in less time and avoided a near-disaster. So avoid the temptation to put all your advertising eggs in one basket until you know from experience what the right basket is.

Myth 4: One shot will do it. Fact: Advertising requires repetition. The fourth misconception about advertising is that a little dab will do you. Advertising is an investment that takes time and repetition. The average American is exposed to hundreds if not thousands of promotional messages every day. As a result, people have learned to screen out all but those messages that effectively claim their attention. This makes advertising a challenge for any business that is operating on a shoestring. Advertising works on what is called the Rule of Seven, which asserts that a message typically needs to be noticed by any given customer seven times before he or she will take action. The corollary to the rule is that it takes an average of seven tries to get noticed once. That means you have to expose a potential customer to your products an average of forty-nine times before he or she is likely to call, come in, or place an order.

For small and home-based businesses with limited advertising budgets, scrounging up the dollars to advertise once can be challenge enough, let alone doing it forty-nine times. However, money spent on hit-and-miss exposures is usually money wasted. For example, when Doris Kay began offering pickup and delivery services to recharge laser cartridges for downtown offices, she decided to spend her limited advertising funds for a half-page ad in a local business journal with a large monthly circulation. She spent her remaining money to buy a thirty-minute block of time on a small-business-focused talk-radio station. The results from both were poor: she got no calls from the magazine ad and only three from the radio show, and no one actually signed up for the service. Following the Rule of Seven, Doris would have been wiser to have invested the same amount of money in a small classified ad in a daily or weekly publication and in shorter radio spots that would have run repeatedly over as many weeks as possible. These small ads could have been supported by public-relations and promotional activities.

No matter what your business is, if you have the budget to keep doing it, advertising can help. In most cases, however, when advertising funds are limited, you have to be selective and creative to obtain a sufficient number of exposures to get results.

Myth 5: Advertising does the work for you. Fact: You can't sit back and wait. The fifth most common misconception about advertising is that it is a totally passive way to get business. Many people think they can simply put some ads in the proper place and sit back and wait for the business to come rolling in. Rarely does that happen.

While advertising can be marketing while you are working, it also demands that you engage in a highly active and interactive process with the prospective clients or customers it reaches. The more active you are in promoting yourself through a variety of marketing activities, the better results you will get from any advertising you do. All your promotional efforts will greatly increase the chances that people will respond to your advertising. And once they do respond, usually you will have to do more than simply take their order. With the exception of direct-response advertising to which people respond by sending in the money with their order, most ads produce leads—people who are interested. Occasionally they will simply want you to write up the sale, but most of the time you will at least have to close the sale.

For example, Dr. John Grable hired a writer to create an ad promoting his new stress-reduction classes. He ran the ad daily for two weeks in the local newspaper. The first day the ad ran, he forgot to tell the secretary about it, and she told the people who called that they must have the wrong number. After this embarrassing episode, the secretary was well prepared the next day to sign people up for the workshop.

Unfortunately, however, they were calling to get more information so they could decide whether to sign up. The secretary didn't know anything about what the seminar covered, so she placed the stack of calls on the doctor's desk to be returned sometime during the day. By now Dr. Grable was very frustrated. The first class was approaching, and his advertising had become a headache instead of a route to new business. Fortunately, he had prepared a flyer about the classes to hand out to patients in the office, so he had his secretary mail a flyer to everyone who had called. There was a total of twenty-six calls during the two weeks, but not one person called to enroll after receiving the flyer. Dr. Grable concluded that advertising was just a waste of time and money.

Had he been aware that advertising is not simply a passive order-taking medium, Dr. Grable could have turned these calls into profits. For example, he could have planned to have someone with sales skills take the calls or make follow-up calls after the mailings had gone out.

He could have arranged to have everyone who called for more information visit his office at one set time for a preview, where they could talk with him firsthand and register for the classes. Since many of the people attending his classes ultimately come to him for treatment, his advertising would have paid off again and again.

While advertising can and often does produce some rapid sales, if you need immediate business, you are best advised to take advantage of the **Stop Gap Measures** described on pages 7 and 8 or use **Direct Solicitation** techniques described in **chapter 9**. Research shows that advertising does a better job of stimulating more business from your existing customers than it does of getting new ones.

Getting the Most Reach for Your Money

Which advertising media to choose from among the options available is a matter of matching your budget with the ability of each medium to reach the greatest number of people who will buy your products or services. For this reason, people who sell advertising space and ad time talk in terms of cost per thousand, abbreviated as C/M, meaning the actual dollar amount you spend in relation to the number of readers, viewers, or listeners the particular medium claims you reach. Cost per thousand is not a bad way to make comparisons among various media, but you need to be sure that the costs are comparable.

Although any medium will give you a C/M number based on its particular audience, it may or may not give you specific demographic information on that audience. For example, suppose the price of a half-page ad in Publication A is $1,350, whereas the price of the same-size ad in Publication B is $1,475. Publication A has a total circulation of ten thousand people, making their claimed C/M $135; Publication B has a total circulation of six thousand, with an apparent C/M of $246. The natural assumption would be that Publication A would be the better buy.

However, a closer look at the circulation figures shows that of Publication A's ten thousand subscribers, six thousand are age twenty-one to thirty-five, two thousand are thirty-five to fifty, and two thousand are fifty and above. In contrast, Publication B's six thousand subscribers break down into five thousand age thirty-five to fifty and one thousand over fifty, with none under thirty-five. If you are looking for potential customers only between the ages of thirty-five and fifty, the original C/M figures change radically. Publication A's effective C/M is $675, while Publication B's becomes $295, and their value to you is reversed.

So here are several factors to take into consideration whenever possible when weighing your advertising choices:

1. ***Verify the claim.*** Find out whether a medium's claimed audience is audited or unaudited. If they are audited, the numbers were confirmed by an independent entity; if unaudited, they come from the medium's management and may not be accurate.

2. ***Get a breakdown of the audience.*** Carefully investigate the specific demographics of the medium's audience. Determine the categories that might truly be potential customers, and work your cost per thousand based on those numbers.

3. ***Calculate the total cost.*** In calculating the cost per thousand, be sure to include total costs, including amortization of your production costs over the span of the advertising period.

4. ***Track your response.*** Once you have run some advertising, despite the inherent difficulties and probable inaccuracies, try to determine approximately how many responses or reactions you got. This information will tell you whether an ad is paying for itself and which ads are bringing in the most business.

5. ***Set a budget.*** Set up an advertising budget based on the percentage of your gross sales that come from advertising; then don't exceed that budget. For example, if your gross monthly income is $10,000, $4,000 of which comes from referrals or networking and $6,000 from advertising, it is sensible to set aside 60 percent of your marketing funds to invest in advertising. So if you have $1,000 to spend on marketing each month, $600 a month will go to advertising and $400 to various networking activities.

Do You Need an Advertising Agency?

The decision to hire an advertising agency depends to a great extent on how much advertising you think you will be doing. If your advertising will primarily be limited to the Yellow Pages, a regularly repeated ad in trade journals, and a few classifieds, involving an agency would probably waste your money and their time.

However, if the best access to your market is through ongoing advertising in a variety of print and broadcast media, you can save time and money hiring an agency to provide a coherent campaign approach to the development and placement of advertising. Keep in mind, though, that most full-service agencies will not give you the time of day unless you expect to have an advertising budget of at least $50,000 a year. The exception would be a young and hungry agency with whom you can grow or a one-person agency that will work with small accounts.

The usual method of compensating an ad agency is to pay 15 percent of the gross amount you spend on preparation and media, which actually works out to 17.65 percent of the net. To illustrate how this works, if a newspaper charged $100 for an ad, the agency would bill you for the $100 and pay the newspaper $85. The fifteen-dollar difference pays the agency. This $15 is 15 percent of the gross, but it is also 17.65 percent of the $85. By the same token, if a printer produces two thousand brochures for you as a client of the agency and bills the agency $1,000 for those brochures, the agency will bill you $1,176.50, or $1,000 plus 17.65 percent. The extra $176.50 is 15 percent of the $1,176.50. Media and some suppliers do, however, offer a 2 percent discount for payment within ten days of invoicing. So if you pay promptly, the agency should pass that discount along to you. In selecting an agency, take into account:

- ***The questions they ask you.*** An agency should want to know a great deal about your business, plans, and expectations.

- ***The responses you get to your questions.*** A good agency will be candid about what they can and cannot do and how they charge for services.

- ***The samples of the agency's recent work.*** Expect first-class work.

- ***The results of advertising they have done*** for other clients. Request and review such data.

For businesses that do not have the size budget that appeals to an agency but still need professional help, hiring a freelance designer or copywriter or using a media-buying service can get you both professional service and save you money.

Of course, whether you do it yourself or get help, you need to give your advertising time to produce for you. Remember the Rule of Seven: You need at least forty-nine exposures to get a true test of the results. That is why you need to be particularly inventive at getting the most exposure for the least money. There is no sense advertising unless you can do it long enough and regularly enough for it to have a chance to work. And be sure your advertising coordinates with your other marketing activities so that all forty-nine exposures get your principal message across.

When a Small Business Should Advertise

The primary reasons to use advertising are to create awareness of your business and knowledge of what you offer, highlight why someone should select you over others who offer something similar, create a favorable emotional reaction to your product or service, remind people to buy, and stimulate impulse purchases. Given these criteria, here is a summary of when advertising would be and would not be the best choice.

When a Small Business Should Advertise

1. When your target market is the mass-market consumer.
2. When your target market is reachable by one or more media.
3. When there is no other method of reaching your prospect.
4. When awareness of your company's existence is an essential preliminary to approaching your customers.
5. When you are expanding your line or moving into a new market.
6. When your budget permits.
7. When you can reach the most people who can and will buy what you offer cost-effectively.
8. When most of your competition advertises.
9. When none of your competition advertises.

When a Small Business Should Not Advertise

1. When there is no medium that reaches your market directly.
2. When it is not cost-effective.
3. When your budget will not permit proper coverage or repetition.
4. When you expect advertising to bring in customers in droves.
5. When there is no way to sell your product or service without one-on-one contact.
6. When advertising would be used as the only way to reach your market.
7. When your advertising cannot compete with your competition's.
8. When you cannot afford to have the preparation done properly.
9. When you cannot express the essence of your product's or service's benefits briefly and dynamically.

Classified and Display Print Ads

Print advertising in newspapers, magazines, and other print media is often referred to as the "Great Mother" of advertising, because it has provided a forum to advertisers of all sizes, shapes, types, and budgets for hundreds of years. The advantage of such traditional print advertising is the wide selection of possible publications you can advertise in and their ability to reach either a broad or a highly targeted base of people.

Traditionally, print advertising refers to buying a portion of a page in the newspaper or magazine of your choice and displaying your ad there. Such display advertising is costly, however, because you are not only paying dearly for the space but must also pay dearly to design the attractive and effective layout and camera-ready art required for your ad. Therefore, instead of making the investment in such display advertising, many successful small and home-based businesses are using more cost-effective methods of print ads, such as classified ads, Yellow Page listings, and directory advertising. Then, when they get a particularly strong response from a particular publication, they may purchase a display ad in that publication.

For many small businesses, the best entry into the realm of advertising is through the classifieds. For example, when Lynn Frances started her cleaning service, she knew her best customers would come from the exclusive community of San Marino, California, so she ran a classified ad in the local San Marino paper. That listing turned out to be her primary source of business—so much so that she continued to run the ad every day of the year.

Newspapers and most consumer magazines, business and trade journals, and even small association newsletters have classified sections where individuals and businesses can advertise products and services for a minimal fee.

The term *classified* refers to the fact that the ads in this section are placed within categories, according to the type of product or service being offered or the type of purchaser sought. Whether your product or service is suited to *Architectural Digest* or *Video Review,* the local American Red Cross newsletter, or a specialized business journal, you will usually find a classified section in which to advertise. Classified sections often consist of the standard "words-only"—no graphics—listings seen in your local newspaper mixed in with varying sizes of display advertising. Other sections consist almost exclusively of mini-display ads, such as those in the Marketplace section at the rear of *PC* magazine.

Pros and Cons of Classified Advertising

One advantage of classified ads is that they are most often utilized by people who are already interested in locating a particular type of product or service. For these people, skimming the classifieds is as important as reading the editorial areas. So, classifieds can serve as a bridge between the more costly display advertising found in most media and the simple listings found in all varieties of directories. When placed in the right publication, you can more cost-effectively reach interested people.

Classified ads can also be used when you're beginning an advertising campaign and want to test whether a particular publication will draw for you before you invest in more expensive advertising They are ideal when you need to advertise consistently in a publication but you can't afford a more costly ad. And they can serve as a way to compare the response from a variety of publications before deciding where to take out display advertising.

On the other hand, classified ads often work best as a way to generate interest. In other words, you shouldn't necessarily expect to be able to sell your product or service directly from the ad. You will probably need to use a two-step process to turn that interest into an order by sending a free catalog, brochure, or other mail piece or by generating calls for further information.

Best Bets. Classified ads work well in selling products or services to consumers. They are excellent when starting almost any mail-order business.

At Home Professions of Garden Grove, California, a business that trains people to become note reader–scopists and medical transcriptionists from home, has built a successful business by placing classified ads in neighborhood shoppers. They use the ads to attract interested individuals to attend free seminars at which they find out about these two high-demand occupations.

To place classifieds in such shoppers on a nationwide basis, you can contact the National Classified Network (see **Resources**). NCN is a media-buying service that specializes in placing nationwide classified ads at substantial savings—as much as 65 percent—in time and money to the advertiser.

Tips for Getting Business from Classifieds

Repetition, repetition. Advertising is a repetitive medium, so, as with display advertising, there is usually a discount if you repeat an ad several times. You should definitely take advantage of such discounts and run your ad multiple times. Think of your own experience with ads. How many times have you seen an ad, thought about it, and looked for it in the next issue? You expect to see it there, and it's most frustrating if it isn't. The first and even second time you advertise are like appetizers building an appetite for your future ads.

Classifieds are usually purchased in one of three forms: by the word, by the line, or by the column inch. Each publication has its own methods of pricing, so to find out what your costs will be for a series, you'll need to check with each publication you're considering.

Pack each word with punch. To take the greatest advantage of classifieds, you must remember that, as in any ad, you have only fractions of a second to grab the reader's attention. Since you have even less space to do this in, your copy must be all the more arresting. Some publications permit artwork, some allow headlines, some permit the first few words to be boldface, and still others allow nothing but straight copy. Before you write your ad, be sure to investigate the requirements of the publication in which you are interested in addition to looking at the publication itself. When such enhancements are permissible, there is most likely an additional charge when you use them. If they fit within your budget, use whatever enhancements are allowed. Even if most enhancements are not available to you, you may be able to use all caps on the first few words or the entire first line. If none of these embellishments are permitted, you will have to rely exclusively on your choice of words to attract attention.

Hit one point. No matter what your design choices are, your choice of words is critical. Unlike display advertising, all classified advertising focuses directly on selling instead of creating an image or providing information. You must select one point, hit it, and hit it hard again. Make your point without using adjectives or qualifiers that will dilute the message. You must have something specific to offer—a specific product, a specific service, a specific discount, a specific gift, or a specific point.

If you glance through the classifieds section of a publication, you can see instantly which ones catch your eye. You'll notice immediately that the best ads focus primarily on one point. If someone is offering a disk copy service, that point comprises the bulk of the copy. That a catalog of diskettes and supplies is also offered may be mentioned, but only briefly.

If you have more than one point to sell, buy more than one classified ad. Instead of trying to crowd all your information into a single ad, think about dividing it and placing two or more smaller ads, each with its own set of power words. Keep in mind, however, that you'll be harder to remember if you confuse the reader with too many different focuses.

Make the first word count. The first word in your ad, especially if you cannot use a headline, is the most important. Skim through *Words That Sell,* by Richard Bayan (see **Resources: Classifieds**) and select the most powerful word that is applicable to what you are selling. Words such as *free, discount, profit, urgent, daring, elite, bold, sparkling, speedy, revitalize, secure,* and *guarantee* all evoke an immediate image in the mind of the reader. They are strong, dynamic words that pull the eye to the next word. Avoid indefinite words like *can, might,* or *may* and impact-losing words such as *the, an, if, a* or any other article. Think of verbally yanking the reader up by the collar.

Call for action. Be sure your ad tells people what to do and motivates them to do it; e.g., "Call for information," "Write for a free catalog," "Call for your free booklet on How to . . . ," "Call for a free evaluation." As we mentioned above, classifieds are best at getting interested people to identify themselves, generating their interest, and getting them to ask for more. So give the reader an incentive to contact you right away.

Now let's take a look at the possible locations for your ads, be they classified or display.

Newspapers

Local newspapers provide the greatest access to the broadest consumer market in a given area. They usually bridge all gaps of social, economic, professional, and ethnic background within the region they cover. This means that if the only common ground your potential customers have is $10 in their pockets, the newspaper is the best and most cost-effective advertising medium you will find. It is the safest and probably the least expensive medium for broad-based retail advertising.

The primary focus and benefit of newspaper advertising is that it sells to individual consumers, not to other businesses. If you are providing a service such as medical transcription or bookkeeping, newspaper advertising is probably not your best bet, but if you provide a baby-sitting referral service, plumbing services, catering, or dog grooming, it might work well for you.

Consumer Magazines

Like newspapers, magazines reach the consumer directly, but unlike them—with the exception of a few general-interest magazines such as *Life* and *People*—these periodicals are targeted to highly specific markets. Whether your potential customer is interested in home improvement (*Home Mechanix*), motorcycles (*American Motorcyclist*), travel (*Travel & Leisure*), fishing (*Fishing World*), computers (*Home Office Computing*), or almost any other area, there is probably at least one consumer magazine published on the subject.

The second major difference between advertising in newspapers and in magazines is the frequency with which they are issued. Although some magazines are issued weekly, quarterly, or even annually, the majority of consumer magazines are published monthly. There is one other major difference. Because of their format, their orientation, and the fact that they are usually printed on coated paper and saddle stitched or perfect-bound, magazines have a more upscale appearance, resulting in a readership on a slightly higher socioeconomic level. And they are likely to be kept around the home or office for a longer period of time.

Business and Trade Publications

Almost without exception, every type of business has at least one major publication dedicated to professionals in that field. For example, there are industry magazines similar to the consumer publications we listed: *Builder*, *Motor Cycle Industry*, *Travel Agent*, *Action Sports Retailer*, and *Computer Dealer*. According to the Society of Association Executives there are 138,000 such organizations nationwide from those we're all familiar with like the American Bar Association or the American Medical Association to much more obscure groups like the Association of Flying Funeral Directors and the Hollow Metal Door Association.

If your primary clients or customers are other businesses or business people, trade publications may be a valuable advertising medium. The business decision-makers you want to reach turn to these publications as their main source of industry news, resources, and other educational material. These publications are considered necessary reading for any individual to function efficiently in his or her particular field.

Therefore everyone with responsibility in a given industry avidly devours the information in his or her trade journals.

Usually you will want to place ads in the trade publications your customers or clients read, not necessarily in your own industry publications. For example, if you are a computer consultant specializing in developing systems for tool-and-die manufacturers, it would be a waste of time and money to advertise in computer magazines. Your best avenue would be to advertise in the journals and publications produced for the tool-and-die industry.

Independent Newsletters

Small special-interest newsletters are a burgeoning avenue for advertising. Some of these newsletters are highly targeted to a specific market. Others are produced by companies to enhance their customer contact; therefore, the market base can be very broad. For example, AT&T has a newsletter it sends to a mailing list of 800,000 home-business customers. Often special-interest organizations and associations produce either local or national newsletters, and some publish both. Many of these newsletters accept advertising.

Since most newsletters are very specialized and some have small subscriber lists, however, they can be difficult to locate. Begin your search by checking all the mail you receive. If you belong to a special-interest group or club, you probably receive a newsletter from that organization. If others in that group would benefit from your product or service, see whether the newsletter accepts advertising. Even if it has not done so in the past, it might start taking ads as a way of increasing revenues or offsetting its costs. It is a lot easier to get people to take your money than you might think.

If you don't find appropriate newsletters in your own mailbox, there are directories of newsletters in the public library to investigate (see **Resources**). The key is digging to locate a newsletter that reaches the exact people you want to reach and then getting short-term contracts. Since organizations start up and abandon newsletter production on a regular basis, never pay for advertising space more than one issue in advance unless the newsletter is one of long standing.

If your product or service complements your customers' businesses, advertise in newsletters they produce for their customers. For example, if you do word processing or bookkeeping for a legal firm that specializes in corporate law, you can advertise in the monthly newsletter the law firm sends to its corporate clients. Your business does not compete with theirs, and the clients would be a market you might not otherwise be able to reach.

If you produce a product that your customers resell in some form and they produce a newsletter, what better way to assist your customers and build your relationship than to buy advertising in their newsletter?

The primary source of information about all types of print media is the Standard Rate and Data Service (SRDS), which comes out in monthly volumes from Wilmette, Illinois. SRDS has separate volumes entitled *Newspapers, Consumer Magazines, Business Publications, Direct Mail,* as well as others directed at additional print media. To begin the process of deciding on specific print media, visit your local library and review what is available in SRDS. There you will find which publications serve your market, how many people they reach, whom to contact,

CONSUMER MAGAZINE ADVERTISING

PROS	CONS
1. Readership generally has a higher average and more discretionary income than newspaper readership.	1. Specialized circulation can miss most of the target market.
2. Most magazine buyers read them to find resources. Ads can be as important as the articles.	2. Cost of space is usually much higher than in other print media.
3. Most magazines cover a greater geographical area than newspapers.	3. Production lead time means ads must be prepared long before publication.
4. Far more time is spent reading magazines than reading any other single consumer-based print medium.	4. Ad clutter means low recall; the average magazine is 50 percent advertising.
5. Magazines are kept, read repeatedly, and passed from person to person.	5. Magazine producers usually do not offer the creative or production assistance that most newspapers do.

what their rates are, the deadlines involved, preparation of materials, and other valuable information. (See **Resources** below.)

Resources: Display and Classified Advertising

Books

Advertising from the Desktop, the Desktop Publisher's Guide to Ads that Work. Elaine Floyd and Lee Wilson. Florence, Ky.: Ventana, 1993.

Directories in Print. Gale Research Inc., 645 Griswold St., Detroit, MI 48226, (313) 961-2242.

Do-It-Yourself Advertising and Promotion. Fred. E. Haun. New York: Wiley, 1997.

One-Minute Designer. Roger Parker. New York: Henry Holt, 1997.

Oxbridge Directory of Newsletters: The most comprehensive guide to U.S. and Canadian newsletters available. New York, annual.

Standard Rate and Data Service. 1700 Higgins Rd., Des Plaines, IL 60018, (847) 375-5000. Monthly volumes entitled *Newsletters, Consumer Magazines, Business Publications, Direct Mail*, and others directed at additional print media where you can find publications that serve your market, how many people they reach, whom to contact, what their rates are, the deadlines involved, preparation of materials, and other valuable information available in libraries and on the Web at www.srds.com

Services

The following services will place your ads in multiple classified sections across the country:

American Publishing Company, 506 W. Potter Ave., PO Box 828, Kirksville, MO 63501, (800) 748-8249.

NRC Media Services Group, 2442 Cerrillos Rd., Ste. 455, Santa Fe, NM 87505, (505) 424-6820.

National Response Corporation, 3511 West Commercial Boulevard, 2d Floor, Fort Lauderdale, FL 33309, (888) 672-4237.

Directory Listings and Ads

The one directory that comes immediately to mind is the Yellow Pages. There are, however, other directories in which you might also want to be listed or consider placing an ad. Directories differ from other forms of print advertising in the following ways:

1. Directories are usually more tightly controlled in terms of who can advertise and the format that can be used than other forms of print advertising.
2. Directories are kept close at hand for extended periods of time.
3. Directories place the seller in contact with buyers who are actively seeking products and services.

Here are some ideas for deciding if directory listings or ads could be a good way to get business coming to you.

Yellow Page Advertising

If you have a business telephone line, you already may have been or will be contacted to buy a Yellow Page listing. One basic listing comes with your business telephone line. However, the free listing you are entitled to is so minimal that if you intend to use the Yellow Pages as a means of getting business, you must consider other possibilities. But would the additional cost be worth your while?

Kenneth McKethan who operates Techni-Lingua LTD, a translation service based in Dunn, North Carolina, thinks so. He uses Yellow Page ads to attract business from several cities. Charlotte Mitchell, who operates Notary on Wheels in San Diego, agrees. She gets a substantial portion of her business from her Yellow Pages ad. The turning point for Patricia Plake's photography studio in Overland Park, Kansas, came when she upgraded her Yellow Pages ad. C. Thomas Fitzwilliam of Arlington, Texas, has had success advertising in an alternative yellow-pages directory for his landscape and irrigation business.

Like these individuals, many small-business operators and self-employed people tell us they get most or a considerable amount of their business from the Yellow Pages. In fact, according to an article in the *New York Times* Business section, 65 percent of Yellow Page advertisers take out no other ads. Others, however, say a Yellow Page listing is of no consequence. Here's why the results are so diverse.

Pros and Cons of Yellow Page Advertising

One big advantage of a Yellow Page ad is that it reaches consumers who are ready to buy now. Also, almost every household or business has a Yellow Pages directory. People expect many types of businesses to be listed in the Yellow Pages and they will look there first. To name just a few, word processing, housecleaning, rug cleaning, plumbing, repair services, window washing, extermination, and notary publics often get a substantial portion of their business from the Yellow Pages. In addition, display ads in the Yellow Pages can be large and varied enough to include the key information someone needs to make a choice among competitors.

Sometimes, even when people would not turn to the Yellow Pages to find someone like yourself, they might look there to confirm an address or phone number or to otherwise check you out when someone has referred them. So having a listing would still be worth your while.

On the other hand, people simply don't look in the Yellow Pages for certain types of businesses such as management consultants, professional speakers, urban planners, architectural design firms, or any niche that is so specialized or unique that there is no Yellow Page category for them to be listed under. In addition, your ad could appear right next to those of your competitors, so comparison may be easy. Also, there may be copy restrictions governing what you can put in your ad and the design you may use. You can only revise your copy once a year, so if you didn't get it right, you'll have to wait a whole year to correct it. Also, because the entire directory is composed solely of advertising, people will only see your ad if they actively turn to the Yellow Pages to shop for what you offer.

Best Bets: Yellow Page ads work especially well when you're offering products and services to consumers that they're familiar with and know will be listed there, like a florist, a window-cleaning service, a picture-framing studio, or a shoe-repair shop. Yellow Page listings can also work well for business services that companies are familiar with and don't require an unusually large expenditure or an extreme degree of risk such as desktop publishing, graphic design, commercial cleaning services, or hauling services.

Tips for Getting Business from the Yellow Pages

First, you must decide whether advertising—as opposed to just being listed in the Yellow Pages—will be worth your while. Then, if so, you will want to create a compelling ad that will lead the right kind of people to select you from among the possibilities. Here are some tips for making such decisions.

Check out if people will be looking for you there. The most important variable in deciding whether Yellow Page advertising will benefit you is whether or not people turn to the Yellow Pages when they buy what you have to sell. As we mentioned, there are many products and services for which people customarily shop through the Yellow Pages and others that people virtually never shop for this way. But most businesses lie somewhere in between these two extremes.

On certain occasions, some people might turn to the Yellow Pages to find a product or service that other potential clients would never think to look for there. For example, as a general rule of thumb, in seeking specialized personal and business services such as public relations or marriage and family counseling, most people will turn to referrals from other professionals, colleagues, or friends. Yet some people will look for these services in the Yellow Pages.

So, to help determine whether your business is one people will turn to the Yellow Pages to find, first see whether there is a category listing there that describes what you do. Then check to see whether most of your successful competitors are there. Contact some of those who are listed to find out what kind of results they have had.

Be sure you're in the right Yellow Pages. If you think you will benefit from advertising in the Yellow Pages, keep in mind that there is not a single Yellow Page directory. Yellow Pages is a generic term for a variety of often competing advertising books. Within a given region, several companies may produce Yellow Page directories that vie with one another for your advertising dollar. In addition to the standard metropolitan-area Yellow Pages in most cities, you will often find separate suburban editions. You also may find as many as three competing Yellow Page companies covering the entire metropolitan area. Sometimes there are also special neighborhood or business-to-business editions and a variety of specialty Yellow Pages, such as the Women's Yellow Pages or the Christian Yellow Pages.

In addition, in recent years telephone companies like GTE, NYNEX, and Southwestern Bell have expanded their Yellow Page market into regions their telephone service does not include. In other cases a metropolitan region may split among as many as three local telephone companies, each with its own Yellow Pages edition, or contract with the Donnelly Directory to produce both a print and a talking version of the Yellow Pages. Increasing the confusion, any one telephone company may produce as many as four different types of directories: *core, overlay, neighborhood*, and *specialty*.

According to Bell Atlantic, the *core* is the principal book of your local phone company, its territory approximately matching that of the telephone company; the *overlay* book generally consists of one or more core books and is used to expand the area covered; *neighborhood* books cover individual market areas such as separate suburbs; and *specialty* books cover either specific areas of interest or specific portions of the population.

So if you wish to use Yellow Page advertising, you will need to select which Yellow Pages to advertise in and whether to advertise in one or more of the supplemental directories. The decision is complicated by the fact that, since each directory is produced and assembled separately, each will often have a different closing date. Therefore, it is more difficult to determine from the lumped charges on your telephone bill what each one is going to cost. Do not let this situation stymie you, however, or intimidate you into purchasing more advertising than you need. Your choice of how many and which Yellow Page editions to advertise in should depend exclusively on your target market, its location, and its likelihood of using the Yellow Pages to find businesses like yours.

When dealing with this proliferation of directories, the prospective advertiser must be fearless in demanding answers from Yellow Pages adspace sales representatives. You also must be just as wary about paying a bill for ad space or production costs. Some directories even send out solicitations for business that look like invoices, and too often these get paid without question.

Beware: Never pay what appears to be a bill for Yellow Page advertising without checking precisely which company you're dealing with. The term Yellow Pages is not copyrighted, so anyone can use it. Some independent sales companies are sending out advertisements for Yellow Page listings that may look just like a bill from your phone company.

Part of any decision you make about Yellow Page advertising will be based on simply looking through the directory you are considering, but the sales rep you speak with should be able to provide some hard figures about which markets the books reach.

Get listed under the right categories. Think about the various listings someone would turn to when looking for a product or service like yours. There may be more than one, and the ones you think of might not be the ones your clients would use. So, ask the Yellow Pages rep to provide you with a list of all the possible categories under which you could be listed. Check out which categories your competitors are listed under. Marketing consultant Pete Silver tells about a word-processing

QUESTIONS TO ASK WHEN SELECTING A YELLOW PAGE LISTING

Here are fifteen questions you should ask any space-sales representative before deciding whether his or her book is the right Yellow Pages for you:

1. Which company sponsors this book? Is it the phone company serving the area in which the book is distributed?
2. How long has this particular book been published?
3. What is the geographical area served by this book?
4. Is this the primary book for the total geographical area your business covers?
5. How many copies were circulated in the past year? (Watch out! Some reps will try to give you the number of books printed rather than those distributed. Also, check to be sure that circulation figures are not inflated by the number of household members instead of the number of books or by huge numbers of employees expected to use one or two directories.)
6. Who gets the directory?
7. How many are provided to each household? Each business location?
8. How often is the directory revised?
9. How is it distributed?
10. How many times per week do people refer to this directory?
11. How many dollars are spent weekly in purchases from this directory?
12. How many of my competitors are in the book already?
13. What kinds of promotions does the publisher do to encourage people to use the directory?
14. What is the publisher's policy concerning rebates for ad production problems such as typographical errors and inaccuracies?
15. How will my ad be billed to me?

service that decided to list under "Typist" instead of "Word Processing," "Secretarial Service," or "Desktop Publishing." To her surprise that was the category customers turned to first, and her business soared. Until you know where your clients will turn, be on the safe side and list under several categories. Then be sure to ask people who call you on which page number they found your name, so you can track which listing is drawing the best response.

Invest in a display ad. Research shows that a one-eighth Yellow Page display ad will triple the number of calls produced from an in-column space ad with a logo.

Have the better ad. The strongest argument in favor of the Yellow Pages is that approximately three out of four people who look something up there will follow up with a telephone call. However, about half the people who start out looking for a specific company are attracted to someone else instead, either because they can't find the listing or because someone else has a better ad. That better ad can be yours . . . but not if you use the same kind of advertising copy that you're using elsewhere.

Yellow Page ads differ from all other advertising (with the possible exception of classified ads) in that when turning to the Yellow Pages, the buyer is actively seeking the seller. So in Yellow Page ads, you're not selling the buyer on the product or service you offer. They're already sold on that. Your ad has to sell the buyer on doing business with *you* instead of with anyone else listed in the same section.

Sadly, despite the fact that Yellow Page advertising is an excellent avenue for many businesses, far too many businesses using it do little to get the most from this medium. Many who do use the Yellow Pages simply purchase a standard ad that they develop on the spur of the moment over the phone. Then they just renew automatically every year when a salesperson calls without investigating the response rate their current ad is generating to determine whether it is working.

Usually the Yellow Pages are filled with flat, bland advertising that isn't geared to sell. Yet it is a fiercely competitive medium. The only possible advantage to appearing in the Yellow Pages lies in being able to win a direct, head-on competition with the competing ads in your section, so a little dynamism in your Yellow Page ad will go a long way toward making it more effective.

You may run into major restrictions on the content and appearance of your ad. Some companies place strict and somewhat arbitrary limitations on the design. Some directories also place restrictions on type size, artwork, and punctuation. Copy limitations often include a ban on any comparative statements (no matter how true the claim might be), unsupported superlatives, and guarantee specifications. However, these limits are not universal, even within the same edition. For the most part, you will find few absolute controls in design, layout, or typeface in display ads other than those imposed by the size, readability, and appeal of the ad.

Companies publishing Yellow Pages offer free assistance in the development of copy, design, and layout. This is helpful as long as you don't allow the salesperson to sell you on a weak, boring ad that won't sell, which unfortunately is highly probable. Remember, the salesperson has to turn out a dozen or so ads every week in addition to doing his or her main job of selling the ads.

Since the Yellow Pages are a directly competitive medium, to be even reasonably effective, you have to put extra punch into your ad. Look through a copy of the Yellow Pages for the strongest ads you can find and emulate those. Here are some additional pointers for designing a winning ad:

1. ***Limit your choices*** to a maximum of one typeface and three type sizes in addition to your logo or company identification.

2. ***Don't waste space*** by stating the obvious, such as repeating what you are if that is the same as your company name or heading.

3. ***Don't crowd the space*** with extra type or unnecessary artwork; make the ad easy to read. Use only artwork that enhances your sales message. But do use bullets to set off different points

4. ***Concentrate on the headline and layout.*** As with any other print advertising, your headline and layout are the most important aspects to work out. They have to draw the reader's eye to your ad and away from all others. Once you have the reader's attention, your copy has to sell. The briefer and more to the point it is, the better, so use as few words and lines as possible. This will allow you to use larger type. The final most important eye-catchers are your company name and address and, even more important, your telephone number. Make these as prominent as your headline.

Don't hesitate to reject a design or layout that doesn't work, even if the deadline is fast approaching. Of course, it is always best to allow yourself plenty of time to plan your ad well ahead of the closing date. That way you have the time to throw out as many unacceptable layouts as you must in order to get a good ad for your investment.

Resources: Yellow Page Ads

Books

Getting the Most from Your Yellow Page Advertising. Barry Maher. San Diego: Aegis Publishing, 1997.

Yellow Page Advertising, How to Get the Most on Your Investment. Jeffrey Price. Pacific Palisades, Calif.: Idlewood Publications, 1991.

On-Line Resources

www.amazon.com lists over 100 specialty Yellow Page directories like the *African-American Yellow Pages*, the *Anglers Yellow Pages*, the *Yellow Pages of Bingo Halls*, and the *Skier's Yellow Pages*.

Trade and Specialty Directories

Trade directories offer an avenue for highly tailored business-to-business advertising. Some of these directories are published as an adjunct to a major trade paper or magazine. Often in such cases, those who advertise in the paper or magazine are offered a free listing.

If your business is primarily geared toward a narrow business market, advertising in the appropriate trade directory is far more important than advertising in a standard Yellow Pages, although listing in a business-to-business Yellow Pages may be equally essential. The right trade-directory listing can be a source of prospects for your company because the readers are already looking for a supplier when they use a directory. And, sometimes of equal importance, just being listed in a directory can confirm that you are who you say you are. Therefore it is definitely worth seeking out these directories and selecting those that will give you the best potential response.

Your best sources for information on such directories once again are your library and SRDS. All questions recommended in the Yellow Pages section on page 449 should be asked of trade directory sales reps to determine which ones will best promote your product or service. Then, in placing your ad, the focus needs to be on what makes you different from all your competitors and on conveying this unique advantage in your directory listing.

Also in most local libraries there is a variety of specialized directories, some of which accept advertising but many of which do not. In fact, there is a *Directory of Directories,* published by Gale Research. Perusing this directory will help you identify other directories to consider, and reviewing those directories will tell you whether they accept advertising and are apt to meet your needs.

Unless it is geared toward a very specific market, advertising in one of these directories will probably not be the most cost-effective use of a small advertising budget. Listing in them, however, can add substantially to a small company's credibility.

Some of these directories have very strict criteria that limit those who may be listed. If these criteria are not stated clearly in the directory itself, a call to the publisher or sponsoring organization will get you this information. At least an equal number of specialty directories are interested in getting whatever listings they can; these often charge for a listing. The price of the listing may be a subscription to the directory, which can range from a few to many hundreds of dollars. Many other special directories, however, are completely accessible to small businesses, and some require only that you submit an application form for a free listing. It is worth the effort to seek them out and get whatever listings you can.

Every trade and professional association has a membership directory, which may take advertising in addition to listing its members. For example, *The National Speakers Association Membership Directory* is not only a membership directory; it is also a resource for any organization seeking to hire a professional speaker. So in addition to a listing, some speakers take out ads in the directory featuring their programs. In addition, other companies will advertise their services to the speakers themselves. This year's directory includes ads by printers, cassette-production companies, training firms, publishers, and other support services for professional speakers. *The American Marketing Association International Membership Directory and Marketing Services Guide* operates similarly; in addition to being a membership directory, it is a resource for companies who need to hire marketing firms, so some members take out ads and other companies advertise to sell their services to the marketing firms themselves.

To determine whether listing in a directory will be worth your time, money, and energy, see who lists in the directories you are considering and phone them to find out whether their listing has helped them and how.

On-Line Directories

Don't overlook the proliferation of on-line directories you can be listed in. Often they are free or sometimes involve a fee, but being included in the right directory is just one more way for you to be in the right place at the right time. Information researcher Seena Sharp, for example, took out a free listing on Helen Burwell's World Directory of Information Brokers on the Web (www.burwellinc.com), and to her surprise was contacted about a substantial piece of business. Profnet (see **Resources**) is a fee-based expert directory composed primarily of college and university faculty, but also open to experts in any field.

You can find on-line directories where you might want to be listed through a hierarchical search engine like Yahoo! where we found 1,304 categories of directories and 576 site matches under "directories" and "trade directories." For example, in looking for directories of Graphic Design Companies we found directories like *The Digital Directory of Graphic Artists* (which offers free listings) and *The Fish Bowl,* a directory of companies providing creative services like design photography.

Creating Your Own Directory

If you don't find an existing directory that meets your needs, you might consider teaming up with others to create your own. In 1994, freelance writer Donna Lewein, who runs Scribe Shop in Oregon, Wisconsin, teamed up with colleague Joyce Feustel, president of For Your Information, to create the *Madison Area Freelance Editors and Writers Directory.* MAFEW's fifty or so members who meet monthly each submit a full-page ad for their annual directory. The ad is one of the benefits of MAFEW's $30 annual membership fee. The directory is indexed by service category and is distributed to libraries, business and communications groups, and interested companies throughout the Madison area.

Resources: Specialty Directories

Gales' Directory of Directories, Gale Research, 645 Griswold St., Detroit, MI 48226, (800) 877-4253, www.gale.com

Profnet, 100 North Country Rd. East Setauket, NY 11733, an on-line fee-based expert directory sent to journalists, legislators, corporations and others seeking specific expertise. (800) PROFNET or (800) 776-3638, www.profnet.com

Standard Rate and Data Service. 1700 Higgins Rd., Des Plaines, IL 60018, (847) 375-5000. Monthly volumes for newsletters, consumer magazines, business publications, direct mail, and other print media where you can find publications that serve your market, how many people they reach, whom to contact, what their rates are, the deadlines involved, preparation of materials, and other valuable information. Available in libraries and on the Web at www.srds.com

Direct-Response Advertising

When you see an ad in a magazine or newspaper or hear a radio or television spot that incorporates a coupon, a postcard, a fill-in-the-blank reply form, words to the effect of "Tell them you saw it here and receive an additional 10 percent discount," or even a telephone order number, you are looking at a form of what is called direct-response advertising. It covers a wide variety of marketing activities like inserts, reply cards, card decks, coupon packs, and bounce backs. These various options are described below.

Pros and Cons of Direct-Response Advertising

The value of this form of advertising lies in its ability to generate not only inquiries but also sales. Including a direct-response element in almost any kind of marketing piece from a sales letter to a direct-mail campaign, brochure, or flyer can boost results. The purpose of direct-response advertising is not just to inform and attract interest but also to push the reader to take immediate action. It also provides a way to turn your advertising and marketing pieces into a two-way communication by openly and clearly soliciting a response.

An additional value of direct-response advertising is that it can provide you with one of the most accurate tracking techniques available. If you use the same ad in two different publications, for example, and receive two hundred responses from one and ten from the other, you can determine that it might not be worthwhile continuing to advertise in the lower-response medium. Unless those ten inquiries lead to high-dollar, high-profit sales, the response is probably not paying the cost of the ad.

Adding a direct-response element does usually add to the cost of whatever marketing effort is involved, however. So you must weigh the potential return with that cost. Also, there may be times when you do not want to be so blatantly commercial, as when sending your marketing materials to the media, in which case you can still include a response element if you wish, but focus on getting requests for information or a free catalog.

Best Bets. Some form of direct-response advertising could work well for any type of business. Business response cards, for example, work well business to business. Card decks, too, are usually focused on reaching other businesses. Coupons, however, usually work better with consumers. With increasing numbers of small and one-person businesses who do all their own purchasing, direct response can be even more effective with business products or services tailored to particular needs.

Tips for Getting Business from Direct-Response Advertising

Print Ads. When a direct-response ad is placed in any print medium, the same rules apply to it as to any other print advertising. The only real difference is the inclusion of some means by which the reader can make a direct response. Usually this is simply a box that allows readers to fill in their name, address, and other pertinent information. Providing a telephone number, especially an 800 or 888 number, for information or ordering will also increase your response and is becoming increasingly important, since people are coming to expect this convenience. Today 800 and 888 numbers are affordable and easy to get. They are offered by all major long-distance carriers. The 800 or 888 number can ring directly into your existing telephone line and cost only a few dollars a month, depending on the number of calls you receive.

Reply Cards A reply card or business response card (BRC) is a postage-prepaid postcard that the recipient can fill in and return to order or request more information. You can enclose one in a sales letter, brochure, newsletter, or direct-mail piece; have a stack sitting on the table at a trade show or exhibit or send them out as a stand-alone double-folded postcard announcing a special discount or a new product or service. For an example of the latter, see the description of copywriter Gregg Siegel's successful direct-mail campaign on page 498.

Having a perforated line to help readers tear off and save a portion of the card can help boost the response to your reply card, as can having check-off boxes where people can indicate what they're interested in. Including an 800 or 888 number and adding a graphic like a telephone or action arrow can help as well.

When you do a large mailing that includes such cards, you can save money by arranging with the U.S. Post Office for a business-reply-mail (BRM) permit so you will pay only for those cards that are actually returned. The post office will usually even supply you with a template to use in printing your cards.

Including an order box on your Web site or as part of an on-line ad is the electronic equivalent of a reply card.

Inserts. Another type of direct-response advertising involves using magazine inserts. Inserts are full pages that are printed by the advertiser and provided to the publication to be "tipped in"—that is, bound in—with the rest of the publication. In most cases all printing costs of the insert are borne by the advertiser, with the publication charging for the inclusion. Sometimes, an insert can be more effective than a print ad.

There is a trick, however, to getting a good response from inserts of which most advertisers are apparently unaware. That is to simply request—and, if necessary, negotiate—to be the first insert in the publication. Research indicates that results decrease with each succeeding insert within a publication. Therefore, you are more likely to pull a strong response if your insert is first.

Card Decks A card deck is a packet of postcards, each touting a different product or service, packaged together in a wrapper by a card deck company and mailed out to large groups of possibly interested individuals. There can be as many as 200 cards in a packet. Generally these postcards do not solicit orders; instead they solicit inquiries for product and service information. The response rate is usually lower than other types of direct replies because yours is one of many sent to people who did not choose to get the card deck. But the cost per piece is very low and you can improve your response by having good copy, a good offer, and an appealing picture or graphic.

As in any mailing, a key to your success will be the list to whom it is sent, so before buying into a card deck check out the source of the list, look over past packs the company has mailed, and talk with several of the other advertisers.

For additional information about card decks, refer to Part III of Business Publication Rates and Data from SRDS (see **Resources: Direct Response Advertising**). There you will find an entire section listing the publishers of card decks. In running through the card-deck information you will find single ad rates ranging from just under $1,000 to around $2,700, with the bulk in the area of $1,500 to $2,000 for black-and-white. Most publishers of card decks offer discounts or lower rates for multiple insertions.

Coupons and Coupon Packs Of course, you can design and hand out or send out your own coupons along with virtually any marketing activity you do. But you can also participate in a coupon pack. A coupon pack works much as a card deck does, except it consists of coupons instead of response cards and is usually sent to consumers instead of to other businesses. For the right product or service, sent to the right list, coupon packs have the reputation of drawing quite well. You will be able to reach many more people by participating in such a pack at a much lower cost than you could do yourself. To boost the effectiveness, however, you might want to send out your own marketing piece to selected recipients as follow-up.

Just as in deciding upon a card-deck company, you should request to review previous coupon packages and talk with previous advertisers. In designing your coupon follow the same principles you would use in creating an effective Yellow Page ad (see page 450).

Ask the distributor to provide you with a print overrun of your color coupons. You can use them as part of other marketing efforts. Any added cost for such overruns should be minimal.

Bounce Backs A bounce back is a card or coupon with a peel-off preaddressed mailing label recipients can send back to you saying they are interested in receiving your information. You, in turn, use the same label and send it right back to them. Obviously a bounce back saves everyone time, but it also identifies the names you want to keep on your mailing list as interested customers. Of course, the more enticing the offer, the more likely it is that someone will peel off the label and send it back to you.

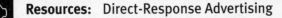

Resources: Direct-Response Advertising

Directories

Standard Rate and Data Service. 1700 Higgins Rd., Des Plaines, IL 60018, (847) 375-5000, (800) 851-7737. Available in libraries and on the Web at www.srds.com

Newsletters and Magazines

The Antin Marketing Letter, Secrets from the Lost Art of Common-sense Marketing. 11001 Delmar, Ste. 1200, Leawood, KS 66211, (913) 663-5775, www.antin@soundnet.com

DM News. 100 6th Ave., 6th Floor, New York, NY 10013, (212) 741-2095, www.dmnews.com

The Levison Letter: Action Ideas for Better Direct Mail and Advertising Communications. Ivan Levison & Associates, 14 Los Cerros Drive, Greenbrae, CA 94904, (415) 461-0672, www.Levison.com

No B.S. Marketing Letter. Dan Kennedy, Empire Communications, 5818 North 7th Street, #103, Phoenix, AZ 85014, (602) 269-3113.

Card Deck and Mailing Companies

Lifestyle Change Communications, Inc., 1900 the Exchange, Ste. 450, Atlanta, GA 30339, (707) 984-1100, www.lifestylechange.com.

Money Mailers, 201 Park Place, Altamont Springs, FL 32701, (407) 831-0022. Call for regional representative.

Val-Pak, 6456 S. Quebec Street, Bldg. 5, Ste. 550, Englewood, CO 80111, (303) 843-0943. Call for names of local brokers or look in the phone book under Val-Pak.

Venture Communications, 60 Madison Avenue, 3d Floor, New York, NY 10010, (212) 684-4800. www.venturedirect.com

On-Line Advertising

While having a Web site of your own (see **Web Site,** below) is one way to advertise on-line, your potential clients and customers may frequent other Web sites in sufficient numbers that you might want to consider

purchasing advertising on their sites, or at least buying a link to your site. At this time there are close to 60 to 80 million Web sites, and their number grows daily. Actually there is a growing variety of ways to advertise on the Web. When Bobby Bhasin wanted to fill more rooms in his London bed-and-breakfast inn, he took out a one-line classified ad on CompuServe and got twenty responses in just two weeks. On-line classified ads are an equally important marketing tool for Mike Holman, an authorized discount reseller of software.

In their book *Advertising on the Internet,* Robbin Zeff and Brad Aronson list over a dozen different forms of on-line ads, eight of which are described below as having potential value to small and single-person businesses.

Pros and Cons of On-Line Advertising

People who see on-line ads have often specifically sought out or subscribed to the E-mail newsletter, lists, or particular sites where the ad has been placed. Therefore, a well-placed on-line advertising message is quite likely to reach the eyes of a dedicated group of highly targeted individuals. Because this is a new medium, advertising costs are often more affordable than advertising in other media, but rates fluctuate. Some classified-ad sites are free, for example. Based on current fees, however, you can expect to pay between \$50 and \$75 for every 1,000 readers of an on-line banner ad.

Unlike other media where the amount of exposure your ad will receive is based on projections of circulation or viewing audience, on-line the exposure is not just projected but also measured precisely by counting the number of times an advertisement is seen as well as the number of times someone clicks on or responds to that ad. Specific demographic information about who is seeing and clicking on your ad may also be available.

On the other hand, many people are still not on-line, so you need to be sure to locate sites or on-line channels that will actually reach the people in your target market. Also, there are many more people who browse the Web than who actually buy from it. The Internet is still thought of primarily as a source of "free" information. And depending on the type of advertising you've selected, people may only see your ad if they choose to do so. Also, as the novelty of the Web wanes and junk E-mail and ads proliferate, people may get fed up with or even hostile toward sites with undue amounts of unwanted advertising. In fact, software is now available that allows Web users to block advertisements.

So, in addition to being carefully placed on sites where people would have an active interest in what you offer, your ad will need to be written and designed to be appealing to Web users.

Best Bets: On-line advertising can be a good route to reaching both consumers and business customers. It works best, however, for highly specialized, niche businesses targeted to clients who are computer literate and who make frequent and regular use of the Internet, E-mail, or on-line services. Selling ostriches and ostrich accessories, creating animated Web designs, and providing on-line publicity services are a few examples of businesses that have done well with on-line advertising.

Tips on Getting Business from On-Line Advertising

As with any ad, you will want to be sure it is reaching the people who need your product or service and that there is sufficient traffic on the site to justify your investment. So before placing an on-line ad, be sure to find out how much traffic the site gets, who the visitors are, and if your ads enable readers to jump to your own site so that your own server can give you the kind of reports you need to determine the effect of your advertising. Knowing exactly how many visitors actually see an ad and thus what you're getting for your money has been one of the concerns about Internet advertising. Software companies like Matchlogic (www.matchlogic.com), however, are working to solve such problems. According to research by DoubleClick and I/Pro, users are more likely to respond the first one or two times they see an ad and then response drops dramatically from there. (For more information on how traffic on a Web site is measured, see page 557.)

One way you can assure that you are reaching the right people is to choose the most suitable Web vehicle for your ad. Here are nine choices for advertising on-line, along with some tips for using them effectively:

Banners A banner is a rectangular graphic ad that runs along the top or bottom of a Web page. Typically the reader can click on the banner and jump to the advertiser's Web site for more information. Banners are the original and still the most common form of Web advertising. But while they were once simply a static bulletin, in an effort to make them more enticing they have become much more interactive and functional. They may fill out a survey or pick topics from a menu of interests, for example.

Banners can be of many sizes, but usually they are seven inches wide by one inch deep. If you want to garner a good response to your banner, you need to place it on a site where people would want to know about what you offer and create a reason for the viewer to click on it for more information. You might offer a discount, give a gift certificate, or offer some other prize. Adding the words "Click here" will help increase the response as will using dramatic color, animation, and rotating a variety of different banners.

Buttons Buttons are small bannerlike ads that can be placed anywhere on a Web page. When anyone clicks on the button, it immediately downloads material from the sponsor into the viewer's computer. Old hands at Web surfing are used to getting free software downloads when they click a button, but anything the reader truly wants and would value will suffice. It could be, for example, a way to distribute your booklet (page 568), a tip sheet, a list of resources, or your newsletter. But, if you want your button to work, make sure the reader doesn't just download an ad.

Create a file of practical, high-value information that can be downloaded to people who click on your on-line ad.

Chat Chat areas offer advertisers a chance to reach people who are discussing specific topics. Since chat participants are spending their time actually "chatting" on-line, it is assumed that their interest in that topic is sufficient that they might also want to look at ads related to that topic. Although it is expected to grow, at the time of this writing, sponsoring a chat or chat site is relatively new. Chatters may not want to leave the discussion to click on a banner or button. People do drop out of chat discussions at random, however, so they could click on the banner whenever they decide to end their participation. Since chats are usually not moderated, though, anything could be said during the course of a chat, including things that would not be in the sponsor's best interest.

An alternative worth exploring would be to sponsor a professionally moderated and well-promoted on-line conference.

Classified Ads Growing numbers of Web publishers are focusing on local content; e.g., AOL's Digital Cities, Microsoft's Sidewalk, Yahoo's city directories. Most major newspapers now have burgeoning on-line sites. Classified ads are a natural for such sites. Independent classified ad sites are also springing up. According to Zeff and Aronson classified ad sites that charge a fee are often of higher quality and get better advertising results than those that offer free listings. For an index of classified ad sites see Boettigener's directory at www.exposure-usa.com/

Content Sponsorship You might also consider sponsoring recurring content on targeted Web pages, like a site with daily updates, tips, or messages. Your ad on a site might itself be a changing daily message. You could explore this possibility by locating and contacting suitable sites and making a proposal to them about such an advertising arrangement.

Discussion Lists and E-mail Newsletters You can sponsor an E-mail newsletter or E-mailing list. There are actually thousands of lists of niched discussion groups who subscribe to get digests or transcripts of messages left from subscribers. Some of these lists accept weekly sponsors who are listed at the beginning or end of the list.

In purchasing advertising sent through E-mail, be certain that the lists are composed of individuals who have actually requested such information or voluntarily joined the list.

PostMaster Direct from NetCreations, for example, is a leader in acceptable direct E-mail (www.netcreations.com/postdirect/). They have over two million E-mail addresses in over 1,500 categories.

E-mail Ads Companies like Hotmail (www.hotmail.com) and Juno (www.juno.com) offer free E-mail to users who see advertisements on a timed basis when they pick up their mail. If you decide to place such ads, be sure that the E-mail company can target your ads to the specific kind of individuals you want to reach and that your ad will be one of only one or two that a reader will see when the mail is picked up.

Broadcast information As is true of ads attached to E-mail and E-mailed newsletters described above, instead of putting an ad on someone else's site and hoping people will see your ad and click on it, you can attach your ad to information that is being broadcast by request to subscribers on a regular basis. This is referred to as push technology. PointCast (www.pointcast.com) and BackWeb (www.ackweb.com) are two examples of many companies that send their clients regular news updates on selected topics. Of course, the more closely what you offer is related to the kind of subjects the receiver has requested, the more likely your ad will be of interest.

Interstitia Interstitia is another version of push technology, but instead of requiring that the viewer click on your ad to see more, an interstitial ad automatically comes on to fill the reader's entire screen in the midst of whatever else he or she is doing. Thus it's more like a television ad, except viewers can click off if they wish. Some such ads are being done, but it is not clear at this time if or how well this type of on-line "commercial" will be received.

Resources: On-Line Advertising

Books

Advertising on the Internet. Robbin Zeff and Brad Aronson. New York: Wiley, 1997.

Cyberwriting: How to Promote Your Product or Service On-line (Without Being Flamed). Joe Vitale. New York: Amacom Book Division, 1996.

Making Money in Cyberspace. Paul & Sarah Edwards and Linda Rohrbough. New York: Tarcher Putnam, September 1998.

On-Line Resources

NetCreations/PostMaster/IPA. Tracks on-line advertising opportunities and rates. www.netcreations.com/

WebTrack. Tracks on-line advertising, showing who is spending money to advertise, who's getting that money, and how much is changing hands. www.webtrack.com/

Articles and Columns

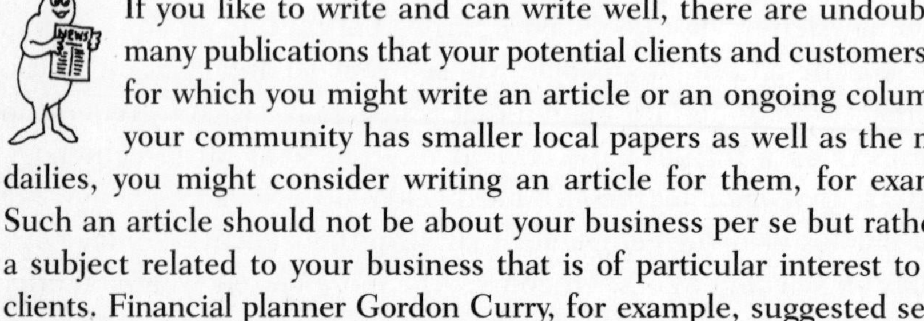

If you like to write and can write well, there are undoubtedly many publications that your potential clients and customers read for which you might write an article or an ongoing column. If your community has smaller local papers as well as the major dailies, you might consider writing an article for them, for example. Such an article should not be about your business per se but rather on a subject related to your business that is of particular interest to your clients. Financial planner Gordon Curry, for example, suggested several ideas to his local paper for feature articles on investing. The editor liked the ideas and commissioned the stories. Ultimately, Gordon was asked to write a regular column.

Almost any business can become a vehicle for a series of articles or a column. A computer consultant might write a series of short articles on the latest developments in computing. The particular focus of each article would depend on the readers of the publication and the consultant's specialty. Or a computer consultant might do a column called "Computer Updates" covering the newest practical breakthroughs in computer technology for home and office. A music teacher might offer to review new classical compact discs; an executive search-and-recruiting firm might do a series on job hunting in a bear market; and a professional organizer might do a series on how to reduce home or office clutter.

Additional outlets for both individual articles, a series of articles, or a column include company newsletters and trade publications, which do not have to be limited to your own trade. For example, if your mailing-list-maintenance firm primarily serves churches, you might consider offering your series "Using the Mail to Stay in Touch" to church newsletters and regional ecclesiastical publications. Often, even when a proposed article is not used for a publication, the writer may later be called upon as an authority to be quoted in other articles and thus acquires immediate status as an expert, as occurred when I, Laura, wrote an article for the AT&T newsletter for home offices. Instead of using my article, AT&T quoted me liberally in an article of their own. I was then free to use my original article for other publications.

Depending on your field, national business or consumer magazines or newsletters may also be a good avenue for an article and column. Marketing communication specialist Bob Burg, for example, writes articles like "Never Stop Prospecting" for *Master Salesmanship* newsletter and "Training Your Networkers" for the insurance industry magazine *The Forum.* New York copywriter Don Hauptman writes articles like "Learning Promotion from Newsletters" for national magazines and newsletters like *Circulation Management* and *Newsletter Association Hotline.* Psychiatrist Mark Goulston writes articles like "You're the Boss" and "Psyched Out" for *Men's Fitness* magazine, "Stupid Résumé Tricks" for *Fortune* magazine, and "Five Steps to Help Children Get Out of Their Own Way" for *Parenting Insights.*

Pros and Cons of Writing Articles and Columns

Writing an article or column for the right publication is an effective way to introduce your name to desired new customers. It also keeps you on the minds of those who already know you. But many other marketing activities can do that. What's most valuable about writing for publications your customers read is the high visibility it provides with people whom you might not otherwise ever reach and the fact that it establishes you as an expert with a particularly significant approach, ideas, thoughts, and point of view. A column or series of articles actually helps you develop a relationship with potential customers. Each week or month they get to know you better.

Your articles or columns have most of the benefits of using an informational brochure (page 479) with the added advantage that your information is seemingly "endorsed" by the publication that runs them. In fact, sometimes providing prospective customers with a copy of an article you've written can be more effective than sending a brochure or flyer. Writing articles or columns also gives you valuable material to include in your presentation materials or proposals.

Writing good articles and columns can be time-consuming, however, so unless you are getting paid adequately for what you write, using this method of marketing could take time away from paying work or cut into already-limited leisure time. Getting a fee for what you write, even if it's a marginal one, can help offset the loss of your time. Also, while you can certainly express your views and expertise, any hint that you are obviously promoting yourself could turn off instead of impress editors and readers as well.

Best Bets: Articles and columns are especially effective when you're offering services or products to businesses. But they can also be quite effective in selling services or products to consumers. They usually work best when your business is either quite novel (e.g., selling Western lingerie on the Web or creating animated CD-ROM presentations for consultants who would rather not incur the cost of traveling out of town to give a sales pitch) or when what your topic relates to is something people are always interested in learning more about (e.g., taking proper care of pets, the latest skin-care or weight-loss secrets, or making the best investments).

Tips for Getting Business from Writing Articles and Columns

There's a knack to writing articles and columns with the intention that they will attract business. Your primary goals, of course, are to inform and provide insights, assistance, or guidance, preferably in an entertaining or thought-provoking way. But in addition, you need to select what you write about and whom you write for so that it will also lead people to want more of what you can offer through your business. Here are several ideas for how to do that:

Know the publication. Before writing or sending anything to a publication, read three or four issues to be sure your area of expertise and the subject you're proposing are appropriate. If you send in something that is way off base, the editor may write you off for future consideration even if you later produce something that would be of interest. Editors have long memories; so be sure their memory of you is a positive one.

If you have a referral or personal contact, you can pitch your idea for an article or column yourself by phone or in person. If you're speaking for an organization, for example, talk with the chairperson about preceding or following up on your presentation with a pertinent article for their newsletter or journal. Without such a lead-in, you will have to either send in your entire article for consideration or write a query letter to the editor suggesting an idea for an article. (See **Resources.**)

Make an offer. Sometimes calling or sending a query letter before you write an article will increase your chances of having the article published, because you can then tailor what you write to the precise interests of the editor. Many people, however, have one or two boilerplate articles that they custom-tailor to publications in different industries. For example, a time-management consultant has a generic article on how to save time on the job, which she tailors on her word processor to produce such variations as "How Secretaries Can Save Time on the Job," "Saving Time for the Sales Professional," and "How Hairstylists Can Squeeze More Time into a Crowded Schedule."

For smaller, more informal publications, some people prefer to send the completed article and hope that the editor will run it. For a larger, more established publication, however, you will be better off sending a query letter suggesting an idea for an article or column. If you have written similar articles for other noncompetitive publications, you can enclose copies of them with your query letter as evidence of your writing style and skill.

Be sure readers have a way of identifying and contacting you. Sometimes, if you are contributing an article or column free or for a nominal fee, the publication will be willing to include your name, address, and phone number as part of the byline at the beginning or end of the article. Sometimes they will even mention that you will send a free booklet on a related topic to interested readers if they send you a stamped self-addressed envelope.

Here's an example: Kathy Keshembert wrote an article for *The Word Advantage,* a newsletter for owners of secretarial services. The credit box read:

> **Kathy Keshembert** has operated Computron in Appleton, Wisconsin, since 1983. She publishes ***Resources!***, a collection of marketing

pieces and operational forms printed on specialty papers which will help any secretarial/resume service owner project a professional appearance on a shoestring budget. For more information, write Dept. TWA, 302 Murray, Appleton, WI 54915 or KathyKC@ aol.com

Some publications won't include an address, phone number, or E-mail address in a credit, however. When this is the case you should try to arrange for them to at least include your city, company name, and title as part of the credit; e.g., "Karen Smith is the owner of Management Consulting Services in Dover, Maryland." Such a byline should be sufficient information for motivated readers to locate you through the telephone directory or the information operator.

Some publications will list your Web address as a way for readers to contact you or provide a vehicle for you to communicate with interested readers through their Web address or at an on-line conference. If the publication does have a Web presence, ask about whether the article will appear there too, and, if you're interested, find out if you could host an on-line conference.

Since all such possibilities vary widely among publications, we suggest that you look at other bylines throughout the publication to see what the norm is and then develop a strategy for how you will make sure interested readers will be able to contact you. Usually the stricter a publication is about such indirect solicitation the more prestigious it is and, therefore, the more desirable it is to have an article appear there. So you always have to weigh the promotional value to you against your investment of time in writing for a given publication.

Keep in mind, if it's a great publication that provides excellent visibility to the very people you want to reach, those who are really interested can always call the publication for information about how to contact you. We (Paul and Sarah) have had this occur on numerous occasions.

Ask if they will include your picture. Sometimes you can arrange to have your picture appear next to your name. Doing so adds both visibility and credibility, so always ask about this possibility or simply include a photo along with the article just in case they're interested. If the publication doesn't want to use a head shot of you, they still might be interested in an amusing or intriguing action photo or illustration that relates to whatever you're writing about. In fact, in newsletters or papers with small budgets and tiny staffs, having a good photo to include with the article may be just the incentive they need to make running your article a priority.

Protect your rights. If you are paid for what you write, the publication may want to keep the copyright on your material. This is referred to as "work for hire" or "first rights." Think carefully before giving any publication the rights to your ideas, especially when they reflect original material that you've developed as central to your expertise, methods, or viewpoint. Giving away your "first rights" prevents you from selling to or using that same article or column in any other publication and allows them to use your ideas, thoughts, and writing in whatever ways they wish with or without crediting you, and without additional payment.

We never do work for hire unless it is to write something so specialized and tailored to a particular publication that we would have no other use for the ideas or the article. We routinely rewrite and renegotiate the "first rights" clause in any writing contract so that we keep the copyright to the material. If you decide to do otherwise, do so with caution and be sure you are ready to turn over ownership of your writing and concepts to the publication.

These days publications will also routinely want to include electronic rights to what you write as part of your fee. This means they have the option of putting whatever you've written on-line, perhaps on their Web site or an on-line service like AOL. This can serve you well in that others who do not see what you've written in the print publication may see it on-line, thus expanding the publicity value to you. This is especially true since often on-line articles are archived—that is, kept around, perhaps indefinitely, for browsers or searches to review. But, if you are being paid for the article, you can and should try to negotiate for a higher fee if they will be using what you write for both media.

Follow up with ideas for future articles or columns. Once a publication uses an article from you, follow up to discuss possibilities for future related articles or with the idea for an ongoing column. For psychiatrist Mark Goulston, the opportunity to write a column began with writing letters to editors. Then he got an op-ed piece in the *Los Angeles Times*. Articles for other publications followed. Now he has three columns: one on mental fitness for *Men's Fitness*, another on parenting for dads, and one related to business for the *L.A. Business Journal*. Goulston says, "Editors need to see that you can write and that you will be dependable. They are also looking for something about you that relates to their audience." His particular advantage, editors tell him, is that although he writes about psychological issues, he does so in a conversational manner, talking "with," not "at" or "to" his readers.

Use alternative routes. Short of writing an actual article, feature story, or column there are several alternative ways to express your views by writing to the targeted media of your choice. For example, you might think about writing a letter to the editor, doing an editorial, a piece for the op-ed pages, or other commentary in a newspaper, magazine, newsletter, or trade publication. Simply make a point of regularly reading the publications where you wish to establish a presence and seize the first opportunity to respond to an article, editorial, or feature story that relates to your niche. Look for something you strongly agree or disagree with. Then write a letter or commentary referencing the article that triggered your response and expressing your viewpoint If your response is cogent and makes a point related to your field, should the editor decide to use it, he or she will most likely include a description of what makes you an authority on this subject along with your name.

For more information on using these alternative approaches to getting published, see **Publicity** in **chapter 10.**

Use your articles in other marketing materials. Once you have had something published—whether it's a story, a feature, a letter, editorial, column, or series of articles—be sure to ask for tear sheets, then photocopy them and add the copies to your presentation materials and future press kits. Keep the tear sheets handy in a file of all your published materials, ready for making future copies. Remember, the more coverage you get, the more likely you are to get additional coverage. If tear sheets are not available, arrange to obtain a copy of the publication and make copies of your material on good-quality paper.

High-Touch Tip: Building a Portfolio of Articles

Often publications will want to see copies of other articles you have written. So, of course, if you have had articles published you will want to include copies of them in your presentation kit. But what if you haven't had any articles published yet? You're in that classic chicken-before-the-egg dilemma. A good way out of this dilemma is to write two or three sample articles and, using desktop publishing software, format them into three columns under a headline as they would appear in a magazine or newspaper column. Include your byline. Then print them out on a white coated stock and include a copy of each in the kit you send out to the media as samples of your writing.

Management consultant Ward Weiman specializes in helping companies navigate rapid growth. He took a humorous approach to enhance the results of an article he wrote for the *L.A. Business Journal.* He sent the following fax to his referral, contact, and client lists:

"The following article I wrote appeared in the November 11–17 issue of *The Los Angeles Business Journal.* They:

changed the title

omitted my picture

lopped off the last paragraph—and

misspelled my name.

Bottom line—"I'm absolutely thrilled they published it and wanted to share it with you."

Resources: Articles and Columns

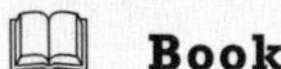

Books

Beginners' Guide to Writing and Selling Quality Features, A Simple Course in Freelancing for Newspapers/Magazines. Charlotte Digregorio. Civetta Press, Box 1043, Portland OR, 97207.

The Complete Guide to Magazine Article Writing. John M. Wilson. Cincinnati: Writer's Digest Books, 1993, (513) 531-2222.

Editor and Publisher International Yearbook. Editor and Publisher, 850 Third Avenue, New York, NY 10022 (available in libraries).

Magazine Writing That Sells. Don McKinney. Cincinnati: Writer's Digest Books, 1994, (513) 531-2222.

Writer's Digest Books, F & W Publications, 1597 Dana Avenue, Cincinnati, OH 45207, (513) 531-2222, provides names, addresses, and phone numbers of magazines along with query letter specifications. Available in bookstores and libraries.

You Can Be a Columnist. Charlotte Digregorio. Civetta Press, Box 1043, Portland OR 97043, (503) 228-6649.

On-Line Resources

A Business Researcher's Interests, Journals and Magazines section provides links to over 800 business-related magazines and research journals. www.brint.com/interest.html

Publicity Blitz Media Directory-On-Disc, Bradley Communications, Box 1206, Lansdowne, PA 19050, (800) 989-1400, lists 20,000 print and broadcast media contacts in seventy-five subject categories.

http://www.enews.com/monster A comprehensive site that allows you to search for on-line magazines by name, subject, and category.

Brochures and Flyers

Paul McDonald is among the growing number of small businessmen who takes his service to his clients rather than having them come to him. He operates Commuter Cleaners, a dry cleaning company that picks up and delivers at commuter railroad stops en route from Connecticut to New York City. In the morning McDonald heads off for commuter stations in his pickup truck with his laundry cart and mobile clothing rack. He picks up clothes from customers before they board the train and delivers their cleaned clothes when they return in the afternoon from work. He gets most of his new business by passing out brochures at the Greenwich station at peak travel times.

While this may be one of the more unconventional ways to use a brochure, whatever your business, chances are potential clients, customers, or referral sources will often ask you for some form of written materials. Having such materials is almost like a theater ticket: unless you have one, you don't get into the show. Even when using advertising and public-relations efforts, you may be asked to submit information about your business. Therefore you need to have some written materials describing your background, your company, and your products or services. These materials may take the form of a promotional kit (see **chapter 3**) or brochure or, more simply, a flyer, circular, or sell sheet.

Although innumerable definitions abound, a flyer or circular is simply a single-page item often printed on only one side with no folds. You may be most familiar with flyers geared to the general public and usually distributed en masse, such as on car windshields, on store counters, posted at bus stops and mass-transit stations, and on public bulletin boards. However, flyers and circulars are also used as part of business presentations. They are generally used on a one-time or short-term basis and are limited in terms of the information they provide to one specific event or item. For example, a flyer might offer a one-time discount or promote an upcoming workshop. A sell sheet might provide the essential benefits and specifications of a single product or service.

Brochures, on the other hand, are more complex pieces of printed matter. The chief differences between a brochure and a flyer are:

1. A brochure is usually folded in some way that is intrinsic to the design of the piece.
2. A brochure contains more permanent information and is used over a longer period of time. For example, a brochure might cover in bulleted points the full breadth of a company's product or service lines, provide more comprehensive information on the products or services themselves, or describe the general benefits of doing business with the company.

A brochure can be any size and any number of pages printed on both sides and is usually, but not always, printed in two or more colors. A simple brochure might be one 8½-by-10-inch paper folded in half or thirds, whereas a more informative brochure might have several pages.

Of course, today, your brochures and flyers need not be printed. You can create audio, video, or digital versions to replace or supplement traditional printed materials (see chapter 12).

Pros and Cons of Brochures and Flyers

Everyone needs something they can leave with or send to a prospective client that provides more information about what they do than can be presented on a business card. A flyer or brochure can be one of the more versatile and cost-effective solutions. To keep costs down, you can easily create flyers and brochures yourself using desktop publishing or graphics software at www.paulandsarah.com. This is an especially good way to test your material to be sure it is effective before investing in more costly and professionally designed printed material Creating your own brochures and flyers also means that you can customize them to the particular needs of each and any potential client.

Also, once you've gone to the trouble of producing a brochure or flyer, you can use it in a myriad of ways from leaving one at every meeting and every personal call you make to tucking one into your presentation materials and/or sending it along with sales or query letters. Once you have created these materials, you can make them available to your potential clients and customers anywhere from trade show booths to office waiting rooms. You can include them as a handout at every presentation you make and in every publicity kit you prepare. Both flyers and brochures can also be mailed to prospective clients or customers as or along with a direct-mail piece.

Unfortunately, however, most brochures and flyers get thrown away, often because of poor design and uninspiring copy. So if you're going to the time, trouble, and cost of producing a flyer or brochure, make it worth the effort.

Best Bets: Even if a brochure may be thrown away, often it is nonetheless expected in doing business with other businesses. Flyers are more popular in selling services or products to consumers.

Tips for Creating Effective Brochures and Flyers

Most of the principles we discussed in designing a good letterhead and business card apply to brochures and flyers as well (see **chapter 7**). Take a look at the example on the next page, produced by Thomas Hudock and his partner, Sean Bickerton, for their company Computer Graphics. It is a simple, single-page flyer printed in black ink on white paper. In this case the business owners wisely chose to use a coated paper to enhance the crispness of the printed image.

Systemax uses this flyer to generate requests for more information. What Systemax wants is for the reader to request a copy of their complete brochure, which, as you see from the copy, is a sample of their work in animated computer graphics. The flyer is sent with a cover letter and reply card, given out at trade shows, and again included in the company's customer presentation packet. As you can see, a little imagination and a clear purpose can produce a dynamic piece of collateral for relatively very little money. Here are a few pointers:

Customize. You are better off creating multiple brochures and flyers yourself that are tailored to specific client and customer needs than to have a general brochure that means little to anyone in particular. For example, the owner of a small software company decided to send out a flyer to dealers and distributors announcing a new product. Since he had created a lot of postcards for announcing his new release to the media, he decided to send this same self-mailing card to his dealers and

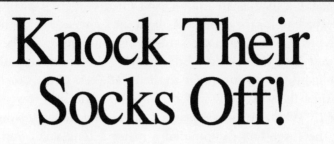

Knock Their Socks Off!

Dazzle your clients and trounce the competition with the power of television packed into a PC. Shimmering color graphics and eye-catching animation will get your message across and your product seen! Introducing the DiscBrochure™ by Systemax Computer Graphics.

Sock It To'em!

Stand out from the crowd - whatever you're selling, don't blend in with the competition. Flat bar-charts on an overhead projector just don't cut it anymore. Make those bar-charts 3-Dimensional, growing right in front of their eyes with firworks bursting in the background in brilliant color. Animated computer presentations are being used successfully by dozens of the most innovative companies worldwide to win the hearts and minds of new customers.

So, throw out that 20-page proposal and put MOTION in your PROMOTION, PIZZAZZ in your PROSPECTUS, SPARKLE in your SELL...you get the picture and they will too!

See for youself how a custom-designed DiscBrochure™ can help you win clients and TRIPLE the response rate to direct mailings. It's so EASY! Just drop the the postage-paid reply card in the mail and we'll send you a FREE copy of our own Electronic DiscBrochure™.

Make Your Next Presentation a Sockcess!

201 East 87th Street, Suite 24E
New York, NY 10128
(212) 348-8756
CompuServe - 71511,1375

The Systemax Electronic Brochure requires an IBM PC or compatible, hard disk, 5-1/4 inch or 3-1/2 inch floppy drive, EGA color monitor, and 385k free RAM. DiscBrochure is a registered trademark of Systemax Computer Graphics. Copyright © 1989,1990 by Systemax Computer Graphics, all rights reserved

Flyer Promotes Requests for Electronic Brochure
This Systemax black-and-white one-page flyer on glossy paper stock is designed to generate requests to see a sample of their animated computer-generated graphics on a disc.

distributors. It detailed all the functions the program could do on one side and offered a free evaluation copy on the other.

Unfortunately, he had given all the important whys for the end user but no reason for the dealer to stock the program. With a little revision, he was able to convey twice as much information for about the same money by using a different flyer altogether designed specifically for dealers and distributors.

Instead of a small postcard, he used a heavyweight paper stock twice the size. The cost for the paper was about the same, as was the press time; even the postage remained the same. This time, however, the headline read "Boost Your Competitive Edge!" giving the dealer something with which to identify—an advantage to them. The rest of the brochure consisted primarily of two rows of three boxes. The first row was boldly headlined, "What Memory Master Can Do for Your Customer," and each of the three boxes contained a major selling point and how the software accomplished it. The second row of boxes was boldly headlined, "What Memory Master Can Do for You!" The three boxes beneath that headline read, "How You Can Increase Your Sales!" "How You Can Lower Your Costs!" and "How You Can Increase Your Profits!" The balance of the piece gave the necessary information about the package.

By incorporating your logo and color theme into your materials, you can cost-effectively customize them in this way or you can use preprinted papers like those available through mail-order companies like Paper Direct or Pueblo. (See color insert and for a list of preprinted paper companies, see **Resources.**)

Decide upon one purpose. Equally important in a successful printed piece is to have one clear purpose—to get prospective customers or clients to take some specific action. The most effective brochures and flyers are designed to elicit one of the following types of actions:

1. an order
2. a request for more information
3. a call for an appointment
4. receptivity to a future contact

Each flyer or brochure should have only one of these purposes as its *raison d'être*. Too often people try to create a flyer or brochure that does it all; but without making a choice as to what response you want and keeping that goal firmly in mind as you prepare your material, you risk getting no response. This does not mean that your printed piece can be used to accomplish only that purpose, but without a clear picture of what you primarily want it to do you will not know how to proceed to make it as effective as possible.

Four ways to get your flyer or brochure to lead to specific orders, inquiries, appointments, and sales follow.

Tell people how you will solve their problem or meet their need. Whatever primary purpose you choose for your materials, incorporate information about how you will address the specific needs you know your clients or customers have. Offer assurance about the issues you know are uppermost in their minds. Once people find out about feng shui, for example, most people are concerned that the consultant will tell them that many of the things that can't be changed about their homes, like the location of the doorway, are unhealthful or unlucky. Therefore a professional feng shui consultant like Charel Morris of Santa Monica, California, always includes information about how she works to enhance the structure and form of your existing home instead of recommending major renovations.

One of the primary reasons people choose to buy your product or service when they read about it is that they have some need or are facing some sort of problem or difficulty that what you're offering can solve. So, don't be afraid of such an approach. Businesses that solve problems succeed; businesses that don't know what the problems are don't get business.

Focus on the benefits, not the features, of your product or service. The most effective printed material focuses on the customer, not on you or your business. This is often a surprise to people who are new to marketing. The tendency is to elaborate on the features that make your product or service a good one, such as your background, your materials, your methodology, what your product does or includes, etc. Effective printed pieces, however, focus on benefits, not features.

A computer consultant, for example, created a brochure headlined "Custom Applications" and was disappointed with the response he got. The problem was that his prospective clients aren't interested in custom applications; they may not even know what the term means. Rather, they are interested in solving their own particular problems.

The consultant's piece would be much more effective if instead the headline read, "Payroll Driving You Nuts?" or "Inadequate Financial Reports Making You Tear Your Hair Out?" These are problems his potential customers recognize and identify with immediately.

No one is interested in how you get the results until they know what the results are. For example, people are more interested in knowing that your cookies are low in cholesterol and chemical free than in knowing that they are made with soy oil and purified water. Clients are more interested in the cost savings for using rechargeable laser cartridges than they are in the method of recharging.

You want your brochure or flyer to hit upon the same kind of heart and head issues we discussed in **chapter 5**. In fact, you can think of your brochures and flyers as the next logical extension of having chosen a business name that describes your niche, developing a file-opening Sound Byte, and a business card that succinctly describes your niche. (See pages 186–87.)

Demonstrate results. One reason people decide to take action is because they begin to anticipate results they would desire for themselves. If someone else they trust and admire talks about the results they've gotten from using your product or service, they feel motivated too. So, whenever possible you should include some form of endorsement or testimonial in your brochure or flyer. A caterer, for example, might offer a prospective client a brochure with the prominently displayed statement "As seen on *A.M. America*," or a security consultant might proudly quote a prominent executive who reports that "this program stopped our security leaks!"

Each of these endorsements adds credibility to the statements and offers in the brochure. But if you use endorsements or testimonials, they must be real and they must be specific. No one believes quotes such as "'Great product!'—Mr. B. R., Des Moines, Iowa." For addition information on using endorsements and testimonials, see **chapter 10.**

Include an offer they can't refuse. Another primary reason customers choose to take immediate action is because they have been made an offer that is too good to refuse. Many doctors and lawyers who advertise on television these days offer a free consultation. If their service is something you need, how can you turn that down?

The same type of incentive can be offered on a product. When a greeting-card company needed to do something to boost sales during their slowest season, they sent out a brief flyer informing their distributors that for a limited time only they would receive a free dozen cards with every twelve dozen they purchased. Their sales jumped 30 percent during that period each year.

Whatever your business, you can offer something too good to turn down: offer a discount, free sample, free trial period, special guarantee, or special sale for immediate action. Provide a telephone number or even a coupon or reply card on your brochure or flyer. For example, Alpaca Pete's has an electronic brochure for their alpaca rugs posted on their Web page. It includes a phone number. When we called, we were delighted to learn that anyone calling from the Web page got a significant discount. It was such a good offer, we decided to buy right then and there without further thought.

The most important thing to remember in preparing a brochure or flyer is that you must know your prospective customers. You must know what will motivate them to use and buy—what will motivate them to take action—or at least keep your brochure until they need to. Dental practice consultant James R. Butler, for example, has used preprinted materials to create his own highly versatile brochure with interchangeable elements presented in a hanging file folder that's easy to save and use. (See color insert.) For more details on how to customize your materials and write motivational copy, see www.paulandsarah.com.

Consider using an informational brochure. There is one other purpose for creating a brochure: as reference material. In this case you are only indirectly attempting to get readers to take any action. You may be introducing them to a new service or product they are unfamiliar with or you may be providing them with the background for how to make an informed decision or why they need what you offer. In other words, you are educating and motivating through facts or illustrations.

Such an informational brochure is not appropriate for all businesses; but it can work far better than a sales brochure for many businesses, and a well-done informative brochure is much less likely than a sales brochure to be thrown away. For instance, the proprietor of a bed-and-breakfast inn needs to have something to mail to those who call requesting information and for guests to take with them and keep as a reference. An informative brochure with pictures, a history of the house, rates, and nearby activities will more likely get filed away than a sales pitch on the inn. A feng shui consultant may want to have a brochure that explains this ancient Chinese art—what it is, how it works, and how she in particular operates to incorporate this service into the needs of American households or organizations. (See color insert, for example)

Like Satu Kristiina Viltanten of Morgan Hill, California, who creates original art screens and wall hangings, an artisan may wish to have a brochure with photographs of some of his or her previous work and text explaining its background or the history of the technique.

In creating informational materials it is important to maintain your company identity throughout because you do not have the luxury of motivating buyers to take some immediate action. So, because you want to be sure those who see your materials keep them until they are actually ready to make their decision, they need to be as appealing and as professional as your budget allows. The All Cajun Good Company,

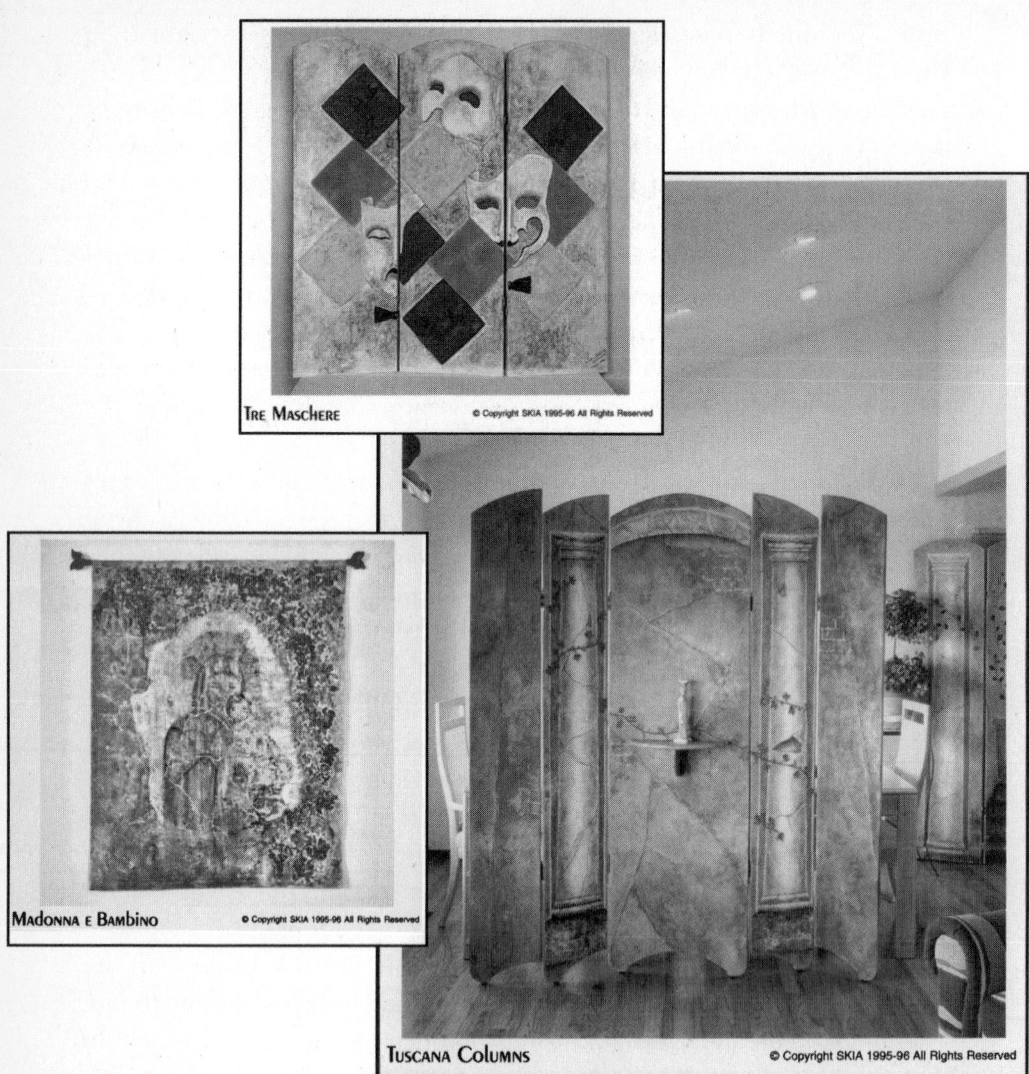

Artist Brochure *Artist Satu Kristiina Viltanten's four-color four-page brochure features a selection of her original art screens and wall hangings accompanied by a description of her background and the history of the process she uses, patination.*

for example, has an eye-catching, informative brochure that relies heavily on graphics to tell humorous stories about how the owner created his various Cajun hot sauce recipes. The material features the company logo, drawings of the bottles the sauces come in, and, best of all, a sample of their seasoning clipped to the back of the brochure, which is filled with recipes that use the various sauces (See color insert.)

SHOULD YOU HAVE A SEPARATE PRODUCT OR SERVICE LIST? HOW ABOUT A PRICE LIST?

If you offer more than one product or service, the question always arises when creating a brochure or flyer of whether or not to list all your products or services along with the prices. Here are several issues to consider when making such decisions.

- **A list of products and services along with the prices will not work as a marketing tool on its own.** Handing out or mailing a list of products or services along with prices is a common error. Such lists are informational only and should always be part of or an attachment to other sales materials like a brochure that explains or illustrates what you offer in terms of the benefits or value you provide.
- **A list is not sufficiently motivational** to stand on its own but it does provide your prospective clients with an inventory of what they can buy and, in some cases, at what prices. The computer consultant we described earlier, for example, could benefit from having a list of the applications he specializes in, and people wanting to order some Cajun hot sauce will need to know the price of each sauce.
- **Having a separate list is usually better whenever your products or services may be changing.** If you feel certain that what you offer will remain constant, you can incorporate a list directly into your brochure. But if, as is more often the case, what you offer will be subject to frequent change—like a caterer's menu, an artist's inventory, or an animal breeder's list of current stock for sale—you should prepare a separate piece that lists what you are currently providing and tuck this piece into or attach to your brochure or flyer. You can desktop-publish this list yourself on less costly paper that is coordinated to complement your company image.

  Jeff Kauzlaric has come up with an innovative alternative for his design studio, the InfoFactory (See illustration on page 261). His fold-out brochure includes a general description of his company on the right-hand side and a series of inserts on the left, staggered in height, to describe each of his services: publications, logos, identify systems, and brochures. To custom-print such a piece would be cost-prohibitive, but Kauzlaric does it himself with *Aldus PageMaker* and he can custom-tailor the inserts as needed.

- **Avoid incorporating your prices into your brochure.** Even if your prices will not change frequently, we strongly recommend leaving prices out of your brochures. There may be many occasions when you will want to provide someone with information about your products or services without introducing the element of cost. So have a separate price list or handle pricing issues verbally.

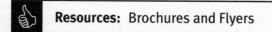

Resources: Brochures and Flyers

Books

Better Brochures, Catalogs and Mailing Pieces. Jane Maas. New York: St. Martin's, 1984.

The Brochure Book. Roger Parker. Paper Direct, 100 Plaza Drive, Secaucus, NJ 07094, (800) A-PAPERS, (800) 272-7377, www.paperdirect.com

Design Eye-Catching Brochures, Newsletetters, Ads, Reports. Jane K. Cleland. CareerTrack, 3085 Center Green Drive, Boulder, CO 80301, (800) 334-1018, www.careertrack.com

Do-It-Yourself Advertising and Promotion: How to Produce Great Ads, Brochures, Catalogs, Direct Mail and Much More. Fred E. Haun. New York: Wiley, 1997.

How to Do Leaflets, Newsletters and Newspapers. Kenneth G. Maugun and Nancy Brigham. Cincinnati: Writer's Digest Books, 1991.

How to Make Newsletters, Brochures & Other Good Stuff Without a Computer System. Helen Gregory. Sedro Woolley, Wash.: Pinstripe, 1996.

One-Minute Designer. Roger Parker. New York: Henry Holt, 1997.

Preprinted Papers

BeaverPrints
Main Street
Bellwood, PA 16617
(800) BEAVER4

Paper Direct
100 Plaza Drive
Secaucus, NJ 07094
(800) A-PAPERS or (800) 272-7377
www.paperdirect.com

Paper Showcase
P.O. Box 8465
Mankato, MN 56002
(800) 287-8163
www.papershowcase.com.

Queblo Images
150 Kingswood Rd.
Mankato, MN 56002
(800) 523-9080

Quill
100 Schelter Road
Lincolnshire, IL 60069
(847) 634-4800
www.quillcorp.com.

Videos

Design Eye-Catching Brochures, Newsletters, Ads, Reports. Jane K. Cleland. CareerTrack, 3085 Center Green Drive, Boulder, CO 80301, (800) 334-1018, www.careertrack.com

Workshops

How to Design Eye-Catching Brochures, Newsletters, Ads, Reports and Everything Else You Want People to Read. CareerTrack, 3085 Center Green Drive, Boulder, CO 80301, (800) 325-5854, www.careertrack.com

On-Line

Writing and Designing Materials That Sell, a free Special Report on www.paulandsarah.com on the Great Ideas for Getting Business page.

Bulletin Board Announcements, Tear Pads, Take-Ones, and Door Hangers

Bulletin board announcements, tear pads, take-ones, and door hangers are quite popular, but less often considered, as formal marketing tools. Yet they are among the most common and easily accessible low-cost ways to advertise. While free advertising is unusual, bulletin boards, tear pads, take-ones, and door hangers are all exceptions. Consider how many times you have found one on your door handle, your windshield, or your seat at a networking dinner—or how often you've seen one at laundromats, restaurants, print shops, grocery stores, banks, bookstores, doctors' offices, employee lounges, and libraries. Perhaps you have even located goods or services from one or more of these materials yourself.

Wayne Orth has found bulletin boards the best way to sell his self-published book. He promotes it with 8½-by-11-inch signs. Some bulletin boards, however, limit entries to the size of an index card. That limitation didn't stop Peggy Glenn, though. She pinned index cards on university bulletin boards to announce her typing service. It was the only advertising she did at first, yet within three months she was earning more than she had as a secretary for the same university. So even with their limitations, bulletin boards have provided essential initial customers to many new businesses.

Pros and Cons of Bulletin Boards, Take-Ones, and Tear Pads

Pros

1. Get your message before the eyes of people who are actively seeking what you're offering, as well as the curious potential shopper.
2. Provide a low-cost, personal touch.
3. Select placement can be highly targeted to your most desired customers.

Cons

1. Some people never look at bulletin boards or other such offerings.
2. Appropriate only for certain types of businesses
3. May cast you as a small-time operation.
4. Some cities or buildings may prohibit distributing such material.

Our local co-op grocery store has a kiosk of take-one slots. It's quite a popular spot; people often are gathered around it. A sampling of material available includes a flyer from a company that creates videos of weddings, special events, fund-raisers, and company promos; a coupon for one free private singing lesson; a promotional piece on an upcoming Artist's Way Creativity Workshop; an informational brochure on therapeutic massage; a flyer offering private and group lessons on learning to surf; and a card introducing miniature water fountains with a phone number to call for a free catalog.

Of course, electronic bulletin board postings often provide even more exposure than the traditional ones. On-line service sites have a vast array of sections with bulletin boards. Many Web sites have bulletin boards as well. To find lists of bulletin boards where you might want to be listed, use a hierarchical search engine like Yahoo! (www.yahoo.com) and search for "Lists of Bulletin Boards." When we searched we got 139 lists plus other search engines and new groups.

Tips: Bulletin Boards

The key to success with bulletin boards or take-one promotions is to locate popular places frequented by your potential customers and clients where your materials will be prominently displayed. For example, the bulletin boards of college campuses and state unemployment offices are ideal places for a résumé service. Print shops, another common spot for bulletin boards, are ideal for a graphic designer's or desktop publisher's card or tear pad. In fact, bulletin boards are so popular that there are now companies that make a business out of posting other people's announcements on them.

Special Warning for Posting on Electronic Bulletin Boards. While electronic bulletin boards may draw as many, or more, readers as conventional ones, they often have strict rules or mores against advertising. Some people are openly hostile to bulletin board postings that are essentially ads. Successful on-line bulletin board postings involve providing valuable information, building relationships, and interacting with others. So, when posting messages on on-line bulletin boards, think personal and think creative. For best results, leave helpful information or advice instead of an overt marketing appeal; e.g., "As a media consultant I have this tip to share from a recent campaign that was most successful. Hope you find it useful, too."

Tips: Tear Pads

Tear pads can range from a simple flyer with tear-off phone numbers along the bottom to a well-produced placard to which is attached a pad of informational slips or requests. You can use a tear pad in place of a simple flyer or index card on bulletin boards to make sure your phone number is retained. The tear-off slip might even be used as a coupon good for a 10 percent discount on a customer's first job or order. Alternatively, you can use sticky pads with preprinted numbers people can peel off.

Use bright yellow paper or a color ink-jet printer to make your announcement stand out from the rest. Desktop-publishing or sign-making software can also help you create a more interesting sign (See **Resources**).

Tips: Door Hangers

There are several things you can to do to induce people to keep rather than toss away your door hanger. You can include a sample, you can include testimonials or incorporate a coupon or discount offer. Additionally you can print something useful on the back of the door hanger: e.g., a calendar with relevant dates marked; a list of vitamins, calories, or fat in various foods; or names and phone numbers of community resources, including yours, of course. Or you can use colorful and attractive mini-gift or shopping bags. You can also create your own customized door hangers using preprinted papers from companies like Paper Direct. (See color insert for an example.)

PROS AND CONS OF DOOR HANGERS	
PROS	**CONS**
1. Cost less than direct mail and produce a higher return (15 percent) from a properly targeted area.	1. Some people find them annoying and most do get tossed out.
2. Can't be overlooked. At least people will see them.	2. Can be illegal in some neighborhoods.
3. Can include a sample.	3. Limited to targeting specific geographic areas.

Best Bets: All three of these methods work best with consumer products and services that people are already familiar with or would be intrigued by and that they experience a need for. The best example, of course, is the pizza delivery shop whose door hangers greet tired, hungry single or dual-career couples coming home late from work.

Resources: Bulletin Boards, Tear Pads, Take-Ones, & Door Hangers

Books

The Desktop Publishing Idea Book, Over 100 Step-by-Step Designs with 250 Illustrations. Chuck Green. New York: Random House, 1997.

Magazines

Boardwatch monthly magazine covers information about on-line bulletin boards. 8500 West Bowles Avenue, Ste. 210, Littleton, CO 81023, (800) 933-6038, www.boardwatch.com

Software

Bannermania, by Broderbund. P.O. Box 6121, Novato, CA 94948, (415) 382-4400 www.broderbund.com. Paper Direct has a selection of acrylic take-one stands and trays for cards, brochures, or flyers. Ask for a free catalog: 100 Plaza Drive, Secaucus, NJ 07094, (800) A-PAPERS, (800) 272-7377, www.paperdirect.com

Catalogs

When Shelley Newman opened her secretarial service, she soon realized that she had little experience in marketing. She was converting only 20 percent of inquiries into clients. Developing a Catalog of Services has helped her turn that figure around. Now 90 percent of incoming phone inquiries lead to client relationships. After an initial consultation, each client leaves with her catalog, which includes samples of the services she offers.

If you have a variety of products or services you, too, may want to create a catalog or arrange to be included in someone else's catalog. A catalog differs from a list of products or services in that it is a standalone sales piece, usually illustrated, that people can shop through, order from directly, and keep for reordering purposes.

Pros and Cons of Catalogs

A catalog is clearly a great way to show off what you do. You can send one out in response to inquiries, offer one for free as a way to generate leads or inquiries, hand out copies at networking events or trade shows and, of course, use it as a separate direct-mail piece that you send out to selected lists of potentially interested customers. On the one hand, a catalog provides a great opportunity for people to read over, look at, and learn about what you offer. On the other hand, designing and printing a catalog is usually expensive, and they can become outdated—and, thereby, virtually useless or even confusing—rather quickly. Every time your line or your prices change, you will need to reprint.

As a result, many people opt to put their catalog on a Web site instead of publishing a printed version (see **Web Site,** page 548), or they find ways to have some of their products or services featured in someone else's catalog. Besides the obvious cost advantages, another benefit of appearing in someone else's catalog is the endorsement value it provides. By including your product in their catalog, someone else is saying, "Here is a good one." The drawbacks of being included in someone else's catalog, however, are that you will be sharing the reader's attention with other products, and most likely only one or a few of your products or services will be featured. Also, you may not be included in the next edition of the catalog, so later when people try to order or reorder, they may hear, "That's no longer available." Once they no longer carry your product, catalog companies will rarely refer interested customers to you.

Tips on Getting Business from Catalogs

Throughout the chapter, we've made frequent references to using promotional materials that are designed to generate requests for a free catalog. Once you've generated such interest, your catalog will need to finish the job by actually getting clients or customers to pick up the phone to call or send in an order. So, you must view your catalog as a sales piece made up of mini-ads for each product or service you are featuring. The way you describe your products or services in a catalog needs to not only inform but also capture readers' interest and motivate them to order.

So, for the most part, creating a successful catalog involves following the basic copywriting and design principles outlined in www.paulandsarah.com and those outlined for other direct mail pieces (see **Direct Mail,** page 493). With today's desktop publishing capabilities it need not be as complex or expensive as you might think. Here are several special issues to keep in mind:

Carve out a niche. As a small, home-based or one-person business, if you are going to create your own catalog you will need to establish a clearly defined niche as David Stockman and Susan Pinsky have done with Reel 3-D, their mail-order catalog featuring 3-D photography equipment—or as Del Howison and partner Sue Duncan did in creating Dark Delicacy, a catalog of horror gifts and books. Otherwise you will find yourself unable to compete with the many large cash-flush mail-order companies.

Elise Casas had worn and collected vintage clothing for years. The design, craftsmanship, and history of the clothing fascinated her. Prompted by comments from friends and acquaintances like "Where can I get one of those great jackets?" and "Could you redesign that in a different color or size for me?" she started the 1909 Company, designing and creating neo-vintage clothing and accessories. She clearly had tapped into a longing for the fashions of bygone times. She now sells her unique line of new clothing based on designs from her vintage clothing collection via catalog.

Define the purpose of your catalog. Knowing the primary aim of your catalog will help you decide if it is cost-effective to create one. How will you be distributing it? Do you want to use it primarily as a handout portfolio or a sales piece? Do you plan to use it as the center of a direct-mail campaign? Will it be an adjunct to your other marketing efforts or the primary way people will find out, select, and order what you offer?

Make sure you can distribute enough of your catalogs. You will need to create a sufficient number of orders from your catalog to justify the cost involved in producing it. So who will be distributing it? Will you be doing it yourself or are their other outlets for getting it into the hands of more people than you could reach yourself? How many people will you be able to reach? Can you afford to reach the number of people you would need to reach?

Get professional help. If you don't feel confident of your copywriting or design skills, hire professionals to help you. An amateurish catalog can do more harm than good.

Charlotte Bradley of Cumberland, Rhode Island, is an example of the latter. She grew up in a family textile business, so she'd always wanted to be her own boss. But for many years she worked as a nurse.

When she had her baby, she didn't want to go back to working the long shifts nursing involved, so she decided this was her chance to start a home business. She turned to one of her own frustrations as the inspiration for her business. "When I was pregnant," she recalls, "I could find nothing to wear over size 16." So two years ago, she started Baby Becoming, a catalog of maternity wear sizes 16 to 48 for "Big, Beautiful Pregnant and Nursing Women."

Using other mom-based businesses as her guide, she set up her desk between the washer and dryer and designed T-shirts, nightshirts, sweatpants, and other items pregnant women need. She found people who would sew one item at a time for her and created her first catalog herself. Later, since she knows she isn't a designer, she found a graphic artist who does the line drawings and layout for her catalog while she writes the copy. At this point she has purchased no mailing lists. She distributes

Getting Your Product in Someone Else's Catalog

There are two ways to get your product into someone else's catalog: You can contact catalog companies yourself, or you can work through a catalog broker.

Do It Yourself

Look through the *Directory of Book, Catalog and Magazine Printers* by Ad-Lib Publications and the *National Directory of Catalogs* by Oxbridge Communications (they should be available at the library) to find catalogs that carry products similar to or compatible with yours. Call these companies and find out if they would consider carrying a product like yours. If so, ask them for their policies and procedures for submitting new products. Follow these carefully. Usually they will involve sending product descriptions, samples, and pricing information. Once you have submitted the requested materials, follow up repeatedly.

Use a Broker

Product brokers (see **Resources**) will find catalogs for you that will carry your product(s), for which they charge either a fee or a commission.

Catalogs that want to carry your products will usually either charge you for ad space or will buy the product from you at wholesale prices. Some companies will *drop-ship* your product, meaning they will take the orders and pass them on for you to fulfill.

SAMPLE CATALOGS *Reel 3-D Enterprises, Inc., Sakiestewa Textiles, and Ltd. Gourmet Gear Chefware*

her catalog at maternity stores, to midwives, and at other places where pregnant women will find them. She has taken out the tiniest of ads in relevant publications like the newsletter of the National Association for the Advancement of Fat Acceptance, and she has gotten listed on a wealth of Internet lists. As a result, people call to request her catalog.

Include visuals. As Charlotte has found, using visuals such as photos, line drawings, or graphics is vital, even if you are selling a service like workshops or training courses. People want to see as well as read about what they will be getting. This is one reason producing a catalog can be so costly, yet effective. Indigenous Designs, of the San Francisco Bay area, has come up with a creative solution to the reprinting challenge. Their catalog consists of a stack of cards, each with a photograph of one of their custom-designed sweaters on it. The cards are linked together by a metal clasped ring. Samples can be added or subtracted from the catalog at any time, or a custom catalog of samples selected for particular customers can be created.

Make it personal. Usually the more personal your catalog, the better. The 1909 Company catalog, for example, opens with a personal message from designer and owner Elise Casas who tells us, "I've collected vintage clothing for years. Not only do I appreciate the excellent craftsmanship, the beautiful fabric, and classic designs, but their history has always fascinated me as well. The idea for the 1909 Company began with compliments ("Where can I get one of those great jackets?"), a suggestion ("Why couldn't you redesign that jacket in different colors and sizes?"), and a longing for fashions seen in books and photos that were lost long ago. The catalog copy includes the history of the designs and information about the kinds of people who wore them, like Amelia Earhart and Katharine Hepburn.

As the copy in this catalog suggests, you want your readers to feel as if they're developing a relationship with you and your company as they read through the catalog. So, collect a lot of the kinds of catalogs you like. Look over your competitors' catalogs. Get a feeling for what you and your customers would like or dislike.

Resources:

Books

The Desktop Publishing Idea Book. Chuck Green. New York: Random House, 1997. Provides a step-by-step guide to creating a simple catalog.

Do-It-Yourself Advertising and Promotion. Fred. E. Haun. New York: Wiley, 1997.

How to Create Successful Catalogs, 2nd ed. Maxwell Scroog. Lincolnwood, Ill.: NTC Contemporary Publishing, 1995, (800) 323-4900.

Mechanics of Mail Order. Mike Rounds and Nancy Miller. Rounds Miller Associates, 6318 W. Ridgepath Court, Rancho Palos Verdes, CA 90275, (310) 544-9502, 1976.

Directories

Directory of Book, Catalog and Catalog and Magazine Printers. Ad Lib Publications, 51 West Adams, Fairfield, IA 52556, (800) 669-0773.

National Directory of Catalogues. Oxbridge Communications, 150 Fifth Avenue, Suite 302, New York, NY 10011, (800) 955-0213, www.mediafinder.com

Catalog Product Brokers

Catalog Solutions, 521 Riverside Avenue, Westport, CT 06880, (203) 454-1919. www.asseenonpc.com

Direct to Catalogs, Inc., 6600 Coffman Farms Road, Keedyville, MD 21756, (301) 432-4410.

Fulfillment Companies

National Fulfillment, Inc., 6960 East Gate Blvd., Lebanon, TN 37090, (615) 449-4433.

Direct Mail

Direct mail refers to sending sales materials of all types to potential customers. Generally the purpose of doing such a mailing—be it a catalog, a brochure, a coupon, a sales letter, or other specially designed sales materials—is to get the recipient either to place an order or request additional information. In addition to generating inquiries and sales, direct mail is used to create awareness of a business or product, to build credibility, and to reinforce one's position in the marketplace.

To achieve these varied purposes, any of the promotional materials discussed in this book can be sent through the mail. Newsletters sent regularly to potential and past customers, flyers and postcards announcing special offers, introductory sales letters, and even news releases sent through the mail can become an element of a direct-mail marketing campaign.

Judi Wunderlich of Schaumburg, Illinois, for example, launched her temporary graphic-design service using direct mail. She sent out 250 letters to local businesses that netted her enough customers to keep her busy for three years, and people actually kept and filed her letter for future use. Two years later, she was still getting calls from the mailing.

Heidi Waldmann, of Minneapolis, also used direct mail to launch her desktop-publishing business. Carefully selecting a list herself from the Yellow Pages and other advertising, she sent double-folded postcards, the back half of which recipients could tear off and return, to five hundred businesses she thought could use her service. She got a 14 percent return from these tear-off return cards. The entire mailing cost her only $150, but it produced several thousand dollars' worth of business.

Tim Mullen, of Loveland, Ohio, built a successful business publishing catalogs of public-domain and shareware software. He sent out twenty thousand pieces of direct mail every other month. Mailings to past buyers got a 20 to 30 percent response, while first-time lists drew a 4 to 7 percent response for him. In comparing his direct-mail costs to the cost of advertising, he found that direct mail does 20 percent better.

These results show what direct mail can do and why it entices so many small and home-based businesses to view the mailbox as the answer to their business problems. Unfortunately, not all small businesses get positive results like these from their direct-mail efforts. Often that is because those who are using direct mail successfully are not doing it in a conventional manner. In this section we will discuss the prerequisites for using direct mail as a small business and provide some basic guidelines for adopting a tailored, customized approach to direct mail that can free your time and bring you more business.

Pros and Cons: Direct Mail

Traditionally, direct mail has come to mean blanketing large categories of people or geographical areas with hundreds of thousands of mass-mailed advertisements. The cost of buying lists and preparing printed pieces—not to mention postage, telephone lines, and personnel to take calls, sort mail, and distribute goods and services—for so many names alone is beyond the budget of most small and home-based businesses. Even when funds for these expenses are available, such mass mailings usually are a waste of time and a major loss of money for most small and home-based businesses, when you consider that the overall average direct-mail response rate is only one-tenth of a percent.

Experience shows that small and home-based businesses who are using direct mail successfully as a source of regular business have actually put together a hybrid of the traditional mass market direct-mail approach. What seems to work best for them is using the mail on a much smaller scale in more customized, specialized, and personalized fashion. In fact, they have redefined the concept of direct mail by devising simple, innovative means of reaching their target audience with small, personalized mailings that feature their unique products or services.

As Miami-based David Groves of Groves Financial Services says of his direct-mail efforts, "With the database/mail-merge facilities of my personal computer and a laser printer that prints directly onto the envelope, I can put out one hundred to four hundred 'personalized' letters a month and turn 7 percent of those names into business. That's where the cottage business has it over the 'bulk mailer.' I can put in whole sentences specific to the individuals on my list and change them from one form letter to the next."

And that is exactly what those who are able to use this hybrid version of direct mail are doing: sending out mailings to small, targeted lists of people who they know buy the type of product or service they offer. Their mailings are highly personalized to the individuals involved and the needs they have. Often the mailings are followed up with a phone call.

Best Bets: Direct mail is clearly not for every type of business. Sometimes, eager to find a simple way to get business fast, business owners will turn to direct mail when some other method of promotion would be more effective. Businesses that do well with direct mail usually meet the following criteria:

___ The business is targeted to an easily definable market that routinely makes similar purchases by mail.

___ The direct-mail piece itself is well written and designed so it won't be thrown out with all the other unsolicited mail. Instead, it will get read and acted on immediately.

___ The mailing is sent to enough of the right people to get a profitable response. The more specialized the list, the better.

___ The expectations for what direct mail can produce are realistic. Many people go into direct mail expecting the moon and the stars, and when all they get are foothills and valleys, they decide it doesn't work.

Here's an example of someone who met these criteria to a tee. Copywriter Gregg M. Siegel of Wilmington, Delaware, developed an eight-month direct-mail campaign using the postcards that follow. A new card was sent each month to creative directors or principals at advertising agencies throughout Delaware, Pennsylvania, New Jersey, and Maryland using a list he has personally developed from agency, club, and organization directories, periodicals, and personal contacts. He did all the copywriting, conceptual work, typesetting, and layout himself. Artwork was prepared based on his instructions by a local freelance artist.

"The purpose of the campaign," he told us, "was to maximize the exposure of my name and services to prospects without incurring the costs of more formal mailing. I wanted each card to be fun, funny, and/or interesting." (See page 498)

Total cost: under $175 per mailing (not including his time).

Results: He has added twelve new clients since initiating the mailing, many of whom provide him with projects on a regular basis.

Is Your Business Suited to Direct Mail?

The more of these following criteria your business meets, the more likely direct mail will work for you. If you meet very few of these criteria, you should look to other methods.

___ 1. Is your market easily definable using finite demographic parameters?

___ 2. Can you actually reach your potential market through a third-party delivery system, such as the U.S. Postal Service, UPS, or Federal Express?

___ 3. Is your prospective customer likely to have purchased a similar product or service as a result of direct mail in the past?

___ 4. Is your product or service one that can be sold without discussion or demonstration?

___ 5. Is your product or service sufficiently visually oriented for the potential buyers to understand its value clearly from a mailing?

___ 6. Is your product or service one that is conducive to impulse buying?

___ 7. Is your product or service highly discounted compared with those of your competitors?

___ 8. Is your product or service one wherein a mistake in purchase will NOT affect the buyer or his company in an especially negative way?

___ 9. Is your product or service one that lends itself to on-the-spot decisions?

___ 10. Can you afford what it takes to produce a sufficiently impressive package to get your prospect to purchase?

___11. Can you afford either the money to buy appropriate lists or the time to create one sufficient to make a mailing worthwhile?

___12. If you are selling to consumers, can you afford to send your package to enough people that a 1 percent return would be profitable?

___13. If you are selling to businesses, are you willing to do the follow-up telephone calls needed to make sure your mailing was received and to discover potential interest?

Tips for Getting Business from Direct Mail

If you decide to use direct mail, **Appendix I** outlines the basic principles for designing an effective direct-mail campaign and other printed sales materials. It's available on-line without charge as a Special Report at www.paulandsarah.com on the Great Ideas for Getting Business page. Here are several other specific issues for creating a successful campaign:

Avoid the Clichés of What Makes an Effective Mail Piece.

• ***Color is not always more effective than black-and-white.*** Sometimes a high-contrast, dramatic black-and-white piece is far more effective than a lovely four-color photograph. The overall design is the key factor.

• ***Short is not always better than long.*** There is more involved in writing a direct-response piece than just keeping it short, even when you are sending out a letter-style promotion. In some cases a rambling, personal style will work better than a succinct and brisk business manner. Any letter needs to be long enough to answer all the questions you would be likely to be asked if you were there in person. The better you know your customers and what they will want to know before they act, the better your response will be.

• ***Paper choice can make or break your piece, so choose wisely.*** Studies done over the years to test the likelihood of a letter's reaching an executive's desk prove that paper selection is important. Not only the look of a piece but also the feel of it can make a substantial difference. Depending on your target market, you may want to consider one of the recycled papers that allow you to use the recycled logo on your piece, showing that you are environmentally aware, or a rag-content sheet

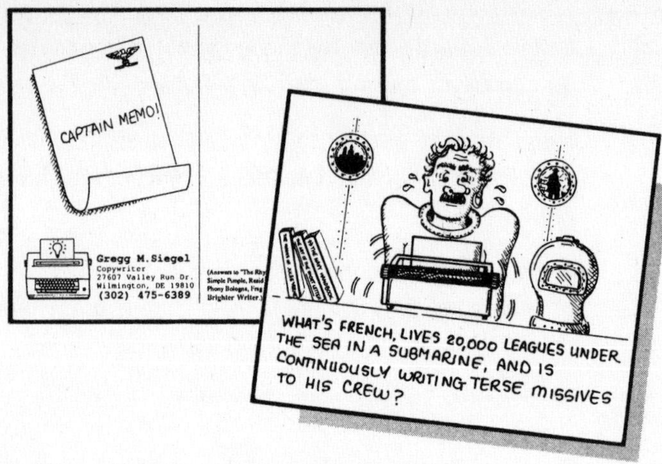

Copywriter Gregg M. Siegel developed an eight-month direct-mail campaign using cartoon-based postcards. He sent a new card every month to a list he compiled himself from directories, periodicals, and personal contacts.

that appears to be more a business letter than a mass mailing. A special weight, texture, or color can add substance and a solid appearance—or it can make your product appear too expensive. A special envelope size, texture, or color can make the piece appear to be social in nature and thus enhance its pull potential, or it can have the reverse effect. Again, you must match your choices to your market.

- ***Messages on the envelope are not always helpful.*** The direct-mail marketing experts often recommend a teaser on the envelope—such as "Open Immediately," "Confidential," "A personal invitation from Joe Blow," or "A special message from John Doe"—that appears to be handwritten. Sometimes the first couple of lines from the piece itself are used on the envelope, followed by "(continued inside)." These phrases can be useful, but they can just as easily work against you because they will alert the recipients that a sales pitch is coming and give them the chance to toss the mailing out unopened. Certainly an expensive professional or business mailing should never utilize a teaser; on the other hand, a mailing that is promoting a contest or a sweepstakes may find it helpful.

- ***Using third-class mail doesn't always save you money.*** Whether to use first- or third-class mail depends on the type of people you are mailing to, the nature and size of the mailing piece, the list you are using, and the timeliness of your offer. If you decide that first class is the way to go, do not use a postage meter, which will negate the appearance of personalization first-class postage can give your piece. Instead use the most attractive stamps you can find.

Test your mailing piece. If you are in doubt about the best choice for any of the above issues and plan to do a large mailing to thousands, test your direct-mail piece with a small list to determine if it works before you spend huge amounts on a larger mailing.

Testing is particularly useful when you are sending several items in an envelope. By placing your coupon or special offer in various locations in the mailing and tracking which placements draw the most responses, you can test how the envelope is likely to be opened and the order in which its contents are removed. Then, with your full mailing, you can make sure your major punch is out in front. If the primary piece isn't immediately apparent, people will probably trash the whole mailing before they even know what it is about.

TIP: Don't include glitter or confetti in your mailer unless you want the recipient to curse you loudly. Your mailer will be noticed, but

THE MARKETING MANAGER

ELEMENTS OF A DIRECT MAIL PIECE

Cherry Valley Press
P.O. Box 836
South Pasadena,
CA 91030

Today's computer revolution opens
a rare 'window-in-time' opportunity to make
your dreams for personal and financial independence
come true....

Dear Computer Owner:

Sitting right there on your desk at home may be your passport to freedom ...fulfillment...financial independence.

Your Personal Computer.

This electronic dream machine can give you freedom from the complexities of today's industrialized world and hassles and frustrations of corporate life, and, best of all, let you reap the rewards of your productivity and enjoy your life and family to the fullest.

"THE TIME MANAGER" is an indispensable one-page planner for work at home that helps you become well organized and totally productive every day.

The "COMPUTER HELPERS" section contains The File Finder, The Electronic Mail Minder and The Database Search Planner -- three important tools you need as you work with your computer.

"THE MONEY MANAGER" is a tested, easy-to-use system for financial records and tax planning, so you'll have everything in one place and you'll know where to find it. It's all here... everything you need to know to turn your home into a fully operable money-making "electronic cottage."

Free 14-Day Trial! Satisfaction guaranteed or your money back!

We're so sure you'll be delighted with your Start-Up Kit that if you're not fully satisfied, we'll gladly refund your money in full within 14 days.

So you have nothing to lose...and everything to gain; your freedom... personal and monetary rewards of untold measure...and the opportunity to run your own business right from home.

You've got half of what it takes now...your personal computer. The other half is ready and waiting for you. Why not get started today? Send for your complete Start-Up Kit now.

Sincerely,

Ben Lizardi

Ben Lizardi
Publisher

P.S. Free Special Bonus! 107+ Ways To Make Money With A Computer! When you order your Start-Up Kit within 14 days, you'll receive FREE 17" x 22" full-color wall poster listing 107+ ... with your computer. Even if ...

INTRODUCING THE COMPLETE MANUAL ON MAKING MONEY AT HOME WITH YOUR COMPUTER.
It's all here...eve... to know to start and operate a h... computer!

BUSINESS REPLY MAIL
FIRST CLASS PERMIT NO. 240

No Postage Stamp Necessary If Mailed in the United States

YES! I want to start making money from home with my computer right away.

Not ready to order the Complete Start-up Kit yet, but send me the full color poster listing 107+ Ways to Make Money with Your Computer.

CHERRY VALLEY PRESS
P.O. BOX 836, SO. PASADENA, CA 91030

DEP. 10/31/84

Amount of order $ 3.70 2.95
Postage & handling .75
Calif. residents add 6½% sales tax .22
TOTAL 3.92

RICHARD VANHOY
1529 GOLDEN GATE DRIVE
SAN DIEGO, CA 92116

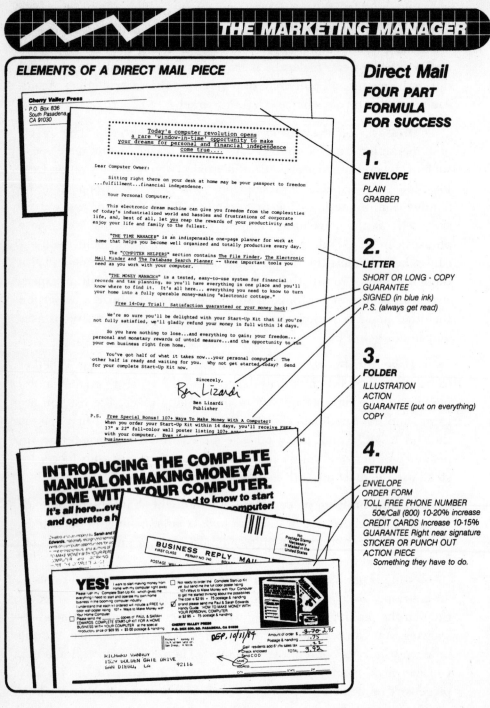

Direct Mail
FOUR PART FORMULA FOR SUCCESS

1. ENVELOPE
PLAIN
GRABBER

2. LETTER
SHORT OR LONG - COPY
GUARANTEE
SIGNED (in blue ink)
P.S. (always get read)

3. FOLDER
ILLUSTRATION
ACTION
GUARANTEE (put on everything)
COPY

4. RETURN
ENVELOPE
ORDER FORM
TOLL FREE PHONE NUMBER
50¢/Call (800) 10-20% increase
CREDIT CARDS Increase 10-15%
GUARANTEE Right near signature
STICKER OR PUNCH OUT
ACTION PIECE
Something they have to do.

Elements of a Direct-Mail Piece

it will also most likely do a great job of unselling your product or service.

Ultimately, the best way to make sure your direct mail is opened and read is to send it to people who are interested in and have an urgent need for what you have to offer and to have a sufficiently high and positive profile for your company that people recognize it and therefore *want* to open mail from you.

Use a good list. Since the way to maximize your response rate is to attempt to reach enough of the right people in the first place, the appropriateness and accuracy of your list will, in great part, determine your response rate. Finding a good list is not as simple as it seems. According to the American Management Association, the overall average response rate to direct-mail advertising is one response from a thousand (.1 percent) pieces sent. Based on this statistic, the average sender gets only one customer from every thousand pieces of mail sent out. The minimum cost of postage alone for those pieces is approximately $185. Unless your product or service costs more than that, one response won't even pay the postage. At this rate, even if you got one response for every five hundred mailings, you could fail royally while getting a better-than-average response!

Direct-mail professionals, however, claim an average response rate of one in one hundred, or 1 percent. But here again, the postage costs alone for those hundred mailings will run in the neighborhood of $18, which is precisely why some businesses conclude they can't afford di-

THE IDEAL DIRECT-MAIL LIST

The ideal mailing list would have these characteristics:

___ The names and addresses are accurate and current. (Many lists have 20 percent inaccuracy.)

___ These prospects need your product or service.

___ They can afford to buy your product or service.

___ They know or have heard of you, your company, your product, or your service.

___ They have a positive regard for you, your product, or your service.

rect mail. With the right list, however, coupled with the right piece, you could do much better than that.

Of course, few lists can meet all these criteria: the goal in building or finding a list should be to come as close to them as possible. The list that comes closest to meeting all these criteria is your own mailing list of satisfied customers. Presuming your product or service is one your customers can use again, or that you can provide some new product or service they need, this list should get far better than a one-in-a-thousand response rate. To draw in new business, however, there are three ways to find a good list: locate and rent one, use a list broker to find one for you to rent, or build your own list.

• ***Renting a List.*** To begin your search, consider which organizations or groups would have a list of your prospective customers. Is there a civic, trade, or professional association to which they belong? Is there a magazine or newsletter to which they subscribe? Is there a manufacturer or retailer who is already serving them? All these sources may be willing to rent you their mailing lists. For example, a company that runs a referral service via a computer bulletin board could approach modem manufacturers and rent the names of people in their geographical area who have purchased modems. Someone who has a mail-order catalog of garden accessories could rent lists from gardening magazines. Or a sales trainer wanting to market to book publishers could investigate renting a list from the Association of American Presses.

Sometimes you can simply contact such groups yourself, ask for their marketing department, and inquire about renting their mailing lists. They will either give you the information or refer you to the list broker who handles their list.

The *Standard Rate and Data Service,* available in many public libraries, is a good resource for identifying lists. Depending on what group of people you want to reach, you can refer to the *Consumer Magazine Rates and Data, the Business Publications Rates and Data,* or the *Direct Mail Lists Rates and Data*. The first two of these are targeted to publications that may or may not rent their subscriber lists. The last one profiles over 12,500 mailing lists that are available for rental. It is updated bimonthly, is arranged by market classification, and describes the lists, rental rates, labeling methods, and related information.

A list consisting of people who have recently responded to mail will be three to five times as effective as an ordinary list. Of course, you pay more for such a list. Before renting one, determine whether the responses represent actual purchases or were simply responses to surveys or offers for free publications. Responders are not always buyers. When you rent a list, it will be sent to you on mailing labels that can be used only once. (For the legal ramifications of reusing a list, see ***Keep it legal***, page 507.)

• ***Using a List Broker.*** If your target market is relatively easy to identify by a specific set of characteristics (age, sex, zip code, income, purchase profile, and so forth), then a list broker is ideal. A list broker will do the research, compile your list from various sources if necessary, and handle the negotiations of renting it for you. These brokers can be found in the local Yellow Pages under a heading such as "Mailing List Services" or on-line

Most list brokers operate in a manner similar to that of an advertising agency. If the list is already prepared and is acquired from a single source, the broker bills you at the rate posted by the source of the list but receives a discount from that source. Most lists rent for between $45 and $100 per thousand names and are guaranteed for 95 percent accuracy—that is, only 5 percent returns or undeliverables. Brokers also build custom lists, negotiating special fees for preparation services in advance.

Also be sure—especially if you are renting several lists, such as credit-card holders and trade-publication subscribers—that your broker does what is known as a *merge-purge* on the lists to help eliminate costly duplications.

• ***Building Your Own List.*** If your budget doesn't cover the cost of renting a list or if you are seeking a new, unusual, or highly specialized group of people, you can build your own list starting with responses to the other advertising methods you are using. There are no better prospects

QUESTIONS TO ASK WHEN SELECTING A LIST BROKER

1. What sources do you use for your lists?
2. Why do you use these particular sources?
3. How often do you use them?
4. What accuracy rate do you guarantee?
5. How often are your lists updated and corrected?
6. How long have you been in business?
7. Are your lists qualified; that is, have the people on them bought similar services or products by mail?
8. Can any of my criteria not be met by your lists? Which ones?

than those who have purchased from you before. You can add to your own list by visiting your public library, which stocks volumes of *Who's Who* for almost every industry. There are also all sorts of other directories that list trade personnel at a variety of levels.

Another way to build a list is to take a booth at a trade show and collect names of interested individuals. To boost the number of names you can collect, hold a drawing. Still another approach is to run a contest as part of a radio advertising campaign (see **chapter 12**). However, be sure your drawing or contest prizes are something that only your market would want so that you don't get a lot of useless names. A low-cost way to run such a contest is to offer your product or service as a free prize to a radio station for their promotions or to a community event in exchange for receiving a copy of the mailing list the contest produces. Or you can contribute a free article to a publication and offer to send some specialized information or a small item to interested readers. If you have selected the right publication and offered the right gift, you will get lots of responses.

Building a good list of your own may take time, perhaps even years, but in doing so through your other advertising and promotional activity you will find these names can be an invaluable resource. For example, Steve Bean, who operates a mail-order software business, over a six-year period found that renting lists produced no results, even though the people on the lists were similar to those who responded to his magazine ads. However, when he built his own list from the magazine-ad respondents, he got a profitable 1 percent response in actual sales.

If you use your own list, be sure to keep it up-to-date. Send out at least one mailing quarterly, purging the names that are not current and adding new names regularly. Have an address-correction request printed on the envelope. For each address correction, the post office will charge you thirty cents at current rates; and when you mail first class, it will return undeliverable envelopes to you at no additional charge. Mailing-list software makes list maintenance a much simpler task than ever before. But if you find list maintenance too time-consuming, you can hire a small or home-based mailing-list management service to keep your list fresh. (For more on how to purge your mailing lists, see page 144.)

One added advantage of building and maintaining your own list is that you can rent your list to other noncompetitive businesses. Take a cue from the major players and salt your list each time you rent it with dummy names at your address or those of friends so you'll know who is using your list and when. However, keep in mind that some of the people on your list may not be eager to get additional direct mail, particularly if the mailings they receive are not of high interest or potential value to them. All they have to do is call the mailer to find out how their name was obtained.

Test your list. Technically, direct-marketing specialists claim that to test a direct-mail concept you must use twenty-five thousand to forty thousand names and, to test a list, a minimum of five thousand names. This is fine if you are using direct mail to approach potentially hundreds of thousands of mass-market consumer prospects. But, the vast majority of small businesses have a targeted market niche that may include fewer than five thousand names. If you plan to send out only a few hundred pieces, consider each mailing itself to be a test.

As with any other marketing medium, direct mail begins as an experiment—although, we hope, a well-thought-out one. You can learn a great deal from each mailing you do about the list, the design elements, and the copy that works best for your business. But if you plan to send out thousands of pieces, a test of between one thousand and two thousand pieces is advisable and may be sufficient. You can test other things at the same time, breaking your test group into segments and offering alternative lead points or sizes, or layouts, length, or approaches. Rather than trying to test too many things at once, however, let testing answer only a few major questions at a time.

Set realistic expectations. Every direct-mail piece is sent out with great expectations. But in reality, the best expectations are realistic ones. With rare exceptions, the vast majority of whatever you send will end up in a trash can without having been opened, so be aware of that before you begin. Again, keep in mind that, as we said earlier, the current overall average response rate for direct mail is one-tenth of 1 percent, so to get one order, you would have to send out one thousand pieces. Of course, if your product or service is appropriate for direct mail and you have been using the methods recommended in this book for designing a creative promotional piece and finding a perfectly tailored list, you could reach a response rate of 30 percent or higher; but that is the exception, not the rule. You will be lucky under any circumstances if your response rate reaches the 5 percent mark, which translates to one hundred orders for every two thousand mailings. So do not expect to slay Goliath with a single mailing.

You should not base your expectations or cost estimates on projections of the highest possible return. You will be much safer and more satisfied if you base both on the lowest probable response. Remember that the vast majority of the best potential customers will not do business with someone they have never heard of. Your mailing has merely introduced you to them.

Expecting too much from a single mailing with no other promotional support only leads to disappointment, especially if you have invested your entire promotion budget in that one mailing. When you have met all other criteria and still don't get the response you need, you should consider a program of multiple mailings rather than expecting a single effort to achieve your goal. Another alternative is to plan to do a mailing in combination with other advertising and promotional methods. Such a multipronged approach is particularly valuable when your product or service is a new one that people don't know about. By introducing yourself through advertising and promotion, you may improve the response to your mailings.

Direct mail, like advertising, must be thought of as part of a campaign—not as a single technique. With rare exceptions, a single ad in a single publication will bring you little but bills; so it is with direct mail. Sometimes direct mail can be even more expensive than advertising. If your budget will not permit a campaign approach or if your break-even point requires a higher response rate than you can reasonably expect, you need to rethink the applicability of direct mail. You may choose, instead, to use other forms of promotion until you build your business to a point at which you can reduce the risks of direct mail.

Time your direct-mail campaign. As with any business, some times of the year are more conducive to pulling a good response rate than others. For mass-market consumer items, pre-Christmas mailers pull the greatest response rates. However, if your product is geared to gardens or water recreation, for example, spring or early-summer mailings are more successful. Similarly, the best season for any product or service geared to income taxes is January 15 through April 15. And late summer seems to be a slow time for most industries. So before you do a mailing, consider when people are most likely to be eager to see it.

An alternative approach is to target your mailing specifically to arrive at a different time from everyone else's, when you have less competition. Someone offering tutoring to children, for example, might have a special promotion during the summer, or a ski school might do a promotion in the summer to sign up early for winter lessons. Reward those who plan ahead with discounts, free gifts, or special offers.

An additional factor of timing has to do with the number of mailings you plan. Most specialists in the field recommend a standard of three. However, the optimal number depends on what you are offering to whom, how you are offering it, and how much it costs. The three-mailing standard is often effective when seeking new clients or customers, especially those who have never heard of you or your company. Your current client list should be contacted on a regular basis by postcard, letter, a simple flyer, or a newsletter, perhaps presenting a special offer or promotion. For example, Mike Chlanda, who provides business-support services from his home in Yellow Springs, Ohio, sends out monthly postcards to his customers, each featuring a different service he provides.

Keep it legal. There are several legal safeguards you should take in using direct-mail. First, make sure you are buying a legitimate list. Work only with a legitimate list broker or publication or develop your own list only from legitimate sources. If you are offered a list on the quick take—even if it is your greatly coveted competitor's list—walk away. All lists are salted with dummy names, to prevent you from using a single-rental list more than once. Any subsequent mailing received by those dummy names opens you up to additional charges at best or even a lawsuit. In some states, theft of a mailing list constitutes a criminal act for which you could pay heavy fines and even go to jail!

Be sure to get copies of all materials about direct-mail regulations from the U.S. Postal Service. Some materials pertain to the regulations on what you may send at third-class rates; others, to business-reply card/envelope requirements. In some cases, the Post Office department handling such matters in your area may require you to submit your mechanicals for approval. They are not interested in approving your design; they only need to confirm that their machines will be able to read your codes properly.

There are also regulations governing the content and types of items you can and cannot send through the mails. Other regulations apply to how third-class mail must be sorted and to weight, size, design restrictions, and quantities. Be sure you are familiar with all such regulations. Post Office personnel can provide you with the information you need. Remember, though, that regulations change constantly and not always logically. Do some homework before each mailing or deal with a printer or letter shop that works with direct marketers regularly.

If you quote from other publications in your mailing piece, be sure to give appropriate credit. If you use more than a simple quotation, get the appropriate permissions required by the copyright laws. Contact your lawyer when in doubt about what is needed. If you include testimonials of any kind, be sure you have a written release or signed permission slip in your files.

Personalize your mailing. The more personal you can make your mailing, the better. Very small mailings can be highly personal, as we suggest in sending out introductory sales letters below. Even with larger mailings, however, with mail-merge software or when using a mailing-list service, there are many ways to make your mailing more personal and thereby increase the likelihood that someone will open and read it. Here are a few:

___Use first-class mail or, to save money, a precanceled third-class stamp, not a postage meter.

___Use your personal or business stationery.

___Print the address directly on the envelope or use a window envelope. To save money, use clear labels now available for laser printers; they are more effective than white labels and will more than pay for their extra cost in results.

___Address the envelope to each individual by name, not "Current Resident," "Occupant," or "Owner."

___Use the person's name and address on the letter and personalize the letter itself in some way by using a mailing-list service or mail-merge software.

___Follow up with a personal call.

Weigh your postage choice. Despite rate increases, the cost of sending your mailing third class is a little more than half the rate of sending it first class. Thus you can mail nearly twice as many pieces for the same postage cost, or you can simply save the difference.

If you have a great many pieces mailing within a narrow band (a minimum of 200 pieces per zip code) and use direct mail on a regular basis, you may also want to consider getting a bulk rate permit. This may become especially important if your piece is larger or heavier than standard. There are a great many regulations attached to bulk mail, but it can save you a great deal of money on large-volume mailings. The best source of information is your local post office.

Of course, sending mail first class does increase the likelihood of its getting read, so many businesses use this service for mailing to smaller lists. Not all third-class mail has to look like your standard idea of bulk mail, however. You do not have to print a permit number in a box where the stamp should be; use precanceled stamps instead.

Beyond budget advantages, the primary issue in choosing among bulk, third-class, and first-class handling is timing. If your promotion is time-dated and cannot survive a delay, do not use bulk or third class.

You also have other mailing options. Not all direct mail is sent through the U.S. Postal Service. Some direct marketers use overnight companies such as Federal Express, Airborne Express, or UPS; others use a messenger service or even their own employees for hand delivery. Your choice depends on your market, what you are sending, and what you are trying to sell.

Include a prepaid response card. Using a prepaid response card can dramatically improve your response rate. Heidi Waldmann used a double postcard to launch her desktop-publishing company in Minneapolis. Half the card was designed so that anyone interested in her business could tear it off and return it after checking one of the following:

___ "Send us more information,"

___ "Call us with information or to set up an appointment," or

___ "We have no need at this time." Space was provided for them to write their name, address, and phone number, along with any comments.

Using such a card can increase the responses and help you follow up more effectively. (See **Direct Response Advertising—Reply Card,** above p. 456.)

Follow up by phone. *"The mail. I never open it,"* electronic newsletter publisher Sarah Stambler was told when she called to see why a friend had yet to RSVP to a special holiday gathering. Having handwritten the address and used a thirty-two-cent stamp on her invitations, Stambler was amazed, but she learned that *"I get so much mail and it's just too hard to wade through."*

Is it any wonder that for many service businesses, the most effective results from direct mail come from combining it with a precall or follow-up telephone call? Obviously this is feasible only when what you are selling is priced high enough that you can afford to invest the time in making phone calls. In fact, the more expensive or customized the product or service, the more likely it is that you will need to combine your direct mail with a phone call and perhaps a personal sales call as well.

There is a rule of thumb in marketing that claims it takes seven contacts to produce a sale. The more expensive the product or service, the more likely this rule of thumb is to apply. Suppose, for example, you are selling a $450 seminar or a $5,000 consulting program. Perhaps some people will call or write to order from your mail piece, but you will get a much higher response if you call first to tell them you will be sending the material and then call to follow up on whether they received it.

A survey of three hundred chief executive officers found that they expect a follow-up to a letter or brochure by either mail or phone. And their response rates are three to seven times higher when direct mail is followed up by a phone call.

When you call to see whether a mailing was received, often people will not remember receiving it. It probably ended up in the wastebasket or in a pile somewhere. Your follow-up call, however, may elicit enough interest that you can offer to send a replacement, after which you can follow up with a second call.

Do follow-up mailings. Follow-up mailings can also increase your response rate. When doing additional mailings as follow-up, however, be sure to purge those who have placed orders from the list to be used for subsequent mailings covering the same special promotion. There is nothing more aggravating for a customer than to place an order for an item and then continue to receive mailings about it. The customer begins to equate your lack of care in this matter with your overall service approach and becomes reluctant to order again.

Respond fast to responses. If your direct-marketing efforts are aimed at finding sales leads or are promoting a service, which usually means the customer will be requesting further information, make sure you make your next contact quickly. If the customer needs additional literature, it should be on its way to him or her within forty-eight hours after receiving the request. If the prospect expects to be contacted personally, the same forty-eight-hour rule applies. As with everything else in marketing, you need to strike when the iron is hot.

Once you have prospects interested, don't waste time in getting back to them. Here again, delay shows a lack of interest or suggests less-than-top-notch organization on your part. And that is the fastest way to lose not only a sale but also a customer, permanently.

Track your results. Whether or not to track a particular direct-marketing promotion should be determined by whatever testing procedures you have already used. If you do not test, consider tracking as a means of preparing your future approaches. Your criteria for tracking could range from whether the list reaches the right people to whether you used benefits that are important to your customers.

For example, suppose you have purchased lists from two diverse trade publications and one credit-card company, each with its own code incorporated in the label. If you make sure to get that code number in your response, the response rate per list can be separated and ranked. Or suppose you wish to experiment with two totally different approaches, but your list is too small for a full-scale testing procedure. You can simply create your own short code to add to the label or to another easy-to-find portion of the return order form. For example, one address could include "Dept. D" and the other, "Dept. K," or, if the headlines are different, you can use the first four letters of each headline as your code.

To make such tracking information as accurate as possible, make sure your printed pieces are alternated one-for-one before labels are placed on them. This will insure the randomness of the distribution among the ZIP codes to which you are mailing. Here again, your response rate for each code will tell you a great deal about how the two approaches were received.

Since tracking is such a simple process for direct marketers, it is foolish not to gather the information available even if it does not interest you right now. Then you will have it on hand when you do need it.

Don't get discouraged. Finally, when using direct mail, remember to keep your expectations within reason to avoid disappointment. A direct-mail piece is little more than a traveling billboard. A billboard can only sell something to someone who is ready to buy. Do whatever is necessary to send your piece to the right people; focus on the benefits to the customer rather than the features you are proud of; be as creative as your product or service allows; make it easy for a customer to respond; and follow up on every contact or request. Do all these things and your return will exceed your expectations.

Resources: Direct Mail

Associations

Direct Marketing Association, 1120 Avenue of the Americas, New York, NY 10036, (212) 768-7277, www.the-dma.org. Has many publications on mailing list practices and guidelines for fair information practices.

Association of Business Support Services International, 22875 Savi Ranch Parkway, Ste. H, Yorba Linda, CA 92887, (800) 237-1462, www.nass.com. Will provide referrals to companies in your area who will prepare mailings for you.

Editorial Freelancers' Association, 71 West 23d Street, Ste. 1504, New York, NY 10010, (212) 929-5400. Has a job bank through which you can find freelance copywriters.

Books & Publications

Do-It-Yourself Advertising & Promotion: How to Produce Great Ads, Brochures, Catalog, Direct Mail and Much More. Fred E. Haun. New York: Wiley, 1997.

Do-It-Yourself Direct Marketing, Secrets for Small Business. Mark S. Bacon. New York: Wiley, 1992.

Domestic Mail Manual. U.S. Postal Service Publication, List ID DOM, File 25, available from the Superintendent of Documents, Washington, D.C.

The Greatest Direct Mail Sales Letter of All Time. Richard S. Hodgson. Chicago: Dartnell Corporation, 1995, (800) 621-5463.

International Mail Manual, List ID IMM, File Code 25, available from the Superintendent of Documents, Washington, DC.

Mail Order Selling, How to Market Almost Anything by Mail. Irving Burstiner, New York: John Wiley & Sons, 1995.

Target$mart, Database Marketing for the Small Business. Jay Newberg and Claudio Marcus. Grants Pass, Oreg.: Oasis Press, 1996 (503) 479-9464.

Mailing List Broker Resources

Standard Rate and Data Service, 3004 Glenview Road, Wilmette, IL 60091, (847) 256-6067, (800) 851-7737, www.srds.com (available in libraries).

The Direct Marketing Market Place and Direct Mail List Rates and Data, 5201 Old Orchard Rd., Skokie, IL 60077, (708) 256-6067 (available in libraries).

Directory of Mailing List Companies, 18 North Greenbush Rd., West Nyack, NY 10994, (914) 358-6213.

Direct-Mail List Catalogs

American Business Directories, 5711 South 86th Circle, P.O. Box 27347, Omaha, NE 68127. They publish:

- *American Consumer Lists:* 82 million households, 4.5 million high-income Americans; available for specified geographical areas.
- *Lists of 9 Million Businesses,* compiled from the Yellow Pages.
- *Online Information Network,* which allows downloading of lists using a personal computer.
- *Nationwide Directory of Business:* 1,200 titles compiled from the Yellow Pages; printed directories from which you can create your own mailing labels and use indefinitely. Phone numbers are included.

Dun's National Business List, Dun's Marketing Services, 49 Old Bloomfield Avenue, Mountain Lakes Corporate Center II, Mountain Lakes, NJ 07046, (201) 299-0181. Covers 8,500,000 American businesses.

The Hugo Dunhill Mailing List Catalog, 630 Third Avenue, New York, NY 10017, (800) 223-6454.

The Polk Mailing List Catalog, R. L. Polk & Co., 6400 Monroe Boulevard, Taylor, MI 48180, (313) 292-3200. Provides over 1,000 indexed complete national lists.

On-Line Resources

Directory of Direct Marketers. An on-line compendium of direct-marketing industry's mailings lists, list managers, list brokers, ad agencies, mail houses and other services. http://mainsail.com/dm-world.htm

SalesLeadsUSA, by American Business Information, 5711 South 86th Circle, P.O. Box 27347, Omaha, NE 68127, (402) 593-4593, www.salesleadsusa.com. Provides access to over 10 million U.S. businesses for sales leads, mailing labels, business profiles, and more.

Software

Mail Tools Database Companion, by MySoftware Company, 1259 El Camino Real, Ste. 167, Menlo Park, CA 94025, (650) 473-3600, www.mysoftware.com. Enables you to add mailing capability to most popular databases, print labels, postcards, and envelopes, automatically correct addresses, add ZIP+4 codes, print bar codes, sort for bulk mail savings, and eliminate duplicates.

My Advanced Mailing-List & Address Book, by My Software Co., 1259 El Camino Real, Ste. 167, Menlo Park, CA 94025, (650) 473-3600 or (800) 325-3508, www.mysoftware.com

Letter Shop and Design Services

ImageDirect™, by Paper Direct at 100 Plaza Drive, Secaucus, NJ 07094, (800) A-PAPERS, (800) 272-7377, www.paperdirect.com will custom-design and print direct-mail materials, rent mailing lists, and prepare mailings.

Tip: Before Faxing the Media . . . Before sending news releases by fax to your Personalized Media List (**chapter 10**, page 385), find out how the individuals on your list prefer to receive material. Some producers, editors, and writers actually prefer to receive releases by fax; other prefer getting your releases via mail, phone, or E-mail.

High-Tech Tip: Fax-Back, Broadcast Fax, and E-Mail

Federal and often state laws prohibit the transmission of unsolicited facsimile, or "junk fax." But, because marketing by fax does not have to be unsolicited, there are still ways you can use your fax to let people know what you're about. You can send a fax to anyone who has asked to be on your mailing list. You can send a newsletter by fax to anyone who has requested it. And, of course, you can send a fax to anyone with whom you have an ongoing business relationship. That includes one of your best sources of future business: your past and present clients.

So your fax can be a great tool for getting out the news about special offers, sales, new services, upcoming marketing events, invitations, announcements, holiday greetings, news releases, and thank-you notes. It has many advantages over other means of getting the word out. It costs less than doing a mailing because there's no printing or postage, and it saves time. There's no printing out material, stuffing envelopes, or putting on stamps, and of course, no trips to the post office. Your material arrives instantaneously, and you know that it got there.

Send your fax by E-mail. You can save on the cost and time of faxing by sending your fax via E-mail, if you wish, using a service like .comfax, the Internet Fax Company. You can send your fax simultaneously to 1,000 sites without ever printing it out. .comfax also enables you to receive faxes in a virtual-fax in-box while you're out of town. You access your fax in-box via the Web.

Broadcast fax capability makes sending out a mass number of faxes even easier. This capability, standard among almost all mid- to high-end machines, allows you to simultaneously transmit the same material to many recipients. You simply enter the document into memory and let the fax know all the locations you want it transmitted to. Your material can even be downloaded directly from your computer. You can send local faxes yourself and use a broadcast fax service (see **Resources,** below) for broadcasting faxes to a long list of long-distance numbers.

Professional speaking coach Sandra Schrift sent a marketing memo via fax to fellow NSA members regarding her services. She got such a tremendous response to the faxed memo that she created an ongoing marketing campaign around sending faxes regularly to those who were interested. Harry Krotowski, who operates a commercial real estate information service in Monmouth Junction, New Jersey, faxes his newsletter to dozens of clients. He finds a fax usually gets read sooner than a four-color brochure that arrives in the mail.

For best results, Sarah Stambler, publisher of *Marketing with Technology News,* a faxed newsletter, recommends the following:

- Be sure your fax messages always look professional and not like an ad.
- Keep your fax to one page.
- If you're using graphics, have them done professionally rather than scanning them in. Stambler recommends Infaxamation's DeskFAX Publishing Service, (800) 329-4632.
- Provide a statement to inform recipients how to get removed from your fax list.

Broadcast E-mail is another way to get your message out. If you have the E-mail addresses of your contacts, you can also broadcast all the above-mentioned types of marketing materials via E-mail. In other words, you can send one E-Mail message simultaneously to many addresses. While junk E-mail is not as of this writing illegal yet, people hate *spamming,* as it's called. So we urge that you also limit your E-mail broadcast to people who have identified themselves as wanting to receive information from you.

Joyce Wycoff, executive director and founder of the Innovative Thinking Network and author of *Mindmapping: Your Personal Guide to Creativity and Problem-Solving,* sends out Monday E-mail messages titled Good Morning Thinkers. The weekly messages also promote Wycoff's upcoming conferences, networking events, and groups creativity products. Occasionally she includes a reader poll. She encourages those receiving her messages to subscribe and fax them on to others. Within months her list grew from 125 to 6,000 weekly readers.

Software like WebMaster allows you to automatically send broadcast E-mail messages to everyone who wants to know when you've updated your Web site.

Fax-back, or what is also called ***fax on demand*** or ***FOD,*** is another way to use your fax for getting the word out. It's a sophisticated version of a voice-mail system. Anyone who is interested in getting certain printed information from you like your bio, product or service list, brochure, prices, schedule of upcoming events, specials, or other announcements can simply call you and by selecting different numbers from a menu immediately receive the desired information from you via fax. This is a great marketing tool for anyone who doesn't have someone to answer the phone or send out frequently requested material.

To offer fax-back you must have a fax modem for your computer, a phone line dedicated to fax usage, and fax-back software. While you don't need a separate computer, if you anticipate getting a lot of calls, you will probably want one you can dedicate to handling your fax-back service. And, by the way, fax-back provides you with a list of the callers' fax numbers, so since they've requested information from you, you can add them to your broadcast fax list.

Fax Cover Sheets. Don't forget, your fax cover sheet is another opportunity to reinforce your image and provide information about who you are and what you do. You can scan letterhead and logo into your computer and create your own custom fax sheet. You might include your mission statement, tag line, or Attention Grabber (see **chapter 5**), for example, along with a news flash, tip for the day, or other special announcement, which could change periodically. Communication specialist Dennis Chambers includes a quote for the month on the bottom of his fax sheet and finds that people like it. They even call to find out when he'll be adding a new one. Vincent Santiago manufactures adhesives. On his fax sheets he adds the company tag line: "We bring people together."

A seminar company increased their recruitment efforts 300 percent with their fax campaign. After placing a call to determine interest, they began following up immediately with a one-page fax announcing that sales materials would be arriving by Priority Mail. The fax sheet included a testimonial from a past workshop attendee who was willing to answer any questions, along with his phone number. The following day, another fax is sent assuring that the Priority Mail package will be arriving that day and describing the bonus available to anyone who signs up immediately.

Resources: Fax and E-Mail Marketing

Broadcast Fax, Fax E-Mail, and Fax-on-Demand Services

.comfax, the Internet Fax Company, 90 John Street, New York, NY 10038, (212) 385-5351, www.comfax.com, E-mail: sales@comfax. com

PC-Xpedite, Xpedite Systems Inc., 446 Highway 35, Eatontown, NJ 07724, (800) 546-1541, (732) 389-3900. Provides database management for fax and E-mail broadcast lists.

Also see Fax Transmission Services in the Yellow Pages.

Newsletters

Sarah Stambler's Marketing with Technology News, 370 Central Park West, Ste. 210, New York, NY 10025, (212) 222-1713, www.mwt.com

Software

WebMaster, by WebMaster, Inc., 1601 Civic Center Drive, Ste. 200, Santa Clara, CA 95050, (408) 345-1800, E-mail: info@webmaster .com

Newsletters

Newsletters have a unique advantage over many brochures, flyers, and direct-mail pieces that end up in the trash unread. When done well and sent to the right people, a newsletter that provides information people want to read will often be saved for later reference, and those who receive it may even look forward to getting new issues on a regular basis.

Direct-mail specialist Ivan Levison mails his two-page monthly newsletter, *The Levison Letter: Action Ideas for Better Marketing Communications,* to 1,200 software marketing executives and encourages them to use and forward the information to their associates and clients. Producing and mailing the newsletter costs him only 75 cents per person each month, which is a minimal expense considering that the newsletter generates about one quarter of his new business or about $40,000 to $50,000 a year.

Of course not every business will get that kind of return on their newsletter, but done well a newsletter can enhance your image and build your credibility as an expert.

Pros and Cons

The greatest advantage of newsletters over other media is the way they can help make sure people open, read, save, and act on your material. In addition, a newsletter permits you to keep in touch with your customers, give them good news, and announce special products or services. It is a good way to offer an incentive, alert customers to important trends in the industry, and, above all, give them an opportunity to know you better. A newsletter is also a great way to convey information you might otherwise find difficult—or even impossible—to report to your customers and prospects, such as news about an award you've received or some outstanding facts about your company.

In other words, having a newsletter provides a chance for you to sell some of the intangible aspects of doing business with you. For example, if there is someone at your office with whom your customers or clients talk by phone on a regular basis, you can ask that individual to write a special column and include his or her photo. There is nothing like being able to put a face with a name and voice.

Two areas that can be especially well handled via newsletter are price increases and product or service problems. Your newsletter provides the opportunity to explain the cause of a price increase and use subtle selling techniques to make such an increase more palatable. It is also a forum in which you can make apologies and explain what a customer can do if he or she encounters any problems. Since such notices can be surrounded by short articles that provide valuable information or positive news about your company, the impact of unavoidable negatives can be softened.

Newsletters are also the ideal way to tell customers about special ancillary products or services you offer that are not usually mentioned in the normal course of your other marketing activities. Furthermore, they can be used to offer special promotions, such as baker's-dozen sales or closeouts, or to promote products or services that haven't moved as quickly as you would like.

On the other hand, newsletters have become such popular marketing tools that your clients and customers may already be receiving many of them every week. You may get a lot of newsletters yourself, and perhaps you've noticed that too many of them are nothing more than sales pieces masquerading as a newsletter. One newsletter we get from a professional speaker and marketing coach is little more than a blatant sales puff piece. One article features pictures and descriptions of her new book, another announces her newest workshop, another describes her coaching services, and another is a calendar of her speaking engagements.

Because of the proliferation of such "pseudo" newsletters, marketing newsletters are no longer automatically opened and read with the eager anticipation they once were. Many of them are getting tossed out right along with other unopened sales material. So you'll need to take the time and energy to make your newsletter truly compelling. And that's another drawback. While producing a newsletter doesn't have to be expensive if you create it yourself using desktop publishing, a high-quality well-written newsletter does take time and energy. Even with the streamlined assistance of today's software, you still must select and compose your material, lay it out effectively, print it, and get it out.

Best Bets: Newsletters work best when you are selling a service that has many complexities or frequent developments like investing or skin care. They are equally effective in any field where your clients and customers simply want or need to know a lot more about whatever you're offering, like the ins and outs of pet care or sales and marketing tips.

Tips for Getting Business from Newsletters

The fundamental purpose of sending out a newsletter is for it to be read, so it's imperative that your newsletter be more than another piece of junk mail. Here are some tips on how to produce a newsletter that will walk the line between compelling content and sales generator.

Define the purpose of your newsletter. To be effective, your newsletter should have an editorial purpose other than to promote yourself. So create a mission statement for your newsletter before you begin. This mission can then guide your decisions about the tone, style, and look of your newsletter.

Paul and Laura Paquet of Ontario, Canada, use their newsletter, *Cornerstone,* as a marketing tool for their communications company, Cornerstone Creative Communications. The purpose is to demonstrate their value and expertise by providing existing and potential clients with high-quality, practical information they can use. The eight-page newsletter is chock-full of valuable tips, reserving only the back page for a tasteful promotion of their services.

Focus on truly valuable information. Limit your first efforts to the number of pages you can fill with practical, useful information that will be of high interest to your existing and prospective clients or customers. Tuck self-promotional items (like a picture of you receiving an award or an announcement of your new discount coupon) into a corner here or there or embed your promotional message indirectly into your informational content. You might use an example from work you've done to illustrate a particular point or include a list of the top-ten problems your clients face with a sentence summarizing how to solve them.

Almost any information of value to your customers and clients can be grist for your newsletter's mill: anecdotes, recipes, industry news, organizational hints, jokes, cartoons, vacation-spot information, and information specific to your business, including warnings about unscrupulous or cut-rate competitors (though with no specific names mentioned). While life skills speaker and trainer Nancy Birnbaum-Gerber of Norcross, Georgia, uses her newsletter to promote her upcoming workshops and seminars, announcements of her programs are embedded in the featured topics like "Setting and Reaching Your Goals," "Managing Holiday Stress," client stories, and reader survey updates.

Information Researcher Pam Geyer of Bellaire, Texas, operates MED-cet-er-a, providing customized research reports on the very latest information available on any medical condition. Her newsletter features short features on topics like "Halogen Lamps and Skin Cancer," "Soft Drinks and Kidney Stones," "Tight Bras and Breast Cancer," and "Arthritis and Chili Peppers."

One way to find compelling information is to read the trade journals in your industry for interesting tidbits you can pass along to your clients. You may also include legislative activity or industry controversies that affect your readers, accompanied by appropriate comments from your perspective. Or contact the Consumer Information Center in Pueblo, Colorado (see **Resources: Newsletters**), for a free catalog that lists many free or low-cost brochures or handouts of public-domain materials that are not copyrighted which you are free to retype, photograph, or send out as a premium.

Select a meaningful name. Your newsletter should have a name distinctive from but recognizable as part of your business. It might be some sort of play on your company name or business, such as Maxwell Paper's *MaxFacts* or information researcher Seena Sharp's *Sharp Information.* Try to incorporate your company's name into the newsletter name, as telecommuting consultant Gil Gordon has done with his newsletter, *Telecommuting Review: The Gordon Report.* The name of Nancy Birnbaum-Gerber's company is SteppingStones. So she calls her newsletter *The Next Step! A SteppingStones Publication.*

Create an effective nameplate. Often mistakenly referred to as a masthead, the nameplate or flag for your newsletter consists of your publication name, graphic identity, and other important publishing information including the date and issue number. Its role is to grab the reader's attention and create an identity for the newsletter. It should be distinctive yet compatible with your overall business image. The goal is to make your newsletter immediately recognizable to those who receive it. Notice in the color insert how the nameplate and design concept of Nancy Birnbaum-Gerber's *The Next Step!* ties into the overall image she has created for SteppingStones.

In addition to tying in to your company name and image, Roger C. Parker, author of *Newsletter from the Desktop,* recommends that your nameplate should be brief, create contrast, and, most important, provide a reason to read the newsletter. He recommends against boxing in your nameplate with a border. Unless you are a top-flight designer, you might want to hire someone to design your nameplate, or use a software package, such as *Bannermania* by Broderbund or *Microsoft Publisher,* to help you design one of your own.

Have a design concept. You also need one overall consistent look for the newsletter itself with recognizable recurring elements, including a format and layout that are both readable and distinctive. The pages should be divided into two or three columns for easy reading. Most desktop publishing packages have newsletter templates to help you select a layout. Pick one that is consistent with your business image (see samples on the next page). For additional ideas on design, refer to **Appendix 1: Creating and Writing Materials that Sell** at www.paulandsarah.com

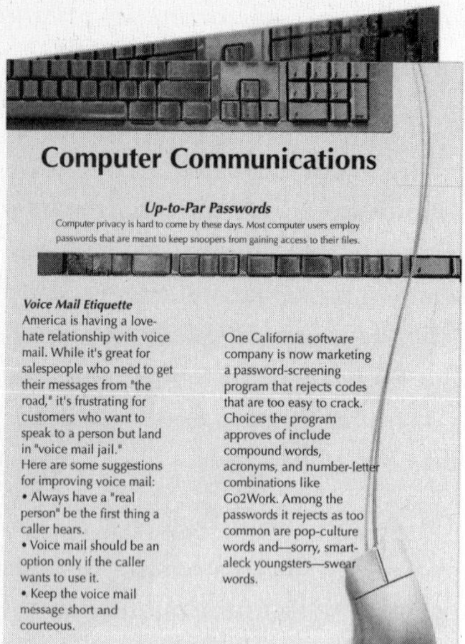

Computer Communications

Up-to-Par Passwords

Computer privacy is hard to come by these days. Most computer users employ passwords that are meant to keep snoopers from gaining access to their files.

Voice Mail Etiquette

America is having a love-hate relationship with voice mail. While it's great for salespeople who need to get their messages from "the road," it's frustrating for customers who want to speak to a person but land in "voice mail jail."

Here are some suggestions for improving voice mail:

• Always have a "real person" be the first thing a caller hears.

• Voice mail should be an option only if the caller wants to use it.

• Keep the voice mail message short and courteous.

One California software company is now marketing a password-screening program that rejects codes that are too easy to crack. Choices the program approves of include compound words, acronyms, and number-letter combinations like Go2Work. Among the passwords it rejects as too common are pop-culture words and—sorry, smart-aleck youngsters—swear words.

Education News

Our Children's Mental Health

Creating a Positive Enviroment

To many of us, the term mental illness carries a stigma. It's something the "other family" deals with. Yet the numbers speak otherwise. It has been found that 22% of the public have some form of mental illness, 13% suffer from anxiety or obsessive/compulsive disorder, and 9% suffer from depression. But of these, less than 5% seek any kind of treatment from a professional. As for treatment, it has been shown to be effective "when taken accordingly." People show measurable improvement by just the eighth session, and 75% show significant improvement by their 26th session. Unfortunately, the average length of

Enterprise News

the Journal of Pre-press, Image Editing and Separations

Today's successful pre-press operations are the ones who display a high resiliency.

This silent revolution may be the hardest for the baby boomer workers of our time. It's harder for them to see the rules changing and accept the new demands as valid. They've invested most of their time into a single career revolving around the old rules of the game. Newer workers are familiar with an unsteady work environment and are not yet set in their ways or dedicated to any one company or profession.

Career Consultant Nancy Woodhull suggests that workers at all levels exchange the image of the proverbial corporate ladder with its orderly rungs, for a sailing ship metaphor. When steering your career, consider yourself as the captain of a ship navigating unexplored waters, and just try to stay on course.

le career revolving around the old rules of the game. Newer workers are familiar with an unsteady work environment and are not yet set in their ways or dedicated to any one com

This silent revolution may be the hardest for the baby boomer workers of our time. It's harder for them to see the rules changing and accept the new demands as valid. They've invested most of their time into a single career revolving around the old rules of the game. Newer workers are familiar with an unsteady work environment and are not yet set in their ways or dedicated to any one company or profession.

Career Consultant Nancy Woodhull suggests that workers at all levels exchange the image of the proverbial corporate ladder with its orderly rungs, for a sailing ship metaphor. When steering your career, consider yourself as the captain of a ship navigating unexplored waters, and just try to stay on course.

le career revolving around the old rules of the game. Newer workers are familiar with an unsteady work environment and are not yet set in their ways or dedicated to any one company o

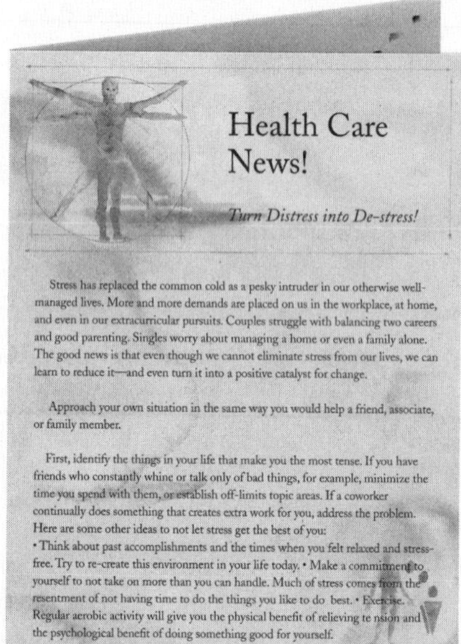

Health Care News!

Turn Distress into De-stress!

Stress has replaced the common cold as a pesky intruder in our otherwise well-managed lives. More and more demands are placed on us in the workplace, at home, and even in our extracurricular pursuits. Couples struggle with balancing two careers and good parenting. Singles worry about managing a home or even a family alone. The good news is that even though we cannot eliminate stress from our lives, we can learn to reduce it—and even turn it into a positive catalyst for change.

Approach your own situation in the same way you would help a friend, associate, or family member.

First, identify the things in your life that make you the most tense. If you have friends who constantly whine or talk only of bad things, for example, minimize the time you spend with them, or establish off-limits topic areas. If a coworker continually does something that creates extra work for you, address the problem. Here are some other ideas to not let stress get the best of you:

• Think about past accomplishments and the times when you felt relaxed and stress-free. Try to re-create this environment in your life today. • Make a commitment to yourself to not take on more than you can handle. Much of stress comes from the resentment of not having time to do the things you like to do best. • Exercise. Regular aerobic activity will give you the physical benefit of relieving te nsion and the psychological benefit of doing something good for yourself.

The flag and overall design concept of your newsletter should be distinctive yet coordinated with your overall company image like these samples on Paper Direct preprinted papers.

Keep the size manageable. Your newsletter may be any size from 5 by 8 (folded and trimmed from 8½ by 11) to 18 by 24 inches (tabloid size). However, the most well-read newsletters tend to use standard sizes such as 8½ by 11.

We suggest that you begin small until you discover how much time and energy you can afford to invest. You might start with a two-page newsletter, on the front and back of one sheet, or if you have enough material, you can begin with a four-page version. An 11-by-17-inch sheet folded in half provides four 8½-by-11-inch pages. If you plan your newsletter to be a self-mailer, you will need to leave a section on the back page for return address, mailing label, and postage information.

If you want to expand, you can do so in increments of two pages. When using more than one sheet of paper, do not staple or paper-clip the pages together at the corner; simply insert an additional single page, or, if you use multiple 11-by-17-inch sheets folded in half, have them saddle-stitched (stapled) together along the fold.

Use color if possible. If you can only afford to print one color, consider using an ink color other than black on a paper stock other than white. Consider matching the colors of your newsletter with those on your letterhead. Or for full four-color effect use preprinted newsletter papers from a company like Paper Direct. (See sample newsletters on the adjacent page.)

Add photos and graphics. In order to keep the newsletter easy to read and interesting, use line art, photos, or cartoons. You can find a wealth of illustrations and graphics available on software or CD-ROMs like *Click Art* by Broderbund, which includes 125,000 such images, and *Popular Photography* by the Learning Company. There are also companies that specialize in stocking photographs of almost any subject, which you can rent. (See **Resources:** Newsletters.)

Keep costs down. To save time, some people are broadcast-faxing their newsletters. Others are sending their newsletters via E-mail or posting them on their Web page or on hospitable newsgroups or forum libraries. Some use a newsletter publishing service that produces the newsletter and customizes some portion like the front page feature for each specific client (see **Resources**).

Permitting your suppliers to advertise can help cover the costs of producing your newsletter. If you decide to do this, be sure that all your suppliers have an equal opportunity and that they advertise without pressure, and don't overload the newsletter with advertising. The point is to promote your company, not your suppliers. Also, be sure you retain final say on the acceptability of ads. You don't want advertising that detracts from the readability of the newsletter or negates the message you're trying to convey. Finally, don't get caught up in attempting to sell a lot of ads, or you will cut into time you need for providing your product or service.

Resources: Newsletters

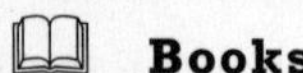

Books

How to Create High-Impact Newsletters. Jane K. Cleland. Career Track, 3085 Center Green Drive, Boulder, CO 80301, (800) 334-1081.

How to Do Leaflets, Newsletters and Newspapers. Nancy Brigham. Boston: PEP Publications, 1997.

Marketing with Newsletters. Elaine Floyd. Newsletter Resources, 6614 Pernod Ave., St. Louis, MO 63139, (800) 264-6305 or (314) 647-6788, 1997.

The Newsletter Book. Roger Parker. Paper Direct, 100 Plaza Drive, Secaucus, NJ 07094, (800) A-PAPERS or (800) 272-7377, www.paperdirect.com

One-Minute Designer. Roger Parker. New York: Henry Holt, 1997.

Publishing Newsletters. Howard Penn Hudson. Rhinebeck, New York: H & M Publishers, 1998, (800) 572-3451.

Starting or Running a Successful Newsletter or Magazine. Cheryl Woodard. Berkeley, Calif.: Nolo Press, 1996.

Winning in Newsletters. Hal D. Steward. Newsletter Clearinghouse, Box 311, Rhinebeck, NY 12572, (800) 572-3451, 1989.

Newsletters on Newsletters

Communications Briefings, 1101 King Street, Ste. 110, Alexandria, VA 22314, (703) 548-3800.

The Newsletter on Newsletters, Newsletter Clearinghouse, Box 311, Rhinebeck, NY 12572, (800) 572-3451.

☞ Directories

Hudson's Subscription Newsletter Directory, Newsletter Clearinghouse, Box 311, Rhinebeck, NY 12572, (800) 572-3451.

Newsletter Directory, Gale Research, Inc., 645 Griswold Street, 835 Penobscot Bldg., Detroit, MI 48226, (313) 877-4253, www.gale.com (available in libraries).

Oxbridge Directory of Newsletters: The Most Comprehensive Guide to U.S. and Canadian Newsletters, 150 Fifth Avenue, New York, NY 10011, (800) 955-0231 (annual, available in libraries).

Associations

Editorial Freelancers' Association, 71 West 23d Street, Ste. 1504, New York, NY 10010, (212) 929-5400. Provides a job bank through which you can locate copywriters.

National Graphic Artists Guild, 90 John Street, Ste. 403, New York, NY 10038, (212) 791-0330.

Newsletter Publishers Association, 1501 Wilson Boulevard, Ste. 509, Arlington, VA 22209, (800) 356-9302.

Seminars

CareerTrack, 3085 Center Green Drive, Boulder, CO, (800) 334-6780, www.careertrack.com

Newsletter Clearinghouse, Box 311, Rhinebeck, NY 12572, (800) 572-3451.

Marketing with Newsletters, Elaine Floyd, Newsletter Resources, 6614 Pernod Ave., St. Louis, MO 63139, (800) 264-6305 or (314) 647-6788.

The Newsletter Factory, 1830 Water Place, Ste. 120, Atlanta, GA, 30339, (770) 955-1600, www.nlf.com

Pattison Workshops, 244 N Crestline Cr., Saint George, UT 84790.

Services

CopySource Quarterly, by Bureau of Business Practices, Simon and Schuster, 24 Rope Ferry Road, Waterford CT 06386, (800) 243-0876 x6, www.bbpnews.com. Quarterly subscription service providing feature articles on business-related topics on disk.

Ideas Unlimited for Editors, c/o Newsletter Services, Inc., 9700 Philadelphia Ct., Lanham-Seabrook, MD 20706, (800) 345-2611, (301) 731-5200. Provides filler articles and clip art.

PhotoSource International, Pine Lake Farm, 1910 35th Road, Osceola, WI 54020, (715) 248-3800, E-mail: info@photosource.com, Web: www. photosource.com. Sells stock photos.

Graphics Software

Adobe Illustrator, Adobe Systems, 345 Park Avenue, San Jose, CA 95110, 800-42-adobe, www.adobe.com

Adobe PageMaker, Adobe Systems, 345 Park Avenue, San Jose, CA 95110, 800-42-adobe, www.adobe.com

CorelDraw, Corel Corporation, 1600 Carling Avenue, Ottawa, Ontario K1Z8R7, (800) 772-6735, www.corel.com

Master Publisher Suite, by IMSI, 1895 Francisco Blvd., E., San Rafael, CA 94901, (415) 454-7101, www.imsisoft.com

Microsoft Publisher, Microsoft Corp., One Microsoft Way, Redmond, WA 98052-6399, 800-426-9400, www.microsoft.com/publisher/

OmniPage Pro, by Caere Corporation, 100 Cooper Court, Los Gatos, CA 95032, (800) 535-7226, www.caere.com

Clip Art and Photos

Adobe Illustrator, Adobe Systems, 345 Park Avenue, San Jose, CA 95110, 800-42-adobe, www.adobe.com

Art Explosion 125,000, by Nova Development, includes 125,000 pieces of clip art on CD-ROM. Nova Development Corp., 23801 Calabasas Road, Calabasas, CA 91302, (800) 395-6682, www. novadevcorp.com

ClickArt, by Broderbund, has 125,000 images, photos, fonts, etc. Broderbund, P.O. Box 6121, Novato, CA 94948, (800) 521-6263, www.broderbund.com

PC Paintbrush Photo Library, by Learning Company, with over 2,500 royalty-free photos from leading photographers, for Windows or Mac. Learning Company, One Athenaeum Street, Cambridge, MA 02142, (800) 227-5609, www.learningco.com

Popular Photography, by Learning Company, is a two-volume collection of royalty-free photographs. Learning Company, One Athenaeum Street, Cambridge, MA 02142, (800) 227-5609, www.learningco. com

Papers

Paper Direct, 100 Plaza Drive, Secaucus, NJ 07094, (800) A-PAPERS or (800) 272-7377, www.paperdirect.com. They have preprinted four-color papers in two newsletter formats, 11 by 17 and 8½ by 11.

Copyright-Free Information

Consumer Information Center lists hundreds of sources of free non-copyrighted material. Contact them at Consumer Information Center, Pueblo, CO 81002, (719) 948-4000, www.pueblo.gsa.gov

On-Line Resources

www.jumbo.com—shareware art programs you can download.

comp.text.desktop—a desktop publishing newsgroup.

Videos

Design Eye-Catching Brochures, Newsletters, Ads, Reports. Jane K. Cleland. CareerTrack, 3085 Center Green Drive, Boulder, CO 80301, (800) 334-1018, www.careertrack.com

How to Create Well-Designed and Highly Informative Newsletters. Jane K. Cleland. CareerTrack, 3085 Center Green Drive, Boulder, CO 80301, (800) 334-1018, www.careertrack.com

Phone and Hold-Button Messages

How many times a day when you call someone are you greeted with a voice-mail or answering-machine message? How often do you end up being put on hold while waiting to talk with someone you're calling? Jeff McNeil of On-Hold Marketing Systems claims that the average executive spends more than sixty hours a year on hold! That's 3,600 minutes, and each of those minutes could be an opportunity for you to create greater interest in what you offer.

In other words, why not use your voice mail or on-hold message as a marketing tool. Television and radio commercials these days are sometimes as short as fifteen seconds, so why not think of these mini-messages as promotional opportunities for informing or updating people about new services, products you're announcing, special sales, or other programs you're running. But, of course, if you don't want to turn your caller off, these messages must be done well.

Pros and Cons: Phone and Hold-Button Marketing Messages

People who call you are already interested in talking to you about something, so why not use the few moments when you have their attention to provide information you think they would be interested in knowing about? Within that question lie both the advantage and the disadvantage of using your phone and hold-button messages as a marketing tool. If you can provide a message that, in fact, is something the people calling will want to hear, you come out ahead; but, if you miss the mark, you run the risk of irritating your callers.

Best Bets: While phone and hold messages can work well with consumers or business callers, they work best when those who call you have fairly common reasons for calling. In other words, the better niched your business is, the easier it will be to use these messages effectively. And conversely, the more diverse your offerings are, the more challenging it will be to neither irritate nor confuse your callers. There is nothing worse than calling someone to give her a referral or book her for a radio show and having to wait through a long message about her upcoming workshop schedule.

Tips for Getting Business from Phone and Hold-Button Messages

Make your message of interest to your target caller. Before putting a marketing message on your voice mail or hold button, spend a week or two tracking who is calling you and why. Then, design your message to be of interest to the target callers you want to encourage to leave a message or stay on hold. Consider that your callers could be existing, past, or potential clients, referral sources, or other marketing opportunities like the media or someone wanting you to speak or do a seminar for their organization. One added advantage of carefully targeting your messages is that it may also help screen out wrong numbers and people to whom you clearly do not want to talk.

When Ellen Parlapiano was writing primarily for magazines addressing the toy company industry, her own children and their friends were instrumental in helping her test and evaluate the play value of the toys she was reviewing. So, she decided to flaunt the fact that she had kids by featuring their voices on her voice mail-message, which went something like this:

"Hi! You've reached Ellen Parlapiano Creative Services and her staff of toy testers. (At this point each child chimed in with his or her name). We can't come to the phone right now, but please leave a message and we'll get back to you as soon as we can. Thanks for calling (here her children chimed in their good-byes)."

For your voice-mail message, you might consider incorporating your **Attention Grabber** (page 182), your **File-Opening Sound Byte** (pages 186–87), a slogan, or tag line. For your on-hold message, you might create an audiotape version of your newsletter, a list of your top-ten tips, fascinating facts, a quiz, survey results, or an audio version of segments from your **White Paper** (page 78), your mission statement, or the titles of any books or booklets you've written, new catalog items, or even a particularly exciting testimonial. Obviously if you have created an audiotape product of interest to your callers (page 574), you should consider using that.

Keep it short and to the point. This applies especially to your opening voice-mail greeting. Listening to a lengthy promotional pitch of any kind can be irritating to someone who is calling to quickly leave a message, place an order, or get specific information. If you want to leave longer or more specific messages like directions to your locale, your workshop schedule, announcement of new products, etc., consider providing a menu.

Even on-hold messages should be composed of a series of pithy, to-the-point segments that convey a key point every thirty seconds. People will most likely not have time to listen to long, rambling descriptions or concepts even if they are interesting.

Consider providing a menu. If you have people calling regularly for a variety of reasons or callers will be interested in different kinds of specific information, you should consider having a voice-mail system that enables you to offer a menu as in:

"If you are calling for directions to our workshops, press 1."

"If you would like information about our new products, press 2."

"If you have questions regarding ______, press 3."

"If you would like to leave a message, please press 4."

Again, however, keep your menu selections short, and always start with the most important reason you want people to be calling. For example, if you are taking orders by phone or requests for service calls, these should always be a caller's first selection, so that they don't get impatient and hang up.

Produce a high-quality professional-sounding message. In selecting your voice-mail system or answering machine, pay particular attention to how the recorded message sounds and the options for length and flexibility of your messages. Ideally you would select a system that allows for a full menu of high-quality recorded messages and that also offers flexibility in terms of the length and nature of what you can record. There is a wide variety of services as well as voice-mail or answering-machine options like the Bogen *Friday* and *Wildfire,* as well as voice-mail options available from your local telephone company.

There are also full-service message and music-on-hold companies like Hallmark Audio and On-Hold Marketing (see **Resources**) that will produce the script, find the music, and provide professional talent who will read your on-hold messages. Such programs cost from a little over $2 a day on up. You need a phone with music-on-hold capability; they provide the digital playback equipment and the finished recording.

Alternatively you can produce your own using a local recording studio, a copywriter, and a voice-over professional. Or, if your call volume doesn't justify this kind of cost, as many small and one-person businesses would not, doing your own messages will usually be quite acceptable. Often, in fact, as long as your equipment has proper sound quality, doing your own messages is preferable for any highly personalized service business.

For under $70, you can purchase an on-hold device like Music-on-Hold by DesignTech that allows you to entertain or inform your caller with your own recorded message. It comes with music options as well.

Remember, if you use anyone else's copyrighted music or information on your message you must get permission and pay any required licensing fees. It's the law.

Fines for ignoring the copyright law are considerable and the music industry has full-time listeners whose only job is to track down unauthorized use of copyrighted music, so beware. This is one reason many people prefer to use a full-service company or special equipment that provides prerecorded royalty-free music as part of the price. Alternatively you can use a product like On-Hold Plus which provides royalty-free broadcast-quality music and professionally recorded hold messages on CDs for small and home offices for as little as $25 up to $300 for customized recordings. (See **Resources**, where you will also find information on how to gain rights to use music of your own choice.)

We, Paul and Sarah, decided to hire someone to write and produce our own theme music, which we own the rights to. There are many home-based songwriters and music-production companies that will provide such services for you.

Resources:

Message-on-Hold Services

Hallmark Audio, 1014 Westlake Boulevard #14-145, Westlake Village, CA 91361, (800) 6 AUDIO or (818) 880-2980.

Marketing-on-Hold, 13023 Polvera Avenue, San Diego, CA 92128, (800) 466-4653, htpp://pages.prodigy.com/voice-pro

On-Hold Plus, 5820 Oberlin Drive, Ste. 203, San Diego, CA 92126, (619) 586-0800, (800) 693-7975.

Musical Rights Licensing Services

ASCAP (American Society of Composers and Publishers), One Lincoln Plaza, New York, NY 10023, (212) 595-3050; 7920 Sunset Boulevard, 3d Floor, Los Angeles, CA 90046, (213) 883-1000.

BMI (Broadcast Music Incorporated), 320 W. 57th Street, New York, NY 10019, (212) 586-2000; 8730 Sunset Boulevard, 3d Floor, Los Angeles, CA 90069, (310) 659-9109.

SESAC, 55 Music Square East, Nashville, TN 37203, (615) 320-0055.

Equipment

Music-on-Hold, by Design Tech, is a manual on-hold device that with a touch of the button allows you to put callers on hold where they will hear music or your own prerecorded message from your radio, cassette, CD, or tape player. Models are available for one- and two-line phones through Damark at (800) 827-6767.

Postcards

Postcards are a highly versatile marketing tool. You can use them to say thanks, extend a holiday greeting, serve as a reminder card, announce a special offer, introduce a new product or service, invite folks to an open house or to visit your trade show booth, or just to say hello. You can send them one-by-one as the occasion arises or tuck them in with a handwritten note along with invoices, clippings, a news release, your brochure or flyer. You can turn them into keeper cards offering a tip-of-the-month or use them to conduct a survey. You can even create an entire direct-mail campaign around them as copywriter Gregg M. Siegel has done. (See illustration on page 498.)

Deborah Durham used a clever postcard to announce the relocation of her company to the West Coast. It features a picture of her heading toward the ocean in a convertible talking on a cell phone. The text announces the new location of her headquarters and reminds people that Deborah Durham & Company will continue "to offer the best spokesperson service no matter where you are. From sunrise to sunset, we're just a fax, FedEx, flight, or phone call away!"

The Expert Connection, an on-line service that "hooks you up with business and professionals who need answers," is a Web-based company. They use an oversized two-color postcard with various color screens to invite professionals to visit their Web site. It features a large fish with glasses swimming toward a computer mouse that's dangling like a fishing pole. The headline reads "How many clients do you have on-line?"

The Envision Group launched a holiday postcard campaign, unveiling their new graphic identity. Each card describes a different Envision Group service illustrated by a graphic icon that could be cut out and used as a holiday decoration.

When CAD-CAM designer Roger Lazier of Arlington, Texas, needed to invite a major client to an on-site demonstration, he knew it was a big opportunity, but he had two competitors scheduled before him. He needed an announcement that would get the design engineers' attention and make him stand out from the others. He turned to his sister Linda Lazier, of Indianapolis, who creates corporate marketing campaigns. She suggested solving the problem by sending postcards created to look like a page from a desk calendar appointment book with a handwritten memo from Lazier reminding the engineers of the time, date, and place of his demonstration along with key benefits of his program. The cards cost only $18 to print but produced a 10 percent return and kept him busy with prospective buyers.

Baderstcher Communications was a small advertising agency up against bigger more established competitors. All the other agencies sent out expensive traditional marketing materials. But Baderstcher decided to hire a copywriter to take an entirely different approach. They arranged for a photographer to shoot a large still-life photo, cut it into fourths, and use each portion as a series of four 4-by-6 postcards. The first three cards arrived unidentified three days apart, carrying three different puzzling questions. The last card identified the agency as one that could provide clients with the big picture, along with an offer to tape, glue, and staple the cards together and return them as a limited-edition poster suitable for framing.

Barbara Levy uses postcards designed to match her brochure. Whenever anyone asks her to send them something, she sends the brochure and then follows up shortly thereafter by sending a postcard reminder. We, Paul and Sarah, like to include a postcard with a handwritten note with whatever printed material we're sending out. We attach a personal note on a postcard to our promotional packages. We pop one in whatever material someone has requested or with an order we're mailing out. This saves us the time and money of writing a formal cover letter, but more important, it provides a way to build the kind of personal relationship we like to have with clients, customers, and associates. Postcards are such an important part of our marketing materials that we have blank four-color cards printed in bulk to match our letterhead, stationery, and business cards.

Pros and Cons of Using Postcards

Using postcards has many advantages. Everyone likes getting them. You can see the entire message at a glance and since no one has to open them up, they almost always get looked at and are less likely to be thrown away. In fact, while many people won't open junk mail, most people will read junk postcards. They're easy to post on a bulletin board, carry in one's pocket or purse, or tuck away somewhere for future reference. You can print them out right from your computer and pop them in the mail, and obviously they less cost than a full-scale mailing piece.

Space is their only limitation. While you can use oversized postcards, even then you will have to fit your message into the equivalent of a display ad. And keep in mind that if you do use larger than standard cards, the price of postage will increase.

Best Bets: Postcards can be effective with businesses or consumers. They are especially effective, however, when the person who will buy what you have to offer is the one who opens the mail.

Tips for Getting Business from Postcards.

For the most part, creating a good postcard will involve following the same principles as creating a good print ad or direct-mail piece (page 497). You can most certainly create your own cards using graphic, clip art, illustrator, and draw programs like those listed in the Resources that follow. You can use preperforated postcard stock available from companies like Paper Direct and Avery Dennison to print out your creations on a laser or ink-jet printer. To make your cards all the more effective, we suggest using color, cartoons, graphics, or even photos, which you can scan into your computer and print out.

For a special mailing, you might even want to use actual four-color postcards like those you get at tourist attractions with your message printed or handwritten on the back alongside the address. For best results, hand-address your cards, but neatly printed address labels sent to specific individuals can be effective too.

Resources: Postcards

Software, Clip Art, Photos, and Cartoons

Adobe Illustrator, Adobe Systems, 345 Park Avenue, San Jose, CA 95110, (800) 42-adobe, www.adobe.com

Art Explosion 125,000, by Nova Development, includes 125,000 pieces of clip art on CD-ROM, Nova Development Corp., 23801 Calabasas Road, Calabasas, CA 91302, (800) 395-6682, www.novadevcorp.com

ClickArt, by Broderbund, 125,000 images, photos, fonts, etc., Broderbund, P.O. Box 6121, Novato, CA 94948, (800) 521-6263, www.broderbund.com

CorelDraw, Corel Corporation, 1600 Carling Avenue, Ottawa, Ontario K1Z8R7, (800) 772-6735, www.corel.com

Master Publisher Suite, by IMSI, 1895 Francisco Blvd., E., San Rafael, CA 94901, (415) 454-7101, www.imsisoft.com

Microsoft Publisher, Microsoft Corp., One Microsoft Way, Redmond, WA 98052-6399, (800) 426-9400, www.microsoft.com/publisher/

OmniPage Pro, by Caere Corporation, 100 Cooper Court, Los Gatos, CA 95032, (800) 535-7226, www.caere.com

PC Paintbrush Photo Library, by the Learning Company, with over 2,500 royalty-free photos from leading photographers, for Windows or Mac, One Athenaeum St., Cambridge, MA 02142, (800) 227-5609, www.learningco.com

Popular Photography, by the Learning Company, offers a two-volume collection of royalty-free photos, One Athenaeum St., Cambridge, MA 02142, (800) 227-5609, www.learningco.com

Preperforated Sheets of Postcards for Your Printer

Avery Dennison
P.O. Box 5244
Diamond Bar, CA 91765
(909) 869-7711

Paper Direct
100 Plaza Drive
Secaucus, NJ 07094
(800) A-PAPERS, (800) 272-7377
www.paperdirect.com

Product Packaging and Point-of-Sale Displays

Often, the labels, displays, and packaging on your product serve as your ultimate sales tool. Whether in a catalog or on the retail shelf, if the package you're offering doesn't grab attention in a pleasing way, your product will be overlooked in favor of others nearby that do. Once buyers pick up your package, your packaging needs to answer any questions they have in making a decision to buy. In fact, experts say that 80 percent of a decision whether to buy or not is made at the point of purchase. So think of your packaging and point-of-sale displays as part of your sales and marketing team.

Suppose, for example, that you have been growing, drying, and supplying herbs and flowers to local craft-supply stores but now you want to create your own potpourris, wreaths, or floral sprays for sale in antique and country-craft stores. You need to take a new look at your current business image and decide whether it is appropriate for your product packaging. If it is, much of your task is already complete. You can use your company name as your product name within your local market if your state regulations permit.

Then you must decide how you will package your products. Will you put your potpourris in cellophane bags, plastic bags, or boxes of some sort? You can approach manufacturers of various boxes and bags to see which stock sizes exist and which size best suits your purposes for both packaging and shipping. The choice of container will dictate the form of closure you will need, such as yarn or ribbon for bags or tape or small stickers for boxes. You will also need to design a simple, pressure-sensitive label with your company name as its framework accompanied by the product name, in this case a specific blend or fragrance. For sprays, wreaths, and the like, you may want a tag with your logo or company name on it.

In the event your company name is not appropriate for your products, you will need to create an entirely new graphic identity for them, following through the same steps discussed previously. For a crafts type of business, the labels and tags for initial samples can be hand lettered. However, you will need to consider printing for most products and higher volumes. Be sure to investigate and register (as previously discussed in **chapter 6**) any new product name, company name, brand, or graphic identity to protect yourself and your rights.

As you can see there are many packaging issues to address, and each one of them can have an impact on how easy or difficult it will be to get business.

Tips for Getting Business from Your Packaging

Packaging and point-of-sale materials are a very specialized business. If you are involved in a product-based business and your products are geared to the general public, it is wise to consult professionals about the design and preparation of these materials. Do not leave this to an amateur, even if the amateur is you. Here are some issues to keep in mind.

Select a good supplier to produce your package. To produce a package that sells, first you need to find a good supplier. If you don't know anyone with a strong recommendation, begin your search with the Yellow Pages. Package designers or packaging specialists often can be found under their own heading. If none of those listed do what you need, try talking to some printing firms, who should be able to guide you to some other sources. Or try getting referrals from commercial artists to a package design specialist.

Don't necessarily choose the first supplier you talk to. Ask to see samples of what the suppliers have done, especially if they have worked in your industry. Discuss your ideas and the approach you want to take. Be ready to explain all the tools you plan to use to get your product seen or known by the public including public relations, advertising, or any other selling activity. Be sure to state your package budget clearly and explain that you want a top-notch package within those parameters.

To help the suppliers understand what you need, you can show them some samples of what your competition is using, explaining what you like and dislike about each package. Give them all the important information about your product, including the benefits you want to highlight or explain on the package. Identify your main themes from the general data you need to convey on your package. If you are producing something that people will decide on in the typical five seconds they give an item at the supermarket, limit the points you make to two or three.

Don't settle for a single package idea—request that your supplier come up with several alternative ideas in rough form, and examine each idea in turn without making quick judgments. If you like aspects of more than one concept, work with the designers to see whether there is some way to combine the good aspects of each into a single package. Don't accept a design that looks cluttered. Coming up with a perfect package is a trial-and-error process.

Once you have a couple of designs that work for you, have some prototypes or mock-ups made to test with various distributors or prospective customers. Take them into the field and experiment. If you sell through stores, ask permission from the manager to set up a display with the various designs, and ask passing customers to complete a short questionnaire about the designs they see. This is as much to the benefit of the distributor and retailer as it is to you, as it enables you to provide your outlets with merchandise packaging that sell the product.

As soon as your package is finished, have it photographed in both black-and-white and color. These package shots are helpful when sending press information or when applying for inclusion in a catalog.

Display and point-of-sale materials are an extension of your packaging and are geared primarily toward product sales. Selection of display materials, whether freestanding or shelf oriented, requires a complex analysis of your distribution network.

Work closely with your packager. Here are several points to keep in mind when working with package designers:

1. ***Packaging can make the difference between a sale and a pass-it-by.*** Wherever you go, packaging competes for your attention. Most purchase decisions are influenced in some way by packaging.

2. ***Big budget isn't essential.*** What is essential is knowledge of both your potential customer and the end user. Expensive packages don't necessarily draw; eye-catching, useful, and appropriate packaging does.

3. ***Packaging provides a golden sales opportunity.*** A good package captivates and educates the buyer. It is one of the best advertising methods available to the manufacturer. When the product inside is more or less indistinguishable from competing products, what will be remembered is the way it was presented.

4. ***Packaging can make or break repeat business as well.*** A purchasing agent doesn't really care how rolls of facsimile paper are packaged inside the box as long as they are properly protected; however, the machine operator who breaks a fingernail or has to cut away several feet of paper to free a glued edge can and will complain long and loudly.

5. ***The packaging on one of your products can affect the purchase of others.*** The more your packaging reinforces your company image, the more likely a purchaser will be to associate one product with another, making for additional selling opportunities.

6. ***Often your label or packaging could bring repeat business*** if you make sure to include your address and phone number on each and every one of them. People often overlook this simple marketing opportunity. When a happy customer decides to reorder, the retail outlet or catalog they originally ordered from may no longer carry your product. So make sure the customer can reach you.

Be sure to include your name, address, phone number, and E-Mail or Web address on both your packaging and your product.

Make packaging and displays practical for the point of sale. Obviously if you will be selling your product through a catalog or by mail, the package itself will be less important than how you picture and de-

Packaging a Service Business

Packaging isn't limited to product-oriented businesses. Movies are commonly referred to as being *packaged,* a term used for the process of pulling together the idea, the talent, the scriptwriter, and other crew to sell to a studio for production. Financial news speaks frequently of stock deals being packaged, referring to the combination of several services into a single integrated product or service. Services are just as packageable as products.

Although the package you use for a service is not cardboard, it is just as important as the box you use for a product. It consists of the people and service elements involved, and it includes your appearance, telephone presence, dress, and manner, as well as every other aspect of what you offer. If you are a service business, the more professional you and the people who work with your customers are, the better your package. All your identity materials—letterhead, business cards, brochures, catalogs, price lists, and any other materials you present to the public—are also part of your package. These materials include your proposal forms, invoices, and statements.

The major advantage to packaging a service is that it doesn't have to cost as much as packaging a product. But, as with all packaging, producing less than the best you can afford will exact an expensive toll in lost sales, even if you cannot see the true cost of that loss. So, you might ask a current client to permit you to place a small display containing your flyers or brochures at his counter or in his waiting room. Some will be happy to help you out. With others you may pay for the privilege, or you might work out an exchange for some of your services.

If you are a software consultant, for example, you may wish to work out an agreement with several local software stores to provide them with a given number of hours of consulting services in exchange for placing your display or point-of-sale materials in public view in their store. Or, if your business is typesetting or desktop publishing, you might pay a local printer with a great deal of traffic a fee to place a special display of your promotional materials on the counter. A nutritionist might request, trade for, or pay for a display of his or her brochures at the reception desk in a medical or dental clinic.

Michelle B. Katz of *Organize This!,* for example, builds her business placing simple plastic business card stands in local shops like nail and beauty salons. Such stands are available through companies like Paper Direct (800-A-PAPERS) for cards, brochures, or flyers.

To get materials that will do the best job for you, work with a single designer to prepare all display and packaging materials. If the designer you are working with is employed by the packaging production firm, be sure he or she sees all your other promotional materials and clearly understands the image and identity you are promoting for your product or service and for your company as a whole. Once you have created a package, the rest of your promotional materials should reinforce the visual image your package creates.

scribe your product in print or on-line. If you will be selling from a retail outlet of any kind, however, from storefront to trade show booth, the way your packaging is displayed could be the difference between its being passed over or taken home. In addition to considerations of cost, appearance, and reinforcement of company image, keep in mind the following:

1. ***Find out if your outlets utilize display materials.*** Not all distributors or outlets can or will use special displays.

2. ***Display materials must suit the space provided by the outlet.*** Not all outlets have the same size or type of display space. A counter display is worthless if an outlet has no counter.

3. ***Display materials should be easy to erect and use.*** The simpler the setup is, the more likely an outlet will be to use it.

4. ***Display materials should be reusable or easy to dispose of.*** Keep your outlet's convenience in mind when creating materials.

5. ***Display materials should neither compete with nor detract from the packaging of the product itself.*** You want to sell product, not a pretty display.

Resources: Product Packaging and Point of Sale

Newsletter and Magazines

POP & Sign Design, Hoyt Publishing, 7400 Skokie Boulevard, Skokie, IL 60077, (847) 675-7400.

Retail Store Image, 6151 Powers Ferry Road, N.W., Atlanta, GA 30339.

WWD, A Business Newsletter for Specialty Stores, Fairchild Publications, 7 West 34th Street, New York, NY 10017, (212) 630-4200.

Organizations

Point of Purchase Advertising Institute (POPAI)
66 North Van Brunt Street
Englewood, NJ 07631
(201) 894-8899.

Display and Packaging Companies

Art Base Works, One-of-a-Kind
1631 East Wilshire
Santa Ana, CA 92705
(714) 723-6642.
Custom-designed art displays.

Innovative Designs
17401 Nicholas Street Unit K
Huntington Beach, CA 92647
(714) 848-0588.

Paper Direct
100 Plaza Drive
Secaucus, NJ 07094
(800) A-PAPERS, (800) 272-7377
www.paperdirect.com

Ruszel Woodworks
2980 Bayshore Road
Benicia, CA 94510
(707) 745-6979.

Tag-It! Pacific
3820 South Hill Street
Los Angeles, CA 90037
(213) 234-9606.

Sales Letters and Proposals

Sometimes it's important to introduce yourself before an initial personal contact. Other times you need to provide more detail for those you've already met. An introductory sales letter is a simple, yet personal, way to introduce you and your company to a prospective customer or client and request an opportunity to discuss specifics personally. A proposal is an opportunity to follow up on a personal meeting with the specifics of how you can help.

They each differ from advertising or direct mail in that while they are clearly part of your marketing efforts they are much more personal in nature. And the more personal and customized they are, the more likely it is that they will get a positive response when you follow up with a phone call.

K.C. Truby offers a variety of corporate training programs at his dude ranch in Wyoming. Because he's located in a rural area, he relies heavily on sales letters to create visibility and attract clients. Since his training programs address pressing corporate needs, his sales letter raises the problems and outlines the solutions to be found through his seminar. One program, for example, trains in-house staff to quickly identify the problem within their mainframe computer that posed problems for all date-driven functions beginning with the year 2000. At the close of the sales letter, Truby provides a reply form so those interested in knowing more about the training program can identify themselves. He faxes his one-page letters toll free and provides a toll-free number for immediate reply.

While proposals are often part and parcel of turning interest into business, for Michael Cahlin proposals are his sales force. Cahlin specializes in providing public relations services for start-up high-tech companies. He gets all his business by cold calling such companies and asking if they're satisfied with their current public relations firm. He finds that most are not, so he offers to prepare a proposal showing them what he could do for them. His winning proposals keep him busy with new business.

Pros and Cons: Sales Letters and Proposals

Because sales letters and proposals should by nature be personalized, unlike most other forms of promotion, you can talk directly about your prospect's specific needs. If you have a clear handle on the difference between the features of your product or service and their benefits to the particular buyer (see **chapter 3**), you can arouse the recipient's interest or solidify a decision without the sense that they are "being sold."

Word-processing, database, mailing-list, and contact-management software makes sending personalized sales letters and proposals possible and cost-effective for even the one-person company. Of course, learning to use the software and making it work can be time-consuming for any one-person business, especially the first time, and is a big headache for any technophobe. Fortunately there is a wealth of cost-effective word-processing and mailing services you can turn to to desktop-publish your proposals and get out your mailings if you don't have the time or inclination to do it yourself.

Best Bets: Sales letters and proposals are most effective when selling services or products to businesses. In fact, often writing an effective proposal is a prerequisite to getting certain types of business—like public relations, corporate training, advertising, Web page, landscape, graphic design, and so forth. Sometimes personalized sales letters sent to the right list can also be effective for selling high-end consumer services, too—like interior decorating, custom-made cabinets, or architectural design. This is particularly so when the person you're sending your letter to has been referred by someone else they know personally, or through a group or organization to which they belong.

Tips for Effective Sales Letters and Proposals

Because a sales letter or proposal is intended to be personal, you should approach each one as if it were unique. This does not mean that you cannot create a form letter or proposal template, but this should never be apparent to the reader once you've tailored and tweaked it to address the needs and circumstances of each person or company you're sending it to. Here are several rules for developing and using effective sales letters and proposals:

Always send the letter or proposal to an individual—never a title. If you don't have a name, make a phone call or look the company up online to get the name of the person who should receive your material. There is nothing more offensive than a personal letter addressed to "Occupant" or "Sales Manager."

Whenever possible, start the first paragraph with the word You. Even when the word *You* can't be the first word (as when starting with a question), make sure you use it in the first sentence.

Use the recipient's name or company name at least once in the body of the letter and repeatedly throughout a proposal. The important issue is transferring ownership of the idea of your company to the buyer. The only way to do that is to create in the buyer's mind a link between him and his company and what you do. Paint a mental picture for your prospective client as if he or she were already doing business with your company. However, you must not force it. If you cannot make it read naturally, opt for fewer inclusions. Too many or awkward constructions will make it look more like a form letter.

Don't insult your potential clients and customers. Many of the poorly designed sales letters we see open with supposedly engaging statements that actually discount the reader's intelligence and capability. One we received, for example, started off with "You're attracting the wrong customers and listening to the wrong people." Another read, "Ever wonder why you're doing so poorly?" Few people like to think they are wrong and even fewer like to admit they're doing poorly, even if they are. Such openings allow no way for the respondent to "save face." By responding to the letter, they have to identify themselves in a negative light. Better to focus your appeal on positive, desired outcomes like "Would you like to clone your best customers?" or "Are you wondering how you could take your business to the next level?"

Limit the benefits you cover. In a sales letter focusing on one benefit is always better, but sometimes you may want to touch on more than just one to adequately address the needs of the buyer. In a proposal, you want to focus on the three most important points, unless otherwise directed by the client or a Request for Proposal.

Even if you offer more than one product or service, focus on one at a time. Don't throw in everything but the kitchen sink. If you want to cover additional products or services, send separate sales letters or discuss the other lines in subsequent interviews. Buyers need to associate you with a single solution in order to become familiar with what you do. When you talk about multiple lines or various services, clients can become confused or frustrated with having to decide which choice would be best for them. Also, your image becomes less clear and your message loses impact. Let a client become familiar with a single product or service that addresses their needs. Once they understand more about who you are and what you do, you can introduce additional lines.

Whenever possible, start with rhetorical questions. The rhetorical question, if it touches a need or a problem to be solved, immediately

Marketing Mistake: Unclear, Unwanted Solicitations

After CPA Janeen McCrevy joined an organization of local merchants, professionals, and other business owners, she decided right off to send a personalized sales letter on her professional stationery to the entire mailing list introducing herself and her multilevel marketing business. She didn't want to turn anyone off by overtly recruiting them, so she decided to report on how rapidly her business was expanding without mentioning just what it was. She then pointed out that she was looking for business partners to associate with and closed by asking the reader to contact her if this sounded appealing.

Many of the members were simply confused by the letter and didn't understand the point of it. They simply tossed it away. Several members, however, read through the lines and thought they were being recruited into an illegal pyramid scheme. They were outraged and called the organization to complain that McCrevy was using false advertising. The few members who contacted her were thinking she had an investment venture of some kind. When they found out she was recruiting them to be part of her downline in a networking marketing business, they too were outraged.

At that point, her name was mud in the organization. She had learned a painful lesson about the importance of clarity and truth in advertising and in more carefully targeting her solicitations to people who would be in the market for her business.

makes you an ally in your prospect's eyes. The right sort of question shows clearly that you understand your prospect's needs and concerns.

Limit your sales letters to one page. Proposals also should be accompanied by a one-page cover letter that summarizes the key benefits the entire proposal addresses. Prospects are too busy to waste time reading long sales pitches. The purpose of your letter is to titillate the imagination and get the reader to take the next step, be it reading your proposal or asking for an appointment. If for some unique reason you *must* write a longer letter, keep your paragraphs short, double-space between paragraphs, and use wider margins.

Ask for the appointment. Never leave a letter open-ended. Explain that you want to sit and talk with them and that you will call them to set up an appointment at their convenience. State clearly when you will call.

Follow up! Follow up! Follow up! Call precisely when your letter says you will. Keep the call short and sweet. Ask for the appointment.

Make sure there are no typos or misspellings and your grammar is correct. The worst thing you can do for your image is send a sloppy letter or proposal. If your customer does not notice or care how perfect it is, precision won't hurt you. However, if someone sees a mistake and cares, you will probably have lost the customer. The presumption is, if you are sloppy in your sales materials or proposals, you are likely to be even more so in your work.

This is especially important when you're working from a template or form letter and risk missing areas that have been properly customized. If you're not good at proofreading, have a professional look at your material. Spelling- and grammar-checking software are helpful but may not pick up some errors.

Resources: Sales Letters and Proposals

Associations

Proposal Management Association, 2111 Wilson Boulevard, Ste. 700, Arlington, VA 22201, (703) 351-5015. Conventions, seminars, and brochures on proposal writing.

Books

The Consultant's Guide to Proposal Writing, 2d ed. Herman Holtz. New York: Wiley, 1990.

The Desktop Publisher's Idea Book, Over 100 Step-by-Step Designs with 250 Illustrations. Chuck Green. New York: Random House, 1997.

The Greatest Direct Mail Sales Letter of All Time. Richard S. Hodgson. Chicago: Dartnell Corporation, 1995, (800) 621-5463.

Sales Letters that Sizzle. Herschell Gordon Lewis. Lincolnwood, IL: NTC Contemporary Publishing, 1995, 800-323-4900.

Successful Proposal Strategies for Small Businesses: Winning Private Sector and International Contracts. Robert S. Frey. Norwood, MA: Artech House, 1997.

Software

Model Sales and Marketing Letters, by ModelOffice, Inc., 804 C Rio Grande Street, Lamor, Austin, TX 78701, (512) 457-1100, www.modeloffice.com. Over four hundred ready-to-use sales letters and memos, for winning new clients, prospecting, proposals, follow-up contacts, networking, trade show demonstrations, strengthening customer relations, and closing sales.

Sales LetterWorks, by CogniTech Corporation, P.O. Box 50019, Atlanta, GA 31150, (800) 947-5075 or (770) 640-3103.

Electronic Yellow Pages

Biz*File, by American Business Information, 5711 South 86th Circle, Omaha, NE 68127, (800) 336-8349, www.abii.com Includes names, addresses, and phone numbers of ten million companies.

Phone Disk USA Business and **Phone Disk USA Residential** by Digital Directory Assistance, Inc., 5711 S. 86th Circle, Omaha, NE 68127, (800) INFO-4636. Includes 9.5 million businesses and 80 million residential listings.

Mailing Lists on the Internet

Usenet/Usegroups

All major Web search engines include lists of newsgroups: You can obtain very specific targeted mailing lists by searching any of the following using the search phrase "marketing mailing lists." We got 6,180 hits for this phrase.

Altavista (www.altvista.com)
Looksmart (www.looksmart.com)
Lycos (www.lycos.com)
Yahoo! (www.yahoo.com)

Videos

Design Eye-Catching Brochures, Newsletters, Ads, Reports. Jane K. Cleland. CareerTrack, 3085 Center Green Drive, Boulder, CO 80301, (800) 334-1018, www.careertrack.com

Proposal Preparation Tools

The following companies have selections of binders, folders, slipcases, notebooks, laminated color-tab divider pages, and plastic sleeves and envelopes for giving your proposals a professional look:

Avery Dennison, P.O. Box 5244, Diamond Bar, CA 91765, (800) 525-7064.

Paper Direct, 100 Plaza Drive, Secaucus, NJ 07094, (800) A-PAPERS, (800) 272-7377, www.paperdirect.com. Ask for the catalog *Wow! What a Great Presentation.*

Queblo, 150 Kingswood Road, Mankato, MN 56002, (800) 523-9080, www.catalog.orders.com

Trade Associations

Association of Business Support Services International, 22875 Savi Ranch Pkwy, #H, Yorba Linda, CA 92887, (800) 237-1462. Will provide referrals to companies in your area who will manage your mailing list and mailings for you.

Editorial Freelancers' Association, 71 West 23d Street, Ste. 1504, New York, NY 10010, (212) 929-5400. Provides a job bank listing to members.

Web Site

Just as it is assumed that you will have some type of written material you can send out or leave behind describing what you do, it is becoming expected that everyone in business for themselves will have a Web site where those interested in what you do can log on and look over or experience what you offer.

The marketing possibilities for a Web site are rich and varied. You can have a simple site of one or more pages with informative content you update periodically that serves much like an electronic brochure. Or you can have a more dynamic site that functions more like a newsletter with daily, weekly, monthly, or quarterly updates. Depending on your business, you can provide some type of sample or experience of what you offer. You can broadcast news of changes in your site via E-mail to anyone requesting updates.

Alternatively, your Web site can be like a multimedia direct sales piece featuring sales and specials and an opportunity to order on the spot. Or it can be like having a twenty-four-hour virtual shop or up-to-the minute electronic catalog through which customers browse and shop. It can even serve as the equivalent of an electronic trade show booth where visitors can see demonstrations of what you have to offer. Alternatively, by building links to and from your site with sites of colleagues and associates, you can create a virtual network for giving and getting on-line referrals. Using contact management software like *Goldmine,* you can automate sending or receiving referrals you get through your Web site. You can even provide actual products or services on-line in real time or you can use your site as a customer service tool offering updates and support to existing clients and customers.

In addition, your site can be an interactive tool, enabling existing or potential clients and customers to respond to surveys, leave personal messages, or make inquiries.

Setting up a Web site turned the tide for Bill Todd and William Holland's business. Their mail-order business, Todd & Holland Tea Merchants, features specialty teas targeted to an upscale clientele. But the response from direct-mail campaigns, advertising in highbrow magazines like *Gourmet* and *Bon Appetit,* and publicity on a top-rated talk radio station, produced only a trickle of orders. Almost as soon as it went up, their site began producing business. Over a six-month period, their site went from producing 30 percent to 53 percent of their business.

Sheila Cuff, owner of The Oaks at Ojai and The Palms at Palm Springs, uses her Web page to give visitors a guided tour of her spas. Instead of clicking on buttons, visitors can view various vacation packages, look over spa menus, shop for health products, and request a brochure (www.keho.com/palms).

Pros and Cons of Marketing via a Web Site

As you can see, one beauty of having a Web site is its remarkable versatility. You can use it for doing promotions, making direct sales, or providing customer service. It can be little more than a business card one month, an animated multimedia commercial the next, all the while serving as an ongoing customer support line. Another plus is that anyone who's interested in exploring what you have to offer can do so at their convenience twenty-four hours a day without your needing to be available or hiring staff to handle inquiries. Thus, you can generate potential new clients and customers or provide customer support quite inexpensively. There's no phone tag. No long distance calls. No postage for sending something out in the mail. No trying to locate the kind of people you're seeking; they find you.

You may be able to pay as little as $300 a year for your site if you create it yourself, using software like *Microsoft Front-page,* Adobe's *PageMill* or Web-page templates like those you'll find on the *Web Marketing Cookbook* CD-ROM. Or you can spend hundreds to thousands of dollars to have a professional service create a highly sophisticated multimedia site with order desk, message board, and chat or conference facilities. (See **Resources** to find Web page developers.) Whichever way you choose to create your site, it can be easily updated and changed, expanding or contracting in accord with your budget and the results you get from it. Here's another substantial advantage:

Overnight you can leap over the limits of offering your products or services on a local basis to having a national or international clientele.

The disadvantages are that not everyone is on-line yet and those who are may or may not find you amid the literally millions of other sites. If you want people to find you on the Web, you will need to promote your site or you may have few visitors. So, having a truly successful site can become time or money intensive. The less you want to spend, the more you have to do yourself, and you may or may not have or wish to develop the skills to do all the work yourself. Even if you have other professionals design, set up, and run your site, you will need to respond to and monitor the results, answer inquiries or complaints, file orders, and update the material regularly.

Karen Capland's, site for Frieda's, her fine-foods company, for example, comes with a Press Room of news releases, pictures, and details of exotic foods along with recipes, nutritional information, and background on each food's history. The By Mail feature links you to their gift baskets sections which you can order by phone or directly from the site via E-mail. Club Frieda is a section where true connoisseurs can sign up to automatically receive advance notice of new items in their area's markets and get discounts on Frieda's baskets and chances to win free products.

As you can see, for those who like exploring new marketing opportunities, there's nothing quite like having a Web site.

Best Bets: Marketing on the Web works best for those who are willing to invest the time, energy, and money to explore how to make this exciting new medium work for them. Of course, your clientele need to be computer literate and have on-line access. A Nielsen survey found that nearly 7 percent of the 30 million Internet users buy products and services directly from the Web. According to Annie Van Bebber of Digital Maven, while most Web sites at this time are addressed to consumers, it is projected that by 2003, 80 percent of business over the Web will be business to business.

Tips for Getting Business On-Line

In general, the basic principles of good promotional copywriting, layout, and design described in **Appendix I: Writing and Designing Materials That Sell** (available on-line without charge as a Special Report at www.paulandsarah.com on the Great Ideas for Getting Business page) apply to creating a winning Web site. The Web is an entirely new medium, however, so it's a mistake to think that you can take a well-written and well-designed newsletter, ad, or brochure and just put it up on your Web site with good results. Therefore, you'll find special tips for designing an effective Web site in **Appendix I**. Here are a few additional steps you'll want to take to create an effective Web site:

Determine the results you want to get. As you can see, there is a wide variety of ways you can use a Web site to get business coming to you. Therefore to be most effective, it's important to identify before you create your site what you want to accomplish with it. It can be any combination of the following or more:

___ Inform

___ Educate

___ Generate leads

___ Take orders and make sales on the Web

___ Display or show products

___ Establish communication andget feedback

___ Update existing clients

___ Provide customer service and support

Select the right ISP. Most small businesses and self-employed individuals do not have the desire, budget, or technical knowledge to purchase and operate their own dedicated Web server. Therefore they rent the services of an ISP, Internet Service Provider. The ISP hosts their clients' sites usually for a monthly fee. What an ISP will provide depends on your needs and what they offer. Most ISPs will reserve your domain name, layout, and design your site around the content you have developed, make site updates you provide and prepare usage reports. Others provide additional services like Internet access, E-mail, and promotion. Fees will vary depending on the size and complexity of your site. Although many ISPs have Web developers on staff, if your site is especially complex, you may need to work with a separate Web developer initially to design your site.

You can use free Web page services. Several sites like GeoCities, Towne Square 200, and Tripod will host your site for free and provide self-publishing tools that let you quickly establish your home page (see **Resources**). Of course, these sites are free because they are advertiser sponsored. So if you're not comfortable with someone else's ad on your site, these services are not for you, but if you want to find advertisers to underwrite your site expenses anyway, this is an option to consider. You would have to build quite a lot of traffic to your site on your own before you could attract your own ads.

The biggest drawback to these free sites is your address. You won't have a tidy www.yourname.com. Instead visitors will have to use a series of slashes and tildes to get to you. And, of course, if the site goes out of business, you'll have to find another home for your page. Generally free sites work best for service businesses that need a way to provide information on-line instead of companies that want to actually sell products from the site, because customers will be limited to phoning or E-mailing their orders.

In choosing a fee site, review such issues as traffic history, member and site search directories, storage capability, E-mail account options, ease of setup, on-line help, visitor counting, search engine links, page creation features, and storage space.

Select a domain name. Your site needs a name, and that name becomes your Internet address by which people find you and access your site. Usually you would want the name of your site to be the same as your company name, so people can become familiar with and use one name to reach you by mail, E-mail, or phone. Sometimes, however, you may want to use the name of a particular product or service instead. Whatever name you choose to use, you will need to reserve it through your ISP, which will first find out if anyone else is already using it and then, if not, reserve its use for you. For information on how to reserve a Web name, see **chapter 6,** Making a Name for Yourself, page 222.

If you have several products, as we, Paul and Sarah, have several books, you might want to reserve several names to prevent anyone else from using their names in the future. You can arrange to do this in a way that whichever of the names you have reserved someone uses, they will get directly to the same one Web site. If your products or services are quite diverse, you may want to have two or more distinct Web sites. A caterer who does both weddings and corporate events, for example, may want to have a Web site with one look and feel for prospective brides and grooms and another with an entirely different look and feel for corporate meeting planners.

Offer something of direct value. In the Internet culture there is an expectation that a site will be more than an ad. Visitors will expect to get something of value for free. So, plan what kind of valuable information you can provide free of charge that will motivate people to want to use your products or services. Here are a couple of examples:

Cindy Eley's business is On-Demand Resources, an information technology staffing and consulting company. Her site (www.ondemandresource.com) has a direct link to MapBlast which pinpoints precisely where On-Demand Resources is located on a scaled map, along with specific driving directions from your location. They also post available positions under an Opportunities section, so it's a great place for someone to go who's looking for technical or computer-related employment. Visitors can also register for employment with On-Demand Resources and submit an application from their Web site. Managers who have positions available in their departments can post them as well.

Mary Schnack provides media services. Along with detailed information about her service, her Web site (www.intrace.com/mary) includes information about what makes the news, creating a communications plan, and how to write a news release, with sample releases included. Feature articles by Schnack like "The Secrets of Successful Communication Under Fire" appear as well as success stories about some of her clients.

Design an inviting, easy-to-navigate site. A Web site is not linear like a newsletter, book, magazine, or booklet. It is literally a site. You can think of it as being like a campus, library, house, or art museum. People approach it like going to an amusement park that has various venues. For ideas on how to design and lay out your site see **Appendix I: Writing and Designing Materials That Sell,** which is available online without charge as a Special Report at www.paulandsarah.com on the Great Ideas for Getting Business page.

Get your site listed on key search engines and browsers. Because there is so much information on the Web and there are so many Web sites, people need a way to find sites related to their particular interests.

That's where search engines come in. Essentially a search engine is an electronic directory of Web sites where someone can locate the addresses of Web sites related to a particular topic. *Yahoo!*, for example, is a popular search engine that indexes selected sites. Others include *Alta Vista, Excite, HotBot, Infoseek, Lycos,* and *Webcrawler*. You should get listed on as many of the major engines as possible. To find other search engines, visit www.search.com where you will find more than 250 Web and usenet search engines alphabetically or by category from one central Web page.

To get your site listed on search engines, you first must identify the key words people would use to search for a site like yours. Actually getting listed on the major search engines can involve long waiting periods, however, and some search engines charge a fee. To avoid long waits and fees for getting yourself listed on search engines, you can get site listed on one or more of the lists that are already listed in the search engines. Or use the services of a submit site like SubmitIt (www.netcreations.com/postmaster) which will list your Web address with eighteen search engines and directories for free.

Also, keep in mind that some search engines do not take applications. They get their listings by sending out automated "robots" that collect information on sites for their directories. To be sure your site gets picked up on the correct categories, make certain that each page includes some of the key words people would use to find you, or have your Web designer embed "metatags" on your site that tell these robots what key words apply.

Getting listed on major browsers like Netscape *Navigator* and Microsoft *Explorer* is also a good idea. A browser is a software programs that enables users to navigate the Web. Each browser has its own home page that pops up on the screen when the user enters the Internet, unless the user has made alterations in the software to do otherwise. At this time the Netscape browser home page is thus one of the most visited sites on the Web. Each browser's home page also has an index or directory of sites by type. Again, to be listed on a browser, you may have to pay a fee.

If this all sounds a bit too complicated and time-consuming for you, some ISPs will take on the task of getting your site listed on the appropriate search engines and browsers. Alternatively you may want to hire a Web Site publicist (see **Resources:** A Web Site).

In addition to getting listed on key search engines and browsers, if you want to stimulate visitors to come to your site, you will need to take other steps to promote it widely, until popularity or word of mouth takes over. You can do this both on-line and off. Here are a few ideas.

10 WAYS TO PROMOTE YOUR WEB SITE

1. List your Web address on your business card, letterhead, brochures, flyers, newsletters, invoices, print catalogs, product packaging, etc.
2. Send out a new release, cards, or flyers announcing your site. Include a picture of your home page (the opening screen on your site).
3. Include your Web address in any advertising you do.
4. Mention your Web address on your voice-mail system, answering machine, or on-hold message.
5. Add your site to your E-mail signature.
6. Include your Web address on your fax transmission sheet.
7. Trade links with other key sites that your clients and customers visit.
8. Leave messages on on-line bulletin boards and participate in relevant newsgroup discussions so you and your site become known to those who would be interested.
9. Volunteer to host live on-line conferences, workshops, or chat sessions where you can refer people to your Web site.
10. Mention your Web site as a way for people to find out more or stay in touch with you whenever you're introducing yourself, presenting, or networking.

Update frequently. Just as people expect a paper or newsletter to have different interesting topics in each issue, visitors to your Web site will expect it to offer something new when they drop by. How frequently you will need to update your site will depend, of course, upon the goals you have for it; but if you think of your site as being like a retail shop people can browse through, you'll want to change the "displays" with some regularity so they will want to come back and see what's new. If people come in and see nothing new, chances are they won't come back.

Updating your site, however, does not need to be a complex undertaking. You should design your site so that you can make changes regularly via your own computer to update the site with new content, new offers, or a new survey or contest, as well as rotate various color schemes or graphics. A simple way to update your site, for example, is to have a *What's New* page that changes every day or week.

Get feedback and capture the names of visitors to follow up with. You will want to have some way to know how many people are visiting your site and who they are so you can find ways to serve them. Your ISP should be able to provide you with a report as to the number of "hits," or visits, also called "page views," you have to your site each day as well as how many buy or respond to what you're offering. These reports provide information like total objects served, total discrete visits, unique visitors, etc. Such information is vital for you to know if your promotion, design, and content are working to attract and keep people coming to your site. If your ISP does not provide such information, you can use the services of an independent tracking service like WebTrack (www.webtrack.com).

In order to get specific information about the people who are visiting, you will have to make your site interactive, so that those who visit are able and motivated to fill out information about who they are and what they are interested in. This is why many Web sites hold contests and do surveys and why adding an E-mail component can be valuable. Of course, if you do this, you will need to have a system in place to respond to and follow up in some way with those who identify themselves. Otherwise, there is no sense in going to the trouble of gathering such information.

Some small businesses are hiring Web site content promotion specialists to help them develop interesting interactive activities like giveaways, contests, free downloads, interactive "guest books," cartoon features, and special on-line events like interviews with experts or other guests.

If you are using your site to generate leads or take orders, you will, of course, need to have a way to respond quickly to the requests made on your site. So far most small businesses still get orders from their Web sites via an 800 or 888 phone number or by mail. Many Web users remain uncomfortable giving out their credit card numbers over the Web, and many small businesses and self-employed individuals still have difficulty getting credit card merchant status from banks and other financial institutions. Most likely both of these restraints will disappear in the near future.

Of course, you can capture inquiries and leads via E-mail, phone, or mail, but one added way to streamline the follow-up process is by using contact management software like *Goldmine,* which enables you to automatically transfer questionnaires or forms that visitors fill out on your Website to your contact management program so you can follow up with the appropriate action.

Protect your site. Don't let anyone rip off your site design or content. Companies like Digimarc Corporation (503/223-0118) offer ways to embed digital watermarks into your images. They will then search the Web for your watermarks and report back to you any uses of your designs or material.

How Web Page Traffic Is Measured

There are several ways to measure traffic to a Web site, including hits, impressions or page views, and click-through. While each of these terms describes a way to measure the number of visits to a site, there are significant differences in what they measure.

Hits

Each Web page is really a document made up of various elements that might include text, graphics, sound, animation, and even video. Each of these different elements is stored in a separate file. Every time someone visits the site all the files that compose the page are sent and each of these files counts as a hit. So, for example, if a Web page that consists of two graphic files, a text file, and the instruction file for how to put it all together is accessed, that page would be counted as four "hits." The server is aware of how many times it sends out each element and keeps a count, which is easily accessible and usually provided without charge to the Web page owner by the ISP.

Impressions or Page Views

Another way to measure Web site traffic is to count "impressions" or "page views." Each time all the elements of a Web page are transmitted to a user, that counts as a single "impression" or "page view." Obviously, tracking page views or impressions is a little tougher than simply tracking hits because you have to correlate the information about each page more carefully. But it more clearly reflects the actual number of visits to a site.

Click-Throughs

Web pages can and should be designed so the visitor can select another Web page or Web site from the page he or she is currently viewing. This is called a "link." The number of times a visitor clicks on the links on the Web site is called the click-through. Click-through numbers are considered the most valuable way to measure Web site traffic because they are seen as active requests for material and therefore show more involvement on the part of the person visiting the site. Click-throughs tell you, for example, which pages of your site are most popular, etc.

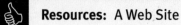

Resources: A Web Site

Associations and Web Publicity Professionals

A1 Web International Commercial Advertising, 1701 Edmonson Avenue, Ste. 204, Catonsville, MD 21228, (410) 788-8298, www.web2.come/homepage/. Access to hundreds of directories, indexes, and catalogs that will list your site for free.

CyberPulse. On-line marketing resource covering newsgroups, mailing lists, promotions, and more: www.cyberpulse.com/ on-line

The Delphi Group. Provides links to Web site development and on-line marketing: www.cam.org/~delphig/index.html

International Association of Professional Web Developers Web: www.webpro.org

Internet Publicity Services (www.olympus.nt/okeefe/PI). Has a large collection of do-it-yourself Internet publicity

NetPost. Specializes in Web site "awareness," including news releases and announcements: www.netpost.com/

Public Relations Society of America, 33 Irving Place, New York, NY, 10003, (212) 995-2230.

Books

Creating the Virtual Store, Taking Your Web Site from Browsing to Buying. Magdalena Yesil. New York: John Wiley & Sons, 1997.

Customer Service on the Internet. Jim Sterne. New York: Wiley, 1997.

Cyberwriting: How to Promote Your Product or Service Online (Without Being Flamed). Joe Vitale, New York: Amacom Book Division, 1996.

Electronic Selling. Brian Jamison, Josh Gold, and Warren Jamison. New York: McGraw-Hill, 1997.

Increasing Hits and Selling More on Your Web Site. Greg Helmstetter. New York: Wiley, 1996.

Making More Money on the Internet. Alfred and Emily Glossbrenner. New York: McGraw Hill, 1996.

The Non-Designer's Web Book. Robin Williams. Berkeley, Calif.: Peach Pitt Press, 1997.

Publicity on the Internet. Steve O'Keefe. New York: Wiley, 1997.

Redesigning Print for the Web. Dr. Mario R. Garcia. 1996. Hayden Books, 201 West 103rd Street, Indianapolis, IN 46290, (317) 581-3833. www.mcp.com/info/1-56830/1-56830-343-2

Running a Perfect Web Site with Windows. Mark Surfas, David M. Chandler, Tobin Anthony and Rick Darnell. New York: Que Corporation, 1996 (also available for Mac).

Spinning the Web: How to Provide Information on the Internet. Andrew Ford. New York, Van Nostrand Reinhold, 1995.

Web Marketing Cookbook. Janice King, Paul Knight, and James H. Mason. New York: Wiley, 1997.

Contact Management Software

Goldmine, (310) 454-6800, 17383 Sunset Blvd., Pacific Palisades, CA 90272, www.goldeminesw.com

Digital Payment Systems

CyberCash. (703) 620-4200 or (800) 929-2371, E-mail: info@cybercash.com, Web: www.cybercash.com

DigiCash. (650) 321-0300, E-mail: info@digicash.nl, Web:www.digicash.com

First Virtual Holdings. (800) 570-0003, E-mail: info@fv.com, **Web:** www.firstvirtual.com

Netbank Payment System. Net Bank, Inc. 950 North Point Parkway, Ste. 350, Alpharetta, GA 30005, (770) 392-4990, (888) 256-6932, Web:www.netbank.com

Directories

Directory of Internet Service Providers, by *Boardwatch* magazine, 8500 West Bowles Ave., Ste. 210, Littleton, CO 80123, (303) 933-8724, www.boardwatch.com

Tracking Page Views

WebTrack, An independent service that tracks Web site visits, from Jupiter Communications and Audit Bureau of Circulation, Web: www.webtrack.com

Web Design Software

Adobe PageMill, (650) 961-4400 or (800) 833-6687.

Art Vault, Art for the Web, by Team Media. Fifteen hundred buttons, icons, patterns, lectures, and Web page templates. 20245 Stevens Creek Boulevard, Ste. 201, Cupertino, CA 95014.

Click Art, by Broderbund, includes 125,000 images from photos and sounds to animation, Web images, and cartoons. Broderbund, P.O. Box 6121, Novato, CA 94948, www.broderbund.com

Kai's Power Goo, MetaCreations, turns photos and graphics into entertaining real-time liquid images. 6303 Carpinteria Avenue, Carpinteria, CA 93013, (805) 566-6200, www.metatools.com

Microsoft's Front Page, (206) 882-8080 or (800) 426-9400.

QuickSite, by Delat Point, (408) 648-4000 or (800) 367-4334.

Visual Page, by Symantec, 10202 Toree Avenue, Cupertino, CA 95014, (800) 971-1564. In Windows or Mac.

Search Engines

Alta Vista (www.altavista, digital.com)
Excite (www.excite.com)
Hotbot (www.hotbot.com)
Infoseek (www.infoseek.com)
Lycos (www.lycos.com)
Magellan (www.mckinley.com)
WebCrawler (www.webcrawler.com)
Yahoo! (www.yahoo.com)

Lists of Newsgroups

news.lists
news.groups
news.announce.newgroups
news.answers

Free Web Site Services

Angelfire Communications www.angelfire.com
GeoCities www.geocities.com/homstead
Towne Square 2000 townsquare.usc.com
Tripod www.tripod.com
Webspawner www.webspawner.com

Resources on Web Sites

NetCreations/PostMaster/IPA. Tracks on-line advertising opportunities and rates. www.netcreations.com/

Sun Microsystems. Web page covers a range of writing and content strategies for the Web. sun.com/styleguide

WEBSight Online magazine. http://websight.com/

WebTrack. Tracks on-line advertising, showing who is spending money to advertise, who's getting that money, and how much is changing hands. www.webtrack.com/

Writers.com. This site offers on-line classes, tutoring, workshops, and writers' groups on a number of writing-related topics, including Web site writing.

Your Own Book

More and more people are discovering the magical marketing power of being a published author. Doctors, public speakers, psychotherapists, consultants, and heads of companies large and small are all writing books as a way to help promote their businesses. So if you've always dreamed of becoming an author, now is a good time to fulfill that dream. Writing a book can open doors that would otherwise be closed to you.

We, Paul and Sarah, were astonished at the difference in the reactions we got from prospective clients, media, and other marketing venues after our first book, *Working from Home,* was published. Even if people had no interest in the topic of our book, the fact that we were published authors resulted in their taking us more seriously than they would have only weeks before. As media consultant Blaine Lee told us, "Your book is your calling card." Here's why.

Pros and Cons of Writing a Book

Books can help enhance your credibility, build your reputation, position you as an expert and authority in your field, and serve as a way to let people experience your expertise firsthand. They open doors to high-quality, difficult-to-get publicity. With a good book as your credential, you can line up interviews on radio and television, get quoted, or have your topic featured in newspaper and magazine articles. The right book can also help you get signed up to give speeches and seminars at the trade and professional organizations your clients, customers, and key referral sources belong to.

Your book can also become a source of additional income to help offset your marketing costs. You can sell it to clients and customers at speeches and seminars and as premiums for companies wanting to add value to what they offer by sending your book to their clients or customers or bundling it in with their products or services.

On the other hand, writing a book can be quite time-consuming, and putting out a bad or a poorly done book can actually work against you. Getting your book published can require more time and energy than you imagined. Also, once your book has been published, some of the information in it may become out of date. An outdated book is useless to you as a marketing tool.

Best Bets: Having a published book is a valuable tool for promoting to both other businesses and consumers. A book is most effective when your business is one in which your personal expertise and point of view are crucial to gaining clients' trust and rapport; e.g., a management consultant, dog trainer, facialist, sales trainer, or motivational speaker.

Tips for Getting Business from Writing a Book

Yes, you can. You may be thinking, Who, me? Write a book? Many people still have the idea that you have to be a highly talented, professionally trained writer to write a book. Generally speaking that is true of writing a novel, which is an art in and of itself. In writing a nonfiction book about your expertise, however, all you need to be able to do is communicate your ideas in a clear, engaging, and organized way. In other words, as long as you are indeed a specialist, expert, or authority in your field, if you can write a useful article, if you can write a compelling sales letter, if you can write an interesting newsletter, then you can write a book. Writing a book will just be longer and take longer.

You can find the time. Most people who are running a full-time business have difficulty finding time to write. But here are several ways to find the time you need to write. To complete their book, many people set aside an hour a two a day, usually early in the morning, to write. Others write on weekends or take an extended vacation to start or finish their book.

Alternatively, you may want to hire a ghostwriter who will work closely with you to do the actual writing. Or, you might want to write the first draft and then hire an editor to polish and perfect your manuscript.

Keep in mind, your book need not be long: 200 double-spaced pages of highly targeted useful information can be sufficient.

Pick a useful in-demand topic about which you have a clear point of view. Your book need not and should not cover everything you know. Obviously you will want to feature one of the crucial issues related to your niche (see **chapter 2**). You should focus on the one key issue that is most compelling to your clients and customers, the one thing related to your niche they want to know about, the one thing that bothers them most, or the one thing they most aspire to. For example, management consultant Cherie Carter-Scott decided to write her book *Negaholics* when she noticed how the chronic negativity of a few employees could undermine the morale of her clients' entire organization. For CPA Richard Schonfeld, the most common trigger for his clients is the fear of being audited by the IRS. His book is *Help! I Owe the IRS.* For marriage and family counselor Coleen Sawyer the key issue for her clients is finding the right mate. Her book is *Fishing by Moonlight, The Art of Choosing Intimate Partners.*

Refer to the work you did in **chapter 5** on getting to the heart of your niche, zeroing in on the key issues, and speaking to where your clients and customers live. The same core issues you identified there are the very ones you should consider addressing when writing your book. In fact, you can think of your book as the ultimate extension of your **File-Opening Soundbyte** (page 186) and your particular point of view on your niche.

Start with what you've already written. Once you begin narrowing down what you want to write to the key issues, you may be surprised at how far along you already are toward having a book. Refer to **Your White Paper** and **Position Paper** in **chapter 3,** for example. Read through your **Mastery Journal.** Look over your newsletters, articles, columns, brochures, speeches, or seminars. There you should find much of the content for your book.

Sometimes you can simply edit and combine articles, columns, informative brochures, and other sales materials you've written into book form. If not, there is still usually some way you can streamline the writing process by incorporating some of what you've already written into sections of your book. Alternatively, if you regularly give a speech or seminar, you can have it taped and transcribed. Then edit the transcript into a book.

Include compelling examples, illustrations, and stories. The most interesting books include many examples, personal stories, and illustrations of your key points. Review your **Master Journal** for key patterns and specific examples. Also, the evidence you've been gathering as outlined in **chapter 3** can come in most handy for filling out the specifics of your book.

Keep confidentiality. When using the names of clients and customers as examples, always get permission. In many cases, you may not want to use your clients' names or have them be identifiable in any way. In such cases, you can use composites or hypothetical cases using made-up names and changing the details so no one can recognize the identity of the individual or company you're writing about.

Consider doing a survey. If you have done a survey of any kind as suggested in getting **Publicity** in **chapter 10,** your book might focus on applying your expertise to what you've found in such surveys. If you haven't done such a survey yet, you might want to consider doing one in conjunction with writing your book. Ph.D. psychologist Al Siebert wrote *The Survivor Personality* based on surveying people who had overcome various tragedies. Management consultant Dr. Jerry Fletcher's and executive coach Kelly Olwyler's surveys of peak performers led to their book *Paradoxical Thinking, How to Profit from Your Contradictions.*

Find a good publisher. There is a variety of ways to get a publisher. Principally, you can either find a literary agent who will represent you in locating a publisher or you can contact publishers yourself. Many of the larger publishers will not accept unsolicited manuscripts; they work only through agents. Some large and many smaller publishers will, however. *Writer's Digest* lists the major publishers and provides information about editors, what kinds of manuscripts they're seeking, and if they accept unsolicited manuscripts (see **Resources** that follow).

You do not need to have completed your manuscript to contact either an agent or a publisher. In fact, we recommend against it. Sending a proposal will usually suffice.

We've found the best way to find an agent or publisher is by getting recommendations from other authors who are happy with their agent and/or publisher or by looking through the bookstores for books addressed to the same target audience your book will be addressing and

Elements of a Book Proposal

Your book proposal should include such things as:

- A cover letter introducing yourself and your book
- A detailed outline of your book
- An explanation of whom the book is written for and how many such people there are
- What similar books, if any, have been written by whom and why these readers would want to read your book.
- Ideas for what you will do to help promote the book
- Two or three sample chapters
- Your bio and promotional kit (see **chapter 8**)

For additional information on preparing a book proposal see **Resources,** below.

finding out who the publisher is, who the editor was, and, if there was one, who the agent was.

Tip: ***Authors who like their agents and editors will usually thank them by name in the acknowledgments at the beginning of their book.***

Consider self-publishing. Often people who want to use their book primarily as a marketing tool decide that they would prefer to self-publish. Or, if no agent or publishing house will pick up your book, self-publishing may be your only route to getting published. The most obvious advantage to self-publishing is that you get to keep all of any profits, and self-publishing can be lucrative. If you have hit upon the right subject, you can earn $10 or more per book. The disadvantage of self-publishing is that you'll not only have to underwrite all the costs of publishing the book, you'll also have to see to it that there are some profits. All sales will be up to you. Otherwise your book will become strictly a marketing expense.

If you anticipate having regular ongoing contact with lots of people who will buy your books, do consider self-publishing. You can write, design, and lay out your book using word-processing and desktop-publishing software. Then you can use a service bureau to produce the

What to Look For in a Publisher

Of course, you want to find a publisher who believes in you and your book and will provide high-quality editorial assistance from someone you can work well with. You also will want a fair advance and royalty arrangement. From the perspective of using your book as a marketing tool, however, here are several additional issues you will want to consider in selecting a publisher:

1. Does the publisher have its own sales force and a distribution system that will get the books out to stores and to you?
2. Will they underwrite book promotion and publicity? How much? For how long?
3. Will they send out review copies to media and others upon your request? How many? For how long?
4. Will they give you a discount on purchasing copies of the book yourself that is sufficiently low that you can afford to use the books for your own promotional activities and for resale at speeches or seminars, through your newsletter, etc.?
5. Do they have a special sales department that will work with you on selling the book or excerpts from the book as premiums to companies that want to give it to their customers?
6. If you do not want to resell books yourself, does the publisher have a special sales department that can efficiently sell books directly to organizations you're working with that want to purchase your books in quantity? Will they offer them a good price?

One of the best ways to get the real scope on these issues is to talk with authors who are published by the publishers you are considering. Also see **Resources.**

pages in high-quality type or your own laser printer to produce camera-ready pages. Finally, you will want to locate a printer who specializes in "short runs" (printings of 3,000 copies or less) who can print your book at less than $2 per copy. You'll find many excellent resources on the ins and outs of self-publishing in the **Resources** that follow.

Keep in mind, however, that to be effective as a marketing tool, your self-published book will need to look and read as professionally as

High-Tech Tip: Paperless Self-Publishing

Using the *Expanded Book Tool Kit,* you can take the paperless route to self-publishing with a Macintosh computer and produce a multimedia book including art, sound, video, and search engines for reproduction on discs, CD-ROM, or for use on on-line services. This software costs $295 plus a 1 percent royalty (see **Resources** for self-publishing).

if someone else had published it. Therefore, unless you're an exceptional writer and have a keen print design sense, you will probably want to hire a professional editor and a packager or designer to help you create the layout and look of your book.

Put your book to work for you. Once your book is out, your work has just begun. You can't let it sit around in your basement, on store bookshelves, or in the publisher's warehouse. Take the following steps at once:

- Make your book a cornerstone of your five-star marketing plan.
- Arrange to order extra copies of your book cover to use as part of your publicity materials. Obtaining such copies should be a minimal cost.
- Order a supply of books to have on hand.
- Send a copy of your book along with your presentation materials to potential clients who are serious about doing business with you.
- Carry a copy of your book with you to all business appointments and gatherings.
- Work with your publisher to initiate an ongoing publicity campaign. If you don't want to do much of this yourself, you should consider hiring a publicist, as most publishers will only do serious publicity upon the release of the book and when a new edition comes out.
- Tie your book into every marketing activity you can; e.g., give it away as a door prize at networking meetings, display it at your trade show booth, build the cost of your book into your fee

Marketing Masterpiece: Creating a Tips Booklet

If you would love to have many of the benefits of having written a book but simply don't have the time or patience to write one, consider creating a tips booklet as professional organizer Paulette Ensign has done. When Ensign decided to move to another city, she was faced with the prospect of having to build a new clientele from scratch. To help ease the transition, she decided to synthesize her eight years of experience into a booklet entitled *110 Ideas for Organizing Your Business Life*. Little did she know that this decision would change the course of her life.

Not only was she able to use the booklet to effectively market herself, but she also has sold over 400,000 copies, and it has been translated into three other languages. The ideas have been incorporated into a laminated product, as well as a calendar and seminar. Whereas writing a book and getting it published might have taken Ensign a year or more, she was able to produce her booklet in only one month. And it has been such a stunning success that she has begun teaching others how to write and develop such booklets.

One of her clients, a matrimonial attorney in Chicago, has created a booklet on divorce which has enabled him to increase his business and entry price point by 50 percent. Another client, Joyce Cooper, is a professional speaker who has created a booklet on her speech topic, *The Enthusiasm Factor in Our Jobs and Our Lives*. She uses the booklet in marketing her services and sells it as part of her training program and at the back of the room after speaking. After hearing her speak companies also buy the booklets for employees who were not able to attend the program.

Michael Wyland assists his clients in grant writing and fund-raising. He now has two booklets: *20 Steps to Effective Grant Writing* for grant writers and *12 Steps to Yes* for fund-raisers. Writing the first booklets was much easier than he imagined. He simply used the outline from his lecture notes.

Ed Voil runs a consulting company, Vertical System Analysis, for property owners and managers on improving and evaluating their elevator service. Of course, he wanted to target the high-rise commercial and residential building market. He turned to marketing consultant Carol Milano of New York City for ideas. She suggested creating a fourteen-page free booklet entitled "Owner's Guide to Better Elevator Service." They sent a new release announcing the booklet to real estate trade publications. Most printed the announcement and the result was an impressive list of new clients.

Chuck Green calls such promotional books Infobooks and provides step-by-step ideas for creating a version of your own in *The Desktop Publisher's Idea Book*. He suggests creating one master copy of your booklet following his template and taking it to a commercial printer to be reproduced in quantity using saddle-stitch binding and eighty-pound uncoated stock for the cover. For additional information on creating such booklets for your own marketing efforts, see **Resources** below. (Also see **color insert** for examples of how you can create your own booklets.)

when you speak at professional meetings, or arrange to sell it at the back of the room after your presentation.

- Include a picture of it in your ads, brochures, flyers, and newsletters; refer to it in your bio and as part of the byline for any article or column you write.

Resources: Writing Your Own Book

Associations

Editorial Freelancers' Association, 71 West 23d Street, Ste. 1504, New York, NY 10010, (212) 929-5400. Provides a job bank through which you can locate professional writers.

National Graphic Artists Guild, 90 John Street, Ste. 403, New York, NY 10038, (212) 791-0330.

National Writers' Association, 1450 South Havana, Ste. 424, Aurora, CO 80012, (303) 751-7844. Consultation and agent referrals for members.

Writers' Guild of America East, 555 West 57th Street, New York, NY 10019, (212) 245-6180.

Writers' Guild of America West, 7000 West 3d Street, West Hollywood, CA 90048, (310) 550-1000.

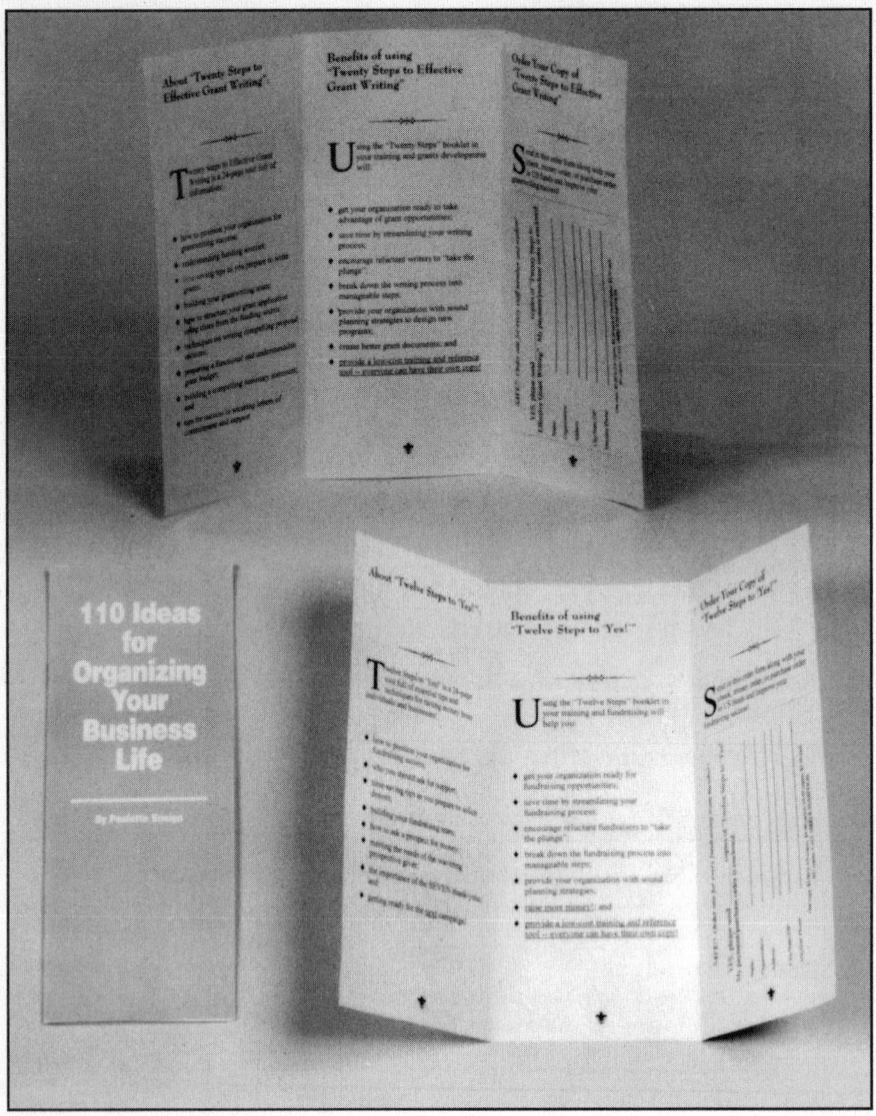

A Tips Booklet

Professional organizer Paulette Ensign provides workshops for how to create promotional tips booklets like her 110 Ideas for Organizing Your Business Life. *Michael Wyland has created two such booklets:* "Twelve Steps to Yes!" *and* Twenty Steps to Effective Grant Writing.

Books

The Complete Guide to Self-Publishing. Tom and Marilyn Ross. Cincinnati: Writer's Digest Books, 1985.

The Encyclopedia of Self-Publishing. Tom and Marilyn Ross. Cincinnati: Writer's Digest Books, 1994.

The Insider's Guide to Book Editors and Publishers and Literary Agents. Jeff Herman. Rocklin, CA: Prima Publishing, 1997.

Is There a Book Inside You? Dan Poynter. Santa Barbara, Calif.: Para Publishing, (805) 968-7277, Web: www.parapublishing.com, E-mail: DanPoynter@aol.com. 1997.

Kirsch's Handbook of Publishing Law. Jonathan Kirsch. Los Angeles: Acrobat Books, 1995.

Paperless Publishing. Colin Haynes. New York: Windcrest/McGraw-Hill, 1994. Includes diskettes with a variety of software to start publishing in a wide range of formats, including multimedia that includes sound and graphics.

Publishing Short-Run Books. Dan Poynter. Santa Barbara, Calif.: Para Publishing, (805) 968-7277, Web: www.parapublishing.com, E-Mail: DanPoynter@aol.com. 1988.

The Self-Publishing Manual. Dan Poynter. Santa Barbara, CA: Para Publishing, (805) 968-7277, Web: www.parapublishing.com, E-mail: DanPoynter@aol.com. 1997.

Writers' Market: Where and How to Sell What You Write. Cincinnati: Writer's Digest Books, Published Annually.

Book Packaging Services

About Books Inc., Box 1500 G, Buena Vista, CO 81211, (800) 548-1876.

Jenkins Group, 121 East Front Street, 4th Floor, Traverse City, MI 49684, (800) 706-4636, www.smallpress.com

Booklet Packaging Services

Paulette Ensign Organizing Solutions, (619) 481-0890, www.booklets@winning.com.

Software

Make-a-Booklet, Paper Direct, 100 Plaza Drive, Secaucus, NJ 07094, (800) A-PAPERS or (800) 272-7377, www.paperdirect.com

Directories and Publishers on Publishing

Dustbooks, 5218 Scottwood Road, P.O. Box 100, Paradise, CA 95967, (530) 877-6110, publishes *The International Directory of Magazines and Small Presses.*

Editor and Publisher, 11 West 19th Street, 10th Floor, New York, NY 10011, (212) 675-4380.

Writer's Digest Books, 1507 Dana Avenue, Cincinnati, OH 45207, (800) 289-0963.

Publishers Marketing Association, 627 Aviation Highway, Manhattan Beach, CA 90266, (310) 372-2732, E-mail: pmaonline@aol.com, Web: www.pma-online.org

Magazines and Newsletters

Publishers Weekly, 245 West 17th St., NY, NY 10011, the leading weekly magazine in the publishing industry, available in libraries or by subscription, (212) 463-6758, www.bookwire.com/pw/

Newsgroups

salt.prose
comp.publish.electronic
comp.publish.electronic.developer
comp.publish
alt.publish.books
misc.writing

Resources: Copywriting and Design for Any Printed Materials

Books

Desktop Publisher's Idea Book. Chuck Green. New York: Random House, 1997. Over 100 step-by-step designs with 250 illustrations for designing Web sites, brochures, books, business cards, tickets, envelopes, packages, signs, presentations, posters, and more.

Do-It-Yourself Advertising & Promotion: How to Produce Great Ads, Brochures, Catalog, Direct Mail and Much More. Fred E. Hahn. New York: Wiley, 1997.

Making a Good Layout. Lori Seibert and Lisa Ballard. Cincinnati: F & W Publications, 1992.

The Non-Designer's Design Book. by Robin Williams. Berkeley, Calif.: Peach Pitt Press, 1992.

The Non-Designer's Web Book. Robin Williams. Berkeley, Calif.: Peach Pitt Press, 1997.

Write Great Ads: A Step-by-Step Approach. Erica Levy Klein. New York: Wiley, 1990.

Words That Sell. Richard Bayan. Chicago: Contemporary Books, 1987.

Trade Associations for Professional Help

Editorial Freelancers' Association, 71 West 23d Street, Ste. 1504, New York, NY 10010, (212) 929-5400. Has job-listing service through which you can find copywriters.

Graphic Artists Guild, 11 West 20th Street, New York, NY 10011. Has job listing service through which you can find graphic designers.

Videos

Design Eye-Catching Brochures, Newsletters, Ads, Reports. Jane K. Cleland. CareerTrack, 3085 Center Green Drive, Boulder, CO 80301, (800) 334-1018, www.careertrack.com

Workshops

How to Design Eye-Catching Brochures, Newsletters, Ads, Reports and Everything Else You Want People to Read. CareerTrack, 3085 Center Green Drive, Boulder, CO 80301, (800) 325-5854, www.careertrack.com

On-Line

Appendix I: Writing and Designing Materials That Sell, available on-line without charge as a Special Report at www.paulandsarah.com on the Great Ideas for Getting Business page.

CHAPTER 12

Showing People What You Can Do

I am not interested in people's claims—only in what they do. The act came first and then the word.

—Alfred Stieglitz

Seeing is believing. What better way for people to understand the benefits of what you can do than to let them actually see or experience your products or services firsthand. Why not let your work speak for itself? But, of course, your work will not sell itself unless you arrange ample opportunities for people to see and experience it. That's what this chapter is about.

In today's multimedia world, there is a growing variety of ways to show off the results of your work from using an audiotape as your calling card to doing demonstrations at trade shows or providing virtual gallery on a multimedia Web page or mailing out video brochures.

Your Goal
Let People See and Experience Your Results

Audiotapes

When someone needs to understand psychiatrist Mark Goulston's specialty of helping people deal with the reality of suicide, he sends them a copy of his audiotape *What Are You Trying to Tell Me?* He slips his business card into the clear plastic cassette case, and the tape becomes an audio business card. It provides the media and potential referral sources with an immediate and highly personal experience of Goulston himself, his point of view, and his approach to working with clients. For any business that has a message to tell, a promotional audiotape is an ideal way to let your work speak for itself.

Whether you create your tape in a studio from a script or record it live from a performance, seminar, or session, a promotional audiotape provides the opportunity to communicate personally and privately with someone about who you are and what you do.

Your Goal: Let People See and Hear What You Have to Offer

___ Audiotapes
___ Business cards as samples
___ Compact disks
___ Demonstrations
___ Displays
___ House parties, open houses, and occasion events
___ Media appearances
___ Multimedia web sites
___ Photos and portfolios
___ Radio and television advertising
___ Samples and giveaways
___ Trade shows and special exhibits
___ Video brochures
___ Your own radio or television show

Audiotape Pros and Cons

Audiotapes allow you to send your message to anyone who wants to listen. They clearly demonstrate your mastery of your subject. They help establish credibility and are newsworthy as they can also be sent to a wide variety of media for review and critique. A well-presented tape or tape series can be sold at events, seminars, through mail, or over the Web and can provide you with a greater regional or national scope, thus helping to offset the cost of using the tapes for marketing purposes.

Creating audiotapes can be time-consuming and costly, however, especially if you're not prepared. They are costly to mail as well and tapes don't lend themselves well to some product-oriented businesses or visual businesses such as desktop publishing, word processing, etc. If you are terribly uncomfortable at the thought of recording your own voice, or if you don't react well to the pressure of reading a script in the recording studio, you may want to professionally record a live presentation and have it edited or consider other options for demonstrating what you can do.

Best Bets: Audiotapes will work best for consultants, teachers, and entertainers who are confident speakers. Audiotapes can also work for certain product businesses if the product can be taught or explained. For example, a gift basket business might create a tape called "Innovative Ways to Thank Customers with Gift Baskets."

Tips for Getting Results from Audiotapes

Write a compelling script. No matter what your subject matter, you will save time, reduce production costs, and end up with a stronger product if you write a well-thought-out, tight script. Write as if you were talking to a single client or customer. Avoid jargon and be sure to include plenty of examples to amplify key points. If you have difficulty writing a script, hiring a freelance writer is a worthwhile investment.

Record your content at a professional studio. When your script is completed, you're ready to record. No matter where you live, you should be able to find a high-quality, reasonably priced recording studio. Today's digital technology has brought prices down and quality way up. Studios charge either by hour or by project. If you are well rehearsed and fairly comfortable in front of a microphone, you can easily record a one-hour tape of material in an afternoon.

Even seasoned professionals make mistakes while recording, so don't worry in the slightest if you do. When you've finished recording, give the engineer a copy of your script so he or she can edit out the mistakes and provide you with a clean "master" tape. Depending on the length of your tape(s), it may take the studio a week or two to complete the editing process.

Have your master tape duplicated. When your master tape is ready, bring it (or send it) to a duplicating house, sometimes called a dubbing house, for mass production. Unless you only plan to send out a few tapes, don't try to reproduce tapes on home stereo equipment. A duplicating house will provide you with everything you need: custom-length blank cassettes, J-cards (the label that's inserted into the cassette case), and cassette labels (the label affixed to the cassette itself). You have two cassette labels options here: printing directly on the cassette shell, or printing a label that will be affixed onto the cassette. Prices vary from facility to facility and, for a limited number of tapes, average from about $2.25 to $4.00 per cassette, depending on length, labeling and J-card. Generally, the per-unit price goes down with quantity.

Package your tape effectively. If you are creating a series of tapes, you may wish to package them together as a complete program series. Although this will add some cost to your project, your tapes will look more professionally presented and create the greatest impression. Professional packaging will also allow you to sell them more easily at your place of business, at events, and through mail or Web order. Packaging prices vary considerably as well. Most packaging companies will also provide assistance in creating the necessary artwork for your package.

Resources:

Books

Billboard's International Recording Equipment and Studio Directory. New York: Billboard Directories, annually.

Digital Home Recording. Editors of *Keyboard* magazine. San Francisco: Miller Freeman Books, 1997.

The Sound Studio. Alec Nisbett. Newton, Mass: Focal Press, 1995.

Online Resources

RealAudio. One of the most widely used standards for putting audio on the World Wide Web. www.realaudio.com

AV and CD Resources Page, A fairly comprehensive list of links to tape duplicators, blank tapes, supplies, and more. http://marrak.com/resource/dupe.html

Newsletters and Magazines

Mix magazine, 6400 Hollis Street, #12, Emeryville, CA 94608, (800) 843-4086. Mix is a magazine for project and studio recording, audio for film and video, and more. www.mixmag.com. Also available on newsstands.

Services

Continental Binder and Specialty These folks provide a number of different single and multiple cassette packaging options. 407 West Compton Boulevard, Gardena, CA 90248 (310), 324-8227.

Business Cards as Samples

As we discussed in chapter 7, for a small or home-based business, a business card is far more than a piece of paper with your name, address, and phone number on it. It is one of your most important marketing tools. It can be a mini-billboard, a

mini-brochure, an advertisement, or even an order form. For some businesses, though, it can also be a sample. Since you will most certainly be giving out business cards on a regular basis, why not turn them into samples of what you do?

That's what facialist Lori Tabak has done. Her card is a pocket mirror on one side and a business card on the other. Metal sculptor James Tanish's card is sculpted from soft aluminum. The business card for Prestige Cover is enclosed inside a bound cover. And Rock Janda, whose company shrink-wraps product packaging for point-of-purchase displays, shrink-wraps his business card in cellophane. Before he came up with this idea, getting in to see purchasing directors when making sales calls was a real challenge. Now, he says, once an assistant presents his card, he always gets a meeting. "They want to meet the person who came up with this card," he told us.

See the color insert for examples of other creative ideas for how people have turned their business cards into samples of what they can offer, from stained-glass angel pins to healthful nutrition drinks.

Pros and Cons of Using Business Cards As Samples

The more your business card stand out from the crowd, the better; and the more effectively it demonstrates what you do, the more successful it will be at getting business to come to you. Incorporating your card into a sample can save you the cost of producing both card and sample. It also makes both your samples and your card more effective, because one item does double duty. People interested in your product can see it firsthand, and those who like what they see have immediate access to who you are and how to reach you. And, of course, since one of the

High-Tech Tip: List your E-mail Address and URL

If you have an E-mail address or Web site, be sure to list them on your business card. But do separate them clearly from your address and phone numbers. You want you address, phone and fax number, and e-mail or Web site address to both stand out and be easy to read. e-Card International of Pacific Palisades, California, offers a unique die-cut business card called an "e-card" that lists only your e-mail or Web address. You can give out this card separately and make an even greater impression (310/230-0384; Web: *www.ecard1.com*).

There are many clever ways to turn your business card into a sample of your work. Rock Janda shrink-wraps the card for his packaging company. Facialist Lori Tabak's metal card is printed on the back of a pocket mirror. Prestige Cover's card is in a mini-bound book. Super Slim NRG's card is stapled to a trial package of three vitamin capsules.

main reasons to give a card is to get a card in return from someone who is interested in your product or service, cards that serve as samples are a great way to make sure those folks will eagerly offer you their card so they too can have a sample. Cards that serve as samples will most likely be more expensive than standard business cards, so you have to determine if the added cost will pay for itself in added profits. You may want to have a smaller supply of sample cards for important presentations

High-Tech Tip: Use Pictures on Your Card

Often a picture is almost as good as the real thing when it comes to showing people what you do. So if turning your card into an actual sample isn't practical, consider using a picture as your card or put one on your card. Many inexpensive software programs, such as *Jasc's Paint Shop Pro,* not only allow you to create original logos and art for inclusion on business cards; they also make it easy to scan in and edit black-and-white or color images, including photos, directly into your card's layout.

and rely on a standard card for general use. Also, if not done well, a card/sample combination can appear too clever or cute, thereby detracting from your being considered a serious business. And you must be careful in designing your sample/card combination so that it isn't so bulky or odd sized that it gets tossed out or placed where no one will see it or find it.

Best Bets: Every business can benefit from giving, sending, distributing, and otherwise disseminating a business card that provides an appealing sample of their work. Business cards as samples work best, however, when your businises is person-to-person in nature, when what you offer can be easily conveyed through a sample, and when that can be produced cost-effectively.

Resources: Business Cards as Samples

Books

1000+ Stationery Designs. Val Cooper. Point Pacific Press, P.O. Box 4333, North Hollywood, CA 91617, (818) 762-1181. 1995. The designs are ready to use and royalty free; also available on disk.

Corporate Identity: Making Business Strategy Visible Through Design. Wally Olins. Boston: Harvard Business School Press. 1992.

Fresh Ideas in Letterhead & Business Card Design 3. Lynn Haller (editor). Cincinnati: North Light Books, 1997.

Print's Best Letterheads & Business Cards 4: Winning Designs from Print Magazine's National Competition (Serial). Linda Silver and Andrew Kner (editors). Cincinnati: Writer's Digest Books, 1996.

Software

Adobe PhotoDeluxe. Add special effects and customize photos for inclusion on your business card. Adobe Systems Incorporated, 345 Park Avenue, San Jose, CA 95110-2704, (408) 536-6000, www.adobe.com

Art Explosion 125,000. Includes 125,000 clip-art images, 850-page image catalog, and 1,500 fonts. Nova Development Corp., 23801 Calabasas Road, Ste. 2005, Calabasas, CA 91302, (818) 591-9600 or (800) 395-6682.

Jasc Ornamatica. Use 5,000 graphic elements to design custom borders and ornaments. Jasc, P.O. Box 44997, Eden Prairie, MN 55344, (800) 622-2793, www.jasc.com

Compact Discs

Interactive media are leading the way into a new electronic age and that includes CD-ROMs, or simply CDs. In the approximately eleven years that CDs have been commercially available, the price of creating them has come down considerably, making them a viable option for small and home-based businesses to use in promoting themselves. CDs are an excellent option for demonstrating your products and services if your market is fairly technologically sophisticated and your products or services lend themselves to the multimedia format.

The best CD programs from a promotional standpoint offer easily searchable text that can be quickly indexed and married with graphics, photos, sounds, and sometimes moving video that amplify the meaning of the content. Here are two of the ways businesses are now using CDs to promote themselves and their products:

• ***Multimedia Catalogs*** Many businesses who offer a diverse product line, such as computer supply houses, parts jobbers of all stripes, and software companies, put their catalogs on CD-ROM. This offers several advantages. CDs are generally cheaper to produce in bulk than large, full-color catalogs. The products in the catalogs can be instantly accessed in any way the user wishes. And with an Internet connection, an order can be placed directly from the consumer's computer to the company's Web site.

High-Tech Tip: Duplicate Your Own CDs

If you don't need to have a lot of CDs on hand at one time, try burning your own. Many companies—such as DynaTek's 4 x 6 CD recorder and Pinnacle's Micro RCD—offer fairly low-priced ($700–$1,200) CD burners that allow you to manufacture your own CDs one at a time. Please note: This is for the manufacturing process only. You will still need to create and program the CD as discussed above.

• ***Corporate Profiles and Product Overviews*** Companies large and small are using CDs to create high-impact profiles of their businesses, products, and services. Used much like traditional corporate training videos, these kinds of CDs present in-depth information on the company, it's history, officers, products, achievements, future plans, etc. Products and services can be presented with the same level of detail. Because of their interactive nature, the information presented on CDs doesn't wash over the user as often happens with traditional media. A good CD will encourage interaction, including using such devices as on-line suggestion forms, requests for further information, even entertaining games and quizzes that relate to the material presented.

The Pros and Cons of CD-ROMS

CDs can be a dynamic way to present what you have to offer. Although they've been around awhile, they are still a road less taken by small businesses in terms of promotional use. This means that if you have a CD for this purpose, it will really stand out. If you are organized, computer literate, and good at managing projects with many steps, creating a CD is a fairly straightforward process. Because they are interactive by nature, CDs actively involve the viewer; they can't be glossed over like brochures and ads or fast-forwarded through like videos. Some of the many other benefits of CD-ROMs include:

• ***Cost savings.*** Creating content on CD can be substantially less expensive than full-color printing. Additional benefits include easy updating of dated material.

• ***True Interactivity.*** The interactive digital format allows viewers to search for the keywords, concepts, or phrases they want to know more about instead of having to read your material in the order you think it should be laid out. This interactivity allows viewers to customize the way they experience your content and gives them much more flexibility and power than an index or table of contents.

- ***Hypertext Linking.*** CD publications allow viewers to jump anywhere on the disc just by clicking a mouse. These "jump points" are called Hypertext Links. The added benefit of Hypertext Links is that they can link your CD to your site or another site on the World Wide Web. Readers of well-designed digital publications can seamlessly switch between links in the publication and the Web.

- ***Multimedia Content.*** Instead of being limited to text and standard graphic images, CDs can include a wide variety of sounds, moving video images, even 3-D images and animations.

If you are not experienced with multimedia, computer programming, or detailed project management, however, producing a CD can be a time- and money-consuming affair. Also, if your market is not related to technology in some way, many of the people you give your CD to may not have the equipment or the know-how to play it. Most offices and many homes still do not have CD players, and you would be surprised at how many 286 and 386 computers without CD-ROM players there still are out there.

Best Bets: CD-ROMs work best as a marketing tools when you offer an extensive inventory or a visually oriented service to a fairly high-tech market. CDs also work for consultants who provide complicated services to other professionals such as financial and business advisors. Graphic artists, Web designers, and video and multimedia producers are tailor-made for promotional CD-ROMs, as most of their work is probably already in a digital format.

Tips for Creating CDs to Promote Your Business

Creating a CD that profiles, presents, or promotes your business is not as complicated as it might sound, although unless you are a computer programmer, it is best left to a professional multimedia author. You can help design the content flow, write the text, provide the images and sound, etc., but an experienced multimedia author will be required to actually program the information into a unified whole that will comprise the actual interactive experience.

Here's a sequential overview of the creation process:

Define the purpose of your promotional CD. Will you be creating a catalog of your products? Will the CD be an overview of a new product? Is this going to be an in-depth profile of your company?

Consult with an experienced CD-ROM author. Finding a good multimedia author who understands the interactive CD-ROM experience is essential. Check with your local Chamber of Commerce, university, or business directory. If you are unable to find someone locally, try searching the Web. Once you've found someone, ask to see some of the titles he or she has created. If everything looks good and checks out, set up an appointment to discuss your project. Based on your initial meeting, he or she will then supply you with a flow chart that outlines the content and the road map that demonstrates how the information will relate interactively.

Provide engaging content. Ask the author to specify which kinds of content he or she would like to receive, and in which order. For example, most authors want the text first, but a few want the images first so they can design the "feel" of the CD. Others may want everything all at once.

Create the programming. When your author has all the required content, he or she will begin programming the CD. This can take anywhere from a few weeks to several months, depending on the complexity of the project.

Do the manufacturing. When the programming is finished, the files must be mastered and "burned" into an actual CD. There are many production facilities across the country who do this for you. Most will provide complete service, such as duplicating the actual CD, providing the jewel box (the CD packaging), designing and printing the booklet which is inserted into the jewel box, printing the CD spine and back cover, and placing the CD into the jewel box and shrink wrapping. Based on an order of 1,000, prices for complete service start at about $2.50 per CD.

Use CD content on your Web site. With some slight modifications, you can post some of the more dynamic, interactive portions of your CD directly to your Web site. The multimedia programming and image/sound digitization will already have been done; you will simply need to have these segments reprogrammed in Java or Active-X. There are many freelancers who can do this for you at reasonable rates. Once your content is reprogrammed, upload it to your Web site. This will increase the attractiveness, as well as the traffic, of your site. If the content is innovative enough, it may well attract the attention of on-line publications as well as all the types of publications we mentioned above (especially if you let them know about it with a news release).

Resources: Compact Discs

 **Books**

Electronic Publishing Construction Kit. Scott Johnson, New York: Wiley, 1996.

Electronic Publishing on CD-ROM. Steve Cunningham and Judson Rosebush. Sebastopol, Calif.: O'Reilly & Associates, 1996.

Getting Started in Multimedia Design. Gary Olsen. Cincinnati: North Light Books. 1997.

 **Newsletters and Magazines**

Multimedia News newsletter. Paradise Software, 7 Centre Drive, Ste. 10, Jamesburg, NJ 08831, (609) 655-0016, www.paradise.com

 **Software**

Adobe Premier. Adobe Systems Incorporated, 345 Park Avenue, San Jose, CA 95110-2704, (408) 536-6000, www.adobe.com

Macromedia Director. Macromedia, Inc., 600 Townsend Street, San Francisco, CA 94103, (415) 252-2000, www.macromedia.com

Toolbook II. Asymetrix Corporation, 110 10th Avenue N.E., Ste. 700, Bellevue, WA 98004, Sales: (800) 448-6543, www.asymetrix.com

Demonstrations

Another powerful marketing tool is an actual demonstration of what you have to offer. This could be a tour or visit to a current or previous customer's operation to show off your work, or a special demonstration at your trade show or exhibit booth showcasing yourself at work. If you love your work, what better way to market yourself than for them to see you doing what you love.

Demonstrations can be especially helpful if your products or services are not easily portrayed in photographs or writing. For example, an Internet or Intranet consultant might personally take prospective clients on a tour through cyberspace, demonstrating the power of the Internet as a communications tool and pointing out specific examples of how the prospect can benefit from his services. A company who staffs heavily with temporary help could make an excellent tour for a temporary agency's prospective clients. An interior designer might show off her work to potential clients through actual visits instead of pictures alone.

Of course, you can always take your show to the prospect. Making appointments for demonstrations at the client's site has been a marketing tack for businesses as long as recorded history. If you are a consultant who offers a complicated service, you could create a demonstration using a multimedia presentation program, load into your laptop computer and hold a desktop demonstration. In either case, your prospective client or customer will not only gain a thorough understanding of your product or service, just as importantly, he or she will get to know you and how you work in the process.

When properly used, such real-life demonstrations can strut your stuff for you better than almost any other method.

Pros and Cons of Demonstration Events

A good demonstration has an air of mystique. Haven't you noticed how people seem drawn to watch someone at work at a trade show or exhibit? They are often entranced. And that is how demonstrations can work for you as well. They also allow you to combine other marketing techniques with them: for example, providing samples, giving out (or selling) audio and video tapes, and networking. Also, unless you must rent facilities or exhibit space, demonstrations cost very little.

The downside of demonstrations is that you really can't control what will happen.

A demonstration event is almost like a dinner party. What if no one comes? What if the souffle falls and the roast burns? At a demonstration there are no guarantees that you will have a good turnout. Despite the best-laid plans you also might not have the effect on the audience that you intended. Also, demonstrations can be time-consuming to plan and cost a fair amount if you need to rent space or equipment, or pay for assistants' fees, and promotional items.

Best Bets: Demonstrations, both on-site and special events, are potentially helpful for almost any business. Having your prospects watch what you or your product does right before their eyes allows them to make their own judgments, independent of your advertising and other marketing efforts.

Tips for More Successful Demonstrations

Organize, organize, organize! The more organized you are, the better results you will have. Period. Planning for every contingency will ensure that, short of an act of God, you will achieve some sort of benefit from your hard work. Instead of figuring out what to do next, you will be able to pay attention to the people you wish to impress. So, to ensure that the event goes smoothly, you should plan and rehearse all crucial elements. Plan how your audience will come in and how they will be seated. Of course, you need to plan the presentation itself. Try to think of all possible contingencies. Will you need an assistant? What if people come late? What will you do if people leave early? How will you compensate if part of the presentation doesn't work or if you encounter technical difficulties with audio/visual equipment or computers?

Scope out the location of the demonstration before the actual event. Always check out the physical space before you begin planning in earnest. Whether at a hotel, a customer location, meeting hall, or wherever, plan where your attendees will sit and where you will speak. If it's a walking tour, take the tour yourself. Can the expected number of attendees fit through the route? If at a customer site, will the tour seriously disrupt the running of the business? Will you have a break? Where will attendees go during break? Where will audio/visual and other speaker's aides be placed? The more you know about the physical characteristics of your event's location, the better able you will be to plan for its success.

Build in some sort of RSVP in your publicity and invitation packages. When promoting the event, always ask potential attendees to RSVP or reserve their space. In this way, you will have an approximate idea of how many people will be attending. If it's a small event, ask your attendees to RSVP by a certain date in your letter or invitation. If you are planning a larger event, make sure that your publicity prominently features a phone number for people to reserve their space for the event. Include the phone number on your direct mail as well.

Make sure to have a handout prepared. Your handout should serve two purposes. For one, it should clearly and concisely list the key informational points that you want your attendees to understand. This part is for them to take home. The second purpose of your handout,

Action Steps: Demonstrating Your Products

1. Select two ways to demonstrate your product or service through on-site visits, trade shows, exhibitions, volunteering, or seminars.
2. Try out one of the ways and track the results.

and it is advisable that this be a separate sheet of some sort, is for you to get information from your audience. In the information sheet, ask them to fill in their names, businesses, addresses, and contact information. Also ask them what part of the demonstration interested them the most. Ask them which of your products or services they would like to know more about. You can even ask them if they would like you to call and set up an appointment. Design this sheet as a questionnaire and provide them with pens or pencils.

According to Gene Call, a professional marketer and marketing trainer for over twenty-five years, "Tell your audience that you will be passing something out at the end of your demonstration. Then, about ten minutes before you intend to close, pass out your handouts. Let them fill out the questionnaire while you wait. After you see that most have stopped writing, tell them you will collect the questionnaires as they leave. Then wrap up your demonstration. When you are finished, ask them to bring up the questionnaires. This will ensure the best response in terms of having an audience actually fill out your form and make sure that you will actually receive them."

Resources: Demonstrations

Books

101 Ways to Captivate a Business Audience. Sue Gaulke. New York: AMACOM Books, 1996.

Business Presentations and Public Speaking (First Books for Business). Peter H. Engel. New York: McGraw-Hill, 1996.

Creating and Delivering Winning Advertising and Marketing Presentations. Sandra Moriarty and Tom Duncan. Lincolnwood, Ill.: Ntc Business Books, 1995.

I Can See You Naked. Ron Huff. Kansas City: Andrews and McNeel. 1992.

Your Public Best : The Complete Guide to Making Successful Public Appearances in the Meeting Room, on the Platform, and on TV. Lillian Brown. New York: Newmarket Press, 1992.

Software

Corel Presentations. Corel Systems. Sales: (800) 836-7274. Support: (613) 728-1990. Web: www.corel.com

Harvard Graphics. Software Publishing Corporation. Sales: (800) 336-8360. Support: (800) 336-8360, ext. 5. Web: www.spco.com

Lotus Freelance. Lotus Development Corporation. Sales: (800) 343-5414. Support: (978) 988-2500. Web: www.lotus.com

Microsoft PowerPoint. Microsoft Corporation. Sales: (800) 426-9400. Support: (425) 637-7098. Web: www.microsoft.com

On-Line Resources

Global Network of Creative Producers. This site provides a comprehensive national listing of venues, audio/visual services, convention and visitors' bureaus, and almost anything else you may need when planning a demonstration event. http://www.california.com/~gnocp/association.html

Displays

There is actually a way to strut your stuff even when you cannot be there to do it personally. Displays have formed the backbone of retail selling for many years. Companies who make or sell products have used various display techniques from small, point-of-purchase (POP) fold-out boxes to giant, room-sized self-running demonstrations.

Not only products benefit from using displays. Service businesses can also use displays to enhance their visibility and show potential customers and clients exactly what they do and how well they do it. For example, suppose you are a graphic designer and your current target market is telecommunications companies. You probably have a portfolio that you take to prospects whenever you have the opportunity. How about making enlargements of these photos to help decorate a booth at a trade show?

A plant service company that maintains green plants in homes and offices might provide green plants (along with a small sign and business cards and brochures) for room displays at furniture stores or for office furniture displays. Maintain them as you would a client's. If you have a carpet-cleaning service, you might work with one of the local carpet stores and have your own display entitled "Maintaining your new carpet," complete with a take-away sheet of tips for new carpet owners (with your name and number prominent on the sheet, of course).

Ask a current client to allow you to place a small display containing your flyers or brochures at his counter or in his waiting room. Some will be happy to help you out. With others you may pay for the privilege, or you might work out an exchange for some of your services.

For example, if you are a software consultant, you may wish to work out an agreement with several local software stores to provide them with a given number of hours of consulting services in exchange for placing your display or point-of-sale materials in public view in their store. Or, if your business is design or desktop publishing, you might pay a local printer with a great deal of traffic a fee to place a special display of your promotional materials on the counter. A nutritionist might request, trade for, or pay for a display of his or her brochures at the reception desk in a dentist's or doctor's office.

Several music teachers we know have worked out mutually beneficial arrangements with their local music stores. The teacher is allowed to display a flyer and business cards prominently. When a potential student calls, the teacher asks where the caller saw his or her ad. If the caller saw the ad in one of the music stores, the teacher sends in a small "referral" fee.

Pros and Cons of Displays

Displays are a helpful technique for almost every business. With a little creativity you can find a way to display what you offer, no matter what it is. Displays can be low-cost if your budget is tight. Displays work well within a larger marketing plan. For example, your ads might reference your display with a phrase like "Check our display at Grundig's Furniture." Displays can also hold your business cards, brochures, flyers, and even audio- or videocassettes and will increase the distribution of these items at no additional cost to you.

Displays can be difficult to maintain. If you're busy, you might not have time to check on that floral arrangement or to see if your POP is out of brochures or cards. Wilted flowers and empty literature holders can be turnoffs to prospects.

Tips for Effective Displays

Work with a Single Designer. To get materials that will do the best job for you, work with a single designer to prepare your display framework and materials. If the designer you are working with is employed by the packaging production firm you use for your products, be sure he or she sees all your other promotional materials and clearly understands the image and identity you are promoting for your product or service and for your company as a whole.

Keep a Consistent Image. Once you have created a display format, the rest of your promotional materials should reinforce the visual image your display creates.

Make It Visual. The key to effective displays is translating what you do into a visual medium. This translation does not have to be quite as direct or as literal as the above examples. Think about how you would create a print ad using only photographs. If your message can be communicated on a purely visual level, a similar display can work for you. The question then becomes Where? Your answer: Whatever locales your potential customers and clients frequent and wherever you can get someone to put what you want on display.

Resources: Displays

Newsletters and Magazines

Display and Design Ideas. Shore-Varrone, Inc., 6255 Barfield Road, Ste. 200, Atlanta, GA 30328, phone: (404) 252-8831 or (800) 241-9034, fax: (404) 252-4436, Web: www.ddimagazine.com

House Parties, Open Houses, and Occasion Events

You might just be sitting in one of the best venues there is for demonstrating what you do. Instead of renting an unfamiliar and costly facility, why not use your own home or office? Many business people have done this to great effect.

As an up-and-coming actor, Jeff Sumner needed a second income to help make ends meet. On the recommendation of a friend, he decided to start his own business selling Tupperware. Tupperware was founded by Earl Tupper in the 1950s and was based on the home demonstration party. Jeff started out by holding parties in his own home, then recruited others to host parties. In the beginning the parties went well enough, but "they were really nothing to write home about," explains Jeff. Then he was struck by a thought. In his acting work he excelled at playing unusual characters. "Why not find a way to bring my

Action Steps: Creating Creative Displays

To help you determine what kind of display might promote your business:

1. In one sentence, write what need your product or service fills.
2. Below that sentence, make a short list of who has the need that your product or service fills.
3. Now make a list of places where these people frequent or can be found. Is it a specific kind of store? On-line? A specific kind of office such as an accountant's, doctor's, or business consultant's? Is it a school or institution? Or maybe an office building. For example, say you offer a typing or desktop publishing service that specializes in typing scripts. Where do scriptwriters often go? Copy shops, for one place. Scriptwriting classes for another. So a copy shop or a local college or university that offers scriptwriting classes would be excellent places to set up a display.
4. Now determine how you can represent your product or service visually. Many products lend themselves to photographs. Many services can be summed up in a simple bulleted list of highlighted points. Better yet, think of a more direct way to represent your business such as the green plant provider or carpet cleaning service we described earlier.
5. You are now ready to create your display and approach the manager or owner of the potential location to allow you to display it. The process of convincing such a manager or owner will go more smoothly if you have something to offer in exchange. You can offer to pay a small fee for each customer referred to you by the display, or promise to send your current and future customers to them if they need that particular product or service sold there. For example, in exchange for placing a display in an instrument sales and repair shop, a music teacher can promise to refer any student who needs to have an instrument fixed or replaced. However, sometimes having you as a way of taking care of needs the store or location does not want to serve may be enough incentive.

acting talents into my Tupperware business?" thought Jeff. After a little more creative digging, true inspiration visited him and a new character was born. Now, instead of Jeff Sumner, his parties are hosted by an "outrageous blonde with really big hair and an attitude as big as a double-wide trailer" named Pam Teflon, Sumner's alter ego. Pam's character is fully developed. She has a "husband named Marvin and two kids named Allen and Sue."

Pam's parties have become all the rage in trendy Hollywood. And the Tupperware "just flies out the door." Jeff/Pam are one of the top-selling Tupperware businesses in the country with gross sales in 1996 of well over $175,000.

Tupperware parties are a classic example of the effectiveness of home parties and special-occasion events. While sales usually are made at trunk sales and home parties like Jeff's, open houses and other events are usually strictly promotional in nature with any sales occurring as a result of follow-up contacts made after the event. Hosting such events allows you to demonstrate not only what you do, but also how and where you do it. Home parties could just as easily be called office parties. Whether your business is run from home or from an office, your guests can see your operations and place of business firsthand. Of course, if you prefer, you can host special events at other locations as well, if your facilities are not suited for entertaining.

There are ample occasions for hosting open houses or other promotional events. Every business celebrates special occasions. Anniversaries, Christmas, Hanukkah, the acquisition of a major new account, and any number of milestones are all occasions that a business can celebrate. When the architectural firm of Brenda Levin and Associates moved into a brand-new office, they invited past clients, current clients, city officials, patrons of the arts, and many others to an open house. This allowed Brenda to thank her clients for helping her attain the level of success she had reached. It also demonstrated to the city officials in attendance that she was successful, too. Placed strategically throughout the new office were large photographs of past projects and enlargements of press clippings and reviews. When DesignTeal, a small but growing design firm, reached their tenth year of business, they decided to throw a party to celebrate. Invited were past and present clients, vendors, colleagues, and a number of prospects that the firm had been pursuing recently.

You begin to see a pattern. By celebrating an event or occasion with clients and prospects, especially a business milestone, you create an opportunity to demonstrate not only what your business can do but also what you have done.

Pros and Cons of House Parties, Open Houses, and Occasion Events

Hosting a promotional social event allows you to do something nice for people. By providing an atmosphere in which guests can celebrate with you, or enjoy themselves in some way, you will definitely create a memorable impression. These kinds of events give you a low-stress platform from which you can demonstrate your business while also demonstrating the kind of person you are.

On the other hand, such events take considerable time to plan and there are costs involved in printing and sending invitations, making your facilities festive, and providing refreshments. If you are not a social person and don't enjoy parties of any sort, you should look for other ways to demonstrate what you do.

Best Bets: Promotional events can work well for any kind of business. If your location isn't adequate to hold such an event, ask a friend or a colleague for help. These situations are excellent networking opportunities and a great way to stay in touch and remain top-of-mind with customers and referral sources.

High-Touch Tip

House parties and occasion events are personal, even intimate gatherings. To ensure a good turnout and create a better ambience for your event, deliver invitations personally. Bring one with you when you visit a client. Bring several with you when you attend someone else's party or event. Handing someone a personal invitation makes that person feel special, and that's the way you want to make everyone feel who attends your party or occasion.

High Tech Tip: Do-It-Yourself Invitations

Consider creating a customized and colorful invitation using software like ***Microsoft Publisher*** or ***Print Artist*** from Sierra and send your invitations by fax or E-mail. Using special software like *Chroma Fax*, you can send and receive color faxes. If you attach a binary file, you can send color files across the Internet. Or create your own invitations using preprinted papers (see color insert).

Tips for Obtaining Good Results from Open Houses, House Parties, and Occasion Events

Include a clear, detailed map to your location on every invitation. A phone number that guests can call if they need directions is essential. Make sure someone can answer the phone before and during the event to give directions to lost or late-arriving guests.

Include an RSVP in your invitations. When promoting the event, always ask potential attendees to RSVP. Provide a phone number, an E-mail address, or a mail-in response card for this purpose. This way you will have an approximate idea of how many people will be attending.

Have the event catered. Remember that you are not only demonstrating the capabilities of your business, you are also demonstrating your skills as a host. For greater impact, try coming up with a subtle theme for your event, such as the American Southwest or a Bavarian Biergarten and have it catered accordingly.

Allow plenty of time for setup. Have your office or house cleaned shortly before the event. Allow time for the caterer to be late. If you are going to give a demonstration, make sure that everything is ready an hour before guests are to arrive.

Keep your perspective as a host.

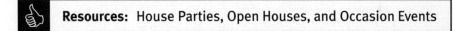

Resources: House Parties, Open Houses, and Occasion Events

Books

Any Excuse for a Party: Hundreds of Fantastic Themes, Invitations, Recipes and Activities for Fabulous Parties. K. Callan. Beverly Hills: Dove Books, 1997.

The Party: Adventures in Entertaining. Sally Quinn. New York: Simon & Schuster, 1997.

Power Schmoozing. Terri Mandell, New York: McGraw-Hill. 1996.

Special Events: Inside and Out. Steven Wood Schmader and Robert Jackson. Champaign, Ill.: Sagamore Publishing. 1997.

Software

Chroma Fax. Compressent Corp. Sales: (800) 400-5568. Support: (500) 442-6567. Web: www.compressent.com

Microsoft Publisher. Microsoft Corporation. Sales: (800) 426-9400. Support: (425) 637-7098. Web: www.microsoft.com

Print Artist. Sierra Online, Sales: (800) 757-7707. Support: (425) 644-7697. Web: www.sierra.com

The Ultimate Event Planner. CR Software Solutions, P.O. Box 40787, Indianapolis, IN 46240-0787, www.softwaresolutions.com

Services

Event Planner. An association that provides comprehensive sources of event planning information, primarily from their Web site. 9114 Town Gate Lane, Bethesda, MD 20817, (301) 365-0470, www.event-planner.com

Media Appearances

In chapter 10 we described how you can get others talking about you and your products and services through publicity in all types of media. If you don't mind doing the talking, however, there are lots of additional media opportunities for showing off what you do. You and your product or service can be featured on radio and television and in cyberspace. Appearing on or in local, regional, or national media is one of the most effective ways to demonstrate what you've got to offer and thereby get business coming to you.

You have undoubtedly seen and heard many guest experts on the media. Makeup artists and hair stylists do makeovers and show us how to look our best. Wedding dress designers show us the spring bridal fashions. Chefs show and tell us how to make fat-free desserts. Dog trainers teach us how to turn unruly pets into well-mannered companions. Psychologists take listener calls on topics from finding the love of your life to surviving the loss of a child. Professional organizers show us how to clear the clutter from our closets, desks, and filing cabinets. Financial planners show us how to invest our money and plan for retirement. Many, if not most, of these guests are small-business owners and self-employed individuals like yourself.

If you would like lots of people to see or hear you doing your thing, there is probably no better way than through the media. You can do this through a well-planned publicity campaign as described in **chapter 10.** The first step, of course, will be creating a presentation kit and using it to capture the attention of the media, as outlined in **chapter 8.**

Here, however, we want to focus on how you can use media appearances, once you get them, to show and tell about what you do. You will want your appearances to attract business, but you will need to do that without alienating the media, who never want you to be commercial—unless, of course, you are paying for advertising. You will find that whatever the medium, be it radio, TV, or on-line, the interview process is surprisingly similar.

Pros and Cons of Media Appearances

Appearing in the media enables you to promote what you have to offer with a power unequaled by almost any other method. It gives you high visibility and establishes your credibility as a successful business person and an expert in your field. You can refer to your appearances in all subsequent advertising and marketing ("As seen on the *Today* show" or "As an acknowledged expert in his field, Joe Mediaguy has been quoted in the *New York Times* as well as . . ."). And other than the time and expense of sending out media kits and talking with producers, appearing on the media will generally cost you nothing.

The only drawback to appearing on broadcast media is if you are incredibly shy or nervous about speaking on camera or through a microphone. Television can be especially revealing. You have undoubtedly seen or heard nervous guests tripping over their tongues or their props as they rush through the limited time most media interviews provide. Any sort of discomfort, or worse, stumbling, detracts from your message. So we generally recommend media appearances only after you have a clear idea of your message, can articulate it with confidence, and feel good about your ability to show off what you do. Even then, we suggest starting small and getting some experience with the media before going for a big-time appearance like the *Today* show. Guest spots on local cable access shows are an ideal place to begin. Sometimes the host will be as nervous as you are, but you can have a fun time together trying out your media legs.

Best Bets: Media appearances are worth the time and expense for any business that wants to show off what it can offer. The more novel, visual, or newsworthy (see **chapter 10**) your message, the more likely it is that the media will be interested in you. Therefore businesses that relate to the needs of large numbers of consumers often do best; however, with growing numbers of niched media outlets, a more targeted business can also do quite well through the media.

Tips for Making the Most of Your Interview

It is important that you make the most of the opportunity to be interviewed by the media, because the more engaging the interview, the more likely it is to lead to business and future publicity opportunities. Here are some tips for making sure your interview sparkles.

Prepare. Write out the key points or message you want to convey to the audience. What do you want people to know about you and your business? It is important to be clear about this and to keep it foremost in your mind during the interview. No matter what the interviewer asks, you should find a way to include your message in your answers. Here are several questions to help you prepare:

1. What is your specialty?
2. How would you describe your specialty in fifteen seconds or less, including whom you provide it to and what it does for them?
3. What problem or problems do you solve?
4. What tips would you give someone facing this problem?
5. What unique solutions do you provide?
6. What examples can you give in which you provided such a solution?
7. What upbeat, encouraging, or funny message can you leave people with?
8. What offer can you make that people can't refuse?

Then write out the most likely questions you will be asked. Think of how you will respond to them in ways that will highlight your unique background, skills, and experience. Include all potentially embarrassing, controversial, or negative questions, and have a good answer even for the things you hope no one will ever ask. However, don't memorize your answers—you want your interview to be lively, spontaneous, and conversational. Practice by having someone else ask you the possible questions you have developed and answering them extemporaneously based on the key points you want to make.

Keep the audience in mind. In answering questions, remember that while you are looking at and speaking to the interviewer, you are simultaneously addressing the audience. In fact, communicating with the audience is your primary goal. When you have succeeded at this, you have done a good job for the interviewer. So find out as much as you can about who will be reading, watching, or listening to your interview.

While you want to use the interview to communicate a message, don't try to sell yourself or your business. Guest appearances and other interviews are not commercials, and the media are quite sensitive to this distinction. Be equally sensitive to the reasons they have chosen to interview you. Usually, your job in an interview is to be informative and to be so in an engaging, and as much as possible consistent with your personality and topic, in an entertaining way. The more informative and appealing you are, the more likely you are to be quoted in an article and invited back on radio or television. The more unusual and valuable the information you provide, the more interested the audience will be in your product or service. Remember, though, that guests who try to mention their business name repeatedly and urge people to buy their product or service will alienate both the audience and the interviewer.

The best way to make sure you get a good plug from the interviewer or host is to provide a lot of useful information that is rich with colorful examples from your experiences in a forthright and moving way. As a caterer, for example, you will get more business from a television guest appearance if your food demonstration looks dramatic and tastes delicious to the host than from trying to make a direct plug for your company. Or, as a tax advisor, you will get a better response by presenting several useful tax strategies than you would from going over your credentials. Watch media guests, such as Dr. Joyce Brothers, who are invited to appear again and again. They are masters at providing a wealth of both practical and entertaining messages.

Arrange in advance for the audience to be able to contact you. If appropriate, ask before the interview whether the interviewer would be willing to let people know how they can contact you for more information. Such a plug will be far more valuable than self-promotion.

Often the interviewer will agree to include your address or phone number in an article or at least will let people know where you are located so they can contact you through the phone directory. Radio and television interviewers will often give out a phone number or address where their guests can be reached at the close of the interview. If the interviewer agrees to give out this information but then doesn't do so, it is perfectly acceptable to volunteer the information at the close of the interview. You should always find out in advance how long the interview will be. Then keep a clock in view so you can provide this information right before the end. Don't, however, get caught checking your watch on camera.

Another way to increase your chances of getting a good plug is to make sure the interviewer has been able to see or use your product or service sometime before the interview. Be sure to send or bring samples, and offer to do a free demonstration. To help assure that your address and phone number will appear, offer to give away something free to everyone who calls in response to the article or show. For example, the caterer could give away recipes for the dishes she demonstrates, and the tax adviser could give away a list of frequently overlooked deductions.

In general, we have found that, if you respect the interviewer's desire to avoid commercialism, he or she will be cooperative about releasing information about you.

Make sure your title and business name are included and are accurate. Interviewers are notorious for mispronouncing names and for confusing titles, so make sure they have the accurate spellings of both your name and your business. Check to see what title will be appearing on the caption below your image on the TV screen and how you will be introduced. Make sure you are described in a way that will promote your business. For example, being introduced as "Janice Jennings, Cajun food chef" is not very helpful, since it doesn't indicate where you cook; "Janice Jennings, Cajun caterer" is better, and still better would be "Janice Jennings, chef and owner of Hot Cajun Catering Service." Should the interviewer give out wrong information, you can correct it as you begin answering your first question.

Restate the question in beginning your answer. This is particularly important for pretaped radio or television interviews, where your answers will be edited. But it also helps to orient a live audience, and it gives you a chance to focus your thoughts and time to formulate your answer regardless of the type of interview. For example:

Question:
"What is the most common cause of fatigue?"

Answer:
"The most common cause of fatigue is . . ."

Reframe the question when necessary. You do not have to answer a question as it has been posed. Your goal is to convey your message in a way that doesn't alienate the audience or the interviewer, so feel free to reframe a question in such a way as to provide the most effective answer. This is true even if you are live on the air. If someone asks you a question that casts you in an unfavorable light or introduces material with which you are not familiar or that is too complex or obscure to answer briefly, reframe the question. Even in a print interview in which the reporter is simply taking intermittent handwritten notes, never say anything you don't want to be quoted as saying. For example:

Question:
"But it takes a lot of money to put on a wedding like that, doesn't it?"

Avoid:
"Yes, a wedding does cost a lot of money but . . ."

Answer:
"A wedding is something people want to cherish for a lifetime. So they will invest as much as they can to make it really special. No matter what the budget, there's always a way to do that. For example, we did a beautiful wedding where . . ."

Keep your answers brief and to the point. Radio and television interviews are a conversation, not a monologue, so if your response to a question lasts longer than thirty to sixty seconds you are probably over-answering. For a print interview, you can give somewhat longer answers, but since you want to be quoted, one or two short, clear points in response to each question are preferable. When an answer requires considerable information, summarize it. For example, if asked how you decided to get into your field, instead of reviewing your entire work history you might focus on one pivotal element such as a customer's suggestion that you go into business on your own.

Short anecdotes told with a twinkle and a smile can be effective. For example, when asked why she started her first business, Peggy Glenn often grins and replies, "Because I got mad!" She then tells how, after years of being underpaid and underappreciated, she walked out on her job in a fit of frustration. With three teenage children and a new husband who had not expected to be the sole support of a family of five, she needed to make some money fast before anyone missed her paycheck. So she started a typing service.

Elaborate beyond "yes" or "no." Make specific points, and use examples that will bring home each point. For instance, when a career consultant is asked whether people have to settle for boring, dead-end jobs, she might respond: "I find there is always some way you can earn a good living doing something you enjoy. For example, I counseled a forty-five-year-old secretary who hated her job but loved to sew. Through our work, she decided to start a business doing freelance custom tailoring for local dry cleaners."

Demonstrate that you are an authority. To build your credibility, use dramatic and startling facts, statistics, and findings to make your point throughout an interview. Enumerate points and call attention to them. For example, you might say, "Here's something to think twice about: Ninety-seven percent of what we say to ourselves is negative!" or "Now here's a sobering thought: At age sixty-five, only one out of twenty people is financially independent!"

Give reasons for the points you make. For example, a personal trainer who is asked about how he helps people lose weight might say, "Many times you don't even need to lose weight; you simply need to tone up your body to look great at your present weight," adding, "Tightening sagging muscles shapes the body and eliminates inches even if you haven't lost a pound."

Talk personally, concretely, and colorfully. Avoid academic, theoretical, abstract, and clinical language. For example, instead of saying "I treated a depressed client who was suffering from the illusion that she was destined to spinsterhood," say "I talked with a young woman who was afraid that her chance of finding a husband was about as good as winning the lottery."

Always look directly at the interviewer when you talk, using his or her name. When answering a live call-in on a radio or TV talk show, address the caller by name, too.

Be positive and speak with enthusiasm and conviction. Don't dwell on the negative aspects of your message. Provide solutions that inspire hope, encouragement, and confidence, and end each segment with an upbeat, summarizing benefit. For example, a drug counselor might talk about the negative effects of drugs but hold out the promise of rehabilitation, closing with an inspiring story of someone who has succeeded in beating the odds and is now living drug-free.

Keep using your best answers. When being interviewed on more than one show or by more than one publication, continue to use the same answers you have taken the time to prepare. You will quickly learn which ones produce positive reactions. You will do better with a clearly thought-out response that works well than by trying to be innovative each time you are interviewed.

Resources: Media Appearances

Books

Dealing Effectively with the Media. John Wade. Menlo Park, CA: Crisp Publications, 1992.

Media Relations in Your Spare Time : A Step-by-Step Guide for Anyone in Business. Laura Brown. Washington, D.C.: National Association of Manufacturers, 1995.

Mediasmart: How to Handle a Reporter by a Reporter. Dennis Stauffer. Minneapolis: Minneapple Press, 1994.

Tidman's Media Interview Technique: Handling the Media and Getting Your Point Across on TV, Radio, and within Your Organization. Peter Theodore John Tidman. New York: McGraw-Hill, 1991.

Multimedia Web Sites

It wasn't so long ago that just having a site on the World Wide Web was a real *fait d' accompli.* It put you ahead of the crowd. But, of course, having a Web site rapidly became like having a fax, answering machine, or voice mail. It is expected that most small businesses and self-employed individuals will have some Web presence, and indeed, as we showed in chapter 11, it is a great way to tell about what you do. For anyone who wants to do more than let people read about what they have to offer, however, a multimedia Web site is the way to go.

Unlike media appearances and publicity, with your own multimedia site you won't have to talk anyone into allowing you to showcase your work in all its glory. You need not be limited to text descriptions. With multimedia capability your site can include video, audio, 3-D images, animation, and interactive graphics. Recent developments in Web and Internet technology now make the transmission of this content faster, better, and easier than ever before.

For example, you can include real-time "streaming" video that allows browsers to click on an icon and instantly see and hear a full-color video segment. Audio content such as voice and music can also be streamed in the same manner, so people can listen to your message in real time when they visit your site. Languages such as Java and Active-X allow programmers to create Web-specific spreadsheet, database management, and indexing applications that can be run right from your Web site. These languages, and a few others, have also led to dramatic improvements in animation and 3-D graphics that can be included in a Web site.

A multimedia Web site can centralize many of the techniques we've discussed in this chapter and include them in a unified source. You can add your video brochure and audiotapes. You can publish pictures of your products. You can even give browsers a 3-D tour of your facility. It is beyond the scope of this book to outline the technical specifics of how to accomplish this, but we will give you an overview of the multimedia capabilities you can include and their benefits.

If you use a Webmaster or Web designer, he or she will no doubt be familiar with what it will take to launch your video into cyberspace. If you designed the site yourself, consult the references listed at the end of this section. Some of the main protocols being used today are VDO, VIVO, and RealVideo. To use them you will need to buy a license from these companies. Contact them at their Web sites (listed in the **Resources** section) for specific information.

In addition to recorded video, you can also broadcast live right from your Web site. With equipment that costs less than $800, you can effectively have your own show that's netcast to a worldwide audience. Since you will be in total control, you can netcast (used like broadcast) as long and as often as you wish. Very few businesses are doing this at the time of this writing. Why not be one of the first?

Pros and Cons of a Multimedia Web Site

Multimedia can add a great deal of depth to your site, making the information you present more easily understood and remembered. Multimedia content also helps your site stand out from the crowd and creates instant credibility. Streamed audio and video can save you money on tape duplication and distribution. It may even cut back on the amount of brochures and printed material you send out.

Multimedia, especially applets and 3-D graphics, can be somewhat expensive to produce however. Your site will have to be redesigned to accommodate all the new content as well. Your monthly server fees are sure to go up substantially, perhaps even to twice or three times what you are paying now. Since not all servers can handle multimedia content, you may need to move your site to another server. This can be problematic. Your new server will need permission from InterNIC (the agency that oversees and manages Web site name registration). Also, if you change servers you will need to resubmit your URL to all the search engines.

Best Bets: If you currently have a Web site and video brochure, audiotape, radio program, or television program, it would behoove you to put this material on your site. If you don't have a Web site, or any of the other multimedia content we just mentioned, you can still benefit from a site that features multimedia. Any business that's visual in nature, or offers a service that people can get a taste of through their computers, is a prime candidate for a multimedia site. Such a site is generally less expensive to produce and maintain than a full-blown video production or series of broadcast ads, yet could bring in comparable results.

Tips For Getting Results from Multimedia Web Sites

Stay focused on your goals. It's easy to be seduced by exciting new technology. Don't get so enamored of the power of multimedia that you forget the main reason you created the site in the first place: to bring in customers and/or serve your current customers. If you add a video, for example, make sure the information it provides is of real value to your browsers, or works hard to sell your product or service. If you offer a 3-D tour of your facility, be sure viewers see your product or service in action. Here are several additional examples of how you can focus the power of multimedia on you and your products or services.

Using Video

Imagine telling a prospect who's calling from across the country to watch a video of your work while you both discuss it over the phone. If you have video on your Web site, you could be doing this all the time.

Marketing Mistake: New Technology Still Needs Old-Fashioned Marketing

Web technology is so new and exciting, it sells itself. This all-too-common trap was fallen into by the unfortunate subject this chapter's marketing mistake. Digibomb, Inc. (the story is real, the name is not) is a small high-tech company located somewhere in the southwest. For ten years their focus was on voice technology. They offered a solid product family and sold it with some success.

Realizing the potential of the Internet and the World Wide Web, they began to focus their attention on cyberspace fairly early in the game, about 1995. After some consideration about how to apply their strength to the new medium they decided, among other things, to develop a high-speed network that specialized in serving multimedia content. Not a bad idea, especially in 1995 when few were actually doing this. Within six months they had the basic technology in place to serve multimedia content. Their aim was to sell space on their server to Web sites whose content was primarily multimedia. Again, this was a great idea as few servers in the market could, or would, provide this service well. In order to sell the idea, Digibomb needed a way to demonstrate the effectiveness of their service.

At the suggestion of an outside consultant, they decided to first produce a corporate video, then incorporate it into their own Web site. This had two inherent benefits. Browsers could see that the Digibomb server indeed served multimedia well. They could also receive a clearer understanding of the company, its capabilities, and its accomplishments from the video itself. The video was produced, and in short order it was on the Web for all the world to watch.

The problem was, no one saw it. Digibomb believed that all they had to do was effectively use the cutting-edge technology of the day and people would beat a path to their door. No one did; not customers, not the media, not even other Web content providers. After six full months of generating nothing in the way of attention, it was their competition who had beaten them. Now, Digibomb is no longer in the multimedia server business.

Digibomb made the mistake that many businesses still make when they create or upgrade a Web site: They thought that the site's very existence would generate interest, traffic, and ultimately sales. They really should have known better. For a Web site to be effective to your bottom line, it has be an integrated part of your overall marketing mix. Even a multimedia Web site. *Especially* a multimedia Web site. Your audience won't find your site all by themselves. You have to point the way. Check the Tips section below for some suggestions as to how to accomplish this.

Having prospects or customers be able to watch you in action on video, twenty-four hours a day, seven days a week, anywhere in the world is pretty powerful stuff. The money you can save in tape duplication and mailing costs will more than offset the surprisingly small price of preparing and streaming your video on the Web.

Using Audio

Audio can be streamed onto your site in real-time and run continuously without interruption while browsers move around within your site. This can enhance your site in many different ways. You can provide a guided audio tour through your business, include regular messages for your customers, or provide a soundtrack that adds to the look and feel of your site. The possibilities are limited only by your imagination.

Audio files have one technical advantage over video files: They take up less memory and bandwidth. This will allow browsers with lower-end modems to still enjoy your multimedia content. It will also make your server happier.

Using Spreadsheet, Database, and other "Applets"

An applet is simply a small application that can run on any platform. Using Java and Active-X, programmers can create small spreadsheet and database programs that run right on your Web site, no matter what kind of computer the browser is using. This allows you to do things like put a catalog of your entire inventory on your site and have it be totally searchable by browsers. When browsers have found what they are looking for, they can place orders right through your site and your inventory record will be updated automatically. Or, you can have a program created that allows browsers to figure out their own potential mortgage or interest rates based upon a set of assumptions and preconditions that they enter. They get their mortgage rate, and you get a detailed profile of each and every browser who utilizes the applet.

Unless you are a computer programmer, leave applet design and programming to a professional. A quick search through the Web or your local Chamber of Commerce, for that matter, will provide you with a good list of candidates. When interviewing a programmer, tell him or her as clearly as possible what you would like your applet to do. Don't worry about the technical stuff; that's his or her job. A good programmer should also be able to offer suggestions about how to increase the power and effectiveness of the applet.

Using 3-D and Interactive Graphics

As compression technologies get better, graphics get more complex and dynamic. VRML (Virtual Reality Markup Language) is a language developed specifically for the Web that allows an infinite number of three-dimensional environments to be created, both real and artificial. You might say, "Big deal, sounds like *Star Trek*'s Holodeck to me." Well, it might be a big deal if your potential customers had the ability to actually "pick up" your products and examine them from all angles—not from your showroom, but on-line from their living rooms. The Los Angeles County Museum of Art (www.lacma.org) offers a 3-D tour through some of its galleries. You can offer a tour through your facility as well. How about demonstrating your product in action, while giving browsers the ability to walk completely around it? All this is possible with 3-D graphics and images.

Again, to implement this you will need professional assistance. Search the Web to find a list of candidates.

Include a mechanism that prompts the browser to take an action. Try to make viewing multimedia material contingent on the browsers' filling out some sort of on-line form. This way you will receive a great deal of valuable information about those who are interested in what you have to offer. The form need not be long. Even just a name, address, and E-mail address will suit your purposes. Include your phone number in easy-to-see places throughout your site and prompt browsers to call. Toll-free numbers are especially effective.

Design your pages, even those containing multimedia, to load quickly. People hate waiting for complex pages to load into their computers. Many will leave your site if they have to wait for more than fifteen seconds for anything. Although multimedia content is complex and therefore will take a long time to load, a good designer will set up pages that at least give viewers something to look at while the rest of the page downloads. Make sure that the pages in your site do this, especially the "home" or "core" page.

Resources: Multimedia Web Site

Books

Creating Killer Interactive Web Sites: The Art of Integrating Interactivity and Design. Andrew Sather, ed., Ardith Ibanez, Bernie Dechant, and Stefan Grunspan. Indianapolis: Hayden Books, 1997.

Database Publishing on the Web and Intranets (Webmaster Series). Kurt Lang and Jeff Chow. Scottsdale, Ariz.: Coriolis Group, 1996.

Instant VRML Worlds. Randall Kennedy and Rich Schwerin. Emeryville, Calif.: Ziff Davis Press, 1996.

Internet Audio Sourcebook. Lee Purcell and Jordan Hemphill. New York: Wiley, 1997.

Java Web Magic. Joseph T. Sinclair and Lee Callister. Indianapolis: Hayden Books, 1997.

The Official Microsoft ActiveX Web Site Toolkit. Alan Simpson. Redmond, Wash.: Microsoft Press, 1997.

Publishing Digital Video. Jan Ozer. San Diego: AP Professional, 1997.

Video

Internet Video: Doing Donuts on the Internet. VVTWV 18732, VHS Video Edition, Baker & Taylor Video, 2709 Water Ridge Parkway, Charlotte, NC 28217, (800) 775-1800, www.baker-taylor.com. 1995.

On-Line Resources

Audio Streaming Technologies:
RealAudio (www.realaudio.com)
Video Streaming Technologies and Protocols:
RealVideo (www.realvideo.com)
VDO (www.vdolive.com)
VIVO (www.vivo.com)

Because of incessant change, we recommend that you do some serious browsing for multimedia sites on the Web and see how others are incorporating technology and ideas.

Photos and Portfolios

A picture isn't only worth a thousand words; it may be worth thousands of dollars or more in business if the essence of what you offer can be captured in a photo. In **chapter 8**, we talked about the importance of including a publicity photo in with your media materials (see page 267). There we listed fifteen business-getting uses for photos from including them in brochures, mailers, and newsletters to sending them along with your presentation kits to the media. Everyone loves pictures, and that is especially true of the media. Here, however, we want to talk about how photos and portfolios of your work can not only enhance your other marketing efforts but also actually become the centerpiece for getting ample business to come to you.

Photos are at the heart of feather artist Lorra Lee Rose's marketing approach, for example (see color insert). She features photos of her feathered art pieces on her business cards, postcards, and brochures, and she has a portfolio of her art pieces with her regularly. So does woodworker Robert Erickson of Nevada City, California, who creates custom-designed chairs. Jackie Austin's phenomenal success with her popular Deva dolls grew from seeing the dolls themselves, or when that wasn't possible from allowing people to peruse a portfolio picturing a collection of these extraordinary dolls. Pictures are a winning way for Denise Carpenter of Janesville, Wisconsin, to let brides and their families see her personalized antique wedding certificates. For many a bride-to-be, to see them is to want one of her own.

While photos are a natural for artists, craftspeople, or any product business, they can be equally successful for the right service or information business. Professional speaker Pam Lontos, for example, lets photos speak to meeting planners for her. The photos in her media kit and promotional materials say it all by capturing her dynamic personality on the podium speaking before lively, rapt audiences in standing-room-only rooms. Triple A Student Painters use photos of a friendly, uniformed student painter on their door hangers. And, of course, before-and-after photo samples like Christine Lauble's for her company, Designscape Landscape Architecture (see page 263), are great for any business people like designers, remodelers, hairstylists, makeup artists, professional organizers, or fitness trainers whose work produces a dramatic change in appearance.

Pros and Cons of Photos and Portfolios

Using photographs and portfolios is an ideal marketing approach for those who prefer to let their work do the talking for them. One of the primary beliefs is that you can carry your portfolio or photos with you virtually everywhere, anytime. So when people ask what you do, you can simply show them! Photos can capture what would be difficult if not impossible to convey with words, and a well-done portfolio can enhance any in-person presentation as well as create a unified business identity for all your materials. Photographs and portfolios can also save money. You can mail or hand them out in place of costly samples, or you can post them on the Web as photographer Ernest Hori does. His photos of nature in the midst of urban life can be viewed on his site, http://www.horizenfoto.com.

On the downside, using photos effectively as the centerpiece of your marketing efforts requires being able to capture the benefits and value of your work visually in an impactful, dramatic way. Of course, that may not be possible for every business. Also, high-quality photographs can be expensive, especially for a start-up and part-time business. Costs do not lie solely in photographer's fees and film processing. The inclusion of photographs, especially color shots, adds considerable cost to producing printed materials, and time and complexity to the design process.

Best Bets: Photographs and portfolios work best for businesses that offer a visually attractive product or a service that can be clearly shown such as gift basket designing, graphic design, restoration and repair services, fashion and makeup design, plastic and reconstructive surgery, landscape architecture, etc. Photos also work well for any sort of consultant, trainer or entertainer because prospects always like to see the face of the person with whom they may choose to do business.

Tips For Getting Results with Photos and Portfolios

In addition to the tips on using photos that you will find in **chapter 8,** beginning on page 265, here are a few tips for using photos to get business coming to you.

Always carry your photos or portfolio with you. Even the greatest of photos won't do you any good stored away in your office, and you never know when you'll have an opportunity to show off what you do.

Buy in quantity. Using photos will be considerably more cost-effective if you order in large numbers. If you are on a tight budget, you might consider having a small supply on hand to use when highly promising opportunities arise and having color copies made for situations like trade shows or exhibits when you will be handing them out en masse.

Use your photos everywhere on everything. Once you invest the time and expense of producing excellent photos, you might as well use them everywhere you can—from your business card to your holiday card, from your brochure to your Web site.

Place them where others can distribute them. Tie in with others who would be willing to let people see your work. A custom woodworker in Montana, for example, did the sales countertops for an outdoor clothing company; and, since many patrons ask about these unique pieces, the company has a stack of the artist's photo postcards, which include address and phone number, available on the counter.

Include a photo with each order or invoice. Providing satisfied customers with a stand-alone photo or a photo business card, postcard, or brochure provides them with an easy way to show others your work and to make referrals.

Resources: Photos and Portfolios

Books

The Do-It Yourself Business Promotions Kit. Jack Griffin. Englewood Cliffs, N.J.: Prentice Hall Trade, 1995.

Look at Me: Images That Photographers and Illustrators Have Used for Successful Self-Promotion. Los Angeles: Books Nippan, 1994.

Portfolio Design. Harold Linton and Steven Rost. New York: Norton, 1996.

Software

PhotoRecall. Create digital portfolios with photos, graphics, text, and more. G&A Imaging Ltd., 975 St-Joseph Boulevard, Hull, Quebec J8Z 1W8, (819) 772-7600, www.ga-imaging.com

Portfolio Materials

These companies offer a wealth of materials that can be useful in creating effective presentation materials and portfolios:

Avery Dennison. P.O. Box 5244, Diamond Bar, CA 91765, (800) 525-7064.

Paper Direct. 100 Plaza Drive, Secaucus, NJ 07094, (800) A-PAPERS or (800) 272-7377, www.paperdirect.com

Radio and Television Advertising

Small and home-based businesses often don't consider advertising on radio, television or cable, making the assumption that these media are far too expensive to fit into a small advertising budget. With network television, this is definitely true. But media outlets such as local radio stations and the world of cable television offer a number of lower-cost alternatives. Cable, especially, is undergoing tumultuous growth and change. Industry experts predict that not far after 2000, 98 percent of all homes in America will be wired to receive up to 500 channels of programming.

There are two excellent ways small, local businesses can utilize the power of television or cable advertising. The first is advertising on locally originated programs such as news programs, talk shows, or "day shows." These programs are only broadcast to your local area, not nationally. They are therefore far less expensive to advertise on and much more targeted to your market. The second feasible avenue is to advertise to a local audience within a nationally distributed cable show. To take advantage of local origination or cable advertising, you can contact your local stations or cable company directly and tell them you're interested in local advertising. Just as a local television station does, they will set you up with an account rep, who will help you plan a strategy that works for you. The cable company can also produce your commercial at a very reasonable rate ($1,500, on average, for a thirty-second commercial).

Radio advertisements, or "spots," are far less expensive to produce and buy than most television commercials and, if used creatively, can also be an effective way to show people what you can do for them. Consider this: Ninety-nine percent of all households have radios. Adults eighteen and older spend more than three hours a day listening to radio. Radio goes everywhere. Ninety-five percent of all cars have radios.

Radio can create a demand for what you offer, and because stations make it more financially desirable to buy a series of spots, the benefits of repetition are built in. The auditory nature of radio also makes a radio message more easily remembered. You should be able to produce an excellent radio spot for under $300, including talent. Often that talent will be station personnel who can be good or bad, depending on the nature of your business and the format of your spot. If you can speak clearly, consider acting as your own talent. Not only will it save fees; it will also give your audience a sense that they know you.

Pros and Cons of Radio and Television Advertising

Radio and television have tremendous power and reach. When people see or hear about a program, product, or service via radio or television, they ascribe a great deal of credibility to it. "I saw that on TV" or "I heard it on the radio" still means a lot to the American public. So either radio or television advertising is a great way to get your message out to the largest number of people in the shortest amount of time. Commercials can support and increase the effectiveness of all your other marketing activities. They also increase your visibility in the community as nothing else can.

Although the benefits of broadcast advertising are great, so is the cost. It can be cost-prohibitive to small businesses, especially start-ups. Getting sufficient exposure at the prime viewing or drive-time listening hours on the popular stations can be especially expensive. Production costs raise the price further because in today's visually overstimulated MTV world, creativity in commercials is everything. But often the most creative ads are the least expensive. One optometrist worked with a local TV station, for example, to produce a claymation (stop-motion photography) spot of dancing eyeglass frames that was put together—complete with voice-over talent, music, and graphics—for $500.

Computer animation can cut talent costs, although it is not inexpensive and requires precise planning. Technologies available today make it possible to create visuals that cost a fraction of what they might have even five years ago. But the key remains the creativity of those designing the ads—and this still isn't cheap: a high-end, broadcast-quality animation sequence costs an average of $1,000 *per second* to produce.

Best Bets: Radio advertising works best for businesses that have products or services that can be quickly and recognizably described in ten to fifteen seconds.

Local television and cable ads work best for businesses who offer a product or service that's visual in nature. If you can afford the airtime for repeat showings, your ads will sell your products or services, generate inquiries about your business, support your other advertising and marketing efforts, and create an awareness of what you have to offer.

Tips for Getting Great Results from Radio and Television Advertising

Select the best station, channel, or network on which to run your ad. In broadcast advertising, you have three choices with regard to your selection. You may select by time of day, by network or station, or by specific show. A financial consultant we know ran limited spots on FNN (Financial News Network, now merged with CNBC). Each spot offered a tidbit of valuable investment information. Within three months, he had been tapped to write a regular column for the business section of his local newspaper. Although he could not distinguish between clients who came to him as a result of the ads rather than the column, he admits that without the ads the column would never have happened.

His success came from choosing the network that his target audience was watching. Get to know the viewing habits of your target audience. Talk to current customers and ask them what station they watch most often. Then ask them what their favorite shows are. The stations you approach will also be able to give you the demographic profiles of their audience and shows.

A station or network's rate kit should also provide you with a detailed breakdown of their listenership by age, income level, occupation, location, and level of education, as well as give you other useful demographic information.

Select the best time to run you ad. Select the most effective programs and times, based on your target audience, before you even develop your spot. Naturally, some times are more expensive than others. But if consumer advertising is a major part of your advertising budget and you have an accurate profile of your target customer, you can select with an eye toward reaching precisely those individuals you need to reach.

Lee Martin of Century Cablevision in Santa Monica gives one piece of advice to first-time advertisers: "Above all else, pick the program on which to advertise." A small jewelry store knew that its customers tended to enjoy intelligent, leading-edge shows. The owner had read in the trade publications about a show that would be a midseason replacement on an independent channel. He bought time on the show before it ever aired. After the first broadcast of *Babylon 5*, the rates doubled, based on viewership, but he had a contract that locked in his prebroadcast rates for the full season. He also tracked the success of his ad by asking all new customers who came into the store where they had heard about him. He followed their purchases over time and discovered that each dollar of time purchased brought in an average of $1.43 of revenue. He not only hit his target, he also hit the bull's-eye. His results, however, came from an intimate knowledge of the customer he wanted to attract coupled with the right medium, the right timing, and an effective advertisement.

Keep your ads focused. The key to successful broadcast advertising is simplicity. You need to get across three things: (1) your name or brand, (2) where the consumer can find you or it, and (3) one benefit of doing so. If you try to cover more territory, you will lose it all. Instead, take your point and reinforce it again and again and don't try to tell your whole story in thirty seconds. You only have thirty seconds, sixty seconds at most, to get your message across. With radio you can only rely on one of the listener's senses: hearing. Therefore, the more direct your message, the more effective it will be. Don't tell the audience that they can save money on taxes by taking full advantage of loopholes in the new tax law, discuss deductions and investments in new IRAs, or say that you are open six days a week for their convenience and that you offer the lowest rates possible. Who's going to remember all that? Instead, tell them that you're an expert in the new tax law and that you will save them money. Period. Tell the audience you have the best prices on sofas. Nothing more; it's too confusing. Tell them you have the best selection of gift baskets. That's it. Stay focused, and your point will be most apt to hit. Save your business's hours, address, and phone number for the end of the ad, or show or mention it throughout.

Most stations have people who can help you develop your spot as well as produce it. If you have a good producer who thinks in terms of copy, get his or her input, but stick to the rule of simplicity.

Be sure that you can handle the increase in business that your advertising will bring you. Media experts tell us it's not unusual for advertisers to see a 30 to 40 percent increase in business from a new broadcast ad campaign. So be ready for such a response. If you are not ready to handle the increase in calls, requests for information, and additional sales, you might as well have put the money you spent on production and air time elsewhere. If you are not prepared, you also risk letting down your newfound customers with poor service and late deliveries, or by not having something in stock—in which case, your ads will actually hurt your reputation and therefore your business.

So make sure that your phone system, and support system, can handle the additional calls. Ensure that you have the time and man-hours required to make the additional sales calls. If you sell products, make sure you have enough in stock and on hand.

Resources: Radio and Television Advertising

Books

60 Second Sells: 99 Hot Radio Spots for Retail Businesses. Michael Redmond. Jefferson, N.C.: McFarland & Company, 1993.

Broadcast and Cable Selling (Wadsworth Series in Mass Communication). Charles Warner and Joseph Buchman. Belmont, Calif.: Wadsworth, 1993.

How to Create Effective TV Commercials. Huntley Baldwin. Lincolnwood. Ill.: National Textbook Co. Trade, 1989.

How to Plan Radio Advertising (How to Guides). Iain Maitland. Cassell Academic, P.O. Box 605, Herndon, VA 20172, (800) 561-7704. 1997.

Radio Advertising: The Authoritative Handbook. Pete Schulberg and Bob Schulberg. Lincolnwood, Ill: Ntc Business Books, 1996.

The Radio and Television Commercial. Albert C. Book, Norman D. Cary, Stanley I. Tannenbaum, and Frank Brady. Lincolnwood, Ill.: Ntc Business Books, 1996.

Radio's Niche Marketing Revolution: Futuresell (Broadcasting and Cable Series). Godfrey W. Herweg and Ashley Page Herweg. Newton, Mass.: Focal Press, 1997.

Newsletters and Magazines

Adweek, ABPI Communications, Inc. (published weekly), 5055 Wilshire Boulevard, Ste. 600, Los Angeles CA 90036, (213) 525-2270.

Electronic Media. Published weekly by Crain Communications, Inc., 740 North Rush Street, Chicago IL 60661, (312) 649-5200.

Organizations

National Association of Broadcasters, 1771 N Street, N.W., Washington, DC 20036, (202) 429-5300, www.nab.org

Radio Advertising Bureau, 261 Madison Avenue, 23rd Flr., New York, NY 10016, (800) 232-3131, www.rab.com

Television Bureau of Advertising, Inc. 477 850 3rd Avenue, 10th Flr., New York, NY 10022, (212) 486-1111, www.tvb.org

Samples and Giveaways

The use of free samples is one of the oldest methods of sales promotion in existence and one of the most effective. Until recent years, the concept was relegated primarily to mass-market consumer items such as cereal, soap, and other household-maintenance goods. In larger manufacturing businesses it was also a common practice to take a few product samples to purchasing agents. Today, however—although you rarely read or hear about it—there has been a resurgence of sampling as a primary marketing method for businesses of all types and sizes. This is especially true for small and home-based businesses.

Recent research by Dr. Avraham Shama and Jack K. Thompson, of the University of New Mexico, demonstrates the business-getting power of samples and other giveaways. They found that giving away business gifts at the close of sales presentations produces a stronger likelihood that those present will become customers and will recommend the product or service. Their research also shows that a pen worth less than two dollars was as effective as a sports bag worth $10. As a result, there is an entire industry, referred to as *advertising specialties,* or *premiums,* that is built around the concept of adding value by giving something away free. While not all advertising specialty catalogs offer particularly creative or unique items, if properly used advertising specialties can serve as effective promotions.

While giveaways are primarily useful as top-of-the-mind reminders, the premise of sampling is that if you try a product or service, you'll like it, and once you like it, you will buy it. We have been amazed at the creative and ingenious ways people have used sampling to start or expand their businesses. Television and radio spots advertising free consultations by law firms, free examinations by doctors and dentists, and complimentary initial visits by weight-loss counselors and health specialists are but a few of the ways small businesses are using sampling to break into their marketplaces.

After years of experimenting to perfect her recipe, nutrition counselor J. B. Morningstar created a line of healthy gourmet chocolates. Her chocolates contain no sugar, butter, or eggs, and some are actually made with oat bran. She uses them as a calling card for her business, offering a taste to anyone who expresses an interest. To launch the line, J. B. took sampling a step further. She sent attractively decorated sample boxes of the chocolates to influential health practitioners, health-food stores, and members of the media. Tucked in each box was a sheet describing her philosophy, the contents of her healthy candies, and a short feedback form for comments on the taste, texture, and appearance of the chocolates for market research. Those who received these delightful treats were intrigued and flattered. Most loved the chocolates, and orders began coming in.

Another person who uses sampling effectively is Mary Ann Jacobs, owner of a thriving gift basket business in Arizona. Her business caters to corporations and professional offices such as hotels, real estate offices, and banks. When a new business opens in her area, she sends them a complimentary gift basket as a "welcome" gift. Her business card and brochure are carefully placed among the many items in her basket. She also includes a personal note suggesting that gift baskets make ideal gifts to premium hotel guests, home buyers, etc. According to Mary Ann, "By sending a sample, I get people not only to see the quality of my work but also to realize firsthand the way a gift basket makes them feel. They immediately translate that as a way to make their valued clients feel the same, and the orders start coming!"

The Internet, and especially the World Wide Web, has given businesses of all sizes an exciting new platform for offering the market a taste of services or products. Many on-line information providers allow browsers access to selected samples of their content. If browsers wish further or more detailed information, they will typically have to pay for it. Filmmakers, video producers, photographers, composers, and other communications professionals include on-line samples of their work in their Web sites. Media professionals are finding that providing on-line samples of their work is far cheaper than making copies and distributing them through the mail—and even more effective. Small businesses who offer products also include free giveaways on their Web sites that people can call or E-mail for.

Pros and Cons of Giving Out Samples or Giveaways

Allowing people to get a taste or feel for what you offer can be an excellent way to entice clients or customers into trying it out the first time. It's also a great way to get them to come back for more. If your products are inexpensive to make, or your service can be quickly and easily rendered (at least enough so to give someone a sense of what you do), giving out samples can be a rather cost-effective way to market. Giving out samples also puts you in closer touch with your market. The very act of giving or sending out samples increases your direct contact with those you market to and increases your presence in their minds. The samples you provide are also a tax-deductible business expense. Of course, when using a sample, for tax and inventory purposes, you will need to keep separate track of what you've given out as samples as opposed to what you've sold.

Providing samples is generally not a good idea, however, for a business whose products or services are costly or time-consuming to make or render. If your business is based on providing a complex service, such as Internet consulting or architectural engineering, it will be difficult to give anyone a sense of what you offer from a quick sample. Providing samples in general can be expensive and time-consuming. In such situations, however, you could still use giveaways that are related in some way to your business.

Best Bets: Whatever your business, consider ways to show it off with strategic use of sampling. Give samples or other reminder gifts to those whose opinions, referrals, or endorsements will lead you to more business, as well as those who are in a position to buy your product or service directly.

Holidays are an ideal time in any field to use gift samples and specialty giveaways. Surprisingly, however, more than half of small businesses polled by *Income Opportunities* magazine say they do not promote their business during the holiday season with business gifts. And those who do most often send calendars (36.5%), pens (31.9%), and paperweights (14.9%). What an opportunity this presents! It means that if you take the time to acknowledge clients, vendors, and business associates during the upcoming holidays with a holiday gift that lets them know you enjoy and appreciate doing business with them, you will stand out from the crowd and distinguish yourself. So sending personalized gifts, gift certificates, samples, or other tokens of expression at special times of the year that will warm the hearts of those you want to continue working with is always a good bet.

Marketing Masterpiece: Sampling Saves the Day

Pattikay Gottlieb has always been creative. That's what drew her into the world of advertising, where she worked comfortably for a few years. On the day of her wedding, she had a unique inspiration. "I got married in my mother's garden. As a joke, my brother decorated it with pink flamingos. Everyone was so impressed with them that it gave me a rather sudden, powerful idea," explains Pattikay.

This "sudden, powerful idea" at first must have seemed ill-advised to her family and friends. Pattikay quit her advertising job and opened Garden Greetings, a business based on setting up lawn decoration displays for special occasions. In addition to the inspiration-inducing flamingos, Garden Greetings offers plastic cupids, cows, and other bestial ambassadors. Along with the animals comes a variety of lawn-sized greeting cards that contain any personal message her clients ask for, within local zoning laws. "Since I come from an advertising background, I believe in the power of advertising. I started out with an ad campaign in the local newspapers." To her surprise, her costly campaign pulled in a whopping "about thirty-nine cents. People can't really understand a business like mine from reading about it. Folks would call and ask if they could buy a single cow."

Pattikay regrouped and decided to get personal. "I drove around to find houses on high-traffic streets in residential neighborhoods. I then sent them a mailing that explained exactly what my business did." In the mailing she also offered to do a complimentary yard-decoration setup. After a few responded to her free offer, she swung into action. "When I finished decorating a yard, I would inundate a three-block radius with brochures and postcards that described my business. When I set up a yard decoration on a high-profile street, I would get anywhere from twelve to thirty-six calls before noon!" The calls have allowed Pattikay to build not only her business but also truly high quality mailing lists she uses to stay in touch with her prospects. "In two years I built up my business from nothing to a comfortable income."

Tips for Getting Results from Samples and Giveaways

Make a statement of value with your sample, gift, or giveaway. If you're going to go to the time and trouble of giving away a sample or sending a gift, don't just choose another calendar, pen, or paperweight imprinted with your business name. Use the opportunity to showcase your business and to show that you understand the needs and interests of those whose business is important to you. An actual sample of your work is always preferable.

Gun Denhart found samples to be a key to her success when she launched Hanna Andersson, her line of 100 percent Swedish cotton knit baby clothing. Besides being soft and adorable, her baby clothes, sold by catalog, were incredibly sturdy. But just from viewing the catalog how were people to know? Denhart decided to attach a cloth sample with each of 25,000 catalogs. To further demonstrate the durability of her clothing, she decided to offer a 20 percent discount for garments her customers return in good condition after their babies outgrow them. As a result she now donates more than 3,000 "Hannadowns" each month to children of needy families through local charities throughout the world.

If providing a sample is not possible, relate your giveaway or gift as directly as you can to your work. For example, one year, we (Paul and Sarah) gave away heart-shaped ornaments with the message *Home Is Where . . .* inscribed on the side. Another year, we gave away ceramic home offices. Both resulted in many positive responses because, if you'll pardon the pun, they got right to the heart of the matter of our business. Whenever we have strayed into using more common giveaways like office items, food treats, or flowers, people seem to enjoy and appreciate them, but we don't get the same enthusiastic results.

Make sure to give out samples only to people who are potential purchasers of your product or service. Giving out free samples of your organic bread at a grocery store where your product is sold is a great way to draw a crowd. But if most of the people enjoying your samples have finished their shopping and are on their way out of the store, you are truly giving your hard work away for free. The greatest impact on your sales will come from those who are still shopping, and still need to buy bread! Jeff Davis, who sells organic sprouts at local farmers' markets, says, "I only offer to give a sample if someone's been looking at my display for a few minutes. I find that if I give them away to anyone walking by, they take them, say thanks, and keep on walking."

If you are providing samples of a service, try to prequalify those who are eager to accept your free service. For example, if you offer a free tax consultation, make sure your prospect isn't already committed to another tax preparer or doing her taxes herself. If this is the case, you are giving away information she can take to someone else or use herself.

Find cost-effective ways to produce your samples. Find ways to produce samples that cost less but still present the quality of your product or service. For example, if you design Web sites, it wouldn't be cost-effective to produce a sample home page for someone. Creating a clever animation that can be used on any page and giving that away, however, is a wonderful, cost-effective way of providing someone with a sample of what you can do without giving away the farm. If you make cookies, or any food item, don't give away your most complex masterpiece. This might show off the full extent of your prowess but drain your cash reserves as well. Instead, develop a simpler version of the recipe with less costly ingredients.

If you have a sample that's been working for you, research ways to have it mass-produced, if possible. When providing samples of a service, develop a script of some sort that outlines exactly what you will do and say. In this way you will be better organized and present your information more effectively. A script will also help you to keep things concise—a very important consideration when it comes to giving away your time.

As far as food items and other perishable consumables are concerned, train others to make them for you and call them in before a giveaway event. If it's a product, having it mass-produced always brings down the per-unit cost.

Consider requesting something in return. Of course not everyone you give a sample to will buy what you have to offer. To maximize the time and expense of providing giveaways, consider getting something in return from those who receive them. Of course this would not be appropriate in all situations, especially when using a sample as a holiday or thank-you gift. When it would be appropriate, however, you might ask those to whom you provide a sample to fill in a quick survey that includes their name, address, and phone number. Or you might ask on your survey for an opinion of your product. You could put these surveys on index cards and hand them out along with your sample. This is a great way to build a mailing list of prospects who already know about you and your product.

When providing a sample of service, you have even more of a cap-

What Makes the Best Sample, Giveaway, or Specialty Gift Item?

The best sample or giveaway provides value and creates goodwill while also accomplishing a specific purpose that ties in with your overall marketing effort. It enhances your sales as well as spreading good cheer without draining your pocketbook. A transportation planning consultant, for example, might give away mini-clipboards that attach to car visors imprinted with her company name, phone number, and slogan—"Put Commute Time on a Diet! Reduce Congestion, Pollution, and Stress." Or a plant-care doctor who goes into his clients' homes and offices to tend to ailing plants might give away imprinted watering cans or sets of gardening gloves.

The best gift is a sample of a client's favorite product or a useful item that reminds them of how pleasant, profitable, and satisfying it is to work with you.

Such gifts, be they given for the holidays, at the close of a sales presentation, along with a thank-you note, or as follow-up to a networking lunch, need not be expensive. It's the thought that counts. Here are several rules of thumb to follow when you create a special sample or select a novelty from an advertising specialty catalog:

1. **The item should be related to your business in some way.**
   - A plant-maintenance firm could give away small plants.
   - A caterer could offer tea mugs with biscuits or coffee mugs.
   - An interior designer could give away clipboards.
   - An editor could give away marking pens or pencils.
2. **There should be some means of imprinting your company name or logo on the item.**
   - Items should be a solid color, or have a pattern that relates to your logo.
   - If there is no space for a logo to be imprinted, use preprinted self-adhesive labels with your logo, name, address, and phone number.
3. **Items should be functional and usable on a regular basis.**
   - Pens, mugs, calculators, pads, reference books, flashlights, penknives, calendars, desktop accessories, and tote bags are all functional.

- Don't purchase any novelty or giveaway until you have a good idea of how your customers work and what they might be able to use.
- Consider choosing several different novelties to be used for clients with differing needs or to give in sequence to especially important clients.

4. **Items should be designed for use at the location where someone is likely to need your product or service.**
   - A clipboard for an auto visor would be great for a telecommuting consultant, but not for someone selling graphic-design supplies.
   - Marking pens or custom Post-It notes would work well for designers.
   - A copy holder would be great for someone doing in-house computer training for secretaries but useless for sales training.
5. **Items should be durable.**
   - Cheap pens leak, cheap mugs crack, and cheap calculators stop working in the middle of an important calculation.
   - Cheap novelties create a negative image; it is better to get fewer high-quality items than a mass order of cheap ones.
   - Remember, your name will be on your items. You want them to last, to work well, and to reflect well on you and your business.
6. **Items should be easy to integrate into your sales efforts.**
   - Take mugs with coffee or tea and a snack on a morning business call.
   - Give a copy holder while the client is sitting at the computer.
   - Give designer marking pens at the drafting tale.
   - Use a knife to open a carton, then hand it to the customer.
   - Use a bonsai in a demonstration and then give it to the client.
   - Give a gardening tool while showing clients what you have done with their shrubbery.
   - Give a calendar during a long-range planning session.

tive audience. Before providing your sample, you could ask people to fill out a more detailed form than the one described above. In addition to name, address, etc., ask them to describe what they are looking for in terms of the service you provide, what kinds of similar services they are currently using or have used, and other useful marketing information. This information will help you determine both how qualified the prospective client is and how to structure your samples more effectively in the future.

If you hand out samples in person, simply include your mini-survey along with them and have plenty of pens or pencils handy. It you mail your samples, enclose your survey with the sample along with a stamped, preaddressed envelope. Or if your budget allows, you can print the survey as a self-addressed mailer.

Resources: Samples and Giveaways

Books

101 Ways to Promote Yourself. Raleigh Pinskey. New York: Avon, 1997.

Present Perfect. Sherri and Larry Athay, Mobius Press, P.O. Box 8, Hyde Park, UT 84318. 1996.

Trade Shows and Special Exhibits

Trade shows and exhibits can be excellent ways to attract business. A study conducted for the Center for Exhibition Industry Research found that well over 100 million people attend trade shows in a given year. But exhibiting at trade shows can also be a big waste of money for small businesses. If that sounds confusing, it can be.

Years ago each industry had one or two major shows, usually produced by the principal trade organization, and every buyer or user of products and services within that industry attended. Nowadays, it seems that each industry has a trade show almost once a month. Some of these shows are for retail customers; others are for vendors. Depending on your business, either kind of show—or both—may be worth considering.

The owners of two computer-accessory businesses, for example, made trade shows work for them. Both were women starting their first business. One was producing computer-related greeting cards; the other was manufacturing a foam-rubber novelty bat she developed for safely clobbering computers in moments of frustration. They decided to share a booth at the fall Comdex (one of the largest shows for the computer industry), where both companies got enough orders to launch their fledgling enterprises. Another person who regularly makes trade shows work for her business is Sandra Wylie, who offers a business opportunity in the gift industry. In fact, she attended her first trade show on an informal basis hoping to get some good industry information, but not expecting to make any sales. She was quite surprised when she closed her first two sales by simply talking about her opportunity to others. Over the phone the following week, she closed another two sales from leads she had generated.

Of course, all shows won't produce such dramatic results, and many are not worth attending either as exhibitor or attendee. But the right one at the right time can make your year.

Trade Show Pros and Cons

Trade shows are a wonderful opportunity to accomplish all in one place many of the marketing tasks we outline in this book. Trade shows are invaluable for networking with prospects, allies, and vendors. Shows allow you to demonstrate what you can do to an audience who came specifically because of their connection to your market. And because many trade show attendees paid to be there, they have already demonstrated their seriousness and viability. Trade shows allow you to practice your sales techniques extensively. Based on real reactions of in-the-flesh attendees, you will know instantly what works and what doesn't in your sales presentation and approach. You can also receive valuable and immediate feedback on your brochures, flyers, photos, videos, and other marketing and demonstration tools you may be using.

Trade shows also help to establish your credibility. When prospects and competitors see you exhibiting with the largest industry leaders in your market, as is often the case in large trade shows, it makes an impression. Trade shows also help to back up your other marketing efforts, such as trade advertising, broadcast advertising, direct mail, etc. Prospects may have seen your ads, read your brochures, and received your direct-mail pieces without acting on them. If they see your booth at a show, however, they will recognize your business name and most likely come over to find out what you're all about.

Trade shows can be very expensive. Renting space, designing and creating an effective booth, manning your booth, and all the travel and shipping expenses involved in most shows can add up to considerable sums. Unfortunately, some shows are misrepresented, underfunded, and, therefore, underattended. A show with a disappointing turnout can end up being a disastrous investment and a very demoralizing experience.

Best Bets: Trade shows are ideal for businesses that are highly visual in nature or for those that require demonstration, illustration, or explanation. They are a great way to gain immediate access to and feedback from potential end users, retailers, suppliers, manufacturers, or reps you might otherwise have difficulty meeting. Some state governments have trade offices that will advise you on trade shows and sublease booth space rented by the state for shows that are relevant to the state's economy. This could be an economical way to exhibit. Contact your state's information office to find out about such opportunities.

Tips for Getting Results from Trade Shows and Exhibits

Your ultimate success with any trade show depends on having a clear understanding of specifically what you expect to gain from exhibiting and whether that trade show is the proper venue for your expectations. Of course the nature of your exhibit will have an impact on your results, as will the location. At many shows, the ideal locations include those near the front door and the lounge and food-service areas. Other good spots are ends of aisles. But to know what your booth should be like, or what you have to measure up to, requires that you attend at least one show before considering whether or not to exhibit. Here are some of the key issues you should consider:

Pick the right show. Is there a trade show that draws the specific customers or contacts you seek? Bear in mind that most trade shows are geared to a specific industry or a specific market, and ask yourself if there is a match between the show and the people you want to meet. A show can draw a lot of people, but to serve your needs it must draw enough of the right people for you.

Do the people who attend a particular show actually come to buy or to browse? Some shows—for example, fashion markets and equipment shows—are the principal showcases for products and services for many industries, and buyers attend with the full intention of placing orders and signing contracts. Other exhibitions—for example, hotel and restaurant shows, general and cross-industry business shows, etc.—are treated primarily as an opportunity for buyers to see what is available in the marketplace and find resources for future purchases.

Determine the most cost-effective way to participate. How much will exhibiting actually cost, and do you have the funds not only to rent the space but also to design, furnish, and staff the booth? No matter how much or how little that space costs, it is only the start. Although there are ways to keep the costs of your display in line, you need to have a clear understanding of all the hidden costs—for example, union or contract rules may dictate that you have to pay the hall staff for assembly, even if you plan to do it yourself. If exhibiting is too costly, consider the following other ways of participating.

WORKING A SHOW WITHOUT EXHIBITING There are three primary reasons to take space at a trade show or exhibition: 1) you are there to meet specific customers and take their orders; 2) you want to find new outlets for your product or service; or 3) you have to be there because your competitors are. Any one or a combination of the three is a valid reason if your budget can withstand the expense. However, there is another way to make use of trade shows that is substantially less expensive: attending the shows to find and talk to prospects who themselves have booths. Simply change the focus of the shows you select. For example, as a wholesaler, instead of taking a booth at a wholesale show, you can visit the booths at a retail show. In this case you will not actually make sales, but you will get a good idea of the selling potential of your product or service from the sales reps and managers at the booths. The information you gather can be helpful when you approach buyers of your product or service in person at a later time.

APPEARING AS A SPEAKER AT A SHOW Still another way of using trade shows is to get yourself booked as a speaker. You may not be able to arrange to receive a fee or to have your expenses paid, but you can negotiate for either or both, as well as for free booth space in lieu of your fee. As a speaker at the event, you can not only show off your stuff but also get the advantage of the preshow publicity, increasing your visibility and positioning you as an expert in the field. To find out whom to approach to get booked as a speaker at a trade show, contact the show management and ask for the program director.

Lay out your booth to best showcase what you offer. Whether you create your own display, rent one, or have one custom-manufactured, you need to arrange your work space to accommodate whatever demon-

Six Types of Booth Displays

If you can't afford to buy or create an appealing booth, you are better off simply attending the show. An amateurish, slipshod booth will not only draw a limited crowd but also create a negative image. With a little ingenuity, however, there's an option for most budgets. Here are six basic types of displays you can use at trade shows in order of increasing expense.

1. A custom-created booth.

This is the simplest, least expensive booth decor. Most shows provide a curtained booth, one or two tables, and chairs and will rent you standard matching table skirting. On this basic background you can mount photographs or promotional materials. An easel or two with framed blowups or a collage of your work can make an attractive display. Plants and flower arrangements can add an elegant touch. Videos, shown with a VCR and monitor or a lively show using a multimedia presentation program like *Lotus Freelance, Harvard Graphics,* or *Microsoft PowerPoint* on a large computer monitor are other ways to catch the eyes of attendees. However, an electrical hookup will cost extra. The primary drawback to do-it-yourself decor is the fact that other exhibitors could have professionally produced displays that can make your booth appear somewhat amateurish in comparison. But when done with creativity and imagination, a custom booth can outdraw a more costly institutionalized one.

In some places, technical assistance and subsidies are available to help craftspeople and other small businesses exhibit at trade shows. One such program for microenterprises in British Columbia is managed by Impact Communications. *www.strategis.ic.gc.ca.*

2. Prefab displays.

The least expensive professional displays you can purchase are prefabricated units, sometimes called portable presentation tools, which consist of some sort of framing, usually aluminum covered by colored fabric. They are available in modular segments that must be assembled. These units allow you to create your own displays, primarily with Velcro attachments, and, with a little forethought, can be configured to be quite appealing. On the downside, these units are on the low end of the impressiveness scale. More often than not, your display will resemble a clever civics project at the school fair, especially when compared with other, more visually sophisticated (and more costly) displays you will surely be competing with.

3. Stock displays.

A stock display is similar to a prefab but is much stronger and more easily adaptable to various show formats. You can assemble special sections such as shelves, enclosed cabinets, and/or pegboard for mounting displays. Most display houses can rent you a stock display, paint it the color you want, and even add your company name and logo to the header.

4. Modular displays.

Modular units consist of several sections that can be combined in a variety of sizes and conformations to suit the available space and your display needs. Although many shows have standard booth sizes, the configurations are not always the same. Some shows standardize on a ten-by-ten-foot booth, some an eight-by-eight, and some an eight-by-ten, or multiples thereof. If you have purchased a rigid format, you can easily find yourself with a beautiful display that is too large or too small for your space. Modular pieces can be reconfigured and adapted to a wide variety of booth sizes and shapes. If you decide to participate in multiple shows, you probably will want to consider a modular display.

Another advantage of modular displays is the fact that they are usually designed to fit in one or more cases that can not only be lifted by almost anyone, but can also ride as luggage on airlines or be shipped via UPS, and be moved into place and set up by the booth manager.

5. Crated displays.

The crated unit is among the most versatile of packaged displays. It is custom-manufactured and can consist of almost any material and design your budget allows. The unit is contained in a huge crate, however, and must be shipped, emptied, and stored for the duration of the show, brought back to the booth, packed, and reshipped. Transporting and storing the crate can become a problem, and you may have less control over it when it arrives at the show.

6. Self-contained displays.

A self-contained unit solves the problems of the crated display by folding up to form its own crate. These units are more expensive than crated displays at the outset, but the savings in shipping, tips, time, and aggravation fully justify the additional cost.

strations or sales activities you plan for the time you are there. You can use tables as counters, islands, demonstration spaces, and sales areas. Try to avoid the standard U-shaped space resulting in people milling past tables around the inside perimeter of the booth. Instead, create areas for the key tasks you want people to engage in while at your booth: browsing, viewing, talking, meeting, and watching demonstrations. For example, divide your booth space into various work areas by placing tables in T-formations or triangles or by creating islands.

Such task areas will make your space more visually interesting and inviting to prospects. They will increase your efficiency and maximize traffic patterns so that your staff and prospects won't be stumbling over one another. Tailor your booth to the needs of those you want to attract. For example, don't try to be too cute and cozy unless such an atmosphere reflects the nature of your business. Including large lounge couches and easy chairs is not an incentive for busy business buyers who are pressed to accomplish their job while at the show. The more efficient you are at helping them do so, the more likely they are to visit your booth. On the other hand, if you are selling stress-reduction courses at a health-and-fitness show or massages and facials to busy executives at a general business show, cozy chairs that vibrate or, as suggested before, free foot or neck and shoulder massages might prompt people to form lines at your booth.

Take steps to attract lots of visitors to your exhibit. Nine out of ten exhibitors at trade shows spend a great deal of money on the off chance that someone interested in their product or service will be attracted to their booth. But there is no need to rely on chance. To ensure that at least those on your current mailing list will look for you and stop by, send a special mailing no later than three to four weeks before the show. This mailing should contain a gift certificate, only redeemable in person, at the show. Add to the list key prospective clients or customers you would like to have visit your booth. A simple mailing like this should almost double the traffic at your booth, and the gift certificate will increase that number by another 50 percent. But if you want to keep a steady stream of people coming by, make the certificate redeemable for a gift item for the attendee's spouse or child.

Another method often used at trade shows to increase booth traffic is to have a raffle or drawing for a prize related to your product or service. Other ideas for generating traffic at your booth include advertising in the trade magazines, business publications, and the show program guide; making up sandwich boards and hiring someone to walk around promoting your exhibit; and donating napkins imprinted with your company name and booth number to exhibit-hall restaurants, receptions, dinners, and other such events. Use your participation in the show as a media opportunity as well. Most shows have open registration for the press. Take a stack of publicity kits to the press room, and watch for people with press badges walking by. They are looking for stories, news, and features to report.

Attend to details. We have spent hours observing traffic patterns at trade shows in order to determine why some booths seem to attract a steady stream of visitors while others remain mostly deserted. We have also talked with exhibitors to determine who are pleased with their results and who are disappointed. In addition to selecting a good show and having an attractive booth, there appear to be certain rules of thumb that produce better results. Here's what works:

Have some visual element or activity that serves as a magnet to catch the attention of everyone walking by. This magnet can be an interesting sign, a photo, a video, or even music. Studies show that a photograph will work 26 percent better than artwork. Your attention-grabber can also be a demonstration, something you say to people who are passing by, or an inexpensive giveaway such as candy, buttons, consultations, mouse pads, or other items. If you give away something like a button or a bag that people can wear or carry, it will attract others to your booth. Be sure, however, that any giveaway you use is sufficiently related to your business that it attracts people who are in your market. You don't want just any crowd; you want people who need and will pay for what you offer.

Have a central theme for your booth. The decor, banners, materials, layout, and design should support one theme, and what you offer should be unmistakable. People give a booth only a three-second glance, and buyers don't stop to figure out a confusing booth.

Arrange to have others available to help work your booth, even if yours is a one-person company. You will need a break from time to time, and having several people working a booth seems to draw people to it. There are at least two key functions that you must be ready to carry out at all times. You can't always do them both: 1) being available to engage people who are walking by and interacting with browsers; and 2) being free to engage in more protracted conversations with serious customers or contacts. So have at least two people present most of the time, and never leave the booth unattended. Often the show you're attending will offer staffing (at a price) for your booth, but this has drawbacks if staff don't know about your business.

Make sure all the staff at your booth are sufficiently familiar with your product or service that they can answer most questions. Experts say that what showgoers hate most are overly aggressive salespeople and personnel who aren't knowledgeable about what is being exhibited. On the other hand, research by Incomm International shows that people won't wait long at a booth; 6 percent won't wait at all, 11 percent wait only thirty seconds, 41 percent wait one minute, 38 percent three minutes, and 14 percent five minutes.

This means you must balance staffing, materials, and activities so that your booth isn't so crowded that passersby are intimidated or feel ignored, yet enough so that they will get attention as quickly as possible. Having a video or some other type of demonstration is one way to handle this dilemma. Often such activities will lengthen the time buyers will spend waiting and will help keep your information in their minds, as well.

Don't waste expensive advertising specialties, four-color flyers, brochures, or complete catalogs on trade shows. Prepare a special, relatively inexpensive brochure or flyer to give to those who request information. Or, even better, respond to requests by cheerfully offering to send information to those who give you their names and addresses. Have a limited supply of your best materials available out of sight for the media or for individuals who become serious prospects.

Never let a prospective client or customer leave your booth without getting his or her business card or at least a name, company, and location. Then be sure to follow up by phone or mail immediately after the show. Running a drawing for a prize is a good way to get people to leave their business cards. To restrict the contestants to serious prospects, make the prize something only people in your market would want to win.

Remain standing and interact with people who pass. People who sit passively at their booths generally have empty booths and get fewer sales. You will miss a lot of prospects if you wait for people to stop and ask questions. Instead, reach out to those who slow down in front of your booth or appear to be looking for something. Make eye contact. Ask whether you can demonstrate something or whether they have seen or used what you are offering. Avoid judging prospects based on how they are dressed; people may wear anything to a trade show. Instead, qualify buyers by asking open-ended, one-line questions about what product or services they have been using. Trade shows require hard work, but studies show that 80 percent of qualified trade show leads become orders.

Prepare several specials to add incentive for buyers to make an immediate purchase. You can offer a discount or other incentives to those who buy at the show only.

Always have plenty of order forms, cards, brochures, flyers, and pens available. Never keep prospects waiting while you dig out something for them to write on. Your name, address, and phone number should appear on every piece of paper you give out.

To save setup time, prepare yourself with a diagram of your booth layout, a checklist of items you will need for display and for use, and a thorough personnel plan. Before the show begins, go over your goals and plans for working the booth with everyone who will be helping you. Goals should be quantified in terms of numbers of leads and sales so everyone knows the target you are aiming for. By spending three to five minutes with each potential customer, you can each plan to talk with ten to fifteen people per hour. Let the people working in the booth know how you would like them to dress. Grooming, posture, and appearance of personnel are all part of the exhibit. Also review how you expect them to handle various circumstances that might arise.

Keep a collection of permanent samples attached to the display. Mount them in such a fashion that they can be used or shown, but not removed.

Make sure every staff person in your booth is engaging with the passersby instead of chatting among themselves. And be sure no one eats, smokes, or drinks at the booth.

Follow up effectively on the leads you gather. Leads are only valuable if you turn them into customers or clients. And the only way to do that is to follow up on each and every one. Do not wait for them to contact you; contact them as quickly as possible. If you held a drawing to collect business cards, you might have a letter and advertising specialty of some sort ready to send each one after the show informing them that they didn't win the drawing but to please accept this small consolation gift. Then set up a schedule to contact each one systematically about your products or services.

Another way to bridge follow-up contacts is to attach a coupon for a special show discount to any information distributed at the show. Then if the individuals don't contact you within a few days, contact them to discuss how you can facilitate their using your show coupon.

Resources

Books

The Complete Guide to Special Event Marketing. Dwight Catherwood and Richard Van Kirk. New York: Wiley, 1992.

Exhibit Marketing: A Success Guide for Managers. Edward A. Chapman, Jr. New York: McGraw-Hill, 1995.

Guerilla Trade Show Selling. Jay Conrad Levinson, Mark S. A. Smith, and Orvel Ray Wilson. New York: Wiley, 1997.

How to Get the Most Out of Trade Shows. Steve Miller. Lincolnwood, Ill.: Ntc Business Books, 1996.

Show and Sell. Margit B. Weisgal. New York: Amacom Books, 1996.

Newsletters and Magazines

Exhibitor. 745 Marquette Bank Building, Rochester, MN 55904.

Tradeshow Week. 12233 West Olympic Boulevard, Ste. 235, Los Angeles, CA 90064-9956, www.tradeshowweek.com

Associations

Trade Show Exhibitors Association. 5501 Backlick Road, Ste. 105, Springfield, VA 22151, (703) 941-3725, www.tsea.com

On-Line Resources

Showsource. Lists events and exhibit products (www.showsource.com).

Trade Show Central. Information on more than 30,000 trade shows, conferences, and seminars, 5,000 service providers, and 5,000 venues and facilities around the world (www.tscentral.com).

EventWeb. Interactive marketing strategies for profitable events. A good place to research the viability of shows in which you are thinking of participating (www.eventweb.com).

Video Brochures

People are becoming increasingly visually oriented. Many prefer getting information from watching as opposed to reading. According to Jay Levinson, author of the *Guerrilla Marketing* series, "People are more inclined to spend five or ten more minutes with a video brochure than a printed brochure. . . . they even feel that they are getting something for free." Marketing experts say response rates to videos are noticeably higher and people retain more of the information presented than from reading material.

You can use videos as demonstrations and giveaways at trade shows, use them to spice up sales presentations, and mail them to qualified prospects who respond to your promotions. In fact, your videos can be used in virtually any situation where printed promotional materials would be the traditional medium. You can even use a video as your calling card.

Universal Aqua Technologies, Inc., produced a video brochure that gave an overview of the company as a whole and demonstrated their water-processing and bottling equipment in action. "We get requests from all over the globe for information about our products," explains Universal Aqua president Marwan Nesicolaci, "primarily from our print ads and Web site. What people really want to see, however, is that our products work like we say they do. That's why we did the video." The fifteen-minute video they had produced cost less than $10,000. In the year and half after they started sending out the video in response to ads, their sales have increased over 60 percent. In the same year Universal Aqua was awarded the Outstanding Export Achievement Award from the United States Department of Commerce and the Small Business Administration.

With some ingenuity and creative thinking any business can create a video brochure that will be informative and entertaining. If you produce or distribute a product, show the product in action and include customer testimonials and success stories. If you provide a service, show yourself working with clients, interacting, offering solutions. Be sure to include testimonials from satisfied customers.

Pros and Cons of Video Brochures

Video brochures are much more apt to be noticed, watched, and remembered than standard printed brochures. Almost any kind of business can benefit from a creative, professionally produced tape that demonstrates a product or service. Videos can be used to add interest to trade show booths, and they can be given or mailed to prequalified prospects of all stripes. They augment the effectiveness of most advertising and marketing efforts. Videotapes lend an aura of prestige to your company. Short of a tour through your facility or a customer installation, video demonstrates what you have to offer far better and in a way that printed materials can only approximate.

Conversely, video may be too expensive for many budgets. A good ten-to-fifteen-minute production can cost between $10,000 and $50,000. And once it has been created, it needs to be duplicated. A fifteen-minute tape duplicated onto NTSC (the American video standard) VHS tape costs between $6.75 and $10 per tape, depending on how many you order. PAL and SECAM (European, South American, and Asian video standards) duplications into VHS tapes cost between $10 and $15 per tape—again, depending on the size of your order. For this reason, many businesses make sure that a prospective buyer is truly interested and able to proceed before he or she is sent a videotape; whereas the lower per-unit cost of printed brochures allows them to be sent out much more freely. If your product or service is low cost, video may not be worth the expense.

Best Bets: If your product or service is best seen or heard in action, a video brochure can do it justice. Videos work for a wide variety of businesses that have the budget to produce the high quality required. Videos are especially effective if sent out in response to requests for further information that come in from other forms of advertising or marketing. They also make sales demonstrations far more powerful and effective.

Tips on Creating an Effective Video Brochure

Ask yourself some key questions first. How will you use a video? Are you currently marketing your business in ways that a video will enhance? Do your products or services change frequently, thereby making your video quickly obsolete or out-of-date? How will you distribute the video when it is complete?

Decide how you want to produce it: by yourself or through an outside producer. Unless you have prior experience or are very confident in your ability to write, produce, shoot, and edit a professional-quality video, we suggest you hire a freelance producer or reasonably priced production house.

Create an engaging script and general "storyboard." When you have determined who will produce your video, the first step in the actual production is writing a good script and producing a "storyboard" (a visual road map that outlines each shot and location in the script). Generally, if you contract with someone, he or she will generate these items. Nevertheless, you will still need to be involved in their completion. You are your own best content and continuity expert.

Oversee all shooting. If the script and storyboard are well written and conceived, shooting your video should go smoothly. The producer will provide all the equipment needed to capture "broadcast-quality" images. Depending on the script, the producer might also hire on-camera talent as well. But be sure that you are on location for all shooting. Again, you are your own best content expert. You know better than anyone what will appear realistic in terms of how your product or service is used. Shooting can take anywhere from one to ten days, depending on the number of shots and locations required.

Edit the footage for maximum impact. When all shooting is complete, the producer will then record a voice-over narration, if required, and obtain all music necessary to round out your video. Please note: Unless you are willing to pay royalties, you cannot use your favorite song or songs on the sound track. You will have to use original music or prerecorded "production music." Check with your producer and make sure he or she understands the kind of music you want in your production. Ask him or her to play samples for you. Nothing's worse than having a video that looks great but contains music that sets the wrong tone for the message you're presenting.

Editing is where your production comes together. Only the best shots will be selected and used to crate a continuous narrative flow. Voice-over, music and any graphics, charts and animations will be created and added during the editing process. When the tape is finished, the producer will hand you the edited master tape. This is the tape from which all copies will be made. Ask the producer to provide you with an additional master that you can store as a backup.

Use high-quality duplication. Take your edited master to a professional duplication house to make copies (called "dubs" in video parlance) of your video. Don't skimp at this phase. Even if your master tape looks great, poor-quality duplication will make your production looked amateurish. Most duplication houses will provide labels for your tapes.

They will give several options as to the boxes into which the tapes will be placed.

Digitize your video for inclusion on a multimedia Web site or CD-ROM. Make the most of your video by using it on your Web site. Interactive digital media such as the Web and CD-ROMs thrive on video content. It really puts the "multi" in multimedia. Having your video digitized (converted to a digital format which can be read by software) is quick, easy, and inexpensive. There are many independent facilities that specialize in converting analog audio- and videotapes into a digital format. Check with your producer or duplication house.

Once you have the converted file, give it to your Webmaster for inclusion in your site. That way it will be available twenty-four hours a day, seven days a week to anyone who is interested. Make sure the video will be streamed in real time, not downloaded (if you don't know what this means, your Webmaster will). Including video will enhance interest and traffic on your site, and may well save you money on duplications as well.

Resources

Books

Basics of Video Production. Des Lyver and Graham Swainson. Newton, Mass.: Focal Press, 1995.

Corporate Video Directing. Howard Hall. Newton, Mass.: Focal Press, 1993.

Marketing with Video. Hal Landen. Slate Hill, N.Y.: Oak Tree Press, 1996.

Producing a First-Class Video for Your Business: Work with Professionals or Do It Yourself **(Self Counsel Business Series)**. Dell Dennison, Don Doman, and Margaret Doman. Bellingham, Wash.: Shelf Counsel Press, 1993.

The Video Production Organizer: A Guide for Businesses, Schools, Government Agencies, and Professional Associations (book and disk). Aleks Matza. Newton, Mass.: Focal Press, 1995.

Writing for Video. Gene Bjerke. 312 Cary Street, Williamsburg, VA 23185, (800) 377-1341. Petrel Publications, 1997.

Newsletters and Magazines

Videography magazine. Miller Freeman PSN Inc., 460 Park Avenue South, 9th Floor, New York, NY 10016, (212) 378-0400.

Videomaker magazine. Mailing address: P.O. Box 4591, Chico, CA 95927; subscription phone: (760) 745-2809.

On-Line Resources

AV and CD Resources Page. A fairly comprehensive list of links to tape duplicators, blank tapes, supplies, and more (http://wwwmarrak.com/resource/dupe.html).

RealVideo. One of the top standards for putting audio on the World Wide Web (www.realvideo.com).

Videomaker Resource Page (http://www.videomaker.com/edit/distrib/index.htm).

Your Own Radio or Television Show

If your business is instructive or entertaining in nature, you might consider having a radio or television show of your own. This is not as extravagant as it may seem. Having a local public-access cable show, for example, costs little or nothing, and for approximately six times the cost of one minute of network time, you can even buy an entire half hour on a local broadcast or cable station. So if you were a caterer, for example, you might host a series of television shows on various cuisines; preparing the foods; giving out recipes; interviewing florists, decorators, or location owners; and showing how to create a dinner party around the theme of each cuisine. Or buy what is called brokered time and host your own weekly half hour or hour-long radio show on cooking.

Marriage and family counselor Dr. Barbara De Angelis of Los Angeles used such a program to build her now nationally known *Making Love Work* seminars for couples. From that show she has gone on to become a best-selling author and network-television commentator, and has hosted her own television show and infomercial. Dr. Murray Susser, who broadcasts his radio show via telephone from his office, uses the show to promote his medical practice. Public relations consultant Ann Schmidt has a show that features her clients, successful businesspeople, authors, or artists. Stockbroker Brian Sheen has a popular investment program in Florida. Dr. Nancy Bonus filled hundreds of non-diet weight-loss classes from her show *The Psychology of Weight Loss.*

Public-access television is an especially appealing opportunity for very small businesses. By law, local cable stations must offer a public-access channel on which they air local programming. Usually this channel is distinct from an educational or governmental channel on which city-council or community-college programming appears. Time on public-access cable is free or very low cost and includes all production, which is done by the cable station. Therefore you don't need to hire a producer. Applicants usually need to submit proposals for the shows they want to produce, and sometimes the cable company requires that you attend a free seminar on how to produce your own shows. A public-access show cannot be a commercial. At the end of the show you can give out your name, telephone number, and address.

Hair stylist Ed Salazar has a weekly cable show that keeps his appointment book filled, and martial arts instructor Steve Grody has such a show where his on-air "urban self-defense" classes promote his private instruction and videotapes. Psychologist Dr. Jessica Schairer gets excellent exposure for her private practice by hosting *Psychological Solutions* on cable access in Santa Monica, California.

Others who might do well by having a radio or television show are:

- Stress management consultants
- Financial consultants
- Fitness trainers
- Business consultants
- Computer consultants
- Web and computer gurus
- Makeup artists
- Public relations firms (which can book their clients on their show)
- Professional organizers
- Image consultants
- Veterinarians

If you don't want the responsibility of a full-blown weekly show but believe you could benefit from having a regular on-air presence, consider purchasing time from someone else's show. For example, financial consultant Dan Silverman ran a regular twelve-minute weekly feature for a year on insurance and investments for small businesses on the *Here's to Success* program in Los Angeles; veterinarian Jeffrey Werber had a daily three-minute spot on pet care on another local program.

The Pros and Cons of Having Your Own Radio, Television, or Cable Show

Although broadcast time can be expensive and often unavailable, public-access cable is a very low-cost option. Being on television or radio regularly provides unparalleled visibility and lots of word of mouth. You can become well known and sought after. And you can use the tapes of your shows to promote in many other ways, as discussed elsewhere in this chapter.

One added advantage of buying time for your show is that you often have the option of recovering your advertising costs by selling advertising spots on your show to your suppliers or to other compatible businesses. Of course this is not an option on public-access cable television. In fact, on cable access you cannot overtly sell your products or services, although you can usually list an address or phone number as part of the closing credits for viewers wishing additional information.

Tips for Getting Results from Your Show

Review similar shows. Effective programs generally come down to three very human elements: good format, great presentation, and capable direction. No matter what your budget, you have the power to affect all three of these elements. Look at other shows that are most similar to yours in tone and presentation and pay careful attention to their format and production. Note how the host sets up a specific theme and presents the subject matter for each show.

Tastefully refer to your business and what you do as often as possible during your show. As we said, no one wants to watch or listen to a half-hour commercial for someone's business. Yet, you still need to reap the benefits of producing a show. Knowing how to refer to your business while presenting guests and information on your show is an art. To begin learning it, study the masters. Notice how the top cooking show hosts will casually refer to their most recent book or reference the top restaurant where they work. They do so while illustrating points they are making. For example, the Frugal Gourmet may say something like, "Don't you just love what the Chinese do with vegetables? In my new book [names book] there's a whole section devoted just to Peking salads." Martial arts instructor Steve Grody often prefaces moves or concepts by reminding his audience he is a private instructor. He does so with statements such as "I was working with a student last week and she made the comment . . ." or "I've been teaching for ten years now, and students always get excited when I show them . . ."

Always include a mechanism that allows your audience to contact you. If you are buying time from a local station, this will be somewhat easier to accomplish. You may want to produce a live call-in show that announces or flashes your phone number continuously throughout the show. You can also build your logo, phone number, or the name of your show prominently into your set. At the end of the show, during the closing credits, always mention or display your business name and phone number, unless the station has rules that prevent it. On public access, the rules are clear. In terms of graphics, you are only permitted to have a graphic in the closing credits that reads: For More Information [your phone number]. That's it. No business name or other information can be included. But there are ways to work the nature of your business and what you do into the program.

Make sure to get tapes made of each completed show. You can extend the value of your investment by creating promotional audio or video brochures from your shows. By using this footage, the cost of producing an audio or video for your business will be a fraction of what you would pay if you had to shoot from scratch. You can also use the shows in their entirety for promotional purposes. If you have a Web site, consider either streaming your show in real-time or digitizing segments that browsers can view. Having a recording of each show also allows you to view and review it for the purpose of critiquing your performance and the show's effectiveness.

Cross-promote. To increase listenership, you will need to promote your show in as many ways as possible. Mention your show in all your advertising and collateral materials. If you can afford it, advertise and promote your show as a separate entity from your business. This not only substantiates your credibility; it will also increase the listenership of your show, and thereby your business. Let your show give you all the credibility you deserve. Always include the fact that you have a show in all your marketing materials and other media appearances.

Increase the scope of your show by broadcasting it through your Web site. If you have a Web site, by all means stream your radio show live so listeners all over the world can tune in. Live shows on the Web are still a novelty and may help you attain additional publicity for your site, your business, and, of course, your show. If your server allows the bandwidth and memory, save your shows in sound files so they can be played at any time. As you can see in the section on multimedia Web sites, you can also include video clips of your show on your site.

Resources: Your Own Show

Books

Basics of Video Production. Des Lyver and Graham Swainson. Newton, Mass.: Focal Press, 1995.

Broadcasting/Cable and Beyond: An Introduction to Modern Electronic Media. Joseph R. Dominick, Barry L. Sherman, Gary A. Copeland and Jo Dominick. New York: McGraw-Hill Text, 1995.

The Essential Television Handbook: What You Need to Know, What to Do and What Not to Do. Peter Jarvis. Newton, Mass.: Focal Press, 1996.

Introduction to Radio: Production and Programming. Michael H. Adams and Kimberly K. Massey. New York: Brown & Benchmark Publications, 1994.

Radio Production: A Manual for Broadcasters. Robert McLeish. Newton, Mass.: Focal Press, 1994.

Radio Production Worktext: Studio and Equipment. David E. Reese and Lynne S. Gross. Newton, Mass.: Focal Press, 1997.

Newsletters & Magazines

Broadcasting & Cable, P.O. Box 6457, Torrance, CA 90504-9865, (800) 554-5729, www.broadcastingcable.com.

Radio and Production. P.O. Box 170265, Irving, TX 75017-0265. Phone: (972) 254-1100. E-mail: info@rapmag.com. Web: www.rapmag.com

TALKERS. A magazine for radio talk-show hosts. P.O. Box 60781, Longmeadow, MA 01116, (413) 567-3189, www.talkers.com

Audio

The Cassette. A monthly audiocassette release of exemplary radio shows and productions, available from Radio and Production Magazine, P.O. Box 170265, Irving, TX 75017-0265. Phone: (972) 254-1100. E-mail: info@rapmag.com. Web: www.rapmag.com

Associations and Organizations

Federal Communications Commission, 1919 M Street, N.W., Washington DC 20554, (202) 418-0200, www.fcc.org.

National Association of Broadcasters, 1771 N Street, N.W., Washington, DC 20036, (202) 429-3925, www.nab.org

National Cable Television Association, 1724 Massachusetts Avenue, N.W., Washington, DC 20036, (202) 775-3669, www.ncta.org.

PART IV

GET GROWING:

Building a Large and Loyal Following

You're in competition with one person only and that is the individual you know you can become.

—MARTHA GRAHAM

Having business come to you feels so great you'll want to make sure it continues. You'll want to turn whatever interest your marketing activities are generating into business and keep your new clients and customers eagerly coming back for more. And once you've developed a loyal following of satisfied customers, they'll not only keep coming back, they'll be more accepting of needed price increases and look to you for additional products and services. And, chances are, they'll be sending others your way. This the easy way to see your business and career grow.

Growing in this way allows you to decide how you will grow. To some growing means getting bigger, adding employees and expanding into increasingly larger facilities. To others, growing means staying small, increasing their income and clientele without having to add employees or move into larger facilities. For some it means expanding their line or raising their prices while avoiding the complexities of building a large business.When your business is based on a loyal following, you have choices about how you grow.

YOUR GOAL
Keep Business Rolling In

This closing section is designed to help you grow from the results of your marketing and ultimately reduce or replace a lot of time-intensive marketing activities. In **chapter 13**, you will see that, by getting business to return again and again, you won't need to be constantly generating as much new business. Then, once you get business coming to you, by making the most of each marketing activity you do undertake, you can incorporate much of your marketing into your ongoing communication with clients and customers.

Are You Going and Growing?

Here is a checklist you can use to monitor if you are optimizing and therefore minimizing the time involved in marketing activities:

___ 1. Are clients and customers calling you as a result of your reputation or the recommendations of others? The higher the percentage of your business that comes from such sources the better.

___ 2. Are you getting compliments and expressions of appreciation and gratitude from your clients? The happier your clientele, the more likely it is to return or seek additional products or services from you.

___ 3. Does most business you do lead to more business with that individual or company? Are clients asking about additional services? Are they suggesting additional ways they could work with you?

___ 4. Are you tastefully and appropriately piggybacking your marketing activities onto your regular transactions with clients and contacts?

___ 5. Do you make multiple uses of each marketing activity you undertake and dovetail any one effort in with a variety of others? The more activities you have undertaken, the easier it becomes to use one to further another.

___ 6. Are marketing opportunities being presented to you rather than your having to invest time and money to seek them out? Are colleagues suggesting joint promotions? Is the media calling you without your having just sent something to them? Are you being contacted to speak or do articles? All such opportunities are a sign that your reputation is spreading and that you are becoming known for your expertise and the value of your product or service.

CHAPTER 13

Turning Interest into Business Again and Again

Nothing sells like sensational results.

—Benjamin Shields

In this book we are focusing primarily on techniques that allow you to do as little one-on-one selling as possible. However, there is no getting around the fact that at some time or other, you will have to turn the interest you've attracted into an order or a decision to do business with you. When someone contacts you, it means she is considering the possibility of trusting you with her business. The hairstylist's clients, for example, must trust him with their appearance; a word processor's or graphic designer's clients must trust her with their companies' image; a trainer, with his employees' productivity; a landscape architect, with the appearance of her home or office.

So, the key word in turning interest into actual business is *trust.* And trust can only be developed one-to-one. If you are marketing yourself as a specialist, expert, or authority in your particular niche, those who contact you will already be predisposed to trust you. But once they express an interest, you must be able to confirm their inclination and help them feel confident about proceeding to do business with you. In this sense you are already a consummate salesperson, although you may not know it yet.

Every day of your life you have been selling someone on something. Think about the last time you convinced your exhausted spouse to go out with you to an evening event. How about the many times you have convinced your child to turn off the television and do his or her homework, enlisted the help of a friend with a chore, talked a colleague into agreeing with your point of view, or convinced your boss to give you a raise. Each of these instances is an example of how in your everyday life you have always been selling something to someone. But, when it comes to doing business, it seems as if "selling" has quotes around it and, therefore, it's easy to forget that we do this all the time.

This chapter will introduce you to some concepts that will make turning interest into business far less intimidating and, actually, fun.

A Great Beginning

Suppose someone you meet at a networking function is interested in talking with you further about what you do. You give her your card and ask her to call you at the office tomorrow, but she never calls. Or perhaps a man comes up after a speech you have given, wanting to find out more about your business. He begins describing a problem he is having, implying that perhaps you can help. You set up a lunch to discuss it further, but an emergency arises and he has to cancel the lunch. He doesn't call back and by the time you contact him weeks later by phone, you discover he has hired someone else.

YOUR GOAL

Make Selling Painless

What's wrong, here? This business should be yours. But these situations point to how easy it is to inadvertently leave valuable business on the table for someone else to pick up. Whenever anyone contacts you or expresses some degree of interest, this is a great beginning. It's evidence that your marketing efforts are working. Each such contact represents potential business, but that usually is as far as your marketing efforts can go. When people respond favorably to any marketing effort, they're seldom sold; they are ready to be sold. They're waiting for details like how much your product or service costs, how it works, and whether you can do something in a way that will meet their needs. They may also want to know whether you have another color, who else has done what you have, what results you have had, and how your product or service can be suited to their specific needs. Sometimes people will ask you these questions directly. That makes your job easier. But more often than not, they don't know what questions to ask, so they simply let you know they're interested and wait for you to take over from there.

If your marketing has truly caught their interest, they want you to convince them that you do, indeed, have what they need. They're hoping you will, but they want reassurance. Once your marketing has developed this positive interest, you must convert that interest into a decision to buy. As sales trainer Joel Weldon says, "Cows don't give milk; you have to take it from them every day." So it is with marketing. Marketing produces the interest; now you have to turn that interest to your advantage. This process is called *closing the sale*.

If, like many others, you dread the word *sale*, keep in mind that your marketing effort has done the most time-consuming and unpleasant part of making the sale. It's created interest. It's predisposed you to success. You won't be talking to or calling on uninterested strangers. Your marketing has found the potential customer; it has qualified the customer to make sure he or she is interested; and it has even made the initial sales presentation. All that remains for you to do once interest has been expressed is close the sale. And this can be the fun part, the part when you get to share your interest in working with your clients, your excitement and enthusiasm about what you can do, and your desire to serve and meet their needs.

Closing a Sale Is . . .

- discovering how you can best meet someone else's needs
- providing additional information
- clarifying concerns
- working toward a win-win agreement
- establishing or building a relationship
- forming a mutually beneficial partnership

Closing a Sale Isn't . . .

- doing a slick con job
- pushing products or services onto someone who doesn't want them
- using high-pressure techniques
- engaging in a win-lose contest
- glad-handing and backslapping
- putting one over on the client
- manipulating someone against his or her will

Seventeen Secrets to Closing a Sale

Turning interest into business is essentially a matter of recognizing and responding positively to someone's desire. Someone has a need that you may be able to meet. Your goal is never to coerce people into buying something from you or even to convince them to buy; it is simply to discover whether in fact you can meet their needs. If you are convinced you can do so and can convince them, too, they will buy.

Here are specific steps you can take to make sure the interest you have generated through your marketing doesn't slip away.

1. Take the initiative to make a follow-up contact. Respond immediately to any signal of interest by proposing that you get back to the interested person by phone. Do not try to close a sale at some meeting or event; you want your customer's full attention without interruption

THE BEST TIME TO PHONE

Avoid the busy hours of the day for the business you are calling.

Business	Hour to Call
Bankers	Before or after banking hours
Dentists	Before their appointments begin, usually about 9:30 A.M.
Doctors	After morning hospital rounds and before they begin seeing patients, usually about 9:00 A.M.
Executives	Before the secretary arrives or after he or she has left for the day, or late morning after startup tasks have been completed—usually around 10:30 A.M.
Trial lawyers	During the noon recess, which may run from late morning to about 2:00 P.M.
Salaried workers	At home after dinner but before prime-time TV
Stockbrokers	Before or after the closing of the stock exchange (open 10:00 A.M.–3:00 P.M. EST)
Teachers and professors	In the late afternoon at home or after 6:00 P.M.

or distraction. If you have been called already, so much the better. Provide whatever information is requested and proceed to set up a further contact or close the sale. But never wait for people to call you back. They probably won't, so why take the chance?

2. ***Determine whether a phone call or personal meeting is called for.*** The more complex the decision involved in buying your product or service and the higher your price, the more likely the purpose of your follow-up call should be to schedule a personal meeting. In such situations, you will want to turn phone inquiries into personal appointments as well.

3. ***When you call, make sure it is a good time for the person to talk.*** If it is not, schedule a more appropriate time. Even when you are calling to set up a personal meeting, your caller may have a variety of preliminary questions that need to be answered before he or she can decide to meet with you. Respond as clearly as you can, but do not try to go into complicated material by phone. Certainly don't quote a price over the phone when you need to meet to determine exactly what will be involved. Emphasize that you will be able to explain everything in more detail when you speak in person.

4. ***Think service, not sales.*** Once you are meeting with someone, whether in person or by phone, focus your attention on finding out what your potential client needs and determining whether it is something you can supply. Find out as much as you can about the results the person is seeking and what interested him or her in your product or service.

5. ***Welcome all questions.*** In contacting you for further information, potential buyers want to determine whether you know enough about how your product or service would relate to their particular business, their life, and their needs. They may ask you questions that were clearly answered in the ad, your speech, or other literature; perhaps the information didn't register, or perhaps they need reassurance. They may even ask you the same question several times. Ultimately, the reason someone chooses your product or company probably isn't because of *what* your product or service provides; someone else almost certainly provides it, too. People will buy from you because of *how* you do whatever you are selling. Particularly when you have an information or service business, the primary reason people do business with you is, in fact, *you*.

In selecting your product or service, buyers must put some aspect of their company in your hands. Therefore they must trust that you truly represent something they can rely on, and whatever happens, you

FOLLOWING UP ON INTEREST

Tips for Follow-Up Meetings

- Bring a brochure or packet of material to leave with customers. Make sure you bring enough for everyone.
- Use visual aids when possible, such as product samples, a video, photos, or a flip pad.
- Have everything you need in a case with you. Know where each item is for immediate access.
- Make sure everything you will be using is in working order before you leave your own place of business.
- Be flexible. Invite questions. Make the meeting a dialogue, not a monologue.
- Keep subtle control of the meeting. Gently bring it back to the decisions at hand when needed.
- Never run over the agreed time for the meeting. Schedule a next appointment if you need to.
- Don't give out information no one needs. Let the questions you are asked guide the focus of the meeting.
- Dress slightly more conservatively than whose with whom you will be talking.

Tips for Follow-Up Phone Calls

- Make the most of your voice. It is the only channel of communication you have on the phone.
- Be pleasant, authoritative, and confident.
- Smile before you dial or pick up the phone. The smile will automatically translate to your voice.
- Always confirm that it is a good time to talk.
- Never read a script, but do write out key words and phrases for the main points you want to make.

- Prioritize your points so that you have a short list of those you *must* make.
- Subtly guide the discussion to cover those main points.
- Have all the information you need at your fingertips—including price sheets, specifications, and resources.
- Place sales calls on a line without call-waiting. You don't want to be interrupted at crucial moments.
- Listen for what is being said between the lines and respond directly to that.

will act in their interest and give them straight answers. With most people such trust does not come automatically. Often, all the questions, delays, doubts, and hemming and hawing you encounter are part of the process a person needs to go through to determine whether you are someone he or she can trust. This is the main reason that, on average, it can take at least seven contacts to make a sale.

6. ***Understand before you answer.*** Although buyers may ask questions about your academic preparation or background or the details relating to your product or service, they are usually not interested in that information per se; they are seeking evidence that you know about, understand, and can do something about what they need. So don't just start answering questions by plunging into a lot of details. If you don't find out everything you can about a person's needs before you answer, you may unwittingly unsell yourself.

For example, suppose you offer a bookkeeping service and someone calls to find out about it. The caller asks how many years you have been in business, what you charge to do a general ledger, and whether you do the work on-site. Instead of jumping in with price information, we suggest answering the first and third questions and then asking questions of your own to determine the person's needs, such as "What type of business do you have?" "How are you handling your bookkeeping now?" and "How many active accounts do you have each month?" By requesting this information, you have conveyed that you are interested in the caller's needs; and, once you have the crucial information you need to answer the caller's questions from an informed position, you can demonstrate how you would tailor your work to meet those needs. You won't be shooting in the dark or hoping your answers are heading in the right direction.

7. ***Know your competition.*** Be prepared not only to address questions about your product or service specifically, but also to demonstrate how it compares with others, what trends it reflects in the field, what research shows relative to the issues involved, and how people similar to your prospect are using what you offer.

8. ***Exude confidence in your skills and in your knowledge.*** In order for others to trust that your product can handle the work they need done, they first need to believe that you are convinced you can do it. So once you have enough information to know that you can handle the work, assert confidently how you will proceed and the benefits that will result.

Never try to act as though you know about something when you don't. Instead, offer to get back to your questioner with additional information. If you try bluffing your way through, you run a high risk of displaying your ignorance and lessening your ability to inspire the necessary trust.

One of the best ways to inspire that necessary trust is to talk about work you have done with similar clients and to offer the names of references your potential client or customer can contact. First, however, be sure to ask questions and listen carefully to the replies so you are certain to be addressing the person's actual needs. Another way to boost your authority is to hold informal surveys or focus groups with potential customers to find out as many of the concerns, questions, and issues that will arise when you talk with potential buyers as you can. You can also hire someone to conduct these for you, or you might want to hire a market-research consultant to review the questions you plan to ask to make sure you are likely to draw meaningful responses. Having such firsthand information will prepare you for objections and provide you with insights into the issues someone may be facing so that you can respond more knowledgeably.

9. ***Build value before quoting the price.*** Often the first thing someone wants to know is how much you charge. While you never want to appear evasive or nonresponsive, it's best not to automatically give out your prices until you've found out just what the person is seeking and taken the time to lay a foundation for what people will be getting for their money—so that when you do quote the price it will seem reasonable and appropriate, if not a bargain. For example, if you have a mailing-list service, before quoting your price to do a mailing, you might want to find out how many pieces someone is wanting to mail; when she needs it to go out; whether her list is already on computer disk, if there will be stapling, folding, and sorting involved, etc.

Then help your potential clients see the value behind your price.

Hiring a mailing-list service to send out a mailing to 1,000 customers might sound expensive, for example, until you explain that because you're working on discounts, using your service will actually cost a company less than doing it themselves, not to mention the time they will save.

10. Offer alternatives. Break down the services you offer into various units so that you can offer price alternatives. Build in a pricing incentive based upon the amount someone purchases. The résumé writer, for example, might have a price for simply typing a résumé, an additional price if someone wants help constructing the résumé, folding it, stapling it, mailing it, etc. An all-in-one price might, however, be considerably less than purchasing each element independently. Another example: A professional speaker might have one price for an hour-long keynote ($4,000), which is not that much less than his full daily price for which he will do a luncheon keynote and morning breakout seminar ($5,000). Additional prices might be available for providing a workbook of handouts and work sheets for each participant or a customized speech tailored to the client's industry.

Such alternatives give you and your client room to find a workable price and, as long as you have priced your services carefully enough, they give you the option of offering more for less as a favor to a client you especially want to work with. One speaker we know, for example, has a reduced price for nonprofits. Another has a lower price for speeches in her own community, where she won't have to spend time traveling, and another reduced fee if the client agrees to purchase a copy of her book for each participant.

11. If possible, offer some type of guarantee. Offering a guarantee—of satisfaction, parts, or accuracy—will short-circuit many objections and serve as proof that you believe in your product. Although a photographer can't guarantee that her customers will get a photo they will love and a therapist can't guarantee that his patients will be cured, there is usually some type of guarantee you can offer, even in a service business. The photographer, for example, can guarantee that proofs will be returned within three days, and the therapist can guarantee that every phone call will be returned within two hours. Among guarantees that work well for service businesses, Roger Lane promises that unless students attending his finance course double their income in six weeks, they can continue in the course free of charge until they do. Word processor Camella Cortez guarantees a 10 percent discount if the customer finds any typing errors and, of course, that she will correct them. And hairstylist Shannon King offers to take back any beauty-care product that doesn't make a noticeable difference. In each of these cases, rarely does anyone actually take the offerer up on the guarantee. Instead, people get hooked on the service.

12. Welcome and respond to objections. Often people dread hearing any fussing, griping, or grumbling, complaints, criticisms, negative comparisons, excuses, or other general reasons why someone doesn't seem to want to buy. All such reactions are referred to in sales parlance as objections. However, you should be delighted when you hear them, for several reasons.

First, if someone is raising an objection, this is a sign that she is still interested but that some concern is preventing her from acting. No one

WHEN AND HOW TO ASK FOR THE ORDER

- The time to ask for the order is when the buyer doesn't have more questions and you don't have any more information to provide.
- Ask directly. Say something like "We can get started tomorrow. Shall I come by in the morning?" or "All that's required is a check. Do you want me to bill you?"
- Offer to make a proposal, bid, or estimate. If what you are selling is complex, offering to provide a proposal, bid, or estimate will give the prospective client time to look over what you can do. (See **chapter 11** p. 542 and the **Resources** that follow for further information on how to develop a proposal.)
- Follow up on the proposal by asking how it seems to the buyer. If the response is positive, all you have to do is say, "Okay, when do we start?" or "How many would you like?" or "When would you like your first shipment?"
- If the person can't give you an answer, you may not be talking to the decision maker. In that case, ask what you can do to make the job easier. For example, you can offer to provide additional information for the decision makers or join in making a presentation to them.
- If the buyer is stalling, you can always ask the one question that usually makes people take notice: "What will it take to get your business?" You are really asking what the real problem is and, if there isn't one, that the sale be completed.

will take the time to raise objections who doesn't retain some interest. Second, these objections can be viewed as someone's internal dialogue that he has decided to voice to you. This gives you a chance to see whether you can help the person get past these concerns.

Objections are the best way for you to know and then to get around any resistance someone has to buying. Think of objections as stated questions. Someone who says "That's an awful lot of money" is essentially asking, "Will this really be worth that much to me?" And "But I need this by Wednesday" means that someone is asking whether she can get it sooner. So whenever you hear an objection, consider how you can answer the question that underlies it. People rarely say what they mean when they object; the objection is a sign of uncertainty. This is why objecting to price is so common. Your job is to draw the buyer out to discover the real problem behind the objection. You may find that it is a very real concern that you can take care of, or you may find out that the concern is based on inaccurate information.

Of course, at times, you may also discover that the objections a particular client has are accurate and appropriate. What you offer will not meet the needs of everyone you attract interest from. In such cases, you can simply confirm what they need instead and see if there is any way you can help them connect with someone who can meet their needs. Such situations are great opportunities to refer to others who can refer to you in the future.

Watch out, however, for the I-don't-want-to-hurt-your-feelings-but-I'm-really-not-interested objection. It can take the form of any other objection, but your sensitivity to picking up gracefully on this kind of objection will determine whether the person will contact you when he does need what you offer or could refer you to others.

Finally, objections are the best way for you to determine whether you can actually meet someone's needs. And if you can't, the sooner you find that out, the better.

13. Find out whether the person is ready to make a buying decision. Once you have addressed the major concerns, ask a question to test whether the person you're talking with is ready to buy. Having explained how your service works, for example, you might ask, "Does that sound like something you want to do?" or "So would you like to make an appointment?" Asking such questions will bring out any remaining objections for you to respond to. If the person no longer seems interested, point out one more time a benefit that originally had appeal, just to be sure your assessment is accurate.

HOW TO HANDLE THE MOST COMMON OBJECTIONS

Business-to-business

Your price is too high.

- "What are you comparing it with?"
- "Is it what you really need (or want)?"
- "Lets consider how this will improve your situation."
- "What we offer differs from what others offer in the following ways. Which of these differences might be important to you or your company?"

We can't afford such a product or service.

- "Let me show you how we can actually save you money."
- "What is your budget? Let me find something in that range."

We can't afford it right now.

- "We can make special billing arrangements for you."
- "With references we would be happy to open an account for you."
- "Can you afford not to?"
- "Will you regret passing this up?"

It won't work for us.

- "Let me show you how it could."
- "We will be happy to tailor it to your specifications."
- "Let me show you how it has worked for others in your situation."

We need it in another form.

- "Exactly what changes do you need?"
- "We will be happy to work with you to meet your needs."

I don't have time to discuss it right now.

- "Your time is very valuable. I promise to be brief. Just answer this one question."
- "Of course, you are busy. When would be a time to show you how we meet your needs."
- "I know your time is pressing, but I don't want you to lose an opportunity."

I'll think about it.

- "Do so. I know you will find it of great advantage to you. I will contact you early next week to see if you need any further information."
- "Are there other questions in the back of your mind right now?"
- "What additional information would be of help to you in making a decision?"

Thanks. We'll call you.

- "I will give you a call next week to see if you need any further information."
- "Let me ask you honestly: does this interest you?"

14. ***Walk the person step-by-step through what is involved in buying.*** As you sense someone's interest growing, explain step-by-step how to order and get the service under way. The more graphically you can describe how simple it is and how soon the customer will have the desired outcome, the better. Such a description enables the person to imagine going through the steps and enjoying the results.

15. ***Ask for the order.*** People often will not actually reach a decision if you don't request them to do so. Mistaking this hesitancy for reluctance, the novice at closing sales may give up on the sale, propose speaking again some other time, or invite the person to think the offer over and talk later. Even sales professionals sometimes miss the sale by not actually asking for the order. In a recent study of professional sales

HOW TO HANDLE THE MOST COMMON OBJECTIONS

Business-to-consumers

I can get it cheaper elsewhere.

- "Can you also get the following advantages?"
- "Are you actually getting the same thing elsewhere?"
- "There are a number of things we can offer. Have you fully considered them?"

I can't afford it.

- "Let me show you why it's worth it in the long run . . . and even now."
- "Let me show you how it will pay for itself in weeks/months."
- "We do offer special discounts under the following circumstances."
- "Let me show you how it would be far less expensive than the alternatives you are considering."
- "Do you want to miss out on this?"

I can't afford it right now.

- "We would be happy to accept your credit card."
- "We do offer the following credit program."
- "The sooner you make the investment, the sooner you'll be able to use (or enjoy) it."
- "You might want to consider that there will be a price increase as of . . ."
- "We do offer discounts or special prices under the following conditions that apply to you."
- "Let me show you how it can start paying for itself right away."

It won't work for me.

- "Tell me a little more about what it is you need."

- "Why do you feel it won't work?"
- "Let me tell you about others who found it solved similar needs."
- "What if I guarantee that I will refund your money if you are not happy with it?"

I don't like the ___ (feature or aspect such as color or location).

- "What is it about that aspect that is not suitable for you?"
- "What would be more suitable for you? Perhaps we can adapt it to meet your needs."
- "That doesn't interfere in any way with the major advantages you're seeking. Let me show you why."

I'll have to think about it.

- "What additional information will you need to help you decide?"
- "Why not try this sample to show you how it would work for you."
- "We are currently offering a special promotion for a limited time."
- "Are there any questions at all that you still have, even in the back of your mind?"

reps during a monitored call situation, only approximately 10 percent of the reps asked for the order. Even when the reps were told that the buyer would be placing an order, still only 17 percent asked for it. The rest didn't and lost the sale.

Don't make this mistake. If there is one thing that will increase your ability to turn interest into business, it is asking for the order. So don't balk when it comes down to the nitty-gritty of asking for business. Before you hang up the phone or walk out of the office, ask for the sale directly.

16. Get the money. No deal is truly complete until the money is in hand or the contract is signed. Spell out and tie down all the financial terms at the time of the sale, and get the full amount or a down payment whenever possible. If you must bill or extend credit, establish the terms of the payment and get what you have agreed to in writing either in the form of a simple contract, a signed purchase order, or a let-

Marketing Masterpiece: Offering Options to Encourage Involvement

Lucinda Kerschensteiner is a career coach and certified Perfect Work consultant in Fort Collins, Colorado. Typically, her coaching process involves approximately six to eight one-hour weekly sessions. She has priced her services so that signing up for the entire process is more cost-effective over time than simply deciding session by session. But sometimes, potential clients still feel hesitant to commit the time and money for the entire process until they know more about its benefits. So Lucinda has created a day-long Saturday seminar for such clients that runs $79 for the day, $69 if they pay in advance.

She finds that having such options allows most people who are interested in coaching a chance to get involved in the process without experiencing price resistance. Her day-long workshop provides ample value for the money. Most people do pay in advance, and of those who attend the Saturday workshops about 50 percent will go on for additional sessions or career services.

ter of agreement. Don't do any work or turn over any product until such an agreement is in place. Be sure you have your customer's authorized signature on some form of agreement that states clearly what is being purchased and under what terms.

Spelling out all terms clearly in a proposal makes this process easier. It is simple for the customer either to sign the proposal form as is or to transfer that information to a purchase order. If the information is transferred to a purchase order, contract, or letter of agreement, be sure it is transferred accurately and that no alterations are made either in substance or appearance.

You can have your attorney draw up a standard contract with blanks for the date and cost figures, or you can write a contract yourself using a form book from a law library or by using such computer software as *Venture* by Star Software, which provides simple pro forma contracts. These can be tailored to your needs. However, be sure to have your attorney review what you create. You are not a lawyer and, even when using standard forms, there may be special laws or circumstances in your state that are not accounted for.

When extending credit, check a new customer's credit rating and/or references thoroughly before you start working or ship a single item.

You can locate credit-reporting agencies in the Yellow Pages or use a computer-based service to obtain TRW and Dun & Bradstreet reports on companies. TRW reports, covering thirteen million companies, are available on CompuServe, Dialog, and the Web at www.trw.com. Dun & Bradstreet reports covering over 9 million businesses are available on CompuServe and Dialog. Its Web site is http://dbisna.com. When you're doing business with another business, you will also want to request a credit application. The customer's bank and at least three credit references may be your most valuable sources of credit information. Just be sure you ask the right quesitons and read carefully between the lines of the answers.

One last point: There will be those few times when you have to assume the unpleasant task of collections. If a customer does not pay you within the time allotted by your agreement (usually thirty days), request payment with a cordial phone call. If you still have not received payment by the forty-five-day mark, call again, firmly but politely making it very clear that the customer will receive no more merchandise or work until the bill is paid. Once they have passed the sixty-day mark, with rare exceptions, customers should be placed on a COD basis only.

One of the greatest mistakes small businesses make is relying on a few very large customers instead of maintaining a broader base of medium-sized customers. If a company that gives you thousands of dollars worth of business doesn't pay for it and on time, you lose money. In addition to the lost payment for your product or service, there are dozens of hidden costs and, therefore, losses in dealing with slow-paying companies. You cannot afford that kind of customer. Make sure people pay on time or put them on COD. Losing a nonpaying customer is no loss.

17. ***Always leave the door open for the next contact.*** Should you not be able to close a sale, you need to determine whether there is suf-

BASIC QUESTIONS TO ASK CREDIT REFERENCES

- How long has the applicant been a customer?
- What is the applicant's highest credit allowed?
- How quickly does the applicant usually pay his or her bills? (thirty days? Slow thirty? Sixty days? Slow sixty? Longer?)
- Are there any currently overdue invoices?

ficient interest to suggest a next step. For example, if a person explains that he or she is moving and unable to make a commitment, you can offer to call again in two weeks. If a company is in the middle of a contract and cannot change suppliers, take advantage of the time to prepare creative selling points for the next proposal period and keep in touch with the buyer to impart information and to show continued interest and reliability. Whenever sufficient interest remains, set up a specific date and time for the next contact. If appropriate, offer to send additional material or a brief proposal and set up your next call or meeting on your calendar. Remember: You need an average of seven solid contacts before a person is ready to buy.

Don't get discouraged. The more work a sale takes, the more committed the eventual buyer will be and the more difficult it will be for someone else to take the client away from you. One company called regularly, though infrequently, on a major wire service for fourteen years, through three different buyers, without completing a deal. But when the wire service finally made the decision to change to the persistent supplier, the deal represented half a million dollars per year in business. Twenty years later, they still have the business.

Even when there will definitely be no sale, thank your prospects for their interest, express your pleasure at having met them, and let them know that you will be happy to serve them anytime in the future should they need your product or service. Keep their names on your mailing list and send materials out at least quarterly so that your name remains in the forefront of their minds.

Communicating Versus Manipulating

Much has been said about selling and manipulation. Some sales trainers point out that most communication we engage in every day is manipulative, because we are trying to get someone else to think or do something we are advocating. Therefore, they suggest, sales is no different, and we need not be concerned about being manipulative. While it may be true that much of our communication is meant to get others to do our bidding, we believe that this argument misses the point.

We have all been pressured at some time into buying something we didn't really want and resented it later. As a result, most people who are new to closing sales feel somewhat self-conscious about selling, wanting to be sure to avoid the discomfort and negative feelings that arise from such manipulation. Manipulation, in this sense, is trying to get someone to buy something he or she neither wants nor needs. In the long run, it never pays off. People won't use the unwanted item; they may even feel angry about it and try to return it or back out on the agreement. You lose their future business, and they won't send any more business your way. They may even bad-mouth you to others. Studies show that people are more likely to denounce a business than to praise one.

If you have a product or service that people need and it does in fact meet that need, you don't have to be concerned about having to manipulate anyone into buying it. Your task in closing the sale is to help each person reach a decision. Customers want to be sure what you offer will meet their needs before they part with their money, so you must address their concerns and doubts. Helping people get past their concerns is not manipulation; it is helping them get what they want.

Getting Repeat Business

Attracting new business costs at least six times more than retaining existing business, according to Carole Congram, editor of *The American Management Association Handbook of Marketing for Service Industries*. That means the best way to get business to come to you is to get your existing clients to keep coming! But here is a shocking fact: When the Small Business Administration asked businesses why they thought customers stopped doing business with them, most said prices were too high. Yet when the agency surveyed customers to find out why they left to buy elsewhere, only 9 percent cited price. Being treated indifferently was the reason 68 percent left.

Once you have business, the wisest marketing investment you can make is to invest in ensuring that your customers come back again and again. Customer service or customer relations is one area wherein you, as a small business, have the advantage. You can do it better than larger businesses because you can offer the personal touch that will make the difference. Martin Wallach, who operates an advertising agency from his suburban Chicago home, is able to say to prospective clients, "You'll never be dealing with an underling. You'll work with top people all the time."

Using Your Greatest Advantage: The Personal Touch

Large companies today often try to rotate personnel in their purchasing departments to prevent personal relationships from forming with suppliers. These companies are under the impression that business is done between institutions rather than between people. They believe that this detachment best fosters the competition between their suppliers and thereby results in lower prices. What these companies don't realize is that there is far more to a business relationship than price. What often ends up happening in such an impersonal buying arena is that the most reputable companies back out of the bidding war, knowing they cannot and will not compete on price alone. This leaves only the less-than-top-flight vendors as the pool from which many of these companies have to choose.

One thing anyone loses who does business with such companies is the assurance of quality. Another is the guarantee that the company will still be in business next week. And the most important loss will be not getting the kind of service that comes from having a close and strong relationship from which to do business. No one is going to stop everything to bail a fickle customer out of a problem or emergency, but most people will go out of their way for someone who has gone out of his or her way for them again and again.

As the owner of a small business, your greatest advantage is that you can provide personal service. Each of your clients is a valued asset, not just another account number. You have the personal touch and can provide service above and beyond that expected. Ultimately, the company with the confidence to stand by its product or service, follow through on day-to-day orders, and assist the buyer if he or she makes a mistake is the company that keeps the business.

The way this trust is developed is by slowly but surely building a history of confidence—a history that shows you will deliver again and again. The more you are able to help someone do his or her job, the more that person will come to rely on you. Part of this trust comes from attention to the details that few others bother with. If you are providing bookkeeping services to the office manager of a law office, for example, the more you apprise that manager of what you are doing, how, and why, the better able the manager is to answer questions from the law partners. Every time a partner asks why the billing was done a particular way, if you have prepared the manager to handle the questions to the partner's satisfaction, he or she looks like a hero to the partner and you are a hero to the office manager.

No matter how long you have had customers, continue to treat each one like a brand-new customer you want to impress. Never take people's business for granted; someone else will most likely be glad to serve them. Impress them again and again.

Eight Ways to Make Sure Your Business Keeps Coming Back

1. ***Do a great job!*** Go the extra mile for each customer. Give people more than they expect. Even if you don't make much money on the first job, do it so well they will want to pay more the next time.

2. ***Deliver on time.*** Meet your deadlines. Don't promise what you know you can't deliver just to get the business. Make sure the deadlines you promise to meet are realistic ones; then see if you can beat them. Coming in ahead of time will be a delightful surprise.

3. ***Solicit feedback.*** Always inquire to make sure the customer is pleased. When possible, check out satisfaction each step along the way, while corrections are easier to make. Let customers know you want to hear any suggestions or complaints.

4. ***Make it right.*** If a problem develops, do whatever is needed to compensate the customer. Reduce the price, redo the job, exchange the item, or throw in something additional of value. Be willing to negotiate, and be flexible and understanding even if it was the customer who created the problem. Don't argue over who caused it; just work to resolve it to everyone's satisfaction.

5. ***Give preferential treatment.*** Let your regular customers know that they come first. Give them whatever preferences you can for time slots or discounts. When possible, exclude them from price hikes.

6. ***Go out of your way to assist your customers' business.*** If possible, refer business to them or provide them with tips that will aid their success. Introduce them to others who could be of help to them.

7. ***Answer phone calls and correspondence promptly.*** Even if this means you need to hire full- or part-time help or work late, make sure you stay current. Whenever possible, phone calls should be returned within two hours, and letters should be answered within the week. Don't be concerned if you have to leave a message. It is less important that you actually reach the customer than that the customer knows you tried to respond swiftly.

8. ***Stay in touch.*** If you don't stay in touch, you lose touch. So, make sure you have some type of contact with past, present, and potential customers—preferably monthly, but at least, quarterly. Depending on the nature of your business, such contact might be offering a special deal, making an announcement, holding an open house, sending flyers,

High-Tech Tip: Databased Marketing

Let's say you get a call or postcard from your veterinarian saying that it's time to bring your dog in for his rabies shot. First, this is a helpful reminder because chances are you would have forgotten. Then when you call for an appointment, the person answering the phone repeats your name and says, "Oh, yes, this will be for your Doberman, Rex." Or let's say that you need to have your dermatologist call your pharmacy and when you call her office, the staff immediately has all the pertinent information at their fingertips. "Yes, that's Drugtown. Their number is 555-1056."

Maybe you've noticed that if you order a golf jacket from a catalog, suddenly you begin getting a raft of golf-related catalogs in the mail. Or maybe you bought your sister a piece of jewelry for her birthday and next thing you know you're receiving mailing about jewelry specials.

These are all examples of what's called databased marketing. The idea is that by creating a database about each and every customer, including the basics like name, address, phone, and fax, but also a record of the time, date, and nature of their purchases, you can increasingly send the right messages to the right people at the right time. You can simultaneously save time and money, increase your business, and, if you do it right, build a better rapport with your customers.

Database marketing became popular with large companies in the 1980s, but small businesses have been slower to adopt it—thinking, perhaps, that keeping track of all these details wouldn't be worth the time, money, and effort. But with computer software and hardware continuing to come down in price while getting increasingly user-friendly, more and more small businesses and self-employed individuals are realizing that database marketing is an invaluable tool for knowing who your best customers are, what they're most likely to buy, when it's best to reach them, what they're likely to respond to, and how best to serve them.

Whether you have 1,000 customers a month or only 10 or 12 a year, database marketing can make your life easier by providing you with the information you need when marketing to them or responding to their calls. It can even help you find the best kind of new customers and let you know if you should spend time trying to reach uncertain or infrequent ones. In fact, virtually everything we're suggesting that you do in this chapter will be simpler if you can easily track and access key information about the who, when, what, and hows of your clients' and customers' needs.

For a simple, fun, and clear understanding of how to decide if database marketing would be right for your business and, if so, how to do it you can turn to *Target$smart, Database Marketing for the Small Business,* by Jay Newberg and Claudio Marcus (see **Resources**). It's a four-color visual guide to database marketing written for people like us who would rather be serving our clients than constructing parabolic charts on the most effective marketing methods. Fortunately, these days, you don't need either a math or computer background to create simple client databases that will help you spend more time with more customers who keep coming back for more.

newsletters, or postcards, making periodical phone calls, meeting for breakfast, lunch or dinner, sending fax or E-mail updates, Web updates, conducting a poll, or sending out a customer survey.

Reminder cards are one great way to stay in touch. If a client orders birthday gifts for his or her top sales personnel one year, for example, the smart owner of a gift-basket business will send a postcard, E-mail, or fax reminder of birthdays next year.

Don't limit your communication to one way only. As important as it is for you to let your clients know what you're doing, it's even more important for you to keep up with what they're doing. It not only shows that you care; it's also how you'll stay relevant to their ever-changing needs. Private practice consultant Gene Call hosts a Dutch-treat monthly Saturday breakfast meeting for his clients. Anyone who's interested can drop by to network or for informal consultation.

Investment counselor Dan Silverman sends a monthly newsletter that features his insights along with tips from clients and client profiles. Marketing specialist Becca Carey polls ten clients each month on a pertinent marketing topic like "What drew the most business for you this month?" and summarizes the results on a Monthly Tip sheet which she sends to everyone on her mailing list.

An insurance agent keeps in touch with her key clients for under $700 a year. Every week she takes one past or potential client to lunch. They talk about his needs and her business. She finds this is a great way to keep abreast of clients' problems and issues and, better yet, she averages about two referrals per luncheon, most of which lead to business. So at about $30 per meal after deducting $50 for taxes, she keeps her marketing costs down to only about $15 a week, all of which she recoups many times over in new or repeat business.

Marketing Mistake: Transferring Your Problems to Your Clients

Joseph started his own environmental testing business after losing his job to downsizing. It seemed like a natural for him because he had a technical background, many corporate contacts, and a real drive to succeed. Getting enough business, however, was tougher than he had expected. Having had no previous experience with marketing, he placed an ad in a local holistic health magazine and, three months later, calls were beginning to trickle in. He was holding on by his fingernails, but nonetheless optimistic, especially when a large company that was involved in completing an environmental impact study was referred to him by someone he knew. They were seeking to test existing buildings to determine whether they would need to be demolished or could be refurbished.

Eager to get the business because it would cover his basic living expenses for several months, he quickly arranged to reschedule several smaller jobs to accommodate the potential new client's "rush" schedule. The morning of the meeting at which he hoped to hear that the project had been approved, the administrative assistant of his contact in the company called to tell him the meeting had been canceled.

Two days later, with no word back from his contact, he was distraught and began calling everyone he knew within the company and his referral source, leaving urgent, desperate messages. When still no one returned his call, he grew angry and left a second round of heated messages accusing the company of being inconsiderate and blaming them for his losing a week's worth of income.

As you might imagine, he never heard back from the company, even though he sent several letters, first demanding and, finally, apologizing. Later he heard the company had called off the meeting because of last-minute legal snags with their project. Six months later, they did proceed and hired another environmental tester. But worst of all, his referral source had lost all confidence in him and was sending business elsewhere, too.

The lesson is clear. Our financial problems as small businesses and self-employed professionals are never of interest to our clients. They're not in business to help us; it's the other way around. We must honor the inevitable quixotic needs of our potential clients. We must take responsibility for any risks we take to get their business and turn to friends, family, or professional consultants for help in handling our disappointments and frustration.

Keep Marketing No Matter What

If you keep promoting, advertising, and trying a variety of methods, two things will happen: first, you will begin to find the concepts and methods that pull consistently for you and can invest more in these avenues; and second, you will develop a marketing momentum. Your various promotional and advertising efforts will begin reinforcing one another. People will recognize you from your promotion and ads and will think about you whenever the need for your product or service arises.

Above all else, remember that promotion does not make good customers; good products and business relationships do that. Promotion can only get people interested in you. Then, you must see to it that they become customers and that they come back again and again.

Managing a Self-Sustaining Business

As your marketing plan begins drawing people to you and you turn their interest into business with greater regularity, you will find that your business begins to develop a momentum of its own. If all goes well, ultimately, satisfied customers will comprise the bulk of your business. Between their return business and new business they refer to you, it will be self-generating. Marketing for new business will become less important, while the importance of customer relations will increase.

At this point, you can begin shifting your budget allocations from lower-cost, time-consuming marketing efforts to smaller amounts of more costly marketing that involves less of your time but continues to provide your business with a high profile within your market. You

☑ **Action Steps:** Develop a Customer Outreach Program

Since staying in touch with your clients is so important, consider having a client or customer outreach program as part of your marketing plan. Ask yourself:

1. How will I contact my past, present, and potential clients monthly or quarterly? Consider all the possibilities, but select methods for staying in touch that are suited to your personality, the nature of your business, your budget, and time schedule.
2. What kind of information do you want to communicate to your clients and customers regularly? What could you inform them of that would be of help or interest to them? Special offerings; new insights; upcoming legislation; trends that could affect their future; technology that might help them; inspirational, informative, or amusing stories, cartoons, or jokes; and pertinent newspaper clippings (including PR of your own) . . . are among the many possibilities to consider.
3. What kind of information do you want to gather from your clients and customers? If you're serving consumers, what changes have their lives undergone? If you're working on a business-to-business level, how is their business doing? What problems are they facing? What good news do they have to celebrate? How are their needs changing? What's working? What isn't? How'd they feel about changes that are taking place relevant to your field? These are just a few examples of the kind of information you can benefit from gathering regularly.
4. How will you make your communication two-way? Surveys, polls, in-person gatherings, luncheon meetings, an interactive Web site, hosting a monthly on-line conference or chat fest, and periodic personal phone calls are several examples of how you can make sure to keep abreast of what your clients are up to so you'll know how you can stay relevant to their needs.

may choose to do more image-building activities and less promotion or direct-response advertising.

You may also find yourself faced with more business than you can handle, and you will be presented with having to make the enviable choice of expanding or containing your business. You can expand by adding staff to carry out the work and devoting your time to continued marketing and sales efforts, or you may contain by raising your prices and referring out your overload business. Whichever you do, we advise that no matter how busy, successful, or comfortable you become, you continue marketing actively to your existing client and referral base and keep up a maintenance level of promotional activity within your specific market.

Building a high profile that will attract business through its own momentum is like following a body-conditioning program. Getting your body in peak condition requires considerable time and energy, but once you have achieved your goal, a maintenance program will keep you there with much less effort. If you stop all workouts, however, your body will revert quickly to its previous state of poor conditioning. So it is with marketing: if you let the excellent program you have developed go, you will quickly lose your market's attention, and others who are marketing aggressively will take your place. Then, should you need to attract more business again, you will have to exert considerable effort to regain a level of recognition that will attract a steady business flow. Supporting a sustained marketing effort, however, takes much less time, energy, and money, and it will enable you to ride out slow periods simply by stepping up your marketing a little.

The more you can incorporate marketing into what you regularly do in the course of offering your product or service through sampling, participating in your community and profession, and providing top-notch customer service, the easier this ongoing process of marketing will be. And you will have become a premier marketer. You will be among the growing number of Americans who wake up every Monday morning to the freedom of being your own boss without having to give up the security of a regular paycheck, because when you get to your desk, there will be as much work for you to do as you can enjoy.

Resources: Turning Business into Interest

Books

The Complete Database Marketer: Second-Generation Strategies and Techniques for Tapping the Power of Your Customer Database. Arthur M. Hughes, New York: Probus, 1995.

Fabled Service. Betsy Sanders. San Diego: Pfeiffer, 1995. Although written for larger businesses, this book reflects lessons on customer service that Sanders, now in private practice as a consultant, gleaned from nineteen years of working at Nordstrom, Inc., where she began as a $2.46-an-hour clerk and rose to vice president and general manager.

High Probability Selling. Jacques Werth and Nicholas E. Ruben. Dresher, Pa.: Abba Publishing Co., 1997.

Selling with Honor, Strategies for Selling without Selling Your Soul. Lawrence Kohn and Joel Saltzman. New York: Berkley, 1997.

Target$smart, Database Marketing for the Small Business. Jay Newberg and Claudio Marcus. Oasis Press, 300 North Valley Drive, Grants Pass, Ore., (541) 479- 9464, (800) 228-2275, 1996.

Newsletters

Art Sobczak's Telephone Selling Report, 13254 Stevens Street, Omaha, NE 68137, (402) 895-9399, (800) 326-7721, arts@businessbyphone.com

Audiotapes

Mind Capture. The mind-opening audiotapes and workbooks from a two-day thousand-dollar seminar with marketing luminaries Dr. Robert Cialdini, Joe Sugarman, and Joe Girard. Steve Dworman Enterprises, 11533 Thurston Circle, Los Angeles, CA 90049, (310) 472-6004.

More Mix-and-Match Tailor-Made Marketing Ideas

101 Mix and Match Ideas for Maximizing Your Marketing Efforts. Paul and Sarah Edwards. Here's How, P.O. Box 5091, Santa Monica, CA 90409, 1998.

101 Ways to Promote Yourself, Tricks of the Trade for Taking Charge of Your Own Success. Raleigh Pinskey. New York: Avon Books, 1997.

301 Do-It-Yourself Marketing Ideas from America's Most Innovative Small Companies. Edited by Dan Decker. Boston, Goldhirsh Group, Inc., 1997.

The Desktop Publisher's Idea Book. Chuck Green. New York: Random House, 1997.

Taming the Marketing Jungle, 104 Marketing Ideas When Your Motivation is High and Your Budget is Low. Silvana Clark. Hara Publishing, Box 19732, Seattle, WA 98109, 1994. An excellent example of a promotional booklet for Clark's own business as a public speaker.

Index